Anonymus

The Westminster Review

July and October 1872

Anonymus

The Westminster Review
July and October 1872

ISBN/EAN: 9783742825308

Manufactured in Europe, USA, Canada, Australia, Japa

Cover: Foto ©Thomas Meinert / pixelio.de

Manufactured and distributed by brebook publishing software
(www.brebook.com)

Anonymus

The Westminster Review

THE

WESTMINSTER

REVIEW.

JULY AND OCTOBER,
1872.

"Truth can never be confirm'd enough,
Though doubts did ever sleep."
SHAKESPEARE.

Menschenliebe prägt sich darin, daß man überall das Gute zu finden und zu schätzen weiß.
GÖTHE.

NEW SERIES.
VOL. XLII.

LONDON:
TRÜBNER & CO., 8 & 60, PATERNOSTER-ROW.
MDCCCLXXII.

CONTENTS.

Contemporary Literature.

WESTMINSTER

AND

FOREIGN QUARTERLY

REVIEW.

JULY 1, 1872.

ART. I.—SOVEREIGNTY: ROYAL AND REPRESENTATIVE.

A Bill to make Provision for Proportional Representation of the People, and otherwise Amend the Laws relating to the Representation of the People of England and Wales. [Brought in and printed 28th February, 1872. Second reading on the 10th July.]

WE have prefixed to this article the title of a Bill which will be debated in the House of Commons in a few days. The first appearance of a measure affecting the principles of representation requires and demands a full justification. We purpose, as far as in us lies, to defend on grounds of philosophical statesmanship, and of political justice and expediency, the introduction; and endeavour to remove the prejudices and antagonistic interests which may hinder and array themselves against the passing of this measure.

For the successful prosecution of a trade or a profession everyone admits that a man must acquire special knowledge and manifest special capacity; and on that admission everyone acts. He who has succeeded by conforming to the conditions of success, requires from all aspirants, who may be influenced by him, a like conformity. And as success and failure are patent and undeniable, and their results are for the most part tangible and at once known, the ways and means, the premises and conditions, of causes leading to either result have been well tested and ascertained. But it is a trite remark that the most part consider themselves to be at once and without thoughtful preparation competent to guide each one his own life, and such also, as if it were a necessary consequence, believe themselves able and

qualified to guide the life of others generally, or of the whole
nation. And of success therein they think that exact knowledge,
wielded by natural ability disciplined and cultivated, is but a
slight cause; chance, opportunity, stratagem, and tact, in their
secret belief, govern all. Perhaps recent events have diminished
the popularity of this view.

In trade and manufactures, in agriculture, in navigation,
in the circulation of goods and passengers by land, in
military and naval warfare, in every legal process, we
are in the region of exact and accurate nomenclature,
wherever in fact, results bear due proportion to the expenditure of
power. But in politics another state of things obtains:
the terminology is so inexact, and the general terms so vague and
unprecise, that, as we daily hear, a man may make a very successful speech to an applauding audience, and yet it may be hard
indeed amid its generalities and platitudes to ascertain what it
was which received approval, or whether speaker or listener had
any clear and knowable meaning at all.

In the business of active life, in war or peaceful industry, in
science—the business of thought, no progress could be made,
nor any course conducted to success, if there were a moment's
doubt as to the terms denoting things or thoughts, or as to the
things and thoughts themselves; yet in politics we find a grand
confusion, so that our royal commonwealth is classed with
monarchies (properly so called), and the present despotic government of France would by most be called a democracy; so that it
might even be thought that a change of our actual into a nominal
republic would be an advance, (whereas all nature teaches that
the more complex and differentiated organic forms are last and
highest); so that measures among us are liberal or anti-liberal
according to the party which takes them up or declares against
them; so that changes which are in their essence conservative
are denounced to the credulous and ignorant as revolutionary;
and that unwise persistence in maintaining that which has
become useless or hurtful is called conservative, though it has
ever been of revolution or rash change the invariable incitement
and cause. It is scarcely needful therefore to defend the expediency of a brief preliminary analysis of government.

The end and object of government either actually is, or is
professed to be, or at least ought to be, the preservation and
maintenance of the National Life in perfect integrity and in
greatest differentiation; or expressed in less abstract terms, to
maintain the unity of national life amid the greatest social and
individual variety; to combine strong government with personal
freedom. And, therefore, the business of government is to protect the individuals of which the nation is composed, as well

individually as collectively, from external and internal aggression. Externally; that is, to prevent the aggressions of other nations: internally; that is, to prevent the aggressions of individuals or classes within the nation upon one another. Government then exists and is created for the sake of Freedom, national and individual.

Freedom, whether national or personal, to be complete or perfect must be limited; if it is unlimited then it is of necessity imperfect and incomplete. To take the case of the individual—for what is true of the individual is true of the nation in this matter—if the freedom is imperfect and unlimited, then the individual may commit unlimited aggression, but he is also liable to suffer unlimited aggression in return. And this by a gross misnomer has been usually called a state of nature; because it, or a state approximating to it, is found among savages and savage tribes; whereas it is adverse to progress and most uncongenial to the nature of man. To distinguish, we may call such unlimited freedom, ungoverned liberty or licence. Complete or perfect, that is, limited freedom, may best be intellectually defined as existing where each one is secured in the full exercise of every faculty in a given subject matter, or in all matters, so long as and provided that he does not prevent a like full exercise on the part of any others. And this in civil matters is called civil freedom; and in religious matters, religious freedom; and in intellectual matters, intellectual freedom; and in commercial matters, commercial freedom; and in social matters, social freedom; and in the whole totality, human freedom, the high prerogative of man. Individuals or nations may be free in one or some and not in others of these matters, or they may be free in all.

It is of principal importance to observe and know whether the limitations on freedom are imposed from within or voluntary, or whether they are involuntary and imposed from without. In the first case, man is either in a given subject-matter, or in all matters self-governed, respecting himself and others according to an adopted rule of conduct, in a word, free: in the second case, he is as to himself ungoverned, and with regard to those associated with him, mutually coerced and coercing. Since what is true of individuals is true of nations, for nations are organic unions of individuals, nations may be divided according to character into two classes: Despotisms, whether autocratic in form or not, the nations of the mutually coerced; and Commonwealths, royal or republican, the nations of the free.

If individual and national freedom is the end of government, and the offspring and parent of civilization, and if freedom means security for each individual in the exercise of his facul-

lies, we have here the standard and criterion by which to
measure and to test all civil institutions, privileges, laws, and
social customs; not alone as to whether they are good in themselves, but also as to whether they are suitable to the character
of the nation in which they subsist. All privileges which tend
or are exercised to curtail the full exercise of perfect or limited
freedom are to be condemned; while privileges, however exclusive,
which tend to maintain and support such freedom, are, so long
as they do so, justified and right. A man will therefore consistently approve in one nation or in one age an institution which
he with equal consistency disapproves in another nation in the
same age, or in the same nation at a different time. To take
an extreme case : the right of sanctuary and benefit of clergy,
two most pernicious institutions, were favourable to progress in a
violent and revengeful age, with a sanguinary criminal law : we
approve them as preparatory, not as final ; they are the vehicle,
not the abiding-place of freedom. So we approve of autocracy
for unruly and despotic nations, yet not for its own sake, but
because autocratic government prepares and as it were compels
nations to freedom; they acquire a capacity and value for it ;
thus misgoverned nations evolve freedom and free government,
but savage tribes must pass through misgovernment or conquest
to become free. Similarly we approve feudal despotism in the
middle ages, because of the prevalent anarchy; and under
certain circumstances, compulsory education, *if effectual and
universal*, because when educated, individuals value education,
and the compulsion then ceases to coerce.

The differences in the character of national governments ultimately and immediately depend on the national character; and
this changes in the course of nature by a slow and irresistible
secular process, which whether in the direction of improvement
or decline, it is impossible by sudden violence to alter or arrest ;
but we can vary the conditions of national life, and by removing
hindrances to progress and initiating beneficial reforms, can
effectually guide and direct, and even gradually by patience,
where it is necessary, completely change, the direction of national
movement. For nations, like national constitutions, are not made,
they grow ; and that which can be done by the Legislator, is to
frame a constitution for, or adapt it to, the actual national state,
and such legislation only will be permanent and natural. In
recent events on the European continent, Cavour and Victor
Emmanuel, and on a great scale Bismarck and the German
Emperor, brought the political arrangements of Italy and Germany into harmony with the life of either nation. The violence
in each case is effective because it was employed to remove obstructions to development. The hindrances were against nature,

the innovations were on her side. The whole political history of England is the record of continual and gradual constitutional adjustment.

In the campaign against Protection and Class-Government, against partiality in commercial and political relations, against Establishment in Ireland, or religious partiality, the victory, being in harmony with nature, has been progress. In the representative reform now introduced, if party-government, which we believe most statesmen in their heart admit has almost out-lasted its time of usefulness—if government based on the counterpoise of local party-majorities and the extinguishment of minorities and honest variety of opinion, is as unsuited to the representation of our highly complex national life as it was well suited to the state of life which gave it origin—if this is so, our movement will succeed, and will be progress towards more perfect freedom, stronger government, wiser and more just laws. On the side of nature, in harmony with the life of England, our victory is sure, even if delayed. And those who aid us are Liberals and true Conservatives—for they conserve good government—and those who are against us, unless they can show that our reform is inexpedient or impracticable, are reactionary and on the side of revolution.

In perfecting representation and defining the sphere of civil government, *Philosophical* Radicals can accord with *Philosophical* Conservatives. Whigs and Tories in party rivalry may take up as a popular measure the mere extension of the franchise. They will take care to retain in their hands the right to "gerry-mander."[*] They may be satisfied with a manipulated expression of the popular voice, but we regard a transfer of the power of government to uneducated multitudes as a calamity; we wish to prevent a course which must end in subjecting government and legislation to a class, none the less despotic because the most numerous. Our aim is to secure for the totality, for every element, the rarest and the highest—for all ranks, all classes, all opinions—the fullest, deepest, widest expression and representation of our whole national life in its most differentiated variety.

If we acquire the habit of regarding national life as a whole,

---

[*] This word is a recent importation from the United States ("American Law Review," Jan. 1872, p. 253 *et seqq.*), where the practice flourishes. When legislators engage in the redistribution of seats, when they define borough boundaries, and divide counties according to justice, and without regard to their own party interests, without bargainings and equivalents and counter-poises, this process is so rare as to be without a distinctive name; when they act as they usually do, they are there said *to gerrymander*, and we, with Dartmouth, Abingdon, Devizes, Aylesbury, Woodstock, Shaftesbury, Wilton, Tiverton, Tewkesbury, Tavistock, and others among us, may borrow the word with intent to abolish the thing.

and as following a path, because from its unity every true nation
has a definite character; in short, if we view it in the only true
light, as a growth and as a force in motion, composed of many
ultimate individual elements combined in one power, we shall
see, as we before remarked, that Government exists and has for
its function the maintenance of that life, and the preservation of
its constituent individuals, and their combined totality in
security from mutual encroachment internally, and from external
violence. Its work is to direct, regulate, ascertain, and give expression to national life. This word Government is used with a
general and also a special meaning. In its general sense it
denotes sovereign power or supreme legislative and executive
authority; in its narrower and special usage, it means the
totality of subordinate, or administrative and judicial functionaries and their multitudinous assistants. For the numerous and
diffused body of subordinates who compose the government in
its narrow sense, are in immediate connexion with, and actively
regulate day by day in details, the general course of the national
life.* And it has not been enough remarked and dwelt upon,
that Supreme Government or Sovereignty exists *for the sake of
directing and regulating this body.* It exists to direct, to
guide, to extend the range or to narrow the sphere, to institute
or abolish, to debate, deliberate, and make rules for its action:
and thereby *to govern.* So that subordinate Government governs,
and sovereign Goverment, royal or parliamentary, directs and
regulates the course of actual government. In its origin or
rudimentary form, tribal chiefs or associated heads of families,
perform all functions pertaining to the tribal life; when most advanced and perfect, government is most complex and developed,
for nature in all living forms works from the simple and general
to the special and differentiated.

We shall begin with a brief sketch of subordinate government, or government in its special sense, as the necessary
active regulator of national life. Taking the more complex forms
as examples, in which the whole is indeed complex but the parts
are each one simple and easy to be compared. The functions of
subordinate government in civilized states are Judiciary and Administrative. I. Judiciary functions are discharged by those
who administer the law with regard to intentional or unintentional aggressions among individuals or against the State. Intentional aggressions, whether by violence or fraud, form the
subject of criminal, unintentional, of all other than criminal law,

---

* Apropos of this, we may quote from the Duc d'Audriffet-Pasquier's
speech, made since these lines were written, "Empires fall, Ministries pass
away, but Bureaux remain."

of which the interpretation of express or implied contracts or
rights secured by documents or customs is the principal part.
IL. Administrative functions divide into external and internal.
1. External : (*a*) Peaceful or ordinary, consist in keeping up communication and facilitating intercourse with other national
governments : Foreign Office and Board of Trade. (*b*) Belligerent
or extraordinary, or maintaining security against external aggression : Departments of Admiralty and War. 2. Internal : (*a*)
Management of Revenue and Expenditure, or what may be
called Treasury functions, including Excise and Customs and
Taxation and Disbursements generally. (*b*) Home Office and
Privy Council functions, or regulation and co-ordination of sub-
ordinate-resident-semi-independent-representative-local-authori-
ties.   3. Superadded functions (the previously mentioned
functions must and can only bo performed by Government, but
these, owing to circumstances, are or may be better discharged
by Government than by private aggregates.   They are therefore
justifiable in theory while and so long as no private organization
exists or can be created to discharge them with equal efficiency).
(*a*) Establishment of Intercommunication, Postal, Telegraph,
and Railway departments : (*b*) Coinage and Currency : Mint
and Bank of England (the latter only so far as it is in relation
with the State).   (*c*) Religious and Educational functions.   (*d*)
Almonary (compulsive) functions : Poor Law Board.   (*e*) Sanitary functions : Privy Council Office, Home Office, Local Boards,
and a whole army of inspectors.   (*f*) Other functions : Charity
Commissioners, Record Commissioners, Greenwich and Kew
Observatories, Ordnance and Geological Surveys, Oceanic
Soundings, British Museum and Library, and the rest.   4.
Colonial.*

Subordinate Government, or Government properly so called,
consists of judges, magistrates, clerks of public legal
offices, policemen, gaolers, and all concerned in the administration of the law ; of the official staff of departments in the
capital, and elsewhere ; of the army, navy (militia and volun-
teers, while in discharge of their duties) ; of the clergy and
national schoolmasters, and of all who in such capacities as are
above mentioned regulate and express the national life.   And
from this general view it will be seen that we have not overrated
its importance : it is from the control and power of directing, or

* Colonial relations are in one aspect best regarded as external, or quasi-
external, and in another as internal ; but though of very great importance in the
empire, the relations of a national centre with colonies and dependencies require,
to receive justice, a separate treatment in more detail than the nature of this
article affords.

from the organization of the national life through this machinery, that civilized states are enabled to maintain and put forth such tremendous force: it makes them emphatically Powers. And for the purpose of regulating the exercise of this power and machinery, sovereignty exists. Let us see how this is done.

Experience has shown that the most effective method of regulating the action of government, as well of subordinate government as also of that supreme government which is called sovereignty, is to divide both into two parts—one *permanent*, the other part *moveable*.

The subordinate government consists of a numerous body of officials, using the word in a large sense, of whom some are collected in the capital and other centres, and others are scattered over the country; but the various subdivisions of this body are connected each with a permanent nucleus of principal officers, men of ability and experience, who reside at the centre of government, and each department is under one or more Permanent Chiefs, or Heads. These chiefs possess knowledge of the details of the business done by their departments, and of the exigencies of administration: they are themselves possible only under settled government. They supply the elements of permanence and continuity. They preserve the traditions of office; they are in the habit of governing. But this very fact of their habitual management, while it eminently qualifies them for superintendence, at the same time unfits them for change. And when the range of departmental activity has to be extended or contracted, or its course and direction altered, new men are best for the work. But new men are without that experience, which is a primary condition of success. The requirements of permanent management, combined with change of direction when necessary, are secured by dividing the headship of each department into permanent and moveable elements. The Permanent Heads administer and regulate the action of the department at each successive moment, but they do not initiate action, or direct or steer its course. New action and change of direction emanate from the Moveable Heads (the Principal and Under Secretaries in each department, and such like). In this way, when the action of a department, or of government generally, requires change or reform, such change is made and superintended by new moveable heads. There is a change in the directors as well as in the direction. If the change is for the worse, and is unsuccessful, the blame is laid on the right shoulders, the moveable heads are changed again, the permanent elements continue.

Now, it is evident, that if the only actual government in a given nation, known to the law, was that body which has been described as subordinate, and there was no supreme government or sovereign, the nation would have to act as pro-sovereign, and exercise sovereign power as best it might. Every substitution or new alteration in the action of government, every change of direction of moveable elements, could only be accomplished by a struggle of parties or factions amid a partial paralysis of the governing power. It would be a grand opportunity for foreign aggression. It would be, in fact, if party differences were great, and party-spirit high, a revolution, either by violence or by form of law. And it is probable that if the party that attempted to seize the direction was weak, and had miscalculated, the party in possession, if the nation was indifferent or favourable, would convert their subordinate position into legally irresponsible government, by the political extinguishment of their opponents.

Sovereignty, whether monarchical or representative, is a contrivance originated and maintained by the necessity of regulating and facilitating this process of transfer, and also for effectually superintending and securing the efficiency of the ordinary and every-day course of government. It fulfils, at times, other almost equally important functions. It supplies a recognised means of effecting and manifesting national action to other nations. It hears complaints, and provides a supreme judge to decide disputes among the classes or individuals of a nation. It presides over legislative changes; it makes war; it ensures peace.

In the course of development, the simplest forms of sovereignty appear first, and the more complex and more perfect later. The object of complexity is to increase security, and ensure the permanence and continuity of political life. National life is maintained by the physical succession of individuals ; political life, or the life of the State, by the continuity of sovereignty or supreme government. And such and so much complexity only is good as serves to maintain permanence, by regulating and facilitating necessary change.

Every nation—except during a period of anarchy, when it may be considered as politically dead, since it is then a mere aggregate of individuals—every nation, during political life, is an organic union of individuals, of whom some are actively governing, and the rest, the great body, are governed. Those who are engaged in active government are divisible into two parts : of which one part exercise supreme, and the other subordinate government. The governed body of the nation, together with the subordinate part of the governing portion, are called politically subject, and the supreme part of the governing portion is called politically sovereign. And this supreme part may be either simple or compound. Just as the moveable heads of

subordinate government may be subject in one capacity, as heads
of departments ; and supreme (as an integral portion of the
sovereign-body) in another, for the individual members of a
sovereign-body are collectively supreme, though subject as individuals ; so also a member, whether individual or aggregate, may
be supreme in one capacity or aspect, without being supreme in
another, or in every aspect.

The criterion, or distinctive mark of Sovereignty, or supreme
power in a nation, whether it be vested in an individual, or in
an aggregate is, firstly, that the sovereign (or supreme individual,
or aggregate) must be determinate ; and next, that it must be
recognised that such determinate sovereign (individual or aggregate) as aforesaid, has authority to command the whole subject
portion, while neither the whole nor any part thereof has
authority legally to command it ; and lastly, it must also be recognised that no external or other power constitutes or maintains,
by legal commands, such sovereign (or supreme person or aggregate) in authority, or has authority to command it.

When the sovereign does not legally or habitually receive
commands, either from within the nation it governs, or from any
foreign power or powers, such sovereign is independent ; and a
nation governed by such sovereign-power is an independent
political society. When it receives no legal commands from
within the society governed by it, but does receive commands
or authority from without, it is a society politically dependent.

In one aspect the sovereign *commands* the nation, directs the
government, controls and guides, or integrates the national life.
In another aspect, the sovereign (whether sovereignty be vested
solely in one, or equally among many individuals, or be vested
in individuals with unequal prerogatives), *represents* the nation
to itself and to other nations, integrates its various elements,
impersonates its national life, and makes manifest the national
vitality. Unfortunately, these two aspects are scarcely ever kept
equally and continually before the mind by political writers.
The true conception of sovereignty, whether individual or
aggregate, is as the General Political Integrator. It receives
influence, it directs energy. Disregarding this, the nations,
especially in modern times, fall into an error, which that great
people, the Romans, always carefully avoided. They agitate to
enfeeble the power of government ; they are driven to extend its
surveillance. Whereas, they ought to limit and define, and
within the defined limits to intensify authority ; while strictly
watching and restraining its exercise. The abuse of authority
is when the magistrate employs his influence or power as magistrate for other purposes than those for which he was appointed,
and is held responsible. But we can only touch upon this
in subordination to our present inquiry.

Nations that are governed are free. Nations among whom government is powerful and clearly defined are free, and well governed. Supreme government, or sovereignty commands, and is not commanded. Before proceeding to the analysis of forms of sovereignty, one observation must be interposed. Most writers take the legal point of view alone, but the statesman's range must be wider than the jurist's. Jurists take law and sovereignty as existing facts, and they proceed to do most valuable work in defining sovereignty, and determining the province of law. But the philosopher should inquire into the conditions of sovereignty, the nature of law, the origin and necessity of government. And the philosophical statesman should bring the results to bear in actual societies.

To the Jurist the supreme individual ruler, or aggregate of individuals ruling supremely, is absolute and irresponsible. It commands, and is not commanded. It receives, it never yields, obedience ; that is, legally, or by law. But the statesman knows that even the most despotic autocrat or democratic chamber is never absolute or irresponsible in fact, and though never, or only in some momentary exigence illegally commanded, yet they may be regarded as receiving *prayers—" preces erant, sed quibus contradici non posset."* They can never be legally commanded ; yet foolish, careless rulers, with small judgment and self-control, are rebelled against and slain or banished, or else dissolved and put to political annihilation. But wise rulers, and all enduring and powerful dynasties and assemblies are wise, govern so as to avoid these prayers and ebullitions. They govern so that occasions for them do not arise.

In the Statesman there inheres, by instinctive tact or by reasoned knowledge, the conviction that, while the sovereign is always supreme and sole in authority to legally command ; it never is, and by necessity of things can never be, supreme in actual strength and force against the nation, for the whole nation, if it puts forth its might, must be stronger than the strongest sovereign body ; that is to say, if the government is of one opinion, and the whole nation of another, and they disagree. But such a divergence ought never to be possible. For in uncomplex national lives the disagreements are plain and patent, and the governors can know and avoid them : and complex national lives should find representative expression.

The object of practical statesmanship is to govern in harmony with the truest and most permanent course of national life ; and the object of philosophical statesmanship is to find, maintain, or improve the form of government which is or may

---

* Quoted from Tacitus, in Austin's Jurisprudence. Lecture I.

be the fullest, deepest, clearest, and most distinct and harmonious expression of the nation and its life. This object, always kept in view by this Review, the promoters of this Bill aim at accomplishing by their present endeavour.

Sovereign power, or supreme government, is divisible according to its nature and character, or according to form. According to its Nature, we divide the concrete instances into Despotisms and Commonwealths, but in scientific strictness this is rather a primary classification of nations. According to Form, they are primarily classified as (*a*) simple: by observing whether the sovereignty is vested in an individual ruling alone, as in Monarchies ; or vests in several ruling together in one aggregate, which we call Pleonarchies ; (*b*) compound: which we call Synarchies, of which among possible forms are (1) two monarchs for life or period, ruling as tenants in common of sovereignty, without a pleonarchy ; (2) two or more pleonarchal chambers bearing joint sway ; while among actual forms are various compound aggregates, in which monarchal and pleonarchal elements are united in the sovereignty, and govern together.

This classification is sufficient for purposes of jurisprudence. Every existing or even possible form of government or sovereignty can, we believe, be described with accuracy by it. But for purposes of statesmanship we must draw two additional distinctions. Both are of great importance. One is between Sovereign-Dignity and Sovereign-Power. The other is between what we will call Actual and Symbolic Sovereign-Power. Although the fact on which both these distinctions are founded has been in the minds of all, and the whole course of English government exhibits them in action, yet, as we believe, they have never before been formally expressed or drawn out into precision in any treatise on jurisprudence or statesmanship. Those masters of political science, Thomas Hobbes and Jeremy Bentham, and that clear thinker, John Austin, demonstrated that the English Royal Person is not a monarch in power ; and that the sovereignty is vested in the Crown and both Houses of Parliament ; but they do not bring into sufficient prominence the fact that in another aspect, that of dignity, the English Royal Person is a true Sovereign-Person ; and the presence or absence of sovereign-dignity is nationally, *in social significance*, almost as great a fact as sovereign-power is politically.

Sovereign-power or supreme government, legislative and executive, judicial and administrative, is with us vested in the Synarchy, which consists of a monarchal-member with hereditary and elected pleonarchal-members, so that the whole power vests in its entirety in every member, while it can only be exerted by the members together. Sovereign-dignity, or supreme honour, vests in the Royal Person alone, as the sole source and fount from which dignity and its expression, rank or title, emanate.[*] No one and no body or order of persons shares this prerogative with the English monarch. By an exercise of the royal prerogative, the Queen or King confers or grants legal dignity or rank upon subjects, so that degrees in the modern, and the right to use degrees in the older universities, diplomas, commissions in the army and navy, as well as patents of nobility, all have origin in grant from the Crown. A peer, as an individual, takes such rank as the monarch has bestowed on him. As members of the Upper House all peers are equal in dignity (as peers, though not in title or rank), as well as equal in power. Each elected commoner, as an individual, takes such rank as the monarch has conferred upon him; as member of the Lower House, every representative is equal in dignity and power. Also the three members are jointly and severally sovereign in the Synarchy.

Let us now turn to the American Synarchy. The sovereign power there is vested, by the written constitution, in a Congress, a Supreme Court of Judicature, and a President; but the functions of sovereignty are vested separately—legislative in Congress, judicial in the Supreme Court, and executive in the President. Freedom is by the constitution maintained with them by checks and counter-checks; with us, by the necessity for harmonious action. The case as to sovereignty, or sovereign-power, is clear; now we will analyse sovereign-dignity. In the supreme government of the United States there is no sovereign-person; the monarchal element is not royal, nor is it supreme. For although the President has a veto-power, yet a two-thirds majority of Congress can supersede the veto, and the House of Representatives can impeach the President before the Senate. It would

---

[*] The great statesmen in the Commons' House, in the reign of Charles I., had this distinction in mind. When the Petition of Rights came back from the Lords amended, by inserting, "with due regard to *leave intire* that Sovereign Power wherewith your Majesty is trusted for the Protection, Safety, and Happiness of the People," in the debate thereupon, "I am not able," said Pym, "to speak to this question, I know not what it is. All our petition is for the laws of England; and this power seems to be another distinct power from the power of the law. I know how to add 'sovereign' to the king's *person*, but not to his *power*; and we cannot *leave* to him a 'sovereign power,' also we never were possessed of it." "If we do admit of this addition," said Sir Thomas Wentworth, "we shall leave the subject worse than we found him, and we shall have little thanks for our labour when we come home. Let us leave all power to his Majesty, to punish malefactors. These laws are not acquainted with 'sovereign power.'" Thus spoke statesmen worthy of England, firm as their Ironside warriors, knowing their own mind, using their words with meaning, valuing the letter as well as the spirit of laws. They were not content with "less accurate" language, and their work endures.

take more space than we can command to show how or why
it is that in the American synarchy the monarchal member is
not equal in dignity to our Royal Person ; but it does not follow
that there is no equivalent, or, to borrow a phrase from comparative anatomy, that there is nothing homologous to our sovereign-dignity.   We must bear in mind that the constitution does
not admit of rank or titles of honour.   America delights to remind her greatest and noblest citizens that the Great Republic
does not honour service.*   In examining the synarchy we shall see
by the peculiar majesty which surrounds *the Senate*, as well
in its origin as in the prerogatives with which it is clothed, that
it is there we find the true homologue of our Royal Person.   Our
sovereign-dignity is monarchal, theirs pleonarchal.

It may perhaps be fitting to trace briefly the synarchal homo-
logies.   Functions which are integrated in the Royal Person
with us, are distributed with them : the Supreme Court of Judicature is homologous with the Queen as supreme judge, exercising her judicial functions through the Privy Council and the
Courts of Law and Equity, especially through the Court of
Queen's Bench ; and the House of Lords, as sharing sovereign
power, in its capacity as Court of Appeal.   The Congress, consisting of the Senate and House of Representatives, exercising
legislative functions is homologous with our royal and pleonar-
chal-elements in their legislative capacity.   The President is
truly homologous, not with our Monarchal-member, as a superficial view might deem, but with the British Cabinet, the Moveable Heads of subordinate government.   When the fulness of
sovereign-dignity disappeared, political power, greater than that
which belongs to our Queen or any Prime Minister, was vested
in the President, but limited in duration to four years ; while,
instead of sitting in Congress, he communicates with it by message.   The homologue of our Royal Person (the sovereign-
dignity being monarchal with us) is the Senate (the sovereign-
dignity being pleonarchal with them), and this is shown especially by the treaty-negotiating and concluding power ; for the
President has, by the constitution, power to treat only when
authorized to do so by Congress, and even then no treaty is valid
until it has been ratified by the Senate.   On all these accounts
we conclude that the Senate is homologous with the Queen, and
the American President with the British Cabinet.   It therefore
seems to us that the British synarchy and nation are at a
disadvantage in negotiating with the American synarchy and
nation, unless the Queen empowers the Cabinet to treat with the
President duly authorized by Congress in that behalf, and then,

---

* Distinguished Americans are esteemed by their fellow-citizens, but from
the nation as a whole they can receive no honour.

on the arrangement of the terms, her Majesty and the Senate make the treaty and exchange ratifications.

It remains for us to observe, that in simple forms of sovereignty, in monarchies the sovereign person is always supreme in dignity, but pleonarchies are generally republican (or unroyal); and we may draw the distinction that in such pleonarchies as would be properly called aristocracies, their members are superior in rank and dignity; while in such as would be called democratic or republican (as contrasted with aristocratic), the members are not superior.

The distinction between Actual and Symbolic Sovereign-power does not exist in jurisprudence. It exists in statesmanship, not in law. Let us take first the case of simple forms of sovereignty. Under a weak monarch, if the minister presiding over the subordinate government becomes so popular that the sovereign dare not displace him, the monarchy may be said to be symbolic. This happened in the case of the French kings of the Merovingian and Carlovingian dynasties (*Rois fainéants*) and the Mayors of the Palace. In Pepin le Bref and Hugh called Capet, the actual rulers acquired full sovereign power by transfer from the symbolic sovereigns. The French sovereignty became an absolute monarchy during the religious wars; it gradually became symbolic during the reigns of Louis XV. and XVI.; after various changes it became a pleonarchy in 1848; but the control of a centralized government in the hands of the Prince President enabled him imperceptibly to make the pleonarchy symbolic, and by the *coup d'etat* to vest the actual sovereign power and dignity in himself, while by the *plebiscite* he placed it on a new and logical basis. Scarcely anything could be more instructive in statesmanship than to trace minutely changes in sovereignty from this point of view.

It is, however, in synarchies that this distinction becomes most important. Where the sovereignty is vested according to constitutional law or established usage in three members, it is evident that in cases of disagreement one member must give way to the other two, or two may give way to one. If space permitted, we would trace in the English synarchy the alternations of actual and symbolic power. As sovereignty with us has rested on the national assent and not, except for brief intervals, and then only partially, on force, we should find that throughout the course of our history each of the three members of the synarchy has become actual in proportion as it has expressed the national will or been an agent of it more efficient than the other two symbolic members. And each member as it has ceased to be in harmony with that will has become symbolic. In the reign of Henry VIII. circumstances had made the monarchal member preponderant. It was necessary to direct the great religious and social changes of the reign. On the death of Elizabeth it developed despotic tendencies, and with an increase of apparent power lost authority. The pleonarchal members together became more and more actual. In the contest for power, in the attempt to change the English synarchal commonwealth into a despotism, the King was executed, the House of Lords dispersed, the Houses having previously obtained legal right to perpetual existence (until they consented to be dissolved), thereby ceasing to represent the nation. True, that is military, monarchy arose and became supreme over the synarchy for a time; but on Protector Cromwell's death the synarchy, restored, though weakened, regained its power. The monarchal member, again actual, became in course of time symbolic, and by a constitutional usage easy to understand, but not easy in short space to explain, was confined to general superintendence and certain important and well-defined functions. But from the coronation of Charles II. the whole synarchy had been gradually becoming the expression of the will of a class or certain classes and interests; and becoming alien to the deepest national life, it became by a necessary consequence symbolic as a whole, and only by the timely passing of the Reform Act of 1832, the repeal of the Test and Corporation Acts, and the series of measures in the same spirit, has it been restored to be that which it ought to be, the complex representative of our complex national life, and the trusty expression of the wisest national will in government.

If our space had allowed us to review at length the events of English history, and to show their significance in philosophical statesmanship, we should have proved that in the synarchy the power of each member exactly as its action was contrary to, or inharmonious with, the course of the national life, declined and became symbolic; while the member which from time to time made itself the exponent and expression of that life acquired a real preponderance, and sooner or later directed the government. Further, that when the general activity of the three members was incongruous with the national action, the governing power declined, and the synarchy *as a whole* became symbolic, or even, to every eye except a lawyer's, was destroyed. Again, when a like fall from a like cause had befallen the new power which had arisen in its place, and the synarchy restored to supreme authority made choice to rest first on the ascendancy of a political and religious party, and afterwards on the support of classes whose common interests were adverse to the national well-being: in the first case, the monarchal member whose duty it was to govern all in the interests of all, failing in that duty, became, and has continued till now, symbolic; and afterwards the Parliament, whose power, once great, had gradually declined, was by a Reform, just in time, saved to recover more than its former authority, and with the Crown to constitute a synarchy which will not easily be overthrown. It is our hope that the reform or rather reinvigoration now proposed will, by making the course and path of government the resultant of all the many and various elements of the national life, strengthen the supreme authority and power of the synarchy, exalt, if it be possible, the dignity and honour of the Crown, and render the Parliament the true and full exponent of the whole manifold life of that which even now, amid drawbacks we do not ignore, is the strong and wise government of a free and therefore a powerful and forbearing nation.

Admitting that practically it is so, it will be said, Why change? For very sufficient reasons. Changes there will be; the first distress or discontent or party rivalry will awaken a demand for a redistribution of seats and for a further enfranchisement. And every change in this direction will make the House of Commons a less and less true representative of the national life, and a more and more true embodiment of the will of one class. And though government by the concentration of all political power in the hands of one class, that class being at once the most numerous, the most sincere and prejudiced, the least inclined to doubt its own capacity to rule, and least wealthy, would not necessarily be bad, yet it would be at all events, to say the least, as objectionable as government by the highest, most educated, and wealthiest class alone, and it would be less likely to be wise. There are other reasons upon which it is not necessary to dwell, because it is useless to reason with those Whigs and Tories alike who are merely influenced in their political action by a desire to keep the preponderant power they have got, and to resist all change. Persons who resist every change as long as they have power to do so, and never learn, are at last compelled to accept any. There are Oligarchical as well as Royal Bourbons.

We must now show the respective functions of the three members of the synarchy, and the nature of the reform proposed as to the election and basis of the third member. For in this question the preliminary introduction and the statement of the case, is of more importance than the litigious argument.

The first member, actual in dignity and permanence, is symbolic in governing power.

The third member, symbolic in dignity and permanence, is actual in governing power.

The second member, is partly actual and partly symbolic. It

has governing power, but less than the third. It has more dignity and permanence, but is subject to renewal and gradual change.

Those ultimate elements which compose the nation, and the
resultant of whose continuous action is the national life, we shall
call *national units.* They are physical individuals, adult men
and women, and children. They are the *factors* of *national
life.*

These ultimate elements, whose action is expressed in the
course of supreme and subordinate government, we shall call
political units. They are electoral constituencies. Their individual constituents are the *political factors.*

The three members of the synarchy, which by their joint
action govern and represent the nation, or in other words inte-
grate the national life, may be called *national political integers.*
The individuals composing each may be called *political coefficients,* the action of each member the *political resultant.*

Her Majesty, in her Sovereign dignity, as the National
Integer, is the Representative of the Nation, and impersonates
its life. As the Political Integer in her individual capacity, the
Monarchal member in the Sovereign synarchy, through responsible advisers, directs the State and gives it continuity. As the
recipient of all representative influence; as the formal centre of
all governing energy; as the embodiment of the abstract State
in ceremonial before the multitude; as holding the threads of
Foreign policy; as, in the theory of law, the supreme temporal
Judge—the Royal Person is an influence and activity whose importance some unphilosophical liberal thinkers have too much
undervalued. But it is not possible within our limits to do
more than touch the functions of Royalty and the hereditary
pleonarchal Member.

In the House of Peers, each Peer as a political coefficient, in
theory represents the whole nation, since the Peerage is unaffected by the alterations of the Suffrage; and the Constitution
seems to have entrusted to them especially the care of those who
are elsewhere in the pleonarchy unrepresented. But, unlike the
Monarchal member, a Peer is not an integer; he does not govern
in his individual capacity. The House is an integer, and governs
or shares in the government, and by its collective action produces its resultant.

In the House of Commons each member of that house, in his
individual capacity, represents, or sometimes more than one
jointly represent, the majority* of a definite local constituency

* The lengths to which majority-worship has been carried by the House of
Commons, may be seen in a letter to the *Times,* appearing May 21, 1872, p. 8,

(the University and the three-cornered constituencies and the City are exceptions), and by his action as a coefficient in the House, in action and reaction with the other coefficients, produces the political resultant.

We propose that henceforth, in the House of Commons, each member of that house shall represent a *personal constituency,* composed of electors who shall have sorted themselves voluntarily, and combined into unanimous political units, or constituencies, according to their political sympathies and antipathies.

The principle of personal as distinguished from locality representation was adopted by the Legislature when it gave members to the Universities. It is therefore in accordance with precedent.

The principle of proportional as distinguished from majority representation was adopted by the Legislature in the three-cornered constituencies and the City, and has been used in an imperfect form in the Metropolitan School-board elections. It has always been our theory. The great variety of the constituencies, as to size and character, has been justified as securing representation for the diverse elements of the whole national life, which it was recognised that equal local electoral divisions would not insure. But the selection and definition of constituencies has been left to party management, or mere party force.

That very complexity which makes synarchy the best form of sovereignty, makes it also the most difficult to describe; for without explanations and qualifications, any description given in the limits of an article must lie open to the charges, either of omissions and inexactness, or of tediousness. But we are compelled to institute a comparison between forms in the synarchy, as to governmental and representative excellence. We will compare the monarchal with the elected pleonarchal form, and in this respect between sole-rule and joint-rule the numerical difference is essential. Take either by itself: that is, compare monarchy with pleonarchy. Monarchy has every capacity for administrative and judicial functions; energy, decision, unity; power to call its agents to instant account, to keep them under the constant sense of responsibility; to accommodate its action

---

col. 3, we give it as a statement of matter-of-fact. "Especially should the practice of the Lords be substituted for that monstrous rule of the Commons, not to hear minorities who protest against a majority, or their representative, bringing in Bills to alter or take away their property or rights. I once found it difficult" (says the writer, Mr. E. B. Denison,) "to convince a very eminent Judge in Chancery that such a rule could exist; and when he was convinced, he required an undertaking that the objection to the minority being heard, should not be taken. I also remember several cases where minorities, and small ones too, have succeeded in the Lords after their mouths had been padlocked in the Commons."

to change of circumstances. In a sudden riot, there is one thing
only to do; there is nothing to find out—a pleonarchy delibe-
rates; a monarch acts. Moreover, there is another great advantage, which we are exceedingly glad to see is patent to all:
the monarchal form *in quiet times* can evoke enthusiasm; exactly what a pleonarchy cannot do. Pleonarchy has every capacity for representation: many men must deliberate, and all distinctions are brought out by full discussion. The nation knows
its own wants more clearly by hearing them stated clearly, and
by competent persons; many plans and courses which at first
seem excellent, are shown by discussion to be open to fatal objections. An assembly has many idiosyncrasies, a monarch one.
It is not so liable to misjudge from want of knowledge; its very
nature, requiring joint action and debate, necessitates deliberate-
ness. Equals cannot act together in any tolerable concert without
forbearance and mutual sympathy. Pleonarchy elicits tact, tests
temper, reveals character. Pleonarchy must be tolerant, hear
argument, follow reason; each member must be responsible, he
may not hand over his judgment to another, though in subjects
on which he is uninformed he must use his judgment as to whom
to trust. In great exigencies, when a nation is full of enthusiasm for a cause, a true representative pleonarchy can sound out
through its many voices the full harmonious chorus of the nation's
purpose. A pleonarchy are irresistible defending law; but in quiet
times a pleonarchy may be dissolved, and another re-elected, it
may politically die, and no one except the election agents
and the members care, except for the inconvenience caused
thereby.

Hence we see that the excellence and capacity of either form
for government (that is, exerting administrative and judicial functions) varies in inverse ratio with its excellence and capacity for
representation.

This may be made still more evident by observing that
monarchs collect round themselves an informing aggregate, to
act representatively and ministerially; they call it sometimes a
Council and sometimes a Divan, and they listen to its advice and
information as it pleases them or not; and pleonarchies do not
govern as a whole, but by a majority of necessity, and through a
chosen one or a few chosen persons, and sometimes a pleonarchy
calls him the Head of the Executive, or in a synarchy they call
him a Prime Minister, and his associates they call a Cabinet, and
in either case the Chief or the Cabinet expresses the pleonarchal
action.

Now, there are many ways of doing this. When a Prime
Minister receives influence from the whole synarchy, and rules

in accordance with the synarchal resultant, we call him a Governor, and his activity governmental ; but when he rules through an acquiescent majority, like a miniature autocrat, we call him a Vizier. Vizierial government acts with a transient energy and gets into scrapes, because, being in character arbitrary, it cannot cause a uniform activity to pervade its subordinate government, and so sudden destruction comes upon it in a moment.*

Leaving viziers and other transient appearances, let us return to permanent manifestations of power. Want of space prevents our giving the theory of the Cabinet, and the theory of the respective functions of the Crown and the hereditary and elected Houses of Parliament.

Proportional representation has been involved in unnecessary complexity by mingling the general principle with the details employed to carry that principle into effect. We shall state the principle, and point out where information as to the details can be found.

The principle is that every voter (or political factor) should exercise his franchise by one vote,† that every elected member (or coefficient in the elected pleonarchy) should be elected by an unanimous constituency, that every constituency should be equal in numbers. To effect this, divide the whole number of votes cast at an election by the whole number of seats to be filled, the quotient will be the number of votes (or quota) required to seat a member at that election. *This principle of proportional representation* was first suggested, in 1859, by Mr. Thomas Hare, in a pamphlet, "The Machinery of Representation," of

* When a powerful party-majority, elected under a party cry to carry out a definite policy, submit on other questions their whole power to the dictation of their leader, the unmanageability of the leader varies inversely with the manageableness of the followers. So much power being confined in an elastic vessel, liable to sudden ebullitions, produces, by its reactions with the recalcitrant and independent portion of the party, and with others, strange results, which may be easily described with clearness and precision. If a powerful government were to result from the co-ordination of Philosophical Radicals with Philosophical Conservatives (that party might as easily become philosophical, as philosophical radicals might with the present distribution of power become conservative), it might be defined as A Governmental Aggregation occasioned by differences growing out of acts committed by an Ambiguous Vessel whose emergence into political supremacy has given rise to that which is generically known as the Submissive Portion of the Liberal Party.

† This is quite consistent with one person's being clothed with several franchises, but he must only have one vote for each franchise ; he might exercise a franchise, as a householder and as a graduate of a university as at present, he might have an income-tax franchise also.

which a second edition was published in the same year; and
with full details subsequently in a treatise.*

The best descriptions in a moderate compass are in chap. vii.
of Mr. J. S. Mill's philosophical treatise "On Representative
Government," a work whose reputation is so high that it would
be unbecoming in us to praise it; and a popular view, in two
eminently clear articles by Millicent Garrett Fawcett, reprinted at
the end of "Essays and Lectures" by Professor and Mrs. Fawcett.

Several plans or ways of carrying out the principle have been
given in full detail. Each has advantages of its own.

The Preferential Voting System, or Mr. Hare's plan. The details for carrying out the principle as given by its originator are
well known; they have been charged with complexity, and they
certainly require as much attention in the reader as would enable
him to master an ordinary act of parliament. Those who expect
to find works of legislation as easy reading as "Lothair" are
naturally disappointed.

These details have been adopted in the Bill at the head of our
article, a Bill remarkable alike for its masterly arrangement and
clearness. Matured in its details and arrangement by its pro-
poser, Mr. Walter Morrison, M.P. for Plymouth, with careful
deliberation, it has been elaborated by the technical skill of an
eminent draftsman.

The Free List, or the Registered Ballot, has been urged with
great earnestness by M. Ernest Naville in Switzerland, and with
modifications in France and the States of Illinois and New
York.†

The Fixed Transfer System, or Mr. Walter Baily's plan,‡ gives
less trouble to the voters than Mr. Hare's, but necessitates a
careful supervision of the clerks at the central office. It effects,
by a very perfect series of additions and subtraction, the appro-
priation of votes and transfer of surplus votes.

The Free Transfer System, or Mr. Archibald E. Dobbs' plan.§
Under this the voter selects the candidate of his choice, and the

---

* The Election of Representatives, Parliamentary and Municipal. Third
Edition, 1865, pp. 350.
  † Breve exposition du système électoral de la Liste Libre. Genève: 1869.
Also : La Réforme Electorale en France, par E. Naville. Paris : 1871 ; and La
Question Electorale en Europe et en Amérique, par E. Naville. Genève et
Bâle : 1871.
  ‡ Advocated with much ability in several pamphlets published by Ridgway,
Piccadilly : 1869-71.
  § General Representation, on a complete readjustment and modification of
Mr. Hare's Plan. Longmans : 1871. Second Edition. 1872.

candidate, if he has surplus votes, deals with them according to his judgment, acting in concert with his supporters, and after consultation with his committee and friends. He will act as the voter would have acted in the new state of affairs arising after the distribution of the votes is made known. It places trust in the candidate to elicit trustworthiness, and exacts responsibility. This plan is the simplest and most flexible; but those who dislike responsibility and trust will dislike it.

Now we refuse to discuss the details of these plans; any one of them is good, and a combination of all would be best. But the very worst, whichever it may be, would be better than the present majority system. One general election would render it safe, and the next general election demonstrate its success. We believe the change, if public opinion were duly aroused and elicited, might be effected as easily as disestablishment in Ireland, without exciting any resentment except among the political wire-pullers and party leaders, and when made would approve itself as thoroughly to the nation as the new Table of Lessons has approved itself to the congregations of the Church of England.

It is not fair to contrast an established method of voting with the first trial of a new principle. But perhaps before these lines are published there will only be the comparison of two new modes. Our old English way of honest open voting, each one before his neighbour and in the face of day, will have passed away, and a new method, noted by Gibbon as accompanying the decline of the great nation which was once the free and law-honouring commonwealth of Rome, a new method of secret voting will have taken its place. We would make the parliament reflect the nation; we would raise the government to the moral level of the governed. Are the constituencies such that a man cannot vote honestly in them? OPEN THEM; let in more light. Are they closed and corrupt? Open them; let in the air of heaven —let in the honest day. It is that cursed love of byways, that fondness for circumlocution, for vague phraseology, for understandings without a plain bottom to them, which, set forth with persuasive tricks of language that would do honour to the Son of Maia, have beguiled the Liberal Party in the House, and for awhile coaxed away the judgment of the constituencies. Let the Bill pass: neither slavery nor secrecy can thrive on the English land.

It is not fair—as we remarked before our indignation got the better of us—to compare a new method with the known course of a working institution. We will suppose the new method has been some time in action, and the little rubs at first start have been surmounted. Each of the plans grapples honestly

with the initial difficulties. We have to deal out justice. Let
us suppose that the second parliament elected on the principle
of proportional representation has been dissolved, and that the
writs are issued for a general election. Let us see what the
electors and the candidates have to do. We shall not enter into
the details of redistribution or machinery. We shall suppose the
members to take their seats as at present, only that the members
have been elected by a sufficient number of voters residing anywhere, the voters being free to vote for any candidate. Throughout the course of the parliament just supposed to have been
dissolved, each voter will have belonged to a personal constituency, composed of the voters whose voting papers were finally
appropriated to the member representing them. They will have
freely sorted themselves, and there will be harmony between
their member and themselves. Each constituency will amount
in number to about two thousand, sometimes more, sometimes
less. Each member will have a nominating committee of about
twenty of the best known among his supporters, whose names
will be a guide to his political opinions, and who during the late
parliament have been a connecting link and means of communication between himself and his constituents. He may also
nominate a committee of parliamentary allies, whose names will
be on his own committee, while his name will be found on theirs,
among whom, or at least with whose concurrence, he will distribute
or transfer his surplus votes, if he should have any. They will also
act in concert with him. Every voter will be free to vote for the
candidate for whom he voted before, or, if he is dissatisfied, to
vote for some one else. In each constituency there will be a
general agreement among its factors, with differences on minor
points. Some will represent localities, their constituents will be
gathered from certain neighbourhoods, some will represent
various political principles, some religious bodies, some trades,
some professions. Where several members differ but little as
individuals, holding the same principles and agreeing generally,
their supporters will unite into a constituency aggregate, larger
or smaller as the case may be, and will vote for their representatives in concert. But each candidate will be under the new
system as anxious to show his individuality and differentiate
himself as he is now to suppress himself and use doubtful or
discreet language. Remarkable individuality is always un-
popular, there is no fear of its becoming too common.

Under this system distinguished men and all leading statesmen
will have sure seats, every man of eminent ability, every man
who can identify himself with an interest possessing two thousand
votes will be returned again and again. There will be no longer

doubt as to whether a great leader may obtain or lose a seat. It seems to us a condemnation of our electoral system that the return of Mr. Gladstone to Parliament should have been for a moment doubtful.

Let us now, instead of examining the action of the con-stituencies upon one another, take them singly, as independent totalities, and view their structure and the way in which their vitality will be maintained. Each constituency or political unit we shall describe, for convenience sake, as consisting of a centre, the representative; a nucleus, the committee ; and constituent substance, the electoral factors or the voters who form the quota. The terminology is convenient and the analogy perfect. Each political unit may be regarded as forming itself by the aggrega-tion of its constituent factors into a nucleated cell, out of the *political blastema*, or totality of enfranchised adults secreted from the adult totality of the nation. The constituencies are personal ; that is, collected by assimilation, and unanimous, or coherent ; that is, organized, and politically *vital :* not at all like those locality-growths which will, we hope, be rejected from and by the political system.

Let us suppose then that certain definite principles are awaiting a candidate to represent them, or that a certain candidate has enunciated definite principles. We will now contemplate the process of *political cytogenesis.* The constituents may aggregate themselves first, the candidate may then be regarded as coming to them ; but a candidate may by the enunciation of principles or policy collect a new aggregate for himself out of the surround-ing blastema, or general mass of electors ; but in either way let there be certain unanimous constituencies, each with a candidate in harmony with it. Every aggregate of about 2000 voters is sure to seat its candidate.. A nucleus has been formed in each composed of about twenty of the most important and prominent leaders among the constituency. Wise candidates, in well organized, that is, strongly vital constituencies, will take care to be in close communication (which need not be constant, if you really agree with a man you do not need continual conferences to ascertain each other's thoughts and actions) with each member of his committee, and will see that each of the twenty can com-municate with one hundred factors, when necessary ; and at any moment, with ten among the hundred, who will each transmit the communication to ten factors, so distributing it through the whole mass. Our organization would be worthless if it did not work as well with the ballot as without it ; we utterly disbelieve that electoral bauble. In dealing with dead matter dead mechanism is a great fact, bear witness all our industrial progress ; but in po-

litical organization the mechanism ought to be alive. Every voter
or factor in each constituency will be certain to have his name and
address entered in books belonging to the committee. These
books will be kept by two or more paid or honorary secretaries
or election agents. Notices and communications will be sent to
or by them. Every voter who keeps his name upon the books
of a personal constituency will, of course, be understood to vote
for the member representing that constituency. Let us suppose
that a parliament is to be elected. Constituencies of 2000
pledged voters and upwards are sure to seat their candidates ;
some candidates will go to the poll with small constituencies,
and will look for support to what we call political blasterna, or to
attract dissatisfied voters from other political cells. These
constituencies will soon become firm and organized, and yet they
must always remain free and perfectly flexible ; and each factor
will have a distinct and undivided interest in his representative.
Let us now suppose the parliament just elected to be dissolved.
Each candidate and his agents will be able to make a good guess
as to the support he will receive. The voters whose names are
on the books of his constituency will nearly all vote for him, and
if a celebrity he will be sure to receive some stray votes. We
hope it is now perceived that these constituencies will have a
real and strong vitality, and that instead of the country being
upset and thrown out of balance by this proposed reform, it will
be much more compactly organized, and far less liable to sudden
and violent changes.

Let us now watch one of these personal constituencies.
Suppose one or two or a few voters take offence at their representative's conduct. They will write to him, or to the secretary,
withdrawing their names. Perhaps they may receive an explanation, or a remonstrance. Very likely the same conduct has
conciliated other voters, who write promising support. Suppose
half a constituency are offended, they with probably a moiety of
the committee remonstrate. This is serious. If the representative has made a mistake, or if he is squeezable, he promises
amendment. If he believes himself right, or is obstinate, he
justifies himself. If they cannot agree, the member and the
dissatisfied portion, at the next election each state their case, and
paint each other black, and the constituency becomes an object
of general interest. Here we may observe a case of spontaneous
fission. There will go to the country the old representative with
his moiety, and a candidate will at once be found, or offer
himself, as representative of the dissatisfied portion. Each will
strive to attract votes, one, perhaps both, will collect quotas, and
be seated. Suppose that nine-tenths of the constituency are

dissatisfied, and only two or three committee members with one-tenth of the constituency are prepared to support him at the next election. The candidate is firm, and prepared to defend his conduct. He will probably give up all claim to represent the individuals composing the constituency, will put forth an address to the electors generally, and supported by his one tenth, consolidate a new constituency on a new basis. If he is a good man in the House he would, under the Free Transfer System, be kept in by surplus votes from his friends until he obtained a quota.

Let us now take the individual voter's point of view. An elector, either dissatisfied with the constituency he has previously voted with, or else about to vote for the first time, looks out among the candidates for one to choose and support. Very likely he fixes on some well-known statesman, or some exponent of the views and wants of the trade, profession, or neighbourhood in which he has most interest. Perhaps he does not choose to pledge himself, although he can change his mind at any moment. If so, he gives his vote, and we will call it a stray vote. But everyone who exerts power likes to have it recognised, and we will suppose he writes to some candidate, or if Parliament is already elected to some member, or his secretaries, desiring that his name should be entered as a supporter. He receives a note, telling him that they are happy to enrol him among the constituency, which, as it already numbers about 4000 voters, is enabled to return not only Mr. A. B., whose powerful advocacy of their principles (or their interest, or the neighbourhood, as the case may be) is so effective, but also to return Mr. C. D., who has proved such a constant ally, and most important coadjutor, and so on. Let no politician be afraid of these aggregations becoming too large. The more numerous a constituency the greater will be its tendency to disintegrate or subdivide. Besides, as Mr. C. D. becomes more known, he will collect a little aggregation of supporters around himself, and finally separate from the parent cell, either in a friendly or unfriendly way to take up, by a process of budding, an independent political existence.

In some cases, a converse process will be taking place. All opinions are not spreading; some are growing less popular. Members and constituencies who honestly hold such principles will first see the number of stray votes diminish, and finally drop off. Next, voters will remove their names, and no fresh voters will fill their places; the candidate will find the numbers he polls will be insufficient to give him a seat, and will be in-

debted to friendly help. Lastly, the committees of some such
candidates will urge their constituencies to coalesce; several
weak constituencies will make common cause, and fuse their
principles. They will adopt a "platform" or "ticket," become
a large and apparently strong aggregate returning several members; still they will decline, and unless they are reinvigorated,
will seat now five, then four, three, two, at last one representative, and finally disappear from political existence.

Each constituency will have a distinct individuality—a definite character of its own. The representative will both give and
receive influence. Voters when they have the power of selection,
will feel an honest pride in belonging to an honourable political
unit. And this influence, acting constantly and imperceptibly,
is most valuable. We acknowledge that we rely greatly on it,
in the new state of things, for the effectual elimination of bribery,
and of dishonest political promises and professions. Now a
necessary result of the change from local to personal constituencies will be to bring out the value of character and trustworthiness. It is a great truth that the untrustworthy cannot
trust. And the power and weight accruing to representatives of
character, honour, high-spiritedness, and ability, will compel
voters to discriminate. It will become a most important means
of education. Everything is tending more and more to cause
people to be valued, not for what they are, but for what they
have. If a man wishes to get the greatest amount of respect
and consideration with the least amount of labour, let him make
a fortune, and perhaps invest it in land. Now this state of feeling leads to national ruin. For though valuable qualities are
necessary for success in the race for great wealth, yet as a rule
they are by no means the highest. Any one can make a fortune
who has fair average abilities, who keeps his word, is temperate,
industrious, has sound judgment, and gives his mind to it.
But he must not be chivalrous, he must not be scrupulous, his
conscience must not be above the average level, and he must be
prompt to take every advantage of his competitors; he must be
sharp, he must be pushing. We are so accustomed to compare
the respectable man of good wealth-acquiring qualities with the
criminal and vicious, that we fail to see what a low level respectability is after all. Even such respectability is often only on
the surface: men of another stamp get on quickest: these are
the lucky speculators, the adulterators, the dealers in shoddy,
the bubble-company floaters, the contractors of scamped work,
and those who delight in the achievers of such exploits. In the
eyes of such prosperous and well-to-do men, who can be more
contemptible than Michael Faraday? He might have made

half a million, and he lived poor. He only enlarged human
knowledge, added honour to the name of England, lived a
blameless life, and died renowned throughout the world.

Was anything great or good ever done by these men of quick-
won wealth, and by these words we mean, in plain English, dis-
honestly acquired riches? Men who have got rich by public
jobbery, political fraud, by short measures, light weights, puffing,
adulteration, unfair use of capital causing unfair use of workman-
organization, lying prospectuses, legal or illegal suppressions,
breakers of implied trusts, false balance-sheets, cooked accounts,
and all the abominations that cause political and national desolation. Upon such men as these comes in honest nations the
good administration of just laws to dock their gains and paralyse
their power; and under base governments upon them bursts the
invader and the communist and the avenging conflagration.

Commerce and manufactures and agriculture and trade must
be honest, and they are honest in the main. But when honour
and respect and social deference is given to mere wealth as
wealth, the endurance of the weak will break down. They will
be corrupted. Honestly won, or well-used inherited wealth, is
rightly honoured; a wealth-acquiring capacity is rightly honoured
in its place. But a man of science, a true thinker, a philosopher,
has every quality for worldly success, and some that are almost
incompatible with it. Men who gain wealth quickly must be
pushing men. But *push* is alien to intellect. Intellect is
power; it is not push. Was ever any man with a talent for
"getting on" noble-minded? A noble-minded man may have
a talent for getting on, but he will use it nobly, that is, for others
as well as for himself, and that is not getting on. These mere men
of wealth, without a thought for anything else—these men of
push, and go, and shrewdness, are mere political scum. What
is most noteworthy in scum? Its way of getting to the top, and
making a great display, mostly frothy. But there are many
ways of rising, and scum rises because good liquor has more
weight.

All our electoral arrangements are constructed for the express
advantage of these men of wealth. And therefore we make war
on our electoral arrangements. The style of people who think the
whole duty of Royalty is to give balls, to lead fashion, a necessary
duty indeed, in its place : those who bring the Crown to the standard of pence-spending, and if it fails in this, away with it ! who
value Royalty for its expenditure, and Government for its penu-
riousness, except when government will do a job for them—to
such the whole function, the whole duty of government is to pour
more money into their lap. The thunder of revolution and the

sacking of the shops of London, would show the true functions
of government if its ceaseless watchfulness were withdrawn for
six hours. What does the House of Commons represent? It
represents money, especially money invested in land or manufactures. What ought it to represent? It should represent men.

If the House should represent men, it must represent them
according to their characters, and so we come again to what we
said before, that each constituency will be individualized, and
will have a characteristic representative. Some will turn their
member into a delegate, they will only have the sort of man who
will submit to act as such. Some will bully. They will have to
represent them a political sneak. Some constituencies will be
purchasable, and such assuredly will sell themselves. Some will
trust their representative, at the same time holding him strictly
responsible. They will have great statesmen for their members,
honourable and trustworthy men.

We would now, in short space, show the effect of this principle
upon bribery and intimidation, the two chief forms of political
corruption. Intimidation is worse than bribery. In our judgment the great guilt is *to be bribeable;* it is in relation to the
moral state a comparatively small matter to be bribed. In fact,
the main fault seems to us to rest with the legislation which forces
votes on those who have no political convictions, who are indifferent. We would wish to see every man who has deliberate
convictions represented. It was remarked to us a day or two ago by
a friend, that although the intimidator is worse than the briber,
yet the man who is bribed is usually worse than the man who is
intimidated. For the bribed takes what, if he chooses, he may
refuse; but the intimidated is often overcome because he fears
for the welfare of those who depend on him. Besides, intimidation is the greatest evil in the State, for it maddens those who
endure, and the honest who hear of it.

Intimidation with proportional representation and open voting
is very difficult; with secret voting it is impossible. It is of no
use. By preventing others from voting a man does not enable
his own candidate to obtain a quota, nor if he has a quota does
he make his return more sure. When members are seated by
voters having qualifications within a limited area, if you drive
an opponent out, you may have seated your man. But by our
plan, if he is driven away, he only retires exasperated to vote
elsewhere. And he can vote anywhere for any one.

Intimidation is a crime; it is an invasion of a man's freedom,
of his political security. A private individual or a mob step in
to prevent the exercise of rights which the law has given, and
which they do not choose to allow. But bribery is wrong in a
different degree and on other grounds. We must take human

nature as we find it. If a man takes a bribe he betrays his
electoral trust, but he betrays it equally—for the vote is entrusted
to his best judgment—if he votes out of social good-fellowship,
or to oblige a friend, or out of prejudice, or from pique. And these
you cannot touch. And a candidate who flatters his party, who
uses sophistical argument to salve an almost acknowledged wrong,
or who appeals intentionally to prejudice, acts quite as injuriously
as the man who gives a money bribe; and legislation cannot hinder
him. We, therefore, look to the gradual and sure elevation
of general morality for the extinction of corrupt influences of all
kinds.

Wherever men who want money are willing to sell their votes,
and men who have money are willing to buy them, bribery will
take place. Let us face facts, and ponder them to reduce the
evil to a minimum without sacrificing principle. We do not
propose to regulate or recognise bribery, any more than we
recognise theft. We acknowledge facts. Some personal constituencies will be constituted on a basis of bribery. The fact
will be known, though it will probably be very difficult to prove
it. But we believe, and can give reasons therefor, that there
will be much less bribery than at present. Let us take one of
these constituencies. There will be an ostensible committee,
and two honorary secretaries, with the usual machinery before-
mentioned, and a go-between in the background. He will be in
communication with the candidate on the one hand, and with
forty or fifty deputy go-betweens, each acting as agent for about
fifty voters or thereabouts. There will be a competition among
bribing candidates and among bribeable voters and their go-
betweens. Each voter will require the market price, and the
agents must receive a commission for their trouble. It will all
be done quietly. There will be constituencies willing to sell
their votes to Liberal candidates, but not to Conservative, and
others willing to do the reverse. But let it never be forgotten
that there will be constituencies which will not sell their votes,
and these will be represented by the men of power.

In many cases men have accumulated fortunes in business at
home, or in the colonies, or in India, or a man has succeeded to
wealth suddenly by inheritance or bequest; and in middle life he
finds he has attained his objects; he retires from his occupation,
or returns home, and he feels in want of employment. He has
vigour, information on special subjects, and capacity. He turns
his thoughts to politics. Men such as he are wanted in the
House. They are good representative men, of sound judgment,
practised in affairs; but they have no standing before the
public, and are unfitted by nature and training to act the
demagogue. Does such an one act very wrongly if he employs a

part of his wealth in getting a seat in the House? If he has
good in him he will have an honest quota at the next election.
Many voters, enfranchised by our law, agree with him politically;
under the local majority system they will vote for him, coerced
or cajoled by wirepullers and election agents; by our plan they
are induced to vote by the plain and unvarnished influence of
two or three pounds sterling apiece.

Facts are facts. We may treat them as men of science, or
as the ostrich in travellers' tales. We admit what we see.
Nevertheless we propose, that if it should be proved before a
court of law that money has passed with a corrupt intent between
a candidate or his committee, or his or their agents acting for
him or them on the one side, and voters on the other, such candidate and voters should be disfranchised for seven years. Let
it be observed that each election fines such representatives, and
does no damage to the unbribing. *Cantabit vacuo.*—The
honest will rejoice.

We have done little if we have not shown the unspeakable
change from false professions forced from candidates, to open
statement of political opinion; from wrangling and electoral
quarrelling, to honourable competition; from intimidation, to
freedom; from bribery in the form in which its influence is
most baleful, to that in which its evil is least injurious. It is a
change from the Land of Bondage to the Free Commonwealth, the
Land of Peace and Safety, the Land of Promise, the Holy Land.
Not in a great march of multitudes, but by an organic growth,
removing wisely every hindrance to the full development of
man; in our legislation welcoming every influence, weighing
every statement, every character, every member, every man:
each co-efficient, every factor, each integer, each political unit
contributing its just proportion to our National Life:—all serving
and all served. As in the great evolution of humanity each
Nation-member dedicates itself a royal gift—English science,
German philosophy, French method: Hebrew religion, Roman
law, Hellenic thought,—Ancient and Modern times alike,
all join and blend in harmony, all form essential portions of one
great and ever-energizing Whole.

Art. II.—English Philology.

King Alfred's West-Saxon Version of Gregory's Pastoral Care. With an English Translation, Notes, and an Introduction. Edited by Henry Sweet, Esq., of Balliol College, Oxford. London: Trübner and Co. (Early English Text Society.) 1871-2.

MANY things indicate that the neglect with which Englishmen have long treated the older stages of their language and literature is gradually disappearing, and that an interest in scientific philology is becoming generally diffused. The elaborate and admirable work of Mr. A. J. Ellis "On Early English Pronunciation" has called attention not only to English spelling and pronunciation, but to general phonetics; and the alphabet published in Mr. A. Melville Bell's "Visible Speech" has afforded the means of representing sounds in a far more simple, exact, and systematic manner than had previously been thought possible. The careful study bestowed by these writers on branches comparatively neglected on the Continent has enabled them to make substantial contributions to philology, so that the English student possessed of a knowledge of the science as far as it has been carried in Germany is placed in a position to discover new principles, and to follow out in new directions those enunciated, but not fully appreciated, by foreign investigators.

That Alfred the Great's translation of Pope Gregory's "Pastoral Care" is now printed for the first time is a proof of Englishmen's neglect of their early history and literature; that it is the first of Alfred's works (indeed all but the first work of his period) printed from contemporary manuscripts is a proof of their indifference to the development of their language. The Early English Text Society, which has in Mr. Sweet's edition brought out its first "Anglo-Saxon" work, has for eight years been carrying out its object of making our early literary and linguistic documents accessible in a cheap and accurate form. Even if it did no more than this, and this much its editors have generally done, it would have done much; for apparently it is only now becoming known that for philological purposes the first requisite is to have correct copies of the only evidence in existence, the writing of the scribes. The support received by the Chaucer Society, which is working in this solid manner, is still miserably small; and the Early English Text Society itself has not as many subscribers as it deserves. While insisting, however,

on mere accuracy, we must not be understood as depreciating
good editing; it is most valuable to the student, and none the
less so from its rarity. But good editing does not consist, as
many German philologists seem to think, in making it so much
the worse for the facts if they contradict theories. If an Old
English, and still more, if a Middle High German work is edited
by a German, the chances are strongly in favour of any word
spelt in a way not considered normal being altered, and it is not
often that the editor thinks it necessary to give the MS. form in
a note. Most of this critical editing, as it is called, involves no
more criticism than the duties of a printer's reader, and can consequently be done by any one acquainted with the elements of
the language; when it does require more, it is necessary to give
reasons for the alterations proposed. Mere mistakes of spelling
in MSS. are not nearly so common as many editors find it
convenient to assume; isolated peculiarities often, common ones
always, point to corresponding peculiarities in the language or
the orthographical system of the scribe of the MS. itself, or of
that from which it was copied. If an editor possesses knowledge
and judgment, the more of his emendations of the text, and of
his reasons for them, the better; but if he wishes his edition to
be of use to philologists, he must give the original text itself.
Unless he thinks that there is nothing more to be learnt in his
branch of philology, and that he is never ignorant or mistaken
about anything it includes, he is not even logically justified in
giving the world only what he thinks the witnesses meant to
say, not what they did.

The present edition of Alfred's work (which comprises, besides
Gregory the Great's excellent treatise, an account of the motives
that led the King to translate it) contains the full text, on
opposite pages, of two of the MSS. written by the King's direction, and the readings of a third. One of these MSS., Hatton
20, in the Bodleian, has fortunately been preserved almost
entire; the second, Cotton Tib. B. xi., which was incomplete,
has been nearly destroyed by fire, so it has been printed from the
copy of Junius (Jun. 53, in the Bodleian), whose accuracy,
wherever it can be tested, is remarkable. The third MS.,
Cotton Otho B. ii., which has also been injured, is later than
Alfred's time; but the first half of it seems a careful copy, and
is therefore philologically valuable. At foot of the text Mr.
Sweet, in conformity with the custom of the Society, has given a
translation, though, as he remarks, the chief result of so doing
will be to prevent proper study of the original. The translation,
though necessarily by no means perfect, has at least the merit of
being in the language it ought to be, the usual prose English of
the third quarter of the nineteenth century, instead of being full

of obsolete and provincial terms, dragged in, with scant regard
for meaning and intelligibility, because they have a real or
supposed etymological connexion with the words of the text.

For linguistic details we refer to the editor's introduction and
notes, in which most of the points calling for notice are carefully
discussed; we would draw special attention to the summary of
the chief differences between the language of the ninth century
and that of the eleventh. The forms of the latter are the chief
part of those to be found in grammars and dictionaries; but
owing to compilers never discriminating between contemporary
MSS. of eleventh century works, and those which are imperfectly modernized copies of older ones, the more ancient forms
are frequently to be met with. In fact, between German editors
who "correct" their texts, and English editors who think accurate
copying beneath them, the ordinary student has been left without proper materials for study, even when the MSS. published
possessed the first requisite of philological trustworthiness, that
of being written in the language of the time and place of the
original author. Even now, a German, Dr. Grein, who has published an edition of all extant Old English poetry, proposes to
reprint all the published prose works from existing editions, without
comparison with the MSS., and of course without at all inquiring
into the linguistic value of the MSS. themselves. The natural
result is, that the history of our language during the first few
centuries of its existence on English soil, and the distinguishing
features of its various dialects, have remained unknown, all attempts at explaining its later stages being thereby rendered uncertain. Mr. Sweet's examination is sufficient to prove what had
been suspected by careful investigators of the history of sounds,
that many modern English forms do not derive from the Late
West-Saxon of Elfric, but from older forms preserved in other
dialects. We join in Mr. Sweet's hope that "the results of these
investigations will help to dissipate the wide-spread delusion
that Old English has been thoroughly worked up, and that
nothing remains for us but to accept blindly the theories of
Rask and Grimm." At the same time it should be pointed out
that ignorance of these theories is not, as some seem to think, a
qualification for correcting them; especially if, as often happens,
they are held to include the facts constituting the correspondence between Old English and the other Germanic
languages.

It will have been noticed that a change in nomenclature,
which some will think wrong, and many useless, has been made
by Mr. Sweet; he has discarded the term "Anglo-Saxon" in
favour of "Old English." As the reasons for this alteration
appear to us both unanswerable and important, and as the

editor has confined himself to the remark that the received
name is barbarous and unmeaning, it may be well to state them.
As to the philological propriety of the name Old English
there can be little question. In the development of our language
three chief periods, with two transition ones, are clearly distinguishable. The first, the one we are now considering, which
extends from the eighth to the eleventh century, preserves the
original Teutonic vowel-quantities, and has the full vowels
a, o, u, regularly in many terminations. Then comes the
transition period commonly known, from its confusion of the
old inflexions, as Semi-Saxon, of which Layamon is an example.
In about a century this gives place to Middle English, which is
characterized by the lengthening of many accented short vowels
in open syllables, the simplification of the substantive and
adjective declensions, the frequent loss of final *n* in inflexions,
and the change to *e* of the vowels of almost all unaccented
terminations. The presence, in the latter part of this period, of
many words borrowed from French, though necessitating a knowledge of Old French on the part of the student of English, has
no influence on the phonetics of the English words, or on
inflexions and syntax, so there is no reason for dividing the
period into two, and calling the first Old English. Middle
English, specimens of which are the Ormulum and the Canterbury Tales, lasts for barely two centuries, the thirteenth and
fourteenth; the northern dialects assume the features of New
English considerably earlier than the southern. The fifteenth
century is, at least for the literary language, the second period of
transition; the final *e* disappears from speech, causing the loss
of many inflexions, the conjugation of verbs is gradually simplified, and the accent of many borrowed French words is thrown
back. This accomplished, we are in the New English period,
during which the most important changes, disguised by the
retention of old spellings, have been in the vowels of accented
syllables. Taking the extremes, the language of the eighth
century is, on the whole, not more different from that of the
nineteenth in England than in Germany; indeed, the development of English is remarkably similar to that of High German,
though the latter language, at every stage, is in some points
more antiquated. English, unlike Latin, has not branched into
several independent languages, so there is no practical or senti-
mental reason against its various periods bearing a common
name. Besides, there is not, as there is with Latin and the
Romanic languages, a part of its development of which we have
no memorial; its history can be traced without interruption for
more than a thousand years, and even the oldest of the other
Teutonic dialects stands to Old English in the relation of sister,

not of parent. A common name, which would be an innovation in the case of the language of the Romans and the so-called Latin races, is just the reverse in this; Alfred and our other early writers call their language *Englisc*, as Chaucer calls his *Englisch*, and as Shakspere calls his *English*. The name Anglo-Saxon for the earliest period of our language was unknown till the seventeenth century, and is founded on an erroneous theory combined with ignorance of facts. The term Saxon was borrowed from medieval Latin writers to denote the language of the Teutonic invaders of Britain; the prefixes Anglo, Dano, and Normanno were used to distinguish three imaginary periods, ascribed respectively to Anglian, Danish, and Norman influence; and as the first period was supposed to be the purest, and as the prefix served at the same time to prevent confusion with continental Saxon, Anglo-Saxon has been for about two centuries the received name. Mr. Cockayne, seeing the absurdity of the term, and finding Old English used for Middle English containing few French words, has chosen "The Oldest English;" but this is clumsy and too limited. As with German, the adjectives Old, Middle, and New are sufficient and convenient for marking the principal periods; Modern is generally used for New, but it causes an awkward confusion with Middle when abbreviations are employed.

To turn to more general considerations: we think the name Anglo-Saxon has exercised a very prejudicial influence on the study of our language, literature, and customs during the centuries of our national existence which preceded the country's recovery from the disturbance caused by the Norman Conquest. We are only now discovering things which ought to have been known long ago, as that the Feudal System found in England well-established legal customs with respect to land, that it was forced to a great extent to conform itself to them, and that absolute private property in land, whatever its merits, is a growth of the last few centuries. Equal ignorance is general on the subject of our early literature, which is usually treated as if "Anglo-Saxon" had as little to do with English as Welsh has, and which is termed rude and barbarous by critics who have not gone through the training necessary to appreciate it. To take only one point, that of the comparative beauty of Old English and Greek (or Latin) metres; it is maintained by some who are equally familiar with both, that the Old English epic metre is decidedly superior in variety and flexibility to the "classical" hexameter, while the question of melody may be set aside until readers of the "Iliad" are in the habit of preserving the original accents and quantities, and are then capable of appreciating the metre by the ear, not merely by calculating the number and arrangement of the syllables they have been taught to call long or short. As to the language, it need hardly be remarked that until quite recently there was more chance of an Englishman knowing Sanskrit or Chinese, not to mention Greek and Latin, than the early form of his own tongue. If that stage had a name indicating, not concealing, its connexion with the later ones, we should not so unconcernedly have left it neglected.

An unexpected and unpleasant proof of how little has been done for Old English, is pointed out in Mr. Sweet's preface. It appears that the basis of all existing dictionaries except Grein's Glossary to the Poems, is the MS. work of Junius made two centuries ago. This was copied, unacknowledged, by Lye, who has himself been copied, directly or indirectly, by all succeeding compilers; so that the learner of the nineteenth century has for sole guide to the prose language a certainly careful, but necessarily very imperfect, glossary of the seventeenth. It happens that amongst the forms in the " Pastoral" overlooked by Junius, and therefore unpublished till now, are the Old English originals of two familiar words which have given etymologists considerable trouble to little purpose. These are *bedegion* and *geon,* of which our *beg* and *yon* are the legitimate descendants. How many other important words exist unknown in other MSS. it is of course impossible to say; and Dr. Grein, notwithstanding his industry, will not help us to find them out. From his reprints mentioned above, he intends to make a dictionary which will not be a mere compilation from others; but we fear it will in many respects be worse than useless for advancing our knowledge of the language. From its appearance of criticalness and completeness a value will probably be attached to it which it cannot deserve, and the mere fact of such a work being published will to a great extent stop the way to any other, good or bad, on the same subject and scale.

In an appendix Mr. Sweet has discussed, chiefly with reference to the Low German languages, the celebrated formula of consonantal correspondence known as Grimm's Law. Many of the literary English public, since the appearance of Professor Max Müller's " Lectures on the Science of Language," must be familiar with the symmetrical table which represents the correspondence as it exists in the minds of most philologists. The chief defects of this striking arrangement are that the same symbols represent different sounds in different places, and that in several cases the real sounds are quite different from anything the symbols were ever supposed to mean; that it does not give half the facts is comparatively of slight importance. It is true that these defects are generally more or less imperfectly pointed out, but as

soon as an attempt is made to account for the law, they are forgotten, the simplicity of the original diagram proving too attractive. It is therefore not surprising that all explanations hitherto
given should involve unsupported hypotheses, and should hardly
apply to what has to be explained. Grimm accounts for the differences of the Teutonic consonants from those of Sanskrit and
Greek, by supposing that the Low Germans, with that abundance
of energy which distinguished them from the degenerate inhabitants of the Roman Empire, changed (to take a single instance) the soft *d* to the hard *t*; and that the High Germans,
similarly distinguished from other Teutonic nations, repeated the
operation by changing the hard *t* to the aspirated *z* (= ts). Professor Müller, seeing that if some of the changes are strengthen-
ings others are weakenings, and not liking the hypothesis of two
opposite phonetic changes occurring simultaneously, boldly maintains that there have been no changes at all, but that the differences—which, it may be remarked, do not exist in all cases—
are original; in spite of having just before demonstrated the
original unity of the Aryan languages, and of proceeding immediately after to show that these different consonants were the
distinctive part of different roots with different meanings. Therefore, believing that when the ancestors of the Hindus used DA
(we do not venture to alter Mr. Müller's notation) to express a
certain idea, those of the Low Germans used TA, and those of
the High Germans THA (or perhaps *za* = *tsa*), to express the
same idea; and similarly that to the TA of the first, with
another meaning, there corresponded the THA of the second
and the DA of the third, and to the THA of the first the DA
of the second and the TA of the third; and believing that these
various ancestors lived together and understood each other's
speech, Mr. Müller manages also to believe, to take two instances out of twenty-seven, that when an original Hindu said
DA, an original Low German must have divined him to mean
TA (for the Low German's DA meant something quite different), and an original High German to mean THA (or *tsa*);
and that if a Low German said DA, the Hindu took it for his
own THA, and the High German for his TA! Now, though the
proposition may seem so self-evident as not to require stating, all
believers in the original unity of the Aryan languages need to
bear in mind that they cannot consistently maintain that there
existed original diversities; or that to the same differences of
sound some people attached one set, and some another, of differences in meaning; or that a theory of strengthening, supposing that any of the phenomena in question are strength-
enings, and that the theory has any external probability, explains
changes which include, on that view, equally great weakenings.

Before any more satisfactory theory could be proposed, it was necessary to state the known facts, and to do this with accurate and unambiguous symbols. The compound sound, that of *t* followed by that of *h*, of the ancient Greek thêta, and the simple one of the Icelandic thorn, the one usually expressed in English orthography by initial and final *th*, must be distinguished in writing; for convenience of printing we must use here Mr. Ellis's symbols—all, for distinction, in parentheses—(tn), (th). The latter of these sounds must also be distinguished from that of the Icelandic crossed *d*, the usual one of medial *th* in English, and of the initial in pronominal words as *the*, *there*, *though*, which may be represented by (dh); and this last again must be carefully distinguished from the Sanskrit true aspirate (dn). These distinctions made, much of the symmetry disappears; but the changes begin to be phonetically intelligible. Mr. Cockayne's observation that some of the earlier Old English MSS. use only ꞅ, led Mr. Sweet to infer that at this period but one of the (th) and (dh) sounds existed, and that this one was (dh). Mr. Sweet afterwards found that other early Old English MSS. use only the rune Þ, and that the earliest of all have the Latin *th*, the representative of the Greek thêta, which in the seventh century apparently had its present sound of (th). When Old English was first written with Latin letters no non-Roman signs were introduced, and for (dh) the symbol for (th) would be the only one available. Afterwards a more exact symbol was chosen; some took a crossed *d*, others borrowed the runic Þ, itself formed from D. That these new signs have as base *d*, not *t*, is a strong alphabetical reason for believing that the sound they represented was then, as that of (d) is, vocal, that is (dh), not (th); equally strong phonetic ones are the frequent interchange in Gothic of *d* and Þ, both corresponding to an original Aryan (t), and the also frequent occurrence of *d* in place of *th* in the oldest documents of the Low German languages. This latter fact points to the sound of Gothic *d*, in cases where it interchanges with that of Þ, being the older of the two, an inference which is confirmed by the general laws of sound-change. The passage from (d) to (dh) is simple and familiar; in Greek, for instance, the delta, whether initial, medial, or final, now represents (dh), not, as in Cicero's time, (d). The change from (t) to (th) may appear equally simple, but few cases are known; that of (t) to (d) is common, at least medially and finally. As to the direct changes of (t) to (dh) and of (d) to (th), both are equally violent and unheard of. One part of Mr. Sweet's theory, then, is this: that at some period after the separation of the Germans from the other Aryans the original (t) became (d), which last is, as we have seen, frequently preserved in Gothic and other Low German languages; and that this

(d) afterwards became (dh), always when initial, generally when medial or final. Dutch and High German subsequently changed this (dh) to (d), thus appearing more ancient than they are; in late Old English generally, in Icelandic always, initial (dh) was changed to (th), which in Danish has since become (t). It is this stage of the changes which is exhibited by the Teutonic words borrowed by the Romanic languages; with hardly an exception these have initially (t), elsewhere (d), for the Germanic thorn. This points to the development of the (th) sound from (dh) having taken place initially at a comparatively early period in those dialects from which the Romanic words were taken. The same change of (dh) to (th) took place afterwards at the end of most English words, and apparently about the same time almost all the remaining instances of (d) between vowels became (dh), the change begun centuries before being thus nearly completed.

There remain to be explained, in the dental series, the change of original (d) to Low German (t), and that of original (dн)—which, not the Greek (tн), is the earliest sound—to (d). These changes are in themselves simple enough; the first is merely the loss of vocality, and the latter, which has occurred in Latin and most other Aryan languages, the dropping of the post-aspiration. The difficulty is to explain how they and the former one took place without at least two of the three original sounds (t), (d), (dн), running together as (t) or (d), in which event the language could never afterwards have separated them in accordance with the original distinctions. The confusion apparently involved in (dн) and (t) both changing to (d) would not exist if the change in the former case were indirect; if, while (t) changed to (d)(dн) became only the assimilated (dd), this afterwards being simplified to (d) when (d) became (dh). This conjecture of Mr. Sweet's as to the double (dd) is confirmed by the shape of the runic letter for (d), which is that of two Ds back to back; it is very probable phonetically, and satisfactorily solves the problem. The other question, how original (t) changed to (d) and original (d) to (t), without both being (d) or (t) at once, is not so easily disposed of. If the changes were successive, there is no means of escape unless we assume intermediate steps, for which at present there seems to be no evidence, direct or indirect; if simultaneous, the dilemma is avoided, but we have two exactly opposite phonetic changes taking place at the same time. Mr. Sweet prefers the latter hypothesis, and considers the phenomenon one of simple interchange, such as is believed to occur with Cockney *v* and *w*, and *h* and no *h*. But these cases are doubtful, and no similar instances are known, so we cannot consider the explanation satisfactory. This appears to us, however, the only weak part of Mr. Sweet's theory of the *lautverschiebung;* though there is

another point, the change of the voiced (dh) to the voiceless (th),
to which exception will probably be taken as contrary to the
general tendency of phonetic change, from strong to weak. The
apparent anomaly, for it is only apparent, is caused by forgetting
that in language a diminution of exertion is possible only in
making sounds, not in hearing them. Vocal sounds, such as (dh),
are softer than non-vocal ones, as (th), because they involve the
additional labour of approximating the vocal cords, and thus
checking the rush of the breath. Any physiological alphabet—
that is, any alphabet whose letters show how the sounds they
represent are made—makes it obvious on inspection that vocal
sounds require a set of motions additional to those required for
their voiceless correlatives, and that consequently the change
from voiced to voiceless, not the converse, is the real weakening.
A clear instance of the change is afforded by those Welsh words
with initial *ll* which have been borrowed from Latin, where
they begin with *l*, the former sound being the voiceless correla-
tive of the latter; as in *lleidr* from *latro.* The frequent examples
of the change from voiceless to voiced are almost invariably due
to assimilation, the necessarily voiced vowel causing the extra
exertion involved in a voiced consonant to be generally felt as
less troublesome than the exertion of changing from a voiceless
consonant to a vowel, or from the latter to the former.

We have examined the theory only so far as it relates to the
dental sounds, but it applies equally to the labial and guttural
series; for differences of detail we refer to Mr. Sweet's appendix.
Setting aside all conjecture, however probable, we give those
parts of the history of the Low German *lautverschiebung* which
we think Mr. Sweet has established as satisfactorily as can be
done with any historical fact. These are, that original (t) became
first (d), and then (dh). before it became (th); and that original
(p) became first (b), and then (v), before it became (f). Any one
who agrees with this will not hesitate to accept the parallel
changes in the guttural series, of (k) through (g) to (gh) and
then (kh)—the German *ch*; though the evidence in this case is
more scientific and analogical than directly historical. The
change, in most Teutonic languages, of all gutturals and labials
before (t) to (kh) and (f) respectively, is comparatively late, the
older (k) and (p) frequently occurring; and the hypothesis
still laid down in the best German philological works (as in
Schleicher's "Compendium der Vergleichenden Grammatik der
Indogermanischen Sprachen," 3te Aufl., 1871), that (t), (p), and
(k) became (th), (f), and (kh) by passing through (th), (ph), and
(kh), is entirely baseless. It was, no doubt, caused by Grimm
(who knew little of sounds, and nothing of phonetics, though he
laid the foundation of the science,) mistaking the digraphs *th*,

ph, ch, now representing (th), (f), and (kh), for the similar
Roman combinations representing the Greek (tH), (pH), and
(kH) ; and the fact that these Greek sounds have undergone the
change required by the hypothesis has helped to keep up its
credit. There is not the slightest direct evidence for the con-
jectural intermediate (tH), (pH), and (kH) ever having existed in
the Low German languages ; that they preceded the New High
German (s), (f), and (kh) arising from Low German (t), (p), and
(k) is hardly doubtful, but this change, affecting also borrowed
Latin words, is too recent to afford more than a presumption in
favour of a similar one having occurred centuries before. Now
that the common early Teutonic changes are proved to have
taken an entirely different course, it is to be hoped that the
symbols of the above-named hypothetical sounds will disappear
from tables of Grimm's Law, where they serve only to keep
up an appearance of analogy between sound-changes which
differ exactly in those points on which the supposed analogy is
founded.

There could hardly be desired a better example of the confusion caused by mistaking letters for sounds, and writing for
language, than the ordinary statement and explanations of
Grimm's Law. Any accurate representation of the facts, even
in the clumsiest orthography, shows the confusion ; but it requires a physiological alphabet to exhibit clearly the relations of
the facts. Yet comparatively few philologists are acquainted
with any such alphabet, and but few of these are in the habit of
employing it for phonetic investigations. This may be partly
explained by the two German ones, Brücke's and Merkel's,
being ill-suited for writing, and having acoustic, not physiological, signs for the vowels. This last defect leaves the relations
of the vowels to each other and to consonants as unrepresented
as by the common Roman letters, so that these alphabets fail
just where their assistance is most needed. But this does not
account for the small progress Mr. Bell's alphabet, by far the
best of the three, has made amongst English philologists. The
merits of this alphabet are twofold. First, the analysis of sound-
formation presented by it is, as to the consonants, but rarely
behind, and often in advance of, any other ; and as to the vowels,
minutely exact, and the only one in existence. Secondly, the
three "Visible Speech" alphabets, for printing, for common
writing, and for shorthand, possess in a higher degree than any
previously existing alphabet the practical requisites of a system
of writing ; they are remarkably legible, and the two last are
still more remarkable for the ease and rapidity with which they
can be written. Being founded on the same analysis of sounds,

knowledge of one reduces the labour of acquiring the others to a little practice; being systematic, they are far easier to learn than the Roman or any other traditional letters. Each of the Visible Speech letters is a combination of two or three of a few simple signs, each of which is a suggestive direction for some part of the vocal organs; so that the learner who is once familiar with them is in little danger of forgetting how to make the sounds the letters represent. Still, great as are the merits, in almost every point, of Mr. Bell's analysis and representation of the modes of making speech-sounds, the phonetic analysis of language has to be carried considerably further before a complete and exact system of universal writing can be devised; and till this is done, no phonetic alphabet can be proposed for general use except as a makeshift, entailing, in addition to the unavoidable inconveniences of any extensive change in popular orthography, the recurrence of these inconveniences at no distant date.

Before, too, any phonetic alphabet can be used by the general public without having its name made inapplicable, a sound knowledge of the elements of phonetics must be generally diffused; and this, notwithstanding the constant and well-founded complaints of bad elocution, public and private, has as yet hardly been attempted. It seems to be thought that there is less need to superintend a child's acquirement of speech-sounds than the growth of its nails, and but few of those who desire to give the superintendence are competent to give it. Not that the subject presents great difficulties; it is much less troublesome than learning to write clearly, another mechanical art which most people seem to wish to prove they never studied. Bad articulation is very easy to acquire, and, unless corrected early, troublesome to get rid of; and seeing that deaf-mutes are now taught to speak better than many of their more gifted brethren, the latter have not much excuse. Without such a knowledge of phonetics as would be general were these hints acted upon, however well the alphabet might be adapted to the language of certain speakers at a given time, the gradual change of that language, and existing diversities, would soon render the alphabet as traditional and unphonetic as our present orthography. And this is far more certain to happen with an alphabet which uses the common Roman letters, whose association with the sounds they represent is purely arbitrary and devoid of system, than it is with one whose signs represent sounds by their formation. For, with a little practice, it is easy to tell whether the sound we make is that represented by the symbol, provided the symbol tells us how its sound is made; but if the symbol gives us no information on this point, how can we tell whether the sound we make is, or is not, that which was associated with the symbol by the original adopters of it ? For acquiring and communicating what is now known of phonetics, as well as for suggesting and recording advances in that knowledge, and by this means preparing an alphabet which may be worthy to supersede its details, though not its principle, Mr. Bell's alphabet is far superior to any other. His notation of phonetic facts of language has the advantages of algebraical and chemical formulas; relations of sound, and analogies of sound-changes, whether previously noticed or not, are presented with a clearness, succinctness, and suggestiveness unattainable in the best verbal description, and impossible with any non-physiological letters. The work ("Visible Speech") which explains the alphabet contains also the phonetic analysis on which it is based, an analysis which, though sometimes imperfect, is very rarely incorrect, and which presents a greater quantity of phonetic knowledge in a more intelligible and workable form than any other treatise on the subject; so that the student who has acquired a theoretical and practical knowledge of its contents will be better prepared than most for phonetic linguistic investigations.

Indispensable as a phonetic alphabet is for philology, it is not therefore inapplicable to general purposes; if it were, the public would be justified in leaving philologists to enjoy its benefits. On the contrary, its immense practical advantages are too obvious, and have been too well expounded by others, to call for much notice here. If each symbol represents but one sound, and each sound is represented by but one symbol, the time and trouble required for learning to read, and still more, for learning to write, would be so much reduced that our notions of what it is possible to teach to those whose schooltime is limited, would be revolutionized. A knowledge of the letters and their sounds would involve the power of reading, and the power of spelling; so that the only difficulty in writing would be the mechanical one of making the letters. That a physiological alphabet possesses these advantages in a greater degree than one founded on the Roman alphabet, and has many of which a non-physiological one is necessarily destitute, is almost equally obvious. Such an alphabet, representing not merely the sounds which happen to be recognized as existing in a single language, but all sounds producible by the vocal organs, is destitute of nationality, and is therefore international. To one acquainted with the symbols of his native sounds, the symbols of foreign ones will, from the systematicality of the alphabet, in most cases explain themselves; the difficulty of acquiring them almost vanishes, their physiological formation being known. Leaving these remarks for the consideration of those friends of education who doubt whether it is advisable that a great part of its elements should continue to consist of learning an extremely difficult, clumsy, and inadequate contrivance, which is of no use in itself, but only so far as it represents something else, we will call attention to a part of the question of orthography which is generally ignored by both the supporters and the opponents of reform in writing and in spelling.

This is the accurate notation of pauses, and of the length, the force (stress, loudness), and the pitch of speech-sounds. These three things are parts of all sounds, as much as their quality is; and it is only voiceless ones, such as *s, f*, which have a fixed tone dependent on their organic formation. In most of the cultivated languages of Europe, a large portion of the meaning of the sounds forming language depends on these elements, and no system of writing which does not mark such important constituents of speech can claim to represent language as it ought to be represented, so as to give the meaning of a speaker as fully and exactly to the reader of the written symbols as to the hearer of the spoken sounds. Formerly, indeed even now in many languages, tones were of little consequence for meaning. In Sanskrit, Greek, and Latin, each word had a definite inflexion of the voice on a particular syllable, which inflexion, though sometimes subject to modification in consequence of the position of the word in a sentence, could rarely be changed to indicate shades of meaning. In most of the Scotch dialects every phrase has the same inflexion; some give to every sentence, whether a question or an answer, a rising tone, others a falling one. It is from this fixity of tone that Latin was obliged to use particles to indicate whether a sentence is a statement or an inquiry, and had hardly any means of calling attention to a word except putting it out of its usual place; and a remnant of the same state in our own language is the inversion of verb and nominative to mark a question, though the now invariably accompanying rise of tone is of itself sufficient to distinguish it from an assertion. In Latin writing tones were rarely marked, because they could easily be determined from the length and position of syllables; but in Greek where tone was, to a considerable extent independent of these other elements, it was found necessary, for the benefit of those learning the language, to mark where and how the tone changed. If such a notation was advisable in a language where the tones of a sentence were independent of its meaning, much more so must it be where the meaning of a phrase is to a great extent dependent on its tones. Our pronouncing dictionaries attempt to give a rough notion of length and force, so far as these are fixed for each word, and our elocutionary manuals do about as much for variable tone and pause; but if a Frenchman ignorant of the meaning of English, and not having heard it spoken, were to attempt reading it aloud

with no guides but these dictionaries and manuals, a perfect
knowledge of the difficult English consonants and vowels would
hardly suffice to prevent his utterances being unintelligible to
an Englishman. And bare intelligibility is generally a very low
degree of that quality ; one that may be sufficient for ordering
what we shall eat, and what we shall drink, and wherewithal we
shall be clothed, but is not at all adequate for scientific and
practical purposes, and is far less so for social intercourse.
Almost every variation of tone, in English at least, excites different thoughts and emotions, which, though generally subordinate to what is known as the meaning of the words, are often
the chief part of the real meaning, and sometimes the whole,
even reversing the apparent one. Except perhaps in a geometrical theorem, a writer wishes to do more, and less, than give a
bare statement of facts and arguments, which few would care to
read but those with a special interest in the subject. He wishes
to excite those various subsidiary thoughts and emotions on
which style mainly depends ; to convey much by hints, rather
than at full length ; to keep alive the reader's interest, if to do
nothing else. A person may do this very well in speaking, but
when his speech is represented in common writing, all the tones,
accents, and quantities, and most of the pauses, are left to be
supplied by the reader. Very likely the reader supplies only a
few, and thinks the printed speech tame ; or he supplies them
wrongly, and mistakes part of the meaning ; or he finds that two
sets, which give different meanings, apply, as far as he can tell,
equally well, and then accuses the author, of the ambiguity
caused solely by the inefficiency of the orthography. And great
as are the mistakes thus caused as to an author's meaning, the
mistakes as to himself are often greater. From reading a writer's
works we not only find out what he intentionally tells us, as far
as his meaning can be conveyed to us by the words and the
orthography he uses, but we draw inferences as to his character ;
and very different estimates of this will be formed, according to
the tones we unconsciously attach to the written phrases. In a
poem or a novel, in which the author's personality is either sunk,
or presented in one of his own creations, this is of less consequence ; if he has ordinary skill, the characters of the personages
will be so unfolded as to admit of little mistake on the part of
any reader capable of appreciating them. But in a political
treatise, for instance, the case is different. What with one set
of tones is a sorrowful statement of a melancholy fact, is with
another an insulting sneer at opponents ; what is meant as the
calm expression of a conviction, may be taken by an unsympa-
thetic reader for absurd declamation. The effect these differences have on the reception not only of the opinions main-

tained in a single work, but of all others advocated by its author,
or by the school to which he belongs, hardly requires to be
stated.

In philology phonetics is gradually assuming its due importance; it is beginning to be known that language is nothing but
sounds associated with ideas, so that to ignore sounds is to ignore
an essential part of it. Teachers of Latin, for instance, are
becoming aware that when we give to the letters which represent Latin words the values they happen to have in our own or
any other modern language, we may have a language, but we
certainly have not the language spoken and written by Plautus,
by Cæsar, or by Suetonius; and that when we read Latin verse
much as if it were English prose, we may have metre, but we
certainly have not the metre of Virgil or Ovid, or anything like
it; and that we consequently have no more right to call our
results Latin than we have to call the result of reading a printed
work of De Musset or Heine with the English values of the
letters, French or German. But the phrase "written language" still exercises that power of confusion for which its
ordinary use admirably fits it. If a man has been photographed,
he may be called a photographed man; but few people would
apply this name to the photograph, and no one would be thereby
induced to take the picture for a human being. Similarly, if a
language has been represented by written symbols, it is appro-
priately called a written language; thanks to travellers and
missionaries, there are now few which have not a more or less
perfect claim to the title. But the term is also universally used
to denote the representation, and, further, to distinguish the
representation from the original, which has therefore acquired
the name "spoken language;" as if the term "photographed
man" came to be applied chiefly and distinctively to portraits,
so that men had to be called "living men." As if this were
not sufficiently confusing, writing is not only called language,
but believed to be language. Many philologists think that when
they have compared those always imperfect and often incorrect
representations of languages which, except with living tongues,
are the sole means we have of knowing them, they have discovered linguistic relations; and if they allude at all to the
sounds which are the real languages, treat "pronunciation" as
an accident of little importance. More accurate results would
be obtained by studying men solely from rough and faded
portraits; little mistake is possible as to the meaning of the
artist's symbols, however conventional they may be, but the
determination of the phonetic values of letters is one of the most
difficult parts of linguistic investigation. If we neglect either

sounds or thoughts we cannot have a better scientific knowledge of language than we can of man if we neglect physiology or psychology.

Of course there is one sense of the word "language" in which it is as strictly applicable to writing as it is to speech, and but for which the above-mentioned confusion could hardly have arisen ; a sense in which it includes a glance of the eye and a deflection of a telegraph needle. In this sense it is possible to have a written language, such as Bishop Wilkins's "real character," which has nothing to do with speech, and which calls up ideas of things directly, not through ideas of sounds ; but it is not in this sense that there exists a science of language, which is the case only with traditional sound-language. Even in practical life the confusion produces much evil ; people think they have but one set of signs to learn, and they have really two, which in English, at least, have very little connexion with each other. Most persons believe that the spelling of English words, with perhaps a few exceptions, represents the pronunciation ; but if there is a question as to how a given word ought to be sounded, they unhesitatingly affirm that the "best," or the "proper," pronunciation is that which follows the spelling. This would be very well if each letter or combination of letters represented but one sound ; but as this is very rarely true in English, which sound is to be chosen in a given case ? And if, as almost always happens, there are several pronunciations of a word, which of them does the spelling represent ? Each individual usually settles these questions as he does many others of greater importance, by laying down what he believes to be his own practice as the rule for all.

Until public opinion on this subject is much more enlightened, it is useless looking for any real reform of our present mode of writing and spelling. People ignorant alike of the history of language, of the history of writing, of phonetics, and of alphabetics, propose or oppose alterations in that chaotic assemblage of inconsistencies known as English orthography ; and whatever part of their plans is specially unphilological is brought forward in the name of etymology. In effect, that orthography which we praise as traditional because it keeps some of the forms of fourteenth-century spelling while abandoning its phonetic principle, conceals from us the state, and therefore the changes, of our language. Strange as some of Chaucer's spellings are to a modern eye, much stranger would his speech be to a modern ear ; and the same is true, to a less extent, of those of Shakspere. But even in the sixteenth century the adherence of printers to the forms they had learnt in youth had caused the theory to be started that the object of writing was not to represent the

language of the day, but that of some centuries before. Even if
those who suggested this theory had been able and willing to
carry it out without error or exception, we should have known
no more, than we do from the scribes of the earlier period; its
adoption, though but partial, has rendered our knowledge of the
language of the period in which the adoption took place considerably more imperfect, and much more difficult to attain, than
it would otherwise have been. Our present spelling does not,
except by a fiction, represent our present language, but rather
that of the fourteenth or fifteenth century; and even this is very
badly represented, because various inconsistent attempts to suit
the orthography to the language of the day, or of some earlier
time, have been partially carried out, and then by the continuing
change of sounds rendered worse than useless. In some cases,
such as *author*, the so-called etymological spelling has actually
led people into giving a sound (th) which is not the descendant
of any that originally existed in the word; so that etymologists,
by inducing a notion to write, not what it speaks, but their own
guesses at what it or some other nation might once have spoken,
have only succeeded in disturbing that regularity of change
which makes general, not merely singular, propositions true in
etymology. When philologists appreciate as well as the least
advanced mathematical student, that it is an essential condition
of accuracy for each symbol to have but one value (however
general) in the same investigation, we may cease to hear some of
them advocating, in the interests of their science, a system which
sacrifices facts in an unsuccessful effort to attain external uniformity.

It is the unavoidable misfortune of philology that almost all
the materials for its study are literary, and that the sole exceptions, living languages, are popular. At the present day it is
usual to find a work on linguistic science classed with poetry
and novels, which have as much affinity with it as with a
manual of zoology, and rather less than with an historical treatise.
Ordinary readers are thereby encouraged in the belief (often
well-founded) that their notions of right and wrong in language
are entitled to as much respect as their opinions on esthetic points.
Many, too, of those who are qualified to pursue literature think
they need nothing else to become good philologists; they might
as well think that taste in arranging bouquets is the chief requisite, or indeed requisite at all, for the successful study of
vegetable physiology. People destitute of any knowledge of the
science consider themselves not merely competent to edit manuscripts in any language they understand at all, but entitled to
claim the attention of the public for opinions and hypotheses

which, even if partially correct, ignore the facts that many philological points have been established during the last half-century, and that discoveries in a science are rarely made without study by those unacquainted with its elementary facts and principles. Others confound knowledge of languages with knowledge of language, a linguist with a philologist; it would be as correct to think that he who can use a word and spear is therefore well acquainted with the chemistry of iron. Some knowledge of languages is of course indispensable for an historical and scientific account of them, and the greater the knowledge the more perfect, other things being equal, will be the theories constructed from it; but a language, as well as a pump, can be used, and used well, by those who know next to nothing of its nature and history.

The natural result of the dilettante way in which philology has generally been studied in this country, is that a philologist has been considered by most people as a cross between an antiquary and a postage-stamp collector; one who accumulates for the pleasure of accumulating, and values things solely because they are old or rare. In enlightening public opinion here, Professor Max Müller, by his " Lectures on the Science of Language," has had no small share ; the really popular way in which he presented the linguistic results of others with his own mythological speculations, attracted many who had thought philology one of the most unscientific and uninteresting pursuits. But the evil effects of thinking that, because it sometimes assists literature, it is merely a branch of this, are still painfully obvious. The derivations in our etymological dictionaries, and to an even greater extent in provincial glossaries, are too often disgraceful and ridiculous absurdities. If the compiler has learnt any language not familiar to all educated people, he generally tries to derive everything from it, without regard to chronology or history. Works on etymology, or on the origin of language, which to one acquainted with scientific philology appear in much the same light as a treatise on alchemy to a modern chemist, stand a good chance in this country of being not merely reviewed, but recommended. Public writers who on other subjects take care to be well-informed or silent, make statements on linguistic points which are excusable only, but fully, because most people, however well educated, have not learnt enough of the science to know from whom to learn more, and are consequently to a great extent at the mercy of any one who appears to know a little. Many even of those who know something of the subject mistake a collection of details for a science, and think that acquaintance with a number of disconnected derivations is sufficient and necessary to make a philologist ; as schoolboys beginning chemistry think more of coloured precipitates and explosions than

E 2

of the law of multiple proportions, they attach greater importance to a few curiosities than to the most striking generalizations. Others, forgetting that special laws of sound-change are empirical, not universal, extend to all languages at all periods every rule which holds good for one; thereby reducing etymology nearly to that primitive condition in which it was correctly defined by Voltaire as "a science in which vowels are of no consequence, and consonants of very little." General laws of sound-change certainly exist, as is obvious when sounds are written according to their formation ; but, like most laws, they state simply tendencies, and our knowledge does not enable us to determine the forms in which they are manifested in any language except from itself.

The important results, in various departments of philology, obtained by those recent investigators—such as Mr. Ellis, Mr. J. A. H. Murray, and Mr. Sweet—who have set about their work in a really scientific manner, are evidence that the science of language is not yet one of those in which long and laborious preparation does not entitle an average student to expect that his contribution to the existing stock of knowledge will be more than a few details. In spite of the great and rapid progress it has made since its birth sixty years ago, philology is only now getting out of the metaphysical stage; phrases which have no meaning unless language is a being, and a sentient being, existing quite independently of those who speak it, are still frequently given as explanations of linguistic phenomena. Indeed, to judge from the fact that an essay by a well-known theologian, whose chief point was the assertion that writing was too ingenious to be of any but divine origin, was published in at least one leading newspaper as an important contribution to science, it would seem that in this country parts of philology are still in the theological stage of development. Many things discovered by those who took a transcendental view of the nature and function of language remain mysterious and unfruitful, awaiting arrangement and explanation by the help of known physical and mental laws. A large quantity of letter-comparison, chiefly, and generally excellently, executed by German philologists, is in existence, but is scientifically useful only as materials for sound-comparison. Numerous facts remain to be collected, and principles to be evolved, in many branches of the science which are generally considered exhausted ; and many other branches have hardly been investigated at all. One of these is that part of comparative philology which treats of language in relation to the ideas expressed, rather than to the sounds which express them. Where, for instance, is anything definite, beyond assertions, to be found respecting the relative advantages of English and Latin for expressing business, or science, or poetry? Indeed, where is there any account of the capabilities of any single language for any purpose whatever? It is as obviously true for philology as for zoology, that to determine the common ancestor of related species we require them arranged according to chronology and affinity; the recognition of this is one of the chief distinctions between scientific and popular etymology. Yet the observations contained in Mr. Sweet's introduction, and appendix on the *th*, are the first important contribution to that knowledge of the history of Old English without which further advance in the philology of our older language is hardly possible. We do not even know at all accurately the language now spoken by well-educated Englishmen; our traditional orthography, the hitherto very imperfect state of phonetics, and the influence of old-fashioned Latin grammars, have combined to make us content with a few rough approximations. That we should be worse off as to our dialects is hardly to be wondered at; the confusion between literature and philology has here helped other obstacles by depriving most of us of the wish for knowledge. Because the works written in one dialect are few, and their contents of little artistic or scientific value, the impression is common that the dialect is of little philological importance in comparison with the one which from political accidents has become the literary language of the country. The only difference of consequence to the linguistic inquirer is that in the latter case the earlier stages of the dialect have probably been written down, thus giving us some materials for their study, while in the other case we have little more than the language of to-day. But there is one group of our dialects, Scotch, to which these considerations do not fully apply; yet Mr. Murray's essay "On the Dialects of the South of Scotland" is the only work containing information of any scientific value. In truth, the number of real philological students is still small, especially in this country. Many of those in Germany who pass under the title are rather literary than linguistic, and many of the remainder, apparently under the belief that the principles laid down by their eminent countrymen who created the science are fundamental, and have been pretty thoroughly followed out, are occupied in working up details to which they apply preconceived theories. With French philologists literature is still more predominant, and many of them resemble some of their English brethren in their ignorance of linguistics. Some other countries are doing good work, but it is chiefly local; here there is a great scarcity even of that. Partly from the wretched way in which languages, their own in particular, are taught to young people, partly from the still prevalent impression that

philology is not a science, and partly from the general belief
that, whether it is one or not, it can give the world nothing more
valuable than a few derivations, almost all of those with an inclination for pure or applied science turn their attention to one
which has been better studied. However, more ground is thus
left for each of those who will cultivate it; and an ample harvest
can be promised to him who brings even moderate attention
and perseverance, provided he will be content to apply them at
first in preparing himself for his work, and ascertaining what
fields have already been gleaned by others.

Art. III.—Greek Lyrical Poetry.

Poetæ Lyrici Græci. Tertiis Curis recensuit Theodorus
Bergk. 3 vols. Leipsic. 1866.

TO compress into a single article all that should be said about
the Greek lyrical poets in Bergk's collection is impossible.
Yet by eliminating the writers of elegies and iambics, who may
be considered separately as gnomic poets and satirists, the field
is somewhat narrowed. Simonides of Amorgos, Archilochus,
Theognis, Solon, not to mention lesser names, are by this process
legitimately excluded. The Æolian lyrists, with Sappho at their
head, and the so-called Dorian lyrists, who culminate in Pindar,
remain. Casting a glance backwards into the remote shadows
of antiquity we find that lyrical poetry, like all art in Greece,
took its origin in connexion with primitive Nature-worship. The
song[*] of Linus, referred to by Homer in his description of the
shield of Achilles, was a lament sung by reapers for the beautiful dead youth who symbolized the decay of summer's prime.
In the funeral chant for Adonis, women bewailed the fleeting
splendour of the spring; and Hyacinthus, loved and slain by
Phœbus, whom the Laconian youths and maidens honoured, was
again a type of vernal loveliness deflowered. The Bacchic songs
of alternating mirth and sadness, which gave birth, through the
Dithyramb, to Tragedy, and through the Comus-hymn to
Comedy, marked the waxing and the waning of successive years,
the pulses of the heart of Nature, to which men listened as the
months passed over them. In their dim beginnings these
elements of Greek poetry are hardly to be distinguished from the
dirges and the raptures of Asiatic ceremonial, in which the

---

[*] An old Linus-song is given by Bergk, p. 1297.

dance and chant and song were mingled in a vague monotony—
generation after generation expressing the same emotions according to traditions handed down from their forefathers. But the
Greek genius was endowed with the faculty of distinguishing.
differentiating, vitalizing, what the Oriental nations left hazy
and confused and inert. Therefore with the very earliest stirrings
of conscious art in Greece, we remark a powerful specializing
tendency. Articulation succeeds to mere interjectional utterance.
Separate forms of music and of metre are devoted, with the unerring instinct of a truly æsthetic race, to the expression of the
several moods and passions of the soul. An unconscious psychology leads by intuitive analysis to the creation of distinct branches
of composition, each accurately adapted to its special purpose.
From the very first commencement of their literature, the Greeks
thus determined separate styles and established critical canons,
which, though empirically and spontaneously formed, were based
on real relations between the moral and æsthetical sides of art,
between feeling and expression, substance and form. The Hexameter was consecrated to epical narrative ; the Elegy was confined to songs of lament or meditation ; the Iambic assumed a
satiric character. To have written a narrative in Iambics or a
satire in Hexameters would have been odious to Greek taste : the
stately march of the Dactylic metre seemed unfit for snarling
and invective ; the quick flight of the Iambic did not carry
weight enough or volume to sustain a lengthy narrative. In the
same way the infinite divisions of lyrical poetry had all their
own peculiar proprieties. How could a poet have bewailed his
loves or losses in the stately structure of the Pindaric ode ?
Conversely, a hymn to Phœbus required more sonorousness and
elaboration than the recurring stanzas of the Sapphic or Alcaic
offered. It was the business, therefore, of the Greek poet, after
duly considering his subject, to select the special form of poetry
consecrated by long usage for his particular purpose, to conform
his language to some species of music inseparable from that style,
and then, within the prescribed limits both of metre and of melody,
to exercise his imagination as freely as he could, and to produce
novelty. This amount of fixity in the forms of poetry and music
arose from the exquisite tact and innate taste of the Greek race.
It was far from being a piece of scholastic pedantry or of
Chinese conservation. No ; the diction, metre, and music of an
elegy or an ode gravitated to a certain form as naturally as the
ingredients of a ruby or a sapphire crystallize into a crimson
or an azure stone. The discrimination shown by the Greeks
in all the technicalities of art remained in full vigour till the
decline of their literature. It was not until the Alexandrian age
that they began to confound these delicate distinctions, and to

use the Idyllic Hexameter for all subjects, whether narrative,
descriptive, elegiac, encomiastic, hymeneal. Then, and not till
then, the Greeks descended to that degradation of art which
prevailed, for instance, in England during what we call the
classic period of our literature. Under the influence of Dryden
and of Pope, an English poet used no metre but the heroic
couplet, whether he were writing a play, an epigram, a satire, an
epic, an eclogue, an elegy, or a didactic epistle; thus losing
all elasticity of style, all the force which appropriate form communicates to thought.

To describe the minute subdivisions of the art of lyric poetry
in Greece, to show how wisely their several limits were prescribed, how firmly adhered to, and to trace the connexion of
choral song with all the affairs of public and private life, would
be a task of some magnitude. Colonel Mure, in a well known
passage, writes: "From Olympus down to the workshop or the
sheep-fold, from Jove and Apollo to the wandering mendicant,
every rank and degree of the Greek community, divine or human,
had its own proper allotment of poetical celebration. The gods
had their hymns, nomes, pæans, dithyrambs; great men had
their encomia and epinikia; the votaries of pleasure their erotica
and symposiaca; the mourner his threnodia and elegies; the vine-
dresser had his epilenia; the herdsmen their bucolica; even the
beggar his eiresione and chelidonisma." Lyrical poetry in Greece
was not produced, like poetry in modern times, for the student,
by men who find they have a taste for versifying. It was intimately intertwined with actual life, and was so indispensable
that every town had its professional poets and choruses, just as
every church in Europe now has its organist, of greater or less
pretension. The mass of lyrical poetry which must have existed
in Greece, was probably enormous. We can only compare it to
the quantity of church music that exists in Germany and Italy,
in MS. and print, good, bad, and indifferent, unknown and un-
explored, so voluminous that no one ventures to sift it or reduce
it to order. Of this large mass we possess the fragments. Just
as the rocky islands of the Ægean Archipelago testify to the existence of a submerged tract of mountain heights and valleys,
whose summits alone appear above the waves, so the odes of
Pindar, the waifs and strays of Sappho, Simonides, and others,
are evidences of the loss we have sustained. They prove that
beneath the ocean of time and oblivion remain for ever buried
thousands and thousands of supreme works of art. To collect
the fragments, to piece them together, to ponder over them until
their scattered indications offer some suggestion of the whole
which has been lost, is all that remains to the modern student.
Like the mutilated marbles of Praxiteles, chips broken off from
bas-reliefs and statues which are disinterred from the ruins of

Rome or Herculaneum, the minutest portions of the Greek
lyrists have their value. We must be thankful for any two words
of Sappho that survive in authentic juxtaposition, for any
hemistich that may be veritably styled a relic of "some tender-
hearted scroll of pure Simonides." Chance has wrought fantas-
tically with these relics. The lyrists, even in classical days, fell
comparatively early into neglect. They were too condensed in
language, too difficult in style, too sublime in imagination for
the pedants of the later Empire. Long before its close, Greek
literature was oppressed with its own wealth; in the words of
Livy, *magnitudine laboravit sua*. Taste, too, began to change:
sophistic treatises, idyllic verses, novelettes in prose, neat epigrams, usurped upon the grander forms of composition. The
stagnation, again, of civic life under imperial sway proved unfavourable to the composition of national odes and to choric
celebrations in which whole peoples took a part. So disdainful
in her almsgiving has fortune been, that she has only flung to us
the Epinikian odes of Pindar; while his hymns to the gods, his
processional chants, his funeral dirges, are lost. Young Athens,
Alexandria, and Byzantium cared, we may conceive, for poems
which shed lustre on athletic sports and horse-racing. Trainers,
boxers, riders, chariot-drivers—all the muscular section of the
public—had some interest in bygone Pythian or Olympian victories. But who sought to preserve the antiquated hymns to
Phœbus and to Zeus, when the rites of Isis and Serapis and the
Phrygian mother were in vogue? The outspoken boldness of
the Erotic and Satiric lyrists stood them in bad stead. When
Theodora was exhibiting her naked charms in the arena, who
could commend the study of Anacreon in the schoolroom? Degeneracy of public morals and prudery of literary taste go not
unfrequently together. Therefore, the Emperor Julian proscribed Archilochus; and what Julian proscribed the Christians
sought to extirpate. To destroy an ode of Sappho was a good
work. Consequently, we possess no complete edition of even a
section of the works of any lyrist except Pindar; what remains
of the others has been preserved in the works of critics, anecdote-
mongers, and grammarians; who cite tantalizing passages to
prove a rule in syntax, to illustrate a legend or a custom, to
exemplify a canon of taste. Imbedded in ponderous prose, these
splintered jewels escaped the iconoclastic zeal of the monks.
Thanks be to Athenæus above all men, to Longinus, to Philo-
stratus, to Maximus Tyrius, to Plutarch the moralist, to Stobæus,
to Hephæstio, to Herodian, and to the host of other Dryasdusts
from whose heaps of shot rubbish Bergk and his predecessors
have sorted out the fragments of extinguished stars! As a mas-
terpiece of patient, self-denying, scientific, exhaustive investigation, the three volumes of Bergk are unrivalled. Every author

of antiquity has been laid under contribution, subjected to critical analysis, compared and confronted with his fellow-witnesses. The result, reduced to the smallest possible compass, yields a small glittering heap of pure gold-dust, a little handful of auriferous deposit sifted from numberless river-beds, crushed from huge masses of unfertile quartz. In our admiration of the scholar's ingenuity, we almost forget our sorrow for so much irreparable waste.

Before proceeding to consider the justice of the time-honoured division of Greek Lyrics into Æolian and Dorian, it will be well to pass in review a few of the principal classes into which Greek choral poetry may be divided. Only thus can any idea of its richness and variety be formed. The old Homeric ὕμνοι, or hymns dedicated to special deities, were intended to be sung at festivals and rhapsodical contests. Their technical name was Proëmia, or preludes—preludes, that is, to a longer recitation; and, on this account, as they were chanted by the poet himself, they were written in hexameters. With them, therefore, we have nothing here to do. Processional hymns, or Prosodia, on the contrary, were strictly lyrical, and constituted a large portion of the poetry of Pindar, Alcman, and Stesichorus. They were sung at solemn festivals by troops of men and maidens walking, crowned with olive, myrtle, bay, or oleander, to the shrines. Their style varied with the occasion and the character of the deity to whom they were addressed. When Hecuba led her maidens in dire necessity to the shrine of Pallas, the Prosodion was solemn and earnest. When Sophocles, with lyre in hand, headed the chorus round the trophy of Salamis, it was victorious and martial. If we wish to present to our mind a picture of these processional ceremonies, we may study the frieze of the Parthenon preserved among the Elgin Marbles. Those long lines of maidens and young men, with baskets in their hands, with flowers and palm-branches, with censers and sacred emblems, are marching to the sound of flutes and lyres, and to the stately rhythms of antiphonal chanting. When they reach the altar of the god a halt is made; the libations are poured; and now the music changes to a solemn and spondaic measure—for the term spondaic seems to be derived from the fact that the libation-hymn was composed in a grave and heavy metre of full feet. Hephæstion has preserved a spondaic verse of Terpander which illustrates this rhythm:

σπένδωμεν ταῖς Μνάμας
παισὶν Μώσαις
Καὶ τῷ Μωσάρχῳ
Λατοῦς υἱεῖ.

In the age of Greek decadence the honours of the Prosodion were sometimes paid to men. Athenæus presents this lively picture of the procession which greeted Demetrius Poliorketes: "When Demetrius returned from Leucadia and Corcyra to Athens, the Athenians received him not only with incense and garlands and libations, but they even sent out processional choruses, and greeted him with Ithyphallic hymns and dances: stationed by his chariot-wheels, they sang and danced and chanted that he alone was a real god ; the rest were sleeping, or were on a journey, or did not exist ; they called him son of Poseidon and Aphrodite, eminent for beauty, universal in his goodness to mankind ; then they prayed and besought and sup-plicated him like a god." The hymn which they sang may be read in Bergk, vol. iii. p. 1314. It is one of the most interesting relics of antiquity.

A special kind of prosodia were the Parthenia, or processional hymns of maidens ; such, for example, as the Athenian girls sang to Pallas while they climbed the staircase of the Parthenon. Aris-tophanes has presented us with a beautiful example of antiphonal Parthenia, at the end of his Lysistrata, where choruses of Athenian and Spartan girls sing turn and turn about in rivalry. Alcman won his laurels at Sparta by the composition of this kind of hymn. A fragment (Bergk, p. 842) only remains to show what they were like: "No more, ye honey-voiced, sweet-singing maidens, can my limbs support me : oh, oh, that I were a cerylus, who skims the flower of the sea with halcyons, of a dauntless heart, the sea-blue bird of spring !" Such Parthenia, when addressed to Phœbus, were called Daphnephorica ; for the maidens carried laurel-branches to his shrine. A more charming picture cannot be conceived than that which is presented to our fancy by these white-robed virgins, each with her rod of bay and crown of laurel-leaves, ascending the marble steps of the temple of the Dorian god. John Lyly, who had imbibed the spirit of Greek life, has written a hymn, "Sing to Apollo, god of day !" which might well have been used at such a festival.

The Prosodia of which we have been speaking were addressed to all the gods. But there were other choric hymns with special names consecrated to the service of particular deities. Of this sort was the Pæan, sung to Phœbus in his double character of a victorious and a healing god. The Pæan was both a song of war and of peace ; it was the proper accompaniment of the battle and the feast. In like manner the Hyporchem, which, as its name implies, was always accompanied by a dance, originally formed a portion of the cult of Phœbus. The chorus described in Iliad xviii. 590, and the glorious pageant of Olympus cele-brated in the Hymn to Apollo, 186, were, technically speaking,

Hyporchems. As the Pæan and the Hyporchem were originally consecrated to Apollo, so the Dithyramb and the Phallic Hymn belonged to Dionysos. The Dithyramb never lost the tempestuous and enthusiastic character of Bacchic revelry; but in time it grew from being a wild celebration of the mystic sufferings of Bacchus into the sublime art of Tragedy. Arion forms the point of this transition. He seems to have thrown a greater reality of passion and dramatic action into his choruses, which led to the introduction of dialogue, and so by degrees to Tragedy proper. Meanwhile the Dithyramb, as a tumultuous choric hymn, retained its individual existence. Its chorus was styled Cyclic, probably from their movement in a circle round the Thymelé. Every town in Greece had its chorodidascalus, a functionary whom Aristophanes ridicules in the person of Kinesias* in the Birds. He is introduced warbling the wildest, windiest nonsense, and entreating to have a pair of wings given him that he may chase his airy ideas through the sky. The Phallic Hymn, from which in like manner Comedy took its origin, was a mad outpouring of purely animal exultation. Here the wine-god was celebrated as the pleasure-loving, drunken, lascivious deity. Aristophanes,† again, our truest source of information respecting all the details of Greek life, supplies us with an instance of one of these songs, and of the simple rites which accompanied its performance. In the Frogs,‡ also, the master of Comedy has presented us with an elaborate series of Bacchic Hymns. Here the Phallic and Satiric element is combined with something of the grandeur of the Dithyrambic Ode; the curious mixture of sarcasm, obscenity, and splendid poetry offers a striking instance of Greek religious feeling, so incomprehensible to modern minds. It is greatly to be regretted that our information respecting the Dithyramb and the Phallic Chorus has to be obtained from a dramatic poet rather than from any perfect specimens of these compositions. Bergk's collection, full as it is, yields nothing§ but hints and fragments.

Passing to the Lyrics which were connected with circumstances of human life, the first to be mentioned are Epinikia, or odes sung in honour of victors at the games. Of these, in the splendid series of Pindar and in the fragments of Simonides, we have abundant examples. We are also able to trace their development from the simple exclamation of ¶ τήνελλα ὦ

* See Frere, vol. ii. pp. 200 and 201.
† See Tr. of Acharnians, Frere, vol. ii. p. 17.
‡ Frere's Translation, vol. ii. pp. 241—245.
§ See however the interesting archaic hymns to Dionysos, pp. 1299, 1300.
¶ Bergk, p. 716, Pindar iz. i.

καλλίνικι, the composition of which was ascribed to Archilochus, and which Pindar looked back upon with scornful triumph. Indeed, in his hands, to use the phrase of Wordsworth, "the thing became a trumpet, whence he blew soul-animating strains." The Epinikian Ode was the most costly and splendid flower in the victor's wreath. Pindar compares the praise which he pours forth for Diagoras the Rhodian to noblest wine foaming in the golden goblet, which a father gives to honour his son-in-law, the prime and jewel of his treasure-house. The occasions on which such odes were sung were various—either when the victor was being crowned, or when he was returning to his native city, or by torchlight during the ending of the victorious day, or at a banquet after his reception in his home. On one of these occasions the poet would appear with his trained band of singers and musicians, and, taking his stand by the altar of the god to whom the victor offered a thanksgiving sacrifice, would guide the choric stream of song through strophe and antistrophe and epode, in sonorous labyrinths of eulogy and mythological allusion—prayer, praise, and admonition mingling with the fumes of intoxicating poetry. Of all these occasions the most striking must have been the commemoration of a victory in the temple of Zeus at Altis, near Olympia, by moonlight. The contest has taken place during the day; and the olive wreath has been placed upon the head, say of Myronides, from Thebes. Having rested from his labours, after the bath and the banquet, crowned with his victorious garland and with fillets bound about his hair, he stands surrounded by his friends. Zeus, in ivory and gold, looks down from his marble pedestal. Through the open roof shines a moon of the south, glancing aslant on statue and column and carved bas-relief; while below, the red glare of torches, paling its silver, flickers with fitful crimson on the glowing faces of young men. Then swells the choral hymn, with praise of Myronides and praise of Thebes, and stormy flights of fancy shooting beyond sun and stars. At its close follow libation, dedication, hands upraised in prayer to Zeus. Then the trampling of sandalled feet upon the marble floor, the procession with songs still sounding to the temple-gate, and on a sudden, lo! the full moon, the hills, and plain, and solemn night of stars. The band disperses, and the Comus succeeds to the thanksgiving.

As a contrast to the Epinikia we may take the different kinds of Threnoi, or funeral songs. The most primitive was called Epikedeian, a dirge or coronach, improvised by women over the bodies of the dead. The lamentations of Helen and Andromache for Hector, and of the slave-girls for Patroclus, are Homeric instances of this species. Euripides imitates them in his tragedies—

in the dirge sung by Antigone, for instance, in the Phœnissæ, and
in the wailings of Hecuba for Astyanax in the Troades. A
different kind of Threnos were the songs of Linus, Hyacinth,
Adonis, and others, to which we have already alluded in the
beginning of this paper. The finest extant specimen of this
sort is Bion's Lament for Adonis, which, however, was composed in the Idyllic age, when the hexameter had been substituted for the richer and more splendid lyric metres. A third
class of Threnos consisted of complex choral hymns composed by
poets like Simonides or Pindar, to be sung at funeral solemnities. Many of our most precious lyric fragments, those which
embody philosophical reflections on life and dim previsions of
another world, belong to dirges of this elaborate kind.

Marriage festivals offered another occasion for lyric poetry.
The Hymeneal, sung during the wedding ceremony, the Epitha-
lamium, chanted at the house of the bridegroom, and many other
species, have been defined by the grammarians. Unfortunately
we possess nothing but the merest *débris* of any true Greek ode
of this kind. Sappho's are the best. We have to study the imitations of her style in Catullus, the marriage chorus at the end
of the Birds of Aristophanes, and the Epithalaminm of Helen by
Theocritus, in order to form a remote conception of what a
Sapphic marriage chorus might have been. In banquet songs
we are more fortunate. Abundant are the Parœnia of Alcæus,
Anacreon, Treognis, and others. Scolia, or catches, so called
from their irregular metrical structure, were also in vogue at
banquets ; and of these popular songs a sufficient number are
preserved. A drunken passage in the works of Aristophanes*
brings before us after a lively fashion the ceremonies with which
the Scolion and the wine-cup circled the symposium together.
Of all these catches the most celebrated in ancient days was the
panegyric of Harmodius and Aristogeiton, attributed to Calli-
stratus. As we have the opportunity of printing from MS. a
translation of this song by the late Professor Conington, we will
introduce it here :—

> " In a wreath of myrtle I'll wear my glaive,
> Like Harmodius and Aristogeiton brave,
>   Who, striking the tyrant down,
>   Made Athens a freeman's town.
> Harmodius, our darling, thou art not dead !
> Thou liv'st in the isles of the blest, 'tis said,
>   With Achilles first in speed,
>   And Tydides Diomede.

---

* Translated by Mitchell, vol. ii. p. 282, in his "Dicast turned Gentleman."

In a wreath of myrtle I'll wear my glaive,
Like Harmodius and Aristogeiton brave,
   When the twain on Athena's day
   Did the tyrant Hipparchus slay.
For aye shall your fame in the land be told,
Harmodius and Aristogeiton bold,
   Who, striking the tyrant down,
   Made Athens a freeman's town."

The whole collection of Scolia in Bergk (pp. 1287–1296) is
full of interest, since these simple and popular songs carry us
back more freshly than elaborate poems to the life of the Greeks.
While on the subject of Scolia, it will not do to pass over the
most splendid specimen we have in this order of composition.
It is a fragment from Pindar (Bergk, p. 327), to translate which
is profanation :—

"O son! 'tis thine in season meet, to pluck of love the blossom sweet,
   When hearts are young :
But he who sees the blazing beams, the light that from *that* fore-
   head streams,
   And is not stung ;—
Who is not storm-lost with desire,—lo ! he, I ween, with frozen fire,
   Of adamant or stubborn steel,
Is forged in his cold heart that cannot feel.

Disowned, dishonoured, and denied by Aphrodite glittering-eyed,
   He either toils
All day for gold, a sordid gain, or bent beneath a woman's reign,
   In petty broils,
Endures her insolence, a drudge, compelled the common path to
   trudge ;
But I, apart from this disease,
   Wasting away like wax of holy bees
Which the sun's splendour wounds, do pine
   Whene'er I see the young-limbed bloom divine
Of boys. Lo! look you well ; for here in Tenedos,
   Grace and Persuasion dwell in young Theoxenos."

It is a pity that the morality of these stanzas, to our modern
notions, is so inferior to their poetry.

Of the many different kinds of lyric poetry consecrated to love
and intended for recitation by single musicians, it is not possible
to give a strict account.   That the Greeks cultivated the
serenade is clear from a passage in the Ecclesiazusæ of Aristophanes, which contains a graceful though gross specimen of
this kind of song. The children's songs (Bergk, 1303–1307)
about flowers, tortoises, and hobgoblins are too curiously illustrative of Greek manners not to merit a passing notice.

After this lengthy, but far from exhaustive enumeration of the

kinds and occasions of lyrical poetry in Greece, we may turn to
consider the different parts played in their cultivation by the
several chief families of Hellas. It is remarkable that all the
great writers of elegies and iambics were Ionians; Theognis of
Megara is the only Dorian whose genuine poems are celebrated;
and against him we have to set the bulk of Solon, Mimnermus,
Phocylides, Callinus, and Tyrtæus, all Ionians. Not a single
Dorian poet seems to have composed iambics, the rigid discipline
and strong sense of decorum in a Dorian state probably rendering the cultivation of satire impossible. We are told that the
Spartans would not even suffer Archilochus to lodge as a stranger
among them. But when we turn to lyric poetry—to the poetry
of stanzas and strophes—the two other families of the Greeks,
the Æolians and the Dorians, take the lead. As a Dorian was
exceptional among the elegists, so now an Ionian will be comparatively rare among the lyrists. So great was the æsthetical
conservatism of the Greeks that throughout their history their
primitive distinctions of dialect are never lost sight of. When
the Athenians developed Tragedy, they wrote their iambics in
pure Attic, but they preserved a Dorian tone in their choruses.
The epic hexameter and the elegy, on the other hand, retained
an Ionian character to the last. The paths struck out by the
Æolians and Dorians in the domain of lyric poetry were so
different as to justify us in speaking of two distinct species.
When Milton, in the "Paradise Regained," catalogued the
poetical achievements of the Greeks, he assigned their true place
to these two species in the line—

> Æolian charms and Dorian lyric odes.

The poets and poetesses of the Ægean Islands cultivated a
rapid and effusive style, polishing their passionate stanzas so
exquisitely that they well deserve the name of charms. The
Dorian poets, inspired by a graver and more sustained imagination, composed long and complex odes for the celebration of gods
and heroes. The Æolian singer dwelt on his own joys and
sorrows. The Dorian bard addressed some deity, or told the tales
of demigods and warriors. The Æolian chanted his stanzas to
the lyre or flute. The Dorian trained a chorus, who gave
utterance to his verse in dance and song.

Though the Æolians were the eldest family of the Hellenic
stock, their language retaining more than any other dialect the
primitive character of the Greek tongue, yet they never rose to
such historical importance as the Dorians and Ionians. Geogra-
phically they were scattered in such a way as to have no definite centre. We find Æolians in Elis, in Bœotia, in Lesbos, and
on the Asian seacoast south of the Troad. But in course of time

the Æolians of Elis and Bœotia were almost identified with the
Dorians as allies of Sparta, while the Æolians of Lesbos and
Asia merged themselves in the Athenian empire. Politically,
mentally, and morally, they showed less activity than their
cousins of the blood of Dorus and Ion. They produced no
lawgivers like Lycurgus and Solon : they had no metropolis like
Sparta and Athens : they played no prominent part in the
struggle with Persia, or in the Peloponnesian war. In the later
days of Greece, Thebes, when Dorized by contact with the Spartans, for a short time headed Greece, and flourished with brief
splendour. But it would not be accurate to give to the Æolian
character the credit of the fame of Thebes at that advanced
period. Yet, for a certain space of time, the Æolians occupied
the very foreground of Greek literature, and blazed out with a
brilliance of lyrical splendour that has never been surpassed.
There seems to have been something passionate and intense in
their temperament, which made the emotions of the Dorian and
the Ionian feeble by comparison. Lesbos, the centre of Æolian
culture, was the island of overmastering passions : the personality
of the Greek race burned there with a fierce and steady flame of
concentrated feeling. The energies which the Ionians divided
between pleasure, politics, trade, legislation, science, and the
arts ; which the Dorians turned to war and statecraft and social
economy, were restrained by the Æolians within the sphere of
individual emotions, ready to burst forth volcanically. Nowhere
in any age of Greek history, or in any part of Hellas, did the
love of physical beauty, the sensibility to radiant scenes of nature,
the consuming fervour of personal feeling, assume such grand
proportions and receive so illustrious an expression as they did
in Lesbos. At first this passion blossomed into the most exquisite lyrical poetry that the world has known : this was the flower-
time of the Æolians, their brief and brilliant spring. But the
fruit it bore was bitter and rotten. Lesbos became a byeword
for corruption. The passions which for a moment had flamed
into the gorgeousness of Art, burning their envelope of words
and images, remained a mere furnace of sensuality, from which
no expression of the divine in human life could be expected. In this
the Lesbian poets were not unlike the Provençal troubadours, who
made a literature of Love ; or the Venetian painters, who based
their art upon the beauty of colour, the voluptuous charms of
the flesh. In each case the motive of enthusiastic passion sufficed to produce a dazzling result. But as soon as its freshness
was exhausted there was nothing left for Art to live on, and
mere decadence to sensuality ensued. Several circumstances
contributed to aid the development of lyric poetry in Lesbos.
The customs of the Æolians permitted more social and domestic

freedom than was common in Greece. Æolian women were not confined to the hareem like Ionians, or subjected to the vigorous discipline of the Spartans. While mixing freely with male society, they were highly educated, and accustomed to express their sentiments to an extent unknown elsewhere in history—until, indeed, the present time. The Lesbian ladies applied themselves successfully to literature. They formed clubs for the cultivation of poetry and music. They studied the art of beauty, and sought to refine metrical forms and diction. Nor did they confine themselves to the scientific side of art. Unrestrained by public opinion, and passionate for the beautiful, they cultivated their senses and emotions, and developed their wildest passions. All the luxuries and elegances of life which that climate and the rich valleys of Lesbos could afford, were at their disposal: exquisite gardens, in which the rose and hyacinth spread perfume; river beds ablaze with the oleander and wild pomegranate; olive-groves and fountains, where the cyclamen and violet flowered with feathery maiden-hair; pine-tree-shadowed coves, where they might bathe in the calm of a tideless sea; fruits such as only the southern sun and sea-wind can mature; marble cliffs, starred with jonquil and anemone in spring, aromatic with myrtle and lentisk and samphire and wild rosemary through all the months; nightingales that sang in May; temples dim with dusky gold and bright with ivory; statues and frescoes of heroic forms. In such scenes as these the Lesbian poets lived, and thought of Love. When we read their poems, we seem to have the perfumes, colours, sounds, and lights of that luxurious land distilled in verse. Nor was a brief but biting winter wanting to give tone to their nerves, and, by contrast with the summer, to prevent the palling of so much luxury on sated senses. The voluptuousness of Æolian poetry is not like that of Persian or Arabian art. It is Greek in its self-restraint, proportion, tact. We find nothing burdensome in its sweetness. All is so rhythmically and sublimely ordered in the poems of Sappho that supreme art lends solemnity and grandeur to the expression of unmitigated passion.

The world has suffered no greater literary loss than the loss of Sappho's poems. So perfect are the smallest fragments preserved in Bergk's Collection—the line, for example (p. 809). ἦρος ἄγγελος ἱμερόφωνος ἀήδων, which Ben Jonson fancifully translated, "the dear glad angel of the spring, the nightingale"—that we muse in a sad rapture of astonishment to think what the complete poems must have been. Among the ancients Sappho enjoyed a unique renown. She was called "The Poetess," as Homer was called "The Poet." Aristotle placed her in the same rank as Homer and Archilochus. Plato, in the Phædrus, mentioned her as the tenth Muse. Solon, hearing one of her poems, prayed that he might not see death till he had learned it. Strabo speaks of her genius with religious awe. Longinus cites her love-ode as a specimen of poetical sublimity. The epigrammatists call her Child of Aphrodite and Erôs, nursling of the Graces and Persuasion, pride of Hellas, peer of Muses, companion of Apollo. Nowhere is a hint whispered that her poetry was aught but perfect. As far as we can judge, these praises were strictly just. Of all the poets of the world, of all the illustrious artists of all literatures, Sappho is the one whose every word has a peculiar and unmistakable perfume, a seal of absolute perfection and inimitable grace. In her art she was unerring. Even Archilochus seems commonplace when compared with her exquisite rarity of phrase.

About her life—her brother Charaxus, her daughter Cleis, her rejection of Alcæus and suit to Phaon, her love for Atthis and Anactoria, her leap from the Leucadian cliff—we know so very little, and that little is so confused with mythology and turbid with the scandal of the comic poets, that it is not worth while to rake up once again the old materials for hypothetical conclusions. There is enough of heart-devouring passion in Sappho's own verse without the legends of Phao and the cliff of Leucas. The reality casts all fiction into the shade; for nowhere, except, perhaps, in some Persian or Provençal love-songs, can be found more ardent expressions of overmastering emotion. Whether addressing the maidens, whom even in Elysium, as Horace says, Sappho could not forget; or embodying the profounder yearnings of an intense soul after beauty which has never on earth existed, but which inflames the hearts of noblest poets, robbing their eyes of sleep and giving them the bitterness of tears to drink—these dazzling fragments—

> "Which still, like sparkles of Greek fire,
> Burn on through time and ne'er expire"—

are the ultimate and finished forms of passionate utterance, diamonds, topazes, and blazing rubies, in which the fire of the soul is crystallized for ever. Adequately to translate Sappho was beyond the power of even Catullus: that love-ode, which Longinus called "not one passion, but a congress of passions," and which a Greek physician copied into his book of diagnoses as a compendium of all the symptoms of corroding emotion, appears but languid in its Latin dress of "Ille mi par." Far less has any modern poet succeeded in the task: Rossetti, who deals so skilfully with Dante and Villon, is comparatively tame when he approaches Sappho. Instead of attempting, therefore, to interpret for English readers the charm of Sappho's style, it is

F 2

best to refer to pp. 874-924 of Bergk, where every vestige that is left of her is shrined.

Beside Sappho, Alcæus pales. His drinking songs and war songs have indeed great beauty; but they are not to be named in the same breath, for perfection of style, with the stanzas of Sappho. Of the other Lesbian poets, Erinna and Damophila, we know but little: the one survives in a single epigram—if we reject the epitaphs on Baucis: the other is a mere name. It is noticeable that of the four Lesbian poets three are women. We may remember that in Thebes, which was also an Æolian city, Myrtis and Corinna rivalled Pindar. To the list of Æolian poets Anacreon, though an Ionian by birth and an Ionian in temperament, is generally added, because he cultivated the lyrical stanza of personal emotion. Into the Æolian style Anacreon introduced a new and uncongenial element. His passion had none of Sappho's fiery splendour, none of the haughtiness and restlessness which distinguished Alcæus. There was a vein of levity, almost of vulgarity, in the Ionians, which removed them from the altitudes of Dorian heroism and Æolian enthusiasm. This tincture of flippancy is discernible in Anacreon. Life and love come easily to him. The roses keep no secrets for his ears, such as they told to Sappho: they serve very well for garlands when he drinks, and have a pleasant smell—especially in myrrh. The wine-cup does not suggest variety of seasons,—the frozen streams of winter, the parched breath of the Dogstar,—as with Alcæus: he tipples and gets drunk. His loves too are facile—not permanent and tempestuous. The girls and boys of whom he sings were flute-players and cup-bearers, servants of a tyrant, *instrumenta libidinis*, chosen for their looks, as he had been selected for the sweetness of his lyre with twenty chords. He never felt the furnace of Sappho, whose love, however criminal, was serious and of the soul. The difference between the lives of these three lyrists is very striking. Alcæus was a politician and party leader. Sappho was the centre of a free society of female poets. Anacreon was the courtier and laureate of tyrants. He won his first fame with Polycrates, at whose death Hipparchus fetched him to Athens in a trireme of fifty oars. Between Bacchus and Venus he spent his days in palaces; and died at the ripe age of eighty-five at Teos, choked, it is reported, by a grape-stone—a hoary-headed *roué*, for whom the rhyme of Walter Mapes might have been written:

> "Meum est propositum,
> In tabernâ mori," etc.

It need not be remarked that of the genuine poems of Anacreon we possess but few [pp. 1011—1045 of Bergk]. His great

popularity in Greece led to innumerable imitations of his lighter
style. These are fully preserved in Bergk's Collection [pp. 1046
—1108].

The Dorian style offers a marked contrast to the Æolian. In
the case of the Ionian satirists and elegists, and in that of the
Æolian lyrists, the national peculiarities of the art resulted from
national qualities in the artists. This is not the case with the
so-called Dorian poets The great lyrists of this school are, with
one exception, of extraction foreign to the Dorian tribe. Alcman
was a Lydian; Stesichorus acknowledged an Ionian colony for his
fatherland; Arion was a Lesbian; Simonides and Bacchylides
were Ionian; Pindar was Bœotian; Ibycus of Rhegium alone
was a true Dorian. Why then is the style called Dorian? Because the poets, though not Dorian by birth, wrote for Dorian
patrons in the land of Dorians, to add splendour to ceremonies
and solemnities in vogue among the Dorians. The distinctive
features of this, the most sublime branch of Greek lyrical poetry,
have been already hinted at: these elaborate Choral Hymns, in
which strophe answers to antistrophe and epode to epode,
chanted by bands of singers and accompanied at times by
dancing, were designed to give expression, no longer to personal
emotions, but to the feelings of great congregations of men engaged in the celebration of gods, and heroes, and illustrious
mortals. Why this species of choral poetry received the patronage and name of the Dorian tribe may be seen by glancing at
the institutions peculiar to this section of the Hellenic family.
The Dorians, more than any other Greeks, lived in common and
in public. Their children were educated, not at home, but in
companies, beneath the supervision of state-officers. Girls as
well as boys submitted to gymnastic training, and were taught
to sacrifice domestic and personal to political and social interests.
Tutored to merge the individual in the mass, habituated to asso-
ciate together in large bodies, the Dorians felt no need of venting
private feeling. Their personal emotions were stunted: they
had no separate wants and wishes, aspirations and regrets, to
utter. Yet the sense of melody and harmony which was rooted
so profoundly in the Greek temperament, needed some outlet
even here; while the gymnastic and athletic exercises practised
by the Dorians rendered them peculiarly sensitive, not only to
the beauties of the human body, but also to the refinements of
rhythmical movement. The spiritual enthusiasm for great
and glorious actions, which formed the soul of the Greek race,
flamed with all the greater brilliancy among Dorians, because it
was not narrowed, as among Æolians, to the selfish passions of
the individual, or diverted, as among Ionians, to meditation or
satire; but was concentrated on public interests, on religious and

heroic traditions, on all the thoughts and feelings which stimulate
a large political activity. The Dorians required a poetry which
should be public, which should admit of the participation of
many individuals, which should give utterance to national enthu-
siasms, which should combine the movements of men and women
in choric evolutions with the melodies of music and the sublime
words of inspired prophecy. In brief, the Dorians needed poets
able, to quote Milton's words—

"to imbibe and cherish in a great people the seeds of virtue and public
civility, to allay the perturbations of the mind, and set the affections
in right tune; to celebrate in glorious and lofty hymns the throne and
equipage of God's Almightiness, and what He works, and what He
suffers to be wrought with high Providence. . . . . Lastly, whatsoever in religion is holy and sublime, in virtue amiable or grave;
whatsoever hath passion or admiration in all the changes of that which
is called fortune from without, or the wily subtleties and refluxes
of man's thoughts from within; all these things with a solid and
treatable smoothness, to point out and describe."

But here arose a difficulty. With all their need of the highest
and most elaborate poetry, with all their sensibility to beauty,
the Dorians thought it beneath the dignity of a citizen to practise the arts. Their education, almost exclusively military and
gymnastic, unfitted them, at all events in Sparta, for studies indispensable towards gaining proficiency in any science so elaborate as that of choral poetry. Drilled to abstinence, obedience,
and silence, dwelling in a camp, without privacy or leisure, how
could a Spartan, that automaton of the State, be expected to
produce poetry, or excel in any fine art? A Spartan king, on
being shown the most distinguished musician of his age, pointed
to his cook as the best maker of black broth. Music, if music
they must have; poetry, if poetry were required by some blind
instinct; dancing, if dancing were a necessary compliment to
the Deity; must be imported by these warriors from foreign
lands. Thus the Spartans became the patrons of stranger artists
on whom they imposed their laws of taste. They pressed the
flexible Ionian, the passionate Lesbian, the languid Lydian, the
acute Athenian, into their service, and made them use the crabbed
Dorian speech. They said: We want such and such odes for
our choruses; we wish to amuse our youths and maidens, and to
honour the gods with pompous harmonies; you, men of art,
write for us, sing for us; but be careful to comprehend our character; and remember that, though you are Ionians or Lesbians,
your inspiration must be Dorian. They got what they required. `
The so-called Dorian lyric is a genuine product of the Dorian
race, although its greatest masters were foreigners and aliens.
Much after the same fashion did England patronize Handel in

the last century; in the same way may Handel's oratorios be
called English music; for though the English are not musicians,
and are diffident in general of the artist class, yet neither Germans nor Italians nor French have seen produced upon their
soil such colossal works of art in the service of a highly intellectual religion.

It is interesting to reflect upon the influence of the Dorian
race in the evolution of Greek art. That, as a nation, they possessed the germs of artistic invention, and that their character
expressed itself very clearly in æsthetic forms, is evident from
the existence of the Dorian style in architecture, and the Dorian
mood in music, both of which reflect their broad simplicity and
strength disdaining ornament. The same stamp they impressed
upon Greek poetry, through the instruments they selected from
other tribes. Had it not been for the strict legislation of
Lycurgus, which, by forcing Sparta into a purely political development, and establishing a complete community of life among the
citizens, checked the emergence of that individuality which is so
all-important to the artist, Sparta might have counted her great
sculptors, poets, musicians, orators, and painters in rivalry with
Phidias, Sophocles, Damon, Pericles, Polygnotus. As it was,
though without hands to paint and carve, without lips to sing
and plead, the stubborn Dorian race set its seal on a wide field
of Greek art.

The elaborate works of the choral lyrists may be regarded as
the highly-wrought expansions of rudiments already existing
among the Dorians. Alcman, Arion, and Stesichorus, the three
masters who formed choral poetry from the materials indicated to
us in the poems of Homer, and who had to blend in one harmonious whole the sister arts of dancing, music, and poetry, so as to
present a pompous appeal to the intellect through speech, and
through the ear and eye, found ready to their hands such simple
songs as may be read in Bergk, pp. 1301–1303. The dithyramb
of the women of Elis: "Come, hero, Dionysos, to the holy sea-
temple, attended by the graces, and rushing on with oxen-hoof !
Holy ox ! Holy ox !" The chorus of the old men, men, and
boys at Sparta: "We once were stalwart youths: we are; if
thou likest, try our strength: we shall be; and far better too !"
The march-song of the Spartans in their rhythmic revels: "Advance boys, set your feet forward, and dance in the reel better
still." From these had to be trained the complex and magnificent work of art, which culminated in a Pythian ode of Pindar!
Alcman was a native of Sardis, and a slave of Agesilaus the
Spartan. He flourished there between 671 and 631 B.C.,
composing Parthenia for the maidens of Taygetus. Who does not
know his lines upon the valley of Eurotas ? "Sleep holds the

mountain summits and ravines, the promontories and the water-
courses ; and creeping things, and whatsoever black earth breeds ;
and wild beasts of the hills, and bees, and monsters in the
hollows of the dark blue deep ; and all the wide-winged birds
are sleeping." Junior to Alcman was Arion, who spent most of
his time with Periander at Corinth. His contribution to choral
poetry was the elaboration of the Dithyramb. But of his work
we have unfortunately not a single fragment left. The piece
that bears his name [Bergk, p. 872,] has to be ascribed to some
tolerable poet of the Euripidean period. His life is involved in
mythology ; most beautiful is the oft-told tale of his salvation
from the sea waves by an enamoured dolphin—a fish, by the
way, which Athenæus dignifies by the title of φιλῳδός τε καὶ
φίλαυλος, and which Aristotle calls φιλάνθρωπος. Rather more
is known about Stesichorus. He was a native of Himera, in
Sicily, but probably a Dorian by descent. His parents called
him Tisias, but he took his more famous name from his profession. Stesichorus is a title that might have been given to any
chorus-master in a Greek city ; but Tisias of Himera won it by
being emphatically the author of the choric system. Antiquity recognised in him the inventor of Strophe, Antistrophe, and Epode,
with the corresponding movements of the dance, which were designated the Triad of Stesichorus. A remark made by Quintilian
about this poet—that he sustained the burden of the Epos with
his lyre—forms a valuable criticism on his style. In the days
of Stesichorus, the epic proper had lost its vitality ; but people still
felt the liveliest interest in heroic legends, and loved to connect
the celebration of the past with their ceremonies. A lyrical poet
had therefore so to treat the myths of Hellas that choruses
should represent them in their odes and semi-dramatic dances.
It is probable that Stesichorus made far more use of mythical
material than Pindar, dealing with it less allusively, and adhering more closely to the epic form of narrative. When we hear
of his ode, the Oresteia, being divided into three books (whatever
that may mean), and read the titles of the rest—Cerberus,
Cycnus, Scylla, Europa, the Sack of Troy, the Nostoi, and
Geryonis, we are led to suspect that his choral compositions were
something of the nature of mediæval mystery plays,—semi-lyrical,
semi-dramatic poems founded on the religious legends of the
past. Stesichorus did not confine himself to this species of composition ; but wrote hymns, encænia, and pæans, like other
professional lyrists that succeeded him, and invented a curious
kind of love-tale from real life. One of these romantic poems,
called Calycé, was about a girl, who loved purely but unhappily,
and died. Another, called Rhadina, told the forlorn tale of a
Samian brother and sister put to death by a cruel tyrant. It is

a pity that these early Greek novels in verse are lost. We might have found in them the fresh originals of Daphnis and Chloe, or the romances of Tatius and Heliodorus. Finally, Stesichorus composed fables, such as the Horse and the Stag, and pastorals upon the death of Daphnis, in which he proved himself true to his Sicilian origin, and anticipated Theocritus. Enough has been said about Stesichorus to prove that he was a richly inventive genius, one of those facile and abundant natures who excel in many branches of art, and who give hints by which posterity may profit. Yet with all his genius he was not thoroughly successful. His pastorals and romances were abandoned by his successors; his epical lyrics were lost in the tragic drama. Like many other poets, he failed by coming at a wrong moment, or by adhering to forms of art which could not long remain in vogue. In his attempt to reconcile the epical treatment of mythology with the choric system of his own invention, he proved that he had not fully grasped the capabilities of lyrical poetry. In his endeavour to create an idyllic and romantic species, he was far before his age.

The remaining choral poets of the Dorian style, of whom the eldest, Ibycus, dates half a century later than Arion, received from their predecessors an instrument of poetical expression already nearly complete. It was their part to use it as skilfully as possible, and to introduce such changes as might render it more polished. Excellence of workmanship is particularly noticeable in what remains of Ibycus, Simonides, Bacchylides. These latter lyrists are no longer local poets: under the altered circumstances of Hellas at the time of the Persian war, art has become Panhellenic, the artists cease to be the servants of one state or of one deity; they range from city to city, giving their services to all who seek for them, and embracing the various tribes and religious rites of the collected Greeks in their æsthetic sympathy. Now, for the first time, poets begin to sell their songs of praise for money. Simonides introduced the practice, which had something shocking in it to Greek taste, and which Plato especially censures as sophistic and illiberal in his Protagoras. Now, too, poets became the friends and counsellors of princes, mixing freely in the politics of Samos, Syracuse, Agrigentum, Thessaly; aiding the tyrants Polycrates, Hiero, Theron, the Scopada, with their advice. Simonides is said to have suspended hostilities between Theron and Hiero by his diplomatic intercession after their armies had been drawn up in battle array. Petrarch did not occupy a more important place among the princes and republics of mediæval Italy. Under these new conditions, and with this expansion of the poet's calling, the old character of the Dorian lyric changed. The title Dorian is now

merely nominal ; and the dialect is a conventional language consecrated to this style.

Ibycus was a native of Rhegium, a colony of mixed Ionians
and Dorians. To which of these families he belonged is not
certain. If we judged by the internal evidence of his poems, we
should call him an Ionian ; for they are distinguished by voluptuous sweetness, with a dash of almost Æolian intensity. Ibycus
was a poet-errant, carrying his songs from state to state. The
beautiful story of the cranes who led to the discovery of his
murderer at Corinth, though probably mythical, like that of
Arion's dolphin, illustrates the rude lives of these Greek troubadours, and shows in what respect the *sacer vates*, servant of the
Muses and beloved of Phœbus, was held by the people. Ibycus
was regarded by antiquity as a kind of male Sappho. His odes,
composed for birthday festivals and banquets, were dedicated
chiefly to the praise of beautiful youths, and the legends which
adorned them, like those of Ganymede or Tithonus, were appropriate to the erotic style. Aristophanes, in the Thesmophora-
zusæ, makes Agathan connect him with Anacreon and Alcæus,
as the three refiners of language. It is clear, therefore, that in
his art Ibycus adapted the manner of Dorian poetry to the
matter of Æolian or Ionian love-chants. Simonides is a far
more brilliant representative than Ibycus, both of Greek choral
poetry in its prime, and also of the whole literary life of Hellas
during the period which immediately preceded and followed the
Persian war. He was born in the island of Ceos, of pure Ionian
blood and breeding ; but the Ionians of Ceos were celebrated for
their σωφροσύνη, a quality which is strongly marked in the
poems of Simonides. In his odes we do not trace that mixture
of Æolian passion and that concentration upon personal emotions which are noticeable in those of Ibycus, but rather a
Dorian solemnity of thought and feeling, which qualified
Simonides for the arduous functions to which he was called, of
commemorating in elegy and epigram and funeral ode the
achievements of Hellas against Persia. Simonides belonged to
a family of professional poets ; for the arts among the early
Greeks were hereditary ; a father taught the trade of flute-
playing and chorus-leading and verse-making to his son, who, if
he had original genius, became a great poet, as was the fate of
Pindar ; or, if he were endowed with commonplace abilities, remained a journeyman in art without discredit to himself, performing useful functions in his native place. Simonides exercised his calling of chorus-teacher at Carthæa in Ceos, and lived at
the χορηγεῖον, or resort of the chorus, near the temple of Apollo.
But the greater portion of his life, after he had attained
celebrity, was passed with patrons,—with Hipparchus, who invited

him to Athens, where he dwelt at amity with Anacreon, and at
enmity with Pindar's master Lasos—with the Scopads and
Aleuads of Thessaly; for whom he composed the most touching
threnoi and the most brilliant panegyrics, of which fragments
have descended to us;—finally, with Hiero of Syracuse, who
honoured him exceedingly, and when he died, consigned him to
the earth with princely funeral pomp. The relations of Simonides to these patrons may be gathered from numerous slight
indications, none of which are very honourable to his character.
For instance, after receiving the hospitality of Hipparchus, he
composed an epigram for the statue of Harmodius, in which he
calls the murder of the tyrant "a great light rising upon Athens."
Again, he praised the brutal Scopas, son of Creon, in an ode
which is celebrated, both as connected with the most dramatic
incident in the poet's life, and also as having furnished Plato
with a theme for argument, and Aristotle with an ethical quotation—"To be a good man in very truth, a square without blame,
is hard." This proposition Plato discusses in the Protagoras,
while Aristotle cites the phrase, τετράγωνος ἄνευ. From the
general tenor of the fragments of this ode, from Plato's criticism,
and from what is known about the coarse nature of Scopas, who
is being praised, we must conjecture that Simonides attempted
to whitewash his patron's character by depreciating the standard
of morality. With Ionian facility and courtly compliment he
made excuses for a bad man by pleading that perfect goodness
was unattainable. Scopas refused to pay the price required by
Simonides for the poem in question, telling him to get half of
it from the Dioscuri, who had also been eulogized. This was
at a banquet. While the king was laughing at his own rude jest,
a servant whispered to the poet that two goodly youths waited
without, desiring earnestly to speak with him. Simonides left
the palace, but found no one. Even as he stood looking for his
visitors, he heard the crash of beams and the groans of dying
men. Scopas with his guests had been destroyed by the falling
of the roof, and Simonides had received a godlike guerdon from
the two sons of Tyndareus. This story belongs, perhaps, to the
same class as the cranes of Ibycus and the dolphin of Arion.
Yet there seems to be no doubt that the Scopad dynasty was
suddenly extinguished; for we hear nothing of them at the time
of the Persian war, and we know that Simonides composed a
threnos for the family.

The most splendid period of the life of Simonides was that
which he passed at Athens during the great wars with Persia.
Here he was the friend of Miltiades, Themistocles, and Pausanias.
Here he compiled his epigrams on Marathon, Thermopylæ,
Salamis, Platæa—poems not destined to be merely sung or con-

signed to parchment, but to be carved in marble or engraved in
letters of imperishable bronze upon the works of the noblest architects and statuaries. The genius of Simonides is unrivalled in
this branch of monumental poetry. His couplets—calm, simple,
terse, strong as the deeds they celebrate, enduring as the brass
or stone which they adorned—animated succeeding generations
of Greek patriots; they were transferred to the brains of statesmen like Pericles and Demosthenes, inscribed upon the fleshy
tablets of the hearts of warriors like Cleomenes, Pelopidas,
Epaminondas. We are thrice fortunate in possessing the entire
collection of these epigrams, unrivalled for the magnitude of the
events they celebrate, and for the circumstances under which
they were composed. When we reflect what would have become
of the civilization of the world but for these Greek victories—
when we remember that the events which these few couplets record transcend in importance those of any other single period of
history—we are almost appalled by the contrast between the
brevity of the epigrams and the world-wide vastness of their
matter. In reviewing the life of Simonides, after admitting
that he was greedy of gain and not averse to flatter, we are
bound to confess that, as a poet, he proved himself adequate to
the age of Marathon and Salamis. He was the voice of Hellas
—the genius of Fame, sculpturing upon her brazen shield with
a pen of adamant, in austere letters of indelible gold, the
achievements to which the whole world owes its civilization.
Happy poet! Had any other man so splendid a heritage of
song alloted to him?

In style Simonides is always pure and exquisitely polished.
The ancients called him the sweet poet—Melicertes—par excellence. His σωφροσύνη gives a mellow tone not merely to his
philosophy and moral precepts, but also to his art. He has none
of Pindar's rugged majesty, volcanic force, gorgeous exuberance:
he does not, like Pindar, pour forth an inexhaustible torrent of
poetical ideas, chafing against each other in the eddies of breathless inspiration. On the contrary, he works up a few thoughts,
a few carefully selected images, with patient skill, producing a
perfectly harmonious result, but one which is always bordering
on the commonplace. Like all correct poets, he is somewhat
tame, though tender, delicate, and exquisitely beautiful. Pindar
electrifies his hearer, seizing him like the eagle in Dante's vision,
and bearing him breathless through the ether of celestial flame.
Simonides leads us by the hand along the banks of pleasant
rivers, through laurel-groves, and by the porticoes of sunny temples. What he possesses of quite peculiar to his own genius is
pathos—the pathos of romance. This appears most remarkable
in the fragment of a threnos which describes Danae afloat upon

the waves at night. The careful development of simple thoughts
in Simonides may best be illustrated by the fragment on the
three hundred Spartans who died at Thermopylæ:—

"Of those who died at Thermopylæ, glorious is the fate and fair the
doom; their grave is an altar; instead of lamentation, they have endless fame; their dirge is a chant of praise. Such winding-sheet as
theirs no rust, no, nor all-conquering time, shall bring to nought.
But this sepulchre of brave men hath taken for its habitant the glory
of Hellas. Leonidas is witness, Sparta's king, who hath left a mighty
crown of valour and undying fame."

The antitheses are wrought with consummate skill: the fate of
the heroes is glorious, their doom honourable; so far the
eulogy is commonplace; then the same thought receives a
bolder turn: their grave is an altar. We do not lament for
them so much as hold them in eternal memory; our very
songs of sorrow become pæans of praise. What follows is a still
further expansion of the leading theme: rust and time cannot
affect their fame; Hellas confides her glory to their tomb. Then
generalities are quitted, and Leonidas, the protagonist of Thermopylæ, appears.

In his threnos Simonides has generally recourse to the
common grounds of consolation, which the Ionian elegists repeat
ad nauseam, dwelling upon the shortness and uncertainty and
ills of life, and tending rather to depress the survivors on their
own account than to comfort them for the dead. In one he says,
"Short is the strength of men, and vain are all their cares, and in
their brief life trouble follows upon trouble; and death, that no
man shuns, is hung above our heads—for him both good and
bad share equally." It is impossible, while reading this
lachrymose lament, to forget the fragment of that mighty
threnos of Pindar's which sounds like a trumpet-blast for
immortality, and trampling under feet the glories of this world,
reveals the gladness of the souls who have attained Elysium:—

> "For them, the night all through,
>   In that broad realm below,
> The splendour of the sun spreads endless light;
>   'Mid rosy meadows bright,
> Their city of the tombs with incense-trees,
>   And golden chalices
>   Of flowers, and fruitage fair,
>   Scenting the breezy air,
> Is laden. There with horses and with play,
> With games and lyres, they while the hours away.
>
>   "On every side around
>   Pure happiness is found,

> With all the blooming beauty of the world ;
> There fragrant smoke upcurled
> From altars, where the blazing fire is dense
> With perfumed frankincense
> Burned unto gods in heaven,
> Through all the land is driven,
> Making its pleasant places odorous
> With scented gales and sweet airs amorous."

What has been said about Simonides applies in a great measure also to Bacchylides, who was his nephew, pupil, and faithful follower. The personality of Bacchylides, as a man and a poet, is absorbed in that of his uncle—the greater bard, the more distinguished actor on the theatre of the world. While Simonides played his part in public life, Bacchylides gave himself up to the elegant pleasures of society ; while Simonides celebrated in epigrams the military glories of the Greeks, Bacchylides wrote wine-songs and congratulatory odes. His descriptions of Bacchic intoxication and of the charms of peace display the same careful word-painting as the description by Simonides of Orpheus, with more luxuriance of sensual suggestion. His threnoi exhibit the same Ionian despondency and resignation—a dead settled calm, an elegant stolidity of epicureanism.

Here we must stop short in the front of Pindar—the Hamlet among these lesser actors, the Shakspeare among a crowd of inferior poets. To treat of Greek lyrical poetry and to omit Pindar is a paradox in action. Yet Pindar is so colossal, so much apart, that he deserves a separate study, and cannot be dragged in at the end of a birds-eye view of a period of literature. At the time of Pindar lyric poetry was sinking into mannerism. He by the force of his native originality gave it a wholly fresh direction, and created a style as novel as it was inimitable. Like Athos, like Atlas, like the Matterhorn, like Monte Viso, like the Peak of Teneriffe, he stands alone, sky-piercing and tremendous in his solitary strength.

Art. IV.—Dr. Newman: the Difficulties of Protestantism.

Discussions and Arguments on various Subjects. By
John Henry Newman, sometime Fellow of Oriel College.
London: 1872.

IN a well-known passage of his Essays, Lord Macaulay has
remarked that it is by no means sure that Roman Catholicism may not be destined to outlive all other ecclesiastical
establishments in the world. We think that it is, at any rate,
destined to outlive the system known as Protestantism. Leaving
out of consideration its superior antiquity, its unity, its matchless
organization and other advantages of an external kind, there are
two internal characteristics in which it far surpasses its rival. Its
promises are more satisfactory to the instincts of the vulgar. The
grounds upon which they are based are, upon the whole, more
satisfactory to the mind of the philosopher. On the former
point it is unnecessary to enlarge. The deity who exhibits himself on the altar of every church is a more immediate deity than
the sublime Being who puts in a momentary appearance in the
reigns of Augustus and Tiberius. The God who remits sins
through the medium of his accredited servants, is a more accessible god than the mysterious spirit of whose pardon and favour
none can feel absolutely certain. Whatever benefits a change of
creed may confer upon a Roman Catholic, it cannot give him—

"Tam præsentes alibi cognoscere Divos."

In the second place, Roman Catholicism is a system very
logically reasoned out from certain premises. These, it is true,
are only assumptions, but they are assumptions in a great degree
common to itself and to its reforming opponents. Whatever
may be thought of its axioms and postulates, its propositions *do*
result from them. Protestantism, on the other hand, with far
better foundations laid for its edifice, finds itself unable to build
in any direction but one, without the risk of seeing the structure
crumble into pieces on the heads of the builders. The corner-
stone is an admirable one for a Temple of Free Thought, and for
nothing else. Granting that God Almighty came upon earth to
found a religious system, we are at a loss to make out where such
a system is to be found if not in the Church of Rome. Granting
the right of free judgment as applied to the Bible, we are equally
at a loss to understand how any one can be called upon to believe
in the inspiration of the Bible; or, in the event of his doing so,
to what part of it he is to be referred for the distinctive tenets of
Protestantism.

It is not by this intended to imply—very far from it indeed—that the Reformation was not of immense service to the world. The logical or illogical character of a religious belief is a question altogether distinct from its beneficial or injurious character. This must be judged of by its effects or tendencies, and these are sometimes of a kind not foreseen by, indeed diametrically contrary to, the intentions of its founders. The great achievement of the Reformation was the establishment of the right of private judgment, as opposed to the dogma of an infallible church. Nothing, to our way of thinking, can be more alien to reason than the idea of a Divine revelation of essential truths from which a dozen conflicting systems can be extracted. Nothing would be more bewildering to our minds (if, to be sure, habit had not accustomed us to the notion) than the idea of God, one of the Trinity, appearing on the earth for a few years, and leaving behind him, so to speak, nothing but a bundle of documents, often contradicting each other, nowhere asserting their own infallibility, and from which not even the dogma of his own Divinity, much less that of the Trinity, is clearly to be obtained. Yet, at the same time—and this history has abundantly proved—nothing could be more beneficial to the world than that men should be freed from the incubus of a despotism which, by claiming authority over their consciences, virtually claimed dominion over everything else. " It is better that men should be free than that they should be sober," said an English bishop not long ago in the House of Lords ; and assuredly it is better that men should be free than that they should be logical. Better that people should leave a fair and commodious, but enslaved and unhealthy city, and pitch their tents upon the mountain heights. It may be that no permanent foundations can be laid there : but a healthier soil and climate will rear a hardier race. Only let it be borne in mind that these are tents, and not buildings, and that the time will come when the temporary settlement must be broken up, and the colonists will have to migrate elsewhere. This is exactly what we think likely to be the destiny of Protestantism.

We have spoken of the right of private judgment as the outcome of the Reformation. But of course, as every one knows, a compromise was adopted. The compromise was to this effect, that every one was perfectly free to exercise his judgment in religious matters, subject to the proviso that, in point of fact, he was not free to do anything of the kind. He must believe in the infallibility of certain writings, and moreover he must consent to see certain dogmas, and no others, inculcated in these writings. These dogmas varied slightly in different regions : but there was for a long while a general agreement or undertaking in Protestant countries to burn all those who persisted in seeing the real pre-

sence in Scripture, or who stumbled in the matter of the Godhead of the Son, or of the Trinity ; while persons who denied
that pædobaptism is to be found in the New Testament, and
minor offenders of that description, were allowed to rot leisurely
in gaols. Ridiculous as this compromise may sound to some, it
may fairly claim the highest merit which can attach to any
arrangement of the kind. It has been successful. It has lasted
for three hundred years. The element which has given it vitality
is the affirmation which it contains of human freedom, a very
misty, confused, and at times self-contradictory one ; still, at the
bottom, a distinct affirmation of this principle. The most fanatical Evangelical bishop, or Methodist tub-thumper, imagines
that he is carrying out this principle of free-judgment. It
seems to him impossible that any one can examine into the subject of Theology without arriving at the same conclusions as his
own. But he admits the right to examine, merely crediting
his opponents with wilful blindness, or perhaps attributing
their perverseness to the special act of the devil. " Look in that
direction, and you will see the same object as I do," is an advance upon " Shut your eyes, and believe whatever I tell you
about the object."

A fair illustration of this kind of compromise may be observed
among the Quakers. And the Quakers, as we think, illustrate
our meaning, when we say that the logical character of a creed
has but little to do with its real value. Moreover, a passing
mention of them is not out of place, since they have pushed
Protestant principles to the extreme limit to which these can be
carried in combination with a belief in the inspiration of the
Bible ; with the result which might have been foreseen, of merely
figuring as an ante-room to Unitarianism and Deism. The
Quakers hold what they call Immediate Revelation and Percep-
tible Guidance. Yet it is certain that if one of their most
respected members were to get up at the meeting-house behind
the National Gallery, and announce that the Spirit had communicated to him the expediency of being baptized with all his
household, he would create a scandal. Revelation, for these
good people, means a revelation not incompatible with the views
of the Society of Friends. Guidance means guidance within the
limits traced by George Fox and Robert Barclay. Nothing can
be more preposterous than this, yet nothing can be more beneficial in its results. For the doctrine of direct communication
between man and his Maker, however disfigured, saves the
Society from a priesthood.

Compromises are, however, from their nature, generally but
temporary expedients ; and we do not think that the one agreed
to in the sixteenth century is likely to form an exception to the

rule. You may seal up the spirit of free inquiry, as the Roman
Catholics do, like another genius in a vase ; but once release it,
and by no arrangement can it be made to assume any but its
natural proportions. Accordingly, the question soon arose, and
still presses for the reply which it has not yet received—" Having
gone thus far, why may I not go further? Why, on your principles, am I called upon to believe in the infallibility of a book,
which nowhere proclaims itself infallible ?" And Protestantism
has no answers to this question which are not beside the mark
or absolutely suicidal. For example, the earliest authority for
the authenticity and genuineness of the four Gospels is Irenæus,
and the value of Irenæus's testimony consists in this, that we
can gather from his language that the Christians of his age held
these gospels for inspired, and the works of the writers whose
names they bear. But if this be taken to be proof, it proves too
much, since the same Father (who, by the way, may have been
in the world with the Apostle John, and who, at any rate, says
that he had known Polycarp), testifies to the foundation of the
Roman Church by Peter and Paul ; teaches the necessity of
conforming to this church "on account of its pre-eminent
authority ;" teaches apostolical succession; the real presence in
the Eucharist ; the co-operation of the Virgin in the redemption
of the world, in the same way as Eve had co-operated in the
fall, and other doctrines which plainly savour of the " Beast."
Or again, the inspiration of Scripture being conceded, it may
fairly be asked by any one who accepts that dogma, " Why
may I not believe what Arius did? Since the New Testament,
from Matthew to Revelation (not even excluding the Fourth
Gospel), seems to me full of the inferiority of the Son to the
Father." Here, again, the Reformation, having conceded the
rights of a supreme tribunal to the individual conscience, has
left itself without a court of appeal. The very act of appealing
to the Church of Rome would be obviously an act of " happy
despatch" for Protestantism. Accordingly, it has been attempted
to erect another court of appellate jurisdiction. It is invoked
by the " Anglican," who admits that many of his peculiar doctrines cannot, without violence, be extracted from Scripture, but
who fails to see that an appeal to anything else on their behalf
is destructive of his own position. This tribunal is to be found
in the " Consensus of the Christian Church during the first three
centuries." But, independently of the fact that all the special
dogmas of Rome may most conclusively be shown to have been
held during these centuries, this compromise (for this is another
specimen of a compromise) would, in any case, rest upon an
assumption of the most arbitrary character. It admits that such
doctrines as the Trinity, &c. are not to be found positively laid

down in Scripture, but that they may be deduced from it, and were logically developed in the early church, and that this process of development went on under divine guidance till the Council of Nice, or the Council of Constantinople, or whatever happens to be the council or epoch most convenient for the theory; and that all the dogmas and practices that were subsequently developed in the same way, were apparently reduced into form under the guidance of the Evil One. The Arian might conclusively reply that he preferred to go further back, and to stop at the beginning of the second century, when certainly neither the equality of the Son to the Father, nor the personality and equality of the third Person were held: and that it was at this point, rather than two centuries later, that the Evil One succeeded to the patronage of the Church, and the task of shaping the Church's beliefs.

Many still more difficult questions than these—questions by no means new, but to which the author's style and mode of treatment have communicated in some cases an air of novelty—are put to the upholder of the Protestant system, in the book before us, or rather in that part of it which we have undertaken to notice. Dr. Newman is doing well in collecting the best of his contributions to periodical literature, and adding them in successive volumes to a uniform edition of his works. Everything that he writes he writes with care. *Non erunt aeterna fortasse quae scripsit, ille tamen scripsit tamquam essent futura.* These papers exhibit the same merits and the same defects as are to be found in his more ambitious works—"The History of the Arians," "The Apologia," "The Grammar of Assent." Seldom has there appeared in the arena a more representative champion of the Romish creed. Grant him his premises, and he will reason from them with almost unexampled acuteness. Whenever he gives us a view of his own fundamental beliefs and his grounds for holding them, he is, to use the expression which he himself applies to some of his opponents, "wasting his efforts in delineating an invisible phantom." It will be recollected how mercilessly, some years ago, he beat and pounded poor Mr. Kingsley; and how in the same breath he favoured us with his views about angels, "as the real causes of motion, light, and life, and of those elementary principles of the physical universe, which, when offered in their developments to our senses, suggest to us the notion of cause and effect, and of what are called the laws of nature;" and how, further on, he tells us that he is a Catholic because he believes in a God, and a believer in God because he believes in his own existence. "Dr. Newman struck upon the method of assailing with logic all who appeal to reason, while assuming that the true faith (his own), being founded on something higher than reason, is not bound to justify itself to reason." This is the judgment passed on him by his own brother, and we believe it to be a correct one. He is in fact like the *retiarius*, cunning at throwing the net and striking his victim with the trident, but when grappled with at close quarters he is found to be himself without defensive armour of any kind. In the present instance, however, we have to watch only his offensive operations, and these, to our mind, are always interesting. The present volume consists of six portions, of which the three most important are "The Tamworth Reading-room," a course of letters on secular instruction, which were first published in the *Times* newspaper during the year 1841; the "Patristic Idea of Antichrist;" and "Scripture and the Creed;" the last-named the longest of the series, and which originally saw the light as one of the famous "Tracts for the Times" in 1838. It is to this Essay that we beg to call the attention of the reader.

We take it that, like other productions of the same writer, it was composed at a time when his mind was principally occupied with the logical weakness of the creed which he had not as yet openly abandoned, and from which a slowly growing conviction of its imperfections was gradually forcing him to a more congenial, if not a surer, resting-place. This is of course a phase through which all thinking men have to pass on their way from one religion to another; and if our estimate of him be correct, it was one particularly calculated to furnish him with an opportunity of exhibiting his powers. The essay is in fact an attack upon the Protestant position, from the Catholic or Anglican stand-point. We are, however, not so much concerned with the banner under which he fights as with the weapons which he uses and his mode of using them. And as his arguments are equally good on behalf of Roman Catholicism proper, to which indeed he himself has been necessarily led by the employment of them, and as, so applied, they would be more intelligible to the general reader, we shall take the liberty of understanding them as brought forward in defence of that system.

Protestants (says Dr. Newman) object on certain grounds to the church system of doctrine. They object that, though professing to rest on Scripture, it can show so little scriptural proof in its favour. I acknowledge the difficulty; but surely you yourselves who raise this objection are in a similar difficulty. You ought, on your own principles, to doubt or disown much which happily you now believe in. For instance, if you deny the Apostolical succession of the ministry, because it is not clearly taught in Scripture, you ought, if consistent, to deny the divinity of the Holy Ghost, which is nowhere literally stated in Scripture.

Examine this objection a little more closely. If Scripture laid such stress, as we do, upon the plenary remission of sin by Baptism, the consecration of the Elements in the Eucharist, Church Union, Apostolical Succession, Absolution, and other rites and ceremonies, why (it is said) is merely indirect mention made of them? Why is the evidence for these doctrines merely a few striking texts which may mean, but need not mean, exactly what they are said by us to mean? I reply that, if these are good arguments, they are good against nearly all the doctrines which are held by any one who is called a Christian in any sense of the word. First, as to ordinances and precepts. There is not a single text in the Bible enjoining Infant Baptism. Our warrant for this practice, as for others about to be mentioned, consists of inferences carefully made from various texts. There is not a text telling us to keep holy the first day of the week instead of the seventh : scarcely a text enjoining our going to church for joint worship, nothing to show that such a practice is necessary for all times, nothing more express than there is to show that an unmarried state is better for all times. The first disciples prayed together, and so in like manner the first disciples practised celibacy and adopted a community of goods. There is no text in the New Testament which enjoins us to "establish" religion, none which allows us to take oaths, none which prohibits polygamy. Again, take the case of Doctrine. If the Eucharist is never called a Sacrifice, nor Ministers Priests, where is the Holy Ghost called God? If Altar, Absolution, Succession are not in Scripture, so neither is the word Trinity. Where does the New Testament declare itself inspired? Where do Protestants derive their notion that every one may gain his knowledge of revealed truth from Scripture itself? May not the doctrine of the Atonement be explained away by those who explain away the doctrine of the Eucharist? If the expressions used concerning the latter are merely figurative, so may be those used of the former. And how shall we prove the doctrine of justification by faith *only*?

More than this, Revelation must surely have been intended to establish a *system* of some kind, and it is equally sure that this system is not on the surface of Scripture. It must therefore be given in Scripture in an indirect or covert way, or given elsewhere, and this can only be in the Church's teaching. There is, indeed, another view, to the effect that there are one or two doctrines to be discovered in Scripture clearly—a message consisting of one or two great and simple statements, and that he who holds these is a Christian. These statements are sometimes called the Essentials, the vital doctrines, the leading ideas of the Gospel. But the great difficulty in the way of this view is that

no great number of persons are agreed as to what are the leading
ideas or peculiar doctrines. Some say the doctrine of the Atonement is the leading idea; others, the doctrine of Spiritual
Influence; others, that love is all in all; others, the acknowledgment that Jesus is Christ; while others deny that His Godhead
is to be found in the New Testament; others, the immortality of
the soul.

The writer thus pursues the subject:—

"But, further, it can scarcely be denied that Scripture, if it does not
furnish, at least speaks of, refers to, takes for granted, sanctions, some
certain doctrine or message, as to be believed in order to salvation; and
which, accordingly, if not found in Scripture, must be sought for out
of it. It says, ' He who believeth shall be saved, and he who believeth
not shall be damned;' it speaks of ' the doctrine of Christ,' of ' keeping
the faith,' of ' the faith once *delivered* to the saints,' and of ' delivering
that which has been received;' recounting at the same time some of
the articles of the Apostles' Creed.   And the case is the same as
regards discipline; rules of worship and order, whether furnished or
not, are at least alluded to again and again under the title of
' traditions.'   Revelation then will be inconsistent with itself unless it
has provided some Creed somewhere.   For it declares in Scripture that
it has given us a Creed, therefore some Creed exists somewhere, whether
in Scripture or out of it."—p. 135.

The Church view cannot be given better than in the author's
own words:—

"Under these circumstances, what excuse have we for not recognising in the system of doctrine and worship existing in history, that
very system to which the Apostles refer in Scripture? They evidently
did not in Scripture say out all they had to say; this is evident on the
face of Scripture, evident from what they do say. St. Paul says, ' *The
rest* will I set in order when I come.' St. John, ' I had *many things*
to write, but I will not with pen and ink write unto thee; but I trust
I shall shortly see thee, and we shall *speak* face to face.' This he says
in two Epistles. Now supposing, to take the case of profane history,
a collection of letters were extant written by the founders or re-
modellers of the Platonic or Stoic philosophy, and supposing those
masters referred in them to their philosophy, and treated of it in some
of its parts, yet without drawing it out in an orderly way; and then,
secondly, supposing there did exist other and more direct historical
sources of various kinds, from which a distinct systematic account of
their philosophy might be drawn, that is, one account of it and but
one from many witnesses, should we not take it for granted that this
was their system, that system of which their letters spoke? Should
not we accept that system conveyed to us by history with (I will not
say merely an antecedent disposition in its favour, but with) a confidence and certainty that it *was* their system; and if we found discrepancies between it and their letters, should we at once cast it aside

as spurious, or should we not rather try to reconcile the two together, and suspect that *we* were in fault, that *we* had made some mistake, and even if after all we could not reconcile all parts, (supposing it,) should we not leave the discrepancies *as* difficulties, and believe in the system notwithstanding? The Apostles refer to a large existing fact, their system—'the whole counsel of God;' history informs us of a system, as far as we can tell, contemporaneous with and claiming to be theirs: what other claimant is there?"—pp. 136, 137.

So far Dr. Newman has been attacking the unfortunate Protestants with weapons which, as we said before, are not new, but which are for the most part dangerous only to his adversaries. He now proceeds to spring a mine, or rather a series of mines, upon them, which may be effective, indeed, for the purpose intended, and also for other purposes presumably not intended. Indeed, it is some time since we have seen an orthodox writer treading so calmly and courageously on the *ignes suppositos cineri doloso* of theology; and this we say with a full recollection of Dr. Irons's recent book, "The Bible and its Interpreters." But the reader shall judge for himself.

Dr. Newman virtually argues thus:—If you reject the Church system on account of its internal difficulties, or its supposed contradictions to or divergencies from Scripture, or want of evidence on its behalf, so, by a parity of reasoning, you ought to reject Scripture itself, in which are to be found the same kinds of difficulties, the same apparent contradictions and divergencies between one passage and another, and against which a like want of external evidence may be alleged. It is evident that this line of argument imposes upon the writer who employs it the necessity of dwelling upon the difficulties, external and internal, of the Canon in exactly the same way as a Deist would dwell upon them. The object of course is different, and the mode of expression may be different, but the process is the same. Thus, starting with his illustrations from the very beginning of the Bible, Dr. Newman carefully points out, what we know to be the fact, that the Elohistic and Jehovistic accounts of Creation entirely differ from each other. If (says he) we had one of these narratives given us in the Bible, and the other came to us from some other source, e. g., the Church, should we not say that the second must be untrue, as contradicting the first? Very well, then; it seems that a statement may seem at variance with Scripture, may wear an improbable exterior, and yet come from God: unless the Book of Genesis is (*what is impossible,—God forbid!*) self-contradictory. We may say, in passing, that we think this fair, as an argument *ad homines*, but let the effect of it be observed—we are not concerned with more than this, at the present moment. Here we have grave doubts on the subject

of the biblical record of Creation inspired in the mind of the
neophyte. It is all very well to say that this book of Dr. Newman's is addressed to particular people. Books are addressed to
everybody. "Certainly, I are," says the young man, "what you
have pointed out to me, for the first time, a difficulty, two contradictory accounts of the same event, in Scripture." "So it
seems at first sight," replies Dr. Newman; "but then, you
know, this is impossible, thank God! And now permit me to
call your attention to another example!"

And he does show other examples, and very numerous ones,
first of all of what he styles "the unstudied and therefore per-
plexed character of Scripture, as regards its relation of *facts*,"—
a strange euphemism. He refers to the two accounts of Abraham's denying his wife, and the similar story told of Isaac; the
contradictory narratives of God's commands to Balaam; the
conflicting views of David's character conveyed in the Books of
Samuel and the Chronicles. But we need not go on with a list
of "difficulties" which, if our memory serves us rightly, make
up the staple of Tom Paine's work. One or two points are,
however, made by the Author which merit a passing notice.
The first three Gospels, he says, contain no declaration of our
Lord's divinity, and there are passages which tend, at first sight,
the other way. He might have added that neither does the
fourth Gospel contain any such declaration of Christ's divinity,
in the sense of his co-equality with God. "I conceive," he continues, with dangerous frankness, "the impression left on an
ordinary mind would be that our Saviour was a superhuman
Being, intimately possessed of God's confidence, but still a
creature." Here we think the Orthodox Protestant is in a
difficulty. For, unfortunately for his case, this impression left
on the ordinary mind by Scripture is precisely what he professes to lean upon, and if he appeals to the voice of the primitive
Church against the sceptic, he is in the situation of the horse
who called in the man to help him against the stag. For certainly at the date of the publication of the Fourth Gospel, or
very shortly afterwards, the distinctive tenets of Roman Catholicism were held by the Church. Again, is the tone of the
Epistle of James the same as the tone of St. Paul's Epistle to
the Ephesians? Might they not as plausibly be put in opposition with each other as the Church system is made contrary to
Scripture? This we suppose is an instance of what the Author
elsewhere calls "the unsolicitous freedom and want of system of
the sacred narrative." Take two more examples. Where are
we told in the Bible that the serpent that tempted Eve was the
devil? The nearest approach to such an intimation is in the
Apocalypse, where the devil is called "that old serpent," and

this is hardly conclusive. Can we be surprised that other truths
are but obscurely conveyed in Scripture, when this hardly
escapes, so to speak, omission? Again, if silence implies
ignorance or denial of the things passed over, if nothing is the
sense of Scripture but what is openly declared, why are we to
say that the Song of Solomon has a spiritual meaning? Either,
then, the apparent tone of passages in Scripture is not the real
tone, or the Canticles is not a sacred book !

It is, however, when he comes to those portions of his essay
specially headed " Difficulties (external and internal) of Canon
and Creed," that Dr. Newman proceeds to grapple at close
quarters with his opponents. " How do you know," he asks
boldly, " that the whole Bible is the word of God? You believe
that it is ; by a happy inconsistency, I say. You ought to have
doubts on your principles, and this I shall proceed to show."
There are two chief heads of objection made against the Catholic
system. The first is external. " It is uncertain what is in antiquity or what not. The early fathers contradict each other ; the
most valuable of them did not live till two or three centuries
after St. John's death ; no doubt there is much of truth and
value in their system, but we deny that it is necessarily *unmixed*
truth ; their views of doctrine were, from the first, corrupted
from Pagan and Jewish sources." Well, but will not the captious spirit treat the Canon after the same fashion ? These
writings are put together in one book. Who put them together ?
The printer. But what authority had those who put them together to do so ? On what authority do we leave out the
Wisdom of the Son of Sirach, and put in the book of Esther ?
Catalogues of these books are given in early times, to be sure ;
but then they do not correspond with each other. This so-called
Canon did not exist till the fourth century. Why should not we
be as good judges as the Church of the fourth century, on whose
authority we receive it ? Why should one book be divine because another is ? Take this case. The first Father who ex-
pressly mentions commemorations for the dead in Christ, is
Tertullian. Tertullian, you say, may have been mistaken ;
errors may have crept in by that time. Granted. But Tertullian
also is the first who refers to St. Paul's Epistle to Philemon, and
he without quoting or naming it. Again, Irenæus, Clement,
Tertullian, and others, invariably speak of the Lord's table as an
altar ; yet these writers are our earliest authorities for the
authenticity of the Epistles to the Thessalonians. Again, that
the Eucharist is a sacrifice is declared, or implied, by St. Clement
of Rome, St. Paul's companion, as well as by St. Justin. On the
other hand, the Acts of the Apostles are not distinctly noticed
till some two centuries after Christ. Which has the best evidence,

the Book of Acts, or the doctrine of the Eucharistic sacrifice?
Lastly, our earliest witness to the existing Canon in anything
like its present form, is St. Irenæus, at the close of the second
century, who quotes all the books of the New Testament but
five. Why may not so learned and holy a man, and so close on
the Apostles, stand also as a witness of some doctrines which he
takes for granted, such as the use of Catholic tradition in ascertaining revealed truth, and the powers committed to the Church?
As to the objection that the doctrinal views of the Fathers were
in many cases borrowed from Pagan and other sources, Dr.
Newman has some observations from his point of view which
well deserve consideration, but which we have not space to notice. "But after all," he asks pertinently, at the end, "do not
the same objections apply to the Canon? Has not Moses been
accused of borrowing his laws from the Egyptians, the Jews of
borrowing the devil from the Babylonians, St. John of borrowing
the Logos from the Alexandrian Platonists?"

The ingenious writer concludes his subject by adverting to the
internal objections adducible against the Catholic system; and
he proceeds to argue that precisely the same objections may be
made to the contents of the Canon. The antecedent exception
taken against the Catholic doctrines is that they are " mysterious, tending to superstition, and to dependence on a particular
set of men." It might with equal truth be said, that there is
much in Scripture which to most men of this generation will
appear "strange, superstitious, incredible, and extreme." We
have not space to follow Dr. Newman through a tithe part of his
illustrations of the apparent incredibilities and unlikely narratives in Scripture; things which we should infallibly reject, if
we were not prevented by "strength of habit, good feeling, and
controlling grace." We are afraid that if this volume should fall
into the hands of Mr. Bradlaugh, who is said not to be subject
to some of these influences, he may make use of it for purposes
of his own. And we consider him thoroughly entitled to do
this, provided he does not fall foul of certain other Canons—
those of good taste. This by the way. We will, however, give
a few short illustrations of the author's mode of treatment.
What, he asks, can be more opposed to science—we beg pardon,
apparently opposed to science, and if we should anywhere drop
the word just italicized, we beg the reader to supply it—than the
whole system of Scripture demonology? Look at the devil
calling out his name, "My name is Legion!" the unclean spirit
walking through dry places and finding none; the damsel possessed of a spirit of divination or Python, that is, of a heathen
god; a serpent being possessed of an evil spirit, and talking to
Eve; the devils and the swine, &c. "If we were not used to

the narrative," these are Dr. Newman's words, " we should be
very unwilling to receive these things." And we think he is
quite justified in adding, " Let those then see to it, who call the
Fathers credulous for recording similar narratives. . . . . Of this
I feel sure, that those who consider the doctrines of the Church
incredible, will soon, if they turn their thoughts steadily that
way, feel a difficulty in the serpent that tempted Eve, and the
ass that admonished Balaam." " Again, what should we say,
unless we were familiarized with it, to the story of Naaman
bathing seven times in the Jordan? or rather to the whole
system of mystical signs:—the tree which Moses cast into the
waters to sweeten them ; Elisha's throwing meal into the pot of
poisonous herbs; and our Saviour's breathing, making clay,
and the like ?" Consider the account of virtue going out of our
Lord, of those who touched the hem of his garment being made
whole, of handkerchiefs and aprons being impregnated with
healing power by touching St. Paul's body. What should we
think of similar narratives—what *do* we think of similar narratives—outside the sacred volume? More than this (and Dr.
Newman puts this point extremely well), what would Protestants
say to these stories if, instead of being found in the Bible, they
had been handed down by Catholic tradition? Not only that
they were ridiculous and profane, but that they had evidently
been concocted with a view to bolster up certain of the Church's
assumptions, such as that of the hands of a bishop or priest
being able to impart a power or grace. " How could a mere
earthly substance be made more holy because He wore it ? *He*
was holy, not *it* ; it did not gain holiness by being near him."
This is what they would say. Nay, on what other ground do
they deny that the Virgin was most holy in soul and body, from
her ineffable proximity to God? He gave to such substances as
wool or cotton the grace of which they were capable ; yet it is
the height of superstition to say that he communicated of His
higher spiritual perfections to her in whose bosom he lay!
Take, further, the well-known difficulties in the way of the
Temptation. " Unless we were used to the passage," we should
certainly stumble at them. " Putting aside other considerations, dwell awhile on the thought of Satan showing *all* the
kingdoms of the world in a moment of time. What is meant by
this ? How did he show all, and in a moment ? And if by a
mere illusion, why from the top of a high mountain ?" What
will a similar spirit of criticism make of Noah and the Ark,
Jonah and the whale, Peter and the fish, the blood and water
that issued from the Saviour's side, the darkness overspreading
the earth, the lion, calf, man, and eagle before the throne
of God, St. Paul's declaration that women must have their

heads covered in church "because of the angels," or his statement that a woman is saved through child-bearing ? But
enough to show the bearing of Dr. Newman's argument. The
objections, external and internal, to "the Church doctrines, are
such as also lie against the Canon of Scripture; so that if they
avail against one, they avail against both." Or thus—"If in
spite of these (difficulties) Scripture is nevertheless from God, so
again, in spite of similar apparent difficulties, the Catholic
system may be from Him also."

We think this argument—it is really Bishop Butler's, with
canon and catholic system substituted for the course of nature
and revelation respectively—a difficult one for Protestants to
answer. The *inspiration* of the whole Bible rests, in fact, upon
the authority of the Church; and this is the case not less with
the Old Testament, if the matter be carefully examined, than
with the New. There is no other argument for it that will bear
a moment's consideration. We may admit the excellence and
sublimity of the books, or of parts of them ; we may rank them,
as a whole, far above all other books ; we may postulate for them
every quality but one ; but, if we put aside this testimony of the
Church, there is no reason whatever for supposing them to be
other than human compositions marked by human imperfections.
As a result of their being human, what follows? The downfall
of orthodox Protestantism. It may seem a very simple thing to
take the dogma of scriptural inspiration from the Church, and at
the same time to discard a variety of the other dogmas of the
Church as so many parasitical growths and impudent inventions. But this course is open to the inevitable retort that if the
Church was fallible in other matters, it may have been fallible in
this one of inspiration.

Of course this was not in the least the way in which the question was looked at by the Reformers of the sixteenth century.
Their view was that of the vulgar in Protestant countries at the
present day. With them the Bible carried its divinity on the
face of it. It was to them as much an idol as any idol that is
worshipped in Madagascar. "Every verse, every word, every
syllable, every letter," was as evidently inspired in the eyes of
most of them as in those of Mr. Burgon. "Give up witchcraft !"
said John Wesley, more than two centuries later. "Never ! It
would be giving up the whole Bible." Modern discoveries, familiar to all, have rendered the sixteenth century theory untenable
to all but the vulgar, and a process of accommodation has been
adopted. It was Professor Agassiz, if we remember rightly, who
said that every new scientific theory passes through three stages.
Firstly, every one says that it is false. Next, that it is contrary
to the Bible. Lastly, that it is quite true, and not in the least

opposed to the Bible. Indeed, orthodoxy has gone beyond this, and after many a vigorous struggle with, and defeat by, science, has represented science as marching under its own banner. *Grœcia victa ferum victorem cepit!* We are most of us familiar with essays and sermons, in which the first chapters of Genesis are represented as sublime anticipations of the discoveries of geology. And not long ago we met with some letters in the *Record* newspaper, the writer of which, avowing himself a disciple of Darwin, announced that the doctrine of evolution was not only not opposed to but actually contained in the Mosaic account of Creation. We entertain no doubt that if the doctrine in question should ever be *proved*, the agreement between it and Scripture will be taught from every pulpit in the land.

It may appear, at first sight, that this faculty of assimilating deadly poison, attributed to the Sacred Volume, must needs be favourable to the vitality of any creed directly founded upon it. But on looking beneath the surface this impression vanishes. The assimilation is found to be only a seeming one. A series of compromises are effected, if indeed that term can apply to an arrangement in virtue of which one side gives up everything. The terms imposed by science are grudgingly accepted, and the theologians proceed to torture the sacred text, as a South Sea islander beats his fetish into a more reasonable mood. A day means an unlimited period; the sun means the earth; the whole earth means Judæa; to be possessed of a legion of devils means to have an epileptic fit; the end of the world means the siege of a fourth-rate city in a corner of the world. Still harder tasks are imposed on the orthodox. Thus, for example, nothing is more clear than that science negatives any such event as a universal deluge; and nothing is more clear than that the Bible describes the Deluge as universal. To effect a compromise between "two and two make four" and "two and two make five" does not seem easy, and can only be attempted by removing the problem into the cloudland of unlimited miracles, or by allegorical interpretation, or by other methods familiar to theologians. "It may have pleased God," writes Dr. Barry, "that as the Deluge was miraculous, it should pass away without leaving its footprints amidst the traces of natural formation." Here, to be sure, is a solution. Only it is not to be supposed that, as knowledge increases, the minds of men will be easy under such arrangements and explanations as these. Evidences of this uneasiness are too patent in Protestant countries and communities—it is of these that we are speaking—to render it necessary to do more than advert to the fact. It is not merely manifesting itself in the pages of a Colenso, a Kuenen, a Réville, and a host of scarcely less able critics; it is fluttering the minds

of many honest fathers of families, who not only go to church,
but help to build churches. In short, it is not to be disguised
from the educated laity, that the creed of the Reformation, sincerely honest at its origin, is becoming profoundly dishonest. Nor
is it strange that an impression of this kind should gain ground,
when we see such subterfuges grasped at by the clergy, as that
the Bible was not intended to convey physical truths; just as if
that covered its teaching of physical untruths. Others of the
clergy, again, to our knowledge, draw a deep line between the
Old and New Testament narratives and miracles. Jonah and
the whale are, after all, "unimportant;" so are the precise circumstances of the Exodus; so are Adam and Eve and the serpent; they are ready to throw all those things to the wolves to
save the Doctrine of the Atonement. This is *their* compromise, and
it is a very favourite one. Just as if the third chapter of Genesis
is not the foundation of the whole Christian system ! Just as if
you could punch a hole in an air-tight vessel with the result of
letting the air into one corner of it ! It will be said that these
doubts have not penetrated to the mass of worthy Evangelical
Christians, Wesleyans, Baptists, and other believers who make
up the bulk of our working and labouring population. Granting
that this is so, and that it may be so for a long time to come,
yet we hold it as a certain law that, in an age of progress, the
conclusions of the educated are ultimately accepted by the crowd.
A conspicuous example of this is to be found in the history of
a belief in witchcraft and demoniacal possession. The lower
classes have never been reasoned out of this belief; their scepticism has been imposed upon them from above. *All* kinds
of knowledge tend to find their way downwards, as the rain per-
colates from the surface through the soil. Without this there
would be no progress in the one case, no cultivation in the other.
We say that a system founded on the supposed infallibility of a
book, cannot survive for ever, even among the most ignorant
(where it will naturally tend to linger longest), a demonstration
of its fallibility to the educated classes. A great deal of the book
may indeed remain, and a great many creeds may be founded
upon it, and these may be styled Protestant Creeds till the end
of the world; but they will not, any of them, be "Protestant"
in the sense in which we use the term.

Approaching the subject from another side, we notice a phenomenon often remarked upon, and which, we think, strongly
bears out our view of the temporary or provisional character of
the reformed faith. Speaking broadly, it may be said that it is
next to impossible, now-a-days, to *convert* any one to it. To
turn a grown-up man into a Protestant, is about as difficult as to
turn him into a Jew. Shoals of people give up Catholicism all
over Europe, but only a few here and there are attracted by the

teaching of Luther and Calvin. Some three hundred years ago, nearly all these people would have become Lutherans or Calvinists. The phenomenon is pointed out by Lord Macaulay, in the essay referred to at the commencement of this notice. No nation, he observes, which did not adopt the principles of the Reformation before the end of the sixteenth century has ever adopted them. And (which seems to some still more strange) "Catholic communities have, since that time, become infidel and become Catholic again; but none has become Protestant." The reason of this is surely obvious, so obvious that it is difficult to state it in terms that will not provoke a smile. The seventeenth and eighteenth centuries were not the sixteenth century. The intellectual atmosphere of the time of Victoria is no more the intellectual atmosphere of the time of Elizabeth, than coats and waistcoats are the same things as doublets and jerkins. The tone of thought, philosophical and theological, of the reigns of Charles the Fifth and Francis the First was that of an epoch, and can only be reproduced by artificial means, that is, by special training. Very few men, and consequently no large body of men, will ever, we may be sure, desert Catholicism for such a system as Protestantism. This consideration applies, to be sure, to a great extent, to all religions. We never hear of large bodies of savages embracing Christianity, as was the case in the first centuries. It makes no progress whatever among cultivated heathens, corresponding to the Greeks and Romans. One would suppose that the Buddhist would delight to exercise his ingenuity upon it, like the Alexandrians of old ; but, on being explained to the Buddhist, it fails to awaken even a languid interest in his mind. The Jews, who contributed so large a section to the early church, now contribute nobody. The same holds good of Christian sects, as related to each other, and indeed of all old creeds. Mahometanism and Wesleyanism make no converts out of their own borders, while Mormonism and Spiritualism do. A change has taken place in the intellectual and moral conditions—whatever these may have been, for on this subject we are to a great extent in the dark—which at one time rendered the rapid spread of these religions possible. This is a point which ought to be attended to, though it will not be attended to, by those excellent and misguided people who encourage missions to the heathen. We think, however, that the consideration in question applies more strongly to Protestantism than to Catholicism, which is our point. We think that such of the heathen as embrace Christianity in any form will be likely to prefer the latter to the former, where they have the choice offered them. Experience has indeed shown that Catholic missions have always been the more successful of the two; but as the fact has been attributed to special causes we forbear to press it. One cause, however, which we have often heard referred to by Protestants, we must notice in a single sentence; this one, that "Roman Catholicism is more suited for human nature," for it appears to us to admit all that we are contending for. What we mean, however, is, that judging *à priori,* we should predict that (say) a moderate-sized town in the centre of China, fairly operated upon by both parties, would yield (if it yielded any converts) a larger number of converts to Rome than to the reformed faith, and that this proportion would be likely to be observed among the upper as well as the lower classes. Our reason for the belief is this, and it has been already in part stated. We look upon it that Protestantism is to Catholicism as the sixteenth century is to the dark ages. The sixteenth century in Europe was a transitional period—a period of unusual intellectual activity, but still, like every other period, transitional—corresponding, probably, in its main features to no epoch that has existed, or will exist, in China or Japan, or anywhere else. The dark ages are impregnated by a theological spirit of much greater vitality, the spirit of "Faith," which can be called into active operation in every country, in every age, and to some extent in every mind. We would back a system elaborately constructed on this basis, to make proselytes against any one that merely presented an arrested development of free-thought. Yet we can suppose some country, as, for instance, India or Japan, passing through a phase in some degree resembling the sixteenth century, and that then Protestantism, "the religion of the Bible," might career through the minds of men, like a fire through an American prairie. Under ordinary circumstances we see no chance of such a result.

It may be asked whether a general conviction of the purely human and uninspired character of the Bible would not prove as fatal to Catholicism as to the Reformed Faith. In the long run we think it would. But we do not think that it would be likely to be so immediately fatal; and this point seems scarcely to have received sufficient attention. Put an extreme case: suppose proof as clear and undeniable as that of any proposition in Euclid, to be forthcoming, that the Bible is a series of purely human compositions. This would be altogether destructive of orthodox Protestantism; to take an example *in limine,* the miraculous conception would instantly disappear. Yet a moment's consideration will show that it need by no means be a deathblow to the Old Creed. The Old and New Testaments are but the title-deeds of the Roman Church, not the soul within its body; and that Church might go on holding its dominion over the minds of men, without title-deeds, as the Earl of Durham and other proprietors hold their landed estates. At the worst, its *infallibility* would receive a shock. It might have to admit that certain early documents (which it has always prudently refrained from putting too much in the foreground) had had a somewhat undue importance attached to them: just as, in all conscience, it must be admitted that the early Church was mistaken in expecting the immediate return of Christ. Putting out of sight the numerous explanations which might be devised on this head, a Church claiming to be divine could very well go on with its prestige for infallibility weakened. Were not the Apostles often, and the great Peter himself, when actually at the head of the Church, mistaken? But a book, convicted of error, though it be the sublimest book that was ever penned on the face of the earth, ceases to be "the Bible;" ceases, therefore, to be a foundation for the Reformed Faith. In any case, the Roman Church might still fairly claim to be the visible representative, through its Head, of God upon Earth: the divine institution which (the possibility of error being even admitted) was supernaturally charged with the office of instructing, comforting, and conveying grace to man. The great body of Catholic tradition would remain unshaken. Though Luke and John were shown to be in error with regard to some of the details of the last Supper, the doctrine of Transubstantiation would remain. It was communicated to the Church, in some way or other, eighteen hundred years ago: tradition shows this, the Church announces it, and therefore people ought to believe in the doctrine unless its falsity can be shown. And people *would* believe in it. The more a system professes to be founded upon reason, the more obnoxious it will be to the assaults of reason, and the surer its fall when assailed by reason. Neither of these dogmatic systems that we are considering can really substantiate its claims; but Protestantism, having so to speak chosen its ground, cannot evade the conflict. Catholicism, like the god Mars, can fly away in a cloud.

Not for ever. The ultimate contest must take place over the admission of the Supernatural, in any form, into the observed phenomena of the universe; and we may be sure that the masses, better instructed, will one day take a part in it. By the time, perhaps a very remote one, when the civilized world is organized for this great contest, there are many reasons which lead us to suppose that the respective combatants will have taken extreme sides. At such momentous periods, compromises which have done good service melt away; those who have supported them, Girondins, Whigs, Protestants, disappear from the stage. We have, more than once, heard in sermons and read in books that the Gog and Magog of the Apocalypse typify "Infidelity" and "Popery" banded together in the last days against the camp of the Saints, comprising, it is to be presumed, Protestant Episco-

palians, together with orthodox dissenters, foreign Lutherans,
Calvinists, and others who at such a crisis will hardly refuse to
fight under Bishops and Archdeacons.   We prefer, however,
another interpretation which has been given of the passage, and
which, though violating in some degree the construction of the
original, does not in so great a degree violate common sense.
According to this view, Gog and Magog will fight against each
other for dominion over the world : and this prediction we think
likely to be substantially correct. Such an interpretation, it will
be observed, seems to involve an eclipse of the system known as
Protestantism.   We deem not only its eclipse, but its disappear-
ance, to be merely a question of time ; yet at no time will the
services which it has rendered to humanity be forgotten.   Incapable from its nature of forming a permanent dwelling-place for
the mind, it has been a temporary construction of the greatest
value, a resting-place which has happily sheltered man on his
way from bondage to freedom, from darkness to light, from
Theology to truth.

ART. V.—THE POLITICS OF ARISTOTLE.

IT is commonly supposed that the writings of ancient authors,
however productive of pleasure, from the grace of their style,
can give but little information of practical value to modern
readers. This opinion, erroneous as it appears to us, is very
probably at the bottom of the agitation which has lately been
raised against classical education. Students of Aristotle are
especially the object of derision, as they cannot claim for their
author the merit of style, unless terseness be considered a merit,
and the invectives of Bacon, who, next to Aristotle, was probably
the greatest thinker that ever lived, have predisposed even educated readers against the works of the latter author. Perhaps
there never was a more unjust judgment than that which Bacon
pronounced, and Bacon's posterity have received almost upon
trust. Were it as profitable as it would be laborious to undertake the task, it might be shown that few of the philosophical
truths uttered by Bacon were not anticipated by Aristotle. But
we are not ambitious of such a labour, and will confine ourselves
to investigating the " Politics" of Aristotle, with a hope of showing
that this work, at all events, of this ancient author, might be

read with profit as well as pleasure. It cannot be denied that a great deal of what Aristotle says on this subject will not impress readers as possessing at the same time novelty and truth; but those things which they have heard before might be read with interest in the author who was the first to say them, and those few things which they consider erroneous will compensate readers by their curiosity. In short, we find in Aristotle the original expression of much that has since been copied or perverted.

The objects in view of which the "Politics" was produced, must be regarded as various and almost conflicting. Aristotle appears, at times, to have despaired of establishing a state, according to his ideal; accordingly, in some passage he gives advice, which, if followed, is to prolong the existence of polities very different from what he approves. Nor is he wholly practical in his views, for we find him seeking for principles in the most abstruse analogies, and giving reasons which nothing but dialectical subtlety could suggest. Sometimes we see the philosopher reasoning on virtue and statesmanship, at other times, the man of the world counselling his benighted countrymen. The Politics is, in a sense, complementary to the Ethics. At the end of the latter work, Aristotle shows how necessary, in his view, is a good state or constitution to produce a good man. Men are either made good, as appears in the Tenth Book of the Ethics, by a natural disposition, over which we have no control: or they become good by instruction in virtue, which, however, in the great majority of cases, is of little value, unless it has been preceded by early training. Children, then, must be habituated from tender years to love right objects, or they will grow up without control over their passions, even though they may be well aware of the difference between right and wrong. To this end it is necessary that the State should interfere more in education and in the regulation of private life, and this presupposes the existence of a form of government which shall be capable of so doing without incurring the enmity of the citizens. But instead of confining himself to demonstrating the kind of state which is most likely to have that effect, Aristotle plunges deep into the subject, and handles the whole art and theory of government. On the threshold of his inquiry, the great work of Plato must be encountered, and from that source are derived most of the theories and maxims which are least true and least valuable in the Politics. Nor can he wholly throw off the metaphysical influence which the prevalence of dialectics in Greece so deeply impressed on all the literature of that age. Finally, he illustrates his conclusions from the past history of Greece. Thus philosophy, history, and the opinions of other writers are all laid under con-

tribution, nor can the work be rightly understood without some
previous illustration being given of the way in which it is affected
by these several influences.

In the first place, then, there is a great deal in common between Plato and Aristotle in their treatment of political subjects.
In both there is a similarity recognised between the State and
the Individual, an analogy which has been very injurious, as
most analogies are, to the proper consideration of the subject in
all times. By Plato the analogy is carried to an absurd excess:
he divides the mind of man into three parts—Reason, Spirit, and
Desire; corresponding to these three parts of the mind are the
three parts of the State—Rulers, Soldiers, and the Common
People. Each section has its appropriate virtue—namely, Wisdom, Courage, and Temperance; while the harmonious union of
these three virtues constitutes Justice. Such, in brief, is the conception of the analogy set forth in the Republic of Plato.
Aristotle was far too sensible to imitate any such whimsical subtlety. With him a man is a limb of the State, dependent upon,
and under certain limitations entitled to take part in its proper
management. Yet he is sufficiently biassed by the Platonic
simile to assert that Courage, Justice, and Wisdom are, as regards both their force and their form the same in a State as in an
Individual (Pol. Book vii. cap. 1); and again, that the happiness
of an individual and of the whole State consists of the same
elements, and depends upon the same conditions (Pol. Book vii.
cap. 2) These propositions are to us idle if not meaningless,
and are due to the colour which has been shed on Aristotle's
work by the mystifying and metaphysical manner in which Plato
deals with the subject. Both the philosophers, again, regard the
relation of the citizen to the State as analogous to that of the
Particular to the Universal in logic; but as in philosophy
Aristotle laid more stress on the Particular, and Plato on the
Universal, so in politics Aristotle has more regard to the individual and Plato to the entire State. An excellent illustration
of this divergence may be found in a passage in the Politics,
Book ii. cap. 5. Socrates, in the Republic, had been met by the
objection that the austere and studious life prescribed by his
system would afford but little chance of happiness to each of the
citizens, however much it might conduce to the wellbeing of the
whole community. To this he answered, that the business of the
lawgiver was not to consider the happiness of persons, but of the
State as a whole. It is obvious that there is a fallacy in this
ingenious reply, and Aristotle points it out. "It is impossible,"
he says, "that the State should be happy as a whole unless the
greater portion, or all, or even some of the citizens in the State

are happy. It is true that a number may be an even number, though all the units that make it up are odd numbers; but though in arithmetic this may be so, it is impossible for happiness to reside in a city as a whole without residing also in the citizens of which it is composed." Here we have the key of the system which not only betrayed Plato into the most visionary and ridiculous speculations on matter-of-fact political inquiries, but which also still later led to the discredit of syllogistic logic and the dissociation of thought from common sense. Plato looks upon men as subordinate machines whose interests may well be sacrificed to the supposed advantage of an abstract entity, which he calls the State; Aristotle looks upon the State as the means of educating and training men to the capacity of realizing their own happiness. Aristotle dwells upon Rights, Plato on Duties. Aristotle proportions the felicity which each man is entitled to enjoy by the extent to which he contributes to the well-being of the community; Plato limits it by the extent to which it will interfere with the happiness of the State as a whole. That there is merit in both points of view, if the mischievous doctrine of Universals above alluded to were not pushed to excess, cannot be doubted. Perhaps both theories, reasonably carried out, would amount to the same thing. The public good should certainly be the measure by which the freedom of the individual ought to be limited; but if we allow ourselves to think of the public good as something quite separate from the community at large, and allied to an abstract and mysterious principle such as Plato's idea of good, we shall be better able to understand the force and reason of Aristotle's revolt from the point of view of his predecessor. It is probable that the influence of Plato is to be traced also in another part of the Politics, to which, although not in itself very important, the form of the book attaches some significance—namely, the description of the Ideal Polis. For a man who is studying forms of government for practical purposes, or for the purposes of research, it seems absurd to draw the outlines of the best State possible, to which it is hopeless to aspire. It would seem as reasonable for a doctor, when consulted how to restore a delicate constitution, to inflame the fancy by drawing a picture of a man in perfect health, in whom all the muscles were developed to the fullest extent, and all the organs were performing their functions in the best conceivable manner. The secret of this weakness, for such it must be called, in Aristotle, is to be traced to the influence of Plato. The latter author, as is well known, has sacrificed common sense to the exigencies of his poetical imagination, and has depicted men rather as what he wishes they were than what they could ever possibly become

He has erased all the habits and antecedents of human nature, and drawn on his fancy for materials wherewith to fill the gap so created. All this, however, is done with so much skill, with so much apparent candour, and in such wonderfully attractive language, that the most logical mind in those days of limited experience could scarcely avoid retaining some of the spirit, even though discarding the doctrines and conclusions of the author. So it seems to have been with Aristotle. Nothing can be more explicit than his declaration that we must consider nature. He positively says that we must not ignore human selfishness, and severely censures Plato for rending family ties and the instinctive aspirations of mankind. Yet from Plato he unconsciously derives the view that human nature is malleable to almost any extent. Both seem to consider, though with Aristotle the delusion is only occasionally put forward, that they may construct a city on paper with the same freedom as they may construct a mathematical figure. Hence it is, that in considering the value of the Politics, no one would take into account the constructive portion of the work. The chief value of the book consists in the dissertations, the historical allusions, and the masterly comments on the existing state of society with which the work abounds. It is, of course, impossible to enumerate severally all the points of resemblance and difference between the two Greek thinkers. Indeed, it would be a task of very questionable advantage, for in every point of view Plato must be looked upon as a poet rather than a philosopher; and though there may be much to interest the curious or the lover of literary merit, there is nothing in Plato's Republic from which a modern reader could derive instruction.

Notwithstanding these flaws, due to his respect for and admiration of Plato, Aristotle has written on the whole in an independent spirit. The method by which he proposes to conduct his inquiry into the origin and requirements of a State has drawn forth loud praises from the advocates of the Baconian and Comtist schools. We shall see presently whether these praises are wholly deserved, and whether in the system which Aristotle wrought out he was not diverted from time to time by theories based upon very different principles. His first inquiry is into the elements of a State. Many writers, he says, have treated a State as if it was merely a large household, whereas in truth there is a difference between them of kind as well as of size. It is necessary, then, to analyse the entire State into its component parts, and consider it with reference to those parts. Society is based, he proceeds, upon certain necessary relations of human beings to each other. The first unions of individuals are those created by various necessities. The continuance of our species requires that men and women should come together;

security requires that the weaker should be governed by the
stronger, or, which is the same thing, that he to whom nature
has given a mind to direct should stand to him who has merely
physical strength in the relation of master to slave ; and thus
the interests of the two are the same. These two relations form
the Family, consisting of husband and wife, master and slave.
From this first association, formed as it is merely for meeting
our daily wants, springs the village or clan, an association in
which more than our everyday wants are supplied. Members of
the same clan are related by blood and consist of several families
connected with each other. The origin of kingship, he proceeds,
is to be traced to this primitive source. In the Family the
husband was king of his own house : when the Family grew
into the Clan the same rule continued, and from the clan it was
introduced into the State or Nation, which was formed from the
enlargement and amalgamation of many clans. Such is in a few
words the account given by Aristotle of the growth of human
society. Now, let us pause here for a little to consider and test
by materials of which Aristotle himself could have had no knowledge the truth of this analysis. The most complete account we
have of the origin and growth of a great people is in the Bible.
There we first meet with Abraham as an owner of cattle,
wandering with his servants and family through a large tract of
territory in search of water and food, fighting with kings, living
in tents, and flying from famine instead of attempting to obviate
it by cultivation. He is an absolute master of the lives and
fortunes of his subjects ; all his dependents are in the position of
slaves, though that position is in no way regarded as ignominious.
Here we see the κώμη or village community of Aristotle in its
most perfect form, for the circumstance of Abraham having led
a migratory life does not in any way affect the question. Later
on in Jewish history we find the princes and elders and heads of
families, all deriving their position from the patriarchal authority,
exercising the same powers among the people, though subordinate
to the chief magistrate in the nation. Indeed, it is by no means
certain that there was at all times, even that restraint upon their
independence. There are grounds for believing that even
Samuel, probably the most influential of the judges, was not
known or recognised beyond a limited portion of the Jewish
territory. Another instance of the family origin and long duration of the village or clan community is to be found in the
history of the Highland clans, all originally sprung from the
same family and devoted to the chief, who wielded in his own
circle the authority of a king. It is needless to refer further to
the many examples of the truth of the family origin of society
and government which are to be found in the history of the

feudal system, or in the present habits of the Arabs, or elsewhere. The theory is conclusively confirmed in Professor
Maine's book on Ancient Law, which shows how all early law was
founded upon this basis, the relics of which survive even in our
own modern jurisprudence. This is not the only instance, as
will be seen presently, in which the judgment of Aristotle,
though pronounced from a much more limited experience than
was open to writers of a later date, has proved more correct than
the opposite opinions deliberately propounded even by eminent
thinkers. The whole doctrine of the social contract, fruitful as
it was of vast enlightenment and indirectly of the greatest revolution ever known in Europe, is refuted by a consideration of the
facts and arguments which have established the Aristotelian
theory of the origin of society.

The next step which Aristotle takes, after describing the
elements and growth of states, is to survey the experience of
past thinkers and past institutions. In this he differs very widely
from Plato, whose work contains little, if any, illustration of his
theories from history. It is obvious, however, that no doctrines
upon political subjects can be worth much, unless they are based
upon such experience. The justification, if any is required, of
this view, is to be found in Polit. Book ii. cap. 5. "We must
not," says Aristotle, "be forgetful of this truth, that diligent
reference must be made to the result of so many generations of
experience. If these doctrines were good" (referring to some
of Plato's vagaries), "they would have been recognised as such
before now. For nearly everything that can be known on such
subjects has been already discovered, though the results of experience have not all been collected, nor have men always
availed themselves even of that which has been ascertained."
Here, then, we have the secret of the enthusiasm with which
Aristotle's method has been received by the disciples of experimental philosophy. He first deduces the laws of the effects from
the laws of the causes, tracing the tendencies of the family and
of the village communities till they are absorbed in the State,
showing how the same elements exist in the larger community,
and then verifying his conclusions as to the nature of States, by
references to history. This is treating politics as a science in
the same way as he would treat physical sciences, and con-
formably to the method pointed out in Mill's Logic. It is true
that the germ of that method, of which so much is now-a-days,
as we believe unreasonably, expected in political and social inquiries, may be found in the treatment of these subjects by
Aristotle. There is, however, no trace in his writings of an
opinion that there can be any analogy between political and
physical science in the exactness of the result to be attained,

though he adopts, in part, the same method of inquiry in regard to both. We venture to think that Aristotle, as well as most thinkers of the present day, would have despaired of ever even approximately reducing so complicated a subject to an exact science. The subject must always be empirically treated, and will always yield, for the most part, changeable and vague con·clusions, though the paths by which the human mind must seek knowledge, will always be the same, whatever be the object in view. However this may be, the illustrations and verifications of his opinions, by reference to history, are certainly among the most valuable parts of Aristotle's work. Occurring, as they do, on almost every page, and treating of almost every kind of political subject, it would be, of course, impossible to collect them and put them before our readers with any advantage. The book must be read in order to appreciate their value; but in some cases we shall be able to refer to those illustrations when we come to deal with a few of the principal social problems propounded and solved in the Politics. But it must not be supposed that Aristotle by any means confined himself to an accurate method of inquiry. Even those who chiefly approved his scientific treatment of the subject must allow that, in many instances, he applies to his study preconceived notions and doctrines. What, for example, is the force of the statement, with which he commences his first book, that all States aim at excellence, unless it be to justify himself in arguing, as he often does, from final causes. Again, we shall find, when we consider his doctrines on slavery, that his views of Nature, as affecting that subject, are both very forced and very much relied on in defence of that institution. The doctrine of Μεσότης also, so familiar to readers of the Ethics, reappears. In distribution of property, we ought not, he says, merely to seek for equality, but should also aim at the Mean. In the fourth book he goes still further, in a most curious and instructive passage:

"If we were correct in laying down in the Ethics that the happy life is the life of a virtuous man endowed with a competence, and that virtue is a mean (or middle) condition, it necessarily follows that the best life is the middle life, that is, the life in which each man attains the mean according to his opportunities. Now the same limitations in regard both to virtues and vices apply also to a state and a constitution, for the constitution is the life of the state. In every state there are three classes of persons, the very rich, the very poor, and the middle classes, who occupy a mean condition between the two others. Accordingly, as we have admitted the superiority of the mean, it is clear that a middle or moderate share of good things is the best for man; such men are the most easily induced to obey reason."

He proceeds to say that those who excel in wealth, beauty,

or anything good, are apt to be insolent, while those who greatly
lack such things are apt to be rogues, and injustice is generally
promoted by insolence or roguery. Thus he arrives at the
conclusion that a State should be governed by the middle classes.
It should be remembered, for fear of causing confusion, that
these remarks of Aristotle do not apply to the Ideal State, which
is of a very aristocratic cast, but to one of the alternative forms
of government, which he considers desirable, if perfection cannot
be attained. However, it is not only a genuine expression of
opinion on a point of statesmanship, but also an instance of the
peculiarity of Aristotle's reasoning. The conclusion is correct,
though the argument is unsatisfactory and imperfect. There is
no better example in the whole book of the degree to which the
writer allowed preconceived theories to influence him. In order
wholly to understand the doctrine of the Mean, which is so
freely applied here, it is necessary to refer to the Ethics, a task
beyond our limits in this paper ; but any who are familiar with
that work will see how entirely alien it is to a political treatise,
however proper it may be in moral speculations. It is, indeed,
a remarkable thing to find in the pages of an author, who lived
in times in which democracy, despotism, or oligarchy were the
only known forms of government, such emphatic approval of
government by the middle classes. So far as we know, there
never has been, except, perhaps, occasionally in the early Italian
Republics, any instance of such government till this country set
the example, after the Reform Bill of 1832. We cannot refrain
from adding the substance of a few more remarks which follow
the passage above quoted. "We wish," says Aristotle, "that
our State should be composed, so far as may be, of men in an
equal condition one with the other. This is best secured by the
government of the middle classes, for thus are we best assured
against the greed and revolutionary tendencies of the poor. The
middle classes, then, ought either to be stronger than both the
rich and the poor combined ; or, at all events, than either separate, so as to be able to side with one or the other, and thus
secure the mastery." Despotism, he continues, is apt to spring
either from a very powerful oligarchy, or a very powerful democracy ; but it is not so likely to occur when the middle classes
rule. Elsewhere, Aristotle points out that military rule is apt
to create a despotism. There are not many epochs of modern
or mediæval history which might not be considered fair illustrations of the justice of these criticisms.

One more instance may be given of our position that Aristotle
did not strictly adhere to his prescribed method. In the First
Book he proclaims his hostility to usury, to the acquisition of
wealth for its own sake. The object of wealth, he says, is to

secure well-being, and just as a doctor seeks to impart unlimited health to his patient, though he does not make use of an unlimited supply of drugs to attain that end, so a householder should seek unlimited well-being, though the manner of reaching it is not to accumulate an unlimited quantity of money. As sound sense this opinion will be accepted by all. Its chief value, however, consists in the quaintness with which Aristotle, in the text, applies the idea of πέρας or Limit derived from Pythagoras, a doctrine which will be found to pervade all that portion of the book which refers to the source and utility of wealth. On the whole, however, considering the enormous extent to which philosophical and religious prejudices influenced actual life in the Greek cities, as well as the intimate connexion between political inquiry and moral philosophy, which until the time of Aristotle consisted of little else than mere metaphysical speculation, it must be admitted that the novel treatment of political subjects which Aristotle introduced was wonderfully logical and sound. It may, perhaps, be said that his method is as logical as that of any subsequent writer on the same subject.

At the time when the Politics was written, Greece had already passed the zenith of her greatness. She attained the highest pinnacle immediately after the Persian invasion and after half a century or so of brilliant civilization, fell rapidly into decay. Philip of Macedon, with his half-Hellenic armies, had humbled the cities which not long before had vanquished the great king. Alexander had led a great army through Asia, and had outdone the feats of the historic heroes of Salamis and Platæa. Henceforward the paths open to Greek statesmen diverged in two opposite directions. The incapacity of small and isolated cities to cope singly with a concentrated power like that of Macedonia had become apparent. If these cities were to remain separate from each other, it must result in the sacrifice of their independence sooner or later. If the Greeks were to preserve their liberties as men, it must be by the sacrifice of their state-system and the subordination of communal to national interests. The growth of their northern neighbour had made it impossible for Athenians or Lacedæmonians to defy each other unless they were willing to make a submission to the common encroacher. On the other hand, Macedonia was not formidable, and even Rome might have been resisted, if by common action the Hellenic cities had consented to merge their differences and form themselves into one united nation. It is certainly strange that Aristotle should not have dwelt upon these dangers, among the most imminent that ever threatened a people. Perhaps his personal connexion with Alexander, whose tutor he was for some time, led him to shun allusion to the altered conditions of states-

manship which had been rendered necessary in Greece by the
exploits of Philip and his son. In one passage only does he
suffer himself to say anything which can be considered to refer
to these events. Speaking of the effect of climate upon national
character, he says in the Seventh Book, cap. 7 :—

> "Nations living in cold countries and in Europe, though full of
> courage, are deficient in adroitness and cleverness; whence it arises
> that, though they preserve their own freedom better, they remain
> without social organization, and are unable to rule over their neigh-
> bours. But Asiatic nations, though adroit and crafty, are deficient in
> spirit; thus they live in a state of subjection and slavery. The Greek
> people, however, situated as they are between the others in point of
> locality, share also in the qualities of both. For they combine spirit
> and intelligence, and thus they live free and with better self-govern-
> ment than any other, nay, they would be able to rule over the whole
> world if they were but embraced within one state."

The subject referred to in the last few words of this passage is
never again mentioned, and indeed it is abundantly clear from
the description which Aristotle gives us of his ideal state, that
he did not contemplate any extension of the existing basis of
government, namely, the separate independence of every considerable city, which was indeed one of the landmarks of
Greek society. It may be assumed, then, that Aristotle knew
of the danger arising from such a subdivision of power, and at
the same time deliberately preferred to look upon that state of
things as embodying the ultimate form of society. Mr. Congreve,
in the Introduction to his edition of the Politics conjectures, by
way of accounting for this attitude of Aristotle, that he "looked
to the peaceful organization of the several Greek states, in themselves and in their mutual relations, under the sheltering presidency of Macedon." We cannot think that such is a correct
explanation. Such a thing as a sheltering presidency was not
familiar in those times; nor can we suppose that the man who
held so high an opinion of the Greek capacity, as it is clear from
the above quoted passage that Aristotle did, would countenance
the idea of their abnegating their rights as freemen. Probably
he did not contemplate the growth of an external power sufficiently strong to keep Greece permanently in chains, and saw
that the best security for freedom, in the absence of such external
coercion, consisted in the municipal form of self-government.
Indeed, in the absence of representation, no city was or could
be free unless it governed itself; and the individual character,
on which Aristotle set great store, could not be developed except
in a free citizen of a free city. However this may be, it is certain
that Aristotle looked upon a self governing city as the highest
model, and as the only form of state into which he need inquire;

and from these premises he proceeds to lay down the principles which should underlie its constitution.

There is some little difficulty in exactly discovering all the particular institutions which Aristotle wished to see established in a State, as for example in the matter of monarchy, but there is no doubt about the fundamental principles on which the State was to be based. There were to be private property, marriage, slavery, and State-education. The point of view from which he regarded each of these institutions requires some little explanation, and in criticising Aristotle's position we must remember that he is in part combating the doctrines of Plato. In the first place he sets himself to inquire whether it is better that property should be private but the enjoyment thereof common, as for example that a farm should belong to an individual and its produce to the community; or secondly, that the land should be common, and worked in common, but the produce distributed to meet the wants of the citizens; or thirdly, that both land and produce should be in common. Plato advocated community of property and produce alike. Aristotle opposes to this view several considerations. In the first place he argues, no one will take an interest in what does not belong exclusively to him. Every man looks best after what is wholly his own, and disregards what is common to himself with others, as we see in large households, where there are more servants than one to do the work, and consequently the work is not done at all. In the next place, unless every one did exactly the same amount of work and received exactly the same in return, there would under this system be constant wrangling between those who were overworked and those who were underpaid. In short, he says, property ought to be private and the produce and fruition ought to be in common in the sense that all should be ready to assist one another; and to that end the government must foster goodwill among men. Besides, it is incalculable how much pleasure there is in feeling a thing to be one's own: nor are we to consider that self-love was implanted in us to no purpose, for it is nature that gives us the feeling; it is only when self-love becomes excessive that it becomes blameable. Lastly, we should destroy at least one virtue by doing away with private property, namely, the virtue of liberality. Against all this, he proceeds, it may be urged that by community of property we should get rid of three intolerable evils, actions at law on contracts, prosecutions for perjury, and the flattery which is paid to rich men. These evils, however, Aristotle prefers to ascribe to sheer wickedness and depravity, and concludes with the remark, that if such a measure was adopted, existence would become simply unbearable. The special dislike which is here exhibited to actions at law must be traced

partly to the extremely unreasonable conditions of litigation in
Greece, and partly to the philosophic horror of money dealings
and money disputes prevalent at that time. It seems strange
that in the argument against the community of property there
is no allusion to what may be called the " Rights of Man "
theory, which had already been proclaimed in Greece at all
events in a limited manner. It seems never to have occurred to
him as worth while seriously to combat the view, that all men
being born equal are entitled to an equal share of the
fruits of the earth. It was reserved for the French " philoso-
phists" to bring forward that argument prominently in favour of
Communism. In another part of the work Aristotle briefly dismisses it by saying that equality consists not in all getting alike,
but in all who are equal getting alike, it being clear in his
opinion that all men are by no means equal. It may be said
that the theory of perfect equality of rights among mankind was
practically ignored by the Greek nation.

Aristotle is equally decided in favour of marriage, an institution, however, which appears not to have been very highly valued
in historical Greece, and which was attacked with great fury by
Plato. Indeed the position of their women was not at all
creditable to the Greeks. They do not appear to have been
educated with any care, or to have been much admitted into the
society of men ; consequently in the whole range of Greek literature we do not obtain much insight into their mode of life. The
Odyssey it is true depicts a Penelope, and the Alcestis furnishes
us with another portrait of conjugal love, but it may be said that
as a rule the ordinary female character is not represented in Greek
literature. Only women of traditional celebrity, or acting under
the influence of exceptional excitement, appear, such as Cas-
sandra in her capacity of prophetess, Clytemnestra as queen
and murderess, Antigone as martyr, Medea as sorceress. In
short the sum of what women were expected to do in Greece is
given in the Funeral Oration of Pericles, who warns them to
seek retirement and thus avoid alike the praise and blame of the
opposite sex. It was probably as a revolt against this unreasonable system of life that Plato put forward his monstrous theory
of Woman's Rights. According to him there is no difference
whatever between men and women except in sex. Women are
equally endowed with mental and bodily capacity ; accordingly
they should be brought up together with men, under identical
influences, and should become rulers and soldiers. There ought
to be, in Plato's opinion, no marriages, but the male and female
soldiers who had chiefly distinguished themselves for vigour and
bravery should at a mature age be deputed by the community
to beget children, in the hope that they might emulate the

virtues of their parents, and thus improve the breed. This proposal, which has provoked a chorus of inextinguishable laughter for two-and-twenty centuries, is uttered with the most complete gravity. It is followed by a detailed account of the manner in which all the children born in the State are to be reared in public nurseries, and suckled by all the women indiscriminately, in order that no mother may know her own child, and no man may know his own father, a consummation which, in Plato's opinion, is devoutly to be wished for. Probably, if such a mad scheme had emanated from any other brain Aristotle would not have condescended to refute it; but proceeding as it did from Plato it commanded his respect. Accordingly he combats it in a manner which is worth recording, rather from the quaintness of some of his positions than from their absolute merit. To begin with, he says, that under such a system every one would claim a youth who had distinguished himself as his own son, and thus a fruitful source of discord would arise. In many cases too it would be impossible to conceal relationships. Children would be fathered by their resemblance, as is the case in Libya, where some tribes have a community of wives, or as the foals are known which have sprung from the celebrated breed of horses in Pharsalus. Again, religious and moral difficulties could not be obviated under the system proposed. Suppose a child were to revile or fight with, or even by accident slay, his parent. This would be of more frequent occurrence if no one knew who his father and mother were; and there would be this further disadvantage, that as the culprit would not know that he had committed a crime he could not make any religious expiation therefor. This, it may be observed, is the only instance in which Aristotle has allowed himself in the Politics to use an argument based upon superstition. Apart from all these reasons, Aristotle further argues that such a system would have the effect of weakening the social tie, and substituting for that family cordiality and fellow-feeling which should pervade the state a " watery friendship," (φιλία ύδαρής). That which we love as our own and that which we love from natural affection are, he says, the objects which are most cherished by mankind.

When we turn to the third principle, namely, that of slavery, on which Aristotle insists as a necessary ingredient in his system, we find his views not quite so decided. In fact, he was only a lukewarm supporter of the institution as it existed in Greece. He considers that the relation of master to slave is a necessary relation underlying the πόλις: its original source was common security. Just as lower animals are in subjection to man for their mutual advantage, so slaves are subject to their masters.

The one is able to rule; the capacity of the other is limited to obedience; and thus, he says, their relative positions are mutually beneficial to each other, and for the common interest of both. Some indeed consider that all slavery is unnatural; but, says Aristotle, implements are necessary to a household in order to enable men to live in comfort, and implements are either lifeless or living. If a distaff could work of its own accord, or if we possessed automata, there would be no necessity for slaves; but as lifeless implements must receive motive power from a living body, slaves are required, and may be defined as "a kind of living property, each slave being, as it were, one implement in the place of many." The slave is a portion of (κτῆσιν), and has no existence except in reference to, his master. Thus those men who are incapable of having a personality of their own, are natural slaves. Having now explained the position of a slave relatively to his master, and the kind of person whom we may make a slave of, he inquires whether there really are any such persons existing. This question he answers by searching for analogies. There are, he says, distinctions in the kind of rule depending on the rulers and the ruled, and in proportion as the persons are better, the rule itself is nobler. "Wherever you have a combination of several parts with a common result, whether those parts be united as in the body natural, or distinct as in the body politic, there you find existing the distinction between ruler and ruled. This subordination is found in all nature, but is found more particularly, is more truly inherent, in the things that have life; though even in those things that have no life there is a certain rule exercised, as in the power of harmony." The first analogy employed to exemplify the application of this doctrine is that of Body and Soul. In a good man the soul rules the body: in a bad man the body rules the soul. In other words, the reason governs the passions, or *vice versâ*, according as the man be virtuous or vicious. Again, in the animal creation, mankind rules over the tame animals. Lastly, in all nature the same applies to male and female; the former being superior rules over the latter who is inferior. All men, then, who are as inferior to other men as the body is to the soul, or lower animals to man, are intended by nature to be slaves; and for the same reason it is better for them to be governed as such. And, says Aristotle, there are some men to that degree inferior. He is confronted, however, by another case, when he considers those captives of war, who are in the position of slaves though free from all slavish qualities. Such persons would not be so inferior as to deserve slavery according to the principle laid down above. Yet, he says, some justify this state of things on the ground that it is a matter of contract, the life of the prisoner being spared

on condition of his becoming a slave. Others arraign the custom
as iniquitous, based as it is merely upon the compulsion of brute
strength, and point out that in this way even noble persons may
become slaves. Aristotle merely observes that victory in battle
argues, after all, some kind of superiority in the conqueror
which may partly justify his assuming the position of master,
and draws a distinction between nobility among the Greeks and
among the barbarians. Greek nobles he considers noble everywhere, while barbarian nobles are only so in their own country.

In summing up the discussion, he concludes that there are
two kinds of slavery—that which is natural, and that which prevails, though unnatural. In the first case, the rule of the master
over the slave is advantageous to both, since this kind of slave
is a portion of his master, and their interests are the same; and
it is well for both that they should be friendly to each other. In
the second case, as the subordination is contrary to nature, hostility exists between the master and the slave. Hitherto we
have chiefly dealt with Aristotle's open arguments in favour of
slavery, which are by no means so emphatic in themselves.
There are, however, mixed up with these arguments in the text
a few passages of peculiar significance, from which we learn how
deep-rooted were his preferences for the slave system.

In the fifth chapter of the First Book we are told, that " a
natural slave is one who partakes of reason just so far as to
recognise it in others though he does not possess it himself,
whereas other animals do not even recognise reason, but are
obedient to passion only." Elsewhere, however (Book I. cap. 13),
he says that those persons are wrong who deny slaves all
reason, and say they ought only to obey. There is a further inquiry as to whether a slave can possess the virtues of temperance, bravery, justice, and the like; or whether all his excellence is limited to the performance of physical services. The
question, he says, is pretty much the same as that about the
capacity of women and children for virtue. All human beings
possess the elements which are comprised in the soul, but possess
them in a different degree. The slave possesses no deliberative
capacity; that is to say, he is incapable of deciding what ought
to be done. In fact, he requires but little virtue, only just so
much indeed as to prevent him from neglecting his work from
want of principle or from cowardice. By way of further illustration, the artisan and the slave are compared in an instructive
passage :—

"One may well doubt," says Aristotle, "whether the artisan (or
working man) also requires virtue, for we often see them neglect their
work from want of principle. Surely theirs is a very different case.

For the slave shares in the family life, whereas the artisan stands farther off, and has a share of virtue proportionate only to his participation in the slave's condition. For the artisans, being degraded persons, are, as it were, unattached slaves; and again, the position of a slave is a natural position, and this cannot be said of a cobbler, for example, or indeed of any artisan."

This explains not only the opinion of Aristotle on the subject of slavery, but also the reason for that opinion. Such, then, is his view, incorrect indeed if measured by the ideas which rightly prevail in modern times, and which have been brought about by the entire change of society since that day; but in the main moderate, if judged by the only fair standard, namely, the condition of the world at the time at which he wrote.

To those who are willing to deal with the now obsolete controversy on the subject of slavery, without having recourse to arguments which are merely addressed to sentiments, the question must always present itself as an historical one. Nothing could, of course, be more abominable than the slave-trade, or the institution of slavery as it existed in our colonies or in the United States. Nothing also can be more abominable in the eyes of just-minded men than the present condition of the English poor, which, however, is witnessed with complacency by almost all sections of society. The latter evil has been produced by the gradual decline of the feudal spirit, without the substitution of better, or indeed of any, provision in its place. The former evil was also produced in a similar way by the gradual decline of the patriarchal system of society. In primitive times the condition of slaves was, comparatively speaking, not at all an unhappy one. The father of the family was master of their lives and fortunes, as he was of the lives and fortunes of his children and grandchildren. Failing issue, his slaves might even succeed to the inheritance, and though this did not often happen, yet the fact that it might happen indicates the light in which slaves were regarded. They were members of the family, and in no sense subject to greater restraints than were all human beings, except the heads of families themselves. In early Rome, for example, the son was exactly in the same position as a slave until his father's death, and the same word, *familia*, included both slaves and the other members of the domestic circle. When the family community expanded into the village community, and that again merged in the city or tribe, all the children of freemen became citizens, and by degrees threw off the shackles of parental tyranny; but the slaves lost by the change. They did not become citizens, and were no longer members of the family united with the children under a common despotism. Thus they remained simply what Aristotle calls them, living implements, valued only as being productive animals and as contributing to the wealth and comfort of their owners. In the Roman Empire of course it is well known how they were aggregated in large numbers on farms, how they often revolted, how they destroyed free labour, and ultimately became one of the sources of weakness which led to the destruction of their masters. In Greece, or at all events in Athens, they were treated with comparative leniency, and we find Helots (the Lacedæmonian slaves) fighting in the wars of Lacedæmon, notwithstanding the cruelties alleged to have been constantly perpetrated upon them. In the Athenian literature slaves are often spoken of kindly and familiarly, though of course it is not pretended that there were not cases of oppression. Nor must it be forgotten that many of the slaves at that time were prisoners of war. It was never disputed that the law of war recognised at that time entitled the conquerors to put their prisoners to death, and thus in a way there was some little justification in the practice of those days for commuting the sentence to that of slavery. Aristotle points out in one passage, which is the last we shall quote on this subject, that "clearly it is the duty of the master to train a slave to the virtues that become him," and that "there must be some reasoning with slaves, nay, more than with mere children." (Book i. cap. 13.) His language here, as elsewhere, is, as Mr. Congreve points out in his edition of the Politics, very conciliatory in regard to slaves, and throws very great light on another considerable difference between the slavery of the ancient world and that of the modern. He recommends that the tie between master and slave should be a friendly one; but as a practical man he could not suggest such a thing as the extinction of slavery at a time when the lower orders of freemen occupied the position they then did occupy. But he was a friend to the partial education of slaves, and in this suggestion the Pagan tutor of Alexander the Great showed himself more humane and liberal than did the Christian slaveholders of the American Republic in the nineteenth century.

The mention of education introduces us to the fourth pillar on which Aristotle proposed to found national institutions. When we consider how short a time it is since the necessity of national education has been practically recognised in Europe, we shall scarcely grudge this great thinker any degree of praise for the foresight with which he wrote on this subject. It is unfortunate that a considerable portion of his writings on education has been lost, but enough remains to show the principles on which he rested his doctrine, and a few of the details of his scheme. It is, he says, the duty of the lawgiver to provide that the citizens shall be good men. Besides, each constitution requires that there should prevail a certain character among the people, and since the state has one end—namely, the welfare of the whole body of citizens, the education must be uniform and public; for no man belongs to himself, but to the state, of which he is in fact a part. It should here be said, that of course these remarks do not wholly apply to slaves or to women; they apply to those citizens who are "capable of taking their turn in obeying while young and ruling when old." Nor would they apply, for the same reason, to the βαναυσοι or tradespeople, for whom Aristotle had a great and abiding hatred. No doubt he would have provided education of a certain kind for them, as he did for slaves, but the particulars do not appear in the portion of his work which is left to us. To return, then, to our author: he divides man into his different elements, each of which he declares ought to be duly trained. The first division is that into body and spirit; and the spirit is subdivided into that part which is reasoning and that which is subordinate to reasoning, or, in other words, into reason and passions, while reason again may be employed either in practical or speculative occupations. Now life involves both activity and repose.

"A man," says Aristotle, "should possess the capacity for fighting, but at the same time should actually be at peace. Accordingly, he ought to be able to do what is necessary and useful, but still more should be able to occupy himself with what is good. Now hitherto teachers in the best states have, in a truly base spirit, confined themselves to imparting to their pupils those branches of knowledge which seem to be useful and productive of material profit; this spirit they have showed in their eulogies of Spartan training. But since peace is the end of war, we must teach both the virtues of peace and the virtues of war. We must teach men to be brave in order that they may procure peace, we must teach them to be wise in order that they may enjoy it, and we must teach them to be temperate and just for the requirements both of peace and war."

Leisure and prosperity, he continues, are peculiarly apt to teach insolence. We must, then, begin by training the body, which exists before the spirit has become developed. Next we must train the passions, which manifest themselves before the reason; and lastly, we must train the reason. This must be done by constant education, which will produce virtuous habits. But although we must not restrict ourselves to teaching what is merely of practical utility, still young men must be taught some subjects of that nature, provided they be not of such a kind as to debase the character and reduce the pupils to the level of βαναυσοι. Aristotle then proceeds to examine the system actually pursued in Greek education at that time. It comprised four branches—namely, Reading with its accompaniments, Painting or designing, Gymnastics, and Music. It is a fair inference from his remarks, that he quite agrees with the propriety of this training. There is no discussion as to the expediency of reading (γραμματική), and little more is said of painting than that it tends to familiarize the mind with forms of beauty. Gymnastics he discusses practically, with a view of laying down rules for the prevention of excessive fatigue; but it is on the subject of music that we find the longest and most complete discussion. It must, however, be assumed that, had all this portion of the work been preserved, a great deal more would have been insisted on as essential to education than the attainments above described. It would have been curious as well as instructive, to have learned from the author of de Cœlo, de Rhetoricâ, and de Animalibus, what was, in his opinion, the relative importance of literary and scientific education. We cannot doubt that one or both would have been insisted on as necessary, for in his preliminary observations he remarks upon the necessity of imparting φιλοσοφία to the citizens, a degree of attainment which could hardly be reached by learning the arts of reading, painting, and music. If any inference can be drawn from his general tone in reference to subjects of study, we are inclined to think he would have preferred a knowledge of facts to a knowledge of theories, and have held a study of nature preferable to a study of books. Such speculations, however, cannot be very valuable, because it is undoubted that Aristotle himself dwells with great emphasis and admiration on Homer and other poets, though he frequently in his philosophical treatises insists on the importance of a familiarity with facts and statistics. The treatise on music is so full, that some critics have considered that nothing on this subject has been lost. However that may be, we are told that music is of the greatest importance in education. It is valuable as an amusement for those who have leisure, as an educational weapon, in order to soften the character, and as a source of intellectual enjoyment to men who have passed childhood and middle life, and have earned honourable rest. It has a deep influence on the character, portraying as it does our feelings in sound, and exciting or soothing us according to the nature of the strains. The student of Greek history will recollect the great and singular influence exercised over the Greeks by means of music. Considering, however, the mutilated condition of the books on education, the details are less worthy of attention than the principles enunciated. We have seen that compulsory education is to be given to all who are capable of taking part in the government of the state; and in a lesser degree even to slaves, who, of course, did not possess that capacity. The object is avowed to be the improvement of individuals, that they may acquire the

character of good citizens. Thus we are led to inquire what is
Aristotle's conception of goodness in citizens, and what that class
is which he considers worthy of wielding the power of the state.

In order to ascertain this, it is necessary to piece together
different passages in the work, for there is a good deal of confusion as to the constitution of the Ideal State, arising partly
from the fragmentary condition of some of the Books, and partly
from the introduction of numerous *θεωρίαι*, or digressive speculations, with which this part of the work is especially loaded. It
must be remembered that there is a deep line between the remarks on the Ideal State and the comments which Aristotle
makes on other forms of government which he recommends as
substitutes for that ideal where it cannot be reached. The object of the state is to make possible a virtuous and happy life;
and it is to be held together by the bonds of amity. There must
be a rotation of rulers. If, indeed, the rulers were as far superior
in body and soul to the ruled as gods are to men, the class of
rulers and subjects ought always to maintain their respective
positions; but since this is not the case, the elders ought to take
turn in ruling. In the best state, the virtue of a good citizen
is the same as the virtue of a good man, which has been described in the Ethics. Accordingly, the object of state education is to produce citizens of the type set forth in the Ethics.
Haughtiness, dignity, valour, temperance, and firmness of character will be found to be the main ingredients in that somewhat
grotesque portrait. There is much that is noble in the good
man of Aristotelian morality, and much also that is foolish.
Those who care to trace the subject farther will find in the description of this noble savage much that is curious and interesting. None who take part in trade, commerce, or agriculture
can be considered citizens in the proper sense of the word, the
only duties of citizens being war in their youth, administrative
and judicial offices in middle age, and sacerdotal functions in
their old age. All who are indispensable to a state, says
Aristotle, are not on that account necessarily citizens. Connected with this distribution of duties is a digression in which
he justifies the position which he has adopted. Where, he asks
as an abstract question, ought the supreme power in a state to
reside? Not in the mob, nor in the few wealthy families, because to allow that would be to acknowledge that might is right.
Nor in the well-to-do classes alone, for it would be unfair
that all the rest should be excluded from civic honours; nor in
the one best man in the state, for that would be still more exclusive. Nor, again, in the law, for that may be framed in the
interest of a particular party. However, it must be admitted
that the mob, unless they are mere animals, ought in some sense

to be sovereign, for a number of men assembled together have collectively more virtue and a better discretion than one good man who combines all virtues in himself; and moreover it would be dangerous to withhold all power from them. They should therefore be entrusted with the privileges of deliberating and deciding the merits of their rulers. In short, to translate into English custom as well as English language, they should enjoy the right of meeting and the right of turning out a perverse government. There are, however, some objections to these views, which Aristotle thinks it necessary to answer. In the first place, it is argued, he says, that just as the skill of physicians can be judged only by medical men, so magistrates ought not to be judged by men who are themselves incompetent to hold the magistracy. The answer to this is, that it is only scientific physicians who require to be judged by medical men, and humorously adds that the skill of mere practitioners may very well be estimated by the patients themselves. Nor is it true that those who know how to do particular work are themselves the best judges of how that work is done: the gentleman at table is a better judge of how a dinner is dressed than the cook who dressed it. What, then, he continues, are the grounds of the claim to superior power which are advanced by the various classes in the state? The rich claim power because of their supposed trustworthiness and superior stake in the country. The aristocracy lay claim on the ground of the ambiguity of the word "noble," which means "well-born," as well as superlatively "meritorious." As they are confessedly noble in the first sense, they claim to be noble in the second sense also, which we cannot admit in all cases, although they will probably be better from being the offspring of better sires. Men of decent lives claim power because of the close alliance between virtue and justice, alleging that those who live virtuously are most likely to govern justly. The weakness of the above claims is pointed out to be that if they were allowed, one very rich or very well-born or very virtuous man, if he excelled each of the other citizens in one particular point, would have a right to the throne. Whereas in truth the legislator ought not to legislate especially for the better or for the more numerous classes without reference to the others, but, striking the average, he ought to legislate for the benefit of the whole body of citizens. If, however, one man or a few men transcend all the rest, not merely individually, but collectively, in virtue and political capacity, they must not be regarded as a part of the state, nor treated as merely equal to those who are their inferiors. If such an individual is found, who so far excels all the rest of the citizens together, we must make him king, as we cannot in fairness either eject him from the state or make

him subject to the rule of others. It was on the ground of this
kind of superiority that the system of Ostracism was originated.
A man was expelled from a state because of his transcendant
merit, just as a painter would not sacrifice the entire portrait in
order to make one limb transcendantly beautiful. From all this
it is clear that, in spite of Aristotle's declared preference for an
aristocratic government, in which the privileged classes were to
take their turn in governing, there might be circumstances in
which he would recommend even for the best possible state a
monarchy or a very confined oligarchy. Perhaps, however, it
was rather a logical necessity that drove him to this conclusion,
for he does not dwell upon the conditions which would arise
under such a contingency. Having laid down as a principle
that participation in government is not a duty, but a privilege
due to those who have proper claims, for that in substance is his
position, he is constrained to admit that if the claims of one individual exceed the claims of all the rest of the citizens put together,
that individual is entitled to be king. As, however, it may
safely be stated that no such superiority has ever been known in
history, or is ever likely to appear, this view of Aristotle would
not practically lead to any serious conclusions, and so may be
dismissed without any further notice.

Whatever was to be considered the best form of government,
the comments in the Politics are by no means confined within
so narrow a range. We are told that in political science men
should consider not only the best condition possible, but also
what are the general rules for selection where the choice is not
absolutely free ; and also, how should be formed, and when
formed, and how preserved, a polity which is neither the best
possible nor the best practicable, but which still is one that is
wished for and acquiesced in by the people (τὴν ἐξ ὑποθέσεως
φαυλοτέραν τίνα), and lastly, we should consider the best
average state. Now it is wholly impossible, within the limits
of this paper, to enter fully into the minute and searching criticisms which are made upon the different forms of government,
and the contrivances used to prop up or destroy them. Generally, it is laid down that there are three healthy forms of
government to be found in existing states, which are placed in
order of merit as follows : monarchical, aristocratic, and constitutional. Each of these forms, when degraded, must be called by
a different name, and the better the healthy form is, the worse
will be the degraded form which corresponds to it. Thus the
spurious or unhealthy forms of government, as placed in order
of merit, will stand thus : democratic, oligarchical, and despotic.
Of each of these forms there are several varieties, into each of
which Aristotle makes considerable inquiries, though not all of

great value in the present day. We must look for the reason of such minute subdivision of forms of government in the fact that Greece was divided into almost as many states as it contained cities, and thereby afforded endless material for speculation and fine-drawn distinctions. In such small communities, also, the least difference in constitution, or in the distribution of wealth or weapons of war, threw a very appreciable weight into one scale or the other, and it was accordingly necessary for a writer who contemplated, as our author unquestionably did, the maintenance of the existing small-state system, to be careful not to omit even the most trivial considerations. From the mass, however, of criticism and illustration on this subject, we will extract—partly as specimens, partly as historic notices—the comments, in first place, on the connexion between forms of government and military systems, and in the second place, on the influence of law in Greece. Aristotle tells us that in Greece, where keeping horses was a matter of great cost, wherever the army of a State was composed of cavalry, the form of government was strictly confined to the very wealthy classes. This he instances by the example of the Eretrians, Chalcidians, and the Magnetes who lived on the banks of the Maeander. There is, indeed, no doubt that in Thessaly and Asia Minor, where the broad plains and extensive pastures led less to the confinement of the inhabitants in cities than did the mountainous districts intersected by arms of the sea so frequent in Lower Greece, levelling ideas did not obtain so much influence, and the power remained long in the hands of the princely families; whereas, in Athens, for example, the great families soon lost their absolute authority. Aristotle points out that after the cities had reached a considerable growth, the lower orders began to take their share of military duties. Drilling became more cultivated, no doubt from the example of Sparta, and this led to the predominance of another class of soldiers—namely, the hoplites, or heavy-armed troops. As the equipment of an hoplite was still a somewhat costly matter, the power, always corresponding in its distribution with the military strength of the respective classes in the state, fell into the hands of what we should call the upper middle class, and thus the form of government was still oligarchical, though less so than under the cavalry *régime.* The last change, according to Aristotle, came when the sailors and light-armed troops became numerous and well-drilled. These men belonged to the poorer classes, and from a remark in the sixth book, it appears that in revolutions the light-armed troops had a great advantage over the heavy-armed and the cavalry, probably because of the narrowness of the streets, which rendered activity and nimbleness the chief ele-

ments of success. The importance of superior capacity for street-
fighting in regulating the form of government will be best
appreciated if we call to mind the law of Solon, which forbade
any citizen remaining neutral in a revolution ; so ready were all
classes to fight out their differences, and so important was it for
the welfare of the state that such contests should end, one way
or the other, as soon as possible. Possibly also, Solon had it in
his mind to prevent more than one civil struggle going on in
the same city at the same time, a disaster of which Athens, in
the time of Pisistratus, had a painful experience.

The importance ascribed by Aristotle to the changing conditions of military knowledge and discipline, as a cause of constitutional changes, leads us naturally to inquire how it was that
in states so highly civilized as Athens there was such constant
necessity for reference to the arbitrament of the sword. Rome was
in a less advanced stage of culture when at all events some blood-
less revolutions were achieved. Why was it otherwise in Greece ?
The answer is, that in the main the Romans had fixed laws, and
respected them.   They were impressed with what we may call a
constitutional morality ; they revered precedents, and if a legal
rule oppressed them, their remedy was to rescind the rule by
legal means, not to resist it while it remained in operation. It
is a fact much noted by writers on Greek history, that this feeling was entirely unknown to the Greeks. They had a few
somewhat vague laws, but had no confidence in them, and their
impulsive characters led them to violate the law when it appeared
unjust, rather than endure the delay and trouble of repealing it,
and enacting afresh. No stronger illustration can be given than
Aristotle's own refusal to allow that the supreme authority
should reside in the law, on the alleged ground that it is liable
to be made a party organ. We must believe, however, that he
deplored this state of feeling, for elsewhere he speaks of law in
very different terms. Law may be likened, he says, to a man
who has reason without feeling. It is inflexible and incorrup-
tible ; but its weakness is that it must apply general principles
to particular cases, which sometimes weighs harshly on individuals. Yet he does not subscribe to the doctrines of those who
deride the law, nor admit their analogies. It is not fair, he
considers, to argue against the utility of laws by saying that sick
people call for a doctor, not for a medicine book ; we must remember that politicians are biassed by self-interest, while doctors
are unprejudiced. Accordingly, he would not allow a judge,
however well-disposed, to decide questions by his unaided sense
of justice. The law, however needs a living exponent, and on
the principle that two heads are better than one, he advocates
the establishment of a board of judges, to decide on cases which
the general principles of law are too wide to meet.

One more sentence, containing his reason for allowing laws to be altered if better can be suggested, is worth recording :—

"Men seek to establish, not what their forefathers practised, but what they find to be advantageous for themselves. Indeed, it would seem that the primitive race of men, whether they sprang from the soil or were preserved from some plague or flood, were on a level with very ordinary or even silly persons of the present day . . . . . so that it would be absurd to abide by their opinions."

This very strong expression of radicalism, if we may apply such a term to those times, seems strange when compared with another passage, in which, speaking of the caste system, he says: "We must consider that pretty near all other political inventions also have, in the long course of time, been often, nay, countless times, discovered before."

In this sketch, necessarily imperfect in so short a paper, of the chief political work of Aristotle, enough we hope will have been said to induce a few who interest themselves in the subject to seek for more in the book itself. It is we believe less frequently read than it deserves. The subject is not one in which new truths are of frequent appearance, and the social or political maxims enunciated by Aristotle are more reliable than the flighty doctrines of men like Macchiavel or Hobbes. Indeed, there is only one important institution advocated in the Politics which a tardy experience has taught us to discard, and that is Slavery. Some remarks have already been offered in mitigation of the sentence which modern thinkers will be apt to pass upon his advocacy of that evil. We will close this paper by noticing another opinion of our author, which would certainly require apology were it not that it is in the main acted upon, if not avowed, by a large number of persons in this country, a circumstance which is of itself an apology. We allude to his estimate of the working classes, for such is a fair general interpretation of the words βαναυσοι and θητικοι. We have noticed the remarkable passage in which the working man is said to possess virtue only so far as he partakes of slavery and thereby has opportunities of approaching his master. Elsewhere Aristotle announces as a distinction between working men and slaves, that the former are necessaries common to all, while the latter serve one master only. In his Ideal State he recommends that there should be a plot of ground reserved for the citizens proper to meet in, and in which no artisan or working man shall on any account be permitted to enter unless he be summoned thither by the authorities. Such was the view of Aristotle on the "equal rights of man." We need not trace the causes which have led to the apparent explosion of such very extreme views, or at all events have made it ridiculous to utter them explicitly : but when we recollect the frequency of the remark in our own day, that "the common people are educated above their position," we think it unnecessary to trouble our readers with any further apology for the prejudices of a thinker who lived more than two thousand years ago.

Art. VI.—André Chénier: Poet and Political Martyr.

1. *Poésies d'André Chénier, avec une Notice par Becq. de Fouquières.* Paris: 1862.
2. *Poésies d'André Chénier, précédées d'une Notice par M. H. De Latouche.* Paris: 1868.
3. *Littérature au dix-huitième Siècle: par Villemain.* Paris: 1838.
4. *La Vérité sur la Famille de Chénier.* Paris: 1844.
5. *Les Œuvres en Prose d'André Chénier, avec une Notice Historique par le bibliophile Jacob.* Paris: 1840.
6. *Various Articles by Sainte-Beuve.*

THE biography of André Chénier contains the parallel stories of the two distinct and strangely dissimilar lives of a poet and of a political martyr—the two never to be confounded or confused, yet, when by death they were finally merged into one completed history, each seeming the fitting complement to the other. As a poet he lived in a cherished retirement, with his friends, his books, his love-longings, and his unuttered hopes, consecrating the days and nights to his writings, and to an intense study which should fit him to be worthy of his art; and yet so adverse was he to the petty jealousies and contests of a literary career, so far removed from the promptings of vanity, so utterly careless of contemporary applause, that he chose to leave his poems unpublished, and, save to a few dear friends, unknown. When, however, the first signals of the great Revolution quickened the pulse and fired the blood of all who were eagerest, most generous, most hopeful, most impassioned in France, André Chénier, leaving the solitude which had to him become a second nature, threw himself into the vortex of political life with a reckless daring that almost savoured of temerity. There were gross abuses to be abolished; crying evils to be hunted down; poor stricken wretches to be set again in God's free air; centuries upon centuries of oppression and wrong-doings and down-crushings and patient long-sufferings to be altered and

amended; and, pen in hand, he fought as valiantly for the pure
ideals of truth and justice as ever with sword or lance did warrior
knights of old. In the great world-drama which was commenced
in 1789, and of which we who live now shall scarcely see the
end, the part played by André Chénier was probably the purest,
the noblest, the most unselfish of any; for not only was he
among the foremost to lead the people onward to rescue all that
was dear to them as men and women from the clutch of a
terribly oppressive authority, but when, as an almost inevitable
reaction, the people themselves, with their mob-laws, their Age
of Reason, their thirst for vengeance and blood, inaugurated the
most appalling tyranny that the world has ever witnessed, he
again dared, this time almost alone, to take the side of the
weakest, to battle for a liberty that should be governed by law,
for a justice that should be tempered by toleration. Nearly
single-handed, he tried to stem the rushing floods of massacres
and madnesses and miseries; he attacked openly—almost
wantonly—men whose scowling hatred foreboded death; and
when at last he found that all his struggles were ineffectual, he
cried that it were better to deserve the guillotine than to enjoy
life in times like these. And, in his death-hour, turning, as if
for consolation, again to poetry—still the strongest passion in his
mind save that of patriotism—he found his loveliest inspiration at
the very foot of the scaffold. Dying with his poems unpublished,
with, alas! too many of them unwritten, it was not until he was
for the last time dragged from his dungeon that he gave utterance to hopes and aspirations hitherto intensely self-contained,
for, smiting his forehead with his hand, he cried, " And yet I had
something there !" Five-and-twenty years after this, when for
the first time his poems were presented to the public, the world
gave a unanimous, though tardy verdict that the words were
spoken not idly nor in vanity, but in the spirit of true prophecy,
in the consciousness of innate genius, of actual performance.

The family of Chénier was originally of Poitou origin, deriving,
indeed, its name from a little hamlet in that province. For generations the eldest son had occupied by a kind of inherited right
the official situation of inspector of mines in Languedoc. Louis
de Chénier, the father of a family that in no less than three of
its members was afterwards to be famous, received from his
ancestors a very slender patrimony, which he generously handed
over to his sister, being determined to seek his own fortunes
abroad. At Constantinople he speedily contrived to found a
business of some importance; but a commercial career was not
at all suited to his eager and ambitious hopes, and he soon quitted
the counting-house, to occupy a place in the French Embassy at

the Ottoman Court. Here his aptitude for diplomacy, and the uprightness and inflexibility of his character, procured him the warm friendship of the Consul-General, who, on his death-bed, nominated young Chénier as his delegate—an office he efficiently executed until a new ambassador was appointed. In Constantinople he married a young Greek lady, Mdlle. Santi l'Homaka —sister, by the way, to the grandmother of M. Thiers. During the ten years of their married life spent in the East, she brought him four sons and a daughter—the third son, André Chénier, being born upon the 30th October, 1762. In 1765, Louis de Chénier returned with his family to France, where he hoped to push forward his diplomatic career, and in a short time he succeeded in obtaining a situation in Africa, which ultimately led to his appointment as *chargé d'affaires* to the Emperor of Morocco; and in 1767, attended by his devoted wife, he again set sail, leaving the children under the care of that sister to whom, as quite a boy, he had behaved with so much brotherly generosity.

The two eldest lads were sent at once to the College of Navarre, at Paris; but André and Joseph passed the most impressionable years of their lives with their aunt, under the lovely sky of Languedoc, beside the borders of the Aude. It was the very country for a poet's childhood—a little romance land, bounded on the south by the eastern Pyrenees, on the north by the Haute Garonne, on the east by the deep blue waters of the Mediterranean. Strangely varied in its scenery—now bleak and desolate round the lofty peaks of Bernard Sauvage, la Glèbe, and Ruse; but in the valley of the Aude itself, a fairy summer haunt set in hills and fed by a hundred mountain streams, two climates seemed absolutely to meet—here summer with its olives and its vineyards, and there the wintry mountains of Alaric, with their massive piles and craters of rocks, with rugged mountain sides and torrentless gorges. Terentius Varro, the Roman poet, had been born here B.C. 116, and hence in the sturdier days of chivalry sprang the trouvères; and the country legends were still full of knightly tales of Moor and Christian. Enjoying the sunshine, playing with the flowers, making childish pilgrimages to the sea or to the mountains, weaving from the songs and ballads that their nurses sung new legends to foreshadow, after boyish fashion, their own individual longings, the two lads spent a happy childhood. The peculiar scenery and imagery of Languedoc, the strong childish recollections of the pastoral innocence of the people, were fixed indelibly upon André Chénier, and are incessantly reproduced in his works. In a manuscript note he himself gives us a charming memory from the many that thronged his brain :—

" The recollection of this lovely country, its lakes, its rivers, its countless rills and streams and torrents, which I saw at an age when I scarcely knew how to see, brings me back a memory of my childhood I would never willingly lose. I could only have been eight years of age, for it is fifteen years ago (ah! how old I am growing!) when on a holiday they led me by the hand to climb a mountain. There were many people there at their prayers. To the right of the road there was a spring, under a hollowed vault, carved out of the mountain side, and under the same little roof there were one or two madonnas. The water was deliciously fresh and sparkling. As well as I can remember this must have been near a town named Limoux, in Lower Languedoc. After walking for a long time we came to a lovely little church, and here there was another and a larger well. I shall tell no one where this was, for I shall have a secret joy in finding it again, when my travels lead me into the country. If ever in a land I love I possess a haven after my own fantasy, I will arrange there if I can a fountain after the same fashion, with a statue to the nymphs, with an inscription like one of those old ones, *de fontibus sacris*, &c.''

About the year 1773, Madame de Chénier returned from Africa and took up her abode at Paris, to superintend the education of her sons, and the two youngest now joined their brothers at the College of Navarre.

Madame de Chénier was a lady of refinement, wit, and even learning. Beautiful she had been with the beauty of old Greece, and endowed with something of the poetical and graceful mobility of the women of ancient Athens. She now willingly exchanged the delights of the song and the dance, in which she had excelled, for the cultivation of letters and the pleasures of the mind. Brought up amid the poetical memories of bygone times, with a keen sense of their beauties and with an accurate knowledge of the grand old language in which they had been embalmed, it seemed as though across the ages it had been granted her to preserve within herself something of the rhythm and perfume of the past, of world-old legends, of eternal loveliness, to cherish the fresh young intellect of her favourite son André, as other mothers supply the physical cravings of their offspring. Aided by her, he made a rapid progress in his classical studies, and at fourteen he was the first Greek scholar in the college, for volumes that to other lads were but dismal threatenings of punishments to come, were to him the relics of a holy fatherland. Turning, as most boys of genius do, to other books than those provided by their masters, he even then began to translate Sappho and Anacreon with feeling and sweetness, for they seemed, heard from his mother's lips, to be his own national songs. At sixteen he was said to have had a perfect knowledge of Greek. At the college he formed boyish friendships—often the most lasting of all—with the les Panges and les Trudaines,

and they already shared his ambitions and acknowledged his
supremacy. At the end of 1779 he left college altogether, and
for the next two years he joined the brilliant circle of which his
talented mother was the centre and the idol.

As soon as Madame de Chénier had taken up her abode in
Paris, her *salon* became the rendezvous of a remarkable assembly.
The future was gloomy with forebodings, for the old world was
drifting by, and on all sides little coteries were formed ; " the
two grand shades of Voltaire and Rousseau seemed to preside
over these gatherings, for all the world, the women above the
rest, had something of the soul of Jean-Jacques and the mind of
Voltaire." Men then celebrated, or to be famous in the mighty
times to come, met together in these rooms—poets and magistrates, diplomatists and painters, musicians and historians. There
was Le Brun, the " French Pindar" of the day, occupying the
throne by an act of courteous usurpation, and requisitioning from
all the pleasant incense of flattery, for the shepherds and shep-
herdesses, the gods and goddesses, his muse put forth in powder
and patches and Watteau skirts and furbelows. Still he had
talent enough to perceive the genius of André, and, though thrice
his age, became a warm and constant companion ; sometimes a
master, often an imitator, always a friend. Many of the faults
in André's compositions are to be traced to this early influence.
There was David, already in the zenith of his fame, who was regenerating French art as André was to regenerate French poetry.
The great painter felt a strong and permanent interest in the
young student's career—had him for ever in his studio, gave him
lessons in drawing, laughed at his efforts, and yet followed his
advice. There were young people, too, in that charming circle—
the brothers Panges and the brothers Trudaine, the Marquis de
Brazais among the most regular ; all dabbling in, at all events
verse-making. Here in the winter evenings, under the joint
presidency of Le Brun and Madame de Chénier, their poems
were read, gently criticised, and warmly flattered. Here mutual
hopes were confided, mutual encouragements given, for all meant
some day to do something very great and very wonderful, and
all tried in the meantime to filch a little pleasure and excitement
from the fame the future had in store ; André alone displayed
a close reserve as to his literary projects ; his study and his own
brain were his only confidants, and much coercion and many
innocent frauds were used before his poems could be brought up
for judgment. An inflexible resolution made him adopt this
course, for his genius was already spontaneously developed, and
was acknowledged far and wide. Nothing would have been
easier than, in the *recueils* of the day, to have speedily out-
distanced Le Brun himself. But he seems to have had no care

whatever for the ephemeral fame that contemporary praise bestows. Not so with his brother Joseph, who was already thirsting for immediate applause, and who, still a boy, had abandoned himself to all the dictates of literary vanity.

André, however, had one passion that could not be concealed —common to that age of great men, to the Voltaires, the Diderots—the burning desire for knowledge, the fever of universality. " To know how to read, to know how to think," are, he tells us, " the indispensable preliminaries of the art of writing." Before the day dawned he was at his books, garnering beauties from ancient poets and wisdom from modern philosophers; laboriously annotating Homer and Plato, yet studying the worthiest works that England, Germany, and Italy have produced ; writing poetry already, he was still deep in the mysteries of science, yet at the same time applying himself to a closely conscientious study of the French language, with the same clearness and exactitude as if it had been a foreign tongue ; then coming from out his world of old books to be the ornament of that distinguished coterie ; loving his friends as earnestly as he shunned all mere acquaintances.

At this time André was nineteen years of age. He possessed the energy and stubbornness of his father's character ; the enthusiasm, the sensibility, the passionate love of the beautiful, of his mother's. He was of a medium stature; his forehead bold and high ; his hair of a light chestnut, clustering round his head in thick crisp curls ; his eyes a grey-blue, small, but very brilliant. La Comtesse Hocquart used to say that he had large features and an enormous head ; was full of a mystic charm, yet positively ugly.

His resolution as to life had been formed from the very first. He says, " Opening my eyes and looking round me on leaving childhood, I saw everywhere that gold and intrigue were almost the only goals towards which all were striving. I resolved henceforth, without examining whether circumstances permitted it or not, to live for ever apart from all business, in retirement and in the most perfect liberty." His father, however, could scarcely be expected to share those delightful and utopian views, and as soon as his son arrived at the years of manhood pressed upon him the necessity of embracing a career, urging him to choose that of diplomacy, in which the family interest chiefly lay. André preferred, since a preference was necessary, a military life, and in the year 1782 he joined the regiment d'Angoumois, then stationed at Strasbourg, as a " gentleman cadet."

The dreary routine of garrison life, the strict discipline, the tedious drills, proved necessarily but little to his liking ; still the long leisure hours permitted him to return with renewed energy to his studies; and in these he was joined by the Marquis de Brazais, one of his boyish friends. At Strasbourg he met

Brunck, the single eminent Greek scholar that France was then able to oppose to the *savants* of England and Germany. Brunck, like Chénier, had been a soldier; and like him, was possessed with a passion for the antique. This love had, however, only been awakened in him at the age of thirty; and, now an official of high standing, he might be seen going, like a schoolboy, with his books under his arm, to attend the lectures of the Greek professor at the university. Few men since the revival of learning have done so much for Greek literature as Brunck; though the idea upon which he always acted, that all the irregularities occurring in the Greek poets were the handiwork of the copyists, led him to make bold alterations of his own, not always of the happiest. Still his love for Greek poetry was familiar, if not reverent. In aftertimes he entered warmly into the cause of the Revolution, and, little by little, sold off his fine collection of Greek books for the benefit of the cause. From that moment Greek literature became hateful to his memory; tears sprang to his eyes when one of his once-loved authors was casually named. With Brunck Chénier formed a lively friendship, and to Brunck's "Analectæ" many of his contemporary and after poems are very largely indebted. To this period are due the earliest of the beautiful imitations and idylls based upon Theocritus and others. In the fine fragment of " Invention," Chénier tells us, with a mingling of bold acknowledgment and loving reverence, how much indebted he was, at all events at this early period, to the inspiration of Greek poetry :—

" Let us change to golden honey flowers whose fragrance aye will last ;— Paint the thoughts that throng the present with the colours of the past ; Let us light our modern torches at the old poetic fires, Sing us songs to rouse and wake us to the tunes of ancient lyres."	" Changeons en notre miel leurs plus antiques fleurs, Pour peindre notre idée empruntons leurs couleurs ; Allumons nos flambeaux à leurs feux poétiques ; Sur des pensers nouveaux faisons des vers antiques."

The epistles to Le Bron and the earliest of the idylls prove how thoroughly he was imbued with this "ancient fire"—they exhibit a wonderful blending of classic memories and modern inspiration. " Le Mendiant" and " L'Aveugle" are, says Villemain, "a page torn as it were from some old Greek manuscript, but written by something more than a modern pen." Of these delicious idylls we can but quote the shortest :—

"MNAZILUS AND CHLOE. *Chloe.* "O flower-strewn borders ! O tall reeds blowing In rhythmic tune to the water flowing !	"MNAZILE ET CHLOÉ. *Chloé.* " Fleurs, bocage sonore, et mobiles roseaux, Où murmure Zéphyre au murmure des eaux,

Oh, tell me is Massilas near your
glades !
Often he comes to your peaceful shades,
And often I wish that the wandering air
Would bring me a message that he is
there."

Massilus.

"O stream ! the mother of flowers, you
hold
This scented dell in your girdling fold ;
Why do you not bring to your winding
thrall
Chloë, the daintiest flower of all !"

Chloë.

"If he but knew that I came to dream
Of love, and of him beside the stream !
Oh, if a glance or a tender smile
Could make him tarry a little while——"

Massilus.

"Oh, if some kind god would breathe a
word
Of the thoughts with which my heart
is stirr'd,
Then dare I pray her, when she was
near me,
To let me love her, at least to hear me !"

Chloë.

"O joy, 'tis he !—he speaks—I tremble—
Be quiet, O lips ! O eyes, dissemble !"

Massilus.

"The foliage rustled — methought I
heard—
'Tis she ! O eyes, say never a word !"

Chloë.

"What, Massilus here ! how strange to
meet
With you in this lonely green retreat !"

Massilus.

"Alone I lay in the shady grass,
And never expected a soul to pass !"

. . . .

Parlez, le beau Massile est-il sous vos
ombrages !
Il visite souvent vos paisibles rivages.
Souvent j'écoute, et l'air qui gémit
dans vos bois
A mon oreille au loin vient apporter sa
voix."

Massile.

"Onde, mère des fleurs, naïade trans-
parente,
Qui presses mollement cette enceinte
odorante,
Amenez-y Chloë, l'amour de mes regards.
Vos bords m'offrent souvent ses vestiges
épars.
Souvent ma bouche vient, sous vos
sombres allées,
Baiser l'herbe et les fleurs que ses pas
ont foulées."

Chloë.

"Oh ! s'il pouvait savoir quel amoureux
ennui
Me rend cher ce bocage où je rêve de lui !
Peut-être je devrais d'un sourire favor-
able
L'inviter, l'engager à me trouver aimable."

Massile.

"Si pour m'encourager quelque dieu
bienfaiteur
Lui disait que son nom fait palpiter
mon cœur !
J'aurais dû l'inviter, d'une voix douce
et tendre,
A me laisser aimer, à m'aimer, à m'en-
tendre."

Chloë.

"Ah ! je l'ai vu ; c'est lui. Dieux ! je
vais lui parler !
O ma bouche ! ô mes yeux ! gardez de
vous troubler."

Massile.

"Le feuillage a frémi. Quelque robe
légère . . .
C'est elle ! ô mes regards ! ayez soin
de vous taire."

Chloë.

"Quoi ! Massile est ici ! Seule, errante,
mes pas
Cherchaient ici le frais et ne t'y cro-
yaient pas."

Massile.

"Seul, au bord de ces flots que le tilleul
couronne,
J'avais fui le soleil et n'attendais per-
sonne."

. . . .

This is a very epitome of first love, with its blushing coyness, its new-born strange, unuttered desires. Of the " Fragments," due also to this period, we quote a specimen, which in the original has a wonderful blending of simplicity, innocence, and *volupté* : —

"I was but a weakly infant, she a stately maid and tall,
Yet with many a smiling promise, many a soft and winsome call,
She would match me to her breast, cradle me and rock me there,
Let my childish fingers trifle with the glories of her hair ;
Smother me a while with caresses—for a moment's space again,
As if shocked with my o'erboldness, feign to chide, but only feign.
Yet it was when lovers thronged her, a confused and bashful host,
That the proud disdainful beauty caress'd and fondled me the most.
Often, often—(oh, how foolish childhood's innocent alarms !)—
Has she cover'd me with kisses as I struggled in her arms ;
While the shepherds murmur'd round us, as triumphantly I smiled,
'Oh what thrilling joys are wasted ! Oh ! too happy, happy child !' "

"J'étais un faible enfant qu'elle était grande et belle ;
Elle me souriait et m'appelait près d'elle.
Debout sur ces genoux, mon innocente main
Parcourait ses cheveux, son visage, son sein,
Et sa main quelquefois, aimable et caressante,
Feignait de châtier mon enfance imprudente.
C'est devant ses amants, auprès d'elle confus,
Que la fière beauté me caressait le plus :
Que de fois (mais, hélas ! que sent-on à cet âge ?)
Les baisers de sa bouche ont pressé mon visage !
Et les bergers disaient, me voyant triomphant :
'O ! que de biens perdus ! O trop heureux enfant !' "

In spite, however, of these pleasant labours, and of severer studies, for these he never abandoned, the routine of duties and pleasures, of watches and balls, incidental to a garrison life, became so insupportable to André Chénier that after a six months' trial he resigned his commission, left Strasbourg, and returned home to enjoy the precious liberty of poverty. But as soon as he reapplied himself to his books, he found that his health had been most seriously injured by over-work. He writes despondingly to one of his friends :—

"I am dying—my brief daytime ended ere the evening gloom,
And my poor rose faded, wither'd, while as yet 'twas scarce in bloom ;
Life for me had many pleasures, lightly, softly flitting by ;
I have scarce had time to taste them—scarce, and yet, behold, I die !"

"Je meurs. Avant le soir j'ai fini ma journée.
A peine ouverte au jour, ma rose s'est fanée.
La vie eut bien pour moi des volages douceurs
Je la goûtais à peine, et voilà que je meurs."

Nor was this alarm uncalled for ; and though, owing chiefly to the tender nursing of his mother, the poet's life was spared, his medical advisers considered it most essential that he should for a while be completely severed from his books. The brothers Trudaine, with a loving solicitude, planned a journey that they thought would tempt him away, and insisted that the invalid should accompany them to the East. The hope of viewing in reality the ruins of that old world he saw so often in his dreams —the glorious relics of Rome and Athens, the gorgeous splendours of the Orient—revived hope, and even health. "Under a lovelier sky," he writes, "my sickness and misery will be charmed away."

They went through Italy, Asia Minor, and Greece, and Chénier was thus the first poet to open the road to the East to Chateaubriand, Lamartine, Byron, Gautier, and others, who have again sung the beauties of its scenery, its grandeur, its magnificence. For his own part, however, he saw much and wrote but little, and in that little an excited admiration is visible, which by its own enthusiasm is compelled to fall back upon memories rather than to create anew. The ultimate effect of this journey upon his art is evident enough; but his contemporary writings consist chiefly of fragments of poetry and prose intermingled, meant eventually to be used in one grand poem, but very beautiful in their rough form, fresh from the quarry of a master-mind.

In Italy, in Greece, lands where the arts were born, his hand tried vainly to fix upon paper the glories of rapidly succeeding images of landscape loveliness, of grass-grown stones and mouldering ruins instinct with the pure art of times now dead, yet still calling up burning thoughts of liberty and glory. At Naples he first heard Italian music, and he continues:—

"The blood rushes to my face, and they tell me that my reason has need of soothing hellebore. But first for things far more important! . . . . I fly to the forum, to the senate. I am surrounded with sublime shadows. I hear the voices of Gracchus, of Cincinnatus, Cato, Brutus. I see the palace where Germanicus and his wife have dwelt. . . . . Perish those who say that admiration for those antique models is a prejudice, who will not confess that those grand virtues which alone are solid and enduring, belong only to lands where liberty is cherished! *Hos utinam inter heroas tellus me prima tulisset.* Ah! if I had lived in those times! . . . . But oh, my two friends, my fellow voyagers! I cannot even wish to have lived in a better world, from which you should have been absent. Would to heaven that we had been there together! We would have formed a triumvirate more virtuous than that. . . . . But let us live now as those great men lived then! Let Fortune act towards us as she please; *we are three to one against her!*"

In the epistle written on quitting France, his affections had been divided between the friends he left behind and those with whom he was to travel, but a genuine joy sparkles through his songs when in good health and glorious spirits he returned.

No sooner was he again settled in his family than he betook himself to his studies with the same energy as of old—rising before daylight and burning the midnight oil ; it being still his primary ambition to master the entire circle of human knowledge, and then to devote this wealth of learning to his art. " Work ! work !" he sings, " dare to achieve this glorious victory ! Still is there need of further proofs, of further reasons ! Work on !—a great example is a powerful witness ! . . . Oh, if I could some day !" . . .

Throughout Chénier's whole career, the distinction becoming more vividly demarcated month by month, there were two sides to his character ; the one belonging to the pursuit of pleasure, to the world of elegance and beauty and sparkling wit, to the discussion of political questions (this last was in graver times to absorb the rest) ; the other, his own inner life, given wholly and solely to meditation, to study, to poetry. And at this epoch study and pleasure seem to have shared his days between them ; the one in no wise interfering with the other. When he could escape from his books it was to fling himself at the feet of Camille ; and the love he felt for her—the joyousness of eager youth, the exuberance of a desire to be caressed—was then celebrated in poetry whose passionate and gracious sweetness has never been surpassed. All the beauty of ancient singers, all the secret mysteries of many years of midnight toil, were used to sound her praises, for " in them he found," says Villemain, " that natural and gracious abandon, that variety of tone, that expressive simplicity and frankness of feeling which has and needs no other ornament than its own vivacity, its own innocent boldness —exquisite qualities, which other writers at the close of the eighteenth century stifled under the tawdry finery of a finnikin elegance." But still the love for Madame de Bonneuil—for "Camille" that is—though ever so beautifully expressed, was the passion of Romeo for Rosaline, not for Juliet—a training merely for young feelings longing for sympathy and affinity. Seeking an inspiration in her arms, he still loved his art more than his mistress. " Camille est un besoin dont rien ne me soulage ;"—a want essential to the perfection of his genius, but not yet an absorbing portion of his very self. It was, however, in vain that his friends urged him to tune his lyre to loftier airs ; love was natural to his age, essentially natural to his genius; and his artistic instincts prompted him to write only upon subjects he could thoroughly feel, for which he had ample knowledge and a perfect training. " Let them whisper," he sings, " each girl, each stripling, ' This loving poet, who knew me so well, when he painted his own heart, had first read mine.' " We quote some lines from an elegy to Camille, beautiful in themselves, exquisite as a pleading of defence :—

"Yet long ago, when burning youth was
      young,
In many a woody glade my thoughts I
      sung;
Fall of vast objects, drunk with war-
      rior's songs,
Breathing of bloody bays and battling
      throngs,
Covering myself with steel, with eyes
      afire,
To combats I attuned my sounding lyre;
Mad with audacious thoughts of high
      emprise,
I left the earth and flew towards the
      skies.

　　　*　　*　　*　　*　　*

"But sometimes now, obedient to your
      will,
Or lured by vagrant fancy I would still
The lofty deeds of 'Plutarch's Men'
      rehearse
In spirit-stirring, generous sounding
      verse;
My voice, accustomed to voluptuous
      charms,
Refuses, struggles, flies in wild alarms;
My hand tormented, tries in vain to
      clasp
The labour'd beauties flitting from its
      grasp;
But if, soon wearied, my dull'd spirit
      flies
Again to those poor nothings you de-
      spise,
If I sing Camille's charms, my loving
      song
In glowing verse flows trippingly along;
Verses to chant her praise around me
      spring,
In clustering crowds to heaven and earth
      they cling;
All things for her have verses, for they
      seem
To sparkle in each wavelet on the
      stream;
They take the birds' sweet voice and
      brilliant hue,
They hide in flower-buds, rich with
      pearly dew;
Her breast has all the peach's ripest
      bloom,
Her mouth the rose's smile and rare
      perfume;
The bee tho' flitting from that flower
      to this,
Bears no such honey as her balmy
      kiss.
All nature brings a poem within my
      reach,
Sweet as her breath, melodious as her
      speech;

"Jadis, il m'en souvient, quand les bois
      du Permesse
Recevaient ma première et bouillante
      jeunesse,
Plein de ces grands objets, ivre de
      chants guerriers,
Respirant la mêlée et les cruels lauriers,
Je me couvrais de fer, et d'une main
      sanglante
J'animais aux combats ma lyre tur-
      bulente;
Des arrêts du destin prophète au-
      dacieux,
J'abandonnais la terre et volais chez les
      dieux.

　　　*　　*　　*　　*　　*

"Si quelquefois encore, à tes conseils
      docile,
On joue d'un esprit vagabond et mobile,
Je veux, de nos héros admirant les ex-
      ploits,
A des sons généreux solliciter ma voix,
Aux sons voluptueux ma voix ac-
      coutumée
Fait, se refuse et lutte, incertaine,
      alarmée;
Et ma main, dans mes vers de travail
      tourmentés,
Poursuit avec effort de pénibles beautés.
Mais si, bientôt lassé de ces poursuites
      folles,
Je retourne à mes riens que tu sommes
      frivoles,
Si je chante Camille, alors écoute, voi!
Les vers pour la chanter naissent
      autour de moi;
Tout pour elle a des vers! Ils renais-
      sent en foule;
Ils brillent dans les flots du ruisseau
      qui s'écoule;
Ils prennent des oiseaux la voix et les
      couleurs;
Je les trouve cachés dans les replis des
      fleurs;
Son sein a le duvet de ce fruit que je
      touche;
Cette rose au matin sourit comme sa
      bouche;
Le miel qu'ici l'abeille met soin de
      déposer
Ne vaut pas à mon cœur le miel de son
      baiser.
Tout pour elle a des vers! Ils me
      viennent sans peine,
Doux comme son parler, doux comme
      son haleine.

Whate'er she does or says, a word, a look,
Would fill the pages of a mighty book.

. . . .

"Oh happy he who breathes in every line
Seductive wishes, like these songs of mine,
Whose glowing muse guide him on his lyre,
In every note he sings, to love's desire !
'Twas last night when I lay at Camille's feet,
I heard her soft lips lovingly repeat,
In pride for me and for herself in shame,
A song, in which I sang my darling's fame.
If these sweet lips had breathed in Virgil's days,
He would have sung of nought but Camille's praise ;
And saved poor Dido from her wild desire
For Eneas' fickle love, and from the funeral pyre."

Quoi qu'elle fasse ou dise, un mot, un geste heureux,
Demande un gros volume à mes vers amoureux.

"Heureux qui peut trouver des muses complaisantes,
Dont la voix sollicite et même à ses désirs
Une jeune beauté qu'appelaient ses soupirs.
Hier, entre ses bras, sur sa lèvre fidèle
J'ai surpris quelques vers que j'avais faits pour elle,
Et sa bouche, au moment que je l'allais quitter,
M'a dit ' Tes vers sont doux, j'aime à les répéter.'
Si cette voix eût dit même chose à Virgile,
Abel, dans ses hameaux il eût chanté Camille,
N'eût point cherché la palme au sommet d'Ilétion,
Et le glaive d'Énée eût épargné Didon."

But even at this time the love for Camille, full of outbreaks and lovers' quarrels as it was, was far from an absorbing passion. "Il veut qu'on aime réellement la beauté qu'on célèbre,"—we cannot doubt the veracity with which he wrote it—and Lycoris and Glycere, Amelie and Rose were often passing rivals.

There was then a strange Bohemian world in Paris of men of letters, artists, grand lords and ladies—noble sometimes, always beautiful and often more than light o' loves. But a few years back and Voltaire, like another Jeremiah, had prophesied the end of all existing order, of every present rule and form of society and rank. They were now standing as it were upon the abyss of a volcano. The air was heavy with the sulphurous fumes of an eruption that might at any moment be precipitated, that could not possibly be long delayed. It was too late to look back, too early to look forward, and pleasure—sparkling as the raillery of French philosophy, mad as the orgies of the Roman Empire, cynical as the innermost thoughts of Diogenes—was the aim of each man's life and each woman's life. It was the time of those famous suppers given by La Reynière, of which Rétif de la Bretonne was the indiscreet historian ; and in his voluminous and garrulous works we find express mention of the presence of André Chénier and les Trudaines in February 1784, and March 1786. At these *noctes coenæque deûm* met all who were most famous in Paris, for wit, for beauty, for thoroughness in some sort, were it only the thoroughness of profligacy. Politics were eagerly debated ; poems that were to make a reputation

were first read, the past, the present, the future of the nation
discussed — and this in the midst of songs and music and dancing,
of mad peals of ringing laughter interrupting orgies unutterably
amorous—men forgetting all but pleasure, women mindful of
nothing but their beauty. Chénier has given us, the spirit of
these meetings in an elegy never to be forgotten, but scarcely to
be quoted here. This same elegy shows us, however, that these
were but passing *éclairs de plaisir* in the midst of a student's
life. "O Gods!" he whispers, "if Camille were to hear where
I have been, what a storm would follow this boasted banquet!
What cries, reproaches, tears, though not even fury could harshen
her low voice; what blows struck with vengeful arms, not strong
for much but loving claspings!"

This period, however, with all its sudden outbursts gave us
some of the finest of the idylls, especially *Le Jeune Malade*,
where says Villemain, "the loveliest memories of grief, the ardours
of maternal affection, the despairs and the joys of love, are
traced with an unequalled pen, with an ineffable harmony."
This idyll gives us the two extremes—a mutual motherly and
filial tenderness, and a first love, young, pure and timid, yet passionate to the verge of the grave. It is, however, of some considerable length and we can only give the outline of the
story.

Watching beside her son's sick couch for restless, feverish
nights together, the mother again implores him to tell her what
fatal malady it is that ails him—to confess to her—to her
only :—

" 'Tis your poor mother's prayer,
'Tis she who rear'd you with a mother's
    care ;
Clasp'd in these arms, and nestling on
    this breast
She sang your childish troubles into
    rest ;
She wiled your pattering footsteps thro'
    the hall,
With many a promised gift and beckon-
    ing call ;
She bade you love her, till your prat-
    tling voice
Mimick'd the sound and made her heart
    rejoice.
O cold pale lips, why should you madly
    shun
To taste this healing potion ! O my son !
Would I could press you to these breasts
    of mine,
And pour my life's warm essence into
    thine !"

" C'est ta mère, ta vieille inconsolable
    mère,
Qui pleure, qui jadis te guidait pas à
    pas,
T'asseyait sur son sein, te portait dans
    ses bras,
Que tu disais aimer, qui t'apprit à le
    dire ;
Qui chantait, et souvent te forçait à
    sourire
Lorsque tes jeunes dents, par de vives
    douleurs,
De tes yeux enfantins faisaient couler
    des pleurs.
Tiens, presse de ta lèvre, hélas ! pale
    et glacée,
Par qui cette mamelle était jadis pressée,
Ce sein qui te nourisse et vienne à tes
    secours,
Comme autrefois mon lait nourrit tes
    premiers jours."

And he replies :—

" O hills of Erymanthus, valleys, glades !
O fresh sonorous winds that stir the
shades,
And make the water tremble, till its
breast
Seems surging 'gainst the charm of too
deep rest ;
For there, my mother, there beside the
lake,
Comes never deep-fang'd wolf nor
venom'd snake :—
Hot damsels, dancing in a hundred
throngs—
O lovely face, O pleasure-days, O songs !
No other place on earth is half so fair,
O twining limbs, and flowers, and flow-
ing hair !
O dainty feet, shall I ne'er see you more !
O mother, bear me to the happy shore—
Oh ! let me see this once before I die—
The still smoke floating in the lazy sky
Above the cot, as in weird shapes it
twines,
And that sweet maid beneath the clus-
tering vines,
Cheering her father with her maiden
wiles,
And sweet home converse, and sweet
home-bred smiles.
O Gods ! I see her as she makes her way
With tardy footsteps, o'er the waves of
hay ;
I see her resting sadly, as she weeps
Above the tomb where her dead mother
sleeps.
Soft yearning eyes, O will you ever
shine
Thro' loving tears, upon a tomb of mine !
And when you see it, darling, will you
wait
To murmur for a moment against Fate ? "

" O côteaux d'Erymanthe ! ô vallons !
ô bocage !
O vent sonore et frais qui troublais le
feuillage,
Et faisais frémir l'onde, et sur leur
jeune sein
Agitais les replis de leur robe de lin !
De légères beautés troupe agile et
dansante . . .
Tu sais, tu sais, ma mère ! aux bords
de l'Erymanthe,
Là, ni loups ravisseurs, ni serpents, ni
poisons . . .
O visage divin ! ô fêtes ! ô chansons !
Des pas entrelacés, des fleurs, une onde
pure,
Aucun lieu n'est si beau dans toute la
nature.
Dieux ! ces bras et ces fleurs, ces
cheveux, ces pieds nus,
Si blancs, si délicats ! je ne les verrai
plus !
Oh ! portez, portez-moi sur les bords
d'Erymanthe,
Que je la voie encor, cette vierge char-
mante !
Oh ! que je voie au loin la fumée à longs
flots
S'élever de ce toit au bord de ce vallon . .
Amine à tes côtés, ses discours, sa
tendresse,
La voir, trop heureux père ! enchanter
ta vieillesse.
Dieux ! par dessus la haie élevée en
rempart,
Je la vois, à pas lents, en longs cheveux
épars,
Seule, sur un tombeau, pensive, in-
animée,
S'arrêter et pleurer sa mère bien-aimée.
Oh ! que tes yeux sont doux ! que ton
visage est beau !
Viendras-tu point aimal pleurer sur
mon tombeau ?
Viendras tu point aimal, la plus belle
des belles,
Dire sur mon tombeau : ' Les Parques
sont cruelles ! ' "

Endeavouring to discover which of the neighbouring beauties
it was, his mother runs through their names, and when with a
disparaging dread she mentions Daphnis, he interrupts :—

" Mother ! what would you say ?
That she is proud and pitiless as they
Who sit on starry thrones ? Yet all
who see
Have loved her madly—loved in vain
like me.

" Dieux ! ma mère, tais-toi,
Tais-toi. Dieux ! qu'as-tu dit ! Elle est
fière, inflexible ;
Comme les immortels, elle est belle et
terrible ;
Mille amants l'ont aimée : ils l'ont
aimée en vain.

O mother, let me die, nor let her learn
With what a dying passionate love I
    yearn.
O death ! O torment ! O sweet mother
    mine !
You see me how I sicken, how I pine—
Seek her before I die, perchance your
    years
Will tell of her loved mother mourn'd
    with tears—
O take this basket fill'd with fruits
    and flowers,
This onyx cup won in Corinthian strife,
This ivory Love—the hamlet's pride and
    ours—
Take my young goats—O take my heart
    —my life—
Throw all beneath her feet, tell her
    that I
With burning passion languish till I die ;
Fall at the old man's feet, with tears
    and sighs
Adjure him by the gods, the sea, the
    skies ;
O mother, start, and if you come again,
Without good tidings you will come in
    vain."

"My son shall live, 'tis fond hope tells
    me this."
She bent her down for one last linger-
    ing kiss ;
On that pale brow, how wan beyond
    its years,
But one long kiss, and then with
    streaming tears
She went her way with aged trembling
    feet
Half falling, and half struggling to be
    fleet.
She came again with panting, bated
    breath—
"O you shall live, my son ! away, O
    death !"
Then fell beside his couch. The old
    man came
And the young damsel, blushing in
    sweet shame ;
Quivering with hope, and joy, the suf-
    ferer hid
His trembling head beneath the cover-
    lid.
With lips that falter'd and with cheeks
    ablaze—
"Dear, you have had no joy for three
    long days,

Comme eux j'aurais trouvé quelque
    refus hautain.
Non, garde que jamais elle soit in-
    formée...
Mais, ô mort ! ô tourment ! ô mère
    bien-aimée !
Tu vois dans quels ennuis dépérissant
    mes jours.
Écoute ma prière et viens à mon
    secours :
Je meurs ; va la trouver. Que tes traits,
    que ton âge,
De ma mère à mes yeux offrent la sainte
    image ;
Tiens, prends cette corbeille et ses
    fruits les plus beaux ;
Prends notre Amour d'ivoire, honneur
    de ces hameaux ;
Prends la coupe d'onyx à Corinthe ravie ;
Prends mes jeunes chevreaux, prends
    mon cœur, prends ma vie,
Jette tout à ses pieds ; apprends-lui
    qui je suis ;
Dis-lui que je me meurs, que tu n'as
    plus de fils.
Tombe aux pieds du vieillard, gémis,
    implore, presse ;
Adjure cieux et mers, dieu, temple,
    autel, déesse ;
Pars ; et si tu reviens sans les avoir
    fléchis,
Adieu, ma mère, adieu, tu n'auras
    plus de fils."

"—J'aurai toujours un fils ; va, la belle
    espérance
Me dit." Elle s'incline, et, dans un
    doux silence
Elle couvre ce front, terni par les
    douleurs,
De baisers maternels entremêlés de
    pleurs.
Puis elle sort en hâte, inquiète et
    tremblante,
Sa démarche de crainte et d'âge chan-
    celante.
Elle arrive ; et bientôt revenant sur
    ses pas,
Ha'etante, de loin : "Mon cher fils, tu
    vivras,
Tu vivras." Elle vient s'asseoir près
    de la couche.
Le vieillard la suivait, le sourire à la
    bouche,
La jeune belle aussi, rouge et le front
    baissé,
Vient, jette sur le lit un coup d'œil.
    L'insensé
Tremble ; sous ses tapis il veut cacher
    sa tête.
"Ami, depuis trois jours, tu n'as d'au-
    cune fête,"

They tell me that a foolish girl, that I
Can save you from your suffering—
Would you die ?
Sweet, live for me, and let our homes
be one !
Your parent have a daughter—mine a
son !' "

Dit elle ; "que fais tu ? Pourquoi veux-
tu mourir ?
Tu souffres. On me dit que je peux
te guérir ;
Vis, et formons ensemble une seule
famille :
Que mon père ait un fils, et ta mère
une fille."

To this period are due also the grand fragments of *Suzanne* and *Hermes*, in the latter of which, from a modern standpoint, he aimed at rivalling Lucretius's *Natura Rerum*. " There would," says Sainte-Beuve, " have been three books, dealing (1) with the creation of the world, with animals and man ; (2) on man, the mechanism of his senses, his intelligence, his errors from first birth to the dawn of civilization and the origin of religion ; (3) upon society politic, the constitution of morals and the discovery of the sciences. The whole to have been closed by an *exposé* of the system of the world according to the most advanced scientific notions of the time."

Such, at five and twenty, were the works written, began and projected. " Nothing," he tells us, " is finished to-day, but all will be ended to-morrow !"

Joseph had already flung himself, with his versatile and irregular talents, into the arena of public writing ; being hissed and praised, and hissed again ; but André had sufficient confidence to wait. His works were, and he must silently have felt it, for the world's wonderment to the end of time, not for the garrulous small talk of contemporary cackle.

The stern necessities of which Horace sings, the *dure necessité* of André's elegies, now put an end to these quiet labours, to this independent standing. His family, though enjoying a good social standing, were far from wealthy ; and his father, a man of intensely active life, insisted that he should embrace a diplomatic career. The elegy of *Liberté* was written in the March of 1787, while hope was struggling with duty, and is, under disguise, a precious revelation of his soul.

La Liberté consists of a dialogue between a goat-herd and a shepherd, the former a free man, the latter a slave. The goat-herd with presents and tender words tries to charm away the brutal ignorant despairing hatred of the other, but his words, his hopes, his own enjoyments only exasperate the shepherd's misery :—

Shepherd.
" Curse them ! Fatherland and Virtue
are but empty sounding names,
Full of subtle bitter giblets at my own
cruel wrongs and shames,

Le Berger.
" Va, patrie et vertu ne sont que de vains
noms,
Toutefois tes discours sont pour moi
des affronts :

For the liberty you prate of and the
happiness you rave,
Make me wish you, too, were fetter'd
with the thraldom of a slave."

Goatherd.

" Nay, poor shepherd, I would wish you
all the pleasures of the free !—
Have the great gods in their mercy no
one remedy for them !—
There are balms and pure lustrations,
of oblivious sweets combined,
Precious unctions for the gaping wounds
and venoms of the mind :
There are magic songs whose music
soothes the bitterness of tears—"

Shepherd.

" Life to me is one eternal circle of unend-
ing fears,
All my days are girt with slavish labour
till the end is come—
Yet I, too, possess a vassal, trembling
terror stricken, dumb—
And to teach the dog I own him, I, in
bitter mute despair,
Pile on him, with blows and curses, all
the wrongs they make me bear."

Goatherd.

" Has the earth, our teeming mother,
with her garnerings of gladness,
Has she not the power to banish
thoughts of dim despair and sadness!
See the landscape, see the summer, now
her journey has begun,
Prodigal of all her treasures, laughing
children of the Sun,
Coming like a lusty lover, with a gay
and happy mien
Caressing all the springtime's colours
with infinities of green.
See the peaches shaping daily, as they
ripen in their bloom,
Till their sun-kiss'd sides are luscious
with the fragrance of perfume !
Mark the white and purple blossoms,
decking every bearing tree,
Coming to announce the glory of the
fruit that is to be !
And beside the grassy borders see the
fields of waving corn—
Golden forests proudly struggling with
a burthen scarcely borne,
Waiting for the joyous harvest for the
sickle and the sheaf,
For the rustic gods of autumn—of
celestial nobles chief—
Peace and Ceres proudly entering with
a look serenely grand—
With wheat-ears round the ample brow,
and with wheat-ears in the hand,

Ton prétendu bonheur et m'afflige, et
me brave ;
Comme moi, je voudrais que tu fusses
esclave."

Le Chevrier.

" Et moi, je te voudrais libre, heureux
comme moi.
Mais les dieux n'ont-ils point de remède
pour toi !
Il est des baumes doux, des lustrations
pures,
Qui peuvent de notre âme assoupir les
blessures
Et de magiques chants qui tarissent les
pleurs."

Le Berger.

" Il n'en est point ; il n'est pour moi
que des douleurs,
Mon sort est de servir, il faut qu'il
s'accomplisse.
Moi, j'ai ce chien aussi, qui tremble à
mon service ;
C'est mon esclave aussi. Mon désespoir
muet
Ne peut rendre qu'à lui tous les maux
qu'on me fait.

Le Chevrier.

La terre, notre mère, et sa douce
richesse
Sont-elles sans pouvoir pour bannir ta
tristesse !
Vois la belle campagne ! , et vois l'été
vermeil,
Prodigue de trésors, brillants fils du
soleil,
Qui vient, fertile amant d'une heureuse
culture,
Varier du printemps l'uniforme ver-
dure ;
Vois l'abricot naissant, sous les yeux
d'un beau ciel,
Arrondir son fruit doux et blond comme
le miel.
Vois la pourpre des fleurs dont le pêcher
se pare
Nous annoncer l'éclat des fruits qu'il
nous prépare.
Au bord de ces prés verts regarde ces
guérets,
De qui les blés touffus, jaunissantes
forêts,
De joyeux moissonneur attendent la
faucille,
D'agrestes déités quelle noble famille !
La Récolte et la Paix, aux yeux purs
et sereins,
Les épis sur le front, les épis dans les
mains,

Coming in the rosy traces of the path where young Hope goes, And emptying out the golden horn, from whence great Plenty flows."	Qui viennent, sur les pas de la belle Espérance, Verser la corne d'or où sourit l'abon- dance.

But the shepherd declares that to slavish eyes the earth is hideous, sterile, and unfruitful, to be tilled with cruel labour, to be reaped for a taskmaster ; not a mother but a harsh step-mother.

In December, 1787, he started for London under the patronage of M. de Luzerne, the French ambassador at the English court, who had been among the first to recognise his talents. Here at once he obtained the situation of secretary to the embassy. There were, however, no special duties attached to the office, and determined to receive no money that had not been fairly earned, he quietly resolved to starve rather than draw upon his salary. He spent months of painful poverty before the ambassador fathomed this reluctance, and his Grace, feigning to be very angry, though secretly admiring the young secretary's independence, made him draw the money forthwith.

André Chénier hated England and the English—a nation he confesses to have been eager, enterprising, calculating, and constant in its projects ; but ready to sell its all to those who had wherewith to purchase. In a few pages negligent in style, but poignant with suffering, he has left us an eloquent testimony of his dreary life here. Alone and uncared for, far away from friends and sympathy, he still studied and wrote during the day, and in the night he went abroad to seek an uncongenial companionship in English taverns and coffee-houses. Wounded by the exclusive pride of the English aristocracy he entered heartily into the great liberal movement then astir, and in the companionship of Priestley and Price, and in their doctrines, he found hopes akin to his own ; and the fellowship of public duties, if not the actual pleasure of private friendship. English literature was scarcely more to his taste. Among our poets he admired only Thomson and Milton ; the others, he declares, "too haughty to be slaves, had rejected the trammels even of good sense," and he bids the French bards "shun the cloying sweetness of the singers of the cloudy north."

Two years of this lonely life became insupportable. One night in April, 1789, in a common tavern, he wrote down the bitter feelings of his heart, rendered all the more desolate by events that were then occurring elsewhere. For this was the most memorable year in the world's history. Day by day the tardy news came of some new movement upspringing to be of the gravest moment to his country. The storm was gathering to a head, and now the political, the patriotic feelings of his double life were intensely aroused. Through the years of work, of study, of dreamings, the ideal of a pure liberty had beckoned him onward, and now he longed more than ever to aid his fatherland, to cheer his fellow-countrymen forward in the glorious march to freedom already commenced. His banishment became daily more painful, and after the news of the days of June, he could bear it no longer, but fled across the Channel. In November, however, his father persuaded him to return to England, and on the 24th November he writes announcing his arrival and his painful suspense :—

"Yesterday the letters tell us that all Paris is in flames, that the tocsin is being sounded in every street. I try as hard as I can to doubt these gloomy tidings, but it is weary work waiting for the truth; for they who have announced this startling news assign no reasons, and add nothing that can give a determined proof to the terrors they have spread abroad. I have no news for you; here as in France, these are the only subjects of conversation."

Early in the spring of 1789, not even his father's earnest injunctions could keep him at his official post, and throwing up his engagement for ever he came back to France; living for a little while in retirement, waiting for events and watching them. But the revolution was, as he says, "big with the destinies of the world," and Chénier, at once a poet and a patriot, loving liberty, justice, and ideal equality, tore himself from his quiet retreat, from the studies he loved so well, and flung himself, heart and soul, into the vortex of political life. But the liberty he dreamed of, and prayed for, "the liberty to think what one will, to write what one thinks," would, he hoped, be brought about immediately without the loss of a single drop of blood, for he detested anarchy equally with slavery, and as he shared the ideas, the dreams of the age, he shared also its generous illusions.

Centuries of down crushing, of the monopoly of land, of wealth, of comfort by the few, who, fortunate through the accident of birth, looked upon the rest as beasts of burthen, or as pretty playthings, created to minister to their comfort or their pleasure; the glaring opposites of tyranny and serfage, of splendour and misery, had driven the minds of every generous youth throughout the world mad with the wildest schemes of liberty. At that period even Wordsworth and Southey were the rankest republicans— were from afar eagerly watching the struggles of a regenerating nation. To the literary men of Paris the crisis was still more intelligible and tangible, for they acknowledged that to their craft, to the writings of the eighteenth century past, present, and to come, all the good and all the bad of the revolution would be due.

Chénier's first step was, together with his immediate friends, to join the "Society of 1789"—a powerful and brilliant club, meeting in the sumptuous rooms of the Palais Royal, and numbering among its members the most enlightened, most moderate, in a word most aristocratic, of the revolutionary party. Doing all that he attempted thoroughly, Chénier entered into all their schemes with ardour and enthusiasm, was the life and soul of the Society, till finally the post of secretary devolved upon him. Changing its title into the "Société des Amis de la Constitution," the club, dreading the excesses that everywhere were foreshadowed, established a journal of their own. Loving Republicanism with all the fervour of a poet's mind, no sooner were its glorious theories smutched and befouled with the taints of anarchy and the threatenings of murder, than he severed himself from those who like the high priests of the Druids thought to celebrate their doctrines, to inaugurate their new social religion, with the blood of many guiltless victims. He abated, however, not one single tittle of the grand and generous principles he had before professed; he clave to them ever with the same energy, spoke of them still with the same eloquence, but while proclaiming aloud the glorious theories of liberty, he attacked with a virtuous indignation the growing lust for anarchy. Was the birth-hour, the time of travail and labour-pangs, the moment for discord and riot and debauchery and murder more hideous in their thoroughness than any the earth had yet suffered to fall upon her?

In No. 18 of the Society's journal appeared the famous "Avis au peuple français sur ses véritables ennemis," signed by André Chénier. Reprinted in a pamphlet form and translated into English, German, and Polish, this *brochure* enjoyed, almost at once, an European circulation, even King Stanislaus sending the author a congratulatory letter with a medal of honour.

"When a great nation," he commences, "after having grown old in error and in carelessness, outwearied by miseries and oppressions, at last awakes from its long lethargy, and by a just and legitimate insurrection re-enters into all its rights, upsetting and reversing that order of things which has violated all, it cannot in a moment hope to find itself quietly and calmly established in that new state which must succeed the old. The strong impetus given to so powerful a mass causes it to vacillate a while before settling in equilibrium. In these times of tumult every human passion is aroused, and, as most men have strong passions and weak judgments, they all of them wish to do something, not for a moment knowing what should be done, and thus put themselves at the mercy of those clever scoundrels whom the wise man follows with his eyes, watching whither they are tending, noting their out-goings and their precepts, and finally unmasking the interested motives that animate all, and branding them as public enemies to the general weal."

The revolution, he declared, was just, and must triumph by just means—the true enemies of liberty being those who wished to establish a hated and unjust tyranny. No invective, no imprudence even, was spared in this onslaught upon the partisans of violence :—

" I take some joy in deserving the esteem of men of worth, in thus offering myself to the hatred and the vengeance of these villains sprung from the gutter; these corrupt professors of disturbance whom I have unmasked. I have thought to serve liberty in rescuing it from their praises. . . . . . If, as I still hope, they will succumb to the weight of reason, it will be honourable to have contributed ever so little to their downfall. If they triumph these are the men by whose hands it were better to be hanged than clasped as friends and comrades."

Even by his own party this manifesto was very coldly received. The hasty blood of the French nation is never in times of excitement to be cooled by advice, however gently given, and the moderation he here preached as an essential doctrine of brotherhood and liberty did but madden their stormy passions the more. The other editors of the paper seceded from him, and the journal ceased to appear. This quarrel with his party caused him to retire awhile, though still preserving his membership in the Society. Not perhaps without a feeling of regret, he cries, " Disgusted with men and things, unknown and poor, and content with being so, I spend my days in retirement, in study, and in friendship." The end of 1790 and the first part of 1791 still belong to the poet. He laboured incessantly at the completion of his poems, and, though separated from the party of disorder, could not suppress his admiration for the glorious conquests of the revolution, which he celebrated in glowing language in " Le Jeu de Paume," dedicated to his friend David, the painter. This was one of the two poems that appeared during his lifetime. With the ringing tones of Pindar, and the fiery spirit of the grand old Greeks, he sung their victories, and yet reproduced the ideas already expressed in " L'Avis." But the hour had not yet come to give the world his poems, and he returned to prose. At the close of the year he presented himself to the electors of La Seine as a candidate for the public assembly, but Chénier was scarcely the man to win the suffrages of a heated mob. He was too proud, too honest, too independent. He is said to have also at this time applied for the post of ambassador to Switzerland. The two defeats, however, were scarcely felt; he was one of those few men who are as far removed from personal ambition as they are from personal fear. France sorely needed earnestness, boldness, thoroughness, and outspokenness, and he was still willing, nay eager, to give up the quiet, which was to him only less dear than the art which it enabled him to cultivate, because he held that " every citizen is bound to this manner of a patriotic contribution of his views and his ideas to the common fund."

When the new year commenced, poetry and study were set aside,
and his time was entirely devoted to politics. From February
to August his letters appeared at least once a week in the
Journal de Paris.

In the feelings that animated his political inspirations during
his short political career there is no tinge of ambition, no longing
to snatch the power from weaker men by proving himself the
stronger; there is only the healthy moral hatred of a man of
cultivation and intelligence against brute strength and blatant
street shriekings; of wisdom against utterest folly; of kindliness
and honesty against rascality and infamous schemings.

André Chénier commenced his first continuous effort in politics
on the 12th February, 1792, by an article in the *Journal de
Paris*, attacking the ridiculous and indecent preface inserted by
Manuel before the "Lettres de Mirabeau et de Sophie." Though
in a manner a journalist he still preserved the independence of
his views. Knowing nothing personally of the editors of the
papers to which he contributed, he made use—then a common
practice—of the convenient method of supplements, open to all
who chose to pay, and boldly replied to those who insisted that
there was a unity of fellowship between him and their editors,
that "there exists no common bond, but that of those who arm
twenty villages against a band of robbers." In the February of
this year began that sad and deplorable dispute between the
two brothers to which such sinister omen has too often been
attached.

Joseph Chénier, younger than André, had, as we have before
stated, long ago given himself up to the excitements and pleasures
of a literary career. Possessed of but a tithe of his brother's
talents, of not a whit of his genius, he had still less of his reticence
and self-control, his avoidance of popularity and contemporary
applause. Having commenced his career while still a boy with
a wretched tragedy he had himself helped to hiss off the stage,
he quickly perceived in the dawning revolution a means of gratifying self-love—of achieving a distinction of some kind. While
André, as a modest student, was silently studying the beauties
of the past, forming a style and cultivating an imagination to
ravish the future, Joseph was obtaining the noisy celebrity of a
stage which had become little else than an arena for the stormy
political passions of the time. From a dramatist he himself
became an actor in the saddest tragedy even yet half played out,
for letters eventually led him to the tribune. Some months since
he had joined the society which under the full-blown title of
Jacobins soon became so famous. Ever as it worstened, he constituted himself its defender, advocate, and pleader. André, on
the contrary, seeing the excesses into which the members were

falling, gradually withdrew from the coterie, and in his article of the 27th February, "Upon the Causes of the Disorders which trouble France, and which retard the establishment of Liberty," declared that this society and all that depended on it were "Usurping brotherhoods, clasping each other by the hands, and forming an electric chain round France—a state within a state, with an organization which is the most complete system of disorganization which there ever has been on the earth :" that to these societies, and such as these, were due the disorders which checked the growth of real freedom—accusations, he declared, only to be denied by rascals or madmen. The club was incensed beyond measure, and Joseph, wounded in his self-love, sent a note to the *Journal de Paris* declining all community of opinion with his brother. Here the dispute would probably have ended but for an editorial note commenting in injudicious language upon the letter. Joseph replied in the *Moniteur*, attacking André's article in tones more vigorous than brotherly, and André, to maintain his position, replied with a piquant allusion to his brother :—" Marie Joseph may perhaps give much praise without much love to a society which disposes of that portion of literary celebrity palatable to one greedy of the multitude's applause." Joseph, who had stood the general attack with tolerable equanimity, now wounded in his sorest pride as an author, retorted in the *Moniteur* that his brother's virtuous indignation was only the despite of a rejected candidate. The family now interfered, but it was long ere the wound was healed, and if at the moment André was attacked by the violent party with the epithet of fratricide, this was a few years afterwards to be brutally retorted by the royalists.

André followed up this deplorable quarrel by another attack, infinitely graver in its consequences—being probably the eventual cause of his condemnation and death. Some soldiers of the Swiss Guard had been condemned two years before to the galleys for mutinying and pilfering the regimental chest. They were now pardoned, and as an insult to the party of order, and as a bitter indignity, the Jacobins resolved to give the guards a fête, in which the municipality was shameless enough to assist. André as a public writer, and as a gentleman who had worn the sword, and knew what was the religion of the standard, revolted from the idea. In letters slashing and bitter, yet full of a dignity which would have become a warrior in Xenophon's army, he denounced this outrageous prostitution of the public honour :—

"The public statues are to be veiled, forsooth, as this procession passes by! I say rather if these wretched orgies take place it is not the images of tyrants that should be covered, but the faces of all honest men ; let the army veil their eyes, lest they see what a reward indiscipline and revolt obtain !   Let the whole country bow its head in shame and sorrow."

In letter after letter he attacked the scandalous Bacchanalian feast, and on the very day it took place he struck a higher chord still, for, again a lyric poet outraged with the shame of his fellow-countrymen, he published *l'Hymne aux Suisses de Château-vieux,* inimitable alike in irony and dignity. "Honour!" he cries "to the clients of Herbois! to Robespierre's forty cherished assassins!" neither of them men to be attacked with impunity. His brother and David—the one as author of the triumphal songs, the other designer of the trophies—and many of his friends took part in the procession, but André fled from this scandalous feast of the Champs Elysées to the country, to breathe the pure air again, to again see Nature in her lovely stillness; to take in fresh vigour, if not fresh hope, for the struggle in which he stood between men for whom he had but little sympathy on the one hand, and men on the other whom he detested and loathed.

Another letter a few days later tells of his return to Paris, and henceforth his daring had no bounds. As if the times were too bad for an honest man to live in, he seems, with a positive pleasure, to have courted a worthy death :—

"It is above all when the sacrifices that must be made to truth, to liberty, to fatherland are dangerous and difficult that they are also accompanied with ineffable delights. It is in the midst of accusations, of outrages, of proscriptions, it is in the dungeon and on the scaffold that virtue, probity, and constancy taste the full joy of a conscience lofty and pure."

His attacks became more personally direct ; there was no traitor, no ignoble designer preparing to steep his hands in blood, whom he did not hold up to scorn and public execration under his proper name. Even friendship, sacred as he ever held it, was forgotten in this Roman-like sense of duty. The comrades of his youth and childhood,—Le Brun and David—were attacked only less violently than the rest. But, at the same time, there was no unfortunate whose career he had not the courage to adopt. Opposing the King while in power, André now, with a rare delicacy and chivalry, congratulated him that, humiliated and insulted, he still maintained an honourable attitude :—

"May he read with pleasure these expressions of respectful esteem on the part of a man without interest as without ambition ; who has never written one single line but under the dictates of his conscience, to whom the language of courtiers must for ever be unknown. As eagerly passionate as any for true equality, he would yet blush for himself if he now refused a signal homage to the virtuous actions by which

our King has endeavoured to atone for all the miseries that so many
other kings have entailed upon mankind."

These were dangerous sentiments to proclaim, and already
Chénier's name circulated upon the private list that the President sent for approval to his followers. Day by day the whole
of young France were deserting to the opposite camp. He almost alone of the Republican party foresaw the heavy calamities
with at all events any feeling of horror and aversion. Weaker
and weaker his party grew, for few men now dared to speak their
consciences aloud. Still like a bugle blast for truth, for fatherland, for human love, in thrilling brazen notes, his voice rang
out undauntedly :—

"Let all the citizens," he cries, "whose thoughts agree with the
writer of these lines, and he has little doubt but that the whole of
honest France is with him, at least break silence, for this is no time
for silence. . . . . Let us one and all raise a deafening clamour of
truth and indignation !"

Under these labours and the excitement that necessarily accompanied them, his health was beginning to break up, and in the
midst of his work he was obliged sometimes to fly to the
country for a few days' breathing time. Even at the beginning of
August, in a week's walk through the laughing valleys of Nor-
mandy, he forgot something of the terrors of Paris—only a stray
ray of light, across a dismal evening; when he returned all Paris
was in arms. The people were ringing through the streets, howling
for blood, for vengeance. Could nothing be done to stem the torrent? Now was the time for prompt action, not for brilliant
writing! He rushed to the Assembly, and with all the lungs
God gave him, tried to gain a hearing; but that one calming
voice was drowned in the roaring hurricane of the revolution.
On the 10th of August his political struggles as a journalist
were ended; the King was in prison; anarchy stalked the open
street; all free discussion was suppressed; the voice of truth
was stifled. In weariness and impotence of spirit he retired from
the battle.

In October, in reply to a question from a brother poet, Wie-
land, as to what part he had taken in the Revolution, André
wrote that he was firmly determined to hold himself aloof, taking
no active part in public matters and attaching himself more than
ever, in retirement, to the profound study of letters and ancient
languages.

This was more than his resolution could maintain. At the
end of the year the King's trial began, and in spite of the sure
hatred, the certain vengeance such a step involved, he begged M.
de Malesherbes to let him share near the King the perils of the

defence; and this, the first favour he had ever asked of the great, was granted. As Malesherbes' secretary the preparation of documents for the defence was entrusted to Chénier's hands; and when Louis XVI. was at length condemned to death, he prepared a letter of appeal to the people. This letter, dated 17th or 18th January, 1793, has the printed proof printed over the minutes in his own handwriting, corrected in several places by M. Malesherbes. Eloquent with a noble fervour, it was unfortunately passed over by the King in favour of a simple note published in the *Moniteur.*

After the King's death the streets ran with blood; still André, at the risk of being assassinated, imprisoned, or dragged to the scaffold, remained in a town from which all were flying as from a plague-stricken city. But his friends, his family, and above all, his brother, prayed him to leave, and to their entreaties he at last yielded. For a few days he went to Rouen, but banishment at this distance from the centre of all his hopes was insupportable; and Joseph soon found him a secure retreat in a little cottage in a bye-lane at Versailles, the district for which Joseph, still with the popular party, had just been elected deputy. In these days of miseries and misfortune, something of the old brotherly love returned again, as if in childhood, to dispel the rancour of the fierce quarrels, the recent bitter bickerings, though in politics they could never, of course, agree. As a further token of affection, Joseph dedicated to his brother the tragedy of " Brutus and Cassius."

For awhile retreat was very grateful. André's health had been terribly shattered from over-work, over-anxiety, over-excitement. It was a marvellous change from the turbulent shrieking crowds of Paris to the peaceful silence of his hidden cottage, the green solitude of his walks. Fevered with the events just passed, it was essential to forget in some degree the wrongs and the passions of men. Though very ill and feeble he took again lovingly to his old world of books; adding daily a learned and laborious note to the *Hermes,* publishing and completing his poems, and mindful of untoward events that might perhaps occur, setting them in due order. It was a return to the days of youth, almost to the innocence of childhood. These were long, dreamy, delightful weeks given up entirely to poetry, to meditation, to love —for at last the poet had met his affinity; at last he was understood; at last he loved with a passion that had in it neither phantasy nor lust.

Madame Pourrat, whose beauty and wit Voltaire had of old admired, had, with her two daughters, taken refuge at Versailles, when the first threatenings of the tempest lowered over Paris, in her country-seat upon the green-crowned Lucienne Hill. Here

all through the troublous times a little court of wit and beauty
was maintained ; and to this circle André, when he used to fly
from Paris for a moment's breathing space, had ever been
most welcome. The youngest of the two daughters, Madame
Laurent Lecoulterne, had inherited the beauty, the charms, and
the graces of her mother. To the poet, heart-sick of the miseries
around him, she brought the balm of smiling consolation, and
brought unwittingly a love—totally unlike the fiery loves of his
youth—a passion chaste and melancholy, hopeless yet not desponding, infinitely tender, but purified from all earthly lust.
Such a passion is only possible to master-minds—in a Michael
Angelo for a Vittoria Colonna, in a Dante for a Beatrice.

Beneath the cares and tender anxieties of "Fanny," in the
delicacy of a new love for a lady who was at once a devoted wife,
a timid loving mother, he again took up his pen ; how different
now his Muse, how fair, how pure, how beautiful ! The loveliest
of all his poems, the "Ode to Versailles," was written at this
period. It has such a subtle beauty, such a delicate rhythm of
its own, standing apart from anything in French literature, from
anything in the world's literature, that to attempt to translate it
would be almost profanation, certainly futile. We can only quote
a portion of it in the original :—

> "O Versailles, ô bois, ô portiques,
>   Marbres vivants, berceaux antiques,
> Par les dieux et les rois Elysée embelli,
>   A ton aspect, dans ma pensée,
> Comme sur l'herbe aride une fraîche rosée,
>   Coule un peu de calme et d'oubli.
>
>   .   .   .   .
>
>   Les chars, les royales merveilles,
>   Des gardes les nocturnes veilles,
> Tout a fui ; des grandeurs tu n'es plus le séjour :
>   Mais le soleil, la solitude,
> Dieux jadis inconnus, et les arts, et l'étude,
>   Composent aujourd'hui ta cour.
>
>   .   .   .   .
>
>   L'abandon, l'obscurité, l'ombre,
>   Une paix taciturne et sombre,
> Voilà tous mes souhaits. Cache mes tristes jours,
>   Versailles ; s'il faut que je vive,
> Nourris de mon flambeau la clarté fugitive,
>   Aux douces chimères d'amours.
>
>   .   .   .   .
>
>   J'aime ; je vis. Heureux rivage !
>   Tu conserves sa noble image,
> Son nom, qu'à tes forêts j'ose apprendre le soir,

> Quand, l'âme doucement émne,
> J'y reviens méditer l'instant où je l'ai vue,
> Et l'instant où je dois la voir.

> Pour elle seule encore abonde
> Cette source, jadis féconde,
> Qui coulait de ma bouche en sons harmonieux.
> Sur mes lèvres les bosquets sombres
> Forment pour elle enco: ces poétiques nombres,
> Langage d'amour et des dieux.

> .   .   .   .   .   .

> Mais souvent tes vallons tranquilles,
> Tes sommets verts, tes frais asiles,
> Tout à coup à mes yeux s'enveloppent de deuil.
> J'y vois errer l'ombre livide
> D'un peuple d'innocents qu'un tribunal perfide
> Précipite dans le cercueil."

His life, for the moment, was perfect happiness. There on the
Lucienne Hill, in its pleasant shady woods. amidst the fragrance
of spring's first flowers, the faint carol of the early singing birds,
the babble and rushing of sylvan streams, would he take to her
and her sister, in the cool calm evenings, the poems he had written
in the morning. He almost lived with her family, for they all
loved him only less than she did, and between them twain the
passion was on either side a combination of the firmest friendship
of manhood with the tenderest love of woman. All their interests were in common ; he mourned as bitterly as any the un-
timely death of her child ; he watched over her delicate health
with a care that savoured of a womanly solicitude. To them the
outside world was like the Italian plague city ; their inner circle
a new and chaste decameron party. Yet waftings of the terrible
doings came hither from time to time ; and when Marat fell beneath the poignard of Charlotte Corday, André, blushing for his
own happiness at such a period, seized up a scathing pen. "This
famous ode breathes," says G. Planche, " an enthusiasm which
has nothing fictitious ; in each succeeding strophe we see that the
author is singing, not as a poet engrossed by the literary beauty
of his work, but with the indignant voice of a citizen, in the interest of imperious duty ; full of the memories of old Greek odes
—without the faintest trace of art, most artistically beautiful."
" Thou alone," cried Chénier, " wast a man ! Thou hast avenged
humanity ; whilst we unmanned, unsexed, a soulless herd of
poltroons, repeated only a thousand womanly and plaintive cries,
for our trembling hands were too weak to grasp the dagger !"
    Human blood was still flowing in Paris, every hour was bur-
thened with crimes, every house in mourning, every other man a

human fiend; but, despairing that his efforts would be of any avail, André kept to his studies and his retirement. As time wore on, the longing to be again in Paris became overpowering. Partially re-established in health, and either careless of events or thinking that in the sweeping changes his name had been forgotten, he returned to Paris, keeping still, however, in careful solitude. Had this secresy been maintained all might yet have gone well, even at Paris; but he was too full of solicitude for his friends to have any personal fears. Early in March, 1794, he heard that M. Pastoret, who had been one of the phalanx to battle for law and liberty, had been arrested. André flew to the house at once to offer consolation and what assistance he could to the sorrowing family. While on his kindly visit a band of officials arrived, who seized all the papers, and, recognising André, declared he was one of the six thousand "suspected" on their list, and carried him straightway to the prison of the Luxembourg; here the gaoler refused to receive him without a regular warrant. But at Saint-Lazare they were less scrupulous, and here for the night he was lodged.

The unfortunate family received the tidings of his seizure at the very moment they heard that his eldest brother, Sauveur, had likewise just been captured. Old M. de Chénier, distracted with alarm, ran off to the *Comité* of Public Safety, demanding in the name of an innocent father the liberation of an innocent son. Barrère, one of the members, formerly an old friend, promised that the request should at once be granted. But next day André's name was formally entered in the prison books, Barrère's friendship extending only so far as to cause his name to be written at the end of the list. There was no hope henceforth but oblivion in the crowd, for his freedom now required a regular order from the National Assembly, and there all the leaders were his personal enemies—for he had sung the heroism of Charlotte Corday, had lashed the evil ambition of Collot d'Herbois with the cutting venom of indignant satire, had dauntlessly attacked Robespierre, who feared his talents, and, himself a poetaster, looked upon his acknowledged genius with a greedy envy and a smouldering hatred. In the meantime his poor old father was uneasily moving heaven and earth to procure his son's liberty, rushing about with frantic fears, invoking the laws, calling aloud to the God of Truth and Justice for aid and succour. Joseph, himself a member of the Comité, but insulted even in the tribune, did what he could, but his efforts were futile; and he now confined his attention to the difficult task of repressing his father's endeavours.

For three months André had to bear this prison life, not altogether unpleasant in itself, for the captives had probably a far less wretched time of it than their anxious friends outside.

St. Lazare had formerly been a priory ; above the door, upon a slab of black marble, was written, in large white letters, the motto of the Republic, the epitaph of those immured :—

> " Unité, Indivisibilité de la République,
> Egalité, Fraternité—ou la Mort."

Never was the careless gaiety of the French character better exemplified, nor its aptitude for pleasure in every situation in life. Within the prison walls he found the very same society that he had so often met in his mother's brilliant circle. It was the same world of rank and beauty, wit and genius, transported intact to the dungeons, the same old *salon*, its futilities, its graces and its faults, its loves, its hatings and its jealousies, its grand aims and its petty. The first sudden seizure had of course been painful, but in the early days of their captivity the prisoners were allowed all the luxuries they chose to pay for—a sub-scription list was opened, to which the wealthy contributed to aid the poor ; the tables were well served, and they were per-mitted pretty constant intercourse with their friends of the outer world. But by degrees their pleasures were taken from them as too great a solace, and then, as Da Broca eloquently describes the scene—

> " A multitude of ladies, married or betrothed, assembled in the gar-den, crowding together, together gazing eagerly in the hope of seeing their lovers or their husbands for one moment at the windows ; — to give, to receive, a look, a gesture,—a fleeting token of ineffable affection. No weather banished these women from the gardens, nei-ther the extremes of heat or cold, nor the tempests of wind and rain. Some were as motionless as statues, others worn out with fatigue and watching, as soon as those they yearned for appeared, fell senseless to the ground. One would come with a new-born child in her arms, bathing it with tears in her husband's sight. Another lady, disguised as a beggar, would sit the whole day long at the foot of a tree, where she could be seen by her husband. The misery of these poor women was extremest when a high fence was erected round the prison, and they were forbidden to remain stationary at any one spot. Then might they be seen wandering like shades through the dark and me-lancholy avenues of the gardens, casting eager, wistful looks at the impenetrable prison walls."

The deprivation of their friends' company rendered the pri-soners all the more dependent upon their own society. A code of rules was drawn up ; the married ladies in rotation acted as housekeepers ; the services of the domestics were shared ; the sitting-rooms were all in common.

All went on as in a fashionable *salon ;* the women dressed as ever ; ties of friendship, love, and pleasure were formed. Every one contributed to the common fund of amusement. Musicians gave concerts ; poets recited their verses aloud, vying with each other to heap indignities upon the *canaille* by whom they were imprisoned, and nevertheless, with a noble enthusiasm, singing the exploits of the French army, which was then ranging France against the world. Softening by art the rigors of captivity, feasting and flirting, happy and careless, never was there such a scene before. When in spite of all this the time hung heavily upon their hands, they had other resources, ghastly and terrible in their light mockery and parody of their impending fate. M. Thiers has given us a description of one of these games. Alfred de Vigny, in that marvellous book "Stello," has given us another. Though appearing in a romance there is no doubt of its comparative truthfulness :—

"I saw at one end of the table a small group amusing themselves with a game of cards. Their soft voices, their reserved and polished tones, told me at once that they belonged to the highest rank of society. They bowed to me from their seats, but rose when they saw the duchess de Saint Aignan. We passed on. At the other end of the table was a much larger group—younger and livelier—bustling, noisy and laughing—a gathering as of a court dancing party *en négligé* on the morrow of the ball. There were young ladies seated to the right and to the left of their chaperons ; there were young men whispering in each other's ears, pointing out this or that with the finger of scorn or jealousy. We could hear stifled laughter and song-airs, and snatches of dance-music, and dance-steps and glidings to clapping hands by way of castagnets and triangles. They had formed a circle, and all were gazing at something that passed in the middle of the thronging crowd. This something caused at first a moment's silence and attention, and then a ringing outburst of blame and of enthusiasm, of murmurs of applause or disapprobation, as if after a good scene or a bad. A head would suddenly be seen and then as suddenly disappear. 'It is some innocent game,' said I, slowly going round the large square table. Madame de Saint-Aignan stopped, leant upon the table, and relinquished my arm to press her girdle with her other hand—her customary gesture. 'O my God! do not go near them ; it is their horrible game again,' she exclaimed ; 'I have so begged them not to play it any more. Where could they have learnt it? It is an unheard of bravado. But I will stay here while you go and look on.' I left her sitting on the bench, and went to see what I could. It by no means displeased me as much as it did her. On the contrary I admired this prison game, comparable only to the exercises of the gladiators. Indeed, without taking matters as gravely and weightily as the ancients, France has sometimes as much philosophy. We are all from father to son Romans in our first boyhood ; and we have never ceased to build us altars, and to worship before the same shrines to

which our fathers prayed. We have all of us at school applauded the
game of 'dying with grace,' which even the slaves of the Roman people practised.   And here I saw these other poor slaves of a sovereign
people do as much, without any pretence or affectation, laughing, jest-
ing, saying a thousand mocking words of their ignoble masters. 'It
is your turn now, Madame de Périgord,' said a young gallant in a
garb of blue silk, slashed with white, 'show us how you can mount!'
'Let us see what you can show,' cried another. 'Order! order!' exclaimed they all; 'you are too free with your tongue, sir, and it is bad
style!' 'Had style as much as you like,' said the accused; 'but the
game was invented to show us which of the ladies could mount most
captivatingly.' 'What childish folly,' whispered a pretty woman of
thirty. 'I certainly wont mount at all if the chair is not better
placed!' 'Oh! oh! Madame de Périgord, it is a shame!' exclaimed
another; 'in our roll-call Sabine Vonville comes before you! Ah!
mount as a Sabine, let us see!' 'Luckily I am not in Sabine costume.'
'But where shall I put my feet?' said the young lady, embarrassed.
Peals of laughter, as every one advanced, stooped, gesticulated, showed,
pointed. 'There ought to be a plank here.'—'No, there.'—'Three
feet high.'—'Only two.'—'No, not so high as the chair.'—'Lower still.'
—'I am sure you are wrong.'—'Who lives will see.'—'Nay, who dies
will see!'—and ringing laughter again. 'You spoil the game,' said a
grave gentleman seriously put about, and eyeing the young lady's feet.
'Well, come, tell me all the conditions,' urges Madame de Périgord in
the midst of the group. 'I have to mount upon the machine?'
'Machine! upon the stage,' interrupted another girl. 'Well, upon
what you like to call it,' continued the first, and without raising her
dress more than two inches above her ankles—'Ah! here I am,' and
jumping into the chair she rested there a moment. General applause.
'And after that?' she asked. 'Afterwards?—oh, that's no affair of
yours,' replied one. 'Afterwards? click! click!' laughed a burly
gaoler. 'Afterwards? oh! don't you harangue the people,' said a
young nun; 'there's nothing in worse taste.'—'And nothing more
useless,' added I. . . . 'Ah, now we shall see something,' they
shouted on all sides. A young, a very young, lady advanced with the
elegance of an Athenian girl towards the centre of the circle. . . .
Her regular profile, her grave mouth, her jet-black eyes, and her eyebrows, severe and arched, after the manner of Circassian women, had
in them something determined and original, which touched and shamed
us all. It was Mdlle de Coigny; she whom I had seen praying to
God in the prison yard. She seemed to think with pleasure upon all
she did herself, not at all of what those who were gazing at her were
doing. She advanced with the sparklings of joy in her eyes. I love
to see that at sixteen or seventeen. It is the best possible innocence.
This joy, so to speak, electrified the worn faces of the prisoners. This
was, indeed, the Young Captive who was 'not willing to die yet.' Her
very air said—

       'Ma bienvenue au jour me rit dans tous les yeux!'

and

       'L'illusion féconde habite dans mon sein.'

She was in the very act of mounting. 'Oh, not you, not you!' cried a young man, in a grey dress, whom I had not remarked before, coming out of the crowd. 'Do not mount, I beg, I pray you!' She stopped, gave a little shrug of her shoulders, like a pettish child, and put her finger on her lips. She regretted the guillotine-chair, and peeped at it sideways. At this moment some one said—' But Madame de Coigny is there.' Directly, with a quick presence of wit, and a rare delicacy of good sense, they took down the chair, broke up the circle, and formed a little quadrille, to hide from her this singular repetition of the drama of the *Place de la Révolution.*"

And thus they played their game through all the least details, even to the shades of the departed coming back, dressed ghost-like in a tablecloth, telling the horrors of hell, and prophesying the ruin of their iniquitous judges, dragging them from their lofty seats into the abyss of some dark recess. And in the midst of all the gaoler at any moment would call out the names of those who were wanted for the actual drama of which this was but the rehearsal. "It was thus," says Rioffe, "that upon the bosom of death, we spoke the truth boldly in our prophetic pastimes, in the midst of spies and traitors."

To Chénier—a poet, a thinker, a dreamer—the scene must have been strangely painful, but even to him the imprisonment had its pleasures. Suvée, the artist, beguiled the tedium by painting the poet, and thus handing down his features to posterity. The two brothers Trudaine, the friends of his boyhood, were there, and they continued the old poetic studies of bygone times. They sang again the woods of Montigny, of Italy, of Greece, and recalled the happy days when the poet, careless of the hand of fortune, had cried out merrily, "we are three to one against her!" Among the noble women, the beautiful young girls, who shed a perfume of hope and love through these gloomy dungeons there was one whose fate excited all the poet's pity and compassion. This was the Duchess de Fleury, better known as Mdlle Aimée de Coigny. Her youth—she was but sixteen—her beauty, her light, exquisite wit, her childish dread of death, all spoke to the poet's heart; and this delicate mixture of pity and love, consoling his captivity and hers, produced "La Jeune Captive." "This," says Villemain, "is one of the chefs d'œuvres of modern poetry, the purest of tender elegies, written in a style whose richness has something of the smiles and freshness of youth." The young captive, even in the prison, is so full of this innocent happiness of youth that she is not ready to die:—

"Let a stoic with tearless eyes hastily clutch at death, But I with my tears and prayers at the chilly N.rth wind's breath	"Qu'un stoïque aux yeux durs vole embrasser la mort, Moi je pleure et j'espère; au noir souffle du nord

Will shiver and hide and flee.
There may be sorrowful days, but then
    there are hours of joy—
Ah! was there ever a sweet but sooner
    or late must cloy,—
      Or ever a stormless sea!

"Illusions and hopes and dreams are
    fluttering thro' my brain,
Till the dreary dungeon walls would
    fetter my soul in vain,
    For I borrow me airy wings;
O joy for heaven's free air, as merrily
    up I fly,
Away from the snarer's nets, to the
    blue fields of the sky,
      Where Philomel soaring sings!

"Why should I die so young, when the
    lingering peaceful years,
Full of soft lulling delights are wait-
    ing to still my tears
    In their dreamless depths profound.
Laughing his love in my eyes, my
    darling kiss'd me to-day,
Till my own joy overflows, to conjure
    and soothe away
      The sorrows of all around.

.   .   .   .   .

"O Death! thou canst wait awhile, for
    a moment let me hide,
There are weary hearts eno', whose
    dolorous shame and pride
    Hail thee with pitiful cry;
For me the summer has still such
    tremulous green delights,
And Love such soft caresses, and my
    songs such wild delights,
      That I do not wish to die!"

Je plie et relève ma tête.
S'il est des jours amers, il en est de
    doux!
Hélas! quel œil jamais n'a laissé de
    dégoûts?
      Quelle mer n'a point de tempête!

"L'illusion féconde habite dans mon sein.
D'une prison sur moi les murs pèsent
    en vain,
    J'ai les ailes de l'espérance:
Echappée aux réseaux de l'oiseleur
    cruel,
Plus vive, plus heureuse, aux campagnes
    de ciel
      Philomèle chante et s'élance.

"Est-ce à moi de mourir! Tranquille
    je m'endors
Et tranquille je veille, et ma veille
    aux remords
    Ni mon sommeil ne sont en proie.
Ma bienvenue au jour me rit dans tous
    les yeux;
Sur des fronts abattus mon aspect
    dans ces lieux
      Ranime presque de la joie.

"O mort! tu peux attendre; éloigne,
    éloigne-toi!
Va consoler les cœurs que la honte,
    l'effroi,
    Le pâle désespoir dévore.
Pour moi Palès encore a des asiles verts,
Les amours des baisers, les muses des
    concerts,
      Je ne veux pas mourir encore.

But it was not love alone that inspired the poet in his imprisonment. In his burning indignation he again and again attacked
the enemies of France with terrible energy. He, too, did "not
wish to die" "Sans percer, sans fouler, sans fletrie dans les fanges
ces bourreaux, harbouler de lois," without surviving these abhorred
brigands long enough "pour cracher sur les noms, pour chanter
leur supplice."

Here in the midst of spies and gaolers he had the same
haughty disdain for safety; he wrote with the same sweeping
audacity, as formerly in the columns of the *Journal de Paris*,
and these things were noted to be hereafter brought against him
—not that there was much utility now in proofs of either guilt or
innocence. Among his papers was found a strange document; a
kind of will, in which he describes himself faithfully before his
conscience and before futurity.

" He is weary of sharing the shame of that vast crowd who, abhorring in secret as much as he can, yet by their silence, at least, encourage and approve these atrocious men and these abominable actions. Life itself is not worth so much opprobrium. When the shambles, the taverns, and the brothels vomit out their thousands of legislators, of magistrates, of generals of armies, upspringing from the mud for their poor country's good, he has in him a vastly other ambition, and he does not believe that his country will one day think it amiss to say, ' This land which produced so many prodigies of imbecility and vileness, produced also a little band of men who renounced neither their reason nor their conscience ; witnessing the triumphs of vice, they remained faithful to virtue, and did not blush at being men of standing. In those times of violence they dared to speak of justice ; in those times of utterest folly they dared to weigh matters calmly ; in those times of the most abject hypocrisy they never feigned to be scoundrels to purchase their repose at the cost of oppressed innocence. They concealed not their hate from those assassins who spared nothing to reward their friends, to pay their enemies—for both cost them only crimes ; and one named A. C. was among the five or six whom neither the general frenzy, nor greed, nor cowardice could cause to bend the knee before these crowned assassins, to touch hands sullied with murder, to seat themselves at a table where men were drinking the blood of brothers !' "

Amid the prison gaieties and love-making—though as the weeks rolled on their pleasures were one by one debarred— Chénier found time to think of his past writings :—

> " Mes parents, mes amis, l'avenir, ma jeunesse,
> Mes écrits imparfaits."

And he set himself carefully to put them forth and complete them as far as he could. Not, however, having the MS. at hand he was compelled to work from memory. He wrote a preface for the volume he could never hope to see published. All this work was written on small scraps and slips of paper in characters so fine that they could scarcely be read without a glass ; when completed he concealed them carefully in the soiled linen which those at home were still allowed to collect.

In the meantime the unfortunate family were still praying for his deliverance. Joseph was now obliged to change his abode every night, and yet he clearly saw that Robespierre's days were numbered, that a week or two gained would be the salvation of his brother. More and more forcibly he endeavoured to impress the necessity of inaction upon his father ; but the poor old man was weary of waiting, sick to the death of his deferred hopes. How could he be calm, he argued to himself, when two of his sons were in prison, when the life of one was in imminent danger. Without saying a word to the family he addressed a petition to the Council—" from an irreproachable father who claims an irreproachable son, deprived for months of his liberty, but who never merited its loss."[1] At first this step consoled his troubles; he thought to rescue his son, and then to triumphantly present him to the family. The petition was not answered, and in spite of Joseph's cheering declarations that the counter-revolution which was to overthrow Robespierre was making immense strides, he again began to fret at this inaction which seemed to him so like indifference. At last he went secretly to see Barrère, who received him coldly and with evasive replies. On the 3rd Thermidor (21st July) he tried to consult André as to what steps could be taken, but he was refused admission to the prison. On the morrow he again visited Barrère, and the wretch, wearied of him and his plaints, said with a cruel significance, "Leave me now, Monsieur, leave me, your son shall come forth in three days from Saint-Lazare." Upon this third day the public accuser made out by instructions the act of accusation against André Chénier.

For many years it was maintained that Joseph had shown great indifference about his brother's fate, that if, even as one of his defenders says, "he had done something, he had not done enough." Rumours of a deeper dye, too, were afloat, and a writer in the *Edinburgh Review* for March, 1821, declares that the facts alleged against Joseph had never been disproved, and communicates them on the authority " of a person who had long been a friend of the family, who had sheltered André Chénier while persecuted by the Revolution, and enjoyed the confidence of his father until his death." The Reviewer's narrative is as follows :—

" He was condemned to die two days before the fall of Robespierre. In the interval between his condemnation and execution his father flew to the Convention, and in one of the adjoining apartments found Joseph C., surrounded by some of his most ferocious colleagues. There he fell upon his knees to implore mercy from one of his sons to the other. Marie Joseph rose from his seat, and leaning his head on his hand, on the chimney, remained mute and motionless, while Robespierre himself seemed to wait for one word from him to grant his brother's pardon. But that word Joseph Chénier did not utter, even when the old man, rising from his knees with all the energy of despair, cried out in a voice of thunder, ' Je te donne ma malédiction !' and burst out of the room. André Chénier was guillotined the next day ; and his father, upon whose authority this story rests, died of grief. . . . It is said, long after the murder of André Chénier, a letter was by some means or other daily conveyed to his brother, containing merely these words :—

' Cain, Cain, qu'as-tu fait de ton frère ?'

Joseph died a natural death in 1813, pursued by shame—not by re-morse."

It is a painful story to quote, worth quoting, however, as it was generally believed, but from all evidence, external and direct, utterly and entirely false.

On the morning of the 6th Thermidor—three days after M. de Chénier's last appeal—there was an unusual stir within the prison walls. About midday the heavy cars—too well known alas !— were driven into the courtyard, but it was not until the evening that the fatal list was read over—none who heard their names once called ever returned—and at the head of the death roll stood the name of André Chénier. It was a moment of eternal farewells, laden with all the bitterness of death ; of the severing of those ties that in the weariness of prison-life had become as love and friendship. André threw himself into the arms of the brothers Trudaine, who were left behind only to survive for a day, and then the gloomy cortége started for the Conciergerie, where Fouquier Tinville sat in judgment. They were too late for trial that evening, and there was thus one night's respite.

Early in the morning of the 7th Thermidor (25th July) he ap-peared at the bar of the tribunal, with forty-four other prisoners. They were allowed to make no defence. A collective accusation was read, an individual statement and an individual interrogation rapidly slurred over, and after two short hours of these formal mockeries thirty-eight of the accused were condemned. At the top of the death-roll stood the names of Roucher, the poet, and of André Chénier. They were found guilty of " having declared themselves enemies of the people, of having taken part in the plots and conspiracies of 'Capet and his family,' of keeping up intelligence with the foes of the Republic, of writing against liberty and in defence of tyranny." In André's case a further charge was added of having satirized the fête given to the Swiss guard—this was the work of his powerful enemy, Collot d'Her-bois. The sentence was " Instant Death."

The trial was over at midday—the executions were to take place in the afternoon or evening. When, wondered the prisoners, when would the hour arrive ! Ah, in those stormy times men were attuned to heroic living—to heroic dying. There were mutual confidences, mutual encouragements ; last wishes, last hopes, last prayers ; not in the silent gloom of a night before execution, but in the full glory of a July sun streaming through the prison bars, as if to remind them all how beautiful, how happy was the life they were leaving. Now it was in his death-hour, face to face with the pallid spectre, that André wrote what must, from its genesis, ever be the most pathetic of his poems :*—

"As the sun's last flashing ray,
  As the last cool breeze from the shore,
Cheer the close of a dying day,
  Thus I strike my lyre once more.
As now by the scaffold I wait
  Each moment of time seems the last,
For the clock, like a finger of fate,
  Points onwards and onwards fast.
Perchance ere the band goes round,
  Perchance ere I hear the beat
Of the measured and vigilant sound
  Of its sixty sonorous feet,
The sleep of the tomb will close
  On my wearied lids and eyes,
Before each thronging thought that glows
  Can have taken fitting guise,
And One, bearing death in his hand,
  Like a grim recruiter of shades,
Will come with his murderous band,
  And, amid the clangour of blades,
Fill all these gloomy corridors
  With resoundings of my name."

"Comme un dernier rayon, comme un
    dernier zéphyre
  Anime la fin d'un beau jour,
Au pied de l'échafaud j'essaye encor
    ma lyre,
  Peut-être est-ce bientôt mon tour ;
Peut-être avant que l'heure en cercle
    promenée
  Ait posé sur l'émail brillant
Dans les soixante pas où sa route est
    bornée,
  Son pied sonore et vigilant,
Le sommeil du tombeau pressera ma
    paupière !
  Avant que de ses deux moitiés
Ce vers que je commence ait atteint la
    dernière,
  Peut-être en ces murs effrayés
Le messager de mort, suivi recruteur des
    ombres,
  Escorté d'infâmes soldats,
Remplira de mon nom ces longs corri-
    dors sombres."

A fragment like his life—a glorious beautiful fragment inter-rupted by the advent of the guard. It was no time then for fear or shrinking. Women and young girls cheered each other onward ; men did not dare to be craven. Far from friends and lovers they clave each to the other. At last, a little before six, the heavy cars drew up. Human life was over, and it befitted all to commence the life immortal with the glory of an heroic death. All was over, yet as he walked up the waggon steps, André gave one last regret to his broken life. "To die, to die, and yet I had something there !" he cried, striking his forehead with his hand. It was the Muse, says Chateaubriand, who in this supreme hour revealed to him his genius.

He was placed upon the same bench as that other unfortunate poet Roucher. Then the cars drove off through a crowd eager for excitement, utterly callous to misfortune—fed daily on bloodshed and massacres, yelling for ever for fresh victims—a crowd insensate, many-headed, brutal, hurling jeers and curses at the prisoners as they passed. Some few wearied with an over-glut of horrors averted their faces and turned aside. None dared to do more, few dared so much. And still the cars drove on ; the two poets meeting at every halt the eyes of a sorrowing friend, who was attending them as at their funeral. As to drowning

---

* "Composé le 7 Thermidor, 1794, au matin, peu d'instants avant d'aller au supplice."

men, to dying men stricken with any sudden death, the thoughts, the events of a whole life crowd into a moment's space, so true to the dreams of their boyhood and their manhood, to the soul-life that could never be guillotined or trampled out, their last thoughts were of poetry and friendship. Let the mob shriek out and surge around with brutal insults to their courage and their innocence! Let the scaffold with its blood-stained axe and bloodier basket loom before! What was that now to them? The pangs of death were over! Quietly amidst the roar they repeated, one to the other, the first scene of *Andromaque;*— André commencing,—

> " Oui, puisque je retrouve un ami si fidèle,
> Ma fortune va prendre une face nouvelle,
> Et déjà son courroux semble s'être adouci
> Depuis qu'elle a pris soin de nous rejoindre ici."

At last the Place de la Révolution was reached, and they mounted the scaffold, still congratulating each other that it were better to die than to live in fiendish days like these. A last grasp of the hand, a last fond dispute as to which should die first, so as to spare the other the horror of seeing a friend butchered, a last look of pride and pity upon the seething crowd below, and all tyranny and wrong and injustice were over for evermore.

"It is so beautiful to die young," so sweet to die for one's country, to give a world of enemies and haters a victim without reproach, to surrender to Almighty God a life still full of the innocent illusions of youth. So died André Chénier on the 25th July, 1794, in the thirty-second year of his age.

Three days after this, at this same Place de la Révolution perished his murderer Robespierre. But three days only, and André Chénier would have been saved!

On the following morning Joseph saw the dreadful intelligence for the first time in the daily papers. His agony and grief were terrible. Uttering nothing but sobs and imprecations, looking nothing but despairs and miseries, he rushed to his brother Sauveur's fiancée, and flinging himself at her feet sobbed, with his face in his hands, "They have killed him! they have killed him!" Madame Landais, pale and motionless as death, stammered, "Who? who?"—"My brother,"—"Which of them?" —"André." Madame Landais clasped her hands in prayer. The dreary silence was broken by Joseph—"Oh! how can I announce it to my father, to my mother! Let us go together at once."

His drawn features, his bloodshot and swollen eyes, drew from old M. de Chénier an exclamation of affright. "My God? what has happened?" "Which is it, speak! Tell us of this new

M 2

misery?' cried the poor mother, clutching hold of Madame
Landais with feeble, trembling arms. Joseph made a superhuman effort, and stuttered in a broken voice, "André has just
appeared at the tribunal." Madame de Chénier threw herself
into Madame Landais' arms, shrieking, "Oh, my God! my God!"
M. de Chénier, with a heart thumping through his breast, with
unutterable dread in his voice, articulated, "Eh! eh! well?"
Joseph remained silent, but the unfortunate old man comprehended only too quickly. Raising his feeble arms towards the sky,
he cried in despair, "The murderers! it was this they promised
me when they said 'three days!'" Joseph, who was supporting
his father, recoiled in affright. "They have promised you?—
who? What do you mean? You have presented a request to
whom, when, how?" Then the unhappy father told what he
could of his unbearable despair, of his secret petition, his stolen
interview. Joseph, maddened with grief and frenzy, cursed his
father as a murderer, hurling reproaches at him. "My son! my
son! do not overwhelm me with woe! Oh, wretch! Oh,
misery!" Then the son as wildly as before begged his father's
forgiveness, and again their tears were mingled.

After Robespierre's death Joseph Chénier recovered his influence in the Assembly, and through his efforts Sauveur was eventually saved. But their father had received his death-blow; he
survived André only ten months.

Having published but two short poems up to the time of his
death, and those in an ephemeral form, André Chénier was yet
acknowledged by all who knew him to be possessed of the rarest
genius. Six months after his execution—a time still poignant
with melancholy memories—"La Jeune Captive" was published
in the *Decade* with this editorial note—"André Chénier had
studied much, written much, but published very little. Few of
us are sufficiently aware what irreparable loss poetry, philosophy,
and ancient erudition have sustained by his death."

This was followed by the publication in the newspapers of two
or three other pieces. But it must ever remain a stigma upon
his brother Joseph—himself a literary man, and something at all
events of a poet—that amidst his own ephemeral labours he did
not make time to fulfil the pious duties of an editor to the poems
in his possession, the worth of which he had certainly sufficient
critical knowledge to perceive. Still he did not conceal the
manuscripts. Far from it; they were lent only too readily, to
be soiled, torn, and stolen. They were repeatedly copied and
quoted, and, in one or two instances, pilfered to make other re-
putations. And in that small and precious circle whose applause
is worth the praise of a world of professional critics, André's genius

was acknowledged—among the most fervent of his admirers being Chateaubriand. By degrees the shorter poems and fragments found their way into print. But it remained for M. Daunon, to whom they had been bequeathed by Joseph, to publish them collectively. The editorship of the volume was entrusted to M. Latouche. From the surviving brother he received some further poems, and he did his pleasant duty well—almost too zealously, for he suppressed some short pieces for fear of marring a reputation already made.

In 1819 the first edition appeared, and a quarter of a century after the poet's death his works achieved a sudden, wide-spread, and lasting reputation. Coming when they did, these poems served as a key-note to much of the poetry of the nineteenth century—were more fittingly introduced then they would have been in the century before ; bringing to that young school, born in the spirit-stirring days of revolution, when great minds come upon the earth—to Hugo, to Lamartine, to de Vigny, to de Musset, a race of poets aflame with the glories of an unknown future—fresh, cool, new thoughts of the old Greek world—a world of loftier art, of purer ambitions, of more unselfish motives than ours, and giving to all mankind, directly or indirectly, fresh glimpses of eternal beauty, new renderings of an art that neither gold nor fame could sully. Bequeathing us all, moreover, as a protest against the materialism that is judged by bankers' balance, that is measured by gratified greed and self-satisfied vanity, the story of a strangely unselfish life, a strangely unselfish death.

Art. VII.—Recent Experiments with the Senses.

1. *Elemente der Psychophysik.* Von G. T. Fechner. Leipzig: 1860.

2. *Handbuch der physiologischen Optik.* Von H. Helmholtz. Leipzig : 1867.

3. *Physiologische Untersuchungen im Gebiete der Optik.* Von A. W. Volkmann. Leipzig: 1863.

4. *Beiträge zur Theorie der Sinneswahrnehmungen.* Von W. Wundt. Leipzig und Heidelberg : 1862.

THE phenomena of sensation constitute in a peculiar manner the borderland of Physiology and Psychology ; for while all mental operations undoubtedly imply physiological conditions, the direct observation of these conditions is in most cases rendered impracticable by reason of their great subtlety and inaccessibility. In the case of the organs of sense, however, physiological observation is specially favoured. The cause to be observed being some external stimulus, as a pencil of rays of light, or an adjusted series of weights, which is wholly in the experimenter's hand, and may be varied or circumscribed at his pleasure, there are presented the most favourable conditions of physical experimentation. Further, the comparative isolation and accessibility of these organs and their nervous connexions, as compared with the deep-lying and intricate structures of the centres, very much facilitate the study of the precise changes to which they are liable under the operation of a given external stimulus. For these reasons the physiology of the senses has attained a very high degree of precision and certainty, and is fast becoming the most elaborate department of the science of organism.

With this increased attention of physiologists to the facts of sensation, psychologists have every reason to be content. It is perfectly true that much of this experimentation might just as readily have been undertaken by the latter in the interests of their particular science as by the former; yet they will hardly regret that their omissions have been made good by the labours of others. Investigations into the precise mode of sensation producible by a given variety of stimulus are just of that nature, that a student of nervous processes, or of mental operations, might equally well have taken them in hand. Of course the aim of the two would not be exactly the same. To the former the mental element is of secondary importance, being simply a co-effect, easily ascertainable, by means of which his inference to the real physiological effect may be corrected. To the psychologist, on the other hand, the mental factor is the essential part of the phenomenon. It is this that he is studying, and the exact conditions of which he seeks to determine. Yet while there is this apparent difference in the claims of the two classes of inquirers, the method of inquiry is really the same for both. The introduction to the several organs of sense, of a large variety of well-ascertained stimuli, and the observation of their effects, while necessary for studying the precise physiological functions of the organs, are just the best means of learning the exact nature of sensation itself.

Simple observation of our sensations by self-reflection, it should be remembered, tells us very little about them. By means of this we learn to compare, discriminate, and classify them according to their several qualitative peculiarities. But there are many other aspects of them which this self-observation tells us scarcely anything about. When we wish, for example, to ascertain the exact duration of a given sensation, or class of sensations, we find it necessary to resort to some objective measure of time. Our mere unaided feeling of the duration of a pain, for instance, is a very vague and feeble means of measurement. We all know how commonly in daily life our individual and subjective impression has to be corrected by a reference to an objective standard. Now, it is just this want of precision in our subjective estimate of sensation which renders its systematic study in connexion with its objective causes a matter of such psychologic moment. In these experiments the external cause, as the stimulus of light, is something non-individual, something determinate and uniform to all minds; consequently, it may be precisely measured. From this it follows that the resulting sensation receives a new mode of measurement. Variations in intensity, duration, &c, which could never have received precise estimation from the mere data of subjective feeling, may in this connexion with nicely determinable causes assume the shape of an exact law. No doubt the indefiniteness and oscillation of individual feeling will still tend to counteract any such effort to quantify sensation. Yet by varying the experiments and by taking different states of the same individual, as well as many different individuals, an approximate estimate of these aspects of sensation, regarded as a mathematical function of the exciting physical cause, may be arrived at.

While these experiments of the physiologist thus directly contribute to the scientific study of sensation, they serve to illustrate very copiously the mental processes and laws previously arrived at by subjective observation. In order to understand this, it must be remembered that the mature sensations here dealt with are the product not only of the present external stimulation, but also of the individual's past experiences. It is impossible to produce, and at the same time obtain an account of what may be called a virgin sensation, such as may be conceived as the impression of an infant's mind; that is, so far as it is capable of existing clearly at all, without an accretion of association. Inextricably interwoven with all our familiar sensations are ideas of connected experiences, so that it is a matter of extreme difficulty to separate the net amount of sensation from the rest of the momentary impression. The physiologist, it is clear, must seek to make this separation if he is to assign the precise character of the effect of the stimulation. Hence these experiments are of no little value in adding to our knowledge of the range of memory and inference in our most rudimentary mental life.

In the following account of some of the most interesting of recent physiological experiments with the senses, we propose to select simply those which bear directly on one of these two results: either serving to render more clear and precise the nature and laws of sensation, or helping to illustrate and confirm some mental law.

The first class of physiological experiments to be noticed here has to do with the measurement of sensation. We have already remarked, that our unaided subjective feeling tells us very little respecting the exact quantity or duration of a sensation. It is only by observing these phenomena in connexion with some fixed and nicely definable objective standard, that we are able to determine their various aspects of quantity. A number of physiologists, chiefly German, have occupied themselves with this method of measuring the sensibilities of our organism; and although many of the results of these investigations appear to add little to our knowledge of the general relation between nervous stimulation and conscious sensation, they are perhaps worth recording as data by means of which such more general principles are to be arrived at.

With respect to the duration of a sensation viewed as the effect of a nervous power, there are several points deserving of attention. First of all, it is clear that the initiating process occupies an appreciable time. It has been estimated that when a muscle is made to contract by communicating a short electric stimulus to the motor nerve, about one-sixtieth of a second elapses before the effect of contraction becomes visible. Yet no method has as yet been discovered of estimating the interval between the application of the external stimulus and the commencement of the resulting feeling. There are two distinct questions involved in this unknown interval. The first relates to the transmission of a nervous impulse from the periphery to the sentient centres. This point has but little psychological interest. The second refers to the minimum duration of the nervous process in the central regions in order that a distinct sensation may result. It is very probable that some limit of duration exists below which a nervous change fails to produce a sensation, and it is supposable that at all times a vast number of such brief and feeble pulses are coursing, so to speak, across the regions of the brain without contributing to consciousness any of its distinct elements. The number of vague fugitive feelings which fill up the interstices of our definite conscious life may be conceived as the immature products of too rapidly ceasing pulsations in the nervous substance. Any advance towards the proof and measurement of this minimum interval would be of great value in helping to determine the minimum duration of a clear sensation. Such a discovery, if possible at all, could only be made by means of just such objective experimentation with the senses as that here described. The physical processes taking place in the hidden structures of the brain, lend themselves to no immediate observation, and can only be approximately determined as the intervening stages between an observable stimulation of a peripheral nerve and a discoverable effect in the subject's mind.

If it be as yet impossible to measure the rate of travelling of an inward nervous current, a good deal has been done to determine the duration of such a current in the central regions. It is a well-known fact, that a nervous change lasts considerably longer than the contact of the external stimulus which occasions it; and this fact is of great significance in accounting for all later or ideal appearances of the sensation. The existence of this self-prolonged sensation is best observed in the impressions of the eye, and it is here that the phenomenon has received the most precise estimation.

It is well known to students of optics, that when a circular disc with alternate black and white sectors is made to rotate about an axis, there is a certain rate of rotation above which all single impressions of the black and white surfaces cease, giving place to a continuous sensation of grey. This is at once accounted for by the persistence of a sensation, just spoken of. The impression left at any given point of the retina by a white sector, continues unabated during the brief interval in which the black sector passes over it, and the effect is the same as if the quantity of light issuing from the white sectors were distributed uniformly over the whole surface of the disc. By ascertaining the time occupied by each rotation, and what fraction the breadth of the black sector forms of the whole circumference, it is possible to measure the exact maximum duration of an impression of light in unabated degrees. Different physiologists in attempting this have reached different results. Thus Plateau found, that in ordinary daylight the time of transition of a black sector, and so of the unchanged impression of light, could be made as large as ·191 seconds. Professor Helmholtz, again, says, that with strong lamp-light the time of transition must not be greater than 1-48th of a second, though in weak moonlight it may be as much as 1-20th.[*] When the light is weaker, it should be added, the time of the unchanged after-impression is greater, there being here less exhaustion of the nerve by the succeeding stimulations. Further, different coloured light appears to have a different duration of after-effect, an impression of blue remaining longer than one of red or yellow. On Young's hypothesis, adopted by Helmholtz,

---

[*] See Helmholtz, "Handbuch der physiologischen Optik." Part II. § 22. "Die Dauer der Lichtempfindung." This work is a complete repository of physiological investigations with the eye, both older and newer, and we shall constantly need to refer to it.

of three classes of fibres distributed through the retina, sensitive only to red, blue and green rays respectively, it must be supposed that the fibres sensitive to blue are most susceptible of this after-effect; that is, retain the longest the molecular movements supposed to be set up in a nerve by an external stimulus. Plateau has also sought to determine the time during which an after-impression of light continues in decreasing intensity. This is found to be greater as the acting light is stronger. From this it follows that a powerful stimulus of light produces an after-impression which begins to fade much sooner than that of a feeble stimulus, though it has on the whole the longest effect. These same experiments with the discs show, too, that the after-impression of a light stimulus depends simply on the quantity of light falling on a given point of the retina, so that it is just the same whether an intense light acts for a brief interval or a faint light for a longer interval.

Another point in connexion with the duration of sensation is the time required for exhausting a nerve. When, for example, a fibre of the optic nerve has been stimulated for some while, instead of the positive effect of an after-impression there appears a negative effect in a temporary diminution of its sensibility. Hence the phenomena of negative images, or after-images (Nachbilder), as the Germans so happily term them. Helmholtz tells us that, for having these negative images most distinctly and persistently, it is best to let the first stimulating light act for a period of five to ten seconds. In this case the positive after-effect is evanescent and inappreciable. A negative image of bright clouds remains, under these circumstances, as long as eight minutes. It is found, further, that different coloured light acts differently in exhausting the nerve. According to Young's view of the classes of optic fibres, the complementary image that succeeds a long impression of a given colour arises from the temporary incapacity of the corresponding class of fibres. Thus, after looking some while at a green object, the fibres sensitive to green rays become exhausted, so that when the eye is afterwards directed to a white object, the part of the retina which received the green rays is unaffected by the green elements of the white light, and the remaining rays produce a sensation of the complementary colour—namely, purple. This exhausting effect is supposed, like that of the positive after-impression, to be of different duration for the different classes of fibres. An impression of white light, as afforded by the sun, may sometimes leave a series of images of various colours, and this effect is probably due both to the various susceptibility of the three classes of fibres to a positive after-impression already alluded to, and also to their unequal liability to exhaustion. At the same time it seems impossible, according to Helmholtz, to assign proportions to these two influences in producing the effect described.

Although both the phenomenon of self-sustaining nervous process and that of temporary exhaustion of the nerve, seem only susceptible of accurate observation in the region of visual impression, they undoubtedly extend to all departments of sensation. Thus it is very easy to observe, at times, a lingering after-sensation of tone left by some external stimulus. Possibly experiments may be extended to these as well as to other classes of our sensations. One question presents itself here of great interest to the psychologist. Does the degree of persistency of the after-sensation vary directly with the degree of facility in ideal reproduction of the sensation? The impressions of the eye, which manifest most conspicuously the first quality, are also among the most recoverable of our sensations. Further, it has been observed by Purkinje and Aubert, that an impression of light fades away much more quickly on the peripheral parts of the retina than at the centre, and it is clear that our visual recollections consist almost exclusively of ideas of impressions projected on the central regions of perfect vision. Hence it is just possible that a more exact method of estimating the duration of this after-effect in the other sensations would show this correspondence to be uniform. It may be presumed, too, *à priori*, that since this after-effect is due to a self-sustained activity of the related parts of the centres when the peripheral stimulation ceases, it will involve the power of central activity without any such peripheral initiation—that is, the appearance of ideal forms of sensation. With respect to the liability of the nerves to temporary exhaustion, this must be considered, in part at least, as a universal property of the cerebro-spinal system, forming the physiological basis of the well-known psychological fact, that conscious life consists in continual change of state, every impression or feeling tending to grow indistinct and feeble after a certain duration. At the same time this need of relief does not present itself in the same form or degree in all modes of nervous action. As seen in the case of visual impressions, the fibres sensitive to one variety of coloured light are much sooner exhausted than those which subserve another kind of sensation. It would be interesting to inquire whether the demand for temporary cessation is not greater in the case of those parts of the nervous system least employed in daily life. Apart from the increased facility of muscular effect arising from repetition of any class of impression or idea, it is quite conceivable that those nervous fibres which are most frequently used come to possess an increased capacity of unbroken work. If, as seems probable, great liability to exhaustion goes with feeble tenacity of after-impression, the fact just mentioned with respect to the peripheral parts of the retina would appear to favour this view of the effect of exercise on the working capacity of a nerve.[*]

Finally, it may be hinted that if liability to exhaustion varies inversely as the power of retaining after-impression, and if this latter varies directly as the power of ideal revival or recollection, we must expect to find among those classes of sensations least susceptible of this revival the least capacity for sustained and unbroken feeling. Thus, for example, tastes ought to be much less enduring sensations than visual impressions. That is to say, a taste would much sooner grow feeble and require variation of impression than a sensation of colour of equal intensity. Whether this is so may well be left to the individual reader to decide from his own experience.

We may now pass to the consideration of another class of investigations into what we may call the dimensions of a sensation ; we refer to the large number of recent attempts to measure the intensive and extensive magnitude of sensation. By intensive magnitude is meant the intensity or force of a sensation, by extensive magnitude, its volume, which, roughly speaking, corresponds to the area of the sentient surface and the number of nervous elements acted upon. In both these aspects of sensation numerous experiments have recently been made, more especially by German physiologists. E. H. Weber led the way in his famous discoveries of the various degrees of tactile and muscular sensibility resident in different parts of the bodily surface. Others have carried similar modes of inquiry into the regions of visual sensations. Finally, the results of these many experiments have been collected and formulated into a general law by Weber's colleague, G. T. Fechner. In giving an account of these investigations we shall be able to quote almost entirely from this author's works[†] We shall first of all discuss the intensity or force of a sensation only, and leave the more difficult topic of its extensive magnitude to the close.

It is clear that the intensity of a sensation, as distinguished from that of its external stimulus, is entirely a matter of subjective feeling. At the same time, as we have already hinted, mere subjective feeling would tell us very little about the

---

[*] On the evolution hypothesis it might be possible to explain any innate inequality in this respect ; for example, between the optic and the gustatory nerve, by supposing them to be the effects of long processes of exercise through many generations.

[†] Fechner has several statements of his general theory in the " Abhandlungen der sächsischen Gesellschaft der Wissenschaften." His most systematic exposition is to be found in his " Elemente der Psychophysik," and from this we have extracted our account of it.

general quantitative relations of our sensations. In order to reduce these scattered and isolated subjective appreciations to something like a general expression, it is necessary to study them in conjunction with certain definite variations in the objective cause. By this means we may learn how the feeling of magnitude in our sensation varies with changes in the absolute magnitude of the object, and so reach a more precise and scientific statement of the relation between nervous stimulation and sensation, body and mind. This is Weber's method as it has been enlarged and explained by Fechner.

By mere introspection of our sensations we know, first of all, the fact of their equality; and, secondly, their mutual relations of inequality, as greater or less. As a general rule it is impossible to say that one sensation is twice or three times as intense as another. We do, no doubt, speak of a light as being twice as bright as another, or a sound twice as powerful; but such numerical judgments are very generally indefinite, and involve for the most part a reference to some objective measure, as, for example, that the sound twice as powerful would produce the same force of sensation as the other at twice its distance. Further, it may be added that, when the sensations are of different orders, any estimation of their relative intensities is very inexact. Thus it is often impossible to say that a sensation of tone is more intense than another of colour. In cases where our judgment is very unwavering, it will be found that we compare the sensations mediately by a reference to the average strength of either class. Thus, when an impression of light is far above the common level of light impressions, and one of sound far below the level of sound impressions, we do not hesitate to pronounce one more intense than the other. In proportion as the heterogeneous sensations have any element in common besides mere force, as a feeling of pleasure or pain, they are of course much more susceptible of direct measurement.[*]

The methods, then, of estimating by objective experiment the force of sensation needed to recognise both these limitations—first

---

[*] Still even here we see the impossibility of reaching exact appreciations of equality or inequality between heterogeneous feelings. A pleasure of light or colour can be much more precisely measured with another pleasure of the same sense than with one of another sense, and nobody probably would attempt to determine the exact equivalent of a sensuous enjoyment in the sphere of imagination. Hence, perhaps, the habit of setting one class of pleasures above another because of an average superiority, even though the intensest of the inferior class are much greater than the feeblest of the other. We think it might be shown that it is this practical device, of great value where exact measurement is excluded, which has led to the supposition that pleasures excel one another by virtue not only of strength and duration, but also of qualitative differences.

of all, that the compared sensations should be of the same genus ; and, secondly, that our immediate appreciation of them is confined to their equality or inequality as greater or less. Acting on this plan, Fechner has sought to construct a standard of quantity of sensibility for the various parts of an organ, or different states of the same part. Fechner's statement is as follows: the sensibility of a particular time, or particular part of an organ, is reciprocally proportional to the magnitude of the stimulus requisite to produce a sensation equal in intensity to a given sensation. Thus, if weights of five and six pounds are required to produce equal degrees of muscular feeling at the same part of the surface at different times, or on different parts of the surface at the same time, we may say that the sensibility in the first case is to that in the second as 6 : 5.

There is one circumstance that greatly favours the employment of this method of measuring sensibility. It is a well-known fact that every stimulus must be of a certain force in order that it produce any sensation at all. Objective light may actually impinge on the retina, yet be of such feeble nature as to be unnoticed. So sounds when travelling from any considerable distance enter the ear without exciting the auditory nerve to sensation. Now, if we can estimate the objective force of two external stimuli which are just adequate to produce sensation on two occasions, or at different parts of an organ, we have in their ratio a very precise measure of the two sensibilities concerned. This measurement of the force of an external stimulus is capable of being made very exact in some instances, according to the principle of the conservation of force and by means of the excellent apparatus of physical science. Thus, for example, Schaflläutl has sought to determine the precise value of the physical impetus requisite to produce a sensation of sound. He has calculated that a piece of cork weighing 1 milligram falling through 1 millimetre on a glass plate produces the faintest observable sound, the observer being ·91 millimetres from the plate. It would be interesting to know how far this represents the average sensibility of the ear to sound, or how far it is coloured by the individual peculiarities of the experimenter. In the case of the eye's sensibility to light it is impossible to determine the exact degree of physical light requisite to produce a sensation in a perfectly dormant nerve, since, even when all external light is excluded from the eye, the nerve is known to undergo a certain amount of "subjective stimulation," resulting in what Helmholtz very aptly terms the *Eigenlicht* of the eye. In the case of weights estimated by sense of pressure, it is very difficult to determine the minimum pressure perceivable, since other tactile feelings, such as a feeling of smooth or rough surface, sense of temperature, &c., interfere with the pure feeling of pressure. Finally, in the case of the so-called chemical senses, taste and smell, we have as yet no method of reckoning the degree of the physical force which forms the stimulus.

The immense value of this method of determining the precise value of the physical force requisite to produce a sensation, consists in its applicability to different individuals. We cannot directly compare the sensations of two or more persons as we can those of two organs of the same individual. Still we may presume that the least perceivable sensation is a sort of constant quantity, the same for all; and in this manner we reach a measure of the relative sensibilities of different persons. These will clearly be in the inverse ratio of the physical stimuli needed to produce a just observable sensation.

From sensibility to stimuli, or absolute sensibility, Fechner distinguishes sensibility to differences in stimuli, or discriminative sensibility. While the former may be measured by the magnitude of the stimulus required for producing a sensation equal in intensity to a given sensation, the latter is to be estimated by the magnitude of the *difference* of two stimuli, needed to produce a certain change of feeling. In both these cases, the greater the objective cause required, the less must the subjective sensibility be supposed to be. Thus, if a greater change of light intensity is needed to effect a difference of sensation at the peripheral parts of the retina than is required at the centre, we may conclude that the latter parts possess the greater discriminative sensibility.

Here, again, we have the all-important fact that a certain amount of change in the objective force of a stimulus is possible without any variation in the feeling produced. That is to say, there is a certain limit of difference below which our various sensibilities are unable to discriminate. This limit, which we have found to exist in the case of both absolute and discriminative sensibility, Fechner denominates by the term threshold (Die Schwelle). Its existence, in the case of discriminative sensibility, is very easily proved. Objective light, sound and pressure may all be made to vary within very small limits, without the subject, who is experimented with, knowing anything of the change. Further, this limit or threshold offers, as in the case of absolute sensibility, the best means of measuring two or more discriminative sensibilities. Thus, in the instance of comparing two parts of the retina, or two regions of tactile surface, it is very difficult to pronounce a change of impression at one part to be exactly equal to a change at another. But the fact of there being a least noticeable difference of stimulation makes this rough method of estimation unnecessary. For example, in

comparing the discriminative sensibility of the palms and backs
of the hands to pressure, it is only necessary to discover, in both
instances, the exact amount of objective change required to produce the faintest sense of difference, and the ratio of the sensibilities will be inversely as that of the two amounts of change.
Similarly this method is perfectly applicable to an estimate of
the relative degrees of discriminative sensibility of different individuals.   The smaller the amount of variation in the stimulus
perceivable, the greater must be the delicacy of the sensibility
concerned.   In this manner, the ear's sensibility to pitch is
found to be of very different degrees of delicacy in different
persons.   It would also be found, probably, that very wide differences in the eye's discrimination of colours exist in different
individuals.   If only the exact amount of objective change, in
the difference of refrangibility of the rays employed, be measur-
able, it is clear that a very fine test would be offered for determining the comparative delicacy of different persons' visual
sensibility.

Hitherto, we have spoken of discriminative sensibility without
any reference to the absolute magnitude of the sensations distinguished.   We have spoken of it just as if this were a matter
of indifference, as if the eye, for example, were able to recognise
precisely the same amount of difference between very powerful
and between very feeble sensations of light.   But a very little
reflection shows that this assumption is incorrect.   Everybody is
aware that he is unable to recognise slight differences in weight,
when the weights compared are very heavy, though these same
differences are very apparent when the constituents are small.
So, too, it is demonstrable that the eye, when looking at a very
bright object, as the sun, is unaware of differences of light intensity, which, existing between feebler constituents, would afford a
striking contrast.   Hence the question arises, what is the relation
of the discriminative power of a sense to the magnitude or force
of the sensations to be distinguished?

This question has been clearly apprehended by Fechner, and
has received at his hands a very complete and systematic treatment.   In effecting this, he has conducted a large series of experiments, varying in every possible manner the absolute magnitude
of the stimuli to be distinguished, and always carefully noting
the ratio of the amount of difference of the stimuli to this absolute magnitude.   The methods of experimentation which he
adopts are three.   The first is that of his predecessor, Weber,
and is named " the method of just observable differences."   It
consists in estimating the minimum amount of difference recognisable at all variations in the absolute intensity of the stimuli,
and in studying the ratio of such difference to the absolute quan-

tity of the stimulation. The second method, named by Fechner "the method of correct and incorrect instances," is more intricate. When two stimuli—say two weights estimated by muscular tension—are very nearly equal, the subject of the experiment will be apt in a large number of trials to make errors as to which is the greater. The greater the objective difference, or the greater the sensibility of the individual, or of the part tested, the greater will be the number of correct as compared with erroneous judgments. It is the object of this method to determine the exact difference between two stimuli, or the relation of the difference to the absolute magnitude of the stimuli, which will produce the same proportion of correct and incorrect instances at all possible values of the stimuli. The third method, that of "average errors," consists in making the person experimented with seek by aid of subjective impression alone to make a stimulus—say a weight, equal to another and fixed one, by gradually increasing or diminishing the former. In doing this, slight errors will be made, and the object is to determine the average error in a large number of trials, and to assign the relation of this error to the absolute magnitude of the stimuli employed.

As the result of experiments according to all these three methods, Fechner arrives at what he calls a general "psychophysical law," and also "Weber's law," since Weber's experiments first distinctly pointed towards it. It may be expressed somewhat as follows. When we have to do with one and the same sensibility, as the muscular sensibility of a given part of the body at a given time, we find that the least recognisable difference between two stimuli is not the same absolute magnitude for all varieties in the magnitude of the stimuli, but is a constant fraction of this magnitude, and that only those differences of stimuli are felt to be equal which constitute equal fractions of their respective stimuli. In other words, the greater the force of stimulation, the less the power of discrimination, as estimated by the absolute amount of difference recognisable. Put another way, and more as a psychological law, we may say that the more intense a sensation, the greater must be the added or diminished force of stimulation in order that this sensation may undergo an appreciable change of intensity.[*]

[*] Fechner gives this law a mathematical expression. If r=stimulus; e= sensation produced by r; de=increment of sensation when r increases by the infinitesimal quantity dr; then if o is a constant, $de = \dfrac{o\,dr}{r}$. That is, the increment of sensation (de) is constant so long as the ratio of the increment of stimulation to the stimulus itself ($\dfrac{dr}{r}$) remains unchanged. Since logarithms

The full import of this law, from a psychological point of view, will have to be spoken of by and by. At present it may be sufficient to say, that it is a most important step in the process of determining and formulating the precise relations of nervous processes and mental life. It is clearly connected with those facts of nervous exhaustion and need of relief, of which mention has already been made. Further, there is little doubt that it might, as Fechner seems to think, be extended to the whole region of consciousness. Provided only that we could estimate the force of an organic or other stimulus in prompting a given form of emotion we should probably find that for every sensible increase of the resulting feeling a greater and greater increment of initial stimulation is requisite.*

Confining ourselves, however, to the facts of sensation, we find that this psycho-physical law comprises a vast number of very interesting facts. These are too numerous to be described in detail here, and for a fuller account of them the reader must be referred to Fechner's work itself.

The most interesting of all our sensibilities is undoubtedly that of the eye. The fact that with variations in the intensity of the light very unequal differences are perceived, has been long known. Stars are seen in the night, and not in the day, although it is demonstrable that in both cases the difference of light intensity between them and the rest of the sky is one and the same. Experiments were conducted, at the end of the last century, by Bouguer and have since been repeated by Fechner and Masson, in order to determine the relation of this visual discrimination to the intensity of the stimulus. Bouguer took two wax tapers of equal flame, placed a rod between them and a white screen, so that two shadows were thrown on it, and then gradually removed one taper till the shadow thrown by it just disappeared. The difference of objective light between the two indistinguishable surfaces (the shaded and nonshaded) would clearly be the point of just appreciable difference. He calculated from this that the eye is able to distinguish 1-64th of a given light intensity. Fechner and his friends, adopting the same method, estimated the discriminative sensibility at 1-100th. Masson employed rotating discs, and judged that the eye can distinguish a change of 1-120th in the intensity of light. Each of these results equally answers to

---

are known to increase in equal degrees when the numbers so increase that the increment has always the same ratio to the magnitude of the number, we may say that "sensation increases in proportion to the logarithm of the stimulus."
* Of course the difficulty in ascertaining this is due to the number of contributing ideal sources of feeling in an emotion which more than outweigh the effect of the initial stimulus and sustain it long after this has ceased to act.

Weber's law of sensibility, and it is possible that the want of agreement points to considerable differences of discriminative vision among individuals. It is only right to add, that Fechner admits the inapplicability of his law to very feeble and to very intense impressions of light. Beyond certain limits, both above and below, a much smaller fraction of change is recognisable. He accounts for these apparent exceptions by supposing that with very blinding light some injury is done to the nervous substance interfering with its regular function, and that when the external stimulus is very feeble the subjective stimulus—the Eigenlicht of Helmholtz—has an appreciable effect in blunting the sense of difference for external stimuli.

A very brief reference to the other illustrations of this psycho-physical law must suffice. With respect to sounds, it has been estimated by Renz and Wolf (Vierordt's Archiv, 1856), that two sounds, whose intensities are in the ratio of 100 : 72, are always clearly distinguished. When the ratio was as 100 : 92, the correct judgments only just exceeded the false ones. Volkmann experimented with the same sensibility by means of a steel ball falling on a steel plate, the weight of ball, height of fall, and distance of listener being varied. The result of his experiments was much the same as that just named, a ratio of 3 : 4 in intensity being sufficient to afford the observer a confident judgment. With respect to the height or pitch of tones, Weber showed that equal intervals always corresponded to one ratio in the numbers of vibrations of the distinguished tones. This fact is very curious, as serving to assimilate pitch with some aspect of force of sensation. It may be added, that the phenomena of light impression do not confirm the view that rapidity of molecular vibration in the stimulus, and so, probably, in the nerve, is equivalent to force or amplitude of vibration. Just perceivable differences of coloured light do not correspond to a constant fraction of the absolute number of vibrations. In the case of the muscular appreciation of weight, Fechner has supplemented the experiments of Weber by applying the method of correct and incorrect instances to the problem. As a result of a series of trials with liftings of one hand in 1856, and with liftings of the two hands in 1857, he finds that as the weight is increased and the difference increased proportionately, being always the same fraction of the first, the fraction representing the proportion of correct to incorrect judgments is pretty constant. At the same time a deviation from this uniformity was discovered at the lower end of the series, when the weight employed was 300 grammes. Once more Fechner has tested the validity of this law in the case of sensibility to temperature, and found that within certain degrees of temperature (20° R. to bloodheat) the differences just observable

N 2

were always proportional to the elevation of the particular temperature above a medium point between freezing-point and blood-heat (147 R.). That is to say, by reckoning the intensity of heat or cold by its distance from a middle and indifferent point, the discrimination was found within certain limits to follow Weber's law. On the other hand, from 20° down to 10° R., the sensibility to change was so great that it was impossible to give the least noticeable difference a precise value, while below 10° this minimum grew larger than was required by Weber's law.

From all this it appears that for all the senses in which the force of the objective stimulus is distinctly appreciable, Weber's law is found to have a certain measure of validity. In order to erect it into a precise general expression of sensibility, it is necessary to discover some method of estimating the force of the stimuli in the case of sensations of taste and smell, and also to account more completely for the slight deviations from this regularity beyond certain limits of intensity in the sensations.

Thus far we have been speaking of the quantity of a sensation in respect of its force or intensity only, and have not discussed another aspect of quantity which belongs in some measure to most, if not all, of our sensations. We mean the extensive as distinguished from the intensive magnitude of a sensation. This property of our sensations is connected, as has been hinted, with the number of nervous elements involved in the sensation. To assume the existence of this aspect of sensation as an ultimate fact involves no theory of immediate perception of extension under any of its aspects. It simply implies that homogeneous sensations—say those of light—are distinguished somehow according to the nervous route along which the stimulation travels, and that there is a clear and marked contrast between a sensation produced by means of one or a few fibres, and one in which a large area of nervous elements takes part, and this contrast is in nowise confounded with that of a great and feeble intensity.

This extensive sensibility, like the intensive, may be regarded as absolute or discriminative. By absolute extensive sensibility we mean any feeling whatever of extent or volume. This, too, has its threshold or limiting condition in the originating stimulus. Every stimulus must act on a certain area of the sentient surface in order that any feeling of extension or volume may arise.* For example, different pencils of rays of very unequal circumference are nevertheless both felt by the eye to be unextended

* In the case of visual impression it is known that some area of operation is required to produce any sensation at all. This fact, however, bears rather on the estimation of intensity than on that of extensive-magnitude.

points. So different points applied to the skin, though of very unequal area, are equally felt to be unextended. This mode of absolute sensibility, it may be added, is susceptible of just the same kind of comparative estimation as that of force or intensity. The hand which felt a surface with the least extent of the applied stimulus, would clearly be most sensitive to this aspect of stimuli.

It is, however, in the form of a discriminative sensibility that the feeling of extension commonly presents itself. In the distinguishing of different points and lines, in the comparison of linear and superficial magnitudes, this feeling plays a very prominent part in our knowledge of external phenomena.

The simplest exercise of this sensibility is the discrimination of two adjacent points. Whenever two stimuli, as two rays of light, two points of a compass, simultaneously operate on the sentient surface, it is found that they must be a certain distance apart in order that two distinct sensations may follow. This mode of determining the relative sensibility to the extension of two parts has been made use of by Weber in his now famous experiments on the tactile sensibility of various parts of the bodily surface. It has also been employed to estimate the fineness of visual sensibility on various parts of the retina. Weber and Helmholtz found that at the centre of the retina two points of light are recognised as such, whose retinal images are from ·0046 to ·0052 millimetres apart. Aubert and Förster discovered that this delicacy of sensibility to extension disappears very rapidly from the centre towards the periphery of the retina, this decrease being most rapid towards the upper and lower parts, least rapid towards the outer regions. All these facts of sensibility to points or extension are supposed to be related to the area occupied by an elementary nervous fibre. Weber supposes that two points applied to the skin, in order to be distinguished, must lie within the circle of two different nervous extremities. Helmholtz, on the other hand, conceives that two points of light can only be distinguished when the distance of their retinal images from one another is greater than the diameter of a retinal element, for otherwise they would fall on the same or on two contiguous elements. In the first case he thinks they would produce one sensation, in the second two, but these would not be recognised as the effect of two points, since they might equally well follow from a single point whose image is projected on the boundary of two elements.

Of much the same character as this discrimination of points are other modes of visual sensibility recently examined by physiologists. We refer especially to the eyes' estimate of the degree of convergence and the amount of dissimilarity of the retinal pictures. The appreciation of distance by one eye by means of the feeling of muscular tension in accommodation has been recently measured by Wundt,* but this is clearly not a case of feeling of extension, since in the experiments alluded to any change in the magnitude or position of the retinal image is excluded, and the judgment is formed solely by means of the degree of intensity of the muscular feeling. On the other hand, in an experiment made by Helmholtz, as to the degree of the feeling of similarity of the two retinal pictures, the basis of the judgment is clearly a feeling of extension. Helmholtz used for this purpose three vertical nails placed at the ends of three small pieces of wood at distances of 12 millimetres from one another and 340 millimetres from his eyes. He then stood with his eyes slightly below the other extremities of these laths, so that the line of union of the nails and wood was invisible. Under these circumstances he could judge whether the three nails were in exactly one vertical plane only by means of the comparison of the two retinal pictures. In so far as they were not, it is clear that their image on the one retina would have a different local arrangement from that of the other. Helmholtz found by this means that a slight deviation of the nails from a plane, such as would cause a local disparity of the two retinal images of ·0044 millimetres, was at once detected, and that thus the delicacy of the feeling of extension in the comparison of the two images of an object is precisely the same as that employed in a single eye's discrimination of points†

Of equal interest are some experiments by Wundt on the visual estimation of distance by help of the variations in the convergence of the two eyes. He used for this purpose a black vertical thread, viewed by both eyes through a horizontal slit, and movable to and from the observer. At a distance of 180 centimetres a change of distance of 3·5 to 5 centimetres was observable. An approach of the thread at this distance by 3·5 cent. implies a shifting of each retinal image through 72

---

* Wundt made the observer look with one eye at a vertical black thread through a slit in a screen. This source of judgment was found to be very vague. At a distance of 250 centimetres nothing less than an approach or removal of the thread by 13 cent. was observable.

† It is necessary to distinguish from this perception of similarity or dissimilarity of the two retinal pictures for stereoscopic vision, the eye's capability of single vision, as measured by the limits of retinal surface within which any two points of the two images must lie in order that the corresponding part of the object be seen single. This appreciation has also been measured by Volkmann. It appears to be of very various degrees of delicacy in different individuals, and is clearly determined less by any original mode of sensibility, such as the discrimination of points, than by the effects of experienced and disciplined attention.

seconds angular measure, and this corresponds pretty exactly to the least distinguishable distances of retinal points. It should be remarked here that one may suppose the eyes to remain fixed while the thread is moved to or from them, so that the first recognition of the change is due to the shifting of the images on the retinæ. At the same time it is possible that the eyes at once follow the moving thread so that the feeling of change of distance is simply a mode of the muscular sensibility.

It remains to inquire whether Weber's law is in any sense applicable to these phenomena of discriminative sensibility as applied to extension. Does the discrimination of two extensions depend on the absolute magnitude of these extensions, so that the greater the magnitude the larger the minimum amount of difference noticeable? In order to answer this question Fechner, assisted by Volkmann, has instituted experiments with sight and touch. In the case of light they both proceeded according to the method of average errors. Fechner employed two pairs of compasses, of which the tips only were visible to the observer. One of these pairs was kept fixed and the legs of the other gradually brought together, or removed from one another, till the observer deemed them to be just as far apart as those of the fixed pair. Volkmann used three vertical threads, stretched by weights and moveable to and from one another, and made the two extremes equidistant from the centre according to the judgment of the observer. As the result of both these sets of experiments it appears that the discrimination of extension depends like that of force on the absolute value of the magnitudes employed. Thus Fechner found that the magnitude of the average error was about $\frac{1}{3}$nd of the sum of the magnitudes compared; and Volkmann found it to be from $\frac{1}{7}$th to $\frac{1}{14}$th of the same. In other words, the amount of error varies directly, and so the degree of discrimination inversely, as the absolute magnitude of the extensions compared. Here again it has been assumed that the comparison of two lateral distances by the eye is effected by means of the various local sensibility of the retinal elements. Probably in this exact measurement this is so, though it is no less true that the amount and duration of the eye's movement in passing along the given distance afford through the muscular feelings a chief instrument of such measurement.

While these experiments appear to bear out the applicability of Weber's law to our various feelings of extension, Fechner and Volkmann both found that with respect to touch no discoverable relation exists between the amount of difference observable and the absolute magnitude of the extensions compared. Fechner hesitates, therefore, to assign to his law any universal validity for this mode of discriminative sensibility.

One other point deserves mentioning before leaving the
subject of quantity in sensibility. We have dwelt on an absolute
and a discriminative sensibility to stimuli. The one is measured
by the amount of objective force needed to produce a sensation
of given intensity, say the weakest possible; the other by the
amount of change, *i.e.*, according to the psycho-physical law, of
the fraction of the absolute stimulus required to produce a
feeling of change of a given amount, say the least observable.
Is there any connexion between these two sensibilities thus
measured? Does sensibility to difference go parallel to absolute
sensibility, so that when the latter is diminished by ill-health or
exhaustion the former falls to a lower fraction? It is proved,
says Fechner, that this is not the case, but that on the contrary
any variation of absolute sensibility which intensifies or weakens
in the same proportion the effects of two stimuli leaves the
feeling of their difference unaffected. Similarly with respect to
the sensibilities of different parts of an organ. Weber's experiments with weights showed that there is no correspondence
between the absolute sensibility of a part and its discriminative
sensibility. Two parts of the bodily surface to which very
unequal weights appeared to be alike, were in spite of this difference of absolute sensibility pretty alike in their power of
discrimination. The fact that the eye loses with exhaustion
a measure of discriminative sensibility is explained by Fechner,
by supposing that the subjective stimulation already referred to
interferes in this case in the estimation of differences in external
light.

The next important result of a general character furnished by
these experiments with the senses, after the increased precision
given to our estimation of quantity in sensation, is to be found
perhaps in the advance made towards the determination of the
ultimate elements of sensation. Our mature sensations, the only
ones we are able to examine immediately, are for the most part
compounded of numerous elements. Thus, the visual impression
received from an external object is made up of a number of
sensations of light, shade, colour, and form. Up to a certain
point subjective reflexion is able to analyze these into their constituent parts. In many cases where a given element occurs
apart from the other factors, whether alone or in other combinations, it is possible to make a mental separation of it. Yet even
here the fusion of the elements may be so complete and the
resulting feeling so unlike its factors that, notwithstanding a distinct knowledge of the elements it contains, the mind fails to
detect their existence in the compound. Still less is it possible
to effect this separation if two given elements of a sensation

never both occur in perfect isolation. Hence we can never be certain by mere subjective knowledge that any apparently simple sensation is not compounded of other and more elementary feelings. The only other way of determining this is by studying the nervous processes. Assuming, as seems legitimate, that some peculiar mode of feeling is effected by every separate nervous fibre, the physiologist may by an exact study of these nervous elements afford important suggestions as to the ultimate elements of sensation.

The naturalist who has recently done most in this objective analysis of sensation is Professor Helmholtz. His now famous doctrine of upper tones is a signal instance of this method of research. From certain physical facts with respect to sound, he was led to infer that in such apparently simple and indivisible sensations as the tone of a violin or a vocal sound, there are many feeble elements present which go to form the peculiar quality of the sound. Since these upper tones never present themselves in isolation from the more prominent fundamental tones, the mind's attention fails to disentangle them from the composite mass of sensation. Yet they are perfectly distinct sensations, produced by means of different nervous fibres, and could easily be distinguished if they occurred in less perfect simultaneity. Indeed, their discoverer asserts that, with considerable discipline in attention, they may be detected even in this close fusion of elements when once the mind is aware of their existence, and consequently able to lie in wait for them, so to speak. The effect of this discovery is clearly to greatly reduce the number of elementary auditory sensations. It resolves all the sensations of timbre as well as those of vowel clang into mere variations of pitch.

Very similar to this discovery of Helmholtz is his revival and amplification of Thomas Young's theory, that all our sensations of colour are compounded out of three elementary modes of feeling, namely, sensations of red, green and violet.[*] The phenomena of colour blindness, and a large number of other facts, both anatomical and optical, favour the hypothesis, that three classes of optic fibres are distributed pretty equally over the surface of the retina, which fibres minister respectively to the three modes of sensation just mentioned. On this supposition our common sensations of colour are never pure elementary feelings, since even the purest coloured light of the spectrum is conceived as exciting more than one order of fibres. Thus the red rays, though they stimulate most powerfully the fibres sensitive to red, affect in a feebler degree the other two classes of fibres also.

---

[*] Maxwell supposes the third elementary sensation to be blue rather than violet.

Hence, in order to produce a pure elementary sensation, it is necessary to incapacitate, temporarily, these other two classes of fibres. This may be done by first allowing the eye to rest awhile on a mass of the complementary colour, in the seeing of which these fibres are chiefly concerned. They then become exhausted, according to the principle already spoken of, and when the eye is turned to the required colour, an approximately pure sensation is obtained. In this way it is possible, by looking for example, at a mass of purple, to obtain a subsequent sensation of green much purer in tone, that is, less whitish than the green of the spectrum. It is needless, perhaps, to point out how impotent mere subjective observation had been to discover any combining feelings in an ordinary sensation of colour. In point of fact, every sensation of colour is, when looked at subjectively, one and indivisible. Yet, by means of physiological investigation, it becomes possible to determine certain more elementary feelings, out of which these *quasi* elements are built up.

It may be well to observe that this physiological method of analyzing sensation has its limits in the number of discoverable nervous elements and processes involved in a sensation. If it be demonstrable that in mediating a given sensation, two or more nervous fibres are employed, it is allowable to assume that the resulting feeling is compound, in the sense that it is the effect of two or more stimulations, which would apart produce distinct modes of sensation. But this does not warrant one in subdividing each separate stimulation into separate time-elements, and inferring that a sensation of colour, for example, is the result of an indefinite number of molecular impulses in the nervous substance, each of which may be conceived as producing some rudimentary mode of feeling, some vague shock of consciousness. Yet this mode of analysis has recently been attempted by so eminent a thinker and naturalist as Mr. Herbert Spencer, and also, and apparently in complete independence, by M. Taine.[*] Such a hypothesis is of great interest to the evolutionist, but it appears to be excluded from psychology by the impossibility of verification by subjective observation. The student of mind may gladly accept a physiological contribution to the knowledge of sensation, such as the doctrine of upper tones, where the alleged elements are in their nature capable of being experienced apart. But how is the human consciousness to experience the ultimate nervous shocks which enter alike into such utterly dissimilar sensations as those of tone and of colour? Müller's doctrine, that every nerve has its specific energy or function, however stimulated, has been con-

---

[*] See Spencer's " Psychology." Second Edition. Part II., chap. i.; also Taine's " De l'Intelligence." Livre troisième, chap. i. and ii.

firmed by all subsequent researches, and it appears only a verbal simplification to speak of the different genera of sensations as various combinations of one and the same conscious element.

Hitherto we have been dwelling on those phenomena of sensation which appear to have equal importance for the physiologist, and for the psychologist. We now turn to those which have a principal bearing on proper psychological laws and truths. Our mature and disciplined senses present to us no longer simple organic effects of external stimulation, but highly composite mental products, perceptions and judgments, in many of which the primordial effect of the organic stimulus is nearly lost in the compact group of cerebral associates. Hence we may expect to find, in experimenting with the organs of sense, numerous illustrations of proper psychological processes.

As a prominent example of this, we may take the great principle of Relativity, or the law of change, to which the whole of conscious life seems to be subject. Every distinct feeling, or state of consciousness, means a transition from some unlike previous state, and an unbroken uniform state of feeling is an impossibility. One part of the physical side of this law was noticed in speaking of the temporary exhaustion of the nervous fibres by stimulation, and the consequent need of alternation, or change of stimulation. This law may be viewed on its negative and positive side. That is to say, we may consider the inoperativeness of uniform stimulation, or the striking effects of sudden and strong contrasts in stimulation. A large number of interesting facts in the region of sensation fall under this head. We will only allude to one or two. We soon grow accustomed to a uniform temperature in the surrounding atmosphere, and after a certain time, are scarcely aware of its existence. Uniform pressure, such as the atmospheric, and in a less degree that of our own body, and our clothes, soon ceases to produce any sensation. In visual sensations we find the same law operative. What are called the subjective phenomena of vision, the effect of the eye's structure and contents on the impression of light, are, for the most part, inoperative on consciousness. It is only under extraordinary circumstances, or in exceptional states of health and nervous energy that we notice these phenomena. A highly characteristic example of this process is to be found in the nonperception of the shadows demonstrably thrown by the blood vessels of the retina on its nervous layer. Ordinarily these shadows fall on the same nervous elements, and so produce no effect. But Helmholtz describes an experiment by which light is made to enter the eye by an unusual route, namely, through the sclerotica, as far as possible behind the cornea, and the effect of this is, that the shadows of the vessels now falling obliquely on new nervous elements, are distinctly perceived.

The increased distinctness and force of sensation due to magnitude of transition are abundantly illustrated throughout the whole region of sensation. This may be viewed under two aspects; first of all, in respect to intensity or quantitative distinctness; and secondly, as to qualitative distinctness. As an instance of the former, we may refer to the psycho-physical law of Fechner itself. That in estimating immediately, and without help from objective measures, the amount of difference or change between one sensation and another, we really start from the magnitude of the original sensation as our standard, is nothing but a restatement of the law of Relativity. Every feeling of quantity is, strictly speaking, relative; we know nothing of magnitude, except by comparison. Hence, in the experiments described by Fechner, since the observer knows nothing of the absolute magnitude of the stimuli, he can only appreciate the magnitude of the new sensation in its relation to the foregoing. In other words, our sensations have no fixed numerical value as to intensity or extension, but acquire, in every new recurrence, a temporary value from the adjacent feelings, with which they are comparable. Hence it follows that a given sensation, that is the effect of a given stimulus, which, coming after a feeble one, seems of considerable intensity, would lose this value when following a much more intense antecedent. At the same time, the precise numerical value given to this law of variation, by Fechner's law, is clearly a great addition to the bare fact of relativity, serving, as has already been remarked, to define much more exactly than had before been done, the mode in which change of stimulation impresses consciousness.[*]

In the eye's estimation of magnitude as well as intensity, there are numerous illustrations of this law. Some of the optical illusions respecting magnitude and direction are among the most troublesome problems of the science, and are very far from being adequately explained. Others, again, clearly rest on the relative character of our visual appreciation. For instance, it is a well-known fact that a line or angle distinctly divided into parts always looks larger than an equal magnitude undivided. The reason seems to be that in the former instance we at once see the whole as a *greater* in relation to its contained parts, whereas in the other this impressive element is wanting.

---

[*] Wundt suggests ("Lehrbuch der Physiologie des Menschen," p. 477) that the proper significance of Fechner's law is psychological. This is scarcely an accurate account of the matter. It embodies and illustrates the law of relativity; but it has a psycho-physical value over and above this.

Very curious, again, is the operation of this principle in the estimation of distinct quality in sensation. We customarily speak as though the psychological effect of stimulation in a given nervous fibre were a fixed and definite phenomenon, and this is approximately true. Yet numerous experiments show that these effects vary, within certain limits, according to their antecedents or concomitants. Nor are these variations altogether referable to the fact of temporary exhaustion of the nerve. When after tasting sweet marmalade my cup of tea seems unsweetened and brackish, it may be presumed that the gustatory nerves have been temporarily rendered less susceptible of that particular mode of stimulation which results in a sensation of sweetness. But when it is found that an impression of colour on a particular part of the retina varies very appreciably according to the other colours of the field simultaneously perceived, this seems to point to a very general mental law, the exact physical counterpart of which it would perhaps be difficult to assign. The phenomena of optical contrast are of very great interest to the psychologist, and will have to be spoken of again presently. As a single instance of the operation of contrast in rendering a visual impression sharp and distinct, we may mention the fact that two adjacent colours in the field of vision always tend to appear too contrasted, and to approximate to complementary colours *along their common boundary.* The effect of this unconscious comparison on the qualitative peculiarity of a sensation is thus seen to be greatest when the loci of the compared impressions on the sentient surface are very close together. This is probably due to the fact that such proximity allows of the most favourable comparison by two consecutive acts of attention, without it being necessary that the two impressions should fall alternately on precisely the same nervous elements.[*]

Another psychological fact that receives frequent illustration in recent experiments with sensation is the influence of attention on our mental life. It is a well-known fact that when the mind is strongly preoccupied and attention engaged, many vague feelings and ideas flit through the mind without leaving any durable trace in memory ; and more than this, nervous processes which would under ordinary circumstances powerfully impress consciousness, remain without any appreciable effect. Thus to a man deeply intent on reading, moderate sounds fail to have any

---

[*] This can only be hazarded as a possibility, for the eye's movements are so rapid, and so involuntary in character, that we can never be certain such an effect is not due to consecutive stimulations on the same nervous elements. It will be seen that the question of the real nature of attention, to be spoken of more fully presently, is involved here.

disturbing effect, and even a serious physical hurt may be unnoticed in the agitation of a fight, or a flight from danger. At the same time this influence of preoccupation has its limits, which it would be very interesting to inquire into. However engaged a person may be, a stimulation of light or sound of a certain force can hardly fail to arouse him.

The directing of attention is a voluntary act, and proceeds according to the influence of some practical end. Where such a motive force is wanting, we find that sensations and feelings escape notice, so to speak, that is, fail to rise into clear consciousness as distinct mental elements. On the other hand, the presence and influence of a powerful inducement, by detaining attention, serves to draw, so to speak, these vague and indistinct impressions into the focus of distinct consciousness.

Each of these processes may be easily traced in the region of visual and other sensation. As interesting cases of impressions escaping consciousness, we may cite the subjective phenomena already spoken of, the lacuna in the field of vision, due to the blind spot, the presence of double images of objects lying far out of the horopter. All these phenomena pass customarily unnoticed, though it is possible, under certain circumstances, to become aware of them by a deliberate effort of attention. It is the same effect of inattention which, as Helmholtz very clearly points out, causes the first net impression in an act of perception to be so often lost to consciousness in the inferred part which has the only practical value for us. The proper understanding of the relations of pure Sensation and Inference, to which we shall presently have to turn, is only possible by remembering how impotent any part of an impression must be which fails, either by its inherent force or by its practical interest, to arrest attention.

On the other hand, a purposed act of attention will frequently extend the borders of conscious life by discovering impressions heretofore obscure and unknown. In this manner any person may discipline himself to observe a number of optical phenomena. So, too, according to Helmholtz, we may bring ourselves to notice the upper tones which blend indistinguishably to the ordinary ear in a rich vocal note. A very curious instance of the effects of attention is to be found in the so-called 'rivalry' (Wettstreit) of the fields of vision. When we look through a microscope at two different colours, we do not, according to Helmholtz and other eminent opticians, receive a sensation of the mingled colours, but see now the colour affecting one eye, now that of the other. The same is true of two perfectly distinct figures or forms. A very slight amount of ideal anticipation, says Helmholtz, is sufficient to bring the one rather than the other into view.

It would be interesting to know the precise physiological equivalent of this effect of attention. It is commonly assumed that attention being a matter of the will, can only be directly operative on the voluntary muscles, adjusting them for a more favourable reception of impression. No doubt this is one chief factor in the process. But there are facts which seem to favour the supposition that an act of concentrated attention effects a flow of energy not only along the *motor*, but also through the *sensory* fibres of the organ, or part of the organ concerned, rendering them highly susceptible of external stimulation. A striking example of what we mean may be found in the ease with which we may "conjure up," to use a colloquial phrase, all manner of subjective tactile feelings, such as prickings, ticklings, &c. The amount of muscular adjustment possible in the case of a great part of the tactile surface is very trifling; and these feelings seem to lend support to the view that attention, by effecting somehow an increase of nervous energy in a particular set of sensory fibres, predisposes an organ or a part of an organ to the reception of impressions. Of course, if this be so, every persistent act of attention has a characteristic danger, since this predisposition may very easily pass into a subjective feeling which is easily mistaken for an objective impression. This source of error ought to be allowed for in such conclusions as those of Helmholtz and others, that upper tones may, by an effort of attention, be distinguished in a musical note.[*]

It only remains to point out, in connexion with the subject of attention, that correctly speaking some measure of attention is a necessary factor of every distinct sensation. No doubt there are myriads of vague feelings constantly flitting through the outer regions of consciousness, which being unnoticed cannot be recalled by memory. Yet even these are scarcely to be dignified by the name of sensations. They lack those elements of discrimination and comparison without which no distinct mental state is possible. Still less is it allowable to speak of "sensations" wholly out of consciousness, the unknown correlatives of those nervous processes which fail to affect the conscious mind. The assumption of any such correlatives appears to us highly unscientific; and certainly they should not be designated by a term which usually connotes a measure of that attention and distinct consciousness which are here supposed to be wanting.

[*] A real instance of this effect of anticipation in misleading perception is quoted by Helmholtz. Goethe and Brewster both asserted that they could see blue and yellow light in green light, though it is now held that green light is elementary in its nature. These observers had a strong predisposition to detect blue and yellow in green from their familiarity with the effects of combining pigments.

The remaining phenomena of sensation to be considered here, involve the distinct effects of past experience through association. These processes reach too deep into the fabric of our mature sensations for the physiological experimenter to overlook them; and the recent investigations which we are more particularly considering here add many new and interesting examples of the mode in which the present bears the impress of the past.

The effects of association are to be found not only in the more passive side of sensation, but also in those numerous and varied movements which, though little observed, accompany and condition sensation. Our voluntary movements are learnt by a very slow process. At first they are probably random and undirected, and they come to be definite through the associations of sensation which grow up about them. Knowing nothing of our voluntary muscles, or the motor nerves by means of which they are made to contract, we are incapable of originating any definite variety of movement, except so far as it is marked off by a particular variety of feeling. These associated feelings are not only those of the muscles themselves, but also the passive sensations which are found to follow the movement. As an example of this process, we may refer to the very elaborate and delicate movements of the eyes, which are scarcely ever noticed, and are guided by the practical ends of distinct impression. It is possible to reproduce in experiment the very process by which these movements come to be learnt and executed. Professor Helmholtz gives us a very interesting example of this. It was shown by Donders, and has been established by the subsequent investigations of Listing and others, that with every change of direction of the axis of vision in relation to the head, there is a definite and invariable amount of rotation about this axis (Raddrehung), though the muscular apparatus of the eye easily allows of a large variety of such rotations for every movement of the axis. That other rotatory movements might be combined with a given direction of the axis, Helmholtz proves by means of an experiment. He uses for this purpose a combination of two prisms, the joint effect of which is to produce a slight amount of apparent rotation in the parts of the object looked at. When these are held before one of the eyes, and an object fixed with both eyes, it is clear that the image projected on the retina of the eye so armed does not fall on the points or nervous elements which, under ordinary circumstances, correspond to the parts of the other retina now affected. The consequence is, that double images of the object are seen. Yet after a number of efforts Helmholtz found that the eye learns to alter its rotation, so as to bring the two retinal images on corresponding parts. In a similar way the customary combinations of adjustment and convergence come to be altered by the use of glasses, and by the constructions of the stereoscope. Even a certain amount of divergence of the axes, and of disagreement in height may be effected when, as in the case just described, these exceptional movements are rendered necessary for distinct vision.

It may be well to point out how these discoveries as to the nature of the eye's movements discountenance the supposition of any innate acquisitions in the region of voluntary action. If an inherited predisposition is ever produced by the accumulated experiences of progenitors, one would expect to find it in the movements of the eye. And yet Helmholtz is disposed to view the whole of these phenomena as the product of many tentatives and effects of association in the history of the individual himself.

Still more plainly, however, do we see the effects of association in the gradual transformation of our elementary sensations into the apparently simple intuitions of our mature minds. No one, we presume, would deny that association enters very largely into our external perceptions; yet there may be very different opinions as to the extent of this influence. Nothing but a long and laborious study of the phenomena of the higher senses, more especially that of vision, can give a just impression of the depth to which it reaches in our mental life.

At first sight, indeed, it may well seem a futile task to attempt to separate the pure elementary sensations from all the added effects of repetition and comparison of impressions, as well as those of associated ideas. As we have already seen, the quality of a sensation may be found by experiment to undergo a change simply in consequence of the absence of some customary foil or contrast by which to bound it. There is little doubt that to the colour-blind the visual impressions received are qualitatively affected by the absence of so many of our elements of discrimination or contrast. How then can we assume the existence of any element in sensation perfectly independent of such extraneous influence, the pure result of a peculiar variety of nervous stimulation?

This difficulty is only an apparent one. It may be impossible to determine the precise boundary line between sensation and inference (in its widest sense), yet they are both known to exist. The sensation of green, for example, which I now receive from an impression of light on a given class of optic fibres, undoubtedly owes much of its clearness and sharpness to rapid and imperceptible comparisons with previous like and unlike sensations; yet these very comparisons involve something fixed in the sensation itself, some property which must be referred to the peculiarity of the nervous process. The visual impression which I receive from a green leaf may be very vague through inattention and the want of the recognising act of consciousness; yet it has that which prevents my confounding it with red, and compels me, on an instant's reflection to classify it with a vaguely defined group of greens, and the next related sensations of colour. The precision of the last or inferential part of the process depends of course on the distinctness of visual recollection, and on the proximity of similar and contrasted impressions. Hence in the experiments alluded to, slight errors occur in the recognition of colours through some unwonted arrangement of the field, whereby the necessary elements of comparison are removed.

Professor Helmholtz rightly finds a negative characteristic of the elementary or instinctive part of a sensation in the inability of any circumstance clearly traceable to experience to overcome and expel it. If a part of an impression, however elementary it may seem, is sometimes overcome and changed into its opposite by a mere element of inference or effect of experience, it is clear that it is not the pure result of the nervous stimulation, but depends, in part at least, on further and cerebral processes.[*] In this way, for example, we know that a person's recognition of a colour is in part an act of inference. The science of optics is full of the most startling illustrations of this displacement of inferences, so rapid and mechanical that they easily appear intuitions to persons ignorant of these facts. What, for instance, seems more of a direct intuition than that I see an object of a particular colour? Even if distance and magnitude be shown to be processes of inference, and so liable to occasional error, one would suppose that in seeing external colour there is not the slightest room for false inference. Yet the phenomena of simultaneous contrast go to show that every projection of an impression of colour into the object-world is an inference, and as such may be erroneous. Thus if, repeating Meyer's experiment, we look at a small piece of gray paper laid on a sheet of green paper, and covered by a thin sheet of white letter-paper of exactly the same size as the coloured sheet, we shall find that the little piece appears no longer to be of a gray, but of a strong rose-red hue; whatever the colour of the under sheet, the gray scrap appears complementary to it. The reason of this illusion seems to be, that we conceive the covering to be greenish instead of white, the green of the under sheet shimmering through the thin covering, and so *reason* that where the gray scrap lies, the pure retinal impression of which must be a dull white, there is a

---

[*] This proposition must not, Helmholtz says, be converted. Not every accretion of inference is capable of being expelled even by the most forcible contradictory evidence, otherwise there would be none of that discrepancy between conception and belief which Mr. Mill has so fully exposed.

red colour beyond the supposed greenish veil. In other words, the actual sensation of white derived from this part of the object is resolved into two elements—namely, those of the complementary colours, green and rose-red, and our attention is fastened to the latter as the contrast to the rest of the field. Such errors of inference in the perception of objective colour are no doubt very slight, and closely limited by certain conditions; yet the very fact of their possibility shows that our supposed intuition of an object's colour is a different thing from our pure subjective impressions or sensation of colour, and being an inference may, in certain cases, be counteracted by other suggestions of experience.

The great field for this disguised play of inference is that of our *quasi* intuitions of space, as extension, distance, magnitude, &c. Nothing seems more clear to a person unaccustomed to analytical reflection, than that our eye has an immediate knowledge of these spacial relations. Yet ever since the famous denial of Berkeley, more accurate knowledge of the eye and its function has been gradually upsetting the popular creed. A large number of the facts thus brought to light—such as the celebrated discoveries of Wheatstone—are now familiar to all psychological students, and we suppose it may be safely assumed by this time that at least distance is no part of the retinal impression, but is only capable of being suggested to the eye by the various feelings of adjustment and convergence and change of retinal picture. As with distance, so with direction. It is provable that the eye has no instinctive knowledge of the direction of a visible object, but that this no less than distance is an inference supplied by associations with our motor and tactual experiences. Helmholtz describes an experiment by which the acquired character of this perception is strikingly shown. If one takes two prisms and places them in the framework of a pair of spectacles, with their angles of refraction both turned left, the optical effect of these glasses is to make all objects appear to be shifted to the left of their actual situation. If one, then, seeks to fix the exact direction of a particular object, and having closed the eyes, tries to reach it with his hand, he will find himself feeling too much to the left. But when these trials have been repeated frequently enough, he will gradually learn to hit the required object. If, when this stage is reached, he removes the spectacles and tries as before, with closed eyes, to reach an object, his hand will wander too much to the right. Further, if, when the right hand has learnt to reach an object first looked at through the glasses, the left hand be tried, the eyes being again closed, the observer will find himself able to reach the object just as easily and certainly as with the right. This appears to prove

o 2

conclusively that it is the eye and not the hand which has altered its appreciation of direction. The newly instructed eye has come to see the object left of its previous direction in exactly the same sense in which it used to see it in this direction, the quasi intuition being in both cases an inference as to motor and other experiences lying outside the limits of visual impression.

Another fact which throws much light on the derivative or acquired nature of our perception of direction has been established by Hering. If, after both eyes have looked at a very distant object, so that the axes were parallel, the right eye be closed, and the other then accommodated for a nearer point in its previous line of vision, this new object will not appear in the same direction, but shifted to the left. Yet the open eye remains fixed in the same direction, and only the closed eye has moved to a state of convergence. It follows from this, that the position of the closed eye helps to determine an eye's sense of direction. Hering and Helmholtz both represent this fact by the supposition of an imaginary eye midway between the two eyes. Each of our real eyes sees objects in the direction of the axis of such a cyclopean eye. This estimation of the direction of all nearer objects from a point midway between the two eyes accords, as Helmholtz says, with the supposition otherwise proved, that direction is not an intuitive perception of the eye, but an inference from the position of both eyes in relation to one another, the real thing inferred being the particular mode of movement which my hand would have to make if setting out from the median plane of my body, or which my body itself would have to make, in order to come into contact with the given object.

Finally, there is the more intricate question as to whether the eye at rest has any immediate knowledge of lateral extension together with form and magnitude. On a first view of the matter it seems self-evident that the retina being itself extended, any impression on its nervous element, will contain immediate information of these special properties. Yet all the facts go to show that the eye's perception of extension is as much derived as its knowledge of distance. All that is required in order to explain the phenomena of optics is to attribute a qualitative difference of sensation of some kind or another to the different nervous fibres of the retina, by which an impression on a particular element will somehow appear unlike those on other elements, the distinguishing quality of each fibre being something constant, so that any new impression on the same element will at once be recognised as like previous ones in this respect. What this difference of local sign (*Localzeichen*) really is we cannot in the nature of the case discover, since *ex hypothesi* it has long ago been buried under associations derived from our other organs. Yet that it exists and is of a very precise nature must be assumed in order to account for the nice discriminations and recognitions of the tutored eye. For instance, it is proved that the comparison by the eye of linear magnitude is only exact when the lines are so situated that the eye, moving according to the laws of rotation already referred to, is able to superpose, so to speak, the image of the second line on exactly the same series of retinal elements as that occupied by the first. In other words, the feeling of duration of muscular movement is much less exact than that of the coincidence or non-coincidence of nerve-fibres affected. The exquisite microscopic fineness of the optic fibres gives to the eye its distinguishing clearness and accuracy of space perception, although in every case these perceptions refer to extra-visual, or, at least, extra-retinal, modes of sensibility.

We are unable to cite all the optical facts which support the derivative theory of visible extension. Professor Helmholtz has done eminent service in bringing them into their right prominence and showing their bearings on the rival theories.* Perhaps the most conclusive refutation of the innate or intuitive theory is to be found in the phenomena of single and double vision. An exact study of the range and limits of single vision, such as are set forth by Helmholtz, shows the enormous difficulties belonging to all theories of identical points in the two retinæ having, *ab initio*, one and the same feeling of extension. Indeed, this supposition is directly contradicted, according to Helmholtz, by some of the newest discoveries in stereoscopic vision. On the other hand, these same phenomena receive an easy and satisfactory explanation from the empirical or derivative hypothesis. The precise situation of the corresponding points of the two retinæ, the margin within which an impression will coalesce with that of a given point in the other retina, the phenomena and limitations of relief,—all these things are fully accounted for on this theory ; and should any of our readers be still in doubt on the point, we can only refer him to the exhaustive treatment of the subject by Professor Helmholtz.†

How the intuitionalist proposes to deal with the host of well-

* "Physiologische Optik." Dritter Abschnitt, § 33. Kritik der Theorien.

† It strikes us as a pity that Mr. Monck did not take the trouble, before writing his ingenious but very hasty essay on "Space and Vision," to look at Helmholtz's masterly work. He could hardly fail, by so doing, to see the meagreness of his few plausible arguments for the eye's intuition of its own retinal space, beside the long array of facts there drawn up against such an hypothesis. This negligence appears all the more singular as Mr. Monck so often expresses his wish to test his theory by the more intricate optical phenomena.

established illusions of the senses we are at a loss to understand. Yet this is certainly his most urgent business. On the supposition that immediate sensation is an infinitesimal quantity, and that a large proportion of what seems to us immediate and intuitive is the product of past experience, it is no mystery that our senses should deceive us. All that is required is to arrange a set of external conditions by means of which the modicum of immediate sensation may be produced apart from those adjuncts which customarily attend it and have become so inseparably associated with it. This device is effected by a large part of those experiments which physiologists have recently instituted. On the other hand, if we are to accept the old theory of an intuitive knowledge of space relations, what is the meaning of all these signal failures of the intuitive faculty? A single instance of error is sufficient to destroy the venerable and amiable notion of an infallible consciousness, and if the phenomena of external perception continue to be referred to this department of knowledge, we shall scarcely envy its possessors the mental comfort which is said to flow from a perfect reliance on the veracity of consciousness.

In conclusion, it may not be amiss to remind the reader that no number of such experiments as those here described can at all affect the question of an independent external world. Physiologists who experiment with an individual's sensations by means of external stimuli necessarily assume the antithesis of the external and internal, which, indeed, nobody questions; and it is not their province to inquire into its final significance, but simply to determine the various aspects of their co-existence and to formulate its laws. Thus, when it is said, for example, by Helmholtz that our sensations are signs which for the most part we disregard, except so far as they indicate objective facts, this statement by no means necessitates a belief in something independent of mind; for, on the Idealist's theory, no less than on the Absolutist's, our single, individual impressions are unimportant as compared with the permanent assurance of impressions to all minds, and a large part of passive sensation is of little account, except as suggesting modes of voluntary action by means of which some evil may be arrested, or the store of our daily happiness increased.

CONTEMPORARY LITERATURE.

The Foreign Books noticed in the following sections are chiefly supplied by Messrs WILLIAMS & NORGATE, *Henrietta Street, Covent Garden, and Mr.* NUTT, *270, Strand.*

THEOLOGY AND PHILOSOPHY.

PUBLISHED sermons do not usually attract the reading public. Still less do they attract that class of readers who think and reason, who thirst for books that instruct. The causes of such disinclination to printed sermons are patent. The pulpit is seldom noted for higher excellences than platitudes, or the repetition of dogmatic propositions remote from men's business and bosoms. As theological sects and parties are numerous, their pulpit effusions necessarily present a diversified character. Even within the range of orthodoxy, sermons differ widely in complexion. They are argumentative, didactic, rhetorical, impassioned, practical, mystical, doctrinal, dull; and the ideas are arranged according to the varying taste of the writers, or that of the audiences addressed. Dr. Mac Ivor's volume[1] presents the substance of several sermons preached in a college chapel. They are therefore of an *ad clerum* nature, not of the popular sort adapted to an ordinary congregation. After defining religion, and showing its origin, functions, and criterion, he illustrates the laws of religious progress, which he calls succession or growth, co-existence or co-operation, unity or life. The instruments which the Holy Ghost uses in developing religion are faith, the church, and the Bible. A wide field is traversed in the discussion of these topics. Dr. Mac Ivor is a man of culture, and has read extensively in books of philosophy. He is familiar with Butler's Analogy, and builds on the basis of its principles. He subjects the Bible to a legitimate process of reasoning, and unfolds what he believes to be its meaning. He is no slave to the letter. His views of theology are liberal to a certain extent. But he is not an exact thinker, and moves awkwardly among the ideas he wishes to express. Encumbered with the leading dogmas of orthodoxy, the materials of his volume lack lucidity of arrangement, largeness of view, and a right apprehension of the Bible as a whole. His philosophy is better than his theology; though the former is not unexceptionable in all particulars. In consequence of the heavy style, which is not counterbalanced by superiority of thought, the reader's task in perusing the volume is not an easy one. Like the majority of ecclesiastics, the author is unacquainted with the best results of modern criticism on the Bible, and adopts the old phraseology which implies that Moses wrote the Pentateuch and David the Psalms. A variety of senses is also wrongly assigned to the words of Scripture. We

---

[1] "Religious Progress: Its Criterion, Instruments, and Laws." By James Mac Ivor, D.D., M.R.I.A., late Fellow and Tutor of Trinity College, Dublin. Vol. I. London: Longmans, Green and Co.

regret to see a man of intelligence and culture ignorant of the first principle of interpretation. The best part of the volume is Note E; that which evidences most acuteness is Note A. But his language about faith, religion, theology, man's *sensibility* to the unseen, should be more accurate. The opinions of the author are in some respects beyond and better than the stereotyped ones; but they are still behind the philosophically true.

Mr. Brooke's "Christ in Modern Life"[1] approaches the model of what sermons should be. The volume contains twenty-seven discourses, written in a graceful style, and implicitly based throughout on that which seems to be the cardinal doctrine of the Broad Church party, the Incarnation. Assuming this doctrine as a fact, the author supposes that the ideas which Christ made manifest are capable of endless expansion to suit the wants of men in every age; and that they do expand with the progress of the race. In them live, as the preacher thinks, the solution of our religious, political, and social problems. The defect under which Mr. Brooke's belief labours is the nonapprehension of what ideas were really Christ's, for the gospels leave this uncertain; and the attaching of ideas which are the result of modern advancement to Christ's, as though they were the natural and necessary outcome of the latter. The sermons themselves are superior specimens of pulpit addresses. They contain good thoughts clothed in appropriate, often eloquent, diction. Those on immortality are beautiful; that on prayer in relation to natural law evinces considerable ability and breadth of view. Judaism and Christianity, the fourth sermon, is less satisfactory. The author's forte seems to lie in the explanation of mental states and emotions under the influence of spiritual motives; in a delicate apprehension of Christ's character; and in the tact with which he presents the best aspects of Christianity to the acceptance of others. The volume may be recommended as a favourable example of Broad Church teaching at the present day. The time, however, must soon come, when the central position of that party will be untenable, and the teaching of Jesus be better understood in its essential distinction from Paul's.

Dr. Newman's Sermons[2] possess many merits. With all the acuteness, subtilty, and vigour of intellect which belong to him, with his varied knowledge of books and of human nature, he discusses a variety of subjects not usually treated in discourses, or fitted for ordinary hearers. In an academic pulpit, however, where university men are the audience, such sermons as the present are appropriate. The chief subject handled is the relation of faith and reason, which is both ethical and theological, involving philosophical as well as dogmatic considerations, and presenting peculiar difficulties. While admiring the ability of the author in explaining such a theme, we feel disappointed

---

[1] "Christ in Modern Life: Sermons preached in St. James's Chapel." By the Rev. Stopford A. Brooke, M.A. London: Henry S. King and Co.

[2] "Fifteen Sermons preached before the University of Oxford, between A.D. 1826 and 1843." By J. H. Newman, sometime Fellow of Oriel College. London: Rivingtons.

with the result. Dr. Newman's philosophy is defective, inexact, erroneous; so that he does not show clearly the mutual relations of reason and faith. It contributes to the unsatisfactoriness of his arguments that *reason* is used by him in three senses. Nor does he throw any fresh light on the nature of *faith*. Rather does he obscure it by making it a principle *sui generis*, and independent of what is commonly understood by *reason*. Had he shown that faith is an exercise of pure reason, the latter being the highest and noblest faculty of the mind, he would have come nearer the right view. As it is, the reader will receive but a vague idea of the dependence or independence of faith on reason, from these discourses. Nor is the subject of miracles set in its proper light by the author, though touched upon in various connexions. The best sermons in the volume are those which treat of less difficult topics, such as the fifth, on personal influence; the ninth, on wilfulness, Saul's sin; and the last, on the theory of developments. The eighth, on human responsibility, is also good. The second, on the influence of natural and revealed religion respectively, though founded on Butler's Analogy, and marked by great ability, is unsatisfactory. The volume leaves a general impression on the mind that the preacher has a settled system of faith, which he has arrived at through mental processes and earnest studies of a peculiar kind; that he is fully satisfied with the belief of doctrines which are clear to himself, without his having the power to persuade others that they are consonant with right reason, or even in many cases with Scripture itself.

Mr. Boulding's sermons[4] present a pretentious wordiness which does not commend them to devout readers. The ideas are of the ordinary commonplace type, and the style is not good. The author strains after an excellence he cannot reach—an originality of expression which degenerates into affectation. The subjects selected are of the very kind that make a poor thinker or writer look more meagre; such as the death of Moses, the religious side of nature, the prophet of the whirlwind, Balaam, Job, the martyrdom of St. Paul, the temptation in the wilderness. What can we say to this beginning of a sermon from Matthew iv. 1. "His *soul* had long dwelt in a wilderness. For eighteen years had the world been growing more uncongenial, and life more lonely, &c. &c."? Or to this, from "Christ, the life;" divided—"I. There was a Fact of Life wanted. II. Christ was that Fact. III. As the Fact of Life He has abolished Death as a Fact. IV. He is the Fact of Life that remains for ever." Sermons like these should not be printed, because they betray mental poverty and ignorance of the Bible, accompanied with an ambitious mode of expression which is signally incongruous.

The sermons of Mr. Baldwin Brown,[5] like those of the Broad Church party, assume and illustrate the Incarnation. They are superior to those of Mr Boulding, who belongs to the same religious body, but are

[4] "Sermons by the Rev. J. W. Boulding." London: Bemrose and Sons.
[5] "The Sunday Afternoon: Fifty-two Brief Sermons." By J. Baldwin Brown, B.A. London: Hodder and Stoughton.

far below the standard of excellence. The author thinks with vigour ; and tries to express his thoughts with corresponding emphasis. He aims at originality of idea and style, without the ability to rise above the ordinary notions of orthodoxy, or to commend them to the cultivated by aptness of language. He moves in an element of exaggeration. Mystical, inflated, positive, he expends artificial energy on a few thoughts, which he invests with a dress more forcible than chaste. The style is bad, bearing on its face an affectation of originality. We are also surprised at the ignorance of Scripture displayed. In this respect the author often offends. Thus he claims the last twenty-seven chapters of Isaiah for the prophet himself, repeating the hackneyd phrase that their ascription to a Deutero-Isaiah springs from the conviction that there is no such thing as prophecy in the Bible ; affirms that Paul calls "faith" what James calls "faith and works ;" that the ancient Jews said so little of immortality because of "the entire healthiness of their belief in it !" He also assumes the Davidic authorship of Psalm li. The sermons abound in big statements, curious words, and anthropomorphisms, as, "men of this strain are of native right the captains of the great host of God ;" "they burst the last barrier which their merciful God had built between them and perdition ; and they went plunging down headlong into the blackness of the pit ;" "there is nothing more inspiring in human history than the long hard struggle of the Lord against the proclivities of the Jewish people ;" "there are times when God seems literally to loose the adversary (Satan) against us ;" "the Apocalypse in its wholeness is a voice from heaven ;" Christ is "the perfect man who explains the manward thoughts and *hopes* of God." Such teaching cannot promote a rational, intelligent, or reverent religion.

Dr. Guthrie's volume[e] contains a number of papers about foreign places resorted to by many from the British isles for recreation, health, or amusement. The essays are well written, and breathe a benevolent spirit ; the piety they recommend being less ascetic than that of Scotland generally. The writer is a sensible and large-hearted man, who has profited by foreign travel. His reflections, which have no pretension to profoundness or originality, are grouped around Aix les Bains, Florence and Savonarola, Venice, La Tour, and the Waldensian valleys.　　•

The writer of "Catholicism and the Vatican,"[f] who is a Roman Catholic, sympathizes with the old Catholic movement in opposition to the recent dogmas of the Vatican. After giving the substance of those dogmas, he states the teaching of the Catholic church in Ireland on papal authority, traces the opposition in Germany under the influence of Döllinger, including an account of the Congress at Munich, describes the effect of the Congress, and concludes with some reflections on the prospect of old Catholicism in Ireland. The volume,

[e] "Sundays Abroad." By Thomas Guthrie, D.D. London : Strahan and Co.

[f] "Catholicism and the Vatican. With a Narrative of the Old Catholic Congress at Munich." By J. Lowry Whittle, A.M. London : Henry S. King and Co.

though small, is interesting in matter and liberal in spirit; the production of an intelligent man, who is awake to the progress of opinion and culture in Europe. His narrative is well told and deserving of wide circulation. Were all Roman Catholics as enlightened as Mr. Whittle his church would soon be reformed.

In the series of "Keys," edited by Mr. Blunt, is one on Modern Church History,[1] describing the rise of the Reformation, the English and Continental Reformations, the English Puritans, the Church of England from the Restoration to the Nineteenth Century, the Continental and Eastern Churches, the principal Sects of Christendom, with the modern spread of Christianity. The information about these various topics is necessarily brief and condensed, since the volume contains no more than 175 small pages. The writer's difficulty must have lain in determining what was most important to be said, omitting much that might have been stated with equal pertinency. The point of view from which he looks at the subject is High Church orthodoxy. The compendium is by no means accurate in all its statements, and is often one-sided. What belongs to the Anglican Church is better told than that relating to sects or men outside it. Thus Matthew Henry is mentioned along with Watts and Doddridge as a Congregationalist; which is followed by the unfounded statement that "Congregationalism generally has been strongly infected with Unitarianism or Socinian error." The account of the origin of the Great Bible, on page 32, is also incorrect. It was not "the translation or rather revision undertaken in A. D. 1535 by the bishops and others," but the work of Coverdale, whom Crumwell employed. Cranmer had no part in its preparation, though the writer would lead us to infer the contrary.

Mr. Jacox has collected a great number of passages, statements, remarks, and sayings, from writings ancient and modern, under several texts of Scripture.[2] Though they throw little light on the meaning of the Biblical passages quoted, they are supposed to have some relation to them, not always pertinent or discernible. His papers are rather gatherings from books, on all kinds of topics, than annotations proper on Scripture; and it would have been better had the author omitted the texts altogether. The range of his reading is wide; the authors cited numerous. Many of the remarks, however, are trivial; and the display of acquaintance with so many writers detracts from any just estimate of the value belonging to the miscellanies. The Greek, French, Latin, &c., inserted is out of place, since it is easy to see that Mr. Jacox is an indifferent scholar. That his selection has not been made with much regard to worth, appears from his citing Mr. E. S. Dallas, Prof. Alex. Roberts, Justin M'Carthy, Miss Eden, Miss Braddon, and others. Yet the reader may find good and interesting matter in the volume mixed with the useless.

[1] "A Key to the Knowledge of Church History." Edited by J. H. Blunt, M.A. London, Oxford and Cambridge: Rivingtons.
[2] "Secular Annotations on Scripture Texts." By Francis Jacox, B.A. London: Hodder and Stoughton.

Some of the preceding remarks apply to Mr. Jacox's analogous volume called " Bible Music," which relates to musicians, instruments, and poetical pieces descriptive of harmonious sounds; but runs off continually into topics, stories, or anecdotes, loosely connected with the main subject. This book is a better one on the whole than the other; though marred by a like display of varied reading and quotation, and loaded with too many notes. The author's own remarks are of small importance; but many citations, especially the poetical ones, may interest others.

Mr. Mackenzie Walcott, who is in thorough sympathy with his subject, has given the "Traditions and Customs of Cathedrals."[11] The work is both historical and archæological, containing a sketch of the cathedrals of the Old and New Foundation, with notices of the ravage or injury inflicted on them, and details of their ancient customs. The author tells us that the volume is designed to be popular, reliable, and instructive. It is certainly both popular and instructive; but all the details cannot be considered reliable, especially those about the ravages attributed to the Parliamentarians. The information collected is worthy of perusal, both as a record of times and men that have passed away, and as a warning for the future. The writer deserves thanks for his fragments of history.

The author of the little book called "Nazareth,"[12] endeavours to set forth the life of Jesus during the thirty years prior to his entrance on a public career. Supposing that he can discover what it must have been, because of the design of the Incarnation, he delineates the outlines of that life. As the Gospels pass over that period, leaving it in all but total obscurity, it is a bold undertaking to fill up the unknown space from imagination and probability. The spirit of the author, however, is devout. He speaks reverently and cautiously. The value of his lucubrations is small, when we observe that he is an orthodox man who takes literally all that is recorded of the birth and infancy of Jesus in the Gospels. The Gospels are to him an inspired source of literal history; and the lessons derived from his imaginary meditations are poor indeed. The work betrays a feebleness of conception and execution which will not recommend it to a thoughtful reader.

The volume written by Dora Greenwell[13] contains musings on the adaptation of Christianity, especially of its primary doctrine, the cross, to comfort, refine, and support the soul in a world where evil abounds. The thoughts are of a feminine type, clothed in a style that is too artificial and florid, though sometimes neat and elegant. We regret that the meditations should be disfigured by a theology which is dishonouring to God or repulsive to reason. "An agonized and dying

---

[10] "Bible Music: being Variations, in many Keys, on Musical Themes from Scripture." By Francis Jacox, B.A. London: Hodder and Stoughton.

[11] "Traditions and Customs of Cathedrals." By Mackenzie E. C. Walcott, B.D. London: Longmans.

[12] "Nazareth: its Life and Lessons." By the Author of "The Divine Kingdom on Earth as it is in Heaven." London: H. S. King and Co.

[13] "Colloquia Crucis: a Sequel to 'Two Friends.'" By Dora Greenwell. London: Strahan and Co.

God," " vicarious sacrifice and satisfaction for sin," and the peculiar views connected with these statements, are antiquated among thinkers. But with such views the Colloquia are impregnated ; and the Father, as is common, gives place to the Son, who appears almost as sole Divinity. In point of matter, the book is rather thin. An elaborate style, aiming at poetic beauty, supplies the place of healthy thought and rational meditation.

The Dean of Westminster has published four lectures on the history of the Church of Scotland, delivered in Oxford and Edinburgh,[1] the first sketching the Celtic, Mediæval, and Episcopal Churches; the second, the Church of Scotland, the Covenant, and the Seceding Churches; the third, the Moderation of the Church of Scotland ; while the fourth touches upon the present and the future of that Church. These have all the excellences of manner and style characteristic of the accomplished author. The national features of the Scottish people and the most favourable elements of their religious character are set forth in an admirable spirit of comprehensive charity. Anxious to say the best things possible of the communities in the North, and to give Presbyterianism all credit for intellectual culture and development, he selects from history the events and men most fit for his purpose. It must be confessed, however, that his glorification of Scottish institutions and Scottish religion is excessive. His treatment is somewhat one-sided, and so far unphilosophical. Though he finds fault with Mr. Buckle, the latter is much nearer the truth than the Dean. He gives but scant credit to the parties who have seceded from the Church of Scotland at different times, amid his predominant desire to exalt the latter even in her days of Moderatism, when religion was all but dead. Some of his judgments are hasty enough— such as "there are several living theologians of the Church of Scotland at whose feet Englishmen might be proud to sit." Sir Walter Scott is pronounced "one of the great religious teachers of Scottish Christendom." We presume that he has not read Rutherford's Letters or Boston's " Fourfold State," or " The Scotch Presbyterian Eloquence," else he would have written more guardedly at times. It is curious to observe, how he avoids a direct censure of Calvinism and the Westminster Confession of Faith, in his auguries for the future of the Established Church of Scotland. With a fine opportunity for counselling Scotchmen to shorten their dark creed embodied in Formularies to which all must subscribe, he prefers instead to deal in generalities, as though a State connexion were the chief means of elevation and freedom. The first step towards the true reform of any church is the abridgment of its dogmatic creed. We prefer subscription to an undogmatic formula to the retention of long and intricate confessions of faith which men must subscribe, since the latter encourage hypocrisy. Above all, they blunt and destroy individual conscience. That liberty is nobler and purer which subscribes only

<hr>

[1] " Lectures on the History of the Church of Scotland, delivered in Edinburgh in 1872." By A. P. Stanley, D.D. London : John Murray.

what is really believed, than that which subscribes as a matter of convenience, and disbelieves.

The Dean of St. Paul's has published the two lectures he delivered in the great National Church last January.[15] The first, on Roman Civilization, expresses thoughtfully in broad outline the leading ideas and characteristics of all that is generally included in the phrase. The second lecture, on Roman Civilization after Christianity, is inferior and unphilosophical. The author attributes to the direct and indirect influence of Christianity far too much of the morality, purity, rectitude, and hopefulness that have been the slow product of human thought. The history of Christian countries shows that their religion has often retarded the improvement of mankind, originated disastrous wars, sanctioned cruelties as horrible as those of paganism, and fettered the mind with degrading superstitions. The Dean has attached certain civilizing influences to Christianity, which have taken place apart from and in spite of it.

In the volume entitled "The Bible and Popular Theology,"[16] Dr. V. Smith gives a lucid exposition of the Bible teachings relating to the more important questions of Christian theology; or, in other words, a summary view of Unitarian opinions about the Bible and its doctrines, with criticisms of Dr. Liddon and others. After the able "Examination of Canon Liddon's Bampton Lectures by a Clergyman," the remarks on passages of that work in the present volume are unnecessary. The sentiments and interpretations propounded are generally correct, but not new. As a reasoner, the author lacks vigour. Sometimes he seems timid, as a few remarks about the authorship of the fourth Gospel evince. Sometimes he is either unacquainted with the best literature on the subject, or ignores it for inferior sources. It is curious to observe how much deference he pays to writers of the Church of England and their books, though the books in question may be poor ones; how he attaches to them laudatory terms which are inapplicable, and contents himself generally with the citation of inferior works. Yet the author sometimes presents good specimens of criticism, as in note E on the Epistle to the Philippians ii. 5–11. Without endorsing all Dr. Smith's reasonings, or assigning much weight either to his judgment or learning, the volume is of more than average merit, notwithstanding the general feebleness it betrays in handling important topics.

The work of a former Balliol student[17] is intended to show that science and theology were originally identical; and that theological teaching rightly understood is merely the development of scientific teaching or the wisdom of the ancients. The contents are exceedingly

[15] "Civilization before and after Christianity. Two Lectures delivered in St. Paul's Cathedral." By R. W. Church, M.A., Dean of St. Paul's.

[16] "The Bible and Popular Theology : a Restatement of Truths and Principles, with Special Reference to Recent Works of Dr. Liddon, Lord Hatherley, the Right Hon. W. E. Gladstone, and others." By G. V. Smith, B.A., Ph.D.

[17] "On Mankind, their Origin and Destiny." By an M.A. of Balliol College, Oxford. London : Longmans and Co.

varied, indicating that the author has read extensively, that he has
studied the Bible attentively and minutely, is acquainted with many
classical writers, and well versed in mythology. He is both destructive and constructive, chiefly the former; attaching little value
to the Bible, and divesting Christianity of all its importance. Ingenious, bold, dogmatic, he pursues his own way through old documents,
mythologies and myths, with a patient analysis which few possess.
The labours of many years are heaped together in a volume of eight
hundred pages, which tries the reader's endurance. The first six
chapters mainly concern the Old Testament, containing a new and
literal translation of the first three chapters of Genesis. The next
eight relate to the New Testament, presenting a critical examination
of the first two Gospels, with all their narratives, an explanation of
the Apocalypse, and a brief investigation of the authenticity of the
Epistles. The Gospels of Luke and John are not unnoticed; and
the Acts of the Apostles are subjected to frequent criticism. After
lists of the Apocryphal Gospels, Epistles, Acts, Revelations, and other
writings, eleven chapters are devoted to the mythologies and cosmo-
gonies of ancient nations. The twentieth chapter concludes with man's
origin, his destiny, and the immortality of the soul. The work is
illustrated by 20 engravings and two woodcuts. Such is the bill of
fare set forth temptingly to the sight of the scholar. A few remarks
will indicate our opinion. The materials are imperfectly digested and
badly arranged, as if the author had added piece to piece without sifting the accumulated mass at its conclusion, and rearranging it in
proper order. His scholarship is inexact and unreliable. With considerable ingenuity he lacks the critical faculty in any superior degree.
He pronounces opinions on very difficult points too summarily, and
errs in consequence. With some exceptions, his reading has been in
an older literature, not the most recent or the best. Hence he ignores
critical results which are now established, and stammers along in
his own path. He is too eager to disparage Bible statements. With
this view, absurd things are cited from apocryphal works—from the
Talmud, the Rabbins, the Fathers, and pagan writers, as if they were
of equal credit with the views set forth in Scripture. The book contains a great deal of extraneous and worthless matter. It lacks condensation. The general system of interpretation applied to Scripture
is crude, perverse, erroneous. A secret meaning besides the literal one
is a nonentity. Hunting after this, he runs into foolish conjectures.
Many excellent remarks occur in the book, but the wheat is outnum-
bered by the chaff. The best part is that on the New Testament,
especially on the first two Gospels. In exposing the contradictions and
unhistorical character of many parts of the Gospels, he is often effective. Thus at pages 328, 329, the facts of the crucifixion and resurrection, as stated by the Evangelists, are well marshalled in all their
diversity. But his account of the sources of Mark's and Matthew's
Gospels, his partition of their component parts, his judgment of later
and earlier pieces, are uncritical. The least valuable portion is that
on the Old Testament, where the secret meaning attributed to Genesis,
the new translations, etymologies of Hebrew words, and speculations

generally, are all but worthless. The Hebrew learning is grotesque. The
author even attributes the invention of the Masoretic points to Ezra,
and adopts the unfounded notion of Irenæus that the primitive
Hebrew alphabet contained but ten letters. Nor is his account of
Moses at all probable—viz., that he was an Egyptian and a polytheist,
who stole some of the secret knowledge of the priests, and put it in
portions of writing, afterwards embodied in the Pentateuch. The last
part of the work, on ancient mythologies and their secret meaning,
bears remotely on the destination of mankind, and is more curious
than profitable. It is matter of regret that this unknown scholar
should not have used the best literature on the Bible, but followed out
his own tedious processes, and fallen into so many errors. Ingenious
as he is at times, one cannot but mark the haste of assertion which
pronounces that when Paul arrived at Rome for the first time, there
was no Christian church there; that Jews, not Christians, met him
at Appii Forum; that Marcion was the orthodox bishop of Pon-,
tus; and that the last supper took place, according to the synop-
tist, on Wednesday, the 12th Nisan. The unscientific criticism that
abounds in the book will repel scholars; especially such as have successfully contributed to a more accurate knowledge of the Scripture
records in recent times.

Mosheh Ben Shealteth, author of a commentary on Jeremiah and
Ezekiel, seems to have lived about the end of the twelfth century in
Spain and Babylonia. Mr. Driver has edited the commentary from a
MS. in the Bodleian Library, with an English translation.[18] The explanations of the Jewish scholar are usually grammatical or lexical,
and add little to our knowledge of the text, though there are occasional
suggestions deserving consideration. Their interest is chiefly historical. Mr. Driver has published the MS. carefully, adding notes to
his translation which show a knowledge of the Hebrew Bible, and of
modern criticism upon it, superior to what commonly exists in
England. His first attempt at literary work is a good omen of future
labours in the same department, which will probably not disappoint
expectation.

The works of Lactantius, rendered into English,[19] form the 21st and
22nd volumes of Clark's Ante-nicene Christian Library. Little is
known of the history of this Christian father, who belonged to the
latter half of the third and beginning of the fourth centuries, except
that he was a famous teacher of rhetoric, who embraced the Christian
faith in advanced life, and wrote his "Christian Institutes" in its defence, demonstrating the falsehood of paganism as well as the vanity
of heathen philosophy. But his knowledge of Christianity was both
imperfect and erroneous. His views were also tinged with Mani-
cheism, notwithstanding Dr. Fletcher's contrary opinion. The trans-

---

[18] "A Commentary upon the Books of Jeremiah and Ezekiel." By Mosheh
Ben Shealteth, edited from a Bodleian MS., with a Translation and Notes, by
S. R. Driver, B.A. London: Williams and Norgate.

[19] "The Works of Lactantius." Translated by W. Fletcher, D.D. Edinburgh:
T. and T. Clark.

lation now presented to the public, taken from Migne's edition,
is excellent; and the notes in that edition are usually appended.
The Latin of ambiguous, difficult, and peculiar expressions, is fairly
given, by which the reader may sometimes correct the translation.
The translator has also furnished a brief and pertinent introductory
notice. The second volume, besides containing short treatises attributed
to Lactantius, authentic and non-authentic, has an English version of
the Testaments of the twelve patriarchs, from the Greek, by the latest
editor of the original, Mr. Sinker. This valuable document will be
welcomed by many. The introductory notice, extracted from his former work, repeats the inconclusive reasoning which fixes the date of
the writing not later than A.D. 135; whereas it should be the latter
half of the second century, not before 170. The volume terminates
with fragments of the second and third centuries, translated partly
from the Syriac, partly from the Greek, by Mr. Pratten. The former
pieces had been already published and translated by Cureton, and Mr.
Pratten builds on his version, changing words here and there. Although he asserts that his own translation differs from Cureton's
"in many and important particulars," there is reason for doubt. The
author's Syriac knowledge is not great, else he would have corrected
Cureton's mistakes instead of copying them. We do not approve of
work which has the appearance of DISGUISED PLAGIARISM.

Professor Lipsius does not publish large works, like many German
scholars, but his monographs and dissertations, though comparatively
brief, are excellent specimens of sound criticism. Not content with a
superficial investigation, he explores with patience the sources and materials, deducing from them such conclusions as appear legitimate.
His work is done thoroughly and exhaustively, so that the results are
seldom questionable. Under his guidance, the reader may confidently
go into corners of ecclesiastical history not previously explored with
the same minute circumspection. The so-called "Acts of Pilate," published in the best form by Tischendorf, are resolved by Lipsius* into five
constituent parts, viz.:—1. The original document beginning with the
words "In the fifteenth year," embracing the first eleven chapters, professing to be a work of Nicodemus, originally composed in Hebrew; 2. A
document relating to the descent of Christ into hell to deliver souls from
Satan's bondage, circulated under the names of Leucius and Charinus;
3. The production of Ananias or Æneas under the Emperors Theodosius
and Valentinian, which added the first prologue and chapters 17-27 to
the first document; perhaps, too, chapters 12-16. This reproduction proceeds on the basis of No. 1. 4. A second elaboration modifying and enlarging the book of Ananias, professedly written by one
Æneas a Jew, and translated by Nicodemus into Latin, is not earlier
in date than the second half of the fifth century; 5. The text, extant
in some Latin MSS. of chapters 12-20, which gives two additional
chapters. Those who believe with Tischendorf that because the Acts

of Pilate are referred to by Justin and Tertullian, they prove the existence of the four canonical gospels at the beginning of the second century, will find substantial proof of the fallacy of such argumentation in Lipsius's masterly essay. It is impossible to prove that either of the fathers had *the present* Acts of Pilate before him.

The second work of the author," on the origin of the legend which makes St. Peter a resident and martyr at Rome, contains an able investigation of the sources from which it sprung, and the forms it assumed accordingly. The older account represents Peter as following Simon Magus into different countries, and finally defeating him at Rome; the younger one makes the apostle travel along with St. Paul to Rome, where they established the church in friendly co-operation, and suffered martyrdom under Nero. Agreeably to the old Jewish-christian view, Simon Magus meant none other in this legend than Paul, who was regarded as a false apostle, and as ultimately overthrown by Peter. Ebionite sources contain the older view, Catholic ones the later. The author enters upon a detailed examination of the Clementine Homilies and Recognitions which give the early Jewish-christian opinion in relation to Paul's apostolic authority, describing his final defeat at Rome, not because it was thought that Peter ever came thither, but because his victory over a hated opponent was all the more illustrious in the capital of the world. After an examination of the Catholic Acts of Peter and Paul, the author proceeds to the Gnostic Acts of those apostles, which exist only in fragments of different recensions, especially in the Passion of Peter and Paul attributed to Linus. It is instructive to observe how all recollection of the anti-Pauline origin of the Simon-legend disappears among the teachers of the Catholic Church as early as the end of the second century. In uniting the two stories, it was desirable to efface the attitude of hostility between the two apostles. But the fusion was not effected in the same way; for some accounts made the apostles meet at Rome for the first time, allowing space for Peter's preaching or presidency there; while others represented both together disputing with Simon, so that his last decisive defeat was brought down to the reign of Nero. The treatise of Lipsius may be confidently recommended as excellent and convincing. It is necessarily full of details, and somewhat dry; but it presents materials for Church History, not a narrative or a biography, and as such has a permanent value.

Mr. Gamaliel Brown's "Sunday Lyrics"" breathe the free sentiments of one who admires God's works in nature rather than the ecclesiastical services of preachers on Sundays. According to him, true devotion excited and cherished by the former, is only hindered by the latter.

Herr Scholl calls himself a free religious preacher, whose object is to promote the religion of humanity. His publications significantly

---

" " Die Quellen der Römischen Petrussage ;" kritisch untersucht von R. A. Lipsius. Kiel : Schwer'sche Buchhandlung.
" " Sunday Lyrics." By Gamaliel Brown. Ramsgate ; Thos. Scott.

entitled "Let there be light,"[10] contain each twelve Hefts or sections, which are reflections, dissertations, or lectures on topics more or less remotely bearing on religion. Oratorical, argumentative, didactic, controversial, the author rejects all that is priestly, maintaining that religion does not rest upon objective faith or doctrinal propositions, on ceremonies, sacraments or mediators; but that it consists solely in a pure heart, in pure morality, in justice, righteousness, active love, in moral freedom and truth; that it rests, in short, in our own self-consciousness feeling itself in union with the Eternal. The author writes intelligently and eloquently. His ideas about the Bible are often just. He illustrates parts of it in the true spirit of an interpreter who knows that letter is inferior to spirit. But he rejects it as a revelation, and abides by the revelation within. Though his views are occasionally extreme, his homiletic addresses have a value, and come home to the bosom of liberal thinkers about God and man. His autobiographical recollections are very interesting, while his pages on St. Paul as a type of the courage and fidelity of conviction, on the worship of Mary and papal infallibility, are excellent. Though he has been suspended long ago from pastoral functions, he can speak and write as a lover of truth emancipated from the yoke of priestly bondage and popular superstition.

Herr Lommel's "Historical Study" respecting Jesus of Nazareth,[11] is a slight sketch of Jesus's person and fate, introduced by a description of the character of the Jews, Romans, and Greeks, because he finds the three national elements reflected in his person. The portraiture of so wonderful a character is neither adequate nor just. It is hardly accurate to depict him as a wandering Essene or Therapeut, a travelling teacher and physician. Nor is the solution of the question, why occurrences so simple have produced world-wide and permanent consequences, sufficient. Herr Lommel dwarfs the significance and mission of Christ too much to afford the means of answering the question which he propounds only to answer perfunctorily. His exposition of the origin of Christianity proceeds on an assumption which contains but a grain of truth.

The second pamphlet[12] contains a brief sketch of Huss, and the proceedings at the Council of Constance, which terminated in his martyrdom. The narrative is concise, but sufficiently extended to give the main points of interest. It is well composed. Herr Lommel has no sympathy with the Christianity that persecutes and murders.

Dr. Lindwurm gives a sketch of things desirable in the establishment of a national Church in Germany, in thirty-four theses.[13] Most of his propositions are practicable and pertinent, deserving the attention of all who desire to see a truly national Church founded on a Catholic basis, with clergymen of culture accountable to God and their own

[10] "Es werde Licht!" Von Carl Scholl. Erster Jahrgang. Nürnberg: 1870. Zweiter Jahrgang: 1871.
[11] "Jesus von Nazareth: historische Studie." Von Georg Lommel.
[12] "Johannes Huss." Von Georg Lommel. Nürnberg: 1871.
[13] "Entwurf zu den Satzungen einer deutschen National-Kirche." Von Arnold Lindwurm, Ph. D. Berlin: Otto Loewinstein.

conscience alone. The defect of the pamphlet in its first paragraph is the not stating what are the few things in all confessions which would form a common basis of belief.

The work of Professor de Coulanges on "Aryan Civilization,"[1] is valuable as a systematic survey of very ancient beliefs embodied in rites, customs, stories, laws. The author supposes that a domestic religion made up of fire-worship and the adoration of dead ancestors gave rise, among the Greeks and Romans, to the family, with its exaggerated paternal authority and its peculiar right of property; that the same religion extended the family through the Gens and the Curia till it formed a city or state where it bore despotic sway, being the source of all rules, customs, and offices; and that new opinions on religion springing up on the decay of old beliefs effected a series of revolutions by which society was transformed. The prominence given to religion as the pervading element of Greek and Roman institutions, is the main feature of the work. Hence the analogy between all ancient cities, which are thought to have passed through the same series of revolution. The chapter at the close on the Roman conquest, is an able and philosophical summary of the course followed by a mighty empire till it was prepared to be set aside. The author's comprehensive sketch is dominated by the leading idea of religious paramount influence amid all the institutions of ancient states. Here perhaps he pushes his theory to excess, not making sufficient allowance for the operation of other causes. But he helps the reader to an insight into the spirit of antiquity; and writes with a good knowledge of the subjects on which he touches. The translator has compressed the original, exercising occasionally an independent judgment, without omitting anything valuable. His work is done indifferently, the sentences being frequently awkward, and the language ungrammatical at times. In abridging and altering, he should have made the marks of translation less palpable.

The papers of Professor Alaux, in his volume entitled "La Religion Progressive,"[2] embrace such subjects as Catholicism and Democracy, including the life, writings, and works of Lamennais; Reason in Faith, represented by Pascal; Philosophy in the Clergy, symbolized by the Abbé Gabriel; the New Public Right, whose text is the work of Mamiani; Pope and King; the Catholic Church and Revolution; the Future Council, now past. The author's object is to set forth such ideas respecting Christianity, or rather Christianity in the form of Catholicism, as would, if carried into effect, make it the permanent religion of humanity. Catholicism, he contends, must be changed into harmony with modern culture, so that it should recognise and respect liberty of conscience without as well as within the Church. Its authority should be solely spiritual, repudiating all pretensions to temporal power or State support. It should insist on morality, not

[1] "Aryan Civilisation: its Religious Origin and its Progress, with an Account of the Religion, Laws, and Institutions of Greece and Rome, based on the Work of De Coulanges." By the Rev. T. Childe Barker. London: Parker.

[2] "La Religion Progressive. Etudes de Philosophie Sociale." Par J.-E. Alaux, Prof. à l'Académie de Neufchâtel. Paris et Genève. London: Nutt.

dogma, requiring of men life instead of doctrine. Whatever doctrine it holds should be reduced to the mere exposition of the facts, psychological and historical, that constitute Christianity, leaving philosophers and others to explain the mysteries which it teaches, without unfolding their secret senses. The application of morality to all public questions and deeds would form an ample field of practical sermonizing. In this way the author projects a free Catholic Church of the future, consisting of brethren equal in rights and immunities, just, charitable, tolerant. It is difficult to see the faintest prospect of these ardent ideal hopes being realized. A united Catholic Church possessing liberty of individual conscience and action, with the ethical element in it chiefly developed in actual life, owning no external authority, but self-contained, is still Utopian. Philosophic Christians, who have emancipated themselves from the intellectual thraldom of Church confessions or organizations, might be attracted by such an institution; but the mass of the people need centuries of education ere they can perceive its desirableness or beauty. The book is written in a fine spirit and style. The essay entitled "Le Nouveau Droit Public," is excellent, and the whole will repay the reader, though the author is too ideal and far-reaching in his views for the present generation of Catholics, or even of Protestants.

Herr Krüger Velthusen adds another to the numerous lives of Jesus published in recent times.[w] His aim is to give a biography accordant with the earnest requirements of critical science as well as the religious needs of humanity. The work is half popular, half critical. The author endeavours to present a connected, comprehensive sketch of Christ's life, based on well-attested facts, and laws of thought considered to be universally legitimate. Distributed in ten chapters, the materials are carefully elaborated into a connected whole. Assuming that the religious life already existing under the Old Testament reached its consummation in Christ, the communications of the Gospels respecting Him are tested and selected which best correspond to the perfect life of faith embodied in Him. Hence the first chapter of the treatise contains a view of the fundamental principles belonging to the Israelite religion and of the condition of the Jews before Christ's appearance. The character and value of such a book mainly depends on the view taken of the Gospels. In this respect Herr Velthusen does not satisfy, because he adopts in substance the opinions of Bleek, which are now superseded. It is too late to maintain, with any probability, that the first appeared in its present form at the time of the destruction of Jerusalem; that the third was written by Luke, afterwards; and that Mark really composed that which bears his name. Nor does it harmonize with the best critical results to assert that the fourth Gospel deserves historical credibility in the main, though it may not proceed from an Apostle. The writer evidently misconceives the genesis of the last Gospel when he speaks of its "Urschrift," and of the large later additions it received; because it did not grow to its

---

w "Das Leben Jesu." Von W. Krüger-Velthusen. Elberfeld: 1871.

present dimensions after the manner of the others, but is rather the outcome of a single original mind. Velthusen's view of the fourth Gospel necessarily moulds the biography he sketches ; not favourably, as we believe. The entire execution of his plan necessarily suggests Strauss's " Die Halben und die Ganzen." The work is not thorough. As a contribution, however, to the literature of the subject, it has a certain value. The author rightly regards many parts of the evangelical narratives as unhistorical, such as those about the baptism, temptation, and transfiguration of Jesus. So, too, those about his resurrection and reappearances in the body. He also relegates most of the wonderful deeds said to have been performed by Jesus to the region of the natural, without, however, furnishing a proper explanation of the miraculous element attaching to them. It is not a philosophical method of procedure to deny myth and fiction, while holding that certain things are narrated as objective occurrences though they really existed only in the domain of the spirit or the invisible world. The book is eminently weak in the part which attempts to bring the synoptists and the fourth Gospel into a kind of harmony respecting Christ's ministry in Galilee and in Judea proper (pp. 128, 129). It also fails in reconciling the times of the Paschal Supper implied in the Synoptists and fourth Gospel. The perfunctory note in pp. 204, 205 shows that the author's strength does not lie in the critical faculty.

Preacher Schulze belongs to the Lutheran school of Theologians in Germany, and therefore adheres to the old orthodox doctrines, as well as the ancient creeds. He is anxious to explain what are commonly meant by Romanizing tendencies," and to defend them, both on the ground of Scripture and antiquity. Yet he is not an extreme man. He writes with moderation, and is an able apologist of the views held by many. His subjects are the usual dogmatic ones on which High Churchmen have decided views: the Church, the kingdom of God, the congregation, church organization, episcopacy and papacy, universal priesthood and its duties, the sacrifice of the Church, justification and sanctification, man's original and intermediate states, absolution, indulgences and the reverence of saints; the object and ground of faith, tradition and Holy Scripture, true and false Protestantism. All these topics are discussed at sufficient length, and with such references to preceding authorities as may serve to instruct the educated Christians whom the writer has especially in view. Most of the opinions advocated are essentially opposed to the spirit of Protestantism. Christianity is looked at as a system of doctrines long since fixed by the Catholic Church ; episcopacy and other institutions are regarded as divine : the sacraments as administered by priests have a mysterious efficacy ; and the Scriptures are the Word of God. It is vain to uphold these and other analogous assumptions. High Churchism is antagonistic to the genius of the age, which insists with increasing energy on the conscientious exercise of individual judgment, instead of merging it in the thing called Church.

" " Ueber romanisirende Tendenzen ; ein Wort zum Frieden." Von F. W. Schulze, Charitéprediger in Berlin. Berlin.

Dr. Ritter von Rittershain, one of the medical professors in the University of Prague, has published lectures on Psychology, which he delivered to a female audience in 1869, under the title of "Spiritual Life;" considerations on the spiritual activity of the human brain, and its development.[u] These lectures are nine in number, ranging over all the mental states with their relation to the conditions of the brain. The feelings and desires; the will and the imagination; memory, reason, understanding, waking and dreaming, self-consciousness, natural egoism and selfishness, are described in intelligible and popular phraseology. The treatise contains little that is new; but the statements are generally judicious. The last lecture on the "Soul and God," is a superior one; and all deserve the attentive perusal of parents and teachers in particular.

Mr. Andrews, who calls the science of the universe universology,[n] dividing its two grand departments into Anthropology and Cosmology, thinks that he has discovered the basis of this new science to be resemblance or unity universalized, *i.e.*, extended to all spheres. He also finds three primitive laws or fundamental principles of universology, which he calls Unism, Duism, and Trinism. "From these three laws," says he, "the whole universe is wrought out, by their successive repetitions in new forms of manifestation, in infinite variety; but in serial order, and traceable regularity of structure, from the lowest to the highest domain; from the basis of the scientific pyramid in the abstract Mathematics, up to its culminating point in Theology, or the Science of God." The large volume, in which the author unfolds his new discovery, contains introductory papers by various writers who sympathize in his system, a copious vocabulary, six chapters, and a digested index, making nearly nine hundred pages. With the new science, we are introduced into a new vocabulary, which is often strange to the ear. The variety of topics is very great. Metaphysics, Mathematics, Theology, Science, contribute to the author's argument, which claims to be a complete demonstration, "a perfect interpretation of the purposes of the Deity in creation, and the entire unfolding of the creative plan of God; not only as expressed in organic forms, but as involved in every sphere of thought, and being in the universe of matter and of mind." Years of reading and thought have been spent upon the scheme here set forth. But though parts of the book are interesting, and tolerably clear, the whole scheme seems to be the product of fancy. The new science, with the uncouth language in which it is explained, is a generalization as intangible and useless for all scientific

---

[u] "Geistesleben: Betrachtungen ueber die geistige Thätigkeit des menschlichen Gehirnes und ihre Entwicklung." Von Dr. Gottfried Ritter von Rittershain. Wien: 1871.

[n] "The Basic Outline of Universology: an Introduction to the Newly Discovered Science of the Universe; Its Elementary Principles, and the First Stages of their Development in the Special Sciences. Together with Preliminary Notices of Alwato, the Newly Discovered Scientific Universal Language, resulting from the Principles of Universology." By Stephen Pearl Andrews. New York: Dion Thomas. 1872.

or theological purposes as Swedenborg's doctrine of correspondence. The book is a monument, not only of the writer's persistent search after the impalpable, but also of his perverted phantasy.

Mrs. Hope's volume on the "Conversion of the Franks and the English,"[m] is divided into three parts : Old Germany, the Franks, and the Conversion of the English. The first describes the origin, organizations, character, and religion of the Germans, with the hostile relations between them and the Romans, their conversion to Christianity, and relapse. The second gives an account of the Merovingians, with the lives of St. Benedict, and many of his order ; of the Irish monks, as also of St. Columba and his disciples. The third narrates the conversion of the kingdoms of England ; with a record of many English kings, bishops, and abbots. The work is written in a pleasing style, which will attract readers. Without pretensions to historical research, or breadth of view, and written from a Romanist standpoint it does not separate legend from fact, but glorifies monks and saints after the fashion of the "Acta Sanctorum." The first part is the best ; the others have an element of the marvellous, which severe history discards. To those who can distinguish the true from the fictitious, it will afford useful instruction ; to others, it will prove an erring guide.

Mr. Sergeant Cox was a member of the Committee of the London Dialectical Society, appointed to examine and report on the pretensions of Spiritualism. His pamphlet[n] is a result of all the observations, tests, inquiries, and experiments connected with the subject. He tells us the conclusions arrived at, and his own opinions also. After describing the proved phenomena, he sets forth reasons for believing that the force emanating from, or directly dependent on the human organization, is a purely *psychic* force, not the work of spirits of the dead. The force, he supposes, to be generated in certain persons of peculiar nervous organization, in sufficient power to operate beyond bodily contact; to whom is given the name *psychics*. The intelligence directing the force is probably the brain of the psychic in the condition of " unconscious cerebration." In the presence of the psychic, motions of heavy bodies, and audible sounds of impact upon them, are produced without contact, or material connexion with any one whatever. The pamphlet is written in a calm spirit, by one who reports the evidence of many experiments, and reasons upon them like a man determined to sift evidence, and believe accordingly. The subject needs further investigation. If there be a force antagonistic to gravitation, or exempt from its influence, or at least operating to counteract gravitation on the bodies in which it is diffused, science should be eager to discover all that can be known about it. We recommend Mr. Cox's most interesting pamphlet to the inquiring and curious.

---

[m] "Conversion of the Teutonic Race. Conversion of the Franks and the English." By Mrs. Hope. Edited by the Rev. John Bernard Dalgairns. London : B. Washbourne.
[n] "Spiritualism answered by Science." By Edward W. Cox, S.L., F.R.G.S., London : Longmans and Co.

The psychologist and physiologist should be equally alive to the statements it contains.

According to Mr. Massey there are, broadly speaking, two kinds of mediumship, the abnormal and the normal." Mediums of the former kind are so constituted that spirits can magnetize them and take possession of their physical organism, make use of their nervous system, speak with their tongues, and become for the time the directing soul of their bodies. The little book published by the author on Spiritualism shows full belief in the system, and is an eloquent defence of its main features. But it is not a process of reasoning, nor an attempt to prove that spirits are the cause of such sounds, motions, voices, answers, as are commonly attributed to their presence by spiritualistic advocates. Mr. Massey assumes throughout what less poetical or imaginative individuals refuse to accept because sufficient evidence is wanting. We do not coincide with his eulogium on Swedenborg, or with the general tendency of his remarks, however well expressed. It would be unjust, however, to deny the truth of some of his judgments, such as that on Mr. Harris's effusions, on the fall of man, total depravity, and eternal punishment. At the end he gives various poetical pieces which show taste and genius.

Mr. Owen has written a book to show that the modern revealings of Spiritualism bringing immortality to light are essential to arrest the growing scepticism of the present day." Believing that there are laws under which men and women have occasionally exercised spiritual powers and gifts; that these powers were extraordinarily developed in the first century, and that their existence is traceable throughout the last seventeen hundred years; he finds evidence of similar gifts and powers manifested among us at the present time. The first part of the volume, entitled "Prefatory Address to the Protestant Clergy," shows that Protestantism has lost ground for three centuries past, and is losing it still; that such retrogression is caused by its adherence to so-called orthodox dogmas which the world has outgrown; that Christianity divested of alien scholasticism, which its Author never taught, is a progressive science; and that the admission of miracles brings us into direct conflict with modern science. The books which follow deal with the more prominent and salient of the phenomena that evidence the laws and characteristics of the spiritual world. The whole is written in a clear style, by a thinking, well-read man, who is evidently in earnest. The address to the clergy is able, and generally conclusive. Calvinism is well exposed, and the salient doctrines of the Reformers censured. It was scarcely necessary, however, while exposing Calvin's intolerance, to enter at length into his treatment of Servetus, since the story has been well told by Dyer, whose life of the Reformer seems to be unknown to Mr. Owen, as is also Kampschulte's able work, else he would not have had recourse instead to inferior authorities, such as Principal Tulloch. The author

* "Concerning Spiritualism." By Gerald Massey. London: James Burns.
* "The Debatable Land between this World and the Next. With Illustrative Narrations." By Robert Dale Owen. London: Trübner and Co.

perceives that the teachings of Christ and those of Paul were not in
many cases identical. Preferring the former to the latter, he rightly
rejects certain orthodox doctrines, denies plenary inspiration, infallibility in man or Church, and holds to law rather than miracles. His
retrospect of the religious past since the Reformation is good. But
when he comes to prove that the teachings of Christ have been supplemented by revealings from a higher sphere of being, and that this
happens in accordance with intermundane laws, his arguments are
doubtful. He fails to explain aright the possessions spoken of in the
Gospels, and the powers said to have been exercised in healing,
prophesying, speaking with tongues, &c. Nor do we suppose that he
judges correctly the patristic evidence regarding miracles. Mr. Owen's
ideas about the times when the synoptic Gospels were written, and
the method in which they grew to their present dimensions, are vague
and inexact. His view of the fourth Gospel is equally so. There was
a sufficient interval between the ministry of Christ and the three
synoptists to allow of myths and legends gathering around it. The
fourth Gospel is later still. The true explanation of what he brings
under the laws of spiritualism in the first century must be sought in
the appetite for the marvellous, the magnifying reverence of an
uncritical age for persons and things invested with a sacred halo.
Some New Testament passages much relied on by Mr. Owen, such as
John xiv. 12, xvi. 12, 13; Mark xvi. 17, 18; Matthew xxviii. 20,
contain sayings never uttered by Jesus Christ. In like manner, he
uses the Acts of the Apostles in an authoritative way rejected by
modern criticism. The collection of cases respecting apparitions,
visions, rappings, revealings, movements antagonistic to gravitation,
is a curious one, whatever philosophy be applied to them. That
spirits good and bad are the active agents in them requires more
proof than has been adduced. The doctrine of immortality is hardly
strengthened by such super-mundane proof. Mr. Owen is more successful in the province of theology than that of spiritualism, though
even in the former he needs to be corrected. In maintaining that the
reign of law is universal and unchangeable, and that conscience is the
supreme arbiter, he serves the cause of modern culture, though we
cannot find with him the nature or mode of the extraordinary communications recorded, worthy of ministering spirits. The proof, tangible
to the senses, of the reality of another life, which they are said to
furnish, has something about it alien to the kind of evidence on such
a subject, which the Deity would probably give.

Dr. Cohen's book on Kant[*] is chiefly directed against Kuno
Fischer, but also against Trendelenburg and Schopenhauer. Hence it
is polemical in character. It is also explanatory of the system and
defensive of the method which the Koenigsberg philosopher followed.
The book shows great acuteness. In consequence, however, of the
ground taken, the perusal is attended with peculiar difficulty. The
points discussed are the most important in philosophy, such as

[*] "Kant's Theorie der Erfahrung." Von Dr. Hermann Cohen. Berlin:
Dümmler.

Perception, Experience, the Phænomenon and Noumenon, the concepts Reality, A priori, &c. The writer also endeavours to bring Kant's theory of Perception into accord with the modern or Herbartian psychology; but is scarcely successful in showing that Kant had any idea of a sound psychology. The volume is a valuable contribution to the proper appreciation of Kant's philosophical principles; though it carries some modern and better notions into them, derived in part, however indirectly, from later metaphysicians who have criticised, not without effect, the writings of one whose merits are universally admitted.

Herr Steudel has published the first part of "Philosophy in Outline,"[*] containing theoretical questions; promising that the second on practical questions will follow immediately. He has pondered long over the subject, and professes to give the ripe fruit of a life's thoughts upon it. In opposition to the prevailing method of synthetic speculation, he adopts the analytical. And he has also striven to write clearly, in language intelligible to the public, not in the technical phraseology of philosophy. After an introduction on the object and form of philosophy, the contents of the volume are divided into four books, the first treating of Perception; the second of Being in general; the third of Man; the fourth of God and the World. The scheme is comprehensive, leaving no question of importance untouched. The object of philosophy is said to be the establishment of the truth, the latter being described as "the agreement of the idea with the actual though non-apparent ground and essence of the objective and subjective world." This is ambiguous, because we know nothing of the unseen nature of things, except by our ideas of them. Materialism and spiritualism, as well as dualism the uniting link of the two, should be cleared away, as Herr Steudel thinks, to make room for a mere "principial identity" of spirit and matter without "dualistic difference." His definitions and conceptions of matter and spirit are neither clear nor good. It is difficult to see how the solution of the soul-problem is attained by regarding matter as the outward formation or development of the "principial spirit;" or to believe that the mode in which he unites these two entities strikes a blow at Pantheism, or proves the untenableness of Materialism, whose opponent the author professes himself to be. The work is written in plainer language than that usually belonging to German works on philosophy. But it neither presents the highest speculative ability, nor contributes to the solution of the profound problems that have exercised so many minds. Its principal use is as a summary of the philosophical views propounded by the leading metaphysicians of the Continent, accompanied by the researches of one who has trod the field of inquiry independently. Though the analytic method seems preferable to the synthetic, as it is more accordant with our English predilections, the author does not arrive, as far as he has yet gone, at more satisfactory conclusions than Schelling, who begins with the idea of the absolute; or Hegel, who believes that the result must be prepared at the beginning of philosophy.

[*] "Philosophie im Umriss." Von Adolph Steudel. Erster Theil. Theoretische Fragen. Stuttgart: Metzler.

POLITICS, SOCIOLOGY, VOYAGES AND TRAVELS.

MR. FRASER RAE'S translation of M. H. Taine's "Notes on England,"[1] is already widely known through the columns of the *Daily News*, from which it is reprinted; but beyond the interest excited by M. Taine's observations of England, this volume claims special attention, owing to Mr. Rae's own admirable criticisms on his author, as well as to M. Taine's Theory of Criticism, which here first appears in English dress. This theory, or system, is wholly comprised in the remark that moral matters, like physical things, have "dependencies" and "conditions." "What is in question here is a form of experiment similar to what scientific men perform in physiology or in chemistry." "A career similar to that of the natural sciences is open to the ethical sciences." Mr. Rae adds to this translation of M. Taine's system his own reply, that there is "a fundamental difference between the positions occupied by the botanist and zoologist, and the critic and historian. The former have no personal and national bias in favour of the results of their observations." And he cites M. Taine himself, in his writings on English manners and customs, as well as on men of note in the world of art and letters, as a proof that the diversity of nationality, character, or condition, must destroy the possibility of an exact science of criticism. "He is noteworthy as a writer, not in consequence, but in spite of his method. Strip off everything relating to it in his several works, and the works themselves will continue to attract and impress; they will still reflect the beauties of his own mind, and be radiant with the splendours of his brilliant style." Mr. Rae's description suffices to attract readers to the pages that follow his own.

It is curious that at the present day, after the writings of Bentham, Austin, and Maine have so completely exploded the countless fallacies that have gathered round the expression "Law of Nature," an erudite Scotch Professor should think it worth his while to devote a closely-printed volume to vindicating the use of the term "Nature," in speculations on the history of Law. Professor Lorimer's work[2] exhibits a genuine love of his subject, and much erudition. It is also fraught with sagacious and valuable observations scattered about up and down. But it is, we conceive, infected with the radical error which Bentham and his eminent successors have done their best to root out—that of banishing jurisprudence to a misty region of purely abstract or merely nominal conceptions, instead of testing its practical value by direct application to the actual problems of making and administering law. The sole purpose of studying "the science of law,"

[1] "Notes on England." By H. Taine, D.C.L. Oxon. &c. Translated, with an Introductory Chapter, by W. F. Rae. London: Strahan and Co. 1872.
[2] "The Institutes of Law: a Treatise of the Principles of Jurisprudence as determined by Nature." By James Lorimer, Advocate, Regius Professor of Public Law and of the Law of Nature and Nations in the University of Edinburgh. Edinburgh: T. and T. Clark. 1872.

is the discovery of what is essential and universal in the laws of all countries, with the ulterior purpose of arranging the laws of each country according to a scientific instead of an accidental and empirical mode of distribution. Professor Lorimer says that "the proximate object of jurisprudence, the object which it seeks as a separate science, is liberty," and "jurisprudence, in realizing its special or proximate object, becomes a means toward the realization of the ultimate object which it has in common with ethics." There is, no doubt, a deep meaning to be extracted from these assertions, but we conceive the form of expression is most objectionable. It is left doubtful whether "jurisprudence" means the study of law, or the existence of law, or a system of actual laws. Again, it is more than questionable whether a "science" can be said to seek anything except truth, and whether liberty can be said to be the proximate—though it undoubtedly is the ulterior—object of laws. It would not be fair to extract a single passage like this for criticism if it did not, with the rest of the book, teach that Bentham, as a jurist, ought to be studied over again by this generation, instead of being only casually, and then disparagingly, alluded to, as he is, by Professor Lorimer.

Jurisprudence is one of those subjects which lie just near enough to the territory of speculative philosophy to be shunned by the practical lawyer and politician, and just near enough to the region of the most intense human action to be unpalatable to the abstract thinker. It is from this cause, perhaps more than from any other, that Law Reform—certainly not the least important opening for national energy—proceeds sometimes so hesitatingly, sometimes so rashly, and rarely indeed with the calm and assured certainty of tread which only convictions, based on scientific conclusions, can give. Professor Sheldon Amos'[1] views of what he calls "The Science of Jurisprudence," are steeped, from first to last, in practical detail. His "Analysis of Topics," which is worked out with considerable precision, is redolent of the thoughts of the lawsuits, the controversies, and the judicial trials with which the daily papers are filled. In the author's eyes, unless the science he cultivates is good to improve the laws of England, and to bring them into harmony with the demands of logical arrangement, as well as with the most approved methods of classification adopted in Foreign Law, that science either does not exist or is good for nothing. Nevertheless, this work is eminently addressed to students. "It is to serious students, professional and unprofessional—men and women—that this book is addressed; though no book—if it serve its purpose as book—can dispense with oral teaching,—if oral teaching also truly serve its purpose as such." The method of the writer is, after a few brief introductory chapters on the scientific claims and place of Jurisprudence, and the nature of Law, to classify, according to their social character, purpose, or importance, all the laws necessarily existing in any highly-developed community. Thus the leading divisions of the work are: "Laws directly relating to the

[1] "A Systematic View of the Science of Jurisprudence." By Sheldon Amos, M.A. London: Longmans. 1872.

Constitution and Administration of the State," "Laws of Ownership,"
"Laws of Contract," "Laws affecting Special Classes of Persons" (as
husband and wife, guardian and ward, trustees and executors, and
certain classes of public corporations), "Laws of Civil Injuries and
Crimes," and "Laws of Procedure." There is a chapter on "Private
International Law," and one of the longest and most elaborate ones in
the book on "Public International Law," in which the nature of this
sort of law, and many of the most abstruse questions attending it, are
discussed at considerable length. In the closing chapter on the
"General Prospects of the Science of Jurisprudence," the topics of
Codification and Legal Education, and others, are treated from a variety
of points of view, in which all sides will find themselves represented.
Englishmen, now-a-days, are mostly acquainted with Jurisprudence
through the works of Mr. Austin and Sir H. Maine. It is a misfortune
that they study Bentham's works so little. The present work starts
with the conception of Jurisprudence which commended itself to Mr.
Austin; and, in fact, the purpose of the work is to carry out, in the
most exhaustive manner, the task which Mr. Austin just sketched out
in his lectures and left unperformed. The historical and antiquarian
achievements of Sir H. Maine, as well as all his keen, suggestive,
logical, though too occasional, criticism, are, of course, laid under
tribute, and, in fact, incorporated. The whole question of codification
is vigorously investigated with especial reference to the existing condition of English Case-law and Statute-law. In the course of the
work, all the most stirring topics of legal interest are thrown into the
crucible, though the author's own views in each case are rather left to
be gathered from the underlying principles of the whole book, than from
any distinct siding with one of two parties in a controversy. This will
be found especially to apply to such topics as Capital Punishment,
the Unanimity of Juries, a Court of Criminal Appeal, the Institution
of a Public Prosecutor, the French Verdict of "Extenuating Circumstances," Difference of Sex, and Competing Modes of Legal Education.

It has been complained in some quarters, not without reason,
that the historical method of studying Roman, and, indeed, all
other law, is threatening to dwarf or supplant the logical method.
Anyway, as the study of Roman Law is now rightly accepted as an indispensable ingredient in a complete legal education, and that study
cannot be detached from that of the meaning of its terms, it is just
as well that a true meaning should be put upon those terms instead
of a false one. We may thus well be thankful to a real scholar like
Mr. E. C. Clark,* who not only explores with laborious assiduity into
the origin of some of the most perplexing expressions by which the
ancient institutions of Regal Rome are represented, but gives in the
most concise and convenient of forms all the authorities of which he
has made a most conscientious use. It will be found, indeed, that
this little work, which is, in truth, one of considerable learning, and
betraying much acuteness of criticism, has a liveliness and freshness

* "Early Roman Law: the Regal Period." By E. C. Clark, M.A. London:
Macmillan. 1872.

about it which could scarcely have been looked for; as, for instance, where an early form of making a will, subject to the sanction of the pontiffs, is compared to the passing of a private act of parliament, subject to the veto of the Episcopal Bench.

Mr. J. A. Partridge' is already well known to the Liberal public by his comprehensive work on " Democracy : its Factors and Conditions," in which he demonstrated that the only perfect system of government is that which results from "the development and organization of the whole manhood and of all men." It is the result of a living organism, not of "constitution," "balances," or "mixtures." Such a government Mr. Partridge explained to be found in a democracy, but the ideal could only be approximated. It is the progressive story of this approximation which is the subject of the present work. " Democracy rises from nationalities to ever vaster conglomerates of power. It becomes the postulate of a new and unknown progress, and is the germ of a universal federation." It must be confessed that Mr. Partridge has a genuine faith in his own principle. He has not a particle of fear as to the consequences of working out that principle to its last conclusion. He is prepared, not only for the greatest possible diffusion, but also for the greatest possible concentration of power. It will be seen from the following passage that Mr. Partridge does not look to checks, minority representation, second chambers, or the like, " to protect the people against themselves," or to secure the claims of the weak against the strong. " Either the government is a majority or a minority. In the latter case freedom is absolutely disregarded; it is a question of force, not of argument. In the former case, the majority must be broken down by appeals to public thought and reason, not by attempts to dictate to the sovereign power. Let the national intellect be open to all influences and opinions, industrial, intellectual, spiritual, natural, and then let it act." It seems to us that though the actual picture which Mr. Partridge presents in this work of a grand and magnanimous democracy is sufficiently attractive, yet that some consideration is due to the fact that the mere number of individuals alone can never be a test of truth or a standard of justice. It is true that, in the last resort, a mere numerical balance of supporters must determine the actual policy to be pursued, and on this ground a mere majority in a legislative assembly will properly carry the day. But for purposes of deliberation, and even for the very purposes, which Mr. Partridge recognises, of letting in "the action of influences and opinions," it may be expedient to secure the adequate representation of even the most isolated fragments of the community.

Mr. Freeman adds to his reputation and to the benefits which he has already conferred on his countrymen by his new volume on the English Constitution,' in which his "object has been to show that the

---

* "From Feudal to Federal ; or, Free Church, Free Schools, the Completest Bases of Equality ; with some of its Results in State, Constitution, and Empire." By J. A. Partridge. London : Trübner. 1872.
' "The Growth of the English Constitution." By E. A. Freeman, M.A., Hon. D.C.L., &c. London : Macmillan and Co. 1872.

earliest institutions of England and of other Teutonic lands are not mere
matters of curious speculation, but matters closely connected with our
present political being . . . . that in many things our earliest institutions come more nearly home to us, and that they have more in
common with our present political state than the institutions of
intermediate ages." " The holders," he continues, " of Liberal principles in modern politics need never shrink from tracing up our
political history to its earliest beginnings. As far as our race is
concerned, freedom is everywhere older than bondage. We may add
that tolerance is older than intolerance. Our ancient history is the
possession of the Liberal, who, as being ever ready to reform, is the
true Conservative." Much of the evil which calls for the energy of
present or future Liberal reformers is ascribed to lawyers, who appear
to Mr. Freeman to be great, though admittedly necessary, evils in a
state of society the disorder of which is largely of their producing.
The nearest approach to the ancient Teutonic constitutions is to be
found, says Mr. Freeman, in the popular assemblies of Uri and
Appenzell and other Swiss cantons, answering to those ancient
assemblies of our shires or hundreds, which are,—almost comically,—
in our days represented by parish vestries, " that unit, that atom, the
true kernel of all our political life." The smaller districts being
gradually welded into larger masses and resulting in the complete
kingdom of England,—though so slowly that until the reign of
Charles II. the county of Durham retained so much of its individuality
as to be counted unfit to send a knight of the shire to the national
Parliament,—the right to vote in the Assembly in all secular and
ecclesiastical matters continued to belong to every freeman, and
" down to the Norman Conquest, the body which claimed to speak in
the name of the nation was, in legal theory at least, the nation
itself," however much difficulties of travel may have kept the members
of the Assembly down and restricted attendance at it to the rich and
leisurely, except in times of popular excitement. This welding
together of the larger aggregates of " political units " brought with
it a change in the title of the chieftain; " it is plain that the king
was the representative of a closer national unity, while the caldorman
represented the tendency on the part of each tribe or district to claim
independence for itself;" the word king being properly traced back to
its relation, cyn, or cyne, and thus meaning " the offspring of the
people." The successive invasions by Saxon, Dane, Norman, brought
no essential changes in the English theory of government, for the
same forms existed with modifications amongst them as among the
English, and thus the right of the nation to exercise a discretion as to
the men who should exercise dominion over it was never lost; " men
never forgot that the king was what his name implied, the representative, the impersonation, the offspring of the people. It was from
the choice of the people that he received his authority to rule over
them." . . . . " And those who gave him his power, and who guided
him in its exercise, could also, when need so called, take away the
power which they had given. At rare intervals,—for it is only at
rare intervals that so great a step is likely to be taken,—has the

English nation exercised its highest power by taking away the crown from kings who were unworthy to wear it. Six times at least" (omitting the instances of Henry VI. and Charles I.) "in the space of nine hundred years have the Witan or the Parliament thus put forth the last and greatest of their powers. The last exercise of this power has made its future exercise needless. All that in old times was to be gained by the deposition of a king can now be gained by a vote of censure on a minister, or, in the extremest case, by his impeachment." Mr. Freeman writes enthusiastically of Simon de Montfort, the great earl to whom, stranger as he was, "we owe that the wonderful thirteenth century, the great creative and destructive age throughout the world, was to us an age of creation, and not of destruction," and to whose burial-place—though he died excommunicated by the Pope—Englishmen attributed miraculous powers; "a pretty convincing argument that the Bishop of Rome hath no jurisdiction in this realm of England." At the same time it should be borne in mind that from the reign of John onward, the alliance was between the whole people and the clergy against the King and the Pope, and that the much vilified "right of clergy" extended to a large part of the population, and meant liability to imprisonment and whipping instead of to the barbarous mutilations inflicted by the king's courts of justice. It is impossible further to notice many most interesting points of constitutional history that are brought into relief in the short space of Mr. Freeman's bright, vigorous, and compendious lectures.

Mr. John Matthews, of Toronto, Canada, gives an interesting review of the state of the Colonial question in a very clearly and ably written volume,[7] in which he advocates as close a junction as possible between England and her colonies, on the principle of a representation of the dependencies of the empire in the British Parliament. Mr. Matthews grapples closely with the adverse arguments of Mr. Goldwin Smith and Mr. Mill, whether based on the commercial, military, and financial aspects of emancipation, or the physical difficulties of federation. The basis upon which the number of colonial representatives, according to Mr. Matthews's plan, would be elected, would be either population or taxation. His own belief is, that neither of them alone would serve for an equitable basis, but that such a basis might be found in a combination of the two. "If population were to be ignored in the distribution of taxation, it would clearly be unjust to make it supreme in the adjustment of representation. To do so would be to arrange burdens according to the system of *relative* equality, and privileges according to that of absolute equality." The whole work is extremely interesting, both for the intrinsic value of the line of thought followed out, and as an exhibition of feeling in Canada.

Mr. Thomas Longman, in a short pamphlet,[8] and a letter already

---

[7] "A Colonist on the Colonial Question." By John Matthews, of Toronto, Canada. London: Longmans. 1872.

[8] "Some Observations on Copyright and our Colonies." By Thomas Longman. London: Longmans. 1872.

contributed to the *Times*, he calls for a repeal of an Act of Parliament
passed in 1847, the purpose of which was to permit her Majesty
by an order in Council to suspend the law of copyright as between
this country and any colony in which "the legislature shall pass an
Act to make due provision for securing and protecting the rights of
British authors in such colony." It is alleged that the working of
this Act is a complete failure; that no provision is made in Canada, for
instance, for securing and protecting the rights of British authors;
and that American copies of all the best works of English authors are
freely imported over the border. Mr. Longman urges that the Act be
repealed, and the English law, as now determined by the Act of
1842, be "replaced in its full effect." The purport of this last Act is
to prevent the selling in any part of the British dominions of any book
for which a copyright has been obtained in any part of the United
Kingdom, and which has been reprinted out of the British dominions.
Canada has lately proposed a compromise on the subject, the adoption
of which Mr. Longman deprecates.

Sir Edward Creasy' has made a valuable supplement to his well
known and extremely useful work on the "Rise and Progress of the
English Constitution," in a new work on the "Imperial and Colonial
Constitutions of the Britannic Empire." The present work, like the
former, is, on a variety of grounds, the highest form of educational
treatise, and on that account likely to be quite as serviceable to the
politician needing reliable information on some special topic as to the
youthful student. The early part of the work expands the notion of
the English Constitution previously given, so as to include the relations of England to Scotland and Ireland; for which purpose the
history of the Union in each case, and the legal consequences of it,
are carefully investigated. In a similar, partly historical, partly legal
spirit, the whole relations of England to her North American dominions, to India, and to the Australian and African colonies, are examined and particularly explained. Sir E. Creasy adheres to the method
which gave so high a value to his former work—that of giving copies
of original documents *in extenso*. Another valuable feature of this
work is presented by some excellent maps.

The existing slave trade in Africa, carried on for the supply of
Turkey, Egypt, Persia, and Zanzibar, seems to vie with all the horrors
of the trade in men to the Southern States of America, which our
fathers finally crushed under foot. It is to be hoped that when once
their offspring are made acquainted with the facts, they will not rest
till they have achieved as decisive a victory. Mr. Joseph Cooper" has
done a service to humanity in translating and preparing in a form
adapted to extensive circulation in this country M. Berlioux's work
on the slave trade in Africa. The miserable story is told by a variety

' "The Imperial and Colonial Constitutions of the Britannic Empire, including
Indian Institutions." By Sir Edward Creasy, M.A. London: Longmans. 1872.
'' "The Slave Trade in Africa in 1872. Principally carried on for the Supply
of Turkey, Egypt, Persia, and Zanzibar." By Etienne Felix Berlioux. From
the French. With a Preface by Joseph Cooper. London: E. Marsh. 1872.

of witnesses, and its locality is extended through the middle and upper valley of the Nile, through Central Africa, and to Zanzibar. Slavery is exhibited in all its wonted abomination, whether as respects the sufferings of the victims, or the reckless greed and cruelty of those who traffic in it. For instance, from the town of Tripoli to Lake Tchad there are nearly twenty degrees, an extent of land more than twice and a half the length of Great Britain. "It is by this route that the convoys of negroes are driven by their pitiless masters, condemned under the burning sun to the tortures of thirst, hunger, and famine." M. Rohfs, who was an eye-witness of these things during his explorings between the years 1865 and 1867, gives the details as follows:—"On both sides of the road we see the blanched bones of the victimized slaves—skeletons still covered by the *katoun*, the clothing of the blacks. The traveller who knows nothing of the road to Bourman, has only to follow the scattered remains, and he will not be misguided." The slave trade at Zanzibar has some features of even still greater atrocity, inasmuch as treaties, signed by British agents with the princes of Zanzibar, have authorized the slave trade by attempting to regulate it. "From Quiloa to Lamoo, Arab merchants may buy, sell, and transport slaves with impunity. English cruisers armed against the slave trade may see all, but they must do nothing." And yet it is asserted that in the passage of the slaves from Zanzibar to Arabia the vessels lose one half of their cargoes during the voyage. The slaves are exposed without shelter to the sun's rays, and to all storms that may arise. Once a day a little water and thick milk is doled out to them. We may certainly re-echo the writer's conclusions, that the only worthy solution England can give is that made by the House of Commons, "that the trade must be entirely suppressed: it must be nowhere authorized, and the treaties must be annulled."

The general apathy of the English public on Indian questions is made vividly apparent by the size of publications put forth by those who would stir public opinion on Indian topics. That statements affecting the welfare of whole kingdoms, or presidencies, or races, or even the entire Indian Empire, should be short and sharp, seems to be necessary if they are to receive any notice at all. To Mr. Chesson's admirable Lecture on the Princes of India attention was called by us last quarter, and Major Evans Bell's last work[11] now affords an opportunity for enlarging on one of the most glaring cases of abuse of power named by Mr. Chesson. It is well that it should be made possible to compare together Major Evans Bell's opinions, to the effect that the problem of Mussulman disaffection is "the most urgent one of the day," and that the wrongs done and proposed to be done to the great Mahommedan family of the Nawab Nazim of Bengal are likely to be felt as race and religious persecutions throughout India, with the opinions expressed in an article on "the Mussulman Panic," in the last number of this *Review*. The Bengal case, as viewed by

---

[11] "The Bengal Reversion, another Exceptional Case." By Major Evans Bell, London: Trübner and Co. 1872.

Major Evans Bell, may thus be briefly sketched. The Principality of Bengal, one of the richest in India, was recognised in 1757 as an Independent State, under the Nawab Meer Jaffier, by the East India Company, and a treaty was made by them with him. In 1765, under his son and successor, the Company became invested by the treaty with the Dewannee, or financial administration of Bengal; and a sum known as the "Nizamut Fund" was agreed upon to cover the expenses of the Nawab's "household, servants, retinue, and the support of his dignity only." Another sum was set apart as tribute to Delhi, and the rest of the resources of the Principality were left for the expenses of administration. In 1793, after (be it noted) the successive long minorities of two Nawabs, the Company appears in possession of all the functions of government, including the judicial department, as well as in the enjoyment of large landed estates which were family property, and of one half of the Nizamut income, of which it had arbitrarily suspended payment during the nonage of the younger of the princes. That suspension was extended indefinitely till it became permanent, and the stipend was reduced to 100,000*l.* per annum, the amount at which it has nominally stood now for a hundred years. For the monthly proportion of that sum the Nawab is required to give a receipt in full, although the shares severally allotted to collateral members of the family are theoretically, and have already been practically treated as lapsing on the death of the receivers, to the Government of India, as trustees of the fund, and not to the Nizam as head of the family. In fact, the Nawab receives 70,000*l.* per annum. As though these pecuniary plunderings, in the face of treaties entered into for the support of the *family*—not of each individual Nawab—"to be inviolably observed for ever," were not enough, it appears from a despatch of June 17, 1864, that the English Government—acting on a policy sketched by Lord Dalhousie, in pursuance of his very remarkable views as to British right of annexation in India, and grounded on an unjust and arbitrary condemnation by him of the Nawab—passing by the incalculable services rendered to England by the Nawab in 1857, which have practically received, according to Major Bell, a singularly scant recognition—resolved to degrade the family from its sovereign position on the death of the present Nawab Nazim, and to conceal this intention from him. A garbled copy of the despatch was sent to him, such as was calculated to assure him that the hereditary dignities of his sons would, as a matter of course, be recognised. He came to England to remonstrate and to press his pecuniary claims. He is met with statements in Parliament which would be made grotesque by the ignorance of the officials supposed to be conversant with Indian affairs, did they not go furth to a House and a public little inclined or able to trouble themselves with such distant and intricate questions, which appear to them to affect only one princely family in India. It is not evident on the surface of things that these misstatements and wrongs affect the principal family of Mahomedan India, the honour of the Mahomedan fifth of the population of Bengal, and of one half of educated Bengal. And yet that there is a subdued uneasiness pervading all India is on all sides admitted. Major Evans Bell points to the opinion of Sir John Kaye, that the great danger of a Mahomedan rising in Bengal—more particularly if it could start from Moorshedabad as a centre, with ostensible countenance from the Nawab—was " very patent," in 1857, " to the minds of our enemies, but no thoughts of this kind disturbed the minds of our people." In the midst of the Mutiny, Mr. Taylor foresaw this danger, and as Commissioner of Patna, arrested the leaders of the Wahabees in Patna. His superiors were tranquil in mind, and disapproved his activity. He was removed, and driven from the service, while the " Wahabee gentlemen" were caressed, honoured, and salaried. In 1864, the principal of them was transported for life to the Andaman Islands for treason. Immediately after his conviction, an unsuccessful attempt was made on the life of his judge by a Mohamedan. Two other Wahabee gentlemen, among others, were arrested, and detained by the Viceroy's authority, just as the others had been on Mr. Taylor's. On the threshold of the Court where they would have been brought that day for judgment by Chief Justice Norman, he was murdered by a Mahomedan. A relative of that Mahomedan, and a fellow-prisoner of the Patna convict, struck down Lord Mayo.

These facts need to be weighed, and their importance is in no degree diminished by the pamphlet" Mr. James Wilson publishes on taxation grievances that press on the poorer populations of India, Hindoo and Mahommedan alike. He only gives us Wahabeeism *plus* oppression as a change from Wahabeeism alone. He strongly denounces the conduct of Lord Mayo's Government, while giving due reverence to the beauty of Lord Mayo's personal character and aims, and suggests as the only excuse for some of the acts of that Government, that they were under the " express sanction" of the India Office,—understood in India itself to mean "express command." When Lord Mayo entered office, Indian finance was " unsatisfactory." The income-tax was proposed as a remedy, and each member of the Council expressed his conviction that it was unsuitable to India, and—with the exception of Sir William Grey—voted for its imposition on all incomes above 20*l.* per annum. The work of assessment was divided among officials who each had an extent of territory which it was simply impossible for them to work themselves, and they have necessarily subdivided—or farmed—it. Those who are able to procure immunity by a bribe, have been found willing to do so. Mr. Reid, senior member of the Board of Revenue, believes that " the natives of India have paid as much in the form of bribes, to escape payment of the tax, as they have paid into the Government treasury as income-tax." Mr. Wilson gives a large number of testimonies on this point, equally, if not more strong. Some of the Calcutta papers have given publicity to notorious instances of oppression within short distances of Government House. From a number given by Mr. Wilson one shall suffice, and the reader will find others substantiated in his admirable and useful pamphlet. This

" " Why was Lord Mayo Assassinated ? The Question considered." By James Wilson, Editor of the *Indian Daily News.* London : Ridgway. 1872. Price 6d.

is extracted from a vernacular paper, and probably "1-2" is a misprint for 12.

"Many days ago, we wrote, a poor man was assessed in the Koomarkhalle Subdivision at Rs 6. Not able to pay it, the judge" (having no discretion in the matter) "fined him Rs. 12, and in default he was sentenced to twelve days' imprisonment. His property was sold, and realized Rs. 1—2" (about equal to 2s. 3d, or, if misprinted, to 1l. 4s. 0d.). "The amount then demanded was raised to Rs. 15, and the man was again apprehended for the remaining Rs. 3. The judge again mulcted him in double the amount, and for Rs. 6 instead of Rs. 3 he was sentenced to twelve days' imprisonment with hard labour." "If his property could realize no more than Rs. 1—2, it is clear that he ought not under the law to have been assessed." "This man supported his family by his daily labour; he is now imprisoned, and what have they to look to? The Mahomedan rulers took away property by force; Biswanath Baboo was a noted robber. But these afflicted the rich, not the poor. Our Government says the tax only affects those who have property; but here we cannot walk on the streets for the crying of the poor."

From the perplexities and distresses laid bare by Major Evans Bell and Mr. Wilson, it is a relief to turn to a scheme[13] for reducing the taxation of India, by diminishing the cost of the British Force, held necessary for the security of British Rule in India, as well as for diminishing and destroying some of the evils inflicted by a military life on the troops themselves, and on the surrounding communities. 65,000 men is the assumed necessary strength of the Army for holding India in times of peace. Besides these a reserve of force is obviously needed for times of disturbance, of drains upon English resources elsewhere, or of both simultaneously. The writer of this pamphlet would supply this needed Reserve by localizing the soldiery through engaging them, after a certain term of service and good conduct, as military settlers, and—in return for stipulated military service, to be continued when needed—advancing money for building houses and settling; giving a retiring allowance, and half the ordinary allowances for wife and children; the land to become absolute property after a short term of years. The plan might be so worked as to offer inducements to enter the Army of India to a higher class of recruits than we have at present; while the various causes here pointed out, of the failure of the military settlements in Halifax in 1749, in the Ukraine in 1737, in Algeria, in New Zealand, at the Cape of Good Hope, and in India among the Himalayas, might, without difficulty, be avoided, and a valuable group of colonies of young, married, disciplined English workers would tend not only to hold, but to raise the populations of India.

Mr. Capper, whose "Wanderings in War Time"[14] were contemporaneously described by him from time to time in the columns of the *Times* and of the *Daily News*, reprints his account of the miseries of

---

[13] "Military Settlements in India." Reprinted from *The Madras Mail.* Madras: 1872.

[14] "Wanderings in War Time; being Notes of Two Journeys taken in France and Germany." By S. J. Capper. London: Bentley and Sons. 1871.

the late war, to which he was witness during a tour made by him, unofficially, between the 11th of August, 1870, and the few following weeks; a tour relieved from all possible accusation of unseemly spectatorship of the woes of foreign lands by the deep and practical sympathy with the sufferers which Mr. Capper not only showed himself, but stirred up in the hearts of many at home by his vivid and impartial writings. Immediately after his return to England, in the end of September, he urged upon the Society of Friends their special duty to undertake the task of relieving the distress of the peasantry around Metz; and six months later was induced to go himself to aid in the distribution of the " War Victims' Fund," " the committee of which, before they closed their labours, had distributed 80,000*l.* worth of relief to the distressed peasantry, and other non-combatant sufferers by the war." Written from a non-military point of view, detailing experiences gained under conditions peculiarly favourable to a knowledge of the real thoughts of the two belligerent parties, and coming from a singularly dispassionate and open-minded man, Mr. Capper's volume has great value as a whole, and many will especially prize the summary on the causes of French defeat and the necessary conditions of French revival, with which Mr. Capper concludes.

Mr. Kingsman's " Over Volcanoes"[15] describes a visit made by him and his friends to Spain at about the same time as Mr. Capper's second visit to France and Germany. But Mr. Kingsman's lacks the serious, earnest tone of Mr. Capper's, just as the objects of the two journeys differed, although the business journey to Spain is attempted to be relieved from all suspicion of spying out the calamities of England's nearest neighbour. Finding it was easiest to go through Paris, Mr. Kingsman does not fail to give utterance to the popular sentiment as to the " truculent set of ruffians" forming the " 100th Battalion of National Banditti," and the dangers of pillage at their hands, which his luggage escaped; as well as to a less popular but facetious account of the conduct of the German military occupiers of Amiens and other towns. Paris is then described, and the journey through France, together with the conversations held by the fellow-travellers on a large variety of subjects, from Republicanism, Standing Armies, the Wine-trade, the possibility of setting up a Water-cure Establishment in the Escurial, the delightful excitement of a Spanish Bull-fight, the chances that King Amadeus would retain his throne, to the state of religious opinion in Spain. It should be added, that for those who like their information in a light form there is a fair amount of detail of facts about Spanish history and literature, with quotations from some principal writers, and some good local description; but more disquisition on things in general than anything else.

Women must not be tempted by the title of " My Wife and I in Queensland"[16] to apply to its writer for information as to what their

<hr/>

[15] " Over Volcanoes; or, Through France and Spain in 1871." By A. Kingsman. London : King and Co. 1872.

[16] " My Wife and I in Queensland: being an Eight Years' Experience in the above Colony, with some Account of Polynesian Labour." By Charles Eden. Longmans : 1872.

chances are in the Australian colonies, unless, indeed, they are content
to be in the position of utter nonentity in which Mr. Eden leaves
" My Wife" as soon as possible and as entirely as possible. They may,
however, gain some information that may be useful from the intensely
masculine tone of the whole society described—if the term " masculine" may for this purpose be used to denote a certain recklessness of
the well-being or happiness of others, incidentally including women,
very positively including " black-boys" and their " gins," and barely
disguised in a rose-coloured account of the extreme happiness of the
life led by certain Polynesian labourers whom, towards the end of his
varied Australian career, Mr. Eden employed on his sugar plantation.
Of these men Mr. Eden says that, under their own chosen leader, they
would work " in a conscientious way that you would seek for in vain
among Europeans. . . . . I have often left them for a fortnight at a
time, having pointed out what was required, and on returning found
they had done considerably more than I had expected of them."
" We never rationed them, giving them as much as they liked to eat,
which was a saving in the end, for they were always contented and
happy, and with a little encouragement grew their own vegetables,
and hardly drew upon the store at all." " Ordinary animal food they
did not seem to care much about, more particularly salt meat; but I
am convinced that they are cannibals—at all events, these Tannamen."

An essay on " Woman and her Social Position,"[17] written in the
pages of this Review thirty years ago by a lady whose opinions have
only been ripened and strengthened by time and experience, presents
an instructive historical episode in the history of the great movement
for the enfranchisement of women. It is for the first time that this
essay has appeared with the writer's name attached, and she has every
reason to take an honest delight in at length divesting herself of her
incognita.

" For this reason," says Mrs. Mylne, " I am pleased to have it reprinted in
my own name; for I feel it would be cowardly at my age to shrink from
avowing that forty years added experience of life has not altered my views,
but rather deepened and confirmed my early impressions. If I once thought
the independence of women desirable, I now think it indispensable as a human,
rather than a woman's right."

The essay itself possesses a high degree of interest from the number
of eminent writers whose views it embodies or criticises, from the
independence and vigour of style which characterizes it throughout,
and from the balance of judgment with which a subject is treated, too
often, in these days, marred by rhetoric and declamation.

The progress of the movement for women's education is demonstrated by an interesting comparative survey, undertaken by a German
writer,[18] of the modes in which the subject is practically dealt with in
England, North America, Switzerland, Italy, France, and, lastly, his

---

[17] " Woman and her Social Position." An Article reprinted from the *Westminster Review*, No. lxviii. 1841. London: G. Green. 1872.
[18] " Mädchenerziehung und Frauenleben im Aus- and Inlande." Von Gotthold
Kreuenberg. Berlin: 1872.

own country, Germany. The writer shows a very careful study of the various grades of educational institutions in this country, from ragged schools to young ladies' academies, establishments, or schools. His strictures upon the most improved methods of education for women in England are that they are devised without sufficient consideration of the different social positions and functions of men and women.

" With the introduction of a well-grounded and methodical education for women, the outgrowths of English life, the errors involved in ' emancipation ' and ' woman's rights ' will speedily vanish, being, as they are, partly the result of a half culture, and partly of an excited condition of fanatical women."

The writer is of opinion that in the lower education of women Prussia has much to learn from England, but not in the higher. It is true that, if men's education be bad and insufficient, to copy it for women is folly, but the question as to how far the minds of men and women must have the same training in virtue of their common humanity, and how far that training must be different in view of their variety of functions, cannot be solved by mere platitudes about " woman's rights."

The writers of " sensation " novels, if no one else, will thank Mr. Browning" for the lucid manner in which he has handled the English " Laws of Marriage and Divorce." It is well known that the greatest possible uncertainty prevails as to the actual English law on some of the more perplexing cases of marriages and divorces of English citizens in foreign countries. It is all the more difficult to ascertain and declare a rule universally binding that England and Scotland have different marriage laws, and in some respects the English laws of divorce differ from the laws of every other civilized country. Mr. Browning's method of treating the subject is the best that its present state admits of. In the Introduction he describes the constitution and general power of the English " Court of Probate and Divorce," and in the first chapter the laws of marriage, the conflict of marriage laws, and the effect of the domicile of the parties in limiting the jurisdiction of the Court. In the succeeding chapters he explains and illustrates by reference to decided cases the law and procedure peculiar to each form of suit.

A curious French squib (though it seems serious enough), on English institutions and customs is presented in a lively little work, entitled " English Liberty laid bare,"* by Jean-Jacques Dauphin, who recounts to his friend, William Tell, " his adventures on a visit to his neighbour and ally John Bull." Jean-Jacques represents himself as having fallen in love with British Institutions, and having visited his friend John Bull in order to acquaint himself with " the secret of his liberties." The result of the visit is a melancholy disenchantment. The survey travels over a considerable ground, and the

---

ⁱ⁸ " An Exposition of the Laws of Marriage and Divorce, as administered in the Court for Divorce and Matrimonial Causes." By Ernest Browning, of the Inner Temple, Barrister-at-Law. London : Ridgway. 1872.

ⁱ⁹ " La Liberté Anglaise mise à Nu." Par Jean-Jacques Dauphin. Paris : 1872.

criticisms are neither devoid of sparkle nor even, at times, of justice. Thus the rush of carriages in Hyde Park during the season—the state of the agricultural labourer, the absurd anomalies presented at times by the operation of our party politics—in which the leader of the liberal party resents a more liberal reform bill than his own—the eccentricities of Murphy and the general circulation of the "Confessional Unmasked," the wealth of the Church, the absurd vauntings of England that her armies have never been defeated—are topics which, at least, have a very quotable and salient side for a pleasant, not to say sardonic, foreigner to turn to very good literary account.

It is rather an ambitious task, though perhaps not too much so for a laborious and erudite German, to attempt to give a history of society, in its several varieties of formal expression, as "Aristocracy, the Middle Classes, and the Lower Classes."[n] Dr. Johann Joseph Rossbach, for each of the main departments of this subject travels over the chief developments of the most characteristic nations in the world. For instance, as to the Middle Classes, he investigates the rise of social order in the East, examining the Babylonians and Phœnicians, together with the grounds and influences of despotism. Passing on to the West, he discovers in the tenure of land and the settlement of warlike tribes, the foundations of society and of liberty. Among the Greeks he traces the passage from the patriarchal condition to that of social ranks, and finds in the institution of a king a mediatorial functionary interposing between the nobility and the people. Rome is then called to contribute her historical light for the solution of the problem, and this is found in the constant struggles of the patricians and plebeians, and in the gradual equalization of the middle classes of society. The problem is then handed on to the modern world. Finally the other elements of the social state are submitted to a parallel historical analysis.

Mr. Ruskin[d] continues his prophetic denunciations against things that are, though some of the objects against which his quaint, half-comical, half-self-conceited, half-satirical, and half-insane battering-ram is directed have already been too much bruised by more potent machinery to be worth the expenditure of Mr. Ruskin's precious time. How precious that time is appears from the following note:—

"Letters addressed to me must be very short and very plainly written, or they will not be read ; and they need never ask me to do anything, because I wont do it. And in general I cannot answer letters ; but for any that come to help me, the writers may be sure that I am grateful. I get a great many from people who 'know that I must be good-natured' from my books. I was good-natured once ; but I beg to state in the most positive terms that I am now old, tired, and very ill-natured."

The main bugbear of Mr. Ruskin in the present letter is the legal

[n] "Geschichte der Gesellschaft." Von Dr. John Joseph Rossbach. Wurtzburg: 1868.
[d] "Fors Clavigera : Letters to the Workmen and Labourers of Great Britain." By John Ruskin, L.L.D. Letter the Sixteenth. Mr. G. Allen, Heathfield Cottage, Keston, Kent.

phraseology, character, and parchment of a Deed of Release he has just had to sign. He contrasts, with rather amusing effect, a short sentence in four or five lines, having exactly the same purport as the deed with the actual language employed in it.

We have great pleasure in calling attention to two works of a class which we hope will become increasingly common. One of these is by Professor Thorold Rogers,[a] and in the smallest possible space, and the simplest possible style, contains "a series of lessons on 'Social Economy' for the upper classes of Primary Schools." No better description of book could be devised for saving children and young persons at the outset of life from the countless fallacies in which the vast majority of people are now-a-days floundering all their lives long. There is scarcely a perplexing topic in the machinery of social life which is not dealt with, and the principles involved in its solution carefully expounded; such topics, for example, as the various rates of wages, the use of gold and silver, public charities, the work of government, the punishment of crime, regulations on professions, poor-laws, and emigration. A similarly useful book is supplied by the "People's Edition" of M. Bastiat's "Essays on Political Economy,"[b] in which a variety of interesting economical and theoretic political questions are discussed in a forcible and telling way, so as to arrest attention and stimulate the beginner to further researches.

The name of Malthus has so long been bandied about from one political party to another, whether as a name of honour or of reproach, that it is high time the present generation should get to know what that name really implied. A new edition of the Rev. T. R. Malthus's[c] "Essay on the Principles of Population," presented in a most attractive and readable form, may, it is hoped, induce many who had hitherto contented themselves with talking about Mr. Malthus' principles, at last to make themselves acquainted with them. It will be seen that Mr. Malthus was the very reverse of the hard, unfeeling, morose, and passionless man he is sometimes painted. The main practical object of his book was, in the interest of the poor themselves, to discredit the existing system of poor relief, and to propose the way for a gradual abolition of poor laws by striking at the root of the doctrine that the poor have any natural "right" to legal relief. "It cannot but strike the labouring classes, that if their main dependence for the support of their children is to be on the parish, they can only expect parish fare, parish clothing, parish furniture, a parish house, and parish government, and they must know that persons living in this way cannot possibly be in a happy and prosperous state."

In the direction of Mr. Malthus's doctrines in disparagement of poor-

---

[a] "Social Economy: a Series of Lessons for the Upper Classes of Primary Schools." By James E. Thorold Rogers, M.A. London: Cassell. 1872.
[b] "Essays on Political Economy." By the late M. Frederick Bastiat. People's Edition. London: Provost and Co. 1872.
[c] "An Essay on the Principle of Population; or, a View of its Past and Present Effects on Human Happiness." By the Rev. T. R. Malthus, A.M., F.R.S. London; Reeves and Turner. 1872.

laws, are the views of Professor Fawcett,[*] as conveyed in an essay on "Pauperism, Charity, and the Poor Law," forming one of a volume of detached essays by himself and Mrs. Millicent Garrett Fawcett on a variety of subjects, economical, educational, and purely political. Professor Fawcett says, "The economic and social condition of England ought to be regarded as radically unsound and unsatisfactory until it becomes the custom, and not as it is now, the exception, for working-men to insure their lives, and to provide themselves with annuities for their old age. The acquisition of these habits of prudence is discouraged not only by the whole tone of public opinion, but also by the sentiments of professed moralists. Those who aspire to be popular, and are anxious to be thought good, are never tired of proclaiming that every man has a right to live, and that the State ought to find work for those who need employment." While candidly adopting Professor Fawcett's repudiation of such principles, we can scarcely believe they are as prevalent as he imagines, and we are rather disposed to attribute the inaction or vicious action, of which he complains, to indolence or inattention, than to anything so formidable as conviction.

SCIENCE.

IT is a remarkable fact in the history of mechanical science that the theory of friction[1] considered as a part of rational mechanics, has hardly ever received the attention which it deserves. Even in the most complete systematic treatises the space given to its discussion is small, compared with that accorded to questions in which the assumption of perfect smoothness forms the basis of all investigations. Great thanks are therefore due to Mr. Jellett, who has in a similar manner, years ago, paved the way for a more extended study of the Calculus of Variations, for having attempted to place the theory of friction on an independent footing; the discussion of the force will thus not only gain in dignity, and may add some day to wider laws embracing all forces, but the results of previous inquirers will at the same time cease to be considered as mere corrections to be applied to mechanical investigations in order to render their conclusions more adapted to practice. The philosophical execution of Mr. Jellett's plan appears to be somewhat fettered by his starting at the outset with the assumption of the proportionality of the force of friction with the pressure. This law, although it represents the facts with sufficient exactness, is not mathematically correct; and although the results of the theory approximate closely to the truth, it seems to us that it should not have been made throughout the leading principle of it. By the adoption of a more correct, although complicated law, the difficulties of the

---

[*] "Essays and Lectures on Social and Political Subjects." By Henry Fawcett, M.P., and Millicent Garrett Fawcett. London: Macmillan. 1872.

[1] "A Treatise on the Theory of Friction." By John H. Jellett, President of the Royal Irish Academy. Dublin: Hodges, Foster, and Co. 1872.

author's work would have somewhat grown, and the results would still have been not quite coincident with facts, but the difference would have been only a final one, not one going through the whole. What is worse, such a giving-in before difficulties, which are perhaps only imagined, cannot be conceded in a more lofty investigation like the present. On the other hand, the author has done everything to give adequate range for either a practical or philosophical extension of the subject. Thus the indeterminateness which often appears in statical questions, where friction is one of the acting forces, is, in Chapters II. and IV., particularly considered, and truly traced to its source, namely, the abstractions of rational mechanics. For there can be no doubt, that all indeterminateness disappears, if the conditions of any problem be stated as they really exist in nature. Throughout the work a great number of distinct problems of high importance is given and well discussed, and we have no doubt that Mr. Jellett's work will attract general scientific attention to the properties of a remarkable force, and will secure for the theory of it a more ample discussion than has yet been given to it.

The manifest tendency of our present science to revise thoroughly even special theories, to subject them anew to the test of experimental comparisons, to give them a wider range by connecting links into chains, and to remodel altogether, or place on a new basis, what appears doubtful, is not only the more deep-seated idea which pervades Mr. Jellett's work, but is also clearly traceable in the work by M. Winkler[*] on a new theory of the pressure of earth upon revetments, and in M. Kötteritzsch's[*] treatise on Electrostatics. It is well known that all the exertions of the most gifted mathematicians as well as of practical men, to embrace the facts connected with the pressure of earth upon walls in a satisfactory theory, have not been crowned with much success. M. Winkler's chapter on the history of this inquiry is the best proof of the variety of views which have been promulgated by the most competent investigators. All theories have one error in common; the approximate formulæ which give the results, start from the assumption of a prism which disintegrates in a plane; but it is absolutely proved, that the surface of separation cannot, in general, be a plane. M. Winkler's theory has this novelty, that certain applications of the law of elasticity are replaced by consequences drawn from that of friction and cohesion: on the action of these latter forces his theory is built, and his experiments deserve, certainly, attention by the close agreement of some results with his theoretical deductions. The author will probably admit that he has not nearer approached to a generally valid and exact solution of the problem than his predecessors, and we are glad to see that M. Winkler possesses the impartiality to admit (page 102) the value of Professor Rankine's labours in the same direction. Indeed, Rankine has, if we are rightly informed, in-

---

[*] "Neue Theorie des Erddrucks, nebst einer Geschichte der Theorie des Erddrucks." Von Dr. E. Winkler. Wien: R. v. Waldheim. 1872.
[*] "Lehrbuch der Electrostatik." Von T. Kötteritzsch. Leipzig: Teubner. 1872.

cluded formulæ in his classical textbook on Mechanics, which cannot rest on any other theory but one in close agreement with that of M. Winkler, whose special merit, however, consists in having devised experimental contrivances for testing it. The work on Electrostatics by M. Kötteritzsch is purely mathematical, and aims principally at reducing the basis of the mathematical theory of Electrostatics to a few experimentally established principles, and at a simplification of the methods of treating electrostatical problems by some processes, which may be admitted to be really original and elegant. The introductory chapter on the potential is not treated with that clearness which we find in the writings of Sir William Thomson and other founders of this branch of Physics; but the second, and especially the fourth chapter, in which a comprehensive view of the sum total of the theoretical results is given, are so interesting and well digested that we earnestly recommend their perusal to anyone who wishes to see for himself to what grand conclusions such theoretical inquiries into physical subjects may lead, even if founded only on a few experimental facts. One cannot help thinking, after having read these portions, that if ever the yet intangible portions of Molecular Physics, or rather the Physics of the Æther, should be capable of being comprehended into one great generalization, it is to Electrostatics that we shall have to look as the true source from which truth will ultimately spring.

Messrs. Fort and Schlömilch[*] are so well known in this country as eminent mathematicians that any production of their joint labour is sure of a welcome reception. Their analytical geometry is a model of a good textbook, written especially with a view to the requirements of technical students, and the applications of that part of mathematical science to constructive applications. Although mere niceties are excluded, the student is nevertheless everywhere made acquainted with a great variety of analytical methods in geometrical investigations. We have especially noticed several remarkably striking demonstrations which are simply founded on the transformation of co-ordinates; thus the proof, instead of deriving its supply of facts from other parts of geometry, is in itself an illustration and application of the original conception which underlies analytical geometry. The reader will be surprised to find how often well known facts are presented to him under a perfectly novel aspect by being quite incidental results of the algebraical processes to which analytical geometry necessarily leads. The authors have throughout avoided that mixing up of ancient and modern methods, which leads, in so many English textbooks on the same branch, the student into a kind of mathematical jungle in which the reader is either lost, or becomes so bewildered that even if he gets out of it the intrinsic beauty of the scenery and luxuriance of vegetation has made no impression whatever on his mind.

Mr. Frost's[*] "Treatise on Curve-tracing" is not only a remarkable work

[*] "Lehrbuch der Analytischen Geometrie." Bearbeitet von O. Fort und O. Schlömilch. Erster Theil. Leipzig: Teubner. 1872.

[*] "An Elementary Treatise on Curve Tracing." By Percival Frost, M.A., formerly Fellow of St. John's College, Cambridge. London: Macmillan and Co. 1872.

in itself, but a welcome sign of modern influences upon the mathematical teaching at our universities. A branch of mathematics, which may be almost termed the poetry of the science, is treated here in a manner at once original and captivating. It is not the least merit of this work that the methods of drawing Polar curves, rolling curves, and the discussion of geometrical loci has been excluded, for the author has with wise forethought aimed at making his work accessible even to those who have a comparatively quite elementary knowledge of mathematics. Another great merit is the exclusion of all historical surveys of the researches which have been made in former times on modes of generation and properties of particular curves, and in modern times on their singularities. It is specially necessary to point out such negative merits of a work at a time, when it not unfrequently occurs that in ostensively elementary works, which ought to give a succinct statement of their subject matter, the exposition of the latter is at every page interrupted by historical data, and even by a discussion of the relative claims of rival discoverers. We have, in looking through Mr. Frost's work, been particularly delighted and struck with the fact that probably, independently of its influence in developing the mental training of every class of mathematical and physical students, no class of readers will derive from it so much lasting and novel enjoyment as ladies who have mastered a few elementary mathematical facts and methods, and can devote part of their time to a regular study of Mr. Frost's Curve-tracing. No other branch of the exact sciences will give them such an inexhaustible mine of pleasure as slow and steady working through page after page of this work. But the practical student of Statics, Engineering, and Crystallography will also find many hints on the subject of Graphical Calculation, which is coming more into use every day, and is applied with so much success to many difficult problems. Mr. Frost has well understood how to avail himself of his wide mathematical research, to point out everywhere to the reader the application also which his subject, or at any rate some portion of it, has in optics and astronomy; and he deserves praise for especially laying stress upon the comparison of large and small quantities of different orders of magnitude, which contains the starting point of many of the most important applications of mathematical analysis; the lunar and planetary theories depending almost entirely upon such considerations of relative magnitude.

A new textbook of Physics has been produced by Professor Weinhold.[*] It is certainly such a work as we have long wished to see in the hands of students, and probably one of the most valuable and excellent treatises on the subject which have appeared for a long time even in Germany, where there is hardly any gap in scientific literature that is not filled up by the best workers. But Professor Weinhold's book has one remarkable feature, hitherto, as far as we know, completely wanting in any textbook that we have seen: it is this, that he directs the student to discover all important physical laws for himself by a series of, in many cases, very delicate experiments, which he may perform quite by himself with extremely little expense. But it must be distinctly stated that these experiments are by no means boyish or superficial; not only are they in many cases quite new and devised with great power of invention, giving proof of a very long experience in the laboratory, but they are such experiments as would not be out of place if publicly performed at the theatre of the Royal Institution, or before a class aiming at high scientific instruction. Professor Weinhold proceeds on the whole thus: he gives first a general description of the experiment; then follows a statement of the conclusions to be drawn from it, and finally there is, in smaller type, a most minute instruction given for the details, which are to be attended to for the successful performance of the particular experiment. There is really nothing forgotten, even the manner of holding a bottle or a tube between the fingers, and there is a full description of all operations of a physicist in the clearest possible language, including everywhere the most sagacious hints for avoiding failure where failure is possible. If this book should appear in an English version we may prophesy for it a great and well deserved success. It will to the student of every age open a true insight into the manner in which physical truths are discovered, and will undoubtedly transform many an English youth's workshop into a physical laboratory.

Mr. Proctor' is a theorizing astronomer; but unlike the majority of those who have given their greater energy and more constant thoughts to speculations built on the facts observed by others, he has brought to his speculations sound knowledge and genuine proficiency in those sciences on which his hypotheses hinge. Besides, his various star-maps and celestial atlases have done undoubted and great services to astronomy and to astronomers. The "New Star Atlas" before us is perfectly delightful to look at. It is the best collection of star-maps we have ever seen: cleverly conceived, practically executed, methodically arranged, and scientifically irreproachable. It will certainly, Mr. Proctor may pardon us the prophecy, bear his name to future times, when, as we fervently hope in the interest of genuine astronomy, his "star depths" will be long forgotten. Turning now to his second work' before us, it appears to us at the present time almost a general conviction, and one growing stronger from year to year, that no real service has ever been done to society by what is usually called the popularizing of scientific facts. A great scientific discovery, a new truth, an ingenious hypothesis can always be stated to the great body of educated people in precisely the same terms in which it is presented to the professional scientific workers; in a few cases only is a translation of symbols into common language required, but in all cases it seems to be now an admitted fact, that the time given to the perusal of the superficial, anecdotic, and often even incorrect

---

' "A New Star Atlas." By Richard A. Proctor, B.A. London: Longmans. 1872.

' "Essays on Astronomy." By Richard A. Proctor, B.A. London: Longmans. 1872.

Journalistic productions on scientific subjects is wanted, and that the information can not only more easily, but in all respects more satisfactorily and lastingly, be obtained by simple and well written elementary textbooks. Mr. Proctor, who is a very clear and reliable writer on astronomical facts, has always avoided the unpleasant flippancy of the "popular" science writers. His articles, speaking at this moment of those only that have appeared in various journals, and are now collected, possess a dignity of tone to which we must accord our admiration, and are perfectly free from those oratorical ornamentations which disfigure so many writings even of our best physicists and astronomers. His articles on Sir John Herschel are written in a manly style, and remind us somewhat of the "éloge" and "Denkrede" of the Paris and Berlin Academies. The various papers on Solar Researches are however, too polemical, and should have been somewhat remodelled on bringing them from the confined, and at the time when they were written, somewhat hot atmosphere of the "Monthly Notices of the Astronomical Society," before, we suppose, calm, pleasant, and gentlemanly people. All the foot notes nearly might have been suppressed with great advantage, especially to the author himself. The papers on Mars and Saturn, are the most admirable specimens of clear and truly scientific statements on the history and results of a particular research, which we have read for a long time.

The general aim of the inquiries into "Air and Rain," by Dr. Angus Smith,[*] is especially to show the fallacy of what has hitherto been believed an undoubted scientific fact, namely, that the composition of our atmosphere is so far uniform everywhere, that the small discrepancies found to exist, are rather to be ascribed to errors of experiment than to fact. Dr. Smith has arrayed a vast collection of data, such as probably has never been presented at one glance at any time, and has also lutely proved that there are impurities in our atmosphere which may be discovered by chemical analysis, and that the senses and general impressions are not at fault when they speak of the peculiarities of a town atmosphere. By a series of experiments, involving not only an application of the best scientific methods known, but often even their extension and adaptation to novel purposes, it is now proved beyond any doubt, that it is not a mere fancy to suppose that air in a crowded room is really "tainted," for the existence of organic matter, capable of nourishing organic forms, is now demonstrated by careful experiment. It would be impossible to discuss here so widebearing investigations upon a subject of the very highest importance to mankind, nor do we think that Dr. Smith has quite completed his labours or brought them to any general conclusions embodying absolute laws on the subject; but while every acknowledgment of genuine services rendered to society is due to the successful prosecution of the inquiry on the composition of air and water, and the causes which govern it in various localities, we entirely fail to see that the author has made out any link whatsoever

---

[*] "Air and Rain. The Beginnings of a Chemical Climatology." By Robert Angus Smith. London: Longmans. 1872.

between Climatology and the chemical constitutions of aerial or aqueous masses distributed over a country or district.

Dr. Aitken has forwarded to us a copy of his able introductory address, delivered at Netley on the opening of the twenty-fourth session of the Army Medical School in April last.[10] It is proverbially difficult to give any air of novelty or even of much permanent interest, to performances of this kind, but the spirited and excellent address of Dr. Aitken is decidedly worth reading. The title, so suggestive in itself, is a good evidence of the character of the contents of this pamphlet, which is devoted to encourage medical men to throw themselves boldly into the stream of scientific progress, and to claim a place beside the forward workers in others of the great branches of human inquiry. Dr. Aitken, like many of the best men of the present century, is inspirited by the contemplation of the great material results of modern western civilization, and is an enthusiastic believer in the capacity of the race for infinite development in the future. "I believe," he says, "in *no limit* (the italics are ours) to the onward march of human progress in the coming time," and thus, full of hopes that burn, he eagerly calls upon those of the profession to which he belongs not to lag behind in the great doings of the present half-century, "which," he thinks, "have not been equalled in any other like period of the world's history." We shall be the last to carp at such noble enthusiasm as this; none can be more conscious than ourselves that such faith is the great motive power needed for the accomplishment of great ends. If, therefore, we were disposed to demur to the too absolute assertion that analogy and sound reason predict a future progress without end or turning, we should nevertheless allow the speaker to be practically right, by admitting, undoubtingly, that great progress in certain directions is now being realized, and that any terms and limitations which may be inherent in it are too indefinite and invisible to have control upon our present hopes and exertions. If again we shrink from granting that man, measured by his mental stature, is higher now than ever before in the world's history, we think that the vantage-ground on which we stand is so much higher as to give us powers beyond those ever before available. We may read, too, with all the warmth of the speaker himself, those eloquent passages in which he urges the rising generation to cultivate the individual intelligence and to master such abstract and technical science as may bear upon their daily duties. Many of us may have our doubts concerning the all-sufficiency of the material prosperity now so pretentiously great, but the more our doubt the intenser our trust in that coincident advance of physical science which is without any parallel in the past, and which as yet serves to strengthen and

---

[10] "The Influence of Human Progress on Medical Education." By Dr. Aitken. Pamphlet. London: Griffin. 1872.

purify a generation which otherwise is not free from some discomforting symptoms of decay.

This little treatise,[11] which in its title at least reminds us of the immortal essay of Hippocrates, is an enlargement of some letters written by the author on the injurious effects of impure air and water on health, and the methods by which such impurities may be detected and removed. This is a handy, useful little book, making less pretence to novelty than many a worse one; and setting forth in a clear and convenient way much information of a kind of the highest importance to the general public.

In his essay[12] read before the Harveian Society last February, Dr. Day puts opportunely and carefully before the profession, some considerations on the true nature of "infantile remittent fever," which, however, can scarcely lay claim to the charm of novelty. Amid much that shows the author to be a skilful and observant physician, and much of interest in the cases recorded and compared, we are sorry to find a number of those inaccurate platitudes which so much disfigure our modern medical literature. The "eliminations" hypothesis, if tenable at all, certainly cannot be used in the crude acceptation of the author; nor would any one who really thinks of the meaning of the words assert, that "the dose of the scarlatinal poison influences the amount of throat, skin, and kidney affections," &c. Surely this is an utterly unproven statement at best, and probability suggests that the quality of the poison and the state of the receiver, are at least of equal importance.

Dr. Lawson[13] begins thus: "A clever friend advises me against writing a preface;" we rather wonder that the clever friend did not advise him against writing the book at all, for few books are more open to the kind of slashing criticism which "clever friends" know so well how to administer. In spite of a good deal of confident dashing through difficult places, and in spite of a firm determination to urge as an infallible, delightful, and somewhat neglected remedy, the hypodermic use of morphia in sciatica, which remedy is neither infallible nor unknown, and is so commonly used as to cause some fear of its abuse, and to many weak vessels is but too delightful; in spite of these little drawbacks the book is really vigorous and instructive, and therefore well worth reading. The author is evidently a man of quick perceptions, and is a lively, if not a profound reasoner; but what adds still more to the value of his treatise, is the fact that he writes upon a disease from which he himself has suffered horribly. From the study of his own pains he, like Anstie, Salter, and many other distinguished writers, has drawn a genuine inspiration. To have felt in one's own person, is a marvellous stimulant to the descriptive powers, and what Dr. Lawson so graphically tells us of the ways of Sciatica, is very valuable to those dull persons who have not enjoyed the stimulant of such experiences as his. We had marked many passages which we had

[11] "The Hygiene of Air and Water." By Dr. Proctor. London and York. 1872.
[12] "The Remittent Fever of Children." By Dr. W. H. Day. Pamphlet. London. 1872.
[13] "Sciatica, Lumbago, and Brachialgia." By Dr. Lawson. London. 1872.

looked forward to as the texts for more than one friendly encounter
with the author, but we feel disposed to forbear, and to take the little
book as it stands, with many thanks, and with sincere congratulations
to the author and the public on his recovery, without which no book
could have been written. On treatment, however, we must, without
argument, take occasion to differ in the most decided manner from Dr.
Lawson. Hypodermic morphia does not always cut short sciatica even
when used as the author directs ; on the contrary, it too often establishes
a periodic recurrence of the pain, with a corresponding recurrence of
insatiable desire for morphia intoxication. On the other hand, the
continuous galvanic current which has been used by ourselves on a
very extensive scale, seems to us to be a far more satisfactory means of
cure. Unfortunately it is but too often out of reach.

Dr. Mackenzie is one of the few physicians who has made a
"specialty" not only inoffensive but useful and honourable. He is
one of the few exceptions which spring to the lips of every one who
is disposed to condemn specialism too sweepingly. Dr. Mackenzie's
own character is partly the reason of this great difference, and the
excellent and thorough quality of his work,[14] which is so free from
any of the parade and flimsiness too often seen in specialists. But
his early bent happened to lead him to the study of a remote subject
which especially needed a prophet. Diseases of the throat were but
little known ; they require a peculiar dexterity for their successful investigation and treatment, and they, like diseases of the eye
and ear, do lie more apart from general disorders than many other
local changes. Nothing can be more adequate and richly instructive
than the present instalment upon "Growths in the Larynx." From
the pathological and diagnostic standpoints, as well as in ingenious
modes of treatment—operative and other—the volume is a most
valuable addition to our knowledge. It will probably stand as a
permanent classic on the subject of which it treats, depending, as it
does, almost entirely upon the author's own personal experience and
but little on compilation. The volume is well got up and is profusely
and beautifully illustrated. The highest praise we can give to
Dr. Mackenzie is that by his lucid and comprehensive writings and
researches he is making his specialty no longer special, but the
common property of all educated practitioners.

Dr. Dobell is one of the most hardworking members of the profession, and his work,[15] generally lies in the direction of practical
clinics and therapeutics. The present volume is of a fragmentary
character, but is apparently intended so to be; we shall certainly
welcome any further instalments of a similar kind. A good point in
the present treatise, is the way in which cases are set forth as the
basis of the whole book, and the points which arise out of these are
argued out and illustrated by the author. The author also undertakes

[14] "Essays on Throat Diseases. No. II. Growths in the Larynx." By Dr.
Morell Mackenzie. London. 1871. Also "Pharmacopœia of the Hospital for
Diseases of the Throat."
[15] "On Affections of the Heart." By Dr. Dobell. London. 1872.

the risk of expressing his clinical experience in the form of aphorisms, and many of these aphorisms are valuable as forcible embodiments of useful hints and cautions. Many of the aphorisms concerning pain at the heart are good and interesting; we would add, what is not generally known, that intercostal neuralgia is sometimes so intense as to simulate true angina, and actually indeed to embarrass the heart itself. Two such cases have occurred within our own notice, and required some careful watching before their essentially superficial character was ascertained beyond doubt. Concerning clubbing of the finger ends, again, the author makes some interesting remarks, and attributes this phenomenon rightly to stoppage of the subclavian veins. He might have illustrated this truth farther by reminding the reader how very greatly the fingers of one hand become clubbed in cases of subclavian aneurism. Dr. Dobell sketches a comfortable and ingenious bed for cases of heart disease, which has been carried out with the pumpkin legs and ugly vulgar detail so characteristic of the British upholsterer.

It is difficult to review such a volume as the following without seeming unkind, or at any rate inconsiderate towards the author, who is no doubt a good surgeon, and has unquestionably taken vast pains to produce a bulky work." Everything, however, must depend upon the circumstances under which the bulky work is produced. Had there been no systematic work on surgery, and had Mr. Gant thrown himself boldly into the gap, we should have congratulated ourselves and the author even on a partial success. But the profession is so well supplied with such systematic works that we become fastidious, and we say if Mr. Gant throws another such a book upon our hands he must justify his temerity. Unfortunately we cannot discover any justification for the existence of the present volume. If there are some paragraphs in it which show that the author has good thoughts here and there, or thoughts which may indeed be really novel and interesting, yet there are scarcely enough of these to furnish out half-a-dozen good contributions to a medical journal, still less to involve their author in the heavy task of instructing his contemporaries in the whole science and art of surgery. In a word, the book is one which might have been written as well by any leading London or provincial surgeon, and by many of them written far better. The only discredit to Mr. Gant in that he has failed in an ambitious and most difficult enterprise, is that he had not better measured his forces before he began. The book as it stands could not have been written by any other than an able and cultivated surgeon, and if Mr. Gant will select a certain few of his chapters, and giving all his intelligence to these, publish them as careful essays on single subjects, he will unquestionably earn that reputation and that right to a favourable reception which his more ambitious labours must fail to obtain.

" "The Science and Practice of Surgery." By F. J. Gant. London: 1871.

HISTORY AND BIOGRAPHY.

WHATEVER may be the destiny which awaits the great and unhappy country which lies so near to our own across the Channel, the present crisis in her history is one that awakes in all friends of progress and culture, the deepest sympathy with her struggles and distress. France more than most nations has undergone rapid vicissitudes and startling changes. At one time under an Emperor she has been amused by visions of military glory never to be realized; at another time under a Commune she has seen her Capital devastated, and her provinces in the occupation of a foreigner. The present time, whilst she is preparing as it were to reorganize the very elements of her existence, is one in which all friends of civilization may well listen to those who are competent to speak of her history and her capacity: and in many respects Mr. Reeve is competent so to speak. The Essays[1] which he now reprints are therefore valuable, inasmuch as they are the work of one who is thoroughly familiar with the French language and the French character, and has had the exceptional advantage of a close and friendly intimacy with the best literary circles of France. At the age of twenty-one Mr. Reeve was already the translator of De Tocqueville, whose friendship he enjoyed until the death of the French writer; and, as he admits, his own opinions "were, no doubt, affected by the influence of that pure and subtle intellect." In the present state of affairs Mr. Reeve sees no comfort. The central event of French history was the Revolution; its causes were of old and necessary growth, its results still prevail, and every stage of the movement has been pervaded with disappointment. The reasons of this disappointment Mr. Reeve traces in the Essays before us, which illustrate certain phases of French history under a Monarchy and under a Republic. The first Essay exhibits the ardour for military glory which animated France in the reign of Louis XIV. That monarch, indeed, by a wily policy not alien from the French nature, succeeded to some extent in aggrandizing the nation, but at the expense of her own real liberty. England, Germany, Spain, and Belgium in various degrees suffered from the guilty diplomacy of his ministers; but in the end France herself was no gainer. This end did not come at once, perhaps it has not even come yet. Mr. Reeve argues from the immoral annals of this reign, that no nation can with impunity neglect the general principles of international justice. Upon this period no writer was better adapted to throw the light of dignified indignant criticism than the Duke of St. Simon, with whom Mr. Reeve's second Essay is concerned. Mr. Reeve shows the sources from which St. Simon found the material for his masterly Memoirs, and illustrates the power with which he infuses life into the doubly-dead mass of details which Dan-

---

[1] "Royal and Republican France: a series of Essays reprinted from the *Edinburgh, Quarterly,* and *British and Foreign Reviews.*" By Henry Reeve. London: Longmans.

geau left behind in the six-and-thirty folio volumes of his diary. Mr.
Reeve makes much of St. Simon's uniform opposition to the king.
He believes that the monarch even foresaw that this noble, whom he
regarded with antipathy, would one day hold up the royal foibles and
vices to the contempt and execration of posterity. If such were
the monarch's presentiments, they have been fulfilled. Mr. Reeve
has amply illustrated the stately independence of the character of
St. Simon; "it is that of a consummate gentleman, who remained
pure when most were corrupt, and erect when all men were prostrate."
But, unfortunately, he has not left the far better picture of an unselfish, devoted man. His partiality does not conceal the aristocratic
cynic, proud of his order, and equally fearless and unconcerned for king
or commons—who disdained in his writings to throw a veil even over
his own weaknesses. In the Essay upon Mirabeau, Mr. Reeve differs
from Von Sybel in his estimate of that statesman's character. He
draws from the letters which passed between Mirabeau and M. de la
Mark, the conclusion that he was an agitator of the most subtle
duplicity, and that far from attempting to establish a Constitutional Monarchy, he sought only to further his personal ambition
by being false both to the Court and to the people. Certainly
no one held so powerful a position between the two parties;
and he died at the right conjuncture for retaining his reputation.
"To the popular cause it seemed, in the anarchy which speedily ensued,
that nothing was wanting but that daring leader; to the Court that the
Revolution might still have been arrested by the counsels of such
a servant." Mr. Reeve's essay on Marie Antoinette opens with a
discussion of the authenticity of the letters attributed to her. The
unpublished letters first collected by the Count d'Hunolstein are specially open to suspicion, and the peculiar circumstances with which
they are surrounded have been commented on with much ingenuity
and more acrimony by Von Sybel. The inconsistencies between this
correspondence and the undoubtedly authentic letters are indeed remarkable. Thus in the authentic letters the Dauphiness speaks to her
mother with natural indignation of the position of Du Barry—"Qui
est la plus sotte et impertinente créature qui soit imaginable." So the
Dauphiness thought, July 9th, 1770. Yet, if the Hunolstein letters are
authentic, she writes, December 7th, 1771:—

"Reste Madame du Barry, dont je ne vous ai jamais parlé. Je me suis tenue
devant *la foiblesse*, avec toute la réserve que vous m'aviez recommandée. . . .
Elle règne. Il pleut dans la moment où je vous écris: c'est probablement
qu'elle l'aura permis."

And this epigrammatic style is attributed to a girl of sixteen!
Mr. Reeve dismisses the Hunolstein correspondence as demonstrably
false; his whole criticism of the letters is admirable and interesting.
Another series of letters, that edited by Fouillet de Conches, also passes
under review. The best part of the essay is that concerned with the
character of Marie and of Madame Elizabeth—"of all the victims
of the Revolution the purest and most innocent." It deepens the
prevalent impression that the Royal family were undeserving sufferers

by the Revolution, and that their martyrdom was borne in a noble spirit. The Essay upon Beugnot is written in an amusing vein, and well depicts the hideous scenes which arose in the times of terror; and the career of Madame Lamotte, who, according to Beugnot, "had a singular love of beer, and who would eat, out of pure inadvertence, two or three dozen tartlets." The story of the diamond necklace is once more told, to the complete exculpation of the Queen; and the terrible stories of the Conciergerie are repeated here. Yet the Reign of Terror, that imprisoned so much of the best and brightest of French life, could not always make its prisoners dull and disagreeable. Even in the Conciergerie there was as much dressing, talking, flirting, and love-making as in the salons of Paris. All these horrors Beugnot saw, and escaped with his life. More, he completely outlived them. In 1830 he was raised to the French peerage, and in 1833 reached the close of a life as honourable, according to Mr. Reeve, as it was eventful. Mr. Reeve's feeling in reference to Napoleon I. is shown by his essay on Mollien. He has no liking for that monarch, and the moral which he draws from the First Empire is an obvious one. The Essays on Chateaubriand and Louis Philippe bring out the salient points of French history from 1815 to 1848. A more interesting paper is that on Alexis de Tocqueville. De Tocqueville ought to be dear to Englishmen, for it is doubtful if any Frenchman of equal intellectual calibre ever had so intelligent an appreciation of our nation. His book on "Democracy in America" made a profound impression here, and became a text-book of constitutional law in the United States. We would draw attention to his remarks, quoted by Mr. Reeve (vol. ii. pp. 115 *et seq.*) on our Indian dependencies. He says, writing to Lady Lewis at the time of the mutiny :—

"There has never been anything so extraordinary under the sun as the conquest, and still more the government, of India by the English; nothing which, from all points of the globe, more attracts the eyes of mankind to that little island whose very name was to the Greeks unknown. Do you conceive, Madam, that a nation which has once filled this amazing space in the imagination of our race can withdraw from it with impunity?"

M. de Tocqueville predicted the fate of the Second Empire and the manner of its fall. We have seen his prediction fulfilled. Mr. Reeve's essay on this great thinker is full of instruction and interest. The remaining chapters of his book on Agricultural France, France in 1870, and Communal France, are more melancholy; but they illustrate the difference between the political conditions of France at different epochs, and the hopes and wishes of her best and wisest spirits for her real development. There has, indeed, never been any lack in France of highminded men, honourable, intelligent, and patriotic; the chief difficulty at the present moment is the formation of a government strong enough to shape the destiny of a country whose traditions of national life and authority have been repeatedly broken, and to erect the edifice of a permanent constitution upon the ruins of shattered and obsolete governments. A perception of this difficulty renders the last pages of Mr. Reeve's book a melancholy epilogue, but it cannot detract from the merits of a work which is thoughtfully and well executed.

Mr. Needham has continued and completed his translation[1] of Herr Rüstow's History of the late War, and, the work faithfully executed, is now open to English readers. These volumes, like the first, show Herr Rüstow's historical impartiality, and are valuable for their clear and accurate narrative. The second volume carries on the history from the concentration of the army of Paris under MacMahon to the fall of Thionville and the occupation of Amiens. Herr Rüstow's remarks on the siege of Strasburg strike us as eminently just, and his account of the military operations before that unfortunate city as clear and authoritative. Nor does he put aside the question: whether the bombardment of the city were in itself justifiable? He supports his affirmative answer from the treatise of a French General of Artillery, whose arguments he summarizes. It is indeed almost impossible not to agree with his conclusions, however much we may for humanity's sake lament their results. Herr Rüstow shares the regret of every feeling man at the fate of the brave old town. In France, of course, the bombardment was looked upon as an act of German barbarity; but, as Herr Rüstow appositely points out, when General Uhrich said that if the Germans succeeded in entering the town he would himself retire into the citadel and from thence destroy the town, the speech was praised in all the French journals as heroic. A great portion of this volume is occupied with the Parisian episode in the war, and will be permanently interesting from a military and historical point of view. The third volume, containing a narrative of the events which led to the proclamation of the Emperor, the capitulation of Paris, and the definite treaty of peace accepted by the National Assembly, closes with an Appendix in which the author reviews and compares the French and German armies, and exhibits the reasons of the superiority of the latter. Herr Rüstow is by no means so hopeful of the permanence of the peace as we should like to see one who has his knowledge of both nations, but we join in his earnest wish that his fears may be in vain. His book is, at all events at present, the most valuable record of the late historical drama; and in Mr. Needham's translation the English reader has as trustworthy a representative of the original work as could be desired.

Herr Winterfeld's book,[2] on the same subject, is one more of the numerous histories of the war; perhaps it is one of the fullest. It begins with the fifteenth century, following, it may be, the example of Thucydides in this respect, though it neglects his example in the matter of bulk, since it contains nearly three times as much letter-press as the Greek historian. Yet Germans will doubtless read it with the national patience and the national enthusiasm. Its distinctive characteristic, however, is a series of more than a hundred wretched portraits and pictures. It has no other noteworthy feature.

---

[1] "The War for the Rhine Frontier, 1870." By W. Rüstow. Translated by J. L. Needham. London: W. Blackwood and Sons.

[2] "Vollständige Geschichte des deutschfranzösischen Krieges." Von Karl Winterfeld. Berlin: Gustav Hempel.

Mrs. Hookham's history[1] of the life of Margaret of Anjou is not so good as it might have been. Our authoress is a lady of inexhaustible patience in collecting her facts, but she has not sufficient power in marshalling and arranging them for a continuous narrative. Her footnotes bristle with the names of authorities whom we suppose she has consulted; but these notes afford no means of verification, and such brief references as "Lingard," "Stowe," "London Chron." "Rot. Parl." &c., give but little assistance to the student. Sometimes her metaphors become a little entangled with one another (as on page 40), but we must admit that confusion of metaphors is not a special fault of her writing. There is no doubt, however, that this history occupies too much space. A long introductory history of more than a hundred pages leads not to an account of Margaret herself, but to the history of her father René's birth, education, and life; and it is only when close upon the two hundredth page that we first hear of Margaret. Another long chapter of English history (which we would not depreciate, for it contains a fair description of the state of England at the time) prepares the stage for the introduction of Margaret upon the scene as Queen of England and France. At this time Henry VI. was in a condition of royal poverty. He had been married by proxy, and had not sufficient funds to receive his bride, who brought him no dowry. He was therefore obliged to pawn his jewels and plate, in order to provide the necessary splendour and equipments. At length the Queen reached England, and in the account of her progress and coronation Mrs. Hookham is really interesting. As early as November King Henry had written to the Goldsmiths' Company. He told them that "he trusted to have our entirely well-beloved wife, the queen, within right brief time," and enjoins them "that they wol prepare to meet her in most goodly wise." Which they did, arrayed with "baudericks of golde about their necks, and short hoods of scarlette jagged." The young sovereign soon obtained great influence, and her energetic character showed itself. Mrs. Hookham repudiates the idea that the War of the Roses resulted from the queen's mismanagement of the reins of government, though she admits that her favoritism and spirit of political intrigue hastened the crisis which was inevitable. We may say, upon the whole, that the book will be interesting to admirers of the character of Margaret of Anjou, and that any student of history may work in these volumes a mine of ill-arranged facts relating to a shameful period of our history, which may be useful to him if he knows how to find them.

Another historical work[2] by a lady presents a great contrast in every respect to the book of which we have been speaking. Mrs. St. John has chosen an interesting period, has read much, and arranged her materials like a true artist. In one volume of 294 pages (we omit the last chapter, as beside her subject), she brings before us many

[1] "Life and Times of Margaret of Anjou, Queen of England and France." By Mary Ann Hookham. London: Tinsley Brothers.
[2] "The Court of Anna Carafa: an Historical Narrative." By Mrs. H. R. St. John. London: Tinsley Brothers.

vivid pictures of a period rich in great names and subtle intrigues—
the period of the Spanish viceroyalty at Naples. She has freely used
the works of the Italian Chronicles, and the *Archivio Storico Italiano*,
and her references are clear and useful. The Princess, whom Mrs.
St. John chooses as her heroine, was a grand-niece of Pope
Clement VII., was sprung from a race distinguished in Italian history,
and was its last direct descendant. Rich, and if poets are to be believed, beautiful, she spent her girlhood amongst those who sought her
favour from interest more than from love; the result of which education was, that she herself grew calculating and insincere. She was, in
spite of her later magnificence, a woman who missed her destiny.
Once she was loved truly by her cousin Diomed Carafa, the best of
the Carafas, and it is probable that she loved him, but she married
the Duke of Medina, and became—— what she was. The government of Naples, under the Spanish Viceroys, Monterey and Medina,
was marked by every conceivable form of falsity and fraud; there was
very little in the character of Anna Carafa, Duchess of Medina, to
redeem her Court. All the Carafas were luxurious; she was luxurious
too; but she was a notable patroness of art and literature. Mrs.
St. John's chapter on the Italian drama is excellent. Under the
Duke of Medina, Spanish influence was naturally felt in the
Neapolitan theatre. Lope de Vega reigned no less upon the
Italian than upon the Spanish stage, and his *Comedias Heroycas*
developed a species of drama which degenerated into performances
of the most degraded type. Alongside of this popular spec-
tacle existed the Mystery or sacred play. Both kinds are fully
described by our authoress. A chapter upon the feudalism of Southern
Italy is equally good, and exhibits the arbitrary despotism of the
Duchess in a vivid manner. And admirably too, in a few words, our
authoress tells of the last desolate untended days of Anna Carafa. She
had lived for herself, and her own selfish, frivolous pleasures; and she
died alone and uncared for, without a single friend. There is a portrait
of the Duchess in the book, which represents her as a lady with a
broad and ample forehead, arched eyebrows, curved and full lips;
beautiful certainly, yet not of a beauty which justified the extravagant
adulation of contemporary poets. She outlived her beauty, and the
evening of her life was dark and sad. Mrs. St. John's book well
brings before us one scene in that splendid, long, accursed drama of
feudal tyranny, which we may now hope will never be enacted again.

The fourth volume of Mr. Ward's translation of Curtius's "History
of Greece"[1] has appeared. The third volume brought the history
down to the close of the Peloponnesian war and the surrender of
Athens to Lysander. The chief characteristic of Dr. Curtius's
history will already be known to the readers of the earlier volumes;
it is that he carries out the invisible connexion which pervades the
whole course of the nation's development. Hence his book leaves the
impression of a pervading unity. It lacks that picturesque treatment
of details which we find in Grote's and Thirlwall's histories; but we

---

[1] "The History of Greece." By Professor Dr. Ernst Curtius. Translated by
Adolphus William Ward. Vol. iv. London: Bentley and Son.

do not heed this in the solemn and stately march of events which
his pages present before us. The most interesting and important period
closes with the third volume, but this fourth volume has much that is
important too. It corresponds to the fifth and sixth books of the
original work, which treat of the supremacy of Sparta in Greece, and
the rise of the Theban power. The victory of Sparta was the defeat
of democracy not only in Athens, but in those states which by their
democratic constitutions had formed under the Athenian hegemony
an anti-Spartan party. Now the bond which united this group of
States was loosened, and it remained in the power of Sparta entirely
to put an end to the divisions which had split Greece into two hostile
camps. Thus to the democracy of Athens there followed a despotism
both general and oppressive. Whether the democracy of Athens had
been a real democracy, or, as it seemed to Thucydides, a government of
the best man, it was now at an end. Athens under the Thirty was very
different from the Athens of Pericles, but her glory had not entirely
departed. This fourth volume has to deal with such names as Sophocles,
Alcibiades, Socrates, and Euripides. The first of these continued to
live in the spirit of the Periclean age, though the symmetry of public
life had been destroyed, but after his death poetry was seized by the
current and swept away into other channels. Socrates more especially
belongs to the changed period. Dr. Curtius's estimate of the philosopher
is admirable, and states well the political reasons which led to his martyrdom. "He became," he says, "the victim of a policy which had for
its object the restoration of the Athens of old without clearly realizing
the means and the end." No advantage could accrue to the State
from his condemnation; but by it the Athenians rendered a real service to him whom they condemned, for they furnished him with an
opportunity of setting the seal upon his teaching, by a free obedience
towards the laws, and a heroic death. The great name of the Spartan
period is Lysander, unfortunately it is not the name of a great man.
He survived, as Dr. Curtius says, his own fame, and died ingloriously.
The sixth book embraces a short but brilliant period of seventeen
years, during which Thebes was the great power of Greece. The
liberation of the Bœotian city dates from the assassination of the
oligarchs, an event which Dr. Curtius chronicles with more than usual
picturesque fulness. It was indeed an event which led to many
momentous consequences. The first task of Thebes was the unifica-
tion of Bœotia, which had been completely disorganized by the peace of
Antalcidas. The Young-Bœotian party at Thebes had adherents in
other towns, and there was a strong feeling amongst the patriots that
the regeneration of Thebes should be followed by that of all Bœotia.
They desired not only that Thebes should become the first and
leading city of the country, but that all Bœotia, blended into a single
whole, should find itself represented in Thebes as Attica was in
Athens. This feeling resulted in the establishment of the "Sacred
Band," a beneficent institution and an honourable monument of the
wisdom of Epaminondas. We have not space to go through the
history of events to the death of Epaminondas, a far greater name than
that of Lysander; but with his death closes this period of Theban

supremacy. Dr. Curtius indeed compares the Theban general with Pericles, and pays a just tribute to his memory as a true Hellene, and an unselfish devoted patriot. With his death the fourth volume of the translation closes. We have carefully compared it with the original, and find it trustworthy, conscientious, and adequate. It is by the title-page alone that we should know it as a translation, for the language is dignified and flowing, and we recommend it to English students as an accurate representation of the German work.

Another translation,[7] but this time from the French of Baron Hübner, is also well worthy of the attention of the historical student. This Life of Sixtus the Fifth is not only interesting on account of the biography itself, but also by reason of the insight it gives into the Italy of three centuries ago. Baron Hübner writes as a diplomatist, and is chiefly concerned with the diplomacy of the reign, but this does not prevent him from adding many graceful pages of literary interludes and episodes. As an historian, however, he confines himself strictly to the authority of official records and documents. "A void," he says, "is better than a fiction." Whether the character of Sixtus was really as great as Baron Hübner thinks it to have been, we cannot say; he certainly does not prove it to have been that of either a great or a magnanimous man. Sixtus never had the power of deciding between his rival advisers, the Ambassadors of Venice and of Spain. Indeed, he was afraid of the latter; as well he might be, if Baron Hübner's theory be correct, that he eventually died of the worry which that distinguished individual caused him. As a politician Sixtus had no definite characteristic; he was weak and vacillating, and unable to avail himself of the opportunities which were then within the grasp of the popedom. As a pope, he abused his patronage without shame, and was tyrannical in success. For the memory of his predecessor he bore an invincible hatred. He ascribed to him all the evils which had occurred from the time that he had mounted the papal throne:

"banditti, Huguenots, and civil war in France. The Gregorian Calendar, which is one of the glories of that pontificate did not escape his censure. He found the innovation contrary to the teachings of the Councils, of the Popes, and of St. Ambrose, and drew his arguments from mathematics, with which he said he was well acquainted. On this subject he was never weary of speaking. His dislike of his predecessor displayed itself even in his dreams. During two consecutive nights he had seen Gregory XIII. surrounded by flames. Happily it was not to hell, but only to purgatory that Gregory had gone.",

We are unfortunately unable to follow our author through the whole of his instructive book. It is one which lends an interest even to historic detail, and is written with both grace and power. The translation is generally well done, but lapses occasionally into a looseness of expression which had better have been avoided.

---

7 "The Life and Times of Sixtus the Fifth." By Baron Hübner, formerly Ambassador of Austria in Paris and Rome. Translated from the French by H. E. H. Jerningham. Two Vols. London: Longman and Co.

We will now turn to Indian literature, which is more than usually
rich this quarter. The biography of Sir Henry Lawrence* will claim
the first place. These two volumes are the work of two authors, each
of them well adapted for the task he has undertaken. Few men were
better qualified for writing the life of Sir Henry Lawrence than his
friend and subordinate, Sir Herbert Edwardes, and few men were
more fitted for carrying on the unfortunately unfinished task than Mr.
Merivale. The first, by personal acquaintance and intimate relationship, the second, by literary power and special capacity, have produced
a biography worthy of their subject. Sir Henry Lawrence was
descended from a family in the county of Derry. Alexander, the
father of Henry and John Lawrence, went to India, and died as
Governor of Upnor Castle in Kent. He had married a lady descended
collaterally from John Knox, the Reformer. Henry was born in
Ceylon in 1800. He passed through Addiscombe, and in 1823 landed
in India, where he was to make his name. In 1824 began the
Burmese war, in which he was actively engaged, but, his health
breaking down, he returned to England in 1827. It was then that
he first met with the lady who was to be his wife—Miss Marshall.
He returned, however, alone to India, and in 1837 Miss Marshall,
whom he had long loved, went out to Calcutta to marry her future
husband. He was at that time surveying the district of Gorukpore,
—an arduous and by no means a pleasant task. The next year he
joined the expedition to Cabul. This campaign lasted until the end
of 1842, when Lawrence was appointed to the district of Kythul at
the recommendation of Lord Ellenborough. Beyond this point in his
history the thread is taken up by Mr. Merivale. Whilst at Nepaul
Sir Henry Lawrence devoted himself to literature. With Sir John
Kaye he started, and more than started, the *Calcutta Review*, which
was to be similar to the *Edinburgh*, *Quarterly*, and *Westminster
Reviews*, but devoted entirely to Indian subjects. He in this work,
as in all literary labours, was greatly assisted by his wife. Mr.
Merivale gives a long list of the articles contributed by Lawrence.
It was at this time, too, that he founded the Lawrence Asylum.
Then follows the history of the Sikh campaigns, in which the tact and
firmness of Henry Lawrence were conspicuous. Mr. Merivale has
told this part of his story well. The differences between himself and
his brother, which eventually led to his retirement from the Punjab,
and his acceptance of the Residentship of Rajpootanah, are impartially
recorded. There, in 1854, Lady Lawrence died. In 1857, as every
one knows, Sir Henry was killed by the mutineers at Lucknow,
whither he had gone to supply the place of General Outram. The
closing scenes of his life are recorded with good taste and reverence by
Mr. Merivale. As a whole, in spite of certain errors of detail, mostly
occurring in the second volume, the biography throughout is admirable. The life of Sir Henry Lawrence is one that was well worth

* "Life of Sir Henry Lawrence." By the late Major-General Sir H. B. Edwardes, K.C.B., and Herman Merivale, C.B. Two Vols. London: Smith, Elder
and Co.

writing, and one that will be interesting to the larger English public than that which interests itself in Indian affairs.

Whatever may have been the value of Mr. Hunter's[9] volume upon our Indian Musulmans (and opinions varied as to the necessity of the alarm which he sounded), there can scarcely be a difference of opinion with reference to the two scholarly volumes which he has published as a sequel to his "Annals of Rural Bengal." Everything which the subject required has been given, official summaries, statistics, and tabulations, and a series of essays upon the province under consideration, which are fascinating from their literary style and the information which they convey. The book is in itself a model of what ought to be done for every province of our Indian empire. For a century, indeed, Government has attempted to collect authorized statistics of the Indian provinces. In 1807 the Company organized special machinery for the work. The Governor-General himself laid out the plans. No expense was spared—30,000*l*. were spent in seven years and—not one page was rendered available to the public or the Government. Isolated attempts followed this gigantic failure with no adequate results. In 1869–70 the Governor-General directed Mr. Hunter to visit the ten local governments, with a view to his submitting a plan for utilizing the materials already collected, and the present work forms the first-fruits of the enterprise thus inaugurated. The book begins with a geographical description of Lower Bengal. Here our author gives the legend of the Chilka Lake, a history of the destructive inundations which are caused by the river overflows, and suggestions for future improvements in the country. We commend to our readers Mr. Hunter's admirable but painfully picturesque description of a Puri flood. Chapters iii. and iv. are devoted to the religion of the province. Mr. Hunter protests against the prevailing ideas of Jagannath, and the missionary exaggerations which are so incessantly iterated in this country. The instances, he says, "of pilgrims who throw themselves beneath the wheels of the car of the god have always been rare, and are now unknown." Official returns place this fact beyond doubt. Mr. Hunter afterwards deals with the history of the primitive races, and discusses the Buddhist rock-temples and caves. These papers are accompanied by interesting illustrations. In the second volume a history of the province under Moghul, Mahratta, and English government is followed by an essay upon those great calamities of the districts, floods and famines, and another essay upon the village system and territorial holdings. Half the second volume consists of official statistics, geological and botanical. It is difficult to know whether the book is most praiseworthy for its literary style, its wide grasp of facts, or its humane zeal.

The unpretending diary[10] which Captain West edits will throw some light upon the progress which English culture is making in India.

9 "Orissa." By W. W. Hunter. Two Vols. London : Smith, Elder and Co.
10 "Diary of the Late Rajah of Kolhapoor, during his Visit to Europe, in 1870." Edited by Capt. E. W. West, of the Bombay Staff Corps. London : Smith, Elder and Co.

The young Rajah who visited us in 1870, and who died shortly afterwards at Florence, was not apparently a man of any intellectual power, but he was a kind and gentle specimen of the "mild Hindoo." During his stay in this country he kept the diary which Captain West gives us. It is naïve and full of wondering admiration for England, and is written in very fair English. It is curious to see the impression which the different sights of the country made upon an utterly unsophisticated nature. The Rajah was as much impressed by the automaton chess-player as he was by the House of Commons. He spends the afternoon eating grapes and drinking champagne with the Archbishop of Canterbury (p. 67), and at 0·30 goes to the Alhambra to see "different kinds of ballets" and "the exercise of two boys," which "is the most difficult and wonderful exercise that ever I saw." It is no wonder if his diary represents a kaleidoscopic variety of events. But perhaps the most significant sentence which the Rajah's diaries contain is this: "I was quite astonished to see the simple and unpretending ways of talking of the Ministers—especially of Mr. Gladstone. They are very gentle in conversation. *They have not got the pride of the Indian officers, though they are the leading men of the English empire. I liked them very much.*"

The third volume of Lord Brougham's Autobiography" is now before us. The introduction contains the directions to his executor: "I alone am answerable for its (the Autobiography's) statements, faults, and omissions. I will have no editor employed to alter or rewrite what I desire shall be published as exclusively my own." And these directions have evidently been followed. Lord Brougham will not so much interest posterity as he dazzled contemporaries. Amazing energy and overflowing animal spirits, together with inexhaustible literary fertility, made him conspicuous in the eyes of those who lived with him, but they will not be sufficient to make him a prominent memory in times to come. But this volume of the Autobiography is characteristic, and may, at least now, be read with much interest. It begins with Lord Brougham's election as Lord Rector of Glasgow University in 1828, and concludes with the year 1835. It thus includes the eventful year of Reform. But that it is really a valuable addition to the history of the period we are not prepared to say. Lord Brougham was a man of energy, he was not a man of enthusiasm. No glamour of personal influence surrounded him. He has chronicled the state quarrels and state manœuvres in which he shared, "*non sine gloriâ.*" But his works will scarcely help to explain the revolution which he aided. Yet his Autobiography is interesting, and will be studied by historians as the key to events otherwise unexplained.

Our next autobiography" is of a different kind. Happily designed and felicitously executed, Mr. Graham's autobiography of Milton will both surprise and please his readers. The book brings indeed no new

---

11 "The Life and Times of Lord Brougham, written by Himself." Vol. Iii. William Blackwood and Sons.

12 "Autobiography of John Milton; or, Milton's Life in his own Words." Edited by Rev. J. G. Graham, M.A. Oxon. London: Longmans, Green and Co.

matter which has not always been at the command of the historian; its peculiarity is that it allows Milton to tell the story of his life in his own words. For this design Milton's prose works, "full of himself, his own plans, aspirations, sufferings, wrongs, and privations," supply sufficient material. By a judicious selection of these passages Mr. Graham has produced a book written in Milton's own "sacred and charmed" words, so full and complete that he is justified in calling it an autobiography of John Milton. Thus, too, the salient points of Milton's character, untinged by the prepossessions or bias of a biographer, are seen with greater clearness than they can be seen in the work of any other historian; since Mr. Graham neither praises nor blames him, "blamed enough elsewhere," but allows him to speak for himself. The materials for the history of his childhood are taken from his "Apology for Smectymnuus," his "Reason of Church Government," and "The Second Defence," and present a clear picture of the studious pure-minded boy, who was as fortunate in his home-training as he was in his natural endowments. The passages connected with his college career are, in spite of Milton's dislike to Cambridge, full of youthful fire and spirit, and they are so arranged by Mr. Graham that they satisfactorily show that John Milton was never subject to the degradation, frequently and gratuitously attributed to him, either of flogging or rustication. Before thirty he had written "Comus," "L'Allegro," "Il Penseroso," and "Lycidas." At that age he visited Italy. The abundant material to be found for this period in his letters and in his prose works renders this chapter unusually full. It includes the history of his Italian friendships, his Italian love, and his intimacy with the great and learned men of the Continent. At the age of forty he was secretary to Cromwell, and at the Restoration was plunged into those political controversies which have enriched our literature at the expense of the happiness of his dark declining days. Those passages of his works which bear reference to his unhappy marriages are perhaps best known. Mr. Graham sees allusion to his matrimonial infelicity in the "Samson Agonistes." It was Milton's last poem, written three years before his death. It little matters now what unhappiness he suffered, his labours have been crowned with inviolable peace and indestructible renown; and if there is much sorrow in the story which Mr. Graham has so skilfully and lovingly brought together, there is much more that is heroic and instructive for all time.

If any other instance were wanted of the fact that a busy and occupied life does not exclude the possibility of catholic culture, that instance is to be found in Dr. Sadler's Memoir of Mr. Field.[13] Mr. Field was a solicitor in large practice; he was connected with every measure of law reform, a Royal Commissioner and pamphleteer for these measures; but he was besides this the friend and benefactor of art and literature. And in both spheres he worked with energy and permanent effect. Mr. Field was the son of a Dissenting minister at

[13] "Edward Wilkins Field: a Memorial Sketch." By Thomas Sadler, Ph.D. London: Macmillan and Co.

Warwick, and a descendant of Cromwell the Protector. (We commend this fact to the notice of Mr. Galton, who has overlooked it in his masterly book.) His youth was one of laborious activity and severe study, and the result was wide general culture and great professional knowledge. This professional knowledge he used for the reform of some flagrant abuses connected with the law, and especially with the Court of Chancery. Some legislation had been attempted before, during the chancellorship of Lord Brougham; but the larger plans of the Chancellor were not carried out. In 1840 Mr. Field wrote a pamphlet on the "Defects in Offices, Practice and System of Costs of the Equity Courts," which attracted much attention. This pamphlet, and an article of his which appeared in this *Review* for January, 1842, seem to have been the main cause of the passing of the Act of 1842, by which the obnoxious offices of the Six Clerks and Sworn Clerks were abolished, and pared the way for further changes, by which the Court of Chancery has been greatly improved in regard both to efficiency and to economy. But other reforms he prosecuted with energy and success. Both in this *Review* and elsewhere he strove to raise the application of the principles of law to the dignified position of an inductive science. "It cannot be right," he wrote, "that we should have one mode in common law, another in equity, another in bankruptcy, another in lunacy, another in the Ecclesiastical Courts." His efforts in this direction resulted in the Act of Parliament for concentrating the Courts of Justice. To the Royal Commission which was issued to obtain and approve a plan for the New Courts, Mr. Field was appointed Secretary, and at his earnest request the secretaryship was an honorary one. Another legislative measure which Mr. Field actively forwarded, was the Dissenters' Chapel Bill. This passed in 1844; and one who was personally active in reference to it, testifies:—"As regards the Dissenters' Chapel Bill, without Field and his exertions I believe it would never have been obtained." But Mr. Field's connexion with art was no less marked by his good and great personal influence than his legal career. Without him the Flaxman Gallery would not have been established, as Mr. Crabb Robinson testifies; the Slade School of Art owes nearly as much to his indefatigable care; and when he died, on the 4th of November, 1871, the Council of University College directed a minute to be entered on their proceedings, which says:—"In this branch of the College (the Slade School of Art), his loss is irreparable." Dr. Sadler gives the history of other benefits which Mr. Field conferred upon art; but we cannot follow him through them all, and will refer only to the formation of a Trust for the purchase of pictures to be presented to the Public Art Gallery belonging to the Corporation of Birmingham. Mr. Field's life was one that was worthy of a biographer, and Dr. Sadler has succeeded in that capacity. His works will speak for his public character; as a man and a friend to art and progress, the sketch which his biographer gives bears witness to his greatness and his goodness. Those who had not the delight of his personal acquaintance may learn to know from Dr. Sadler's pages a character as amiable as it was useful.

Mr. Robertson's book[14] is hard to read, and difficult to criticise. It is full of varied and recondite learning, combined with accurate and close reasoning, and leads to results which are important, if history is to be concerned with obsolete land customs and measurements and standards of weight and currency, that have long ceased to be in use. Such subjects have, as Mr. Robertson observes, few attractions for the general reader; but these essays are not for the general reader. As a work of reference, however, it will be undoubtedly useful for historical investigations, since it includes much information upon obscure points, which is well brought together in these pages. The titles of some of the Essays will indicate their contents. "The Roman and Byzantine Pounds," "Talents of the Classical Era," "Currency of the Early Franks and the House of Capet," "Early Germanic and Frison Currency," "Norwegian and Irish Currency," "Early English Currency and Standards." Mr. Robertson shows that the Cologne weight was the origin of the English sterling, and that the German standard was derived from the Constantinople measure, which even yet continues to exercise a theoretical influence in every mint and goldsmith's shop in Europe. "Twenty-four carats fine," is the expression still applied to gold of the finest quality; meaning, originally, that every *keration* in the twenty-four that made up the weight of the standard coin of Constantinople, was of the purest gold unmixed with alloy. Mr. Robertson explains further the origin of that double system of weights which has prevailed, and traces it back to the time when Constantine adopted the heavier pound of 84 *soldi*, instead of the ordinary pound of 72 *soldi*, known as the *Libra Occidua*. To this heavier pound may be referred *Troyes-weight*. Mr. Robertson has given some curious examples of the early substitutes for coinage. Cattle passed for money, so did cloth, and personal ornaments, as the Celtic *torque* and the Teutonic *beag*.

The second part of the book deals with the inheritance of land. The papers on The Acre, Land gavel, and the Shire, are valuable contributions to the history of the subject, and the position of the King's kin among the Saxons, the Policy of Dunstan, and the relation of the Normans to the Saxons, are well brought out. Mr. Robertson shows that the superiority of the great families was chiefly owing to their superiority in discipline and equipment. The book has an excellent index, which is, in itself, an example of diligent and learned research.

Mr. Larwood has produced a history of three London Parks:[15] Hyde Park, St. James's Park, and the Green Park. The first volume is devoted to Hyde Park, as the most important, and contains many anecdotes of the company who frequented it, from the days when Henrietta Maria walked barefoot through the park to the gallows at Tyburn, down to our own times. In the earlier portion of the history of these parks we constantly meet with the inextinguishable diarist

---

[14] "Historical Essays in Connexion with the Land, the Church, &c." By E. W. Robertson. Edinburgh: Edmonston and Douglas.
[15] "The Story of the London Parks." By Jacob Larwood. Two Vols. London: John Camden Hotten.

Pepys, who has assisted our author to realize the spirit of early London society. The later fortunes of the Parks are told in a light and gossiping manner. The book is, perhaps, scarcely open to serious criticism, or we might be startled at the frequent inaccuracies which meet us. Thus we find the "School for Scandal" attributed to Fielding (ii. 102); wrong dates (*e.g.* that of the American Revolutionary War, vol. ii. 211), meet us not unfrequently; and the book is written in a careless, slipshod style, which is at times unpleasant, and which the subject does not wholly excuse. But it may be read not without amusement, by people to whom these Parks are familiar. Some few caricatures, from the pencil of Cruikshank, enliven the pages, which, to the general reader, are without interest, and which are not free from sins against good taste.

We can only briefly refer to the remaining books upon our table.

M. Guizot's "History of France"[16] continues to appear as a monthly publication by Messrs. Low. It is a book whose merits are well known; we can say nothing new in its favour. But one thing we should like to know, why are the accompanying pictures so inferior to the letterpress as they are? They have neither historical accuracy, which they might have had, nor artistic value. A more authentic representation of costume would have been more valuable, and would have really assisted the student.

Major Jones has written a small and unpretending book[17] upon the Conquest and Settlement of Britain by the Saxons, Danes, and Normans. It is an honest and good little book, and worthy perusal. It is intended to give a general view of the military and political events which accompanied the formation of the British nation, and it does so in a clear and attractive style. Major Jones apologizes unnecessarily for the military tone of his pages. We can honestly recommend the book to those who wish to become acquainted with the early history of the country, and are prevented from studying more voluminous works.

The Annual Register for 1871,[18] is a summary of the events of last year, and compresses into one volume the more permanently interesting topics of the journals. The Literary Retrospect is especially well done, and notices all the remarkable books which appeared during the year. The Science section is not so happily dealt with.

Our next work of reference[19] is a remarkable instance of painstaking industry. It is a volume of 1487 pages, crowded with dates, and, as far as we have tested it, correct dates. We have taken the trouble to

[16] "The History of France, from the Earliest Times to the Year 1789." By M. Guizot. Translated by Robert Black. London : Sampson Low, Marston Low and Searle.

[17] "Conquest of Britain." By Major W. P. Jones. London : Bemrose and Sons.

[18] "The Annual Register, 1871 : a Review of Public Events at Home and Abroad." London : Rivingtons.

[19] "Encyclopædia of Chronology : Historical and Biographical." By B. B. Woodward, late Librarian to the Queen, and W. L. R. Cates, Editor of the "Dictionary of General Biography." London : Longmans, Green and Co.

count the number of dates on a page, and find them to average 150.
This gives a total of nearly 225,000 dates—"a thing imagination
boggles at." The book was commenced twenty years ago, and has
taken a year and a half in the printing. It will doubtless be useful,
and we cannot but be grateful to Mr. Woodward, who has not lived to
see his work ended, and to Mr. Cates, who has completed this serviceable volume.

Mr. Levi's "History of Commerce"[a] is not a book to be dealt with
in a paragraph, but we unfortunately have no more space. It contains
in a clear arrangement the history of the economic progress of the
British nation during the last century, from the end of the Seven
Years' War to 1870. The influence of the French Revolution upon
our foreign trade—Mr. Huskisson's reforms—the Corn Laws—and the
effects of the Russian war upon commerce, pass under review. There
is also a statistical appendix, which is likely to be of value; and the
book concludes with a good general index.

Mr. Yonge's book[b] is intended to give the youthful student some
idea of the general history of Continental Europe in modern times.
It begins with the fifteenth and closes with the eighteenth century.
Mr. Yonge says there can be no more interesting study than that of
history; he fails, however, in supporting his theorem. This book,
like his "History of Literature," is full of inaccuracies. Whether
they are his own, or, as he has recently asserted in a weekly paper, the
inaccuracies of his printer, does not much matter; we cannot recommend his book.

BELLES LETTRES.

MR. SHAND[c] has partly fulfilled the promise which his first
novel, "Against Time," held forth. He writes with the same
freshness, power, and knowledge of places and men. From an artistic
point of view he has made considerable advances. The parts cohere
together. Incidents give birth to other incidents in a natural way.
The story grows, and is not pieced together by a number of chapters
of accidents. The hero is consistent in his folly, and plunges on from
one species of gambling to another, and no lucky investment in Peru-
vian mines, no backing some dark horse, no marrying some rich hei-
ress, no breaking the bank at Homburg, is permitted to gild the last

[a] "History of British Commerce, 1763-1870." By Leone Levi, F.S.A. F.S.S., London: John Murray.
[b] "Three Centuries of Modern History." By Charles Duke Yonge, Regius Professor of Modern History in Queen's College, Belfast. London: Longmans, Green and Co.
[c] "Shooting the Rapids." By Alexander Innes Shand, Author of "Against Time." London: Smith, Elder and Co. 1872.

scenes of his wasted life. Further, Mr. Shand has evidently been at
great pains to work out particular scenes, on which the action of the
story chiefly depends, and to throw minute details into the background.
Generally speaking, the ordinary novelist reverses this order of things.
He tells, in an offhand way, perhaps in half a dozen lines, an event
which goes either to the making or marring of the hero's fortune.
Mr. Shand, on the contrary, possesses the artist's true perception of the
fitness of events, and their true bearing upon one another. And it is
especially necessary to dwell upon this excellence, for it is generally
the last gained by the novelist. Further, Mr. Shand, like a true
artist, contrives to keep continually bringing his own strong point to
the foreground. And Mr. Shand's strong point is that in which most
novelists are the weakest—the Stock Exchange. Mr. Shand has here
broken new ground. He contrives to give a new interest to the Stock
Market. In his hands "Peruvians," "Egyptian Seven per Cents,"
and the "Khedive Mortgage Bonds," take a literary aspect. Figures
become eloquent. We have said, however, that Mr. Shand has only
partly fulfilled the high expectations which "Against Time" raised.
Over and over again we find ourselves reading a passage, with the
thought uppermost,—how much better Mr. Shand could have done
this had he chosen, or had he given himself more leisure. Mr. Shand
seems to be always writing at full speed. This rough and ready style
undoubtedly has its advantages. The bold broad stroke undoubtedly
contributes more to the effect of certain pictures than any quantity of
minute touches, ever so carefully coloured and ever so carefully laid on.
But then, it is only certain effects which will bear handling in this
way. Mr. Shand, for instance, shows a master-hand in describing a
journey in the old coaching days (vol. i. p. 175), a horse race, the wild
bits of mountainous country round Schloss Heppenstall (vol. i. pp. 124—
128), or the equally wild, though very different, scenery of the Che-
viots. The swift style suits him. His brush is juicy. But a great
deal more than this is required. We want tenderness, delicacy, and
repose. So, too, with Mr. Shand's conversations. In their way they are
excellent. But the countrymen of Miss Austen and Thackeray have
been trained to admire " the dazzling fence " of words rather than mere
cudgel-playing. We make this criticism, because we feel satisfied
that Mr. Shaud has really the right stuff in him to form a novelist, if
he would but give himself fair play. We trust that his next novel will
show as great an advance upon "Shooting the Rapids," as this has
done upon "Against Time." In the mean time we can most strongly
recommend the present tale, as containing sketches not merely of
English country life and scenes, written by one who thoroughly en-
joys them, but of foreign sharks and adventurers, who are to be met
in every street at the west end of town.

"Strange Folk"[1] is about as different a novel from "Shooting the
Rapids " as it is possible to conceive. In the one we are whirled away

---

[1] "Strange Folk." A Novel. Translated from the German of Hermann
Oelschlager, by Lieut.-Colonel Grant. London: Longmans, Green and Co.
1872.

into the very vortex of modern society, in the other we are taken into what the Germans themselves would describe as Schlaraffenland. A pleasant dreaminess pervades "Strange Folk." Authors, actresses, and monks are its chief characters. We alternately exchange the stage for the cloister, and step at one stride from the greenroom to the green wood. Dr. Anselmus is a German author who suffers from extreme nervousness. The least noise prevents him from writing. He flies away from home with his niece, to a little town in Franconia. He finds a house there beautifully situated. Everything is charming. His book progresses. He feels the inspiration of the scenery. Summer comes. The grass in the meadows changes from its varying shades of green to its last purple tints. From that moment there is no more rest for the Doctor. From morn till night sounds the eternal sharpening of the scythes. He flies from his new quarters to the Convent of the "Fifteen Holies." His niece, disguised in the dress of a student, accompanies him as secretary. Here the real story begins. Of the characters, that of the Doctor is, perhaps, the best drawn. Marion is more interesting and less vulgar than most actresses are. Dr. Breitman is one of those odious hangers-on, to be found at every theatre, who sponge upon every one alike. We fancy, however, that Dora's unconventional habits may prove some bar to the popularity of the story.

No such objection is likely to be taken against "The Rose Garden." ² The tone is pure and sweet throughout. In the way of art it is a perfect triumph. There is not a character too many, and each one plays their part to perfection, and advances the action of the story. Even the very dog Coquin is a character, and contributes his fair share to the plot. In fact, without Coquin there is no plot. His misfortune makes the fortune of the heroine. Coquin may fairly take his place beside Shakespeare's Crab and other historical dogs. Renée and Gabrielle are both of them, in their different ways, charmingly sketched. Mdme. Dalbarade is very natural, but to M. de Savigny must be given the first honours. The book, in short, is, in these days of vile sensationalism and meretricious daubing, a perfect godsend. There is a natural sweetness about it like that of a rose-garden. No amount of quotation will fairly display its beauties and charms, and yet we are tempted to make one or two extracts. Here, for instance, is a subtle description of spring as seen by the eyes of love.

"She did not answer him this time. Something of change in his voice seemed as if he, like her, had been led on a little further than he intended. They walked on quietly. The rain which had fallen in the night had freshened everything; there was no dust, but a smell of earth and growing things; every shade of green among the trees, which yet showed their beautiful dark branches: soft white clouds with depths of intense blue between them; birds singing in the gardens,—a great burst of spring everywhere. Gabrielle's heart was singing with the birds; she wanted nothing better than to walk on for ever in this delicious silence.'—pp. 68, 69.

² "The Rose Garden." By the Author of "Unawares." London: Smith, Elder and Co. 1872.

But it is not in isolated passages like this, however beautiful, that the charm of the book lies; but, as in all good works, in its pervading tone. But we must, however, give one more quotation, because it reveals something, we believe, of the writer's philosophy :—

"The divine law is one of softening; age and time bring with them tender tints; over the graves grow grass and flowers; after the injury comes soft healing. But we will have none of this. If there has been a convulsion, an ugly scar in the rock, the birds that sweep over may let drop seeds, the sweet air carry them to us on its wings; but we—and we only—love to frustrate the merciful law, and to root up the tiny blossoms that would spread themselves to cover it."—p. 274.

With this quotation we must close our notice of a very beautiful book, but not without again earnestly recommending it to all those who are puzzled to find a novel fit to be put in the hands of young girls.

How some novels ever come to be written, and then to be published, and lastly to be read, is a puzzle. "Tottie's Trial"[1] is one of them. Here is a specimen of a conversation :—

"Who else is there?"—"Your cousin Joanna."—"Oh, don't ask her."— "I must, dear, if the other cousins are invited."—"She is so disagreeable."— "You must cultivate forbearance, my dear Tottie."—"I have, auntie darling. But I wish there were no disagreeable people."—"So do I."—"Why need there be?"—pp. 16, 17.

This twaddle actually fills up half of one page and a portion of another. Here is a specimen of the author's reflective style :—

"There is something very awful in the wild power of fire, when it breaks away from the restraining hand of men and works its own mad will, mocking at his puny efforts to subdue it, and engulfing all around in its resistless fury."—p. 143.

On the whole we prefer the vulgar proverb—"Fire is a good servant but a bad master," to Kay Spen's verbiage.

"A Novel with Two Heroes"[2] opens with the rather stale incident of a pair of runaway horses dragging a carriage with its load of terrified occupants towards a chasm in which roars a foaming river. Of course we know, before we turn over the first page, that a mysterious stranger, probably of "noble mien," will spring forward, and, at the moment when destruction appears inevitable, check the foaming horses with that firm restraint yet gentle manner which were the characteristics of all the heroes of the late Mr. G. P. R. James. But the author of "A Novel with Two Heroes" does not do this sort of thing badly. His best and most lively chapters are probably those in the sixth book, entitled "The Carnival," "The Streets," "The Procession," and "The Ball." Whenever he describes life from the outside, he succeeds. He has an eye for colour. He seizes upon the telling points of a story, and paints in the picturesque details of a passing

[1] "Tottie's Trial." By Kay Spen. London: Strahan and Co. 1872.
[2] "A Novel with Two Heroes." By Elliott Graeme. London: Charles Griffin and Co. 1872.

scene. The great fault of the work is a tendency to vulgarity. As an instance of what we mean we may point to a conversation at page 125 of the first volume. The whole scene is marred, not merely by want of taste, but by an absolute blunder. To represent an Oxford professor decrying education on the Continent, on the ground that a young man would forget his own language, is the height of absurdity. The conversation which immediately follows this extraordinary statement, with the rector, about Shakspeare, is equally grotesque. If the writer will be at the pains to check this tendency to vulgarity, and to represent English gentlemen as not quite such boors, he may win no mean place amongst the novelists of the day.

"Jane Eyre" still continues to exercise an influence upon our younger novelists, especially if they are ladies. Into the causes of the popularity of that very remarkable book we need not enter. It simply stands alone in literature; and whoever endeavours to imitate its style, and its tones of feeling, courts most certain failure. This is the case with "Lucy Fitzadam."[*] Had the authoress relied upon her own powers, which are of no mean order, her knowledge of character, her delicate sense of humour, her quiet power of painting natural scenery, she might have obtained a success. Instead of that she has deliberately chosen to sacrifice all these gifts to write a second-rate imitation of Miss Brontë. No form, too, is so difficult, especially for a beginner, as the autobiographical. Many a one can tell an excellent story about others, but the instant that he begins to narrate his own adventures, he becomes dull and prosy. And this is the case with most novelists. They can describe with effect the good or bad fortune which befalls others, but the spell deserts them when they write in the first person. We might, were it worth while to do so, easily illustrate these remarks from "Lucy Fitzadam." The best parts of the story are decidedly some of the minor sketches, which are full of quiet humour. The picture of old Mr. Munday, at the Westford Institution, is excellent. We trust the authoress will at once burn "Jane Eyre," and in her next novel trust entirely to her own powers.

"Thomasina"[†] may be recommended with a clear conscience to all young ladies who are in want of a novel this summer on a wet day. Without making any pretensions, the book fulfils all the requirements which the most exacting subscriber to Mudie's is likely to demand. The plot is fairly probable, the characters are good, the incidents are natural, and the conversations—those crucial tests of a novel writer—best of all. The tone is struck in the first chapter, and is sustained to the last. We have not for a long time read a novel descriptive of English country life, seen from its very best points, so genuinely interesting, and so evidently sketched from careful observation. In justice, too, we are bound to add a word of praise to the publishers for the excellent style in which the work is brought out. It is a per-

---

[*] "Lucy Fitzadam: an Autobiography." London: Smith, Elder and Co. 1870.
[†] "Thomasina: a Biography." By the Author of "Dorothy." London: Henry S. King and Co. 1872.

feet relief to the eye, after wading through pages of cheap paper, with close, small type, to light upon these soft, delicate cream-coloured sheets, with their handsome, bold-cut print, and spaced lines. Messrs. King and Co. we hope will not stop at their present improvements in novel-printing, but follow the example of the best publishing houses in America, and give us their novels with the leaves cut. This would be a real boon.

Mr. Freeland's well-written and painstaking novel will,' we fear, not meet with that success, which it certainly deserves, from English readers. An historical novel, unless the subject is very well chosen, labours under heavy disadvantages. The reader must, in the first place, take an interest in the leading characters, and be thoroughly well up, not merely in the history of the period, but in the very topography of the district where the scene is laid. If he is not, then all the details, so valuable in themselves and so telling in the narrative, are not merely lost upon him, but actually weary him. Scotchmen ought to take an interest in "Love and Treason," but then novels, unless they are guaranteed by the name of Sir Walter Scott, are on the other side of the Tweed, generally regarded as "Deil's books." Mr. Freeland possesses many of the requirements which make a novelist; a clear perception of character, an incisive style, and a deep love of nature. We should, however, advise him to tone down the colouring of his pictures. His descriptions of morning (vol. iii. p. 179), and of the Lanarkshire river (vol. iii. p. 121), smack a little too much of the vein of the late Mr. Alexander Smith and King Cambyses.

It is, of course, perfectly superfluous to praise from an artistic point of view, the "Story of the Plébiscite."' Those who have read the "Conscript," and "Waterloo," will here find the same old charm of style, the same clear-cut descriptions, and the same delicate tender pathos. But we must say, that a heavy responsibility lies upon the authors. The book will do more than any other to deepen the hatred of the French against the Prussians, and to rouse a never-dying cry of vengeance against the conquerors. Naturally enough, Frenchmen regard the war and its results in a different light to mere neutrals; but we trusted that MM. Erckmann-Chatrian would have displayed a nobler temper in defeat, and a higher patriotism than preaching the crusade of vengeance. Of course it is open to them to say that this is not the intention of the book, but it will certainly be its result.

Mr. Henry Kingsley" still continues his old happy-go-lucky style. His first story, "Hornby Mills Garden," begins with a discussion on flowers, and ends with a tale of some bankrupts. His next story, "Why Lady Hornbury's Ball was postponed," is simply a piece of

* "Love and Treason: a Novel." By William Freeland. London: Tinsley Brothers. 1872.

' "The Story of the Plébiscite." Told by one of the Seven Million Five Hundred Thousand who voted "Yes." From the French of MM. Erckmann-Chatrian. London: Smith, Elder and Co.

'⁰ "Hornby Mills: and other Stories." By Henry Kingsley. London: Tinsley Brothers. 1872.

preposterous nonsense, and much the same may be said about an
"Episode in the Life of Charles Mordaunt.'" Mr. Henry Kingsley
appears to inhabit some world of his own, where people are in the
habit of calling one another "old girls" and "old boys," and where
the most wonderful pieces of luck are always turning up. His heroes
are, as we are always told, marvels of either strength or learning, or wit.
Of the Rev. Charles Mordaunt, we learn that he possessed the most
"withering oratory," that he spoke "stinging and never-to-be-forgotten words," and further, that "the lash of the man's satire brought
blood, and blood which took a long time in healing," (pp. 93, 94).
But when we come to look for his "withering oratory," we discover
nothing but loud-sounding common-places, and when we seek for his
"stinging and never-to-be-forgotten words," we are met by such play-
fulness as calling his wife "old girl." The most remarkable feat,
however, which this clerical Juvenal performs, is bringing blood, and
then healing the blood which he has brought. But this is not a whit
bigger nonsense than many other passages in his life. Criticism is,
however, simply wasted on Mr. Henry Kingsley. He has adopted a
loud, vulgar style of his own, which he will never leave off. He mistakes declamation for eloquence, and what we must call—for there is
no other term to be used—"chaff," for humour.

When the thrifty housewife has a little dough left over on her
paste-board, she generally kneads it up into little lumps and cakes for
children. Holme Lee" has apparently had some dough left over from
her heavy novels, with which she has lately been feeding the public,
and has worked it up into a number of short childish tales. She has,
as a kind of "makeweight," as bakers would say, flung in a little
poetry, principally about the months. The poetry is somewhat
heavier than the prose.

"Essays," by Véra," is one of those few light books which may
always be taken up with pleasure and laid down with profit. The
tendency of lightness of style is, we need scarcely say, to beget flippancy. But there is not a trace of this, the great besetting sin of
our day, to be found in the volume. Most of the papers have appeared
in the *Edinburgh Review*, and, when we say that they are quite
worthy of that journal, we give them no small praise. Of course, when
an author deals with subjects so varied and so different as we find in
the present volume, there are sure to be some weak places in his
armour. The best papers are those upon art, and the least satisfactory
upon poetry. The article "English Vers de Société," requires some
supervision, and the one "On Some Christmas Carols," some additions. The writer has evident sympathy with both subjects, but be—
or ought we to say she—is hardly strong enough in his facts. An
impression of thinness is conveyed by both. For instance, the writer
seems to know nothing about "All under the Leaves, and the Leaves
of Life," and "As I sat on a Sunny Bank," and many other Christmas

---

" "Country Stories, Old and New, in Prose and Verse." By Holme Lee.
London: Smith, Elder and Co. 1872.
" "Essays." By the Author of "Véra." London: Smith, Elder and Co.
1872.

carols, which are so popular in the wilder parts of Derbyshire and Yorkshire, and which are hawked about the country in broadsheets. In conclusion, let us say that this is not a book which the reader should send for to Mudie's, but should buy for his library.

The title, "Men of the Second Empire,"[13] is a little misleading. We at first hoped that it was some account of that gang of conspirators who raised the Man of Sedan to the Imperial Throne, and reduced France to its present condition. No one could have described them so well as the author of that remarkable book, "The Member for Paris." He possesses all Kinglake's power of satire with a far greater knowledge of French affairs. The present book, however, is a reprint of some of those brilliant sketches of Frenchmen, taken generally from a social point of view, which have so often delighted the readers of the *Pall Mall Gazette*. Any one who wishes to gain some general idea of the condition of France during the Second Empire should certainly read these twenty chapters, which describe as many different types of character, photographed with wonderful accuracy. Perhaps some of the clerical photographs are the best. Here, for instance, is the Abbé de Vernis, who when being taunted with being a Jesuit, does not rant or rave, but meekly folds his hands, fixing his eyes devoutly on his almond-shaped nails, and proceeds to give a short sketch of the Jesuits, dwelling especially on their many good deeds. Then when everybody expects to hear him sum up in their favour, he quietly adds, "But the Jesuits have been guilty of many crimes, and they are reproached with being hypocrites. This being the case, I can only rejoice that I have nothing to do with them." The Abbé de Vernis is not, however, exclusively French.

With the preceding work should be compared "Eight Months on Duty."[14] The testimony which it bears is especially valuable as coming from a French officer. It confirms in every particular what impartial Englishmen have already said concerning the organization of the French troops during the late war. One of the most hopeful signs for the regeneration of France is the publication and popularity of such a book. We most cordially thank Dr. Vaughan for having introduced us to a work which, apart from professional considerations, should for its high tone and manly bearing be studied by every English officer.

Our poets are as prolific as usual. Mr. Longland,[15] has put the Boscobel Tracts into the shape of a drama. The value may be judged by the following extract, describing Charles taking refuge in the famous oak. "Colonel Careless, we must conceal ourselves at once. Look here—this is a capital tree to screen us. Jump up here—don't breathe, nor stir a limb. . . . . the higher up the better" (p. 30). Mr.

[13] "Men of the Second Empire." By the Author of "The Member for Paris." London : Smith, Elder and Co. 1872.

[14] "Eight Months on Duty. Diary of a Young Officer in Chanzy's Army." From the French of Roger de M. With a Preface by C. J. Vaughan, D.D., Master of the Temple. London : Strahan and Co. 1872.

[15] "King Charles the Second : an Historical Drama, in Five Acts." By Joseph Longland. London : Longmans, Green and Co. 1872.

Longland has evidently taken great pains to insure historical accuracy. There is, however, one passage upon which we feel some doubts. Can Mr. Longland produce any authority for the following speech, which he puts into King Charles's mouth?—"Thank you, I have just had an excellent meal, for which I must pay my host." This seems, we must confess, thoroughly out of keeping with the popular idea of the merry monarch, who apparently believed in Panurge's maxim, "to lend is divine, to owe is heroic."

Mr. Maccrom's[16] attempt is worse doggrel than even Mr. Longland's. Here is his idea of poetry: "Viewed from the elevation of my place, the landscape was an admirable one before me, stretching many a league away; 'twas very fair, and wild variety" (p. 78). This stuff is cut into lines, and so at a distance looks to the eye something like poetry. This, however, is the only resemblance.

The author of "The Bride"[17] appears to possess a comic vein. We are led to this conclusion by his poem on "The Laying of the Cables," where we find such a stanza as—

"Then lent America her ship ' Niagara,'
   To bring the cable half the ocean o'er;
And the 'Agamemnon' sent from the English side, was meant
   To conduct it to the shore."—p. 145.

If this is poetry, what did Shakspeare and Milton write?

If the term "New Writer" be synonymous, and there are some grounds for thinking so, with a "Young Writer," then "Songs of Two Worlds"[18] contains genuine promise. The writer possesses not merely poetical feeling, which is common enough, but here and there shows, what is so rare, real imaginative power. For instance the second poem in the collection, "Love's Mirror," or as Herrick in his "Hesperides" would have said—

"Babies in the eyes,
   In their crystal nunneries,"

recals a love-strain of our Elizabethan poets, but idealized by the writer's imagination, and purged of that grossness which the same idea degenerated to in the hands of Cleveland and his contemporaries. Further, the writer shows a generous enthusiasm, as may be seen in a piece, "The True Man." Lastly, he possesses a descriptive power of no mean order, which has evidently been carefully cultured. In no recent volume of poetry have we seen the delights of simple English country life in the summer time, touched with so much tenderness and real feeling as in some stanzas in the "Young Mother." We must, however, warn a "New Writer" that at present his poems can only be regarded as an earnest of future success, and that if he would reach that ideal which he has so well painted in his lines "On a Young Poet," he must exercise a far more rigid power of self-control. Had his volume been reduced by one-half it would certainly have gained in value. Let him take a lesson from the "Sibyl."

[16] "Unseen and Idealities." Poems by J. S. Maccrom. London: Smith, Elder and Co. 1872.
[17] "The Bride, and other Poems." London: Smith, Elder and Co. 1872.
[18] "Songs of Two Worlds." By a New Writer. London: Henry S. King and Co. 1872.

"Poems Narrative and Dramatic"[19] are written by a man who could evidently do anything else better than write poetry. Here is a specimen:

> "Sir, of my eldest sister now
> The fate you have heard, and I proceed
> Of our loved Annaline to speak.
> Worthy was she of better meed
> Than fate decreed she should obtain."—p. 103.

For our own part we should say that a list of articles in an auctioneer's catalogue was quite as poetical as this.

We now come to a different class of writers, who always, at least, command our respect for their culture and liberal tone. But unfortunately, as has been so often said, mere culture and good taste will not make poetry. If this were so the author of "Fra Angelico"[20] might take his place amongst the first poets.

And the same words apply with equal force to the author of "Delhi."[21] Nor must it be thought that because these books do not make their mark in the world that they are entirely without value. On the contrary, they show the increase of refinement and of a higher tone and spirit of liberalism, which is making its way in the world. No one can read either of these two books without being persuaded that their authors in their own circles must exercise a vast amount of beneficial influence upon all those with whom they come in contact. If the complete gift of poetical expression is denied, yet the power of true poetry in its influence on life and our social relations one with another remains.

Mr. Piatt has, if we may judge by the American papers, obtained considerable reputation in the United States. We think, too, that we have seen a statement that some of his poems have been, or are going to be, translated into German. That Mr. Piatt's poems should be popular in the States is by no means extraordinary. They deal in a popular way with popular subjects, with which Americans are familiar. He can for instance, as in "Western Windows,"[22] describe such a scene as is common in the far West, of burning the last year's stubble previous to breaking up the ground in the spring for a fresh sowing, with considerable vigour. Again, he can, as in "Landmarks,"[23] describe such a scene as apple gathering, just before the Indian summer sets in, with a fulness of detail and a picturesqueness which are certainly impressive. We doubt, however, if he will be as popular in England as in his native land.

[19] "Poems, Narrative and Dramatic." By the Author of "Poems by L." London: E. T. Whitfield. 1872.
[20] "Fra Angelico, and other Short Poems." By I. G. S. London: Longmans, Green and Co. 1872.
[21] "Delhi, and Other Poems." By Charles Arthur Kelly, M.A. London: Longmans, Green and Co. 1872.
[22] "Western Windows, and other Poems." By John James Piatt. New York: Hurd and Houghton. London: Trübner and Co. 1872.
[23] "Landmarks, and other Poems." By John James Piatt. New York: Hurd and Houghton. London: Trübner and Co. 1872.

We have reserved for the last the two most notable books of poetry. The lady first. We deeply regret that Mrs. Webster should have chosen a dramatic form for her new poem.[14] In these days a closet-drama has become associated with weariness of the flesh. We are apt to regard a reading-play as an intellectual feat, which it is a duty rather than a pleasure to read. Our stage has sunk so low, that there is no chance of writers of Mrs. Webster's genius turning their attention to play-writing. Her dramatic instinct, which is so strong, finds therefore its only outlet in a shape like the present. The subject which she has chosen is a fine one, and she has treated it in a noble way. We cannot now analyse the plot, which turns upon the charge of witchcraft, or of the beauty with which such characters as Dorothy, Amy, and Father Gabriel are drawn, though we hope to do so on some future occasion. Our chief aim just now will be to point out the quality of the poetry. It may be a very fair question, whether the masque at the beginning of the play had better have been omitted or not; but there can be no doubt as to its extreme beauty. We must go back to the days of our Elizabethan poets for its match. And we call especial attention to its warmth and colouring, and gay sprightly movement, because there seems to be some notion abroad that Mrs. Webster's poetry is of that cold, intellectual kind which would be better in the form of an essay. For instance, the following song, sung by the Nymphs, appears to us perfect, as pure and as sweet as May blossom:—

> " One star only for Love's heaven;
> One rose only for Love's breast;
> One love only to be given.
>
> Star that gathers all stars' glory;
> Rose all sweetness of the rest;
> Love that is all life's glad story."—p. 19.

Surely the secret of love—its undying constancy—has never been told in our songs in sweeter lines than these. As a song-writer, Mrs. Webster is always seen at her best. She has the true lyrical power of expression. Take, for instance, one more song on this same subject of love:—

> " Where found Love his yesterday?
> Where is Love's to-morrow?—say
> Love has only now.
> We can swear it, we who stand,
> In Love's present, hand in hand,—
> Thou and I, dear, I and thou.
>
> *By-and-by* and *Long ago*,
> Last month's buds, next winter's snow,
> Love has only now.
> Do we wot of rathe or sere
> In Love's boundless summer year,
> Thou and I, dear, I and thou?

> Suns that rose and suns to set;
> *Gone for ever* and *Not yet*—
>   Love has always now.
> Do we count by dawn and night,
> Dwelling in Love's perfect light,
>   Thou and I, dear, I and thou ?"

Surely, we must repeat, that that old sweet burden, "They two, and they two, and they two for aye," has never been set to tenderer or truer words. If the colouring, the lyrical sweetness, the passion, and above all, the truth of these lines, will not send readers to Mrs. Webster's new poem, then no words of ours can possibly do so. We will merely add, that in our opinion "The Auspicious Day" shows a marked advance, not only in art, but, of what is of far more importance, in breadth of thought and intellectual grasp.

Mr. Payne's[23] new volume of poems is far more likely to be popular than any of its predecessors. Mr. Payne is less shadowy and less mystical. He lives less in that dreamland which he peopled with shadows of his own creation. It is a perfect delight to meet with such a ballad as that of "May Margaret" in the present volume. The art of ballad-writing has long been lost in England, and Mr. Payne may claim to be its restorer. Nor has Mr. Payne sacrificed any of those qualities, grace of style and delicacy of thought, which first of all won him so many admirers. He still writes with the same delight of the fields and the flowers and the spring, and still, like his contemporaries Rossetti and Morris, goes to the storehouse of our elder English poets for their old expressive words, which we have forgotten, and sets them with fresh beauty to modern thought.

On our table lie a number of reprints and new editions, which we can only briefly acknowledge. Every one will rejoice to see that the handsome edition of Tennyson[24] is progressing; all lovers of Horace will welcome Lord Lytton's[27] new edition of his translation of the Odes and Epodes; and all Scotchmen hail with pleasure a convenient reprint of Tennant's "Anster Fair."[28] We have, too, also to acknowledge a quantity of schoolbooks. As we had often said, nothing but the actual test of experience can prove their value. The names of Heslop[29] and Sidgwick[30] may be taken as guarantees for the excellence of any works which they may edit. Mr. Cranstoun's translation of Tibullus[31] is both

---

23 "Songs of Life and Death." By John Payne, Author of "Intaglios : Sonnets," "The Masque of Shadows," &c. London : Henry S. King and Co. 1872.

24 "The Works of Alfred Tennyson, Poet Laureate." Vols II. III. London : Strahan and Co. 1872.

27 "The Odes and Epodes of Horace. A Metrical Translation into English. With Introduction and Commentaries." By Lord Lytton. New Edition. London : Longmans, Green and Co. 1872.

28 "Anster Fair." By William Tennant. Edinburgh : John Ross and Co. 1872.

29 "Demosthenis Orationes Publicæ." Edited by G. H. Heslop, M.A., Head Master of St. Bees. The Embassy. London : Rivingtons. 1872. (Catena Classicorum Series.)

30 "Scenes from Aristophanes" (Rugby Edition). By A. Sidgwick. The Plutos. The Knights. The Clouds. London : Rivingtons. 1872.

31 "The Elegies of Albius Tibullus." Translated into English Verse. By James Cranstoun, B.A. London : Blackwood and Sons. 1872.

poetical and scholarly, whilst Mr. Donne's Euripides[22] is in places
somewhat too flippant for our taste.

"Your beans look bad," said one neighbour to another. "Yes, but
Farmer Brown's are as bad, and that's some comfort!" was the reply.
Much the same may be said about English and German novels. Both
are on the average equally bad. "Der neue Abälard"[23] is a fair
specimen of the second-rate novel, which is common enough in both
countries, written by a man of decided ability, who has a quick eye for
character. But a novel requires something more than a little smart
comic writing and a plentiful supply of tears. The hero is one of
those beings who tries all callings, and as a last resource takes to
love. He has been actor, lecturer, and tutor. In his last capacity,
the modern Abelard falls in love with Heloise, or Heloise with him,
for it does not much matter. We need not say that he is super-
humanly virtuous and painfully good. His love-suit, however, does
not, at first, turn out much better than his other undertakings. The
lady's father will not hear of the match, and carries her off from the
scene. Abelard proceeds to console himself with a work on the popular
songs of the Fatherland, and in some curious speculations on Providence, and an original Faith of his own making, and some vague
metaphors. Then he proposes to go after his beloved. The thought,
however, luckily occurs to him that he has no money, and further,
that he does not know where she is; two difficulties not to be got
over by metaphors. Finally, he takes to lecturing on the "Rights
of Women." So great is the enthusiasm which his eloquence arouses,
that the audience present him with a silver goblet; and those hard-
hearted wretches the German publishers, and even those still harder-
hearted wretches the English publishers, literally thrust money into
his hands. A man who can perform such a feat as this is sure
to succeed in the world. We feel no further anxiety about
him. And when we read on the last page of the last chapter
of the first volume, that he is going "to take the bull by the horns,
and beard the lion in his den," or, in other words, compel the
father to sanction the marriage, we are quite sure that he is the man
to keep his word. Of the other characters, Herr Sommervogel, of
the druggist's shop, who told you, as a great secret, that Easter was
coming, and who had the satisfaction of buying his medicines cost-
price, is an amusing scamp. Frau von Ribbeck is the usual stage
Madonna with deep melancholy eyes. Little Walter is natural
enough as a boy, and plays yeoman's service in forwarding and retard-
ing the action of the story during its early stages, by interrupting the
lovers at precisely the right moment. With his eternal Onkel, Onkel,
we may venture to call him a Deunculus ex machinâ.

Of the other German novels of this quarter we can say but little.
Herr von Strauss's[24] collection of stories may, however, be recommended,

[22] "Euripides." By William Bodham Donne. (Ancient Classics for English
Readers Series.) London: Blackwood and Sons. 1872.
[23] "Der neue Abälard." Roman. Von Julius Grosse. Leipzig: Ernst
Julius Grünther. 1871.
[24] "Novellen." Von Victor von Strauss. Leipzig: F. Fleischer. 1872.

for if one tale does not suit the reader's taste, another probably will.
There is a healthy out-door tone about some of them. "Letzte Reste"[20]
contains two pretty little tales, more especially for children, overflowing with a poetical spirit. "Fritz Ellrodt"[21] is one of those long-
winded romances which is sure to find more popularity in Germany
than in England. Lastly, we have to acknowledge a new edition of
"Christian Klebauer und Compagnie,"[22] by Dr. Fritze.

The faults of "Gundel vom Königssee"[23] lie on the surface. Some
of them may be attributed to the hexameter metre, which in German
and English seems to peculiarly adapt itself to Tupperisms and commonplaces. We feel particularly thankful when some of the personages finish their harangues, for there is no earthly reason why they
should stop. Further, the men indulge in far too much stage rant.
They smack, in their talk at least, far too much of the conventional
theatrical brigand in spangles and feathers. Ignaz, instead of being
a villain, is simply a "boer," whilst Thomas, in spite of his wrongs and
sufferings, hardly excites our interest, much less our sympathy. The
best drawn character is, without doubt, Gundel. She is sketched
with firm strokes. Only once or twice does she rant or rave. The
descriptions of mountain scenery are particularly good, and are evidently painted by one who is well acquainted not only with the
natural beauties round Salzburg and the Königssee, but with the
country-people and their customs, and is thus enabled to throw in a
local colouring which has a peculiar charm of its own. The description of the old farm (p. 24), situated in the valley, amongst its
meadows and brooks, shadowed over by elms, with its great roof and
its balcony covered with flowers, and its rows of beehives, is nearly
a perfect picture. The boat race and the various hunting exploits are
described with vigour and life, which admirably contrast with the
quiet idyllic scenes by the side of which they are set. We have already
noticed the local colouring in the tale, and we may add that the author
has very rightly added a glossary of all the provincialisms which he
has used. Further, it is but bare justice to say that the book is
brought out in a style highly creditable to the publishers. The paper
is excellent, and the head and tail-pieces and initial letters are really
artistic. But why cannot German binders stitch a book together so
that it shall not fall to pieces with five minutes' handling? Long
before we had read the poem through, the first and last leaves were
mixed in inextricable confusion; and the sins of the binder are apt to
be visited upon the head of the inoffending author.

We in vain look, in Herr Rogge's "Westminster-Abtei,"[24] for any-

[20] "Letzte Reste. Ein Cyclus von Novellen-Skizzen." Von Hermine Weigelt.
Bremen: J. Kühlmann. 1872.
[21] "Fritz Ellrodt." Roman von Karl Gutzkow. Jena: H. Costenoble. 1872.
[22] "Christian Klebauer und Compagnie." Roman von Dr. Hermann Eduard
Fritze. Zweite Ausgabe. Jena: H. Costenoble. 1871.
[23] "Gundel vom Königssee." Erzählende Dichtung aus dem bayrischen Hoch-
land in sieben Gesängen, von Julius Grosse. Berlin: Franz Lipperheide. 1872.
[24] "Aus Westminster-Abtei." Von Friedrich Wilhelm Rogge. Leipzig:
Otto Wigand. 1872.

thing like the power which Beaumont showed in his small poem " On
the Tombs in Westminster Abbey."

> " Here's an acre sown indeed
>   With the richest, royallest seed,"

but Herr Roggo is evidently not the poet to celebrate that " world of
pomp and state buried in dust." He writes something like a poetical
undertaker :—

> " Hier in St. Benedict's glanzvollen Raum
>   Schläft Lionell von Middlesex in Frieden,
>   Ein Siebziger."—p. 13.

Herr Meyer's poem" is very welcome. His verse is rough-hewn,
but it suits the subject. It is, in short, such verse as the poet-warrior
who is here celebrated would have hailed with delight. There is not
only vigour, but picturesqueness and humour in these short pieces,
which remind one of the times which are portrayed. There is a hearty
ring about the verses. Nothing can be more to the point than such a
little poem as " Feder und Schwert," when we remember how Zuingli
wrote that Hutten left behind him nothing in the world but a pen.
These poems should be read with Strauss's " Life of Hutten," a new
edition of which appeared last year. Herr von Kobell's little volume"
appeals more to philologists, and Germans in particular, than to the
general public. Copious notes, however, illustrate all the provincialisms, and so smooth down the difficulties. The author is, we may
add, very popular in Germany, and no less than ten years since some
of his provincial poems had attained the honour of a sixth edition.
" Der deutsch-französische Krieg"" is the title of one of those innumerable little volumes of war-songs of which we are heartily tired.
The present volume appears to give both German and French songs
with great impartiality.

Englishmen who have been puzzled at the reverence with which
the middle-class Germans, especially along the Rhine, regard the
" Kölnischer Zeitung," may find some explanation of its popularity
in a paper on Heinrich Kruse, by Herr Lindau," in his volume of
miscellaneous essays. We have an interesting sketch of his early life
and opinions, and of the particular talents which he afterwards brought
to bear with such good effect in the columns of that paper. His style
appears to belong to the sledge-hammer school, depending rather on
mother-wit than refinement and argument. Those who are interested
in the state of the German daily press, and of the writers to the
" Tretmühle der Gedanken," as it has been called, should turn to
another paper in the same volume—Ein Fest der Berliner Presse.
We are glad to learn from it that the discovery has been made in

* " Hutten's letzte Tage." Eine Dichtung. Von C. Ferdinand Meyer. Leip-
zig: H. Haessel. 1872.
† " G'schpiel." Volkstücke und Gedichte in oberbayerischen Mundart. Von
Franz von Kobell. München: C. A. Dempwolff. 1872.
‡ " Der deutsch-französische Krieg 1870-1871." Herausgegeben von Adolph
Enslin. Berlin: Th. Enslin. 1871.
§ " Literarische Rücksichtslosigkeiten." Feuilletonistische und Polemische
Aufsätze. Von Paul Lindau. Leipzig: J. Barth. 1872.

Prussia as well as in England, that genius is not incompatible with clean linen. Many of the miscellaneous articles are not without interest. In "Heiter in ernster Zeit" will be found the Temptation of Bismarck, which, although witty, sounds rather profane to English ears. Of course, Benedetti figures as the devil. The papers on various German translations of foreign authors are all good. The author notices a curious blunder in a recent version of Tartuffe, where in a famous passage the translator mistakes "fumier" for "fumée," and renders it "rauch." If, however, Herr Lindau should ever come across our English translation of Molière in 1739, he will find some still more curious blunders. In his paper on different translations of Shakspeare, Herr Lindau presses we think rather too severely upon the shortcomings of the new Bodenstedt version, which in some renderings we certainly prefer to the Schlegel and Tieck edition.

The interest which the Germans take in Shakspeare is inexhaustible. The late Otto Ludwig's work" possesses one most valuable characteristic—it regards Shakspeare from the dramatist's point of view—a point of view nearly totally neglected in England. Nor is this neglect a matter of wonder, when we consider how few critics are capable of judging his plays from this stand-point. The perfection of Shakspeare's art is perhaps the last quality realized, because it is the least showy, and can only be appreciated by dramatists of a high order. Such a criticism as that entitled "Das Shauspielerische in Shakespeare," (pp. 42, 43) goes to the heart of the matter. Had the author's life been spared, these reflections and notes would doubtless have assumed a more consistent shape. But even as they stand, they form a volume of criticism of the very highest order.

Herr Kreyssig's little work" addresses itself to an audience of a very different kind. Its substance, originally delivered in the shape of essays, is essentially popular in tone. The first three parts contain all that is known of Shakspeare's life, put together in a small compass, and compiled with evidently great care from the best and most recent authorities. The remainder of the volume is devoted to criticisms on the plays, written in the same popular yet painstaking style. It is much to be regretted that we have no corresponding class of book in England to familiarize the people with the works of their greatest poet.

ART: MUSIC.

THE tendency of modern educational works is to simplify the matter taught, and convey it by the most direct way to the learner's mind. This is especially the case with regard to music, a knowledge of which could only be gained, not so very long ago, after sore trouble with obstacles imposed by the ignorance or pedantry of former generations. In the theoretical department a great work of simplification has recently been done, and is still doing; but till the

" "Shakespeare Studien." Von Otto Ludwig. Aus dem Nachlass des Dichters herausgegeben von Moritz Heydrich. Leipzig: C. Cnobloch. 1872.
" "Shakespeare Fragen. Kurze Einführung in das Studium des Dichters." Von F. Kreyssig. Leipzig: F. Luckhardt. 1871.

appearance of Madame Sainton Dolby's "Tutor"[1] no effort was made
to popularize the principles and practice of vocalization. We have
had manuals in plenty, it is true, but, for the most part, they have
"darkened counsel," or shown themselves best fitted to increase the
number of tenth-rate imitators of Italian singers. Under these circumstances Madame Sainton could have rendered no better service than
by the publication of a work meant to guide English vocalists in their
study of music dear to English taste, and carrying out its intention
with plainness of speech as well as directness of method. As to the
competency of Madame Sainton not a word need be said. A long and
illustrious career in the very front of the profession is a guarantee that
her words are words of wisdom. Madame Sainton's remarks upon the
"formation, production, and cultivation of the voice" deserve careful
study by all who are practically interested in the subject. Here, for
example, is a sentence calculated to upset a most mistaken and
mischievous notion :—" It is not the compass which decides the
character of a voice." Ignorance of or disbelief in this fact has ruined
many a noble organ, and Madame Sainton wisely cautions her readers
against trusting the classification of voices to anything but the judgment of a good professor. In this case, as in many others throughout
the work, she clearly indicates where the province of a manual ends
and that of a living teacher begins, thus guarding herself against mis-
conception and the pupil from inevitable disappointment. The purely
technical advice given in the first portion of Madame Sainton's work is
pregnant with "sound doctrine;" but we come upon still more
valuable remarks in the division which treats of "expression, style,
and taste." It is insisted, for example, that the student should have
regard to his personal sympathies in the selection of music. The old
counsel, "know thyself," needs to be acted upon before individual
qualities can be turned to best account. Yet few vocalists ever give
this matter a thought, and the result is that for one natural expression
of musical ideas we have ten which are the reverse. "Many singers,"
observes Madame Sainton, "affect an originality they are far from possessing, and that in art which is artificial is always offensive." The sentence should be inscribed in golden letters upon the walls of every music
class-room. Equally valuable are the remarks concerning that peculiar
quality of a great singer which, for want of a better word, Madame
Sainton calls "inspiration," and upon which she insists as necessary
to perfection, while frankly owning that it is incommunicable. Where
it exists, however, the professor can guide its development, and prevent untutored impulse from violating the rules of art. On that much-
neglected branch of vocal training, elocution, Madame Sainton expresses
herself with characteristic plainness and strong common sense; urging
that the effect of the purest voice is impaired by malpronunciation,
and that half the charm of vocal music is lost unless the audience can
hear every syllable. This is emphatically true, yet no truth was ever
ignored with such unanimity and persistence. Even professional
singers of rank sometimes need to take elementary lessons in elocu-

---

[1] Madame Sainton Dolby's "Tutor for English Singers (Ladies' Voices). A
Complete Course of Practical Instruction in the Art of Singing." London:
Boosey and Co.

tion; while as for amateurs, it is rarely that they give the matter
a thought. The foregoing remarks serve to show from what a high
artistic stand-point Madame Sainton surveys the ground her work
is intended to cover, and with what honesty and thoroughness her
task has been accomplished. As regards the course of exercises forming
the bulk of the volume there cannot be two opinions. Anything more
complete of its kind, or better adapted to make study pleasant, we do
not know. A special and most valuable feature is a collection of arias,
songs, and ballads, accompanied by plain hints upon the best method
of interpreting them.' This section of the "Tutor" is worth the price
of the whole, and cannot fail to obtain wide popularity among really
earnest amateurs. Madame Sainton, we say again, has done well to
place within easy reach a full exposition of that system which,
having given her fame as an artist, is bringing her more and more
into repute as a teacher. Madame Sainton, it should here be observed,
is affording the best possible illustration of her theory, and of her own
power to reduce it to practice, by the success of the Vocal Academy
over which she presides. We do a real service to art in prominently
noticing this fact, because we see in Madame Sainton's method of
instruction the beginning of a most valuable reform. Collective study
has long been a rule in other branches of knowledge; but with regard
to music, for reasons which it is scarcely worth while to specify, the
individual system has held, and still holds ground. Madame Sainton
now seriously threatens its existence by basing her practice as a
teacher upon the obvious considerations that collective study not only
offers the highest incentives to perseverance, but adds to the pupil's
knowledge of his own merits and defects a knowledge of the merits
and defects of others. In class the pupil must necessarily be always
learning, and the larger the class the greater his opportunity, while
the moral influence of association with others in a high pursuit is of
priceless value. We feel sure that Madame Sainton has no reason to
doubt the soundness of her method, so far as its results have yet
appeared, and the only fault possible to be found with it is its limitation to ladies only. It would be well if some bold teacher recognised
and acted upon the fact, that even in the matter of acquiring knowledge the sexes are the complement of each other. Of course there
are details of instruction in music which cannot have a common application: but, generally speaking, there is no reason why men and
women should not carry on their study of the art together. In fact,
reason and observation alike point to an opposite conclusion. But,
pending greater reform, it is well to know that a teacher so distinguished as Madame Sainton is applying to musical instruction those
common-sense ideas which have long regulated instruction of other
kinds. In this respect her Vocal Academy is worthy of public notice,
and of every kind of support which can legitimately be given to it.

We have spoken above of the work of simplification going on in the
theoretical department of music, and Dr. Stainer's thoughtful book[2]
gives the best possible proof of its extent and completeness. In dis-

---

[2] " A Theory of Harmony founded on the Tempered Scale, with Questions and
Answers for the Use of Students." By John Stainer, Mus. Doc., M.A. Magd.
Coll. Oxon. London : Rivingtons.

cussing a subject so purely technical, it is hard to find expressions
which shall be intelligible to the general reader ; but we may nevertheless, hope to make Dr. Stainer's system understood, at least in its
main points, by those whose knowledge of music is elementary only. In
the first place, he gets rid at one swoop of the mathematical musicians,
and their enharmonic scale ; accepting the tempered scale, with all its
deficiencies, as being the basis of musical literature, "from the works
of Bach to those of Wagner." This is an immense clearance of the
ground, and one upon which practical musicians will congratulate our
author. The mathematicians, with their notion of a perfect scale for
every key, have in view an ideal perfection ; not perhaps unattainable,
but certainly not necessary, seeing that Haydn, Mozart, and Beethoven could express themselves without it. Dr. Stainer recognises
this fact, and, accepting things as they are, he has developed a theory
of harmony described as generalizations, "which shall help the student
to place clearly before his mind the chords which a composer has at
his disposal ; how they have hitherto been used, and how they may in
future be used." In other words, our author accepts the recognised
language of music, and adapts his grammar to it, rather than seeks to
make the actual conform to the ideal. So far, he has analogy upon
his side. Every spoken language existed before its grammar. It is
quite refreshing to find Dr. Stainer, at the outset of his book, throwing the light of common sense upon the needless obscurity created by
older theorists. The merest tyro in harmony knows how the intervals
of the fourth and fifth have been exalted to perfection, while the third
has taken secondary rank as imperfect. Our author demolishes this
theory, and, at the same time, defines the basis of his system in words
which deserve quotation :—

"The old veneration for the perfection of the fourth and fifth, hardly yet
extinct, helped to degrade thirds by calling them imperfect intervals ; yet the
greater number of those lovely chords which ravish us so much and furnish us
with an endless source of modulation (such as the chord of the diminished
seventh and its inversions), contain neither the interval of a fourth or fifth
between any of the component notes. All are thirds, or their inversions,
sixths. If any interval ever deserved to be called perfect it is the third. A
major fifth by itself does not give us the means of judging whether we are in
the major or minor mode. Except in barbarous music, the bare major fifth is
never used, unless a composer, for the purpose of producing special effects,
wishes to foster the impression of doubtfulness of mode. The fourth is less
entitled to be called a harmony-producing interval than the fifth. The only
simple interval, then, which may be said to form harmony is the third, both in
its natural and inverted state."

The major part of these propositions could not be denied by the
sternest believer in the old theorists. Yet Dr. Stainer is almost alone
in taking the third as the basis of harmony, and raising upon it a
simple, because natural superstructure. There is an odd perversity
in human nature which often leads men to reject that which is clear
in favour of that which is obscure ; and to this we attribute the fact
that while untutored instinct makes harmony in thirds, or their inversions, science has dubbed these very intervals as "imperfect," and
gone floundering about in a very slough of difficulty to find some
better foundation. Having defined chords as neither more nor less

than combinations of thirds, Dr. Stainer developes his theory in a
very logical and complete manner. We cannot, for obvious reasons,
follow him through its ramifications, and must be satisfied to refer
those who are curious in the matter to a concise summary (pp. 118-
120), which puts Dr. Stainer's leading principles in the clearest light.
Our own conviction is, that the new organist of St. Paul's has done an
immense service to the theory of his art by the publication of this
work; stripping that theory of many superfluous appendages, and giving
it not only light but liberty. The examples, taken from great masters,
with which the work abounds, and the numerous exercises forming an
appendix, are most useful, and do great credit both to Dr. Stainer's
research and skill.

That the world knows nothing of its greatest men has passed into a
proverb; but with regard to at least one great man, Felix Mendelssohn Bartholdy, the world will soon know all. It is not likely to be
satisfied with anything short of all, so great a charm attaches itself
to the composer, his works and ways. In such a case it seems un-
gracious to complain as revelation after revelation is made of Mendelssohn's public or private life. But really there is a medium even
in gratifying legitimate hero-worship; and it does not follow that
because Beethoven wrote the Choral Symphony, his notes of invita-
tion to dinner should be printed; or because Mendelssohn composed
St. Paul, it should be announced to the world that at seven years old
he loved marmalade as much as music. Yet analogous absurdities are
often done; and we are inclined to place Dr. Karl-Mendelssohn's book[a]
among them. *Primâ facie*, nothing could be more interesting than
the relations between such men as the composer of *Elijah* and the
author of *Faust*, but an acquaintance with those relations, even when
gained through the medium of the great musician's son, proves eminently disappointing. It appears that when Mendelssohn was twelve
years old, his music-master, Zelter, took him on a visit to the sage of
Weimar, who was pleased with the boy's precocious genius and viva-
cious ways. But Goethe's first recorded utterance with regard to him
is very much like "In the name of the prophet, figs." "You know,"
he said to Rellstab, "the doctrine of temperaments; every one has all
the four in him, only in different proportions. Well, this boy, I
should say, possesses the smallest possible modicum of the phlegmatic,
and the maximum of the opposite quality." Very likely, but so do most
boys of twelve. It would be easy to make a string of truisms which
Dr. Mendelssohn quotes from Goethe as though they were the
essence of hitherto concealed wisdom; and it would be still more easy
to laugh at the poet's remarks upon an art of which he knew scarcely
anything—music. "Make a little noise for me," was his manner of
asking Mendelssohn to play; and once, when the musician had revealed to the poet, as far as could be done on a pianoforte, the majesty
of Beethoven's C minor Symphony, Goethe could find nothing better
to say than a common-place " That is very grand—quite wild enough
to bring the house about one's ears; *and what must it be when all the*

[a] "Goethe and Mendelssohn (1821-1831). Translated, with Additions, from
the German of Dr. Karl Mendelssohn-Bartholdy." By M. E. von Glehn.
London: Macmillan and Co.

people are playing at once!" The fact was, and Dr. Karl Mendelssohn confesses it, that Goethe cared nothing about either music or musicians. He loved Mendelssohn for his personal qualities, and appears to have tried hard to get up an interest in his art, but with no great success. On Schiller and his works the poet was more competent to speak, for which reason a conversation between himself and Mendelssohn relative to the author of *Wilhelm Tell* is perhaps the most valuable portion of the book. With regard to Mendelssohn himself, so far as he is here revealed, we can only wish that the picture were more agreeable. At twelve years old the lad's natural modesty was struggling hard against a priggishness engendered by the well-meant but most mischievous system of training to which he was subjected. Thus we find him writing home from Weimar about a Polish pianist whom Goethe enthusiastically admired: "People set the Szymanowska above Hummel; they have confused her pretty face with her not pretty playing." Again, he says of the lexicographer Riemer:—"He seems to thrive on the making of lexicons. He is stout and fat, and as shiny as a priest, or a full moon." "From all that I see," remarked Goethe to Eckermann, "I gather that the Berliners, as a class, are such a forward set that delicacy is thrown away upon them;" and having this impression, it was well, as Dr. Karl Mendelssohn intimates, that the old poet did not know all the pertness in which his young guest indulged. This objectionable quality, here termed "independence of mind and real originality," grew with Mendelssohn's growth and strengthened with his strength. In 1825, being then sixteen, he was taken to Paris for a consultation with Cherubini, who received him most kindly. In return the "forward" Berliner, anticipating Mr. Disraeli's Manchester sarcasm on the Treasury Bench, compared the author of *Medea* and *Les Deux Journées* to "an extinct volcano, still throwing out occasional flashes and sparks, but quite covered with ashes and stones." He even went so far as to parody the old master's style in a sacred piece, whereupon poor foolish Zelter, his Berlin guide and friend, if not philosopher, cried out, "Clever fellow." Nothing in musical Paris satisfied this young German gentleman of sixteen, and in particular was he irritated by Auber's opera *Léocadie.* Here are a few of his criticisms upon the illustrious Frenchman's work:—"anything so miserable you really cannot conceive;"—"most miserably tame music;"—"no breadth, no life, no originality;"—"no vestige of seriousness or spark of passion, no power, no fire;"—"in short, the whole thing might be capitally arranged for two flutes and a jew's-harp *ad libitum.* Oh dear!" All this vituperation, be it remembered, had for its object one of Auber's most charming operas,—a work Mendelssohn could not have written by trying ever so hard. We might go on with extracts of a like character, but enough has been said to raise a question as to the propriety of making these revelations. The public have an insatiable appetite for details about great men, it is true; nevertheless, that appetite is satisfied at too heavy a cost when the result lowers genius by showing its alliance with personal foibles or weaknesses. It is matter for regret that modern book-makers do not bear this in mind to a greater extent. *De mortuis nil nisi bonum* applies even to particulars which, if not absolutely bad, have a tendency to make their object less a hero. In other respects the volume is chiefly noteworthy " as an example of book-making." So slight were the actual relations between Mendelssohn and Goethe that it seems to have been necessary to fill fifty pages—nearly one-third of the whole—with letters written by the composer on a variety of topics to a variety of people. Some of these are interesting; especially the series addressed to Mr. G. A. Macfarren, and having reference to an edition of Handel's works. But there are others, especially that wherein Mendelssohn records a visit to Queen Victoria at Buckingham Palace, which ought not to have been made public; and we may ask, in view of them, whether the printing of letters addressed, in confidence, by the composer to his friends, has not gone far enough ? At any rate, the case of Mendelssohn is a warning to famous persons, and will induce them to pose for the world even in the privacy of the cabinet—not a desirable consummation.

Whether language be or be not given us for the purpose of concealing our thoughts, it is a fact that the titles of books are often but little indicative of their contents. Mr. Haweis's " Music and Morals"* supplies an example. Touching but lightly upon morals, it is really a dissertation on musical things in general, from the Choral Symphony to Low Country carillons, and from Beethoven to "nigger" melodists. The reverend author trips over this wide extent of ground with obvious enjoyment to himself; and if it cannot be said that he much increases our knowledge, he is, beyond question, both readable and amusing. Mr. Haweis classifies his observations under four heads :—Philosophical, Biographical, Instrumental, and Critical. The first section contains all that justifies the title of the book, and is well worth reading as the result of an intelligent amateur's experience of contemporary music and musical society. We cannot here follow Mr. Haweis's numerous excursions into the region lying round about the art of which he treats, nor can we pretend to distinguish the plan by which his observations are regulated. Enough that the first division includes forty-four subjects, all duly indexed, and that one succeeds another without necessary connexion, while all, with a few exceptions, are treated in a gossiping, superficial style. The fact is, that Mr. Haweis here, as well as elsewhere in his book, attempts too much ; and to get through the work is compelled to touch but lightly that which, if touched at all, should be exhausted. He finds opportunity, however, to make some pertinent remarks upon the abuses existing in musical circles. Here, for instance, are truths told with refreshing plainness :—

"I declare that musical taste in England is degraded and kept low by jealousy and time-serving, and that musical criticism is so gagged and prejudiced and corrupt, that those whose business it is to see that right principles prevail, seem too often led by their interest rather than their duty. When it comes to judging a new composer, the truth is not told, or only half told ; when a new player is allowed to appear, his success depends, not on his merits, but on his friends ; and, whilst it is of course impossible to quell first-class merit, second-class merit is constantly ignored, and many

* "Music and Morals." By the Rev. H. R. Haweis, M.A. London : Strahan and Co.

sound English musicians are often compelled to stand aside and see their
places taken by young quacks or foreigners inferior to themselves."

This testimony is not borne for the first time, nor will Mr. Haweis's
voice of reprobation affect the evils of which he complains one jot;
but it is nevertheless good to meet with such plain speaking at a
time when the art of making things pleasant is better understood
than ever. In his biographical section, Mr. Haweis simply brings
together the results of extensive, if not always accurate reading. After
a prologue, which rushes through the centuries from Ambrose to
Handel at headlong speed, come sketches of Handel, Gluck, Haydn,
Schubert, Chopin, Mozart, Beethoven, and Mendelssohn; the biographical details being interspersed with remarks explanatory or analytical upon these masters' compositions. We must caution the reader
to take a good deal that Mr. Haweis sets down *cum grano salis*, because there are not wanting in his work many proofs of that credulous
spirit which is the greatest drawback to an historiographer. All the
"good stories" about Handel are gravely retold, for instance; and even
his imaginary conversation with Arne and Pepusch appears in the
dignity of large type; only a brief foot-note, easily overlooked, guarding the reader against believing it. To follow Mr. Haweis through
his sketches of the great masters would be unprofitable work. He
adds nothing to the common stock of knowledge; and though his
grandiloquent style may possess attraction enough to excite the
general reader's interest, we fail to see why so much of a book on
"Music and Morals" is given up to diluted extracts from the "Dictionary of Musicians," with twenty-six pages of analysis of *Elijah*, by
way of *coda*. As Mr. Haweis contends that "it is difficult to contemplate
a fine old violin without something like awe," we are not surprised that
he should discuss that class of instrument at length in his third section.
His remarks, it is only fair to add, are interesting as well as enthusiastic; but, *per contra*, we do not find much to praise in the chapters on
pianofortes and bells; the latter of which, seventy pages long, owes a
good deal, if we mistake not, to a series of articles on campanology, first
printed in the Belgian *Guido Musicale*. Passing this by, as having
little to do with music and nothing to do with morals, we come to the
last and "critical" division of the book, which treats of thirty-one
indexed subjects. A majority of these themes, though essential it
may be, to Mr Haweis's plan, are scarcely worth discussion, and we
dismiss at once the lively sketches of musical amateurs, organ-grinders,
street singers, and Ethiopian serenaders, which follow each other with
characteristic rapidity. Our author is more worthy of attention when
writing upon the present state of music in England; though we are
far from agreeing with all the opinions he expresses, and though it
would be difficult to compress into the same space a greater amount
of loose or absolutely inaccurate statement. When, for example, Mr.
Haweis asserts that "music in England has always been an exotic;"
that the English idea of music does not go beyond a "pleasant noise
and jingling rhythm;" and that English people are insensible to the
emotional effects of music, he asserts that which we might safely
challenge him to prove. Again, Mr. Haweis exclaims, after b lending
his favourite German public, "Fancy the frequenters of Cremorne

encoring a symphony by Mozart!" Why not? The frequenters of
M. Jullien's concerts used frequently to encore Beethoven, to say nothing of Mozart; and we believe that no people are more susceptible
to the influence of good music than our English "masses," though
they may have but a vague notion as to what good music is. Mr.
Haweis is inexact again when he sneers at Jullien as "knowing little
about the science of music," and getting other people to arrange his
polkas, &c. He is inexact still more—but why go on through
an almost interminable series of reckless statements? Enough if we
quote one remark, which could hardly be paralleled for flippant impertinence. After his contemptuous review of English musical taste Mr.
Haweis observes: "However, the people have their music; and it is of
no use to deny it; and the marks of patronage bestowed upon ballad-
mongers, one-eyed harpers, asthmatic flutes, grinders, and bands from
'Vaterland' are sufficient to inspire the sanguine observer with hopes
for the future." After this no English reader will need more of Mr.
Haweis's book; but we cannot close this notice without asking what
good end is likely to be served by works so discursive, superficial, and
amateurish? Serious matters—and all art is serious—should be handled
thoughtfully and exhaustively, not as though they were simply an
excuse for the gossip of an idle hour.

It is now hardly a matter of surprise to Englishmen that their
German cousins assign a very high rank among composers to Robert
Schumann. Essentially Teutonic in mind, temperament, and mode of
expression, Schumann was promptly understood by his countrymen,
and fairly distanced the more cosmopolitan Mendelssohn in a race for
their highest favour. This was natural, and natural also was the cold-
ness shown by musical England to a composer whose utterances were,
if not couched in a strange tongue, marked by much strangeness of
manner and form. It was long before Robert Schumann made any
way in a country wholly devoted to Mendelssohn; but of late his
progress has been rapid indeed. Acquaintance with his music has got
rid of doubtful or hostile impressions to a large extent, and revealed
beauties unsuspected before. To prophesy how this movement in
Schumann's favour will end would be dangerous; but the end, whatever its character, may be furthered by the dissemination of such
thoughtful and eminently critical works as that of Herr Reissman.[*]
The book, which we are glad to see has reached a second edition, is
less a life of Schumann, in the ordinary sense of the term, than an
analysis of his genius, as shown in his compositions. To this task
Herr Reissman brought special qualifications—among them high
critical ability, a dispassionate temperament, and intimate acquaintance with the subject. For the sake of English readers, we regret
that the volume has not been translated. It sets forth, perhaps, the
most careful investigation of Schumann's claims ever made, and follows
his career from *das Vaterhaus* to *das tragische Ende*, with a discrimination beyond praise. This is the kind of musical literature we want;
and it may be hoped that ere long the "Robert Schumann," of Herr
Reissman, will appear in an English dress.

---

* "Robert Schumann, sein Leben und seine Werke," dargestellt von August
Reissman. Berlin: Guttentag.

CONTENTS.

THE

WESTMINSTER

AND

FOREIGN QUARTERLY

REVIEW.

OCTOBER 1, 1872.

Art. I.—The Heroes of Hebrew History.

Heroes of Hebrew History. By Samuel Wilberforce, D.D.,
Lord Bishop of Winchester. Fourth Edition. London:
1871.

THIS is a noteworthy book, not so much on account of its
merits, though it has certain merits, as owing to the condition of mind which it indicates on the part of its author, and of
the purchasers of the four editions through which it has already
passed. Here we have the reflections which are suggested by
parts of the Old Testament narrative to a Bishop of high reputation, deliberately penned and dated from Winchester House,
enthusiastically reviewed by the leading journal, and now, we
doubt not, read and re-read with ever-increasing admiration by
crowds of the faithful. We were of course aware that there is a
public which this kind of composition eminently suits, and which
creates a demand for it, not inadequately supplied from the pulpits
of the land; but we did also think that among the higher-placed
and more thoughtful of the clergy there was now-a-days a tacit
agreement to forbear dwelling upon some of these Old Testament
narratives; to defend them, indeed, if attacked, but not to parade
them before the world more than the lessons and services of the
Church require; in short, to remit them to a convenient twilight.
This is the kind of policy indicated in a recent number of the
orthodox *Guardian*, where we were told that certain chapters of
Genesis "should not be pressed too closely as literal narratives
of facts;" and again, in a speech by one of the Bishops in the
House of Lords, in the course of which some portions of Holy
Writ, now happily excluded from the Table of Lessons, were

minute, will furnish him with "practical observations," such as
good old Thomas Scott used to weave by the yard; just as every
supernumerary that stalks across the stage of the Bible may be
immediately seized and dressed up as a "type." He will draw
promises or threats, warnings or consolations from the same
passages, as the Wizard of the North poured different kinds of
wine from the same bottle. He is not even subject to the condition which is imposed on public speakers, of "sticking to
the question," but may ramble unchecked from Shakspere to
the musical glasses. He is, to use an expression of Mr. Disraeli's
with a slight variation, "the chartered libertine of monologue."
As a wag once said of Horace Vernet that he would undertake,
if required, to paint the whole façade of the Rue de Rivoli with
battle-pieces, beginning at the Place de la Concorde, and not
ending till he came to the Hotel de Ville, so a fluent preacher
gives us the idea of being able to spin this not altogether unpleasant sort of compound into a good-sized library. The one
condition imposed upon him is to interest people as much as he
can, which means, in most cases, to bore them as little as possible.
We are bound to say that those sketches, especially if delivered
in the pleasant voice, and with the agreeable manner of their
writer, would have interested an educated congregation. And
since, on that supposition, they would have fulfilled their chief
purpose, we should hardly have felt justified in criticising them,
if, "at the request of many," they had subsequently appeared in
print. But the case appears to us to be entirely different with
compositions intended primarily, indeed solely, for the closet; to
be read, not to be listened to. We have just called them
sketches, because the author has so styled them in his short
preface, but they are assuredly not always *historical* sketches.
We take it that it is not admissible to introduce into historical
sketches, any more than into history proper, expressions, ideas,
or incidents which the original documents give no authority for:
and less than any other documents, at least so we think, do the
Scriptures lend themselves to this kind of treatment. Minute
as is often the painting of Lord Macaulay, we do not recollect
that he has introduced a single touch into any of his scenes or
portraits, for which he had no authority. We know very well
that the contrary practice is at the present day habitual, especially among the French; but the frequency of a bad practice
only furnishes an additional reason for stigmatizing it whenever
it is met with. And this is a very bad practice indeed, outside
of a poem or a historical romance. A writer who describes Cæsar
as confronted on the banks of the Rubicon by the image of his
trembling country, then seized with a sudden faintness, and after
a pause clapping spurs to his horse and dashing into the stream

with a convulsive effort, is writing romance in prose (as Lucan
in a similar passage was writing it in verse), not history. Surely
the same remark applies to such writing as this: "Even as he
(' the prophet from Judah,') paced the streets of Jerusalem, the
engrossing strife within had made him feel himself soutterly alone,
that its crowded thoroughfares were to him as a desert." . . . .
"He looked upon his left, and saw the blue sea brightly speckled
with the ships of Tarshish, and swelling in its might under the
breath of God; and he saw before him the outstretched rod of
his prophet ancestor, and those waves at his command parting
themselves asunder and standing as a wall on this side and on
that." Then we are told how a variety of other ideas occurred
to his mind, the stones which Jacob had taken to be his pillow,
the oak of weeping, and so forth; and how the trees of the forest,
as they swayed under the breeze of the morning, seemed to be
uttering God's sentence, and helped to nerve him to his task.
"With such thoughts burning within him" he treads the crowded
thoroughfare, he passes through "the self-opening circle" of the
idol-worshippers, he stands "in threatening silence" in the
presence of the King. Where does the Bishop find all
these pictorial details in the simple narrative contained in
the First of Kings? Again, what earthly authority have we for
the following statement about the Old Prophet, who seems to
have been the innocent cause of the good man's death? The
words of Scripture are simply these: "Now there dwelt an old
prophet in Bethel." This is how we find them amplified: "The
old prophet was one of those whose souls had once been visited
by the visions of the Most High. But they seem to have
vanished from him. Probably a life of worldly compliance had,
as it is wont to do, dulled the receptive ear, and made dumb the
prophetic voice. . . . . In such an one, *painfully conscious of
the fading away of the prophetic power*, there would of necessity be a craving for acknowledgment by a brother in the great
company of the prophets, *even for the satisfaction of his own
uneasy conscience ;*[*] and much more to the same effect. Again,
we are told what Samson was thinking about in the last moments
of his life. "All his great soul is turned inward. He scarcely
hears or sees anything around him. His thoughts are with the
past; with the days of his Nazarite youth; with his early associations. . . . . What is there yet that he can do for the Lord?
. . . . he prays his last prayer," &c., &c. So David, as he goes forth
to fight Goliath, "hears the whispers of the trembling soldiery;
his heart shudders as he hears the words of blasphemy." Elijah

---

* The Italics in this and other quotations from the author are our own.

is furnished with "great limbs exhibiting gaunt strength;" "a defiant stride," and "a grand, deep, capacious brow."

Let it not be said that we are hypercritical. We are not in the least objecting to the Bishop's smart style, or to the graphic touches in which he presents great scriptural events, often in the present tense, after the manner inaugurated by the late Charles Dickens. We are too grateful for any variation on the conventional language used by most writers on these subjects to quarrel with his mode of treatment in this particular. We don't object to the introduction of Queen Elizabeth in the very first page. "Abram's birth was but two hundred and eighty years after the Flood: a shorter period than has passed since Queen Elizabeth sat under a tree which is still alive in Hatfield Park, and saw the approach of the royal messenger who brought her, instead of the expected warrant to a dungeon and a scaffold, the tidings of her succession to the throne of England." Nor have we anything to say to the appearance of the Duke of Wellington, and some dozen lines from Tennyson's Ode, in the chapter on Joshua. Where every character is shown to have been a type of Christ, it is a relief to meet with one character who seems at the same time to have been a type of some one else. These kinds of illustrations would be very much in place in a child's history; and the bulk of the orthodox, for whom books of this sort are written, are childlike in their whole spirit, as well as in their credulity. What we object to—and we should not make the objection in the case of a sermon, or a popular lecture, or a religious romance, or a Seatonian prize-poem—is, we repeat, the insertion of imaginary details and additions in sketches which profess to be historical. No sensible grown-up reader would like to see any ancien author, Herodotus for example, treated in this fashion. No one would care to be told how Crœsus on the pyre, before he fell into the reverie which induced him to call out the name of Solon, suffered his mind to ramble over the antecedents of his family from the time of Gyges, and the events of his own past life, his reception of Adrastus, the death of his son Atys in a boar-hunt, the wars he had fought, the oracles he had consulted, the presents he had sent them. No serious Historian or Essayist would talk of "the grand deep brow" of Æschylus—by the way, he would have some authority for using the words in the case of Aristophanes—though we should not be surprised to meet with the expression in an article in the *Little Pedlington Gazette* on the decline of the drama.

This, however, is a very small matter. It is the general method of treatment adopted by the writer which will astonish those unacquainted with the processes of theology. Not that he is chargeable with the invention of this method. He is only adopting a system of interpretation which has been in existence for ages, and applying it with more or less ingenuity to particular cases. For aught we know, these very applications may be not new, and indeed the probability is that they are not. The early fathers and others who worked this mine, in days when such researches were deemed worthy of serious minds, must, we should think, have succeeded in unearthing nearly every hidden type which can lie under the surface of Scripture. And as many as have escaped their notice must have come to light in the shape of answers to scriptural conundrums, such as we see propounded to good Sunday-school children, in the pages of religious magazines, " What Old Testament characters are typical of John the Baptist ?" "What is meant by the two pence which the good Samaritan left with the innkeeper ?" and the like. We notice the present book chiefly as furnishing a conspicuous example of the employment of this method of "Gnosis" by a conspicuous personage. In the eyes of its followers the Scriptures are essentially cabalistic. There is not a single incident from which there may not be drawn some portentous doctrine or dogma, or which is not a "parable," or a "foreshadowing," or an "emblem." There is not a single passage of any kind which is not in some sense mystical, or we should rather say mystical in any sense that may suit the operator. In the words of an old song, "Everything is anything but what it seems." Thus, to quote one example out of many given in a volume of excellent sermons preached by Dr. Adler in the Bayswater Synagogue, which has recently met our eye ; a well-known passage in Psalm cx., "He shall drink of the brook in the way." Nothing can be plainer than the *primâ facie* sense of these words, to the effect that David, who is to be otherwise blessed in his wars, shall not suffer from want of water in his expeditions. "One of the greatest dangers which threatened warriors in the East was lack of water ; one of the greatest hardships they had to endure was the fearful thirst they suffered after the fatigues of the battle," says Dr. Adler, who quotes Judges xv. 18, and 2 Samuel xxiii. 15. And he might have quoted a still more remarkable passage in 2 Kings iii. 9. This is how orthodox commentators torture these words. Henry and Scott interpret them, "We have here the Redeemer saving his friends and comforting them for their benefit. He shall be humbled, He shall drink of the brook in the way, of that *bitter cup* the Father put into His hand. *The wrath of God running in the curse of the law*, may be considered as the brook in the way of His undertaking." The Rev. Stanley Leathes, in the Boyle Lectures for 1868, tells us that this brook means "*the ever-open fountain of the grace of God.*" It is obvious that this kind of exegesis may land us in any interpreta-

tion that perverted ingenuity can invent. Similarly, all the
leading characters in the Old Testament are, as we see David is
here, distinctly typical of Christ. Even when they are not
engaged in typifying him, their smallest actions are as full of
meaning as Lord Burghley's shake of the head. This system
has been carried, in modern times, to its extreme limits by
Swedenborg, and the Bishop of Winchester is scarcely inferior
in his "correspondences" and "applications" to Swedenborg. If,
according to the latter, Adam signifies the most ancient church
and the Flood its dissolution, and Noah the ancient church
which was superseded by the Jewish, this does not seem to us
nearly so violent as to see the story of the Church in the history
of Joseph; or to trace a "strange similitude" between Samson
and Jesus, in that immediately after his marriage "came first
the display of Samson's might against Philistia," and so, "at
a marriage in Cana of Galilee the power of the Son of Mary
was first miraculously manifested!" Why not complete the
parallel by informing us that Samson going in to Delilah is a
foreshadowing of the unfolding of the Gospel scheme to the
Gentiles? Though we confess that the shaving of his head would
rather puzzle us. Perhaps, however, this is typical of the weakening of the Christian spirit in the world, through the artifices
of that harlot Rome. Or a Catholic may take it differently, and
represent the cutting off of the seven locks as a denial of there
being seven sacraments, and the Philistines will stand for Luther
and Calvin. But it is bad enough to have to notice this kind of
rubbish; we will not charge our conscience with the guilt of
adding to it.

Of course, wherever there is the worship of an idol—and surely
the Bible, the most venerable of all books, and the one most
profaned by such treatment, has been debased into one—this, or
an analogous process, is sure to be gone through. What the
pushing forth of a fresh leaf by a sacred tree, or the mystical
response of an oracle, or the wagging of a snake's head—

"Cum movisse caput visa est argentea serpens"—

what these signs are to the heathen votary, such to the orthodox
are the mysterious and recondite meanings continually evolved
from Scripture texts by the laborious efforts of those who consult them. An idol has, so to speak, to be kept in motion, to
be made to give signs of vitality, either directly or indirectly,
through the messages of its priests, to the worshipper. A book,
which cannot be made to undergo this process physically is tormented into undergoing it in another way. The Christian priesthood—not indeed with the express intention of deceiving, but
yielding themselves up blindly, often unconsciously, to the spirit

of their craft—take care to flaunt before us the Book of which they are the custodians, as something unlike any other book, something perpetually growing, and pushing out unexpected shoots, and yielding unsuspected perfumes under cultivation. Of course the same might be said of any book in the world—the Iliad of Homer, the Metamorphoses of Apuleius, the Arabian Nights, Alice in Wonderland ; and in the event of any of these books coming to be worshipped, we may be sure that it would be said, as in the case of the Bible, the Koran, the Vedas, and no doubt the book of Mormon. But however effective this sort of manipulation may have been in the days of Augustine and Gregory, we see some danger in practising it, at any rate as to parts of Scripture, in the present day. The temper of the educated British public with regard to the dogma of the plenary inspiration of every syllable of the *Old* Testament, is rather one of silent acquiescence than of enthusiastic acceptance ; and without the help of this dogma, the system we are considering cannot hold its ground. We have been taught it, it works well, it is taken to be part of the law of the land, like hereditary legislation, the easy-going citizen does not trouble his head much about it. But we think we are correct in asserting that not one layman in a thousand would go to the stake in its defence, as Christians would certainly have done in the days of Nero or Diocletian. Paterfamilias at morning church listens without mental objection to a lesson in which Jared is represented as having lived nine hundred and sixty-two, and Methuselah nine hundred and sixty-nine years. The next evening he reads without any disapproval, perhaps with a strong internal sense of acquiescence, an article in *Fraser's Magazine*, in which one of the greatest of living naturalists, Professor Owen, demonstrates the absurdity of the whole story; an article which an early Christian would have set down as distinctly and unmistakeably the work of the devil. The precise conclusions which paterfamilias arrives at we cannot inquire into; probably he does not know them himself ; but we are sure that he would rather wince under a sermon which should deal with the longevity of the patriarchs as a literal fact, such as to admit of a superstructure of applications and inferences, and to warrant a hunt after types, and other Will o' the wisps. He does not absolutely reject the narrative, but he does not *assimilate* it. That this is the state of mind on these points of the bulk of the educated there cannot be the slightest doubt. We have seen even the " Speaker's Commentary," which was to be a mighty engine for careering through the ranks of the sceptics and crushing them into small powder, pausing to let off its steam on the subject of Balaam's ass. It seems that after all the ass did not speak ! Bishop Wilberforce, with much greater honesty,

though with questionable prudence, presents himself to us as
one prepared to assimilate everything. In his very first page
we are told that Noah lived for sixty-two years after the birth of
Abraham. The sun and the moon "stand still" with no more
disturbance to the writer's equanimity than to the solar system.
Parts of Hebrew history which we should have thought it judicious to keep in the background, are boldly dragged into the
light of day, and commented on with no apparent suspicion that
they are open to any other observations than those in the style of
the Bishop. His lordship's "heroes" are mildly rebuked for
their peccadilloes (such, for instance, as the murder of Uriah by
David), and then gently dismissed to their respective stations in
the great army of types. The Bishop would doubtless reply, that
his book is addressed to his own co-religionists, that it treats of
topics on which he and they are agreed, and that the plan of
his work does not call upon him to meet objections. We quite
admit this. At the same time we conceive ourselves entitled to
address our observations upon it to those who agree with us—
and to call attention to the extraordinary matter in which these
good people find a recreation, and particularly to the chase after
types—which we should think the more sensible among the
orthodox would repudiate—an occupation which the irreverent
will look upon much as people contemplate boys blowing soap-
bubbles.

Of the twelve personages brought before us in this volume,
the first, Abraham, is we need hardly say typical of Christ.
Why, it would be difficult to pronounce beforehand. What we
mean is, that it would be difficult to guess the particular qualities
of Abraham, or the incidents in his career, which might be selected
by the author to found the likeness upon. For the science of
Typology would certainly admit of a likeness being established,
not only between Abraham, but between every person who existed
before the Christian era, and Christ. It appears that it was because
"he obeyed the will of God." Similarly, his tent was the type
of the Church. It was visited by three mysterious strangers,
who were no other than the Trinity! We wish that the Bishop
had explained to us verses 19 and 20 of the xviii. of Genesis, and
we really think that, having introduced the subject, he was called
upon to do this. Though we do not hold him bound to meet
every objection, yet we do hold him bound not to slur over every
difficulty, as he does throughout these pages. "And the Lord
said, Because the cry of Sodom and Gomorrah is great, and
because their sin is very grievous; I will go down now, and see
whether they have done altogether according to the cry of it,
which is come unto me; and if not, I will know." If this
passage had occurred in the Zendavesta, or in a fragment of

Berosus, and Dr. Wilberforce had been led to approach it, would he have passed it without comment? We are quite sure that he would have done nothing of the kind. We can picture to ourselves his eloquent remarks on the subject of an anthropomorphic deity, who comes down upon the earth to ascertain the truth about rumours which had reached him, and the contrast he would draw between this conception, and that of an all-seeing and all-pervading God. And this "consecrated tent" was, further, the type of the Church, in that "there, in vision, in dream, and by voice, vouchsafed to the watching patriarch, was all which should grow under the prophetic breathing of the future, into the lively oracles of God." Without being quite sure that we understand this, we think that we can decipher a kind of hazy meaning attached to it. Again, Joseph is a type, not only of the Church, but also of Christ, in that he saved his brethren "through the sacrifice of himself." Where, and when, did Joseph sacrifice himself? We had thought he was thrust into the pit against his own inclination, and if the reference be to what the Oxford undergraduate styled "that unpleasant little affair with Potiphar's wife," to refuse to commit a crime, and in consequence of such a laudable refusal to be subjected to an unexpected false accusation, is not an example of "self-sacrifice." Moses, Joshua, and David are, of course, conspicuous types of Christ. So are all the Judges, inasmuch as they were "saviours of their brethren." So was Samson, for the whimsical reasons already given, and also because he suffered himself to be bound with cords. So was Elisha. We note, with some surprise, that Elijah is not entrusted with a similar part. For surely in his mode of leaving the world he foreshadowed the Saviour much more closely than Samson in any part of his career. To ascend to heaven on one occasion is much more like ascending to heaven on another occasion, than killing a lion is like being tempted by the Devil. It appears, however, that Elijah was wanted as a type of John the Baptist. This is a specimen of the way in which the parallel is worked out. The persecution of Elijah by the King of Israel "drove him, as it were, *for refuge to the fiery chariot.*" That of John by Herod "ended his sufferings under the sword of the executioner and *sent him to his rest.*" Surely this mode of torturing the Scripture narratives into a far-fetched resemblance with each other will be as objectionable to the sensible churchman as it is to ourselves. We may be permitted to ask, moreover, accepting the Bishop's system,—since Joseph is represented as being at the same time a type of Christ and a type of the church, why should not Elijah stand for a type of Christ as well as of the Baptist? Here seems to us to be an opportunity thrown away.

The reader will have had enough of these puerilities of interpretation. To our way of thinking, it is absolutely lamentable to observe a man of the Bishop's intellect and influence deliberately consuming time in weaving these cobwebs. We would rather see him sit down like a Spanish or Italian (we forget which) romance-writer of a past generation, to concoct a story in which the vowels *a* and *e* should never occur, and another one from which two other vowels should be similarly absent: very much rather see him, like a certain German enthusiast, devoting his evenings, for a whole year, to solving the problem of King, Rook and Knight, against King and Rook. Our consolation is that this type-building must be, after all, a very easy art. "From first to last, all Holy Scripture is full of Christ. In direct prediction, in type, in example, He is ever reappearing. It is the perpetual presence of this one master-figure, the marvel that throughout the ten thousand mysterious characters which are inscribed upon *that still unrolling scroll* the same image ever recurs, which to the eye of faith, makes up the mighty wholeness of the prophetic record." The marvel would be if to these good people the image of Christ did *not* perpetually reappear. In such cases as these, to seek is to find. To a mind on the lookout for types and predictions, everything will wear a typical or prophetical aspect. We may go further and say that, as we understand the orthodox system in this matter, undoubted types &c., may be exhibited to everybody. For the rule, or at any rate the practice, in this kind of conjuring with texts seems to be that when any two objects have one common quality or characteristic, one may be made typical of the other. Thus Jesus was poor and lowly. Every one in the Old Testament who was poor and lowly becomes immediately a type of Jesus. Jesus suffered. Every one who suffered is a type of Jesus. On a similar principle of interpretation, the passage of the Red Sea and the Jordan foreshadow baptism. The dropping of manna from heaven foreshadows the divine food given in the Communion. Here the chief elements of resemblance are the presence of water in one set of parallels and of some kind of food in the other. And as it would be impossible to find in Scripture or elsewhere any two personages or events without some feature in common, so everything may be worked up into a prediction of anything. This may be theology, but—or perhaps rather *and*—it seems to us very like nonsense.

We will here take the liberty of giving what we consider a useful hint to the clergy, though with the fate of so many benefactors of their species before our eyes, we are not sure that it will meet with the gratitude which it deserves. There is a general complaint among the laity of a want of novelty—indeed, not to mince matters, of a dreadful sameness—about the

sermons of the period. Many very devout persons who follow
with unwavering attention the church-service are unable to
"stay" through the discourse. Their thoughts are apt to ramble
during that dreary half-hour: their owners are pleading causes,
or concocting companies, or sanding the sugar, or doctoring the
beer-barrel, or sticking the family pig, or "trowling" at Giles's
legs. On sultry afternoons, the farmers of our own parish fall
asleep, with uneasy snortings and gruntings, which at such a
time terrify their wives and daughters. And who can wonder
at this result, when, on the last occasion of our attending the
parish-church, the vicar, whom we take to be in all respects a
favourable specimen of country vicars, occupied some forty
minutes in establishing a resemblance between the mother of
Sisera awaiting his return ("Why is his chariot so long in
coming?") and the Christian awaiting the return of Christ.
When Sisera (who, by the way, never *did* return) is pressed into
the service as a type of Christ, one sees that this system of interpretation is worn threadbare. There is indeed what would be a
strikingly novel kind of discourse which might be introduced
into our pulpits, and which, we are quite sure, would arrest the
attention of the congregation. We say we are sure of this,
because we have observed over and over again, that whenever a
preacher comes down from the clouds, and points a moral from
some event of the day, or some occurrence in the parish, his
hearers immediately evince great interest. But it is not with
regard to this that we have a hint to offer. We feel that it
would be altogether a hopeless undertaking to urge the clergy
to enforce upon their flocks, from the pulpit, the plain duties of
every-day life in intelligible language; to tell them to avoid the
pot-house, to eschew finery, to further their children's schooling,
to keep out of debt at the shop; to furnish them with some
plain sanitary rules, and directions what to do in ordinary forms
of sickness, and the like. To adopt such a course would be, we
suppose, to prostitute the pulpit to secular purposes: all this is
not "Gospel-truth," or "Saving truth;" and, to be sure, being
very plain, unmysterious, and practical, and being calculated to
be of patent benefit, it is as unlike theological teaching as anything can be. What we would suggest is, that "applications"
and "improvements" and "correspondences" in Scripture being
by this time rather used up, some novelty might be introduced
by occasional type-hunting and shadow-hunting excursions upon
virgin-soil. These expeditions, conducted by explorers able to
apply theological instruments of observation, would, we feel sure,
greatly enlarge the domain of Typology. For instance, there is
the whole volume of Nature, which is admitted by all who
believe in the volume of inspiration to be from the same hand.

If Christ is "for ever reappearing" in Scripture, we should expect from analogy that he would be for ever reappearing in nature. And so, to be sure, he may be made to do, literally as well as figuratively. There is hardly a natural object on which the mark of a cross may not be deciphered, if only one's eyes are sharp enough. And many of the processes of nature are distinctly typical of Christ. For example, we are all of us preserved in early life, i.e. saved, through the instrumentality of others. We forbear from pursuing the subject; indeed the field for the exercise of ingenuity in this direction is boundless. Yet one more example of what we mean. As the Trinity is revealed to us in the very first chapter of Genesis, and again on the occasion of the "mysterious visit" to Abraham, so we should expect to find this great dogma announced, its "image recurring," in nature. And that this is the case has been repeatedly pointed out. "All life is developed in three terms, all being subsists in three phases: our conceptions are regulated by a trinal law; in the simplest figure there are three lines; in every body three dimensions; three words constitute a proposition; three propositions constitute a syllogism," &c., &c.

This, however, is not altogether virgin soil, though it is soil which has been very inadequately worked. The hint we wish to give to orthodox preachers concerns the personages and incidents of heathen mythologies. The early Fathers could not turn them to any good account, since in their eyes the gods of Egypt and Babylon and Greece and Rome were real existences, but demons; and consequently all the mythical stories of these countries smelt of brimstone. This view has long been given up. It has long been admitted that such countries as Egypt and Greece were agents employed by Supreme Wisdom for the civilization of the world; and their legends, which God has permitted to form part of the religious belief of large and cultivated portions of humanity for many centuries, must surely have had some meaning underlying them. Why not, among others, a mystical one, unsuspected at the time, but now revealed to "the eye of faith?" If Christ is to be found everywhere in the Bible, so, we repeat, judging from analogy, he is to be found everywhere in the world and its history, and these legends form part of the world's history. Take the story of Jason. Why should not the Argonautic expedition be treated as an allegory of the Christian's life? We think it lends itself to such an interpretation much more easily than Samson to a parallel with Jesus. The search after the golden fleece is the search after "the pearl of great price." It will be observed that, in the New Testament, figurative language is used of a spiritual treasure. And indeed "fleece" is a more direct image than "pearl" of the thing intended, since it is con-

nected with a sheep, the very term applied to the Saviour in the
prophetic utterances of Isaiah. The Symplegades which so nearly
crush the vessel represent the world and the flesh. The dove
which guides it safely through is of course the Spirit. Hylas,
who wanders off from the party and is dragged by a nymph into
the water needs no explanation. Aetes is the Law, that hardest
of taskmasters, and Medea is Faith, born under the Law, but
destroying the power of the Law. The dragon which guards the
sacred fleece speaks for himself; he is of course that old serpent
the Devil. Hercules, again, is most distinctly typical of Christ.
He is exposed to peril in his cradle. He saves a number of
people by his labours. *He slays a lion,* which, as we have seen,
is symbolical of an encounter with the Evil One. And an event
which is infinitely more symbolical of such an encounter, to our
way of thinking, than the destruction of any wild beast, marks
his career. He meets with Pleasure and Virtue, and chooses the
latter. He acts the part of a good shepherd, and tends sheep.
"A strange similitude looks out upon us"—as Bishop Wilberforce, if he adopts our suggestion, will one day put it—between
the twelve labours upon which his reputation rests, and the twelve
Apostles upon whom, as pillars, the Church is founded. As his
crowning work, he descends into Hades, and worsts the powers
there, carrying off captive the guardian of that dreary abode.
Finally, he ascends a mountain, and is carried up to heaven in a
cloud. Surely this is more like Christ than anything in the life
of Elisha is like Christ. We say that if one part of the work of
God be a texture of mystery, woven into which the theological
microscope can everywhere reveal the sacred letters I H S, there
is no reason whatever why the same should not hold good of
everything in the universe, with the result of letting in these
legends. We commend them therefore to the attention of the
clergy. They would be new to most congregations. Many of
them will be found much easier of manipulation than the general
stock of Old Testament narratives used for the same purpose.
We are sure that their introduction would keep town and country
congregations awake; whilst the scoffer could see in their employment only an extension of the present practice, and no
violence or absurdities that may not be matched in the present
practice.

To return to the Bishop. One of the most marked characteristics of his book, as of all similar books, is, as we have already
intimated, its quiet avoidance of difficulties. We are not speaking
of scientific difficulties, but of such as lie on the surface of the
sacred text, and must present themselves to the reasonable among
the orthodox. A preacher on the twenty-second of Numbers is
not bound to notice the objections to an ass speaking—a miracle

which, *pace* the Speaker's Commentary, we decline to give up, at least until all other miracles are given up. But if in one passage a horse were represented as speaking, and in another passage an ass; or if the same scene were laid in two different localities, then we think that here are circumstances of variation which the preacher is bound to notice. Now, as is well known, there are in Scripture two accounts of Abraham denying his wife, and one of Isaac denying his wife. In the second and third of these narratives, Ahimelech, king of Gerar, figures. We are far from saying that all these narratives may not be literally true: but a word might have been given to the undoubted difficulties which attach to them, even at the cost of stopping the Bishop's flow of rhetoric. As it is, the first is dwelt upon, and the others quietly ignored. A famine drives Abraham into Egypt, where "the tented wanderer shrank as the Arab of the desert shrinks from the crowded city life . . . . felt himself forsaken and alone in the more depressing isolation of being immersed in the full busy stream of a life which was separated in every sympathy from his own. In this depression his great heart sank within him, and he sought to save his life, endangered through the coveted beauty of Sarai by the denial of his wife." But God is better to him than his fears, delivers him, and he departs "safe under the shadow of the Almighty hand." Not one word, either, as to the *moral* difficulties presented by these two passages in Abraham's life. But moral difficulties are "cantered over" in every page of this volume. Every event is looked upon from one point of view. The colour of the spectacles is communicated to the landscape, and everything is complacently described as green or blue. Thus Pharaoh, who seems to have acted with perfect propriety according to the usage of those times, and indeed of all times, is plagued, while Abraham gets off scot free. "God delivered him from the danger which he dreaded." So Bishop Wilberforce canters over this transaction. Again, the faith of Abraham in offering up his son is, as usual, highly extolled. "This was the last great act of his discipline." "His noble, single-hearted faith was perfected." We do not wish to appear captious, but for the life of us we cannot help asking, by the way, in what did the immense faith of Abraham consist? God Almighty, the Creator of heaven and earth, with whom he had long been in constant intercourse, appeared to him and ordered him to perform a particular action. There has never existed a sane man in the world who, under the same circumstances, would not have done precisely what Abraham did. However, granting Abraham's faith, how comes it that one who was conscious of the Divine companionship, conscious that he and his were the subjects of so many promises, should

again fall into the same dastardly course of conduct in the land
of Abimelech? Here really was an instance where faith might
have come into operation, yet it is entirely wanting. Not a word
about all this in a sketch of Abraham's career. The next
"hero," Jacob, offers a difficult subject to the orthodox commentator.
Never, we should think, has a less heroic figure presented
itself in the world's history. Even Dr. Wilberforce is obliged to
be a little cross with him at times. He condemns his purchase
of Esau's birthright and, still more strongly, his perfidious conduct
in the matter of his father's blessing. Yet his lordship
has a word of excuse for him. "Rebekah is the tempter. Her
son more timid, perhaps less deceitful, than herself, shrinks from
the perfidy of abusing the darkened sight of his aged parent."
We see nothing of this in the original. The only doubt expressed
by Jacob is as to the success of the stratagem; his only fear is a
selfish fear that he may bring on himself a curse instead of a
blessing. "Rebekah has now persuaded herself that it is well to
lie for God, that the great, just God of truth can be helped in
the government of His world by a cunning devil-born falsehood;
and she succeeds in her plot, and the younger son secures the
blessing." But it seems that Rebekah was right, and that the
God of the Hebrews *was* helped by this lie; for it was in consequence
of his father's blessing that Jacob obtained the priority
over his brother. If this had been otherwise, if the blessing had
gone for nothing, we should certainly have expected to be informed
of the fact; we should have expected some word of
remonstrance or blame to be addressed to the authors of this
useless crime. Yet nothing of the kind appears in Holy Writ.
There is something in this affair which merits the attention of
the purchasers of four editions of the "Heroes." According to
all sound ideas of morality, the title-deeds of Jacob to the special
favours of Heaven were forgeries; the blessing was no more his
than are goods obtained by false pretences, the property, by law,
of the person who holds them. But this was not the idea of the
period. Blessings and curses were supposed to have an inherent
force, against which even the gods were powerless; to be, in short,
in the nature of incantations. This notion is an example of what
Mr. Tylor calls "survival" from savagery. It still exists among
savages, and is to be found in the religions of India. When the
word of blessing had once gone forth from Isaac, it attached
itself mysteriously to the person to whom it was actually addressed,
and became henceforth irreversible. Of course all this is
beneath the lofty sweep of the Bishop's flight over history. But
we may say of it, parodying the answer of Ben Jonson on a well
known occasion, "It is not rhetoric, but it is true." Further on
we have a characteristic trait of this same Jacob's nature in the

shape of a prayer which he puts up. "If God will be with me, and keep me in this way that I go, and will give me bread to eat, and raiment to put on, so that I come again to my father's house in peace: *then shall the Lord be my God.*" (Gen. xxviii. 20, 21.) Bishop Wilberforce remarks upon this, "Everywhere God was around him. Everywhere God was beside him. The great training of his spirit had begun. That close perpetual presence of the personal God made life another thing;" though he admits that Jacob's prayer betrays "much remaining darkness." Yes, much of that kind of darkness which leads savages to pamper their idols with offerings when victorious, and to pitch them into the river when they are defeated. "You give me what I want, and I will serve you: if not, good morning!" Considering the circumstances of Jacob's life and parentage, and the history of his family, as presented to us in the Bible, we hold this to be the meanest and most contemptible prayer on record. After this, we hardly know whether it be more amusing or painful to read the Bishop's remark, when he is comparing together the careers of Jacob and Esau. "It is best, after all, to be indeed on God's side in His world!" No doubt it is very agreeable to be marked out for prosperity, and increase, and dominion from the cradle; but this we should rather call having the Deity on our side than being on his. Surely the writer should hesitate, in the interests of morality, before holding up a life of fraud, meanness, and chicanery,—a life marked by all the vices, and few if any of the virtues of the Arab character, as a godly one, as one exhibiting "the regenerating, renewing influences of the Holy Ghost," merely because he finds it in the Bible, because it was crowned with affluence, because the person who lived it has been credited with uttering prophecies on his death-bed. Of these, by the way, the Bishop of course cites "The sceptre shall not depart from Judah," &c., without the slightest allusion to the historical and other objections which lie against the orthodox interpretation of the words.

Where every page is full of matter calling for comment, we scarcely know where to choose. We should have imagined—though to be sure we are no authority as to the feelings and views of orthodox people—but we should have imagined that the utmost that could be made out of some of these stories was, that they are inspired, and somehow or another must be swallowed; not that they could be "improved" and glossed over. Take the story of Agag. The crime of Saul in sparing Agag is not such as to avert all sympathy (at any rate, human sympathy) from him. If crime it was, it pales before those committed by his successors, David and Solomon. After the whole population of Amalek had been "utterly destroyed by the edge

of the sword," one would have supposed that some forgiveness
for his weakness in this one instance might have been extended
to Saul when he cried, "I have sinned, for I have transgressed
the commandment of the Lord;" a forgiveness which was immediately extended to David when he utters the same words,
"I have sinned against the Lord," in acknowledgment of a cold-
blooded murder. Yet for this offence Saul and his family are
deposed. We should have thought that this was precisely one
of those passages "not particularly suited for edification." Not so
the Bishop. He devotes several grandiloquent pages to it: the
following sentence may serve as a specimen :—"And forthwith,
like the darting down of the brightness of the lightning's flash,
the prophet's voice gathers itself up into one of those magnificent utterances which, belonging to another and a later dispen-
sation, antedate the coming revelation, and are evidently launched
forth from the open ark of the testimony of the Highest!"
What an appropriate "antedater" of the gospel of peace do we
here see in the figure of Samuel, cursing his sovereign for having
spared from the otherwise universal massacre *one* human victim,
whom he himself proceeds to hew in pieces! To cite but one
more instance, here is a sentence from the turgid utterances
in which we suppose the believing reader loves to see improved
the very awkward story of Elisha and the children and the
bears :—"The message of the Lord was not to be despised, and
there fell upon the prophet the inspiration of judgment; and
the curse which he pronounced upon them in the name of the
Lord was forthwith executed on the mockers by *the savage
denizens of the neighbouring wood!*"

Sometimes, on the most unexpected occasions, the Bishop
treats us to a little bit of what might almost be called rational-
izing. The evil spirit which tormented Saul was madness. He
is a trifle squeamish, too, about the proper character of Joseph's
dreams :—

"While we must not class them with those visions of Daniel, in
which the strong and direct breath of the Divine Spirit swept before
his sleeping eyes the course of dynasties and empires and ages; nor separate them altogether from the inborn prophecies wherewith great
minds forecast their own future; neither can we altogether deny to
them the character of being inspirations from the Spirit of God."

What, in the name of goodness, were they, after all? Further
on we are told that—

"God gave Joseph, by means which we call natural, however unusually quickened, the intuition to read what would have been illegible
to a shallower or less observant or less enlightened mind. His
natural gifts had enabled him to gather *first* from his communion with

the state-prisoners whom he tended the probable restoration of the one, the probable execution of the other."

Then came the dream of each, "presenting to his eye in airy imagery the shadow of the coming crisis." It would seem from this that Joseph's predictions were lucky guesses. A man who can guess that there are to be seven good seasons, followed by seven bad seasons, comes, however, very near to a prophet. Surely for an orthodox writer to haggle about the purely supernatural character of these communications to Pharaoh, &c., is an example of straining at a gnat. We wish we had space to notice the Bishop's speculations about dreams generally. The following may be commended to the attention of psychologists :—
"Are they (often) purposes and desires of good or of evil which have been wakened up by the sweeping over the waters of our soul of the *breath of the unseen enemy*, or of the gusts bred of past passions; or, on the other hand, by the sweet, healing, and enlightening presence of that blessed Spirit which bloweth where it listeth?" We should like also to notice the Bishop's definition of prophecy, as well as other passages in which he indulges every now and then in an excursus of his own : notably one on "Micaiah the son of Imla," in which we are told that the vast deserts of Africa abound in large carnivora, the vast northern ocean in huge whales, the highest mountain-tops in great vultures; and that here we see so many material types of great sins calling forth marked interference, and great sinners being met by great witnesses of God. But we have only space to refer the reader to them, and must pass on.

Such, then, is the kind of rendering of the Hebrew narratives, free enough in some respects, but as a general rule abandoning itself blindly to every miracle, portent, prodigy, and extravagance on its path, which is put forth with authority in the latter half of the nineteenth century. We say "with authority," for we are not now criticising the sermons of the Reverend Mr. Crawley to his parishioners in Mungelwurzelshire, but the utterances of a State-appointed chief-teacher of great weight, influence, and authority. These are the lucubrations of a bishop, who must be credited with the knowledge that there are such sciences in existence as astronomy, geology, physiology, philology ; and however much he may wish that these might all die, so that you do "but leave us still our old *Theology,*" yet he must know by this time that they do not die, but increase in strength, while the myths to which their conclusions are fatal are rapidly losing their hold on the minds of men. Or is all this, after all, only the conventional language which people, at a period of crisis, love to repeat to each other as a kind of talisman against defeat, and which the leaders accept and shape into high-sounding pro

clamations, as a useful means of stimulating the spirits of their
followers? Whatever useful results such a course may be attended with, there is one result which it rarely accomplishes. ·
It rarely imposes on the outsider.

With the object of showing the Bishop that there are such
outsiders in the present case—in other words, that there are
persons who by no means accept his commentaries for history,
we shall conclude this notice by giving *our* view of one of these
Hebrew heroes. We shall select David, the subject of the
apparently last written, and in some respects most characteristic
of these sketches. The enthusiasm of the Bishop for David
finds its vent in language which we should think must have
shocked that not particularly thin-skinned personage himself, if
he could have heard it from one of his own prophets or priestly
courtiers. "More by far than any other saint in the Old Testament does he stand before us as the type of Him who hath
suffered being tried." "He ever drew nigh to God, the just,
the righteous, the almighty, the all-living" (what, by the way,
is meant by "all-living?") "God, in whom he lived and moved
and had his being." In him was prefigured "the great image of
the One only man who was ever *perfectly* after the heart of
God." "The history of his life is the record of his education in
this high grace by the hand of God." Even when he was a
shepherd-boy tending his father's sheep, "doubtless the angels
of God met him" (where does the author find this?). Every
page teems with this kind of fulsome panegyric, till at last,
"grey as an autumn evening ends the life of the great saint, of
the man of love, of passion, of fervour, of inspired insight, *of a
woman's tenderness,*" &c. &c.; and "bright as the beauty of
the morning shall be that resurrection day when he shall rise
up after the likeness of his son and of his Saviour, and be satisfied with never-ending joy."

Now, what are the chief facts of David's career, as they stand
plainly disclosed to us in the Old Testament narrative? He
was born in an obscure station, but gifted with great qualities, a
warrior, a poet-minstrel, precociously prudent in speech and
conduct. As not unfrequently happens in Eastern countries,
this remarkable youth was before long introduced at court. The
story of his having been privately anointed by Samuel seems to
us extremely doubtful; it was probably an after invention of the
parti prêtre, whose favourite candidate he was, and whose pens
have supplied the world with his history after their fashion. If
the story be true, it will be difficult to acquit David of something very like treason to his lawful sovereign, and if the story
became known to Saul, Saul's conduct towards him is explained
and in great degree justified. Be that as it may, some great

warlike achievements soon turned the attention of all Israel to him, and he appears to have entered into some sort of alliance with the heir apparent, about the nature of which there is considerable obscurity. This young prince, Jonathan, had been condemned to death by his father on a previous occasion, and had only been saved by a popular rising. We do not like to indulge in conjecture; but it is certainly far from impossible that Jonathan may have borne his wrongs in mind, and further, that foreseeing the ultimate success of David, he may have deemed it the most prudent course to make terms with him, with the view of sharing the kingdom, or at least of providing for his own safety. And that this course would really have been a prudent one is shown by the fate which befell the descendants of Saul at the hands of the victorious David. Such a view is by no means inconsistent with the statement that a real friendship existed between the two young men. It is at any rate to be noticed that Saul at a subsequent period openly charged his son with having incited David to his treasonable attempts. Escaping from Saul's court, David fled to his friends the priests; first to Samuel, and afterwards to Ahimelech. After a short sojourn at the court of Achish, where he feigned madness, he betook himself to Adullam, a place in Judah which has not been identified, but the supposed site of which—great limestone cliffs excavated in various directions—would offer a convenient hiding-place for a band of free-lances. Such a band David soon succeeded in gathering around him.* A single story which has come down to us serves to reveal their modus operandi. One Nabal, a wealthy country gentleman, had the misfortune to find himself in their vicinity. On his refusal to pay black-mail to the robber-chief, the latter formed the immediate resolve of slaughtering him and all his household. He was deterred from this atrocity, for which he could not pretend a "command from God," and the moral guilt of which still rests on his memory, by a visit from Abigail, Nabal's handsome wife. Whether anything passed between them beyond the interchange of beautiful sentiments in which "the Lord God of Israel" as usual figures, we do not know. What is certain is that a few days after the return of Abigail to her husband, the latter died, and David, "blessing the Lord" for his death, married the widow. We are not told what became of the property. At times, the band was so strong that they were able to beat off detachments of the Philistines and to hold strong cities in open revolt against their sovereign.

---

* "David, the *unwilling* head of such a following," &c.—Bishop Wilberforce, p. 248.

After terrorizing over the respectable inhabitants for some twenty years, and finding the country too hot to hold him, David, in fear of Saul, passed over to the enemy. He had long been a traitor to his king: he did not shrink from the thousandfold greater guilt of turning traitor to his country.[*] He lied, as all through his career he seems to have lied, to Achish, king of Gath, and became a hanger-on of that heathen monarch. To keep his hand in, and to supply the wants of his followers, he plundered and massacred various outlying tribes, persuading the king that his forays had been directed against Judah. Not that he was not prepared to fight against his own countrymen, or indeed against any one else, if the occasion favoured his interests. When a battle which seemed likely to be a decisive one for Israel was impending, David is found making importunate offers of his services to the enemy! They appear to have known him, and to know him was to distrust him. He was perfectly capable of lying in wait for a critical moment, and then falling on the weaker party. Dismissed with some oriental compliments by the king, he occupied himself in exacting a bloody revenge from the Amalekites, having first consulted a magical image which his priestly followers had plundered from a sacred shrine, and which he and they manipulated to signify " the will of God." It is remarkable that in his case the will of God always permitted him to carry off the plunder, after murdering the women and children : the very act for which Saul had been deposed. Saved in this way, not indeed from the moral guilt, but from the actual guilt of assisting in the overthrow of Saul and Jonathan, David consoled himself by composing a beautiful hymn over their remains, and then proceeded to usurp their inheritance. Eleven of the twelve tribes adhered to their rightful allegiance, but it is not surprising that he should have succeeded in seducing his own tribe, the powerful one of Judah. There never was a crisis in their history when it was more necessary that the Israelites should remain united. What may have been the exact reasons which prevented the Philistines from following up their decisive victory we do not know, nor is it necessary here to enquire. But what we do know is that, only a few years before this, the Israelites were virtually subject to the Philistines, who would not suffer a smith in the land, for fear of weapons being manufactured, and we may be sure that, especially after such a defeat, a

---

[*] " His hard and restless life drove him into settling *reluctantly* amongst the heathen people."—Bp. Wilberforce, p. 250. How adroitly are these words which we have italicized, slipped in : and what, we would ask, is the authority for them ?

disunited country would be in great peril from a powerful neighbour. Not one straw did David care for such considerations as these. For seven years he distracted his land with civil war, fomented for his own selfish purposes. When at last treason and assassination had brought to a successful issue his guilty designs, he proceeded to make himself secure by putting to death the sons of Saul in cold blood (which he had sworn in the most solemn manner to Saul that he never would do) on a flimsy pretext, which does not bear investigation. The only person that he spared was a miserable cripple, in whom it was impossible that he should find a serious rival, and who was the son of his bosom friend Jonathan. Even this poor creature he treated with gross unfairness. If we look at his wars, no conqueror has ever behaved with more ruthless cruelty to the vanquished. He always plundered, and sometimes reduced them to slavery; but his general course was to massacre man, woman, and child (as he had proposed to treat the household of his own countryman, Nabal), submitting them to the most refined torments when their resistance to his arms had been such as should have merited his esteem. In such a career, the murder of Uriah and the adultery with Bathsheba sink into insignificance, yet for reasons which we cannot now enter upon, they evidently attracted contemporary attention, and are now styled the "one blot on David's life." The one blot! The last act of the disreputable old man was to summon to his bedside his son Solomon, and to communicate to the youth a dying charge. This Solomon had been named his successor through some palace intrigue, in which we may be sure that sultanas, eunuchs, prophets, and persons of that description were mixed up. Indeed we are told how Nathan, from interested motives, persuaded Bathsheba to allege to David a certain promise, supposed to have been given by him, Nathan at the same time undertaking to back the lie. The dying man fell an easy victim to the conspiracy. He roused himself, however, sufficiently to urge, with great deliberation, upon Solomon the duty of violating in spirit if not in the letter an oath which he had once sworn before God to one Shimei, to the effect that Shimei's life should be spared. Having thus entrusted to his son the care of his own posthumous dishonour, he expired, almost literally, possibly quite literally, with the word "blood" (it was the blood of an innocent man too!) upon his lips. Whether, as the Bishop tells us, he be destined "to rise up at the resurrection," and then "to be satisfied with never-ending joy," is a point on which we can form no opinion. But until that event shall have happened, we must object to his receiving the appellation of a saint, unless by the figure of prolepsis or anticipation.

What nobody will deny is, that he was a man of genius, a
born ruler of his kind, a great warrior, a powerful administrator
—in short, that he was what is commonly called "a great
monarch," if not, according to modern ideas, a good one. He
established a Jewish kingdom in the proper sense of the word,
and gave it a metropolis and a dynasty and a stable position
among other kingdoms. He suppressed what we may call the
constitution, and set up an absolute monarchy and a standing
army. He also instituted a harem. In short, he converted the
pastoral rule of Saul into an oriental despotism of the most
approved type. Whether these achievements were for the good
or the evil of his country, they have at any rate thrown over
his memory a halo which still blinds the spectator. He has
long enjoyed, and will probably always enjoy, among his
countrymen, the same sort of reputation which Napoleon the
First has acquired among the French. His crimes are forgotten
or glossed over: his great deeds, which have carried captive the
popular imagination, remain.

Not that he was altogether and irredeemably depraved. Not
that there have not been worse men. We are bound, too, to
take into account the time and the circumstances in which he
found himself. Our contention is against his being decorated
with the title of a saint. He was attached to his own worthless
family, and generous on occasions to his friends; he was beloved
by the masses for his popular manners. He really seems to have
had views on the subject of the Deity in advance of his age,
though whether this lessens or enhances his guilt it is for the
reader to determine. "Then he composed such beautiful
psalms!" This is generally held to be a complete answer to
everything which can be alleged against him. But, granting
that he wrote them all, this kind of defence reminds us of what
we have heard said in relation to a distinguished living lawyer—
"If any one remarks that So-and-so has made a false statement
in opening his case, the answer always is, 'Oh, but he teaches in
a Sunday-school!'" This contrast between a deeply religious
instinct, breaking out in hymns and spiritual songs and passionate confessions of sin when the soul's eye is turned inwards
in moments of seclusion, and conduct the reverse of religious
under the influence of the world's contact, is to be met with
every day. In David this instinct was united to poetical powers
of the highest order, enabling him to give utterance to the lofty
thoughts which moved his soul in the closet, but had little effect
upon his active life. Not that we suppose him for a moment to
have been a hypocrite. He doubtless felt all that he composed
at the time of its composition. Some of the sublimest moral
dissertations in existence are from the pen of Seneca, and

Cranmer assisted in the compilation of a Liturgy which ranks deservedly next to the Bible. We think it would be a mistake to charge these two men with hypocrisy when they wrote: yet certainly the life of neither of them can be held up as an example. Sir Samuel Baker has given us the spoken meditation of an Arab Sheik, worthy of insertion in the Book of Job; yet we should not be surprised to learn that the Sheik in question immediately afterwards rode off to pillage a caravan. Yet, after all, in these beautiful compositions which bear the name of David a great deal of the writer's worse self makes its appearance. Every species of destruction is invoked upon his enemies, who are at the same time the enemies of the Lord. Everywhere the ignorance natural to the age manifests itself. God is essentially the God of David and of the Hebrew race. The rest of the world are so much vermin, created to be hunted down and worried and knocked on the head by Israel. God is to be propitiated with fatlings and rams and bullocks and goats. However, we are not disposed to deny that the existence of the Davidic Psalms does certainly constitute a phenomenon when compared with the life of the writer as it has been handed down to us. Our own explanation would be one favourable to David, for we do not believe that he was in reality so bad a man as the priestly historians have unwittingly painted him: though in speaking of him we have felt ourselves bound to adhere strictly to their narratives. Not the least singular part of this phenomenon is to be found in the fact that a man who could utter such sublime thoughts about the Deity should at times fall a victim to superstitions worthy only of a savage. He seems—though this is not absolutely certain—to have been one of the company who "prophesied" in a state of nudity with Samuel and Saul and other "prophets" who had received what the Wesleyans term "a call;" a filthy practice, afterwards imitated by Isaiah and Micah. However, if he did this, it was in his youth. In his mature years we have seen how he consulted on his expeditions a magical ephod, containing there is strong reason to suppose, the image of a scarabæus, or mystical Egyptian beetle. Later on we find him dancing, again naked, and this time in public and before females, in honour of the ark, and very properly rebuked for thus "shamelessly uncovering himself" by his wife Michal, whom the priest-historian records to have been struck with barrenness for this utterance of sober sense and womanly decency! We should not have been surprised to read of such a performance as this last on the part of Rehoboam or Manasseh. But we are surprised to meet with it in the history of David. We are accustomed to contemplate him as savage and bloodthirsty, but we are conscious of a kind of shock on observing him to be ridiculous. And yet it might

have been well for him if he had never done worse than lower
the dignity of the crown and outrage the feelings of respectable
people; if he had danced naked in public a little more often,
and put under the harrow and the axe fewer of his enemies—if
absorbed in his dervish-like yells and capers he had forgotten
to murder his legitimate princes and to corrupt his son with
his last breath, like a Parthian dart of wickedness shot behind
him—

> Atque utinam his potius nugis tota illa dedisset
> Tempora sævitiæ claras quibus abstulit orbi
> Illustresque animas impune et vindice nullo!

ART. II.—PINDAR.

1. *Pindari Carmina.* DISSEN, revised by SCHNEIDEWIN.
2. *Bergk. Poetæ Lyrici Græci.* Pars I. *Pindari Carmina.*

PINDAR, in spite of his great popularity among the Greeks,
offers no exception to the rule that we know but little of
the lives of the illustrious poets and artists of the world.
His parents belonged to the town of Cynoscephalæ; but
Pindar himself resided at Thebes, and speaks of Thebes as
his native place—Θήβα μάτερ ἰμά. That his father was called
Daiphantus appears tolerably certain: and we may fix the date
of his birth at about 522 B.C. He lived to the age of seventy-
nine; so that the flourishing period of his life exactly coincides
with the great Persian struggle, in which he lived to see
Hellas victorious. He had three children—a son, Daiphantus,
and two daughters, Eumetis and Protomache. His family was
among the noblest and most illustrious of Thebes, forming a
branch of the ancient house of the Ægeidæ, who settled both at
Thebes and Sparta in heroic times, and offshoots from whom
were colonists of Thera and Cyrene. Thus many of the heroes
celebrated by Pindar, and many of the illustrious men to whom
he dedicates his odes, were of his own kin. Genius for the arts
seems to have been hereditary in the family of Pindar, as it was
in that of Stesichorus and of Simonides: therefore, when the
youth showed an aptitude for poetry, his father readily acceded
to his wishes, and sent him to Athens to learn the art of composing for the chorus from Lasos, the then famous but now for-

gotten antagonist of the bard of Ceos. Before his twentieth
year, Pindar returned to Thebes and took, it is said, instruction
from the poetesses Myrtis and Corinna. To this period of his
artistic career belongs the oft-told tale, according to which
Corinna bade her pupil interweave myths with his panegyrics,
and when, following her advice, he produced an ode in which he
had exhausted all the Theban legends, told him τῇ χειρὶ δεῖν
σπείρειν ἀλλὰ μὴ ὅλῳ τῷ θυλάκῳ, that one ought to sow with the
hand and not with the whole sack. Against both Myrtis and
Corinna, Pindar entered the lists of poetical contest. Corinna is
reported to have beaten him five times, and never to have been
vanquished by her more illustrious rival. Pausanias hints that
she owed her victories to her beauty, and to the fact that she
wrote in a broad Æolic dialect, more suited to the ears of her
judges than Pindar's Doric style. The same circumstance which
ensured her this temporary triumph may have caused her ultimate neglect. The fragment we possess of Corinna—

μέμφομαι δὲ κὴ λιγούραν Μούρτιδ' ἰώνγα
ὅτι βάνα φοῦσ' ἴβα Πινδάροιο ποτ ἔριν.

"I blame the clear-voiced Myrtis for that, a woman, she contended against Pindar," is curiously at variance with her own
practice. Its Æolisms prove how local and provincial her language must have been.

The history of Pindar's life is the record of his poetical compositions. He was essentially a professional artist, taking no
active part in politics, letting out his muse for hire, and studying to perfect his poetry all through the perilous days of Salamis
and Platæa—like Michael Angelo, who went on modelling and
hewing through the sack of Rome, the fall of Florence, the decline of Italian freedom, with scarce a word to prove the anguish
of his patriot soul. Pindar, unlike his fellow-countrymen, did
not side with the Persians, but felt enthusiasm for Athens, the
ἔρεισμα Ἑλλάδος, as he calls her in a dithyramb[*] (fr. 4). For
this he was made Proxenos of Athens, and received a present of
10,000 drachmas. It is also said that the Thebans fined him
for his implied reflections upon them, and that Athens paid the
debt. These facts, if true, testify to the post of honour which a
mighty poet occupied in Hellas, when the *vox et præterea nihil*
of a bard, inspired indeed by muses, but dependent on a patron
for his bread, was listened to with such jealous ears by the rulers
of great cities. The last Isthmian ode shows in what a noble
spirit Pindar felt the dangers of Hellas during her deadly strife

---

[*] This and all references are made to Bergk's text of Pindar.

with Persia, and how he could scarcely breathe for anxiety until
the stone of Tantalus suspended over her had been arrested.
In the Proemium he says:—

"For Cleander and his prime of beauty let some one, O ye youths,
bear the glorious meed of toil to the splendid portals of his sire Tele-
sarchus, the revel-song, which pays him for his Isthmian victory and
for his might in Nemean games. For him I too, though grieved in
soul, am asked to call upon the golden muse. Freed as we are from
mighty griefs, let us not fall into the bereavement of victorious crowns,
nor nurse our cares: but ceasing from vain sorrows, spread we honeyed
song abroad thus after our great trouble: forasmuch as of a truth
some god hath turned aside the stone of Tantalus which hung above
our heads—intolerable suffering for Hellas. Me verily the passing away
of dread hath cured not of all care: yet it is ever better to notice what
is present: for treacherous time is hung above the lives of men, rolling
the torrent of their days. Still, with freedom on our side, men can
cure even these evils; and it is our duty to attend to wholesome
hope."

Pindar passed his time chiefly at Thebes, where his home was.
But he also visited the different parts of Greece, frequently stay-
ing at Delphi, where the iron chair on which he sat and sang,
was long preserved; and also journeying to the houses of his
patrons—Hiero of Syracuse, and presumably Theron of Agrigentum, and perhaps, too, Alexander of Macedon. Olympia must
have often received him as a guest, as well as the island of Ægina,
where he had many friends. Odes were sent by him to Cyrene,
to Ceos, to Rhodes—on what tablets, we may wonder, adorned
with what caligraphy from Pindar's stylus, in what casket worthy
of the man who loved magnificence? The Rhodians inscribed
his seventh Olympian—that most radiant panegyric of the sea-
born isle of Helios—in letters of gold on the walls of their temple
of the Lindian Atheno. In the midst of his artistic labours, and
while serving many patrons, Pindar, as we shall see, preserved
his dignity and loftiness of moral character. The sale of his
poems failed to reduce him to the level of sycophancy or flattery.
He mingled panegyrics at so much the strophé with sharp
admonitions and rebukes. Pindar is said to have died in the
theatre at Corinth, in the arms of Theoxenos, a youth whom he
loved greatly, and whom he has praised in the most sublime
strains for his beauty in a Skolion, the fragment of which we
possess. Anacreon choked by a grape-stone, Sophocles breathing
out his life together with the passionate lamentations of Antigone, Æschylus killed on the sea-shore by the eagle whose
flight he had watched, Empedocles committing his fiery but
turbid spirit to the flames of Etna, Sappho drowning her sorrows
in the surf of the Leucadian sea, Ibycus the poet-errant, mur-

dered by land robbers, Euripides torn to pieces like his own Pentheus, Archilochus honoured in his death by an oracle that cursed his battle-foe, Pindar amid the plaudits of the theatre sinking back into the arms of his Theoxenos and dying in a noontide blaze of glory—these are the appropriate and dramatic endings which the literary gossips among the Greeks, always inventively ingenious, ascribed to some of their chief poets. *Se non son veri, son ben trovati.*

Some purely legendary details show the estimation in which Pindar was held by his countrymen. Multitudes of bees are said to have settled on his lips when he was an infant. Pan chose a hymn of his and sang it on the mountains, honouring a mortal poet with his divine voice. The Mother of the gods took up her dwelling at his door. Lastly, we have the famous story of the premonition of his death in dreams—a legend of peculiar significance, when we remember that Pindar, like Sir Thomas Browne, believed that "we are more than ourselves in our sleep," and wrote:

> " All by happy fate attain
> The end that frees them from their pain;
> And the body yields to death,
> But the shape of vital breath
> Still in life continueth;
> It alone is heaven's conferring;
> Sleeps it when the limbs are stirring.
> But when they sleep, in many dreams it shows
> The coming consummation both of joys and woes."[*]

Just before his death, then, Pindar sent to inquire of the oracle of Ammon what was best for man. Ere the answer came, Persephone appeared to him in his sleep, and told him that he should shortly know by experience—indeed, that he had already solved the doubt in his last ode. Thereby Pindar knew that death was in store for him; since he had written that it was best for men to die. Persephone added, that he should praise her in her own realm, though on earth he had not done so. The hymn which Pindar composed for Persephone in Hades, was dictated to a Theban woman by his ghost—so runs the tale—and written down. After his death, Pindar received more than heroic honours. They kept his iron chair at Delphi; and the priest of Phœbus, before he shut the temple gates, cried, "Let Pindar the poet go in to the banquet of the god." At Athens his statue was erected at the public cost. At Thebes his house was spared in the ruin of two sieges:

---

* Translated by Conington, from Fragment ii. of Dirges.

> " Lift not thy spear against the Muse's bower;
> The great Emathian conqueror bid spare
> The house of Pindar, when temple and tower
> Went to the ground."

At Rhodes, as we have seen, an ode of his was sculptured on the
temple walls of Pallas. Throughout the future, as long as
Greek poetry endured, he was known emphatically by the title
of ὁ λυρικός.

Pindar was famous, as these semi-mythical stories about his
infancy and old age indicate, for piety. Unlike Horace, who
calls himself *Parcus deorum cultor et infrequens*, Pindar was a
devout and steadfast servant of his country's gods. He dedicated
a shrine or μητρῷον near his own house to the Mother of the
gods, a statue to Zeus Ammon in Libya, and one to Hermes in
the Theban agora. The whole of his poetry is impregnated
with a lively sense of the divine in the world. Accepting the
religious traditions of his ancestors with simple faith, he adds more
of spiritual severity and of mystical morality, than we find in
Homer. Yet he is not superstitious or credulous. He can afford
to criticise the Myths like Xenophanes and Plato, refusing to
believe that a blessed god could be a glutton. In Pindar
indeed we see the fine flower of Hellenic religion, free from
slavish subservience to creeds and ceremonies, capable of extract-
ing sublime morality from mythical legends, and adding to the
old glad joyousness of the Homeric faith a deeper and more
awful perception of superhuman mysteries. The philosophical
scepticism which in Greece, after the age of Pericles, corroded
both the fabric of mythology and the indistinct doctrines of
theological monotheism, had not yet begun to act.

Passing to the poetry of Pindar, we have a hard task before
us. What can be said adequate to such a theme? What can be left
unsaid of the many thoughts that ought to be expressed? At the
time of Pindar's youth, lyrical poetry in Greece was sinking into
mannerism. He, by the force of his originality, gave it a wholly
new direction, and, coming last of the great Dorian lyrists, taught
posterity what sort of thing an ode should be. The grand pre-
eminence of Pindar as an artist was due in a great measure to
his personality. Frigid, austere, and splendid; not genial like
that of Simonides, not passionate like that of Sappho, not acrid
like that of Archilochus; hard as adamant, rigid in moral firmness, glittering with the strong keen light of snow; haughty,
aristocratic, magnificent—the unique personality of the man
Pindar, so irresistible in its influence, so hard to characterize, is
felt in every strophé of his odes. In his isolation and elevation
Pindar stands like some fabled, heaven-aspiring peak—a Matterhorn of solid gold conspicuous from afar, girdled at the base with

ice and snow, beaten by winds, wreathed round with steam and vapour, jutting a sharp and dazzling outline into cold blue ether. Few things that have life dare to visit him at his grand altitude. Glorious with sunlight and with stars, touched by rise and set of day with splendour, he shines when other lesser heights are dulled. Pindar among his peers is solitary. He had no communion with the poets of his day. He is the eagle, Simonides and Bacchylides are jackdaws. He soars to the empyrean; they haunt the valley mists. Noticing this rocky, barren, severe, glittering solitude of Pindar's soul, critics have not unfrequently complained that his poems are devoid of individual interest. Possibly they have failed to comprehend and appreciate the nature of this sublime and distant genius, whose character, in truth, is just as marked as that of Dante or of Michael Angelo.

Since we have indulged in one metaphor in the vain attempt to enter into some *rapport* with Pindar, let us proceed to illustrate the Pindaric influence — the impression produced by a sympathetic study of his odes upon the imagination saturated with all that is peculiar in his gorgeous style—by the deliberate expansion of some similes, which are by no means mere ornaments of rhetoric, but illustrations carefully selected from the multitude of images forced upon the mind during a detailed perusal of his poetry. One of the common names for Pindar is the Theban Eagle. This supplies us with the first image, which may be conveyed in the very words of Dante :[*]

" In dreams I seemed to see an eagle hovering in air on wings of gold, with pinions spread and ready to swoop. I thought I was on the spot where Ganymede was taken from his comrades and borne aloft to the celestial consistory. I pondered—peradventure the great bird only strikes this hill, and peradventure scorns to snatch elsewhere his prey. Then it seemed to me that, after wheeling awhile, it swooped, terrible like lightning, and caught me up into the sphere of flame; and there I thought that it and I both burned; and so fiercely did the fire in my imagination blaze, that sleep no longer could endure, but broke."

This simile describes the rapidity and fierceness of Pindar's spirit, the atmosphere of empyreal splendour into which he bears us with strong wings and clinging talons. Another image may be borrowed from Horace,[†] who says:

" Fervet immensusque ruit profundo Pindarus ore :"

likening the poet to a torrent, unrestrained, roaring to the woods and precipices with a thundrous voice. This image does not, like the other, fix our attention upon the quality peculiar to

---

* Purg. ix. 19.   † Carm. iv. 2.

Pindar among all the poets of the world—splendour, fire, the
blaze of pure effulgence. But it does suggest another characteristic, which is the stormy violence of his song, that chafes
within its limits and seems unable to advance quickly enough in
spite of its speed. This violence of Pindar's style, as of some
snow-swollen Alpine stream, the hungry Arve or death-cold
Lutschine, leaping and raging among granite boulders, has mis-
led Horace into the notion that Pindar's odes are without
metrical structure:

> " numerisque fertur
> Lege solutis:"

whereas we know that, while pursuing his eagle-flight to the sun,
or thundering along his torrent-path, Pindar steadily observed
the laws of Strophé, Antistrophé, and Epode with consummate
art. A third figure may be chosen from Pindar* himself.

" As when a man takes from his wealthy hand a goblet foaming
with the dew of the grape, and gives it with healths and pledges to
his youthful son-in-law, to bear from one home to the other home,
golden, the crown of his possessions, honouring the feast and glorifying
his kin, and makes him in the eyes of the assembled friends to be
admired for his harmonious wedlock: so I, sending outpoured nectar,
the Muse's gift, to conquering heroes, the sweet fruit of the soul,
greet them like gods, victors at Olympia and Pytho."

Then too he adds: " With the lyre and with the various voices
of flutes† I come to Diagoras across the sea, chanting the wave-
born daughter of the Cyprian goddess and the bride of Helios,
island Rhodes." In this passage we get a lively impression of
some of the marked qualities of Pindar. Reading his poetry is
like quaffing wine that bubbles in a bowl of gold. Then too
there is the picture of the poet, gorgeously attired, with his
singing robes about him, erect upon the prow of a gilded galley,
floating through dazzling summer-waves toward the island of his
love, Rhodes or Sicily or Ægina. The lyre and the flute send
their clear sounds across the sea. We pass temple and citadel
on shore and promontory. The banks of oars sweep the flashing
brine. Meanwhile the mighty poet stretches forth his golden
cup of song to greet the princes and illustrious athletes who
await him on the marble quays. Reading Pindar is a progress
of this pompous kind. Pindar, as one of his critics remarks, was
born and reared in splendour: splendour became his vital atmosphere. The epithet φιλάγλαος which he gives to Girgenti, suits

* 7th Ol.
† Compare this with the passage in Pythian, iii. 120—136, where Pindar
describes himself ioníar νέμων θαλάσσας.

himself. The splendour-loving Pindar is his name and title for all time. If we search the vocabulary of Pindar to find what phrases are most frequently upon his lips, we shall be struck with the great preponderance of all words to indicate radiance, magnificence, lustre. To Pindar's soul splendour was as elemental as harmony to Milton's. Of the Graces, Aglaia must have been his favourite. Nor, love as he did the gorgeousness of wealth, was it mere transitory pomp, the gauds and trappings of the world, which he admired. There must be something to stir the depths of his soul—beauty of person, or perfection of art, or moral radiance, or ideal grandeur. The blaze of real magnificence draws him as the sun attracts the eagle; he does not flit moth-like about the glimmer of mere ephemeral lights.

After these three figures, which illustrate the fiery flight, the torrent-fulness, the intoxicating charm of Pindar, one remains by which the magnetic force and tumult of his poetry may be faintly adumbrated. He who has watched a sunset attended by the passing of a thunderstorm in the outskirts of the Alps, from some height like the Rigi or the Monte Generoso, or from the meadow-slopes of Berchtesgaden—who has seen the distant ranges of the mountains alternately obscured by cloud and blazing with the concentrated radiance of the sinking sun, while drifting scuds of hail and rain, tawny with sunlight, glistening with broken rainbows, clothe peak and precipice and forest in the golden veil of flame irradiated vapour—who has heard the thunder bellow in the thwarting folds of hills, and watched the lightning, like a snake's tongue, flicker at intervals amid gloom and glory—knows in nature's language what Pindar teaches with the tongue of art. It is only by an inflated metaphor like this that any attempt to realize the *Sturm und Drang* of Pindar's style can be communicated. Go still farther afield in search of similes: fancy yourself playing such a motette as Mozart's *Splendente te Deus* in the Chapel of Mont St. Michel, which is built like a lighthouse on a rock, at the bottom of which the sea is churning in a tempest—and perhaps the imaginative equivalent will be still more complete. But a truce to this fanciful building up of similes! In plain critical language, Pindar combines the strong flight of the eagle, the irresistible force of the torrent, the richness of Greek wine, the majestic pageantry of Nature in one of her sublimer moods.

Like all the great lyrists of the Dorian School, Pindar composed Odes of various species—Hymns, Prosodia, Parthenia, Threnoi, Skolia, Dithyrambs, as well as Epinikia. Of all but the Epinikian odes we have only inconsiderable fragments left; yet these are sublime and beautiful enough to justify us in believing that Pindar surpassed his rivals in the Threnos and the Skolion as far as in the Epinikian Ode. Forty-four of his poems we possess entire—fourteen Olympians, twelve Pythians, eleven Nemeans, seven Isthmians. Of the occasions which led to the composition of these odes something must be said. The Olympian games were held in Elis once in five years, during the summer: their prize was a wreath of wild olive. The Pythian games were held in spring. on the Crissean plain, once in five years: their prizes were a wreath of laurel and a palm. The Nemean games were held in the groves of Nemen, near Cleonæ, in Argolis, once in three years: their prize was a wreath of parsley. The Isthmian games were held at Corinth once in three years: their prize was a wreath of pine, native to the spot. The Olympian festival honoured Zeus; that of Pytho, Phœbus; that of Nemea, Zeus; that of the Isthmus, Poseidon. Originally they were all of the nature of a πανηγύρις or national assembly at the shrine of some deity local to the spot, or honoured there with more than ordinary reverence. The Isthmian games in particular retained a special character: instituted for an Ionian deity, whose rites the men of Elis refused to acknowledge, they failed to unite the whole Greek race. The Greek games, like the Zwing-feste and shooting matches of Switzerland, served as recurring occasions of reunion and fellowship. Their influence in preserving a Panhellenic feeling was very marked. During the time of the feast, and before and after, for a sufficient number of days to allow of travellers journeying to and from Olympia and Delphi, hostilities were suspended through Hellas; safe conduct was given through all states to pilgrims. One common religious feeling animated all the Greeks at these seasons: they met in rivalry, not of arms on the battle-field, but of personal prowess in the lists. And though the various families of the Hellenic stock were never united, yet their games gave them a common object, and tended to the diffusion of ideas.

Let us pause to imagine the scene which the neighbourhood of Olympia must have presented, as the great Derby-day of the Greek race approached—a Derby-day, however, consecrated by religion, dignified by patriotic pride, adorned with Art. The full blaze of summer is overhead; plain and hill-side afford no shade but what the spare branches of the olive and a few spreading pines afford. Along the roads throng pilgrims and deputies, private persons journeying modestly, and public ambassadors gorgeously equipped at the expense of their state. Strangers from Sicily or Cyrene or Magna Græcia, land from galleys on the coast of Elis. Then there are the athletes with their trainers—men who have been in rude exercise for the prescribed ten months, and whose limbs are in the bloom of manly or of boyish strength. Sages, like Gorgias or Prodikus or Protagoras, are on their way,

escorted by bands of disciples, eager to engage each other in
debate beneath the porticoes of the Olympian Zeus. Thales or
Anaxagoras arrives, big with a new theory of the universe. Historians like Herodotus are carrying their scrolls to read before
assembled Hellas. Epic poets and rhapsodes are furnished with
tales of heroes, freshly coined from their own brains, or conned
with care from Homer. Rich men bring chariots for racing or
display; the more a man spends at Olympia, the more he honours
his native city. Women, we need not doubt, are also on the
road—Hetairæ from Corinth and Cyprus and Ionia. Sculptors
bring models of their skill. Potters exhibit new shapes of vases,
with scrolls of honeysuckle wreathing round the pictured image
of some handsome boy, to attract the eyes of buyers. Painters
have their tablets and colours ready. Apart from these more
gay and giddy servants of the public taste, are statesmen and
diplomatists, plenipotentiaries despatched to feel the pulse of
Hellas, negotiators seeking opportunities for safe discussion of
the affairs of rival cities. Every active brain or curious eye, or
wanton heart, or well-trained limb, or skilful hand, or knavish
wit may find its fit employment here. A mediæval pilgrimage to
St. James of Compostella or St. Thomas of Canterbury was nothing to this exodus of wit in Greece.

As they approached Olympia, a splendid scene burst upon the
travellers' eyes—the plain of Elis, rich, deep-meadowed, hoary
with olive trees. One cried to the other, There is the hill of
Cronios! There is the grove of Altis! Thither flows Alpheus
to the sea! Those white and glittering statues are the portraits
of the victors! That temple is the house of everlasting Zeus;
beneath its roof sits the Thunderer of Pheidias! Every step
made the journey more exciting. By the bed of the Alpheus,
tawny in midsummer with dusty oleander-blossoms, the pilgrims
passed. At last they entered the precincts of Olympian Zeus:
the sacred enclosure is alive with men; the statues among the
trees are scarcely more wonder-worthy in their glittering marble
than are the bodies of the athletes moving beneath them. The
first preoccupation of every Greek who visited Olympia, was
to see the statue of Zeus. Not to have gazed upon this master-
piece of Pheidias was, according to a Greek proverb, the unhappiness of life. In this, his greatest work, the Athenian sculptor
touched the highest point of art, and incarnated the most sublime
conception of Greek religious thought. The god was seated on
his throne; but, even so, the image rose to the height of forty
feet, wrought of pure ivory and gold. At his feet stood figures
symbolical of victory in the Olympian games; among them the
portrait of Pantarkes, himself a victor, the youth whom Pheidias
loved. In designing his great statue the sculptor had in mind

Y 2

those lines of Homer which describe Zeus nodding his ambrosial locks, and shaking Olympus. That he had succeeded in presenting to the eye all that the Greek race could imagine of god-like power and holiness and peace, was attested not only by the universal voice of Hellas, but also by the Romans who gazed as conquerors upon the god. Lucius Paulus Æmilius, we are told, after the battle of Pydna, swept Greece, and coming to Olympia, saw the Pheidian Zeus. He shuddered, and exclaimed that he had set mortal eyes upon the deity incarnate. Yet Paulus was a Roman trampling with his legionaries the subject states of fallen Hellas. Cicero,* too, proclaimed that Pheidias had copied nothing human, but had carved the ideal image existing in an inspired mind.

Zeus, it must be remembered, was the supreme god of the Aryan race, the purest divinity of the Greek cultus. He was called Father, Sire of gods and men. Therefore his presence in the Panhellenic temple was peculiarly appropriate and awe-inspiring. We may imagine the feelings of an athlete coming to struggle for the fame of his own city, when he first approached this statue in the august Olympian shrine. The games were held at the time of a full moon; through the hypæthral opening of the temple-roof fell the silver rays aslant upon those solemn lineaments, making the glow of ivory and gold more solemn in the dimness of a wondrous gloom.

Presidents chosen from the people of Elis and named Hellanodikai, awarded the prizes and controlled the conduct of the games. From their decision, in cases of doubt, there was a final appeal to the assembly of Elis. In the morning the heralds opened the lists with this proclamation: "Now begins the contest of the noble games; time tells you to delay no longer." When the runners were ready, the heralds started them with these words, "Put your feet to the line and run." At the end of the day they cried, "Now ceases the contest of the noble games; time tells you to delay no longer." The victor was crowned with wild olives, and led by his friends to the temple of Zeus. On the way they shouted the old Archilochian chorus, τήνελλα καλλίνικε, to which Pindar alludes in the beginning of his 9th Olympian: "The song of Archilochus sounded at Olympia, the triple cry of Hail Victorious! was enough for Epharmostos, leading the revel by the Cronian hill with his bold comrades. But now, from the far-darting bows of the Muses approach Zeus of the blazing thunder and the holy jutting land of Elis with these mightier shafts." Sacrifice and banquet took place in the evening; and happy was the athlete who, in this supreme moment, was greeted by Pindar with atten-

* Orat. ii. 9.   † Bergk, Poetæ Lyrici, p. 1301.

dant chorus and musicians of the flute and lyre. Three Olympians, which seem to have been composed and chanted on the
spot, survive—the 4th, the 8th, the 10th. The Proemia to
these odes, two of which are remarkably short, indicating the
haste in which they had been prepared, sufficiently establish this
fact. "Supreme hurler of the thunderbolt that never tires,
Zeus! Thy festival recurring with the season brings me with
sound of lyre and song to witness august games." "Parent of
golden-crowned contests, Olympia, mistress of truth," &c. But
it could not be expected that the more elaborate of Pindar's compositions should be ready on such occasions. It usually happened
that the victor either found Pindar at Olympia, or sent a message
to him at Thebes, and bespoke an ode, adding gifts in accordance
with the poet's rank and fame. Then Pindar composed his
Epinikian, which was sung when the conqueror returned to his
own city. The ode would be repeated on successive anniversaries
at banquets, sacrificial festivals, and processions in honour of the
victory. The 9th Olympian, which has been already quoted,
was, for example, sung at a banquet in honour of Epharmostos
of Opus, after the altar of Ajax, son of Oïleus, had been crowned.
Pindar, as we find from frequent allusions in the odes, had such
a press of work that he often delayed sending his poems at the
proper time, and had to excuse himself for neglect. In the
second Isthmian he records a delay of two years. We may add
that he did not disdain to accept money for his toil. In the
11th Pythian he says: "Muse, it is thy part, since thou hast
contracted to give thy voice for gold, to set it going in various
ways." In the Proemium to the second Isthmian he somewhat
bitterly laments the necessity that made him sell his songs.

"The men of old, Thrasybulus, who climbed the chariot of the
gold-crowned Muses, and received a famous lyre, lightly shot their
arrows of honey-voiced hymns in praise of boys, of him whose beauty
kept the summer bloom of youth, that sweetest souvenir of Aphrodite
throned in joy. For the Muse as yet loved not gain, nor worked for
hire, nor were sweet and tender songs with silvered faces sold by
Terpsichore. But now she bids us keep the Argive's speech in mind;
and verily it hits the truth; that Money, Money, Money makes the
man. He spoke it when deserted of his riches and his friends."

Yet we must not suppose that Pindar sang slavishly the praise
of every bidder. He was never fulsome in his panegyric. He
knew how to mingle eulogy with admonition. If his theme be
the wealth of a tyrant like Hiero, he reminds him of the dangers
of ambition and the crime of avarice. Arkesilaus of Cyrene is
warned* to remit his sentence of banishment in favour of a

* Pyth. iv. 263.

powerful exile. Victors, puffed up with the pride of their achievements, hear from him how variable is the life of man, how all men are mere creatures of a day. Handsome youths are admonished to beware of lawlessness and shun incontinence. Thus Pindar, while suiting his praises to the persons celebrated, always interweaves an appropriate precept of morality. There was nothing that he hated more than flattery and avarice, and grasping after higher honours than became his station. In him more than in any other poet, were apparent the Greek virtues of εὐκοσμία, σωφροσύνη, and all the qualities which were summed up in the motto μηδὲν ἄγαν. Those who are curious to learn Pindar's opinions on these points may consult the following passages :[*] Nem. viii. 32 ; Nem. vii. 95 ; Pyth. xi. 50 ; Isthm. vii. 40 ; Isthm. v. 14 ; and lastly, Pyth. x. 22, which contains this truly beautiful description of a thoroughly successful life, as imagined by a Greek :

"That man is happy and songworthy by the skilled, who, victorious by might of hand or vigour of foot, achieves the greatest prizes with daring and with strength ; and who in his lifetime sees his son, while yet a boy, crowned happily with Pythian wreaths. The brazen heaven, it is true, is inaccessible to him ; but whatsoever joys we race of mortals touch, he reaches to the farthest voyage."

With this we may compare the story of happy lives told by Crœsus to Solon, and the celebrated four lines of Simonides :— "Health is best for a mortal man ; next beauty ; thirdly, well-gotten wealth ; fourthly, the pleasure of youth among friends."

---

[*] "Hateful of a truth, even in days of old, was treacherous blandishment, attendant of wily words, designing guile, mischief-making slander, which loves to wrest the splendour of fame and to maintain the unreal honours of ignoble men. Never may such be my temper, Zeus, our father! but may I follow the plain paths of life, that, dying, I may leave no foul fame to my children. Some pray for gold, and some for vast lands ; but I to please my countrymen, and so to hide my limbs beneath the earth, praising where praise is due, and saving blame for sinful men. Virtue grows and blooms, like a tree that shoots up under fostering dews, when skilled men and just raise it towards the liquid air." . . . . . "Among my fellow-citizens I look with brightness in my eye, not having overstepped due bounds, and having removed from before my feet all violence. May future time come kindly to me." . . . . . "May I obtain from heaven the desire of what is right, aiming at things within my powers in my prime of life. For finding, as I do, that the middle station in a city flourishes with more lasting prosperity, I depreciate the lot of kings, and I aspire to excellence within the scope of all." . . . . . "Passing the pleasure of the days I gently glide toward old age and man's destined end : for all alike we die : yet is our fortune unequal ; and if a man seek far, short is his strength to reach the brazen seat of the gods : verily winged Pegasus cast his lord Bellerophon, who sought to come into the dwellings of the heaven, unto the company of Zeus." . . . . . "Seek not to be Zeus . . . . . mortal fortunes are for mortal men."

Closely connected with Pindar's ethical beliefs were his religious notions, which were both peculiar and profound. Two things with regard to his theology deserve especial notice—its conscious criticism of existing legends, and its strong Pythagorean bias, both combined with true Hellenic orthodoxy in all essentials. One of the greatest difficulties in forming an exact estimate of the creed of a philosophical Greek intellect, is to know how to value the admixture of scientific scepticism on the one hand, and of purer theism on the other. About Pindar's time the body of Hellenic mythology was being invaded by a double process of destructive and constructive criticism. Xenophanes, for example, very plainly denounced as absurd the anthropomorphic Pantheon made in the image of man, while he endeavoured to substitute a cultus of the One God, indivisible and incognisable. Plato still further developed the elements suggested by Xenophanes. But there was some inherent incapacity in the Greek intellect for arriving at monotheism by a process of rarefaction and purification. The destructive criticism which in Xenophanes, Pindar, and Plato had assailed the grosser myths, dwindled into unfruitful scepticism. The attempts at constructing a rational theosophy ended in metaphysics. Morality was studied as a separate branch of investigation, independent of destructive criticism and religious construction. Meanwhile the popular polytheism continued to flourish, though enfeebled, degenerate, and disconnected from the nobler impulses of poetry and art. In Pindar the process of decadence had not begun. He stood at the very apex which it was possible for a religious Greek to reach—combining the aesthetically ennobling enthusiasm for the old Greek deities with so much critical activity as enabled him to reject the grosser myths, and with that moderate amount of theological mysticism which the unassisted intellect of the Greeks seemed capable of receiving without degeneracy into puerile superstition. The first Olympian ode contains the most decided passages in illustration of his critical independence of judgment:

"Impossible is it for me to call one of the blessed ones a glutton : I stand aloof: loss hath often overtaken evil speakers."

Again :

"Truly many things are wonderful; and it may be that in som cases fables dressed up with cunning fictions beyond the true account falsify the traditions of men. But Grace of Song, which is the author of all delicious things for mortals, by giving to these myths acceptance, ofttimes makes even what is incredible to be credible: but succeeding time gives the most certain evidence of truth; and for a man to speak nobly of the gods is seemly; for so the blame is less."

These two passages suffice to prove how freely Pindar handled the myths, not indeed exposing them to the corrosive action of mere scepticism, but testing them* by the higher standard of the healthy human conscience. When he refuses to believe that the immortals were cannibals and eat the limbs of Pelops, he is like a rationalist avowing his disbelief in the doctrine of eternal damnation. His doubt does not proceed from irreligion, but from faith in the immutable holiness of the gods, who set the ideal standard of human morality. What seems to him false in the myths, he attributes to the accretions of ignorant opinion and vain fancy round the truth.

The mystical element of Pindar's creed, whether we call it Orphic or Pythagorean, is remarkable for a definite belief in the future life, including a system of rewards and punishments, for the assertion of the supreme tribunal of conscience,† and finally, for a reliance on rites of purification. The most splendid passage in which these opinions are expressed by Pindar, is that portion of the second Olympian, in which he describes the torments of the wicked and the blessings of the just beyond the grave:—

"Among the dead, sinful souls at once pay penalty, and the crimes done in this realm of Zeus are judged beneath the earth by one who gives sentence under dire necessity.

"But the good, enjoying perpetual sunlight equally by night and day, receive a life more free from woes than this of ours; they trouble not the earth with strength of hand, nor the water of the sea for scanty sustenance; but with the honoured of the gods, who delighted in the keeping of their oath, they pass a tearless age: the others bear woe on which no eye can bear to look. Those who have thrice endured on either side the grave to keep their spirits wholly free from crime, journey on the road of Zeus to the tower of Cronos: where round the islands blow breezes ocean-borne: and flowers of gold burn some on the land from radiant trees, and others the wave feeds: with necklaces whereof they twine their hands and brows, in the just decrees of Rhadamanthus, whom the father, the son of earth, has for a perpetual colleague, he who is the spouse of Rhea throned above all gods.

---

* Compare for a similar freedom of judgment Antigone's famous speech on the unwritten Laws.

† The conscience forms a strong point in the ethical systems of many of the ancients, especially of Plato, of Lucretius, of Persius—authors otherwise dissimilar enough as representing three distinct species of thought. In Mythology it receives an imperfect embodiment in the Erinnys, who, however, are spiritual forces acting from without, rather than from within, upon the criminal. Purifying rites belonged to the Mysteries or τελεταί; they formed a prominent feature in the Ethics of Empedocles and Pythagoras, and an integral part of the cultus of Apollo and the nether deities. Philosophers like Plato rejected them as pertaining to ceremonial superstition.

" Pelœs and Cadmus are numbered among these ; and thither was
Achilles brought by his mother when she swayed the heart of Zeus
with prayer ; he who slew Hector, the invincible firm pillar of Troy,
and gave Cyonus to death and Eo's Æthiopian sou."

The following fragments from Threnoi* translated by Professor
Conington:

"They from whom Persephone
　　Due atonement shall receive
　　For the things that made to grieve,
To the upper sunlight she
Sendeth back their souls once more,
Soon as winters eight are o'er.
From those blessed spirits spring
Many a great and goodly king,
Many a man of glowing might,
Many a wise and learned wight :
And while after days endure,
Men esteem them heroes pure."

And again :

"Shines for them the sun's warm glow
When 'tis darkness here below :
And the ground before their towers,
Meadow-land with purple flowers,
Teems with incense-bearing treen,
Teems with fruit of golden sheen.
Some in steed and wrestling feat,
Some in dice take pleasure sweet,
Some in harping : at their side
Blooms the spring in all her pride.
Fragrance all about is blown
　　O'er that country of desire,
Ever as rich gifts are thrown
　　Freely on the far-seen fire,
Blazing from the altar-stone.
　　*　　*　　*　　*　　*
But the souls of the profane,
　　Far from heaven removed below,
Flit on earth in murderous pain
　　'Neath the unyielding yoke of woe ;
While pious spirits tenanting the sky
Chant praises to the mighty one on high."

For Pindar's conception of the destinies of frail humanity, take
this sublime but melancholy ending to an ode† which has been
full of triumphant exultation : " Brief is the growing time of joy

for mortals, and briefly too doth its flower fall to earth shaken by
fell fate. Things of a day! what are we—the great man, and
the man of nought? A shadow's dream is man. But when the
splendour that God gives descends, then there remains a radiant
light and gladsome light for mortals." Compare with this the
opening of the sixth Nemean:

"One is the race of men, and one the race of gods; from one
mother we both drew breath. But a total difference of force divides
us, since man's might is nought, while brazen heaven abideth a sure
seat for aye. Nevertheless, we are not all unlike immortals either
in our mighty soul or strength of limb, though we know not to what
end of night or day our fate hath written down for us to run."

Passing to the consideration of Pindar purely as an artist, we
may first examine the structure of his odes, and then illustrate
the qualities of his poetry by reference to some of the more
splendid Proemia and descriptions. The task which lay before
him when he undertook to celebrate a victory at one of the Greek
games, was this. Some rich man had won a race with his chariot
and horses, or some strong man had conquered his competitors
by activity or force of limb. Pindar had to praise the rich man
for his wealth and liberality, the strong man for his endurance of
training and personal courage or dexterity. In both cases the
victor might be felicitated on his good fortune—on the piece of
luck which had befallen him; and if he were of comely person or
illustrious blood, these also offered topics for congratulation. The
three chief commonplaces of Pindar, therefore, are ὄλβος, ἀρετή,
εὐτυχία, wealth or prosperity, manliness or spirit, and blessings
independent of both, god-given, not acquired. But it could not be
that a great poet should ring the changes only on these three
subjects, or content himself with describing the actual contest,
which probably he had not witnessed. Consequently Pindar
illustrates his odes with myths or stories bearing more or less
closely on the circumstances of his hero. Sometimes he celebrates
the victor's ancestry, as in the famous sixth Olympian in which
the history of the Iamidæ is given; sometimes his city, as in the
seventh Olympian where he describes the birthplace of Diagoras,
the island Rhodes; sometimes he dwells upon an incident in the
hero's life, as when in the third Pythian the illness of Hiero
suggests the legend of Asklepios and Cheiron; sometimes a
recent event, like the eruption of Etna, alluded to in the first
Pythian, gives colour to his ode; sometimes as in the case of
the last Pythian, where the story of Medusa is narrated, the
legendary matter is introduced to specialize the nature of the
contest. The victory itself is hardly touched upon: the allusions
to ὄλβος, ἀρετή, εὐτυχία, though frequent and interwoven with
the texture of the ode, are brief: the whole poetic fabric is so

designed as to be appropriate to the occasion and yet independent of it. Therefore Pindar's odes have not perished with the memory of the events to which they owed their composition.

Pindar's peculiar treatment of the Epinikian ode may best be illustrated by analysing the structure of one or two of them. But first take this translation of one of the shorter and simpler of the series—the twelfth Pythian:

> " To thee, fairest of earthly towns, I pray—
> Thou splendour-lover, throne of Proserpine,
> Piled o'er Girgenti's slopes, that feed alway
> Fat sheep!—with grace of gods and men incline,
> Great queen, to take this Pythian crown and own
> Midas; for he of all the Greeks, thy son,
> Hath triumphed in the art which Pallas won,
> Weaving of fierce Gorgonian threats the dolorous moan.
>
> She from the snake-encircled hideous head
> Of maidens heard the wailful dirges flow,
> What time the third of those fell Sisters bled
> By Perseus' hand, who brought the destined woe
> To vexed Seriphos. He on Phorkys' brood
> Wrought ruin, and on Polydectes laid
> Stern penance for his mother's servitude,
> And for her forceful wedlock, when he slew the maid
>
> Medusa. He by living gold, they say,
> Was got on Danäe: but Pallas bore
> Her hero through those toils, and wrought the lay
> Of full-voiced flutes to mock the ghastly roar
> Of those strong jaws of grim Euriale:
> A goddess made and gave to men the flute,
> The fountain-head of many a strain to be,
> That ne'er at game or nation's feast it might be mute,
>
> Sounding through subtle brass and voiceful reeds,
> Which near the city of the Graces spring
> By fair Cephissus, faithful to the needs
> Of dancers. Lo! there cometh no good thing
> Apart from toils to mortals, though to-day
> Heaven crown their deeds: yet shun we not the laws
> Of Fate; for times impend when chance withdraws
> What most we hoped, and what we hoped not gives for aye.

Here it will be seen that Pindar introduces his subject with a panegyric of Girgenti, his hero's birthplace. Then he names Midas, and tells the kind of triumph he has gained. This leads him to the legend of Medusa. The whole is concluded with moral reflections on the influence of Fate over human destinies. The structure of the sixth Pythian is also very simple. " I build an indestructible treasure-house of praise for Xenocrates

[lines 1—18], which Thrasybulus, his son, gained for him ; as
Antilochus died for Nestor [19—43], so Thrasybulus has done
what a son could for his father [44—46]: wise and fair is he
in his youth; his company is sweeter than the honeycomb
[47—51]." One of the longest odes, the fourth Pythian, is constructed thus : " Muse! celebrate Arkesilaus [1—5]. Cyrene,
Arkesilaus' home ; its foundation and the oracle given to Battus
[5—69]. The tale of the Argonauts, ancestors of the founders
of Thera and of Cyrene [69—262]. Advice to Arkesilaus in the
interest of Demophilus [263—299]." Here the victory at Pytho
is but once briefly alluded to [line 64]. The whole ode consists
of pedigree and political admonition, either directly administered
at the end, or covertly conveyed through the example of Peleus.
The sixth Olympian, which contains the pedigree of the Iamidæ,
is framed on similar principles. The third Pythian introduces
its mythology by a different method : " I wish I could restore
Cheiron, the healer and the tutor of Asklepios, to life [1—7].
The story of Koronis, her son Asklepios, and Hippolytus [7—58].
Moral, to be content and submit to mortality [58—62]. Yet
would that Cheiron might return and heal Hiero [62—76]! I
will pray; and do you, Hiero, remember that Heaven gives one
blessing and two curses, and that not even Cadmus and Peleus
were always fortunate [17—106]. May I suit myself always to
my fortune [107—115]!" The whole of this ode relates to
Hiero's illness, and warns him of vicissitudes: even the episode
of Koronis and Asklepios contains a covert warning against arrogance, while it gracefully alludes to Hiero's health.

The originality and splendour of Pindar are most noticeable in
the openings of his odes—the Proemia, as they are technically
called. It would appear that he possessed an inexhaustible
storehouse of splendid imagery, from which to draw new thoughts
for the commencement of his poems. In this region, which most
poets find but barren, he displayed the fullest vigour and fertility
of fancy. Sometimes, but rarely, the opening is simple, as in the
second Olympian : " Hymns that rule the lyre! what god, what
hero, what man shall we make famous?" Or the ninth Pythian :
" I wish to proclaim, by help of the deep-girdled graces, brazen-
shielded Telesicrates, Pythian victor," &c. Rather more complex
are the following: Nem. iv. " The joy of the feast is the best
physician after toil ; but songs, the wise daughters of the Muses,
soothe the victor with their touch : warm water does not so
refresh and supple weary limbs as praise attended by the lyre ;"
or again: Ol. xi. " There is a time when men have greatest
need of winds ; there is when heaven's showers of rain, children
of the cloud, are sorest sought for. But if a man achieves a
victory with toil, then sweet-voiced hymns arise as the beginning

of future fame," &c. &c. But soon we pass into a more gorgeous region. " As when with golden columns reared beneath the well-walled palace-porch we build a splendid hall, so will I, build my song. At the beginning of the work we must make the portal radiant."* Or again : " No carver of statues am I, to fashion figures stationary on their pedestal ; but come, sweet song ! on every argosy and skiff set forth from Ægina to proclaim that Pytheas, Lampon's son, by strength of might is victor in Nemea n games, upon whose chin and cheek you see not yet the tender mother of the vine-flower, summer's bloom." † Or again : " Hallowed bloom of youth, herald of Aphrodite's ambrosial pleasures, who resting on the eyelids of maidens and of boys, bearest one aloft with gentle hands, but another with rude compulsion !"‡ Or once again, in a still grander style :

" Listen ! for verily it is of beauty's queen, or of the maiden-goddesses of triumph, that we turn the glebe, approaching the rocky centre of the deep-voiced earth : where for the blest Emmenidæ and stream-washed Acragas, yea, and for Xenocrates is built a treasure-house of Pythian hymns in the golden Apollonian vale. This, no voice of winter, driving on the wings of wind the pitiless army of the rushing cloud, no hurricane, shall toss, storm-lashed with pebbles of the up-torn beach, into the briny ocean caves : but in pure light its glorious face shall speak the victory that brings a common fame on thy sire Thrasybulus and thy race, remaining in the windings of Crissæan valleys."§

We have already seen how Pindar compares his odes to arrows, to sun-soaring eagles, to flowers of the Muses, to wine in golden goblets, to water, to a shrine which no years will fret away. Another strange figure‖ may be quoted from the third Nemean [line 76] : " I send to thee this honey mingled with white milk : the dew of their mingling hangs around the bowl, a draught of song, flowing through the Æolian breath of flutes." It will be perceived that to what is called confusion of metaphor Pindar shows a lordly indifference. Swift and sudden lustre, the luminousness of a meteor, marks this monarch of lyric song. He grasps an image, gives it a form of bronze, irradiates it with the fire of flame or down-poured sunlight.

To do justice to Pindar's power of narrative by extracts and translations is impossible. No author suffers more by mutilation and by the attempt to express in another language and another rhythm what he has elaborately fashioned. Yet it may be allowed us to direct attention to the rapidity with which the burning of Coroni (Pyth. iii. 38), and the birth of Rhodes from

---

* Ol. vi. † Nem. v. ‡ Nem. viii.
§ Pyth. vi. ‖ Compare too, Nem. vii. 11, 63, 77.

the sea (Ol. vii. 54), are told in words the grandest, simplest,
and most energetic that could be found. This is the birth of
Iamos, (Ol. vi. 39):

> " Nor could she hide from Æpytus the seed
>   Divine: but he to Pytho, showing care,
> Journeyed, to gain for this great woe some rede;
>   She loosening her crimson girdle fair,
> And setting on the ground her silver jar,
> Beneath the darksome thicket bare a son,
> Within whose soul flamed godhead-like a star;
>   And to her aid the golden-haired sent down
> Mild Eleithuia and the awful Fates,
> Who stood beside, while from the yearning gates
>
> Of childbirth, with a brief and joyous pain,
>   Came Iamos into the light, whom she therewith
> Sore-grieving left upon the grass: amain
>   By gods' decree two bright-eyed serpents lithe
> Tended, and with the harmless venom fed
> Of bees, the boy; nor ceased they to provide
> Due nurture. But the king, what time he sped
>   Homeward from rocky Pytho, to his side
> Called all his household, asking of the son
> Born of Evadne, for he said that none
>
> But Phœbus was the sire, and he should be
>   Chief for his prophecy 'mid mortal men,
> Nor should his children's seed have end. Thus he
>   Uttered the words oracular; and then
> They swore they had not heard or seen the child,
>   Now five days old; but he within the reed
> And thick-entangled woodland boskage wild,
>   His limbs 'mid golden beams and purple brede
> Of gillyflowers deep-sunken, lay; wherefore
> He by his mother's wish for all time bore
>
> That deathless name. But when he plucked the flower
>   Of golden-wreathéd youth, he went and stood
> Midmost Alpheus, at the midnight hour,
>   And called upon the ruler of the flood,
> His ancestor Poseidon, and the lord
> Of god-built Delos, praying he might bear
> Some honour 'mid the people. Then the word
>   Responsive of his sire upon the air
> Sounded :—" Arise, my son, follow the voice,
> Yea, to the land wherein all men rejoice!"
>
> So came they to the high untrodden mound
>   Of Cronios; and there a double share
> Of prophecy on Iamos was bound,
>   Both of the voice that knows no lie to hear

Immortal words, and next, when Heracles,
Bold in his counsels, unto Pisa came,
Founding the festivals of sacred peace
And mighty combats for his father's fame,
Then on the topmost altar of Jove's hill,
The seat of sooth oracular to fill.

After so much praise of Pindar's style, we must confess that
he has faults. One of these is notoriously tumidity—an over-
blown exaggeration of phrase. For example, when he wants to
express that he cannot enlarge on the fame of Ægina, but will
relate as quickly as he can the achievements of Aristomenes
which he has undertaken, he says:—"But I am not at leisure
to consecrate the whole long tale to the lyre and delicate voice,
lest satiety should come and cause annoy: but that which is
before my feet shall go at running speed—thy affair, my boy—
the latest of the noble deeds made winged by means of my art."[*]
The imaginative force which enabled him to create epithets like
Φιλάγλαος. παμπόρφυρος. and to put them exactly in their proper
places, like blocks of gleaming alabaster or of glowing porphyry—
for the architectural power over language is eminent in Pindar—
the Titanic faculty of language which produced such phrases as ἰξ
ἀδάμαντος ἢ σιδήρου κεχάλκευται μέλαιναν καρδίαν ψυχρᾷ φλογί.
did also betray him into expressions as pompous and frigid as
these—ποικιλοφόρμιγγος ἀοιδᾶς...... σχοινοτενεία τ' ἀοιδὰ
διθυράμβων. These, poured forth by Pindar in the insolence of
prodigality, when imitated by inferior poets, produced that inflated manner of lyrical diction which Aristophanes ridicules in
"Kinesias." The same may be said about his mixed metaphors,
of which the following are fair examples:—

τόξαν ἔχω τιν ἐπὶ γλώσσᾳ ἀκόνας λιγύρας
ἅ μ' ἐθέλοντα προσέλκει καλλιρόοισι πνοαῖς.—Ol. vi 82.

Κῶπαν σχάσον ταχὺ δ' ἄγκυραν ἔρεισον χθόνι
πρῴραθι χοιράδος ἄλκαρ πέτρας
ἐγκωμίων γὰρ ἄωτος ὕμνων
ἐπ' ἄλλοτ' ἄλλον ὥτε μέλισσα θύνει λόγον.—Pyth. x. 51.

Nor are these the worst, perhaps, of the sort which might be
chosen : for Pindar uses images like precious stones, setting
them together in a mass, without caring to sort them, so long as
they produce a gorgeous show. Obscurity is another of his
faults—due partly to his allusive and elliptical style, partly to
his sudden transitions, partly to the mixture of his images.
Incapable of what is commonplace, too fiery to trudge, like

---

* Pyth. viii. 40.

Simonides, along the path of rhetorical development, infinitely more anxious to realize by audacity the thought that seizes him than to make it easy to his hearer, Pindar is obscure to all who are unwilling to assimilate their fancy to his own. Voltaire called the Divine Comedy *une rhapsodie informe:* what, if he had found occasion to speak the truth of his French mind, would be have said about the Odes of Pindar? Another difficulty, apart from these of verbal style and imagination, is derived from the fact that the mechanism of his poetry, carefully as it is planned, is no less carefully concealed. He seems to take delight in trying to solve the problem of how slight a suggestion can be made to introduce a lengthy narrative. The student is obliged to maintain his attention at the straining point if an ode of Pindar's, even after patient analysis, is to present more than a mass of confused thoughts and images to his mind. But when he has caught the poet's drift, how delicate is the machinery, how beautiful is the art which governs this most sensitive fabric of linked melodies! What the hearers made of these odes—the athletes for whom they were written, the handsome youths praised in them, the rich men at whose tables they were chanted—remains an impenetrable mystery. Had the Greek race perceptions infinitely finer than ours? Or did the classic harmonies of Pindar sweep over their souls, ruffling the surface merely, but leaving the deeps untouched, as the soliloquies of Hamlet or the profound philosophy of Troilus and Cressida must have been lost upon the groundlings of Elizabeth's days, who caught with eagerness at the queen's poisoned goblet or the by-play of Sir Pandarus? That is a problem we cannot solve. All we know for certain is, that even allowing for the currency of Pindar's language and for the familiarity of his audience with the circumstances under which his odes were composed, as well as with their mythological allusions, these poems must at all times have been more difficult to follow than Bach's fugue in G minor to a man who cannot play the organ.

Art. III.—Free Public Libraries.

IT is now about twenty years since the first Free Town Library
was established in this country, under the permissive law
that had been passed in 1850, entitled "Public Libraries Act,
1850." The towns that first adopted this Act were Liverpool,
Manchester, and Salford. The example set by these three
Lancashire towns was not eagerly followed in other parts of the
country. There was no strong interest felt in the subject, and it
was only at somewhat irregular intervals that one town here, and
another there, took up the matter, and sought to avail itself of
the advantages of this Act. In several places the proposal to
adopt the law was negatived by the vote of the ratepayers.
During the ten years that elapsed from the passing of Mr. Ewart's
Act in 1850, we believe it was adopted in about fifteen or sixteen
places. Soon after the formation of the libraries at Salford,
Manchester, and Liverpool, accounts of their operations began to
be made public through the press. These reports were favourable:
they showed that Free Libraries in these towns might be regarded
as successful, and likely, when fully developed, to be an important
educational agency among all classes of the community. Still,
notwithstanding the diffusion of facts of this nature, and the
amendment of the law in 1855, Free Libraries did not rapidly
multiply. In the ten years from 1860 to 1870, the Act was
adopted only in about the same number of places as had put it
in force in the preceding decade. In a few of the larger towns,

branch libraries were established, while in several places where
the Act had been formally adopted, it was not carried into effect
for some years. Up to the present time, the law has been
adopted in about forty towns.

It is interesting to find that these libraries have been established among different kinds of population, and in almost every
sort of town; in large manufacturing and sea-port towns; in
smaller manufacturing places, in metropolitan, university,
cathedral, and agricultural towns. Some of these forty libraries
have a history extending over nearly twenty years, and others
over shorter periods, varying from fifteen to two or three years.
These institutions have thus already existed among us for some
time, and under considerable diversity of local circumstances.
These considerations may, perhaps, warrant us in saying Free
Libraries have had a fair trial, or they may authorize the conclusion that they have been at work so long, and under such
varied conditions, that the facts brought out in their experience
will enable us to judge of their character and utility,—of the
work they are adapted to accomplish, and of the way in which
they may best effect this object. It appears to us that the time
has arrived when a free inquiry may be instituted respecting the
origin, nature, working, management, and results of our Free
Town Libraries. Materials for such a discussion are not wanting.
In the reports which have been published yearly by the managers
of most of these libraries, in the numerous papers and pamphlets
that have appeared on the subject during the last fifteen years,
and in the elaborate and valuable work of Mr. Edward Edwards
on their history and development, ample materials have been
accumulated to assist us in forming an estimate of the general
nature and influence of these institutions. We therefore propose
to examine, as fully as our space will allow, some of the most
salient points which the history of Free Libraries presents for
consideration.

The first step towards the establishment of Public Free
Libraries in England is usually said to have been taken when,
on the 15th of March, 1849, Mr. Ewart moved for a Select
Committee of the House of Commons to inquire into the desirability of forming such libraries in this country. Mr. Ewart was
an enlightened educationalist as well as a genuine philanthropist.
He took a deep interest in whatever tended to improve the social
condition of his fellow-countrymen, and he seems to have been
led to move in this matter by the following circumstances. He
had carried, in 1845, a measure "for encouraging the establishment of museums in large towns." This Act was a permissive
law, and very few towns availed themselves of its provisions. In
1848 Mr. Edward Edwards, then of the British Museum, published

a paper in the *Statistical Journal* entitled "A Statistical View
of the Principal Public Libraries in Europe and the United
States of North America," from which it appeared that English
towns were much less adequately provided with public libraries
than were the large towns of most other countries. This paper
attracted the notice of Mr. Ewart, and seems to have suggested
to him the desirability of trying to connect town libraries with
town museums in this country. As both were much needed, and
as he found they were sometimes combined in the same establishment on the Continent, Mr. Ewart concluded that it might be
advantageous to connect the formation of public libraries with
his project for the establishment of museums. Feeling that it
would be vain to hope to carry a bill through parliament for this
purpose without the previous collection of information, he was
led to propose the appointment of a Select Committee of the
House of Commons "on the best means of extending the establishment of libraries freely open to the public, especially in
large towns in Great Britain and Ireland."

In submitting this motion to Parliament, Mr. Ewart first
dwelt on the fact that our large towns were almost wholly without public libraries, and that similar towns in most countries of
Europe possessed libraries that were freely accessible to the
public. He contended that our literature had suffered from this
circumstance, and referred to a well known complaint of Gibbon
to this effect. Continental writers, he said, could consult large
collections of books on whatever subject they might be pursuing,
whereas English authors had not access to such assistance. He
showed that inquiry into English libraries was necessary, as,
under existing regulations, they were not rendering the service
they might do; they were not freely open to the public, although
a number of them were assisted by public money. He next
referred to the work which he hoped would be accomplished
through the labours of the Committee he proposed. By this
inquiry, he contended, attention would be called to the question,
and its simple agitation would do good, because it would awaken
interest in the matter, and would undoubtedly lead to efforts
being made for the formation of public libraries. Mr. Joseph
Hume seconded the motion. On behalf of the Government, Sir
George Grey spoke disparagingly of the proposal, but did not
positively oppose it. He modified the proposition so that the
range of the inquiry was more restricted than Mr. Ewart had
suggested. On this Committee were many gentlemen well
known to the public, as Mr. Brotherton, Mr. Monckton Milnes
(Lord Houghton), Sir G. C. Lewis, Mr. Disraeli, Mr. Kershaw,
with Mr. Ewart as chairman. The Committee sat from the
15th of March to the 12th of July, 1849, and on the 23rd of

z 2

July its report was presented to the House. The evidence taken constitutes a blue-book of more than 300 pages. This volume supplies a large amount of valuable and interesting information on all points connected with the nature, extent, management, and workings of existing libraries on the Continent, in the States of America, and in the United Kingdom. The evidence presented in this blue-book fully sustained the statements advanced by Mr. Ewart in proposing the committee, as to the miserable provision of public libraries in our large towns, as compared with that existing in similar towns on the Continent and in America. It appeared that Paris possessed 7 open libraries; Brussels, 2; Berlin, 2; Vienna, 2; Milan, 2; Dresden, 4; Munich, 2; Copenhagen, 3; Florence, 6; London, 0. It was also shown to be the judgment of men practically acquainted with the habits and tastes of the people that the formation of public free town libraries would be a great boon to all classes, as a means of helping forward the intellectual progress of the community. It was said by these witnesses that the progress of education was retarded, and the early instruction of workers often rendered unproductive of good through the want of access to books in the periods of life subsequent to the school age. As embodying the drift and spirit of the evidence, the report of the Committee is an interesting document, and contains important suggestions and recommendations respecting the nature and working of public libraries. The Committee were able to state "that every witness examined on the subject has given an opinion favourable to the grant of assistance, on certain strict and clear conditions, by the Government, for the formation of public libraries." They distinctly recommend "that a power be given by Parliament enabling Town Councils to levy a small rate for the creation and support of town libraries." In reference to the general nature of libraries, the Committee say :—

"They have recognised in the establishment of libraries the general principles that they should be based on a firm and durable foundation ; that they should be freely accessible to all the public ; that they should be open during the evening ; that they should be, as far as possible, lending libraries. The last consideration is one of great importance. Many men, in order to derive the fullest advantage from books, must have them not only in their hands but in their homes. A great public library ought, above all things, to teach the teachers ; to supply with the best implements of education those who educate the people, whether in the pulpit, the schools, or the press. The lending out of books, therefore, which is a general characteristic of foreign libraries, should be an essential element in the formation of our own."

The result of this inquiry must have been gratifying to Mr. Ewart. The substance of the evidence taken, and the spirit of the Committee's report, were well calculated to encourage him in his design to obtain legislation on the subject, because they went directly to strengthen the case he sought to bring before Parliament. With such a body of favourable evidence, it might, perhaps, have been expected that the passing of a measure for the establishment of public libraries would be smooth and easy. Such a thing was not, however, possible in the British Parliament, and Mr. Ewart was sensible of this. As a practical man, he lost no time in bringing it before the House. He prepared a short bill, adapted to realize the principal recommendation of the Committee—"enabling Town Councils to levy a small rate for the creation and support of town libraries." This he laid before the House on the 14th of February, 1850. In introducing the measure, he contented himself with a brief and plain statement of the grounds on which he conceived Parliament would be warranted in sanctioning the proposal, and with a simple explanation of the provisions of his bill. He referred to the facts established before the Committee, that scarcely any country was so inadequately provided with public libraries as England; to the accessibility of the town libraries on the Continent and in America; to the assistance which these libraries were giving to the student, the author, the man of research, and thus to every department of science and literature, as well as to their agency in diffusing knowledge among all classes. He said the evidence went to "prove that our labouring population would be far more advanced if they had such opportunities as were afforded by means of public libraries to the working classes of the Continent." In reference to the more direct bearing of these libraries on education, he remarked that "there were two kinds of education—that imparted in schools, and that acquired by individuals themselves, and, in public libraries, the opportunity of self-teaching would be afforded to the labouring classes." In reply to the question, was such a bill called for by the people? he thought it was, and referred to facts brought out in the evidence as to the growing desire of the people for books. Mr. Brotherton seconded the motion, and leave was given to introduce the Bill. On its second reading, March 13th, there was a debate and a division. When Mr. Ewart had briefly moved the second reading, Colonel Sibthorpe spoke against it on various grounds, and proposed that it be read that day six months. Mr. Brotherton defended the Bill in a sort of apologetic strain, alleging that it was permissive, and only such towns would adopt it as were willing to be taxed for such a purpose, and that it only proposed to levy a rate of one halfpenny in the pound. Mr. Goulburn, Lord John Manners, Mr. Miles, Mr. Spooner, Sir R. H. Inglis, and Mr. Roundell Palmer, and other Conservatives opposed the measure. On a division, the second reading was carried by 118 votes against 101. It is worthy of note that the division was virtually a political and party division; the supporters of the Bill were nearly all Liberals, and its opponents, with few exceptions, were Conservatives. In Committee, some features of the measure were modified, and the effect of these alterations was to impair its character. It required much patience and tact on the part of Mr. Ewart to ensure its passage through Parliament, even in its mutilated state. The Bill received the Royal assent, and became law on the 14th August, 1850.

In the Act thus passed Mr. Ewart had incorporated the provisions of the law he had carried in 1845 for encouraging the establishment of museums in large towns, and all the subsequent amendments of the Libraries Acts also authorized the formation of museums as part of the same establishment. The Act of 1850 could only be adopted in corporate towns whose population exceeded 10,000. In such boroughs the proposal to adopt the Act was to be voted upon by the burgesses, in a way similar to that in which votes were taken at a municipal election. The burgesses might vote for or against its adoption; and unless two-thirds of those who voted were in favour of its adoption the act was rejected. When adopted the Town Council could provide buildings, fuel, lighting, fixtures, furniture, officers, and servants, from money raised by a rate of one halfpenny in the pound on the rateable property in the borough. The Council could not, however, purchase books; it could only provide and maintain a house for the library, not the library itself. Admission to all libraries formed under this Act was to be free. Since the obtainment of this law of 1850 five other Acts of Parliament have been passed respecting Public Town Libraries. Some of these have only slightly modified the first, or extended its provisions to Ireland and Scotland, while others have effected material changes in the law. In 1853 an Act was carried mainly to extend that of 1850 to the municipal boroughs of Ireland and to the parliamentary burghs of Scotland. In the next year another Act was passed to amend the law as applicable to Scotland. By this change better facilities were given for its adoption; if a poll was not demanded the vote of two-thirds of a meeting of qualified electors was sufficient, and further, it authorized the levying, in Scotland, of a rate of one penny in the pound, instead of one halfpenny. The Act of 1855 effected some material alterations in the details of the law. It supplied greater facilities for the establishment of libraries. It applied not only to municipal towns, but to all towns, places, districts, and parishes whose population exceeded 5000 at the preceding census. The Act could be adopted in any such town, district, or parish or union of parishes, by the vote of

two-thirds of the ratepayers present at a meeting duly called for
that purpose. The Council or Board was now authorized to purchase books, newspapers, specimens of arts and sciences, as well
as to provide buildings as before. The rate might now be levied
to the extent of one penny in the pound. The law was again
amended in 1866. This amendment authorized the adoption of
the Act in any place, irrespective of its population, at a public
meeting of ratepayers, called by the Council or Board, or on the
requisition, in writing, of ten ratepayers. A simple majority of
those present at such meeting was now sufficient to decide for or
against its adoption. The Libraries Act of 1867 only relates to
Scotland, and is chiefly an extension to that country of the
English law. In one of the pamphlets mentioned at the head of
this article the following summary is given of the chief provisions of the law now in force :—

"1. Any town, district, parish, or union of parishes, whatever its population, may now adopt the Free Libraries Act. 2. It may be adopted
by the vote of a majority of ratepayers at a meeting duly called for
that purpose. 3. This meeting may be called by the Town Council,
local board, or commissioners, or on the requisition in writing of ten
ratepayers. 4. The expense of calling a meeting convened to consider the propriety of adopting the Act must be defrayed from the
borough fund, whether the Act is adopted or rejected. 5. After a
vote of the meeting, duly called, in favour of its adoption, the Act may
at once be put in force. 6. When adopted, the Council or local
authority is required to appoint a committee for the management of
the library, and this committee can frame regulations for the library.
7. The managing committee may consist partly of members of the
Town Council or Local Board, and partly of other suitable gentlemen
in the locality. 8. All the property belonging to the library or museum must be vested in the Corporation or local governing body.
9. The rate levied for the purpose of this Act must not exceed one
penny in the pound on the annual rateable value of the property in the
town. 10. Admission to the library or museum must be free. 11. If
the meeting, called to consider the propriety of adopting the Act,
negatives the proposal, no further attempt can be made until the expi-
ration of a year. 12. The provisions of these Acts authorize the
establishment of museums or galleries of art, as well as libraries.
13. Town Councils or local bodies can borrow money for the purposes
of these Acts on the security of the rates." *

Such is the existing law respecting the establishment of Public
Town Libraries. Let us now see to what extent the Act has
been adopted, and in what way its provisions have been carried
out in the towns of the United Kingdom. As already intimated,
the formation of Free Libraries under law was not a subject in

* "Free Libraries: their Nature and Operations," pp. 12, 13.

which the people of this country evinced much concern. There had been no popular cry for the measure of 1850. The Act had not been demanded by the voice of the nation, or urged upon Parliament by pressure from without. It had rather been carried by a few enlightened advocates of social reform like Mr. Ewart, Mr. Brotherton, and others. Under these circumstances, it could hardly be expected that the burgesses of our large corporate towns would make haste to adopt its provisions. The truth is, no feeling of this kind was manifested, and the fact will not surprise us if we bear in mind one or two features of the statute as it first stood. It could only be adopted in corporate towns whose population exceeded 10,000; a rate of one half-penny in the pound could be levied, but no part of the proceeds could be applied to the purchase of books, but merely to the providing of rooms and the payment of librarians. All books had to be obtained either as donations, or to be purchased with money raised by subscription. Hence the Act could only be carried into effect where a feeling was strong in favour of the object, and where there was public spirit enough voluntarily to provide funds for the purchase of books. In some few places, as Warrington, Winchester, and Salford, museums had been formed under the Act of 1845, and these towns were almost inevitably led forthwith to adopt the Libraries Act, as the latter law virtually included the former. To the populous towns of Lancashire must be accorded the credit of first taking up the subject and carrying the law into effect with spirit. Liverpool began to move in the matter in 1850. The corporation gave 1000l., and a like sum was subscribed by gentlemen of the town, with which to make a commencement. Books, also, were freely given, and the library was opened in 1852. Other donations followed, and ultimately the late Sir William Brown gave 30,000l. for the erection of the splendid building now used as the central library. In Manchester the late Sir John Potter entered into the movement with much zeal, and chiefly through his liberality and exertions a sum of 10,000l. was subscribed to start the project. Of this amount about 800l. was collected by working men from twenty thousand workpeople. The library was opened in 1852. In Salford a committee of gentlemen, unconnected with the Corporation, obtained 12,000l. for the project, besides numerous gifts of books and objects for the museum. At Bolton the Act was adopted in 1852, and here also a sum of 3246l. was subscribed by the inhabitants, towards which working men contributed a considerable amount. These were the towns that first brought the Public Libraries Act into operation. In the next year, 1853, Cambridge adopted the Act, as did also Sheffield and Blackburn, although in the two latter towns the libraries were not actually

formed for several years, until after the law had been modified
in 1855. In 1854 Oxford followed the example set by
Cambridge.

From 1855, one penny in the pound could be levied instead
of one halfpenny as before, and the amended law also authorized
the purchase of books with the rate-money. This was an important alteration, as the towns had no longer 'to rely upon
voluntary subscriptions for the purchase of books, or upon donations of books. In the years following these changes, the law
was brought into force at Kidderminster, Hertford, Airdrie, Westminster, Birkenhead, Leamington, Norwich, Lichfield, Walsall,
Birmingham, and Cardiff. Within the last ten years, the Act
has been adopted at Maidstone, Canterbury, Warwick, Coventry,
Nottingham, Paisley, Doncaster, Dundee, Exeter, Leicester, Wolverhampton, Leeds, Rochdale, Bradford, and a few other places.
There are public libraries at some other towns, such as Lynn,
Sunderland, Stirling, Preston, &c., where libraries have been
established and supported by private gentlemen, but they are
not all regularly under the Act, and we have no report as to
their operations. In considering this somewhat tardy progress
in the formation of public town libraries, it should be remembered that large numbers of patriotic thoughtful Englishmen
hold on this subject, as on that of popular education, that this
work is not within the legitimate province of the Civil Government. Persons of this way of thinking were opposed to the
adoption of the Act on principle; many were indifferent as to
the principle, but were against the establishment of libraries on
the score of economy. From these circumstances it happened
that, in many towns, a considerable proportion of the inhabitants
were opposed to the formation of these libraries. And as under
the first Act burgesses could vote for or against it, and as two-
thirds of those who voted must vote for the proposal, or the law
did not come into operation, it was not a difficult matter in some
places for the opponents of the measure to defeat a proposal for
its adoption. It is not easy to ascertain the number of places in
which this proposition has been negatived; but it is known that
in the following places it was rejected:—Exeter, March, 1851;
Birmingham, April, 1853; Cheltenham, September, 1853; City
of London, November, 1854; Islington, November, 1855; Hull,
January, 1857; Haslingden, and Mary-le-bone, on dates not
known. In most of these places the Act was not adopted, because a majority of the burgesses were unwilling to submit to an
increase of local taxation for such an object. It may also be
mentioned that the propriety of establishing Free Libraries has
been considered in several other towns where the Act has not
yet been brought into force. In these cases information respect-

ing its working has been collected; preliminary meetings held, and the matter fully considered, and the result has been that it was deemed expedient to abandon the design of forming a library. This was the case at Edinburgh. Then in some towns where the proposal was carried, it was strongly opposed. It was so in Leeds. Here an active agitation arose on the subject, and numerous meetings were held in various parts of the borough, where the question was freely discussed in its different aspects and bearings. Ultimately the adoption of the law was carried at a large meeting in the Town Hall, by a narrow majority.

If we now pass to the working of the Free Libraries that have been formed during the last twenty years, it will soon be evident that all have not been equally successful; nor have they all taken the same course in seeking to carry out the provisions of the law. Several of these Free Libraries have been eminently successful; the number of books on their shelves has regularly increased; these books have been well chosen, have yearly been more widely read, and it may be fairly affirmed that the libraries have become every year more powerful for good. This is particularly true of the libraries in the populous towns, although it is satisfactory to know that it is also true of some of the middle-sized and of one or two of the smaller places. But in reference to a goodly number, it must be admitted their progress has not been as satisfactory as could be desired. In most of the articles and pamphlets on Free Libraries, the writers have dwelt for the most part upon the facts connected with some half-dozen of the largest and most successful, while the statistics and operations of the smaller libraries have been scarcely noticed. Where the object of the writer has been simply to show what Free Libraries might be under favourable circumstances, this special attention to the larger was perhaps just and useful. This, however, is not the object of the present article: we intend to ascertain how the law is operating as a whole—what it is accomplishing, or is adapted to effect as a national measure, and how the Act is really working under varied circumstances. Now while information respecting the operations of the larger libraries is abundant, it is difficult or impossible to obtain complete or accurate statistics in reference to the smaller institutions. The following table exhibits the statistical particulars of free library work under the specified heads:—

TOWN	Population	Act Adopted	Vols. in Libraries — Reference	Lending	Total	Vols. to 100 of Population	Issues — Reference	Lending	Total	Issues per vol.
Warrington	32,083	1848	3,250	7,100	10,350	32	...	...	7,224	.69
Salford	124,805	1851	18,297	16,843	34,140	29	35,621	149,704	186,525	5.42
Winchester	14,705	1851	1,600	...	1,600	10	2,000	...	2,000	1.40
Liverpool	493,346	1850	58,124	89,621	82,746	18	507,835	426,408	933,743	10.00
Manchester	355,065	1852	45,003	60,573	105,466	29	263,611	643,523	917,163	6.68
Bolton	82,854	1852	17,014	10,502	27,516	33	49,164	94,100	143,262	5.20
Sheffield	239,947	1853	2,702	30,644	33,346	13	17,646	140,716	158,362	4.74
Cambridge	30,054	1853	4,841	11,298	15,639	52	6,620	44,927	50,447	3.22
Oxford	31,354	1851	4,000	3,000	7,000	21	1,903	12,003	13,906	1.98
Kidderminster	19,463	1855	950	...	1,800	5	No record	record.	...	...
Hertford	7,161	1855	...	2,350	2,350	23	...	...	6,000	3.33
Alnwick	13,487	1856	...	8,000	8,000	17	...	11,103	11,103	4.72
Westminster	246,413	1856	2,254	12,390	14,644	...	...	43,028	43,028	5.43
Birkenhead	65,930	1856	...	8,500	8,640	21	18,421	50,821	69,242	4.72
Leamington	22,730	1857	...	...	4,700	33	...	30,895	30,895	3.63
Norwich	80,390	1857	...	...	2,530	6	769	24,350	25,116	5.34
Lichfield	7,380	1860	...	...	...	34	...	...	...	...
Birmingham	343,696	1860	28,559	31,788	60,347	17	133,678	302,867	138,445	7.23
Blackburn	76,337	1862	7,904	6,886	16,790	22	3,210	37,659	40,869	2.43
Cardiff	39,070	1862	...	5,836	6,936	15	...	17,671	17,671	3.01
Warwick	11,001	1865	...	...	2,237	20	...	...	13,760	7.91
Coventry	39,470	1867	1,296	9,091	10,377	20	4,000	54,252	68,262	5.71
Nottingham	86,048	1867	3,860	13,319	17,209	20	8,074	129,608	137,628	7.99
Paisley	48,257	1867	4,228	8,067	12,292	25	not open little used	66,833	66,833	5.43
Doncaster	16,758	1868	8,400	9,510	14,940	79	...	15,200	15,200	1.01
Dundee	118,974	1868	2,500	21,000	24,500	20	50,290	122,457	172,857	7.01
Exeter	34,646	1868	...	...	9,717	28	12,998	12,047	23,015	2.57
Leicester	95,084	1869	2,868	6,151	8,019	10	1,148	...	...	...
Wolverhampton	68,270	1869	800	11,000	11,800	17	...	108,408	104,553	8.87
Maidstone	26,198	1865	3,500	...	3,506	13	...	...	6,460	1.52
Canterbury	20,901	...	...	...	2,600	12	1,500	...	1,500	.57
Tynemouth	38,900	1869	2,410	12,259	14,079	57	5,316 Just opened	67,740 opened	72,842	4.96
Rochdale	46,556	1870	4,600	7,000	11,600	23	...	...	...	...
Leeds	259,201	1869	14,000	14,000	30,000	11	...	...	...	...
Bradford	145,827	1871	6,000	Not opened	...	...	...	...	...	...
Walsall	46,459	1869	...	...	...	...	...	...	...	...
					8,500	12			39,200	7.00

In connexion with this table, it will be needful to offer a few observations to render the figures truly serviceable to the reader, and to prevent their misinterpretation.

1. The statistics given are as complete and accurate as it has been found practicable to make them. It will, however, be seen that they are defective in a few cases. Some of the managing committees do not print reports, and the reports of others do not always supply the specific information on all the heads. In the case of a few of the smaller libraries, the officers are unable to say what number of volumes the library contains, or what are the issues; no proper records, seemingly, are kept of these matters. Then, from a few of the institutions the information desired could not be obtained, although repeated applications were made, with distinct printed questions and schedules supplied, ready to be filled up.* At some of the towns in the list, as Leeds, Rochdale, Bradford, the libraries have been so recently opened that no statistics of annual issues can yet be made. In Leeds there is abundant evidence that the library will be a useful and successful one; and the probability is that both in Bradford and Rochdale the libraries will do a useful work.

2. Most of the libraries consist of two branches—a Reference department, and a Lending department. This is not, however, the case in every town. At some places it is only a reference library, as at Winchester, Kidderminster, Maidstone, and Lichfield; at others it is only a Lending Library, as at Airdrie and Walsall; while in a few instances, as at Leamington, Exeter, and Westminster, there are not two distinct libraries, but all the books may be loaned, and they may also be consulted in the reading-room, if upon the shelves, so that the same books form both a Reference and a Lending Library.

3. The slightest examination of the figures in columns 4 and 5 will suffice to show that different notions prevail at different places as to the nature and objects of a reference library. In several towns, as Salford, Liverpool, Manchester, Birmingham, Bolton, and Leeds, it will be seen the reference library is large, usually much larger than the lending library; while in most others, as Sheffield, Cambridge, Birkenhead, Coventry, Nottingham, Dundee, Tynemouth, and Leicester, it is much smaller than the lending branch. The aim of the managers in the former in-

* This applies to a very small number. From the librarians and officers of free libraries the writer has experienced the greatest attention and courtesy. His inquiries, either in person or by letter, have been readily and fully answered, and he is greatly indebted to them for reports and documents, which have been cheerfully supplied. He gladly embraces this opportunity of acknowledging the great assistance they have rendered him, and of expressing his thanks for their kindness.

stances has evidently been to make the reference or consulting library a collection of the best books in the various departments of science and literature, so that the student, the inquirer, or man of research might always find on the shelves the books he might desire to consult, in order to aid him in whatever field of thought he might require assistance. In the latter cases, we apprehend the term "reference library" is used in a narrower sense, and simply means a collection of books of reference strictly so called.

4. The figures in the 6th column represent the gross number of volumes in all the departments of the free library establishments of each town—in the reference and lending libraries, and in the branches, where branches exist.

5. In summarizing the statistics of European public libraries in 1849, Mr. Edwards adopted the plan of stating the number of volumes in each town to every 100 of population. This mode of indicating the amount of public library provision was also used in the report of the Select Committee of 1849. It has been followed here, and the 7th column exhibits the number of volumes provided by the free libraries of the respective towns for every 100 of the population.

6. It should be stated that the issues are not taken on the same principle at all places, or recorded in one uniform way. Thus, at some places the issues of Patent Specifications are counted and included in the statistics, whereas in others they are not included; again, at some places the issues of periodicals in the reading-room are counted and included, while at others they are not so reckoned. Take the case of the Liverpool reference library. Here the number of issues is very great—proportionately larger, for instance, than at Manchester or Birmingham; but it must be stated that this reference library contains a considerable amount of Fiction; and further, the issues of periodicals at Liverpool are counted, and, we believe, entered under the class "General Literature." The issues under this head are 202,984, and under "Works of Imagination," 151,643, making together in the two heads, 354,627.

7. The figures in the 9th column show remarkable differences in the amount of provision when estimated as explained above. As might be expected, the proportionate amount is largest in small and moderate sized towns. This large proportionate supply proves nothing, however, as to the character of the books, or as to the use made of them by the inhabitants. The figures in the 11th column will better help us to conclusions in this direction. These illustrate the use made of the books by indicating the number of times a book has been taken out; thus, in the case of Manchester, it appears the issues have been equal to the

circulation of every book in all the libraries more than eight times. Now, if columns 7 and 11 be compared, it will be evident that in towns where the proportionate number of volumes is the largest, the use made of the books is sometimes the least. If we take Warrington, Oxford, Hertford, Leamington, Doncaster, and Exeter, we shall find the provision large, while the issues are low; and, on the other hand, if we take the populous towns of Liverpool, Manchester, and Birmingham, where the proportionate supply is small, we find the use made of the books is much greater.

8. This fact may undeniably be regarded as some indication of the reading habits of the different populations; but we apprehend it is equally important as significant of the character of the books and of the skill exercised in their choice. In several of the smaller towns a considerable proportion of the books have been given; or the collections forming the libraries are largely made up of old libraries of little value. These books are not the result of "systematic purchase," and are thus of less interest to readers.

9. Besides a reference and a lending library, and a reading-room properly so called, many of the free libraries have also news-rooms, which are plentifully supplied with daily and weekly newspapers, representing all political parties, as well as with an abundance of periodicals. It is so in Manchester, Salford, Birmingham, Cambridge, Cardiff, Nottingham, Tynemouth, whereas in other places periodicals are provided for the reading-room, but not newspapers.

10. In several of the larger towns, as Manchester, Liverpool, Salford, Birmingham, and Sheffield, branch lending libraries have been established. These are located in those districts of the boroughs where the people chiefly reside, and which are at a distance from the central library. In Manchester there are four branches, in Liverpool two, in Birmingham four, in Salford one, in Sheffield one, and in Leeds two. These branches are doing a capital work among the residents of the localities in which they are situated. They constitute a very important feature in the free library movement in large places, and are indeed essential to its success in such boroughs.

11. Our statistical table supplies the facts of these libraries for the last year, or for as recent a year as the information could be obtained. The history of some of the larger libraries has been marked by a development that is at once interesting and instructive. Like other institutions, even some of the more successful have at times slightly fluctuated, though upon the whole there has been a real and steady progress. The subjoined tables will show the increase of books and issues in six of the largest free

libraries.* The first gives the number of volumes in the libraries
of these towns at the dates mentioned :—

	1852.	1857.	1862.	1867.	1871.
Manchester . .	10,013	30 000	60,347	83,0 9	105.600
Liverpool . .	13,456	40.090	67,693	80.4. 2	92.745
Salford . . .	17,758	20,509	27,441	30,0 0	34.140
Bolton . . .	12,239	16,341	20,125	22,420	27,516
Sheffield . .	...	7,784	18,020	23,3 4	33.316
Birmingham .	...	...	...	10,158	60,347

The next furnishes the gross number of issues in all the
libraries of the same towns at the same dates :—

	1852.	1857.	1862.	1867.	1871-2.
Manchester . .	138,312	198,108	472,686	673,432	917,103
Liverpool . .	111,723	100 246	456,372	673,470	933,743
Salford . . .	35,116	137,814	161,808	122,578	184,225
Bolton . . .	88,472	94,284	100,157	63,401	143,202
Sheffield . . .	...	114,275	154,501	162,573	158,302
Birmingham .	...	...	...	112,557	430,445

12. The history of the libraries in the smaller places presents
nothing analogous to this in reference to their progress. The
money which the managers of these libraries can yearly apply to
the purchase of books is limited, and in some cases is very small
indeed. The increase of books is consequently very slight, and
the readers do not increase in number where there is not a fresh
supply, and old readers cease to frequent the library as often as
at first.

From this inquiry as to the numerical extent of existing
libraries, and the general circulation of their contents, we advance to ask—What kind of books do these libraries contain?
What is their character as collections? The selection of books
is the most vital question connected with a library in relation to
its character and utility. In free libraries the law vests the choice

* In Mr. Axon's capital pamphlet, "Statistical Notes," &c., will be found
many very interesting facts illustrative of the development and progress of
free libraries.

of books in the managing committee, and these committees are
appointed by the Town Council or Local Board. As the amount
of the funds which the different committees can apply to the
purchase of books varies greatly, so we find almost as much
diversity in the nature of the collections as in their numerical
extent. Considering the circumstances under which these
libraries have been formed, they are just what might be expected—often very unsystematic collections. In reference to
several of the largest, there can be no hesitation in saying these
libraries are collections of great value, and are admirably adapted
to the purpose for which they were designed. They have been
formed with a distinct aim, and they reflect great credit on the
knowledge, judgment, and exertions of the managers and librarians. But in reference to free libraries as a whole, we regret
we are unable to speak so confidently of their character as collections. We gladly recognise and rejoice in one feature of these
libraries—as a rule they are not sectional, but really general collections. So far as we have been able to ascertain—and we may
say we have examined the catalogues of a large proportion of
them—no department of literature, and no species of good books,
appear to be excluded. They have, for the most part, been
formed on a broad, catholic basis; they contain all classes of
useful works, including theological, political, and speculative. In
the best of them, all parties, sects, denominations, and schools
seem to be represented, as well as all branches of science, art,
and literature. In a country like this, where sectional feeling
affects detrimentally so many useful institutions, we regard this
as a great good. If we pass beyond this general remark, and
attempt to speak more definitely of the collections forming our
free libraries, we are stopped by preliminary questions like the
following:—What constitutes a good free library? What is the
just conception of what such a library should be? Then we are
met by the inquiry—How far have these conceptions been realized
in the libraries already formed? Again, it would be needful to
view this inquiry in two aspects, as applicable to a reference
library and a lending library. Now we readily admit that it is
most desirable that these questions should be answered. The
investigation of these points would be most instructive, and we
venture to think it will be necessary to institute some such inquiry before we can reach exact knowledge of the various collections forming these public libraries, or satisfactorily answer
certain queries as to the specific value of each. Into such a discussion, however, we cannot now enter. The materials are not
at hand. But still we may offer a few general remarks that relate to some of the points just mooted.

The formation of a good library, either on a larger or a smaller scale, is not a work of accident or chance. There cannot be a greater mistake than to suppose that a really good collection of books can be brought together without a combination of knowledge, skill, experience, and much labour. Whatever may be the extent of a library, if it is to be truly valuable, it must be formed after some fixed aim or design. To buy books at random, and bring them together haphazard, or without an intelligent aim that constantly determines their selection, is merely to form what Mr. Edwards calls "a heap of books," and not a library properly so termed. It has been well said by Mr. Burton, in his "Book-hunter"—

"A great library cannot be constructed—it is the growth of ages. You may buy books at any time with money, but you cannot make a library like one that has been a century or two a growing, though you had the whole national debt to do it with."*

If we paraphrase Mr. Burton's first sentence, it will express a great truth directly applicable to our purpose. Let us say, a good library cannot be formed by accident; it is the product of a determinate purpose, of special knowledge, peculiar talents, and persistent effort. This truth is fully recognised in more than one of his works by Mr. Edwards, when he refers to the "systematic collection of books" as distinguished from "a mere chance aggregation of books." And Mr. Axon expresses the same thought when he speaks of "a carefully chosen collection of books" as opposed to "a fortuitous conglomeration of books." It is to be feared that this important truth has not always been sufficiently understood and practically acted upon in the formation of free libraries. Do not the facts connected with the history—particularly the early history—of many of them, show that there has too often been a confounding of "a systematic collection" with a "mere chance aggregation"? Have not too many of them been formed by the latter rather than by the former process?

Now, what should be aimed at in forming a reference, or a lending department of a free library? Answers to this question, sufficiently definite for our purpose, may be found in the works named at the head of this article. Speaking of the Manchester libraries, Mr. Axon says:—

"It will be seen that from the commencement the Manchester library was divided into a reference and a lending library, each having a distinct aim. The reference library was intended to place at the disposal of every student, rich or poor, the best books in the various domains of human thought, whilst the lending library was intended to be of a more popular character, and whilst containing elementary books of a scientific nature, consisted chiefly of works of history, poetry, and fiction, including serviceable editions of really all the greater English writers." [*]

But perhaps the question, so far as it relates to a reference library, could not be better answered than in the following statement of the principles which have guided the Birmingham committee and officers in forming their reference library. They say :—

"The collection has been formed on the following principles :—
  "I. That the library should, as far as practicable, represent every phase of human thought, and every variety of opinion.
  "II. That books of permanent value and of standard interest should form the principal portion of the library, and that modern books of value and importance should be added from time to time as they are published.
  "III. That it should contain those rare and costly works which are generally out of the reach of individual students and collectors, and which are not usually found in provincial or private libraries." [†]

Acting on these principles, the Birmingham committees have formed a consulting library of some 28,000 volumes, which, though not so large as that of Liverpool or of Manchester, may be regarded as unequalled for its choice collection of works. But how few of the reference libraries have been brought together on such principles, or under the influence of a definite guiding aim, in how few cases have the managers ever endeavoured to realize such a design in forming a reference library, let the character of many of these collections answer. It will at once be said, all towns have not the means which the Birmingham committee have had. This is true ; but then is it not also a fact that very few of the towns have levied the whole amount of the rate allowed by law, or have ever attempted with what means they had to secure a consulting library on the principles indicated in the Birmingham statement ? The inspection of the figures in our table which exhibit the extent of the reference libraries, not simply at small places, but even at many considerable towns, as Sheffield, Birkenhead, Coventry, Nottingham, Dundee, Wolverhampton, Leicester, and Tynemouth, will suffice to convince the reader that the parties who have formed the consulting libraries at these places have not been guided by a conception of their nature similar to that which has produced the Birmingham library. Further, if we consider how largely the libraries of the smaller places are made up of books obtained

---

* Statistical Notes, p. 333.   † Catalogue of Reference Department, p. vii.

by donation, or even to what an extent those of some of the larger towns have been "enriched" in this way, or through the incorporation of old libraries, we shall easily understand the part which "chance aggregation" or "fortuitous conglomeration" has played in the formation of these collections. At first, books could not be purchased by rate-money, and at the establishment of the earlier libraries, even in some of the populous towns, as Liverpool, Manchester, Salford, and Bolton, books were "begged," and considerable quantities were obtained in this manner. According to trustworthy information, at Bolton 3240 volumes were thus got; at Norwich, 2500, out of a library now only reaching 4700; at Lichfield, 2300, out of a library of 2500; at Winchester, "the greater portion;" at Blackburn, "a large number;" at Cambridge, "two-thirds;" at Oxford, "nearly all the books in the reference library;" at Warrington, "a large number;" at Kidderminster, 750 out of a library of 950. And in reference to some recently established libraries, it appears that at Coventry the free library took some 10,000 volumes from the Coventry Library Society, on paying off the debt of that society, amounting to 180*l.*; at Doncaster, the free library may be said to have been partly formed through the failure of the Doncaster Subscription Library, and into it was also absorbed the library of an unsuccessful Mechanics' Institution. From these two sources the free library got about 10,000 volumes. At Leicester the free library took the library of an unsuccessful Mechanics' Institution, on paying off the debt of that institution and buying the building. At Paisley, the free library took 8000 or 10,000 volumes from the Paisley Library. In other towns similar incorporations or purchases were made.

Now we are not condemning donations of books to free libraries, nor the absorption or purchase of existing libraries; nothing of the sort. Where libraries that have been carefully selected and are in good condition can be obtained for the nucleus of a free library, it is most desirable that they should be purchased for this purpose; but worn-out subscription libraries, or the books of an unsuccessful Mechanics' Institution, are not likely either to have been skilfully chosen or to be of much worth. Donations of books must be welcomed, as they are sometimes very valuable; but again, as a rule, gifts of books obtained by solicitation are of questionable value. In the cases of libraries of collectors that may be bequeathed, that is a very different thing : such additions are always most desirable, and are frequently invaluable to the institution to which they are left. At Birmingham comparatively few books have been obtained through donation; their books have mostly been obtained by what Mr. Edwards calls "systematic purchase." Speaking of

A A 2

"the special circumstances which have marked the formation
and growth of the Birmingham library," Mr. Edwards observes:—

" The Central Consulting Library has been selected by systematic
purchase. It has not been left to the chances of casual donations,
supplemented now and then by casual purchases. Too often the
books that are given to libraries (otherwise than by request) are the
mere weedings of private collections; they sometimes remind us of an
inscription which often meets our eyes in the purlieus of our watering-
places—'*Rubbish may be shot here.*' In order to a better result at
Birmingham, the Town Council has devoted a large proportion of the
rate money to book-buying. At this early stage of the business,
therefore, it is already really a library, and not merely a heap of
books."*

As already stated, the 10th column of the table given above
exhibits the gross issues of the books in all departments of the
free libraries of the respective towns. These figures say nothing
as to what sort of books are most or least read, or as to the extent
to which the books of any class are circulated. This, however,
is an interesting question, in trying to estimate the work that is
being done by free libraries. As in other cases, the books in
free libraries are mostly classified. The classification varies at
different towns, although there is some general resemblance in
the grouping of a number of them. Important as is the subject
of classification, it is one into the discussion of which we
cannot enter. For the ordinary purpose of ascertaining the
number of volumes circulated in the different departments it is
not desirable to have a great number of classes ; nor, on the
other hand, should the number be very small. If the classes are
very few several kinds of books are necessarily included under
one class, and then the statistics of issues fail to bring out the
precise character of the reading. Thus at Manchester the books
are divided into five classes, and the fifth, "Literature and
Polygraphy," includes works on widely different subjects, as
Essays, General Literature, Poetry, the Drama, Prose Fiction,
and "Collected Works." The defects of this classification are
felt at once when we attempt to determine that important
inquiry,—What is the proportion in which works of fiction are
read in the Manchester libraries ? In other classifications, not so
faulty as this, we encounter difficulties on the same score,
because, in some cases, the class " Fiction" includes the drama and
poetry, as well as novels and tales; and in other cases the class
" Works of Imagination" includes the last mentioned kinds of

---

* Free Town Libraries, p. 153.

books, together with others. The classifications are so various that we are utterly unable to bring the issues of the different towns into any tabular form. We subjoin statistics as to the issues of the different classes of books at the various towns named below. It must be remembered that these issues refer to the lending department, except in cases where the issues from the two branches are not distinguished in the reports:—

MANCHESTER.—Gross issues, 649,522: Theology and Philosophy, 11,035; History, Biography, Voyages and Travels, 63,246; Politics and Commerce, 6020; Science and Art, 25.735; General Literature and Polygraphy, 516,517; Books for the Blind, 65. Percentage of General Literature, 84.0. Percentage of issues of General Literature, &c., in Reference Library, 15.3

LIVERPOOL.—Gross issues, 420,408: Theology, Morals, &c., 8209; Natural Philosophy and Mathematics, 4456; Natural History, 3045; Science and the Arts, 0790; History and Biography, 20,162; Topography and Antiquities, 1940; Geography, Voyages and Travels, 10,000; Miscellaneous Literature, 35,855; Jurisprudence, Laws, and Politics, 408; Social Science and Political Economy, 1196; Education and Language, 4100; Poetry and the Drama, 3432; Prose Fiction, 323,172; Latin and Greek Classics, 390; Books for the Blind, 140. Percentage of Fiction, 75.7. Percentage of issues in Works of Imagination and General Literature in Reference Library, 60.0.

BIRMINGHAM.—Gross issues, 302,807: Theology, Moral Philosophy, &c., 5247; History, Biography, Voyages and Travels, 25,400; Law, Politics, and Commerce, 645; Arts, Sciences, and Natural History, 12,045; Poetry, Drama, Fiction, Periodicals, &c., 240,070; Juvenile Books, 19,390. Percentage of Fiction, &c., 70.2. Percentage of Fiction, &c., in Reference Library, 18.5.

SHEFFIELD.—Gross issues, 142,875: History, Biography, and Travels, 25,874; Arts and Sciences, 11,238; Theology and Philosophy, 4025; Politics, &c., 918; Poetry, 4851; Fiction, 68,941; Miscellaneous, 27,028. Percentage of Fiction, 48.1.

COVENTRY.—Gross issues. 58,252; Theology and Philosophy, 508; History, Biography, Voyages and Travels, 4520; Law, Politics, and Commerce, 213; Science and Art, 1235; Miscellaneous, Fiction, Poetry, 30,328; Juvenile Books, 11,140; Magazines and Reviews, 4200. Percentage of Fiction, &c., 62.3.

BIRKENHEAD.—Gross issues, 60,821; Theology and Philosophy, 2203; Natural Philosophy, &c., 1110; Natural History, 1279; Arts and Sciences, 1802; History and Biography, &c., 4633; Topography, Archæology, &c., 414; Geography, Voyages and Travels, 3130; Miscellaneous Literature, 5005; Law and Political Economy, 296; Classical Literature, 80; Education, 1182; Poetry and the Drama, 1054; Novels and Tales, 23,000; Books for the Young, 4330. Percentage of Novels and Tales, 47.2.

BOLTON.—Gross issues, 55,524: Theology, 760; Philosophy, 194; English History, 650; Foreign History, 814; Biography, 2380;

Topography, 718 ; Voyages and Travels, 2103 ; Law, Politics, &c., 700 ; Sciences and Arts, 1007 ; Poetry and Drama, 918 ; Novels and Romances, 39,158 ; General Literature, 4715 : Percentage of Fiction, 70.5.

SALFORD.—Gross issues, 73,469 : Theology, 330 ; History, 4887 ; Science, 1341 ; General Literature, 3404 ; Novels, 63,501. Percentage of Fiction, 86.4.

BLACKBURN.—Gross issues, 40,869 ; Theology and Philosophy, 292 ; History, 4783 ; Politics and Commerce, 210 ; Science and the Arts, 1092 ; Miscellaneous Literature, 33,601. Percentage of Miscellaneous Literature, 82.2.

NOTTINGHAM.—Gross issues, 129,608 ; Theology and Philosophy, 2887 ; History, Biography, Voyages and Travels, 13,450 ; Science and Art, 5428 ; Law, Politics, and Commerce, 340 ; Poetry, the Drama, Fiction, Collected Works, &c., 107,503. Percentage of Fiction, &c., 83.2.

EXETER.—Gross issues, 12,047 : History, Biography, Voyages and Travels, 2455 ; Science and Art, 484 ; Literature and Polygraphy, 8001 ; Theology and Philosophy, 102 ; Politics and Commerce, 15. Percentage of Literature and Polygraphy, 74.5.

TYNEMOUTH.—Gross issues, 67,710 ; Theology, &c., 2298 ; Political Economy, 317 ; Biography, &c., 2817 ; History, 2536 ; Voyages and Travels, 2725 ; Miscellaneous Literature, 7744 ; Arts and Sciences, 2900 ; Novels, Tales, &c., 35,836 ; Poetry, 1302 ; Books for the Young, 0508 ; Books for the Blind, 123. Percentage of Fiction, 63.

DUNDEE.—Gross issues, 122,213 ; Theology, Philosophy, Education, &c., 4263 ; Law and Jurisprudence, 545 ; Physical Science, 1589 ; Natural Sciences, 1801 ; History and Biography, 9871 ; Geography, Voyages and Travels, 7326 ; Politics and Commerce, 668 ; Science and Arts, 2470 ; Miscellaneous Literature, 12,912 ; Novels and Works of Imagination, 74,020 ; Poetry and the Drama, 3340 ; Classical Literature, 108 ; Books of Reference, 253 ; Periodicals, 2087. Percentage of Fiction, 61.3.

CARDIFF.—Gross issues, 17,871 : Theology and Metaphysics, 235 ; Natural Philosophy and Mathematics, 200 ; Natural History and Geology, 438 ; Science and Art, 259 ; History and Biography, 2010 ; Topography and Antiquities, 100 ; Geography and Travels, 1849 ; Miscellaneous Literature, 2065 ; Law and Politics, 142 ; Commercial Statistics, 42 ; Education, 55 ; Poetry and the Drama, 430 ; Light Literature, 9904 ; Books for the Blind, 136 : Percentage of Light Literature, 55.4.

CAMBRIDGE.—Gross issues, 44.927 : Theology and Philosophy, 874 ; History, Voyages and Travels, 2721 ; Biography, 970 ; Law, Politics, and Commerce, 924 ; Science and Art, 070 ; Natural History, 095 ; Poetry and Drama, 1020 ; Fiction, 31,111 ; Periodical Literature, 4823 ; Miscellaneous Literature, 1400. Percentage of Fiction, 69.2.

In reference to the smaller libraries, they either print no

reports, or their reports furnish no information as to the way in which the different kinds of books are read. This is the reason we are unable to supply details on this point respecting such libraries. The statistics just given relate to different sized libraries and to libraries located among differing populations; and may thus be taken as fairly representing the general reading in free libraries. The facts here presented will enable any attentive reader to form a tolerably correct judgment as to the sorts of books borrowed from these institutions. To all that feel concerned in the working of these libraries, and in the mental improvement of the community, these facts are full of significance and interest. They demonstrate that through the agency of free libraries a great educational work is being carried on—a work that must in time tell on the general intelligence and culture of our town populations. These statistics prove that in some of the most important departments of human thought the issues in these lending libraries are numerous; and the facts, as a whole, afford abundant evidence that these institutions are largely resorted to by the thoughtful and inquiring in every town where they have been established.* It has frequently been objected that free libraries are only or chiefly resorted to for amusing and light books.† This allegation is disproved by the figures just placed before the reader; it is dictated by ignorance or prejudice. It is of course undeniable that works of fiction are extensively issued from free libraries; the facts now brought together show this. It would be folly to attempt to deny that the demand in these institutions runs strongly on works of this class. Here, however, it must be observed: 1. This is only just what might be expected. It is the inevitable consequence of the reading habits of the age and the character of our current literature. The same thing is found in every other library in the country of a general nature. 2. But a fair question here is this—Is the proportion of issues of books of this kind from free libraries greater than from the libraries of other institutions? Let us see. Again we must say that in consequence of the

---

* Nothing could more conclusively establish this than the accounts presented in the Birmingham and other reports of the books "most in demand," with a record of the number of times these books have been issued in one year. Let any sceptic as to the utility of these libraries in promoting mental improvement, consult these lists, and he will find abundant evidence of what we have said.

† The *Publishers' Circulars* for June, July, and August, contain a series of letters on this point. The writers that condemn free libraries on account of novel-reading, &c., seem to have taken no pains to inquire into the real working of these institutions, or if they have looked into them at all, they must have taken very one-sided views, or they have been under the influence of some strong prejudice.

different kinds of classification adopted it is difficult to state exactly what is the proportion of issues in prose fiction; but if the figures given above are examined, it will perhaps be admitted that these statistics warrant the conclusion that the issues in prose fiction range from 40 to 70 per cent. of the whole issues. Speaking of the earlier years of the Manchester lending library, Mr. Edwards says :

"The issues to borrowers stood somewhat in this proportion : Three-fourths of the whole issues were in the class 'Literature and Poly-graphy.' And of the issues in that class about *four-fifths* were books of prose fiction. In other words, the circulation of works in prose fiction in the fourth year was nearly *five-eighths* of the whole circulation of that year in all classes."

Now this is about 63 per cent. Let us now take the reading in a few of our Mechanics' Institutions of reputation. In recent reports of the Manchester, Leeds, and Bradford Mechanics' Institutions, we have the following facts :

MANCHESTER MECHANICS' INSTITUTION.—Gross issues, 20,412 : History, 1310; Biography, 1070; Geography and Travels, 1101; Science, 1903; Economy, 288; Theology, 238; Philosophy, 182; Finance, 65; Poetry, 600; Fiction, 17,001; Blue-books, &c., 83; Periodical Literature, 793; Foreign Languages, 123; Miscellaneous, 1260. Percentage of Fiction, 64·0.

LEEDS MECHANICS' INSTITUTION.—Gross issues, 60,327: Geography and Travels, 1236; History and Biography, 1049; Philosophy, 150; Poetry and Drama, 533; Theology, 138; Languages, 487; Education, 13; Mathematics, 47; Medicine, 111; Political Economy, 154; Fiction, 43,401; Literature, 3561; Fine Arts, 185; Arts and Manufactures, 65; Natural Sciences, 751; Mechanics, 211; Collected Works, 150; Unbound Periodicals, 1504; Books overnight, 214; Periodicals, 1059; Works of Reference, 99. Percentage of Fiction, 77·5.

BRADFORD MECHANICS' INSTITUTION.—Gross issues, 43,534; Philology, Logic, Education, 468; Theology and Philosophy, 242; Mathematics, 104; Natural Philosophy, Mechanics, 505; Chemistry and its Applications, 190; Anatomy, Physiology, &c., 191; Natural History, 608; History and Antiquities, 1614; Biography, 1502; Geography, Voyages, and Travels, 2803; Political Economy, Politics, &c., 347; Poetry and Drama, 1213; Fiction, 20,932; General Literature, 2784; Fine Arts, 615; Works of Reference, 115; Periodicals, bound, 2568; Periodicals, unbound, 6139. Percentage of Fiction, 48·08.

If the reader will carefully compare these figures with those given above, he will be satisfied that the reading of the free library lending departments is equal in solidity and instruction to that of our best Mechanics' Institutions. Upon the whole the issues in these institutions very much resemble those of the lending departments. 3. In the case of free libraries, where

access to the books is free, it might naturally be presumed that
the issues of amusing works would be more numerous than where
the members have to pay for the loan of books ; but it does not
appear to be so. 4. Then it should ever be remembered that
the works of prose fiction in the free libraries are the best of
their class. Only works of reputation, the productions of the
best authors, are admitted, and the demand is met by providing
several copies of these books instead of supplying works of
inferior character. For instance, it will be found that it is usual
for these libraries to contain four, six, or eight copies of the
works of Scott, Dickens, Thackeray, Trollope, Cooper, Lytton,
George Eliot, Mrs. Gaskell, and others. 5. Further, it is only in
the lending libraries that works of fiction are provided in any
considerable quantity. As a rule, in the reference or consulting
libraries, the amount of amusing literature is small. 6. Finally,
in the case of most of the large libraries, the writer has been
assured by experienced officers, that the reading habits of borrowers always improve in relation to this point. They begin
with taking light, amusing works, and if they continue borrowers,
a taste is created for more solid and instructive books. Numerous interesting facts, illustrating this tendency, have come
under the notice of librarians and their assistants at almost
every institution.

Who use free libraries ? What classes of the community avail
themselves of the books thus provided out of the rates? To
whom are these libraries useful ? The consideration of the very
nature of these libraries, and the facts brought out in their
operations, alike enable us to answer these questions, and to say,
ALL CLASSES. Free libraries were designed for all classes, and
all classes use them where good libraries have been formed.
This is the answer we ought to be able to give, and, it is satisfactory to know, it is the answer which facts actually do give.
As working people cannot purchase many books for themselves,
or pay high subscriptions for the use of books, there is a sense
in which it may be said, free libraries are especially useful to
them. This circumstance, and the term "free," have led many
persons to conclude that these institutions were designed especially or exclusively for working people, and the poorer classes.
This is a great mistake. It may, perhaps, be called a popular
error. All the inhabitants of a town are equally required to pay
the library rate, as in the case of lighting or watching the town,
and, consequently, these libraries should be adapted for the use
and benefit of all. If they are good, or what they should be,
they will be alike serviceable to the higher, the middle, and the
poorer classes of society. For instance, if a consulting library of
any town be what we have seen it should be the aim of the

managers to make such collections, we may rest assured persons of every class will resort to it. It has been said :

" In such cases the free library will be the largest and best collection of books in the town, and therefore the ablest thinkers and teachers in that community, clergymen, ministers, officials, lecturers, speakers, school-masters and all others whose mission it is to guide and form the public mind, will resort to those libraries, because they are the best source of the knowledge they want. Again, thoughtful, inquiring, studious persons, that require the assistance of books, will naturally resort to these libraries because they are the most easily accessible."[*]

Facts confirm this reasoning. These libraries are of daily assistance to all classes. Probably free libraries will prove of more signal benefit to the intelligent, thoughtful, inquisitive, gifted of the workers, just because this class most needs the help they supply. The workers cannot command the books that are frequently wanted to enable them to contribute of their ability towards the extension of human knowledge, or the improvement of the useful arts.

The reports of many of the free libraries supply full particulars as to the occupations or professions of their borrowers. The details are very interesting, and although they refer almost wholly to lending libraries, yet they clearly prove our statement that all classes make use of these institutions. We cannot give these lists or analyses of the borrowers of every institution in full, but shall give examples or specimens belonging to the following institutions :—

SALFORD.—Analysis of the 901 borrowers at Peel Park library ; Females, 256 ; youths, 216 ; artizans, 176 ; clerks, 160 ; professional 2 ; others, 91. The 2294 at the Greengate branch are thus classed : —Scholars, 650 ; workmen, 648 ; clerks and warehousemen, 844 ; miscellaneous, 198 ; females, 440.

BIRMINGHAM.—The 10,550 borrowers of the Birmingham lending libraries are arranged under sixty-six kinds of employment. Samples : —Accountants, 21 ; actors, 10 ; agents and collectors, 68 ; apprentices, 71 ; architects and surveyors, 12 ; artists and draughtsmen, 46 ; assistants and salesmen, 254 ; bakers and confectioners, 61 ; barmaids, 12 ; bedstead-makers, 97 ; booksellers, 27 ; boot and shoe makers, 114 ; brass-founders, 224 ; bricklayers, 90 ; carpenters and joiners, 109 ; casters, 20 ; chemists, 64 ; clerks, 1329 ; commercial travellers, 57 ; domestic servants, 52 ; dress-makers, 151 ; engineers and machinists, 293 ; engravers, chasers, &c., 235 ; errand and office-boys, 203 ; foremen, 13 ; gunmakers, 154 ; lithographers, 37 ; scholars and students, 1458 ; and so on.

COVENTRY.—The 883 borrowers are here classified according to 65 sorts of occupation. Specimens :—Assistants, shopmen, 15 ; cabinet-

* "Free Libraries : their Nature and Operations," p. 30.

makers, &c., 11 ; chemists and druggists, 5 ; clergymen, 2 ; clerks, 20 ; drapers, 13 ; engravers, 8 ; gardeners, 0 ; manufacturers, 4 ; metal-smiths, 10 ; painters, 11 ; schoolmasters, 11 ; scholars and students, 123 ; watchmakers, 60 ; weavers, 64.

NOTTINGHAM.—The 4027 borrowers are here put into 65 classes. Artists and designers, 34 ; boiler-makers, 3 ; clergymen, 8 ; clerks and warehousemen, 160 ; commercial travellers, 5 ; domestic servants, 20 ; drapers, 21 ; engineers and fitters, 41 ; fish-salesmen, 3 ; gentlemen, 3 ; grocers, 18 ; hosiery-trade, 60 ; joiners, 45 ; labourers, 42 ; lace-trade, 167 ; music-teachers, 7 ; printers, 48 ; students, &c., 00 ; surgeons, 4 ; teachers, 44.

BOLTON.—The 653 male borrowers for the last year are placed in the following classes :—Artisans and labourers, 256 ; warehousemen, 24 ; cotton operatives, 85 ; bleachers and dyers, 8 ; assistants in shops, 93 ; clerks and book-keepers, 82 ; pupils, 85 ; shopkeepers, 14 ; clergy, 6 ; and females, 153.

BIRKENHEAD.—The 4664 ticket holders are placed in upwards of 00 classes. Examples ; Apprentices 142 ; Agents 40 ; Architects, &c. 11 ; Attorneys and clerks, 25 ; banker's clerks, 12 ; blacksmiths, 42 ; boiler makers, 72 ; bricklayers, 35 ; boys in employment, 219 ; book-keepers and clerks, 393 ; engineers and fitters, 81 ; gentlemen of no employment, 233 ; joiners, 133 ; labourers and porters, 215 ; ladies, 50 ; police constables, 26 ; surgeons, 5 ; teachers, male, 27 ; watch-makers, 33.

TYNEMOUTH.—The 4377 ticket holders are placed in similar classi-fications to those in the places mentioned above. Examples : Appren-tices, 206 ; bakers, 16 ; boys at school, 277 ; butchers, 45 ; black-smiths and shipbuilders, 80 ; druggists and assistants, 56 ; females, 1124 ; gentlemen, 120 ; joiners, 137 ; licensed victuallers, 43 ; manu-facturers, 10 ; merchants, 40 ; master mariners, 89 ; mariners, 101."

In reference to smaller places, and those whose reports give no information of this kind, the question has been distinctly put to librarians—What classes of people mostly avail themselves of the library ?—and although the answers vary to some extent, they substantially agree in reporting "*All classes ; but chiefly the working classes.*"* It should be remembered that these answers come from small libraries, where important reference libraries do not exist, and where the lending libraries are neither extensive nor remarkable for the character of the selection.

The character of a free library, and the efficiency of its opera-tions depend very largely on its management. In connexion with the management of these libraries, there are two points on which it is important to note how the Act has been worked. One of these is the constitution of the Committee. The law entrusts the appointment of the library committee to the Town Council or Local Board, and, as we have seen, gives these local

* "Free Libraries : their Nature and Operations," p. 35.

bodies the privilege of making these committees "mixed committees." These "mixed" committees have generally been composed of some definite proportions, as one-half, two-thirds, or three-fourths of the members from the Town Council, and the other half, one-third, or one-fourth from gentlemen of the town selected on account of their suitability for such duties. It would appear the great majority of existing libraries are managed by mixed committees. At Manchester, Leeds, Bradford, and a few other places, the committees are chosen exclusively from the Town Councils; but at Liverpool, Salford, Bolton, Birmingham, Warrington, Airdrie, Norwich, Leamington, Oxford, Cambridge, Cardiff, Blackburn, Coventry, Birkenhead, Winchester, Hertford, Sheffield, Leicester, Paisley, Rochdale, Doncaster, and Nottingham mixed committees have been appointed. In the judgment of Mr. Edwards and other experienced men, this was a wise provision of the law, and has worked well for the libraries. It is stated by the most competent men that the success of the library in many places may be traced to the knowledge and labours of these outside members. Another point in the management of free libraries deserving attention is the amount of rate levied for the library. In boroughs, the Town Council is the rating authority; in certain other townships and districts the fund is to be provided from the "Improvement or District Rate," and in parishes the money is to be taken from the poor-rate. The amount of rate to be levied for the purposes of the library must not exceed one penny in the pound for any one year. Has this amount of one penny in the pound always been levied to create and maintain free libraries in the places where they have been formed? We regret to say that in a considerable number of cases the lawful rate has not been levied, or so appropriated. In some places, as Liverpool, Manchester, and Birmingham, the whole penny has long been taken; in others, the library rate has only been one halfpenny, and in some it has been three farthings. In several towns, no specific rate is applied to the library, but a certain sum is voted yearly by the Council from the borough fund. In consequence of these different modes of providing the money, it is not easy to ascertain with certainty what amount in the pound is actually levied in each place. It is, however, well known that the full amount is not taken in a goodly number of cases. Mr. Edwards says, "Of the larger towns, few have yet levied for free libraries or museums the whole sum that the Act permits them to levy."* We regard this as one of the most unfortunate and unsatisfactory circumstances connected with the working of these institutions; because it has been the source of

---

* "Free Town Libraries," p. 33.

much of that inefficiency which has marked the history of several of them. At any rate, had the full amount been levied, and had these libraries been well managed, they would have been far more powerful for good than they have been; in the past, they would have accomplished more, and would be capable of effecting greater things in the future. To us it appears that our Town Councils have, in this respect, sadly neglected their duty. At Liverpool, Manchester, Salford, Birmingham, Airdrie, Birkenhead, Leamington, Lichfield, Dundee, Wolverhampton, and some other places where libraries have been recently formed, we believe the full amount of the rate is now taken. At Sheffield it was formerly one halfpenny, then three farthings, but now it is one penny; at Bolton it was formerly a halfpenny, and is now three farthings; at Cambridge it is about a halfpenny; at Oxford, less than a halfpenny; at Blackburn, a halfpenny; at Canterbury, a halfpenny; at Nottingham, not quite a penny, and one-fourth of the sum voted goes to the museum, and three-fourths to the library; at Cardiff, formerly a halfpenny, now a penny; at Exeter, a penny, but the yield is appropriated to three things—library, museum, and science school; at Paisley, a penny, but the produce is divided between the museum and the library; at Coventry the net produce obtained is somewhat less than a penny; at Tynemouth, a penny, but a part goes to the museum and classes.

Had our space permitted, we might here have given some account of the numerous Town Libraries on the Continent—in Germany, France, and Italy—as well as of those in the United States and Canada. Mr. Edwards, in his different works, has, with much labour, collected a mass of interesting facts illustrating the nature, history, and operations of these libraries. The American libraries are especially worthy of the study of English educationists, and we would particularly call attention to the wonderful development of the Boston public library, as this is exhibited in the elaborate reports of the trustees. We regret our inability even to glance at its short but extraordinary history.

Such is the general nature of the Free Libraries established under the provisions of the different Public Libraries Acts. In the preceding account we have been chiefly anxious to afford our readers the means of understanding what these libraries are, and what they are doing, and thus of reaching sound conclusions as to their character and utility. It is almost unnecessary to say that their history shows faults of management and failure to realize the full hopes of their founders. No sensible man will be surprised that such is the fact. It must be remembered that the oldest free library is only twenty years of age. In 1852, when

the first was formed, the project was altogether new and untried
in England. It is through practical experience that we come to
find out the best modes of working new institutions, and that we
are able to discover their excellences and defects. Perhaps we
ought to say this movement has been passing through its infancy
and youth, and that hitherto our efforts should be regarded as
chiefly experimental or tentative. The history of these libraries
is, however, full of instruction. It abounds in useful lessons, and
it now becomes our duty to see that these suggestions of experience are not lost, but turned to account for the improvement
of future libraries. But while it is readily admitted that there
have been errors and defects in several of our free libraries, we
submit that every candid person must acknowledge that they
have already effected a great and good work, and are capable of
still greater things. In small places these libraries have been
feeble enough, but in the larger towns, and in some of a
moderate size, facts demonstrate that they have done much to
awaken thought and inquiry, to spread useful knowledge, to
create a love for wholesome reading, and to raise the tastes of
large numbers of the community. Let any one reflect on the
daily, weekly, and yearly issues from the libraries of Liverpool,
Manchester, Birmingham, Salford, Leeds, Bolton, Sheffield,
Nottingham, Birkenhead, Paisley, Wolverhampton, Dundee,
Tynemouth, and he must be sensible that these hundreds of
thousands, nay, millions of volumes, cannot be read by the inhabitants of those towns without producing a most salutary intellectual and moral effect.

These libraries are interesting to us not solely on account of
what they have already accomplished, but also on account of
what they are capable of effecting in the future. Would it be
just to estimate the value of these young institutions by what
they have done in the period of their infancy and adolescence?
Surely not. It seems to us that it would be far more philosophical
to look at what they promise, and at what they may do when
fully understood and efficiently managed, than to confine our
attention to the results already accomplished. Their full power
for good has yet to be developed. Still, the statistics and facts
contained in the preceding part of this paper are deserving of the
closest examination, because they help us to a knowledge of the
capabilities of these institutions. For this purpose we would
bespeak special attention to the operations of the most prosperous
and successful. We do this on the principle that we are fairly justified in concluding what an institution may do from its workings
under conditions favourable to the development of its full strength,
and in circumstances calculated to secure for it free play and
efficient management. In proceeding to offer a few remarks on the
capabilities and value of free libraries as educational agencies, it

must be understood that we waive altogether the theoretical question of the legitimacy of state interference in such matters. It may be taken for granted that, practically, the question has been settled in this country for the present, in reference both to strictly elementary and to other forms of educational work.

1. In the first place, we take it that all will admit that the formation of good consulting and lending libraries in our towns, that shall be freely accessible to all, will constitute a means of diffusing knowledge—scientific, historical, literary and entertaining. Experience proves that if the books provided in these libraries are well chosen, they will be read. Is the spread of knowledge, then, a desirable thing? Is it not idle to ask such a question? And would it not be absurd to attempt to argue it? Then comes the inquiry:—Are free libraries constituted and used for this purpose? The facts already presented conclusively show that such is the case. These libraries, especially in large towns, contain the best standard works in every department of science and literature, and the figures given above prove that such books are largely read and consulted.

2. But then comes the old objection: These libraries are chiefly frequented by idlers, and such as seek amusement in novel reading. The extent of this kind of reading has already been dealt with, and the facts in every report prove that such an allegation is unfounded. Without arguing the question of novel reading, we may, in passing, be permitted to say that, as the prose fiction in these libraries is the best, as it comprises the productions of the most gifted men of the age, if it be said the perusal of these works is injurious, must it not be held that the study of the works of those great authors of fiction, Homer, Æschylus, Sophocles, Dante, Chaucer, Shakspeare, Spenser, Milton and Goethe, is also pernicious? Will not all thoughtful men allow that the reading of the works of Scott, Dickens, Thackeray, Lytton, Trollope, George Eliot, Charlotte Brontë, and others must awaken, expand, and elevate every mind that can appreciate their excellences? The indiscriminate and excessive reading of fiction may be an evil, but we venture to think that it would be an unspeakable blessing to this country if the thousands that frequent our beershops and dramshops, daily and nightly, were to spend a portion of their leisure time in the perusal of the writings of the authors we have just mentioned. It should never be forgotten that in these days, when the division of labour is carried so far that almost every occupation is monotonous and mechanical, some systematic provision for the amusement and rational recreation of the people is a necessity of our social state; and further, that, as yet, how to provide it is an unsolved problem in our social philosophy.

3. We contend that books are now, and are becoming more so

every year, the great instructors of the world. Mr. Carlyle has
forcibly enunciated this truth in his striking remark that collections of books are the universities of our time. He says:

"In books lies the *soul* of the whole Past Time; the articulate
audible voice of the Past, when the body and material substance of it
has altogether vanished like a dream. . . . . The Universities are a
notable, respectable product of the modern ages. Their existence, too,
is modified to the very basis of it by the existence of Books. Universities arose while there were yet no Books procurable; while a man,
for a single Book, had to give an estate of land. . . . . Once invent
printing, you metamorphosed all the Universities, or superseded
them! The teacher needed not now to gather men personally around
him, that he might *speak* to them what he knew; print it in a book,
and all learners, far and wide, for a trifle, had it each at his own fire-
side, much more effectually to learn it. . . . . If we think of it, all
that a University, or final highest School can do for us, is still but
what the first School began doing—teach us to *read*. We learn to
read, in various languages, in various sciences; we learn the alphabet
and letters of all manner of Books. But the place where we are to
get knowledge, even theoretic knowledge, is the Books themselves!
It depends on what we read, after all manner of Professors have done
their best for us. *The true University of these days is a collection of
Books.*"

The last sentence appears to us to be no rhetorical flourish, but
a sober verity. Is it not a literal fact that all good teachers
either send their pupils to books for fuller, or it may be, better
knowledge, or they themselves draw the knowledge they impart
from books? It is so, and it must be so, because the inventors
and discoverers, the thinkers, the gifted, the men of learning and
research, of speculative power and philosophical insight, the
theologian and moralist, the poet and the seer, embody the
results of their efforts in books: in short, books are the agencies
through which the great spirits of the race help their fellow-
men. To some extent it has been so in past ages, but it is more
emphatically so now. Every branch of science or department of
thought has its one, two, three or more great men, who have so
enriched it by their labours that they are the accredited ex-
pounders of its truths; their works represent the highest form it
has attained. This is carried further now than formerly, because
of the division of labour even in science and learning. One man
is the highest authority, not, perhaps, in a whole science, but only
in one particular branch of it, to which he may have devoted
special attention. Well, does not every good teacher of this
branch and its allied departments send his pupils to the works
of this master? There may be elementary books, but do not
the compilers of these aim to embody in them the views of the

representative cultivator of that department? Would not a professor of physics direct his pupils to the writings of Prof. Tyndall? or of geology to those of Lyell and other great authorities? Certainly. Hence it is that Carlyle's remark is a truth which our every-day life practically recognises.

4. From this we argue that good libraries, freely accessible to all, are essential to the spread of the best knowledge, to the efficacy of teaching in every branch of inquiry, and to the carrying forward of the culture of the country. We are not, of course, speaking of elementary instruction, but of education after 15 or 16. If education is to unfold the faculties, to influence the tastes and habits, and to tell on the formation of character, efforts must be made to carry it forward, or to supplement the instruction received in boyhood and girlhood. Great things are now attempted for the extension and improvement of the elementary education of all classes. But if education is to do anything to influence society, it must develop mind, teach men to think, and lead to the acquisition of knowledge in its highest forms. This can only be accomplished through the agency of the works of the best thinkers, in every sphere of thought and action. And how are the minds of persons who leave school at 14 to be brought into immediate contact with these productions? It can only be through libraries; by means of those "collections," which are "the universities" of these days.

5. Take, as an illustration of this point, the effort now making by the government to diffuse scientific knowledge through classes. In every part of the country classes for the study of Science are formed, under teachers holding certificates from the Science and Art Department. The design here is not simply to promote mental culture, but to advance the "material" interests of the country; because it is found needful to train our artizans in science as a means of advancing our commercial and industrial prosperity. How is the elementary knowledge imparted in these classes to be kept up or enlarged, carried forward, and rendered practically useful in our industries? How is the taste for scientific knowledge, thus created, to be fostered and satisfied? This cannot be realized unless we provide an easy access to the best scientific books for the young men and young women who have acquired a smattering of science in these classes. The same may be said of history, of literature, and of other departments of knowledge.

6. On these grounds we hold that good libraries,—not "heaps of books,"—must accompany all our other efforts to enlarge and improve the education of every class. The labours of all sorts of teachers, professors, and lecturers must be supplemented by easy

access to the best books. Without this, these other agencies will
be comparatively ineffectual and abortive.

7. It may be said all this may be admitted, but still it does
not prove that libraries supported by rates should be formed.
These arguments only show that books are required, but they
settle nothing as to the particular way in which they should be
obtained. In the first place, we answer, suitable libraries have
not been supplied in any other way. As a matter of fact, such
collections do not exist in our towns, and there is no probability
that they will be provided by any other agency. And secondly,
if libraries did exist, or were projected, what guarantee is there
that a condition so essential to their utility as easy or free access
to their contents could be secured? We venture to assert that
there is no other way practicable in which the want could be
met except by rate-supported libraries; and certainly none that
would be so simple and equitable. As in America, so with us,
the rate-supported library must be the concomitant and supplement to the rate-supported school.

8. It may be, and indeed constantly is,' urged, that in many
towns there is no need of free libraries, because numerous libraries—subscription libraries, proprietary circulating libraries,
libraries connected with scientific, literary, or educational institutions, or with religious bodies—already exist. Here, again,
the primary objection to these is, they are not public libraries;
they are only accessible to particular classes, or on certain pecuniary conditions. But the second objection to these libraries is
stronger than the first; and it is, the character of these libraries
is not that which is wanted. Our existing libraries, even the
town subscription libraries, have mostly some sort of a sectional
character; they are either chiefly supported by some particular
party, and thus books are selected to suit this section, or, through
deference to certain parties or sects, their contents are shaped,
and so, either directly or indirectly, these collections are coloured
by sectional feeling and interest. Denominational libraries are,
of course, formed on a narrow principle. In some degree this
sectional peculiarity dominates in the libraries of our literary
and educational societies, although these professedly stand on
what is called neutral ground. Unfortunately, it is almost impossible, in this country, to exclude the influence of narrow views
in the management of libraries supported by subscription. Even
in the libraries of such societies as our Mechanics' Institutes,
this principle shows itself, and works a practical narrowness.
Either by some fundamental constitutional law, or through a
fear of offending influential parties, or indeed through actual
want of breadth of soul, the managers of these societies yield to
this spirit, and exclude from their libraries works of the highest

power in some of the most important departments of thought. This is one ground on which we contend for public libraries, that shall rise above all the petty and narrow feelings that now spoil other collections.

9. If public libraries are effectually to assist the continuous education of the country, or to promote the general culture of the people, they must be framed on a broad, comprehensive basis. This is essential to their highest work, and to their complete success. If the reader could examine the Catalogue of the Reference Department of the Birmingham Library, and compare it with the contents of proprietary libraries, or the libraries of the institutions referred to above, he would at once understand what is meant by a comprehensive, well-chosen library, as distinguished from what Mr. Edwards calls a "heap of books." As we have repeatedly said, libraries like this at Birmingham are resorted to regularly by the studious and the inquisitive of every class, because these persons find in such a collection the assistance they need. We want, in every town, a library similar in character, if not in extent. Here every student might come; here the schoolmaster, the professor, the preacher, the divine, the scripture-reader, the missionary, the public speaker, the lecturer, the author, the essay-writer, the editor, might also come and find assistance in his work; indeed such a library would materially aid all persons called upon to impart knowledge to others, or influence the thinkings and opinions of the public. Then there is a kind of literature that is furnished in the best free libraries which is not found in those of other institutions: we refer to what Mr. Edwards calls "the literature of public questions"—blue-books, and all public or national documents of every kind. In this way alone can a means be provided in every town for the thorough investigation of all the vastly important questions connected with the political, international, foreign, colonial, legal, administrative, statistical, social, educational, sanitary, commercial, manufacturing, and industrial interests of the community, and which are daily engaging the attention of Englishmen. Works of this class, and those which the Birmingham Committee style "books of permanent value and standard interest," and their "rare and costly books," cannot be provided in ordinary libraries, such as those of Mechanics' and similar institutions. The mention of such works in the committees of these societies would instantly call forth questions like these:—"Will they be read by the members?" "Who will read them?" "Do our members want such books?" This is the commercial principle, and it inevitably determines the choice of books in such institutions. These societies are the last places in the world where a comprehensive concep-

tion of a library can be practically realized, or where broad views or bibliographical knowledge can guide the selection of books.

Are the free libraries of this country accomplishing the work here set forth as their mission ? Are they capable of doing it ? We have sought to show what these libraries actually are, and if we do not sadly misinterpret facts, these point to the conclusion that many of our free libraries are practically doing what has here been claimed for them; but then it is admitted that some are not. Attention has frequently been directed to the operations of some of the larger, and we have spoken of them as exemplifications of what free libraries should be. If others are not so efficient, why is it ? If many fall short of the ideal, how does this happen ? What are the causes of failure, and is there any remedy ?

Want of efficiency may be traced to various causes : in some cases it has arisen from difficulties inherent in the very circumstances in which the libraries have been formed. In other cases the shortcomings are mainly due to the errors and faults of the managing bodies. In the first class must be placed those instances where the funds raised by the rate are wholly inadequate for the maintenance of good libraries. This has been the state of things in a few small towns. At Lichfield the penny rate produces about 100*l.* a year ; at Airdrie it yields 75*l.* 16*s.* 4½*d.* With these sums the managers have to provide room, fire, light, librarians, and—purchase books ! In places where the rate produces small sums like these, it is simply impossible to purchase many books. At Lichfield 40*l.* is paid for wages. Notwithstanding its very limited income, the library at Airdrie is noteworthy as a remarkable instance of what may be accomplished with small means. It is simply a lending library. This consists of about 2400 volumes; and, having examined the catalogue, we are able to say these books have been chosen with sound judgment. For its extent the collection is a capital one. The books have not been obtained by donation, but have nearly all been purchased ; and further, they have been bought with funds raised by the rates. The borrowers last year were 600, and the issues 11,103. In 1867 the number of volumes was 2200, the borrowers 700, and the issues 14,000. Probably the decline has arisen from the want of an adequate supply of fresh books. The library is open in the evening from five to nine o'clock. The room is a shop belonging to the town, and the sum of 22*l.* 1*s.* 9*d.* is paid annually as librarian's wages. We should rejoice to see more such libraries in our small towns.

But there is a greater number of places where the full amount of the rate has never been levied by Town Councils for the

libraries. In some of them the amount which the full penny in
the pound would yield is only small, but this has not been raised
and applied to support the library. At Winchester the rate is
one halfpenny in the pound; it raises 108*l.* a year, which has to
support both the museum and library; at Kidderminster the
Council votes 70*l.* a year for the library, and out of this the rent
takes 25*l.*, and the librarian's salary 35*l.*; at Canterbury the
penny rate would yield about 272*l.*, but only about one-half of
this is applied to the library; at Warrington some 250*l.* a year
is allowed for the museum and library; at Cambridge 350*l.* is
granted by the Council, which Mr. Edwards says is "a fraction
more than one-third of a penny in the pound;" at Oxford less
than one halfpenny in the pound is granted for the library, and
Mr. Edwards remarks, "So niggardly is the annual grant of the
local board that it yields absolutely nothing towards the expenses
of the lending library. These expenses are restricted to the
scanty annual product of the sale of catalogues and borrowers'
tickets." As we have seen, at Bolton, Sheffield, Blackburn,
Cardiff, Nottingham, and other places, the full amount of a
penny in the pound has not been appropriated to the purposes of
the library. These facts clearly prove that whatever the free
libraries at these towns are, they are not what they might have
been if the Town Councils had been willing to appropriate
the lawful rate for their support. The responsibility of the
defect here manifestly rests with the local rating authority.
These circumstances lead to the more general inquiry—How far
have Town Councils taken up this work in a satisfactory manner?
Their unwillingness to appropriate the product of the penny rate
constitutes the most tangible and striking evidence of their want
of zeal; but there are many other significant facts in the history
of these libraries which point in the same direction, and which
deserve the grave consideration of all interested in the subject.
It will be remembered that the law can be adopted, in any
place, on the vote of a majority of a meeting of ratepayers called
for that purpose; such meeting may be convened by the Town
Council, or at the request of ten ratepayers. Thus any Town
Council can take the *first step* towards putting the law in
motion; but how few Corporations have actually taken this first
step! In England and Wales there are some two hundred and
fifty municipal boroughs, and yet during the twenty years that
have elapsed since the passing of the first Free Libraries Act
libraries have only been established in just over thirty! Is not
this satisfactory evidence that Town Councils are averse to move
in this matter? At Derby the Town Council actually prevented
a meeting of ratepayers from being held to consider the propriety
of adopting the Act. This was under the old law; now these

bodies have no such power. Further, when the Act has been
adopted on the motion of the ratepayers, and its working
devolved upon Corporations, these bodies have often seemed to
regard the work as something beyond their true province, and
which did not belong to them. In the case of one large town,
where the Act had been adopted at the meeting of ratepayers, a
portion of the Council were so opposed to it that they were
anxious to upset the decision of the meeting of burgesses, and
were deeply mortified when they found they had no power to
undo what the meeting of ratepayers had done. Town Councillors are primarily chosen to manage the lighting, watching,
paving, and cleansing of towns, and other matters of the nature
of police regulations; they are selected on account of their
fitness for work of this kind, and not on account of their knowledge of books, literary tastes, or interest in the diffusion of
knowledge. These Councillors are, for the most part, successful
tradesmen, clear-headed, shrewd, practical men of business, with
little special fitness for the work of managing libraries. Hence
the indifference they have shown in many places respecting the
operation of these institutions. All who have watched the
working of free libraries know that this indifference, nay, more,
hostility, has manifested itself in a variety of ways. Even in
Manchester, although the Act was adopted by a vast majority of
ratepayers, Mr. Edwards says. "There was a certain amount of
strenuous opposition to the proposal, and the leaders of it were
at that time Town Councillors." Sir John Potter remarked,
"These persons tried repeatedly to put obstacles in his way."
Mr. Edwards speaks of the necessity of Corporations entering
into the spirit of the Libraries' Act, and certainly nothing can
be more essential to the effectual working of its provisions; but
this is precisely what Town Councils have not done: they have
not taken up this work cordially, with zeal, intelligence, and a
determination to make the libraries as useful and successful as
possible. It is cheerfully and thankfully admitted that a few
Corporations have entered into this work in a right spirit, but
then it must be added there are very few such.
  Besides the evils of indifference and hostility in Town Councils,
these libraries have suffered through the inaptitude of Corporations for the work, and through the baneful influence of party
feeling that operates in these bodies. It was in view of unsuit-
ableness in Town Councillors for the duties imposed upon them
by the Act, that the legislature provided for the election of
"mixed" committees. In relation to the character and success
of the library, the choice of the managing committee is a very
important matter. It seems needless to say the election should
be made with sole reference to fitness—to some sort of qualifica-

tion in the members for the work. We fear, or rather, perhaps, we should say, incontestible facts render it certain, that those party interests which have spoiled the working of so many of our noblest institutions, have sometimes been allowed to determine the constitution of library committees. Unfortunately, political parties exist in Town Councils, and every party has a policy of its own, and objects of its own. Where party spirit runs high, party ends have to be promoted in all their proceedings, and so it is that frequently these interests have to be considered in appointing a library committee, rather than the efficient working of the library. To some, perhaps, this may seem almost incredible, but clearly-established facts render it unquestionable. Take a well authenticated instance. In appointing the library committee in a populous borough, where the Act has recently been adopted, the majority of the Council, on purely party grounds, excluded from the committee members of the Council that had taken the deepest interest in the question, who had made themselves acquainted with the workings of free libraries, and whose pursuits had given them a practical knowledge of books, and preferred to these, for party objects, persons who had been opposed to the formation of the library, and who possessed no fitness for the duty; such as retired publicans, and others whose employments and acquirements had in no way qualified them for the work. Thus, these Town Councillors were prepared to sacrifice the welfare of the undertaking to party and personal ends. We are satisfied that the apathy, hostility, ignorance, niggardliness, and party-feeling of Corporations have done much to prevent the proper development of many of the existing free libraries.

With the library committee rests the appointment of librarian, the choice and purchase of books, the arrangement of the contents of the library, the determination of the point, what shall be the character of the library, and what the guiding aim in its formation, with all the other matters constituting library economy and connected with the details of its working. For this work very special knowledge and peculiar qualifications are required, if it is to be done satisfactorily. For the right performance of these duties few Town Councillors have shown themselves to be fitted. And we may rest assured, that if these duties are not well discharged, the result will be, not a library properly so termed, but what Mr. Edwards calls "a mere chance aggregation of books," or what Mr. Axon describes as "a fortuitous conglomeration of books." When a number of Town Councillors are constituted a library committee, they are required to enter upon duties which, in all probability, are entirely new to them. The chances are that they have had no experience whatever in similar work ; perhaps they possess no bibliographical knowledge and small literary taste, and being actively engaged in business, have little time to devote to the subject. In these circumstances, their first business is almost sure to be the appointment of a librarian. What sort of a man should they seek to fill this office ?* Not surely a mere clerk ; not simply a person who is capable of entering issues. This is purely mechanical work, and can be performed by any intelligent youth. What they also-solutely require, especially at first, when everything is new to them, is a man with a practical knowledge of bibliography, of literary acquirements and tastes, with experience in the collection and arrangement of books, that can assist them in their arduous task of forming a library. It is essential to their success to secure the services of a person of this sort, and they should therefore be prepared to pay for the services of such a servant. This is the course which common sense and all experience pre-scribe, and it is the course which is invariably followed in other fields of action, where special or professional knowledge is re-quired. It is the cheapest course, because it is that alone which can save committees from irretrievable mistakes and waste. We are glad to say this is the course which has been taken where our most successful libraries have been established. In Liverpool, Manchester, Birmingham, and other large towns, the committees have had the sense to secure the assistance of able and expe-rienced men as librarians. But many of our Free Library Com-mittees have not acted thus, and we regard this as one reason why several of them have not been more successful. In many places the managers appear to have reached no higher concep-tion of what they want in a librarian than that he should be an ordinary clerk ; a man fairly competent for the clerkly duties ; or, perhaps, capable of entering the issues in some peculiar mode, or some mechanical manner. This has too often been their ideal. We know what the comment of some of these committees will be on our remarks ; they will say they have not the funds with which to command the services of persons of this kind. Our answer is simple : these very same Town Councils

---

* Mr. Edwards's remarks on this point are worthy of attention. "Next to the choice of the library committee in order of time, but even before it in intrinsic importance to the good working of the institution, stands the choice of libra-rian. The day will come when in Britain we shall have courses of biblio-graphy and bibliothecal economy for the training of librarians, as well as courses of chemistry and physiology for the training of physicians. But as yet there is no such training, either in London or Edinburgh, though it is pro-vided at Naples. In the interval, the proof of adequate qualification will some-times be difficult. But the two main things to be looked for in a librarian are, 1. A genuine love of books ; and 2. An indomitable passion for order."—" Free Town Libraries," p. 30.

did not levy the amount of the rate allowed by law, but only some fractional part of it; and further, in some cases, they spend considerable sums in providing news-rooms. News-rooms in connexion with Free Libraries may be very attractive, but they are surely secondary to the formation of a good library. We very much question the policy of spending money on news-rooms where there are not funds sufficient to realize the primary object of the Act—the formation of a good library. Of course there are some places where the penny rate will not enable the Committee to take the course we have indicated ; but it is not to cases of this exceptional kind that our remarks apply. We allude to what has been done in moderate-sized and in some rather large towns. As an illustration of what we mean, look at the course pursued to obtain a librarian at Bradford—a town where the penny rate will produce more than 2000*l.* a year. On being first appointed, the Bradford Library Committee advertised for a librarian, and offered the magnificent salary of 100*l.* a year for a gentleman to assist them in the arduous and responsible labour of forming reference and lending libraries in a borough where 2000*l.* a year can be devoted to the institution! This fact speaks for itself, and it speaks volumes as to the conception this Committee entertained of the nature of the work before them, and of the qualifications that were required for its right performance. Unfortunately, many of these committees have not the faintest notion of the extreme difficulty of forming a really good library. They do not know what is involved in it.* They seem to think it is about one of the easiest things in the world ; whereas, on the contrary, every competent, experienced man knows that the formation of a good library is a work of extreme difficulty, and requires the exercise of rare qualifications. As an experienced man, Mr. Edwards speaks on this point with great force and truth, in his "Memoirs of Libraries," vol. ii. pp. 628, 9. In reference to the appointment of competent librarians, to the conception of what is involved in the systematic formation of both reference and lending libraries, and other

---

* A notable illustration of this came within the writer's knowledge. When a candidate for the appointment of chief librarian of one of our free libraries was before the committee, and questions were being put and answered as to the difficulty of making a good selection of books, one member asked the candidate if they would not have catalogues and publishers' lists from which to choose books? This was said with an air to convey the impression that if they only had catalogues and lists before them, no special knowledge or ability would be required to make a proper selection : anybody could do this, and anybody could do it equally well! Do catalogues, then, supply the knowledge and skill that will insure their being used aright? Is it so in trade? Perhaps this committee-man could answer the question in the case of his own business. We wonder if this worthy alderman ever read that exquisite satire, Lucian's Dialogue addressed to "An Illiterate Book-buyer."

points of detail, it appears to us that many of our library committees have sadly erred, and these errors are exercising an unfavourable influence on the character and usefulness of many Free Libraries.

Having spoken thus freely of the defects in some of our Free Libraries, it seems only reasonable that we should point to the sources of remedy for these shortcomings. Into any lengthy discussion of this part of our subject we have not space to enter, and perhaps it is not necessary to dwell upon it, as the foregoing strictures will, in a large degree, suggest the reforms needed. Remedies for the defects noticed must relate mainly to two points—the funds, and the management of the libraries.

It is obvious the penny rate is inadequate for small towns. Except on some such scale as the library at Airdrie, we do not think a library can be maintained unless there is at least an income of 200*l.* a year. This would seem to be the smallest sum with which a committee could, under ordinary circumstances, support a library of any character. In places where the penny rate will not produce 200*l.* a year, the rate should be higher than a penny in the pound. With regard to larger towns, it should be imperative that they levy the whole amount of the rate. This should be done in all cases. The largest towns require it, and, indeed, say it is too little, where they have to provide good reference and lending libraries, and establish branches in their outlying districts. The smaller towns assuredly require it, if they will only do their duty, and establish libraries of high character. It has been held by some writers that this penny in the pound should be supplemented by a grant from the Imperial Government, because free libraries are as truly national institutions as schools. This is a point on which men will differ. For ourselves, we rather incline to an increase in the local rate in preference to obtaining aid from the National Government. In all towns or parishes where the penny rate will not raise 200*l.* a year, we suggest that it should be three-halfpence.

The great reform, however, that is needed in our free libraries, must relate to their management. What change is practicable here? While we gladly acknowledge that, in several large towns, which have been repeatedly mentioned, the Town Councils have entered fully into the spirit of the Public Libraries Acts, and are now carrying out their provisions in the noblest way, we must say that, as a rule, Town Councils have not done their duty in this matter. We hope this position has been established by the foregoing facts and considerations. That these bodies are not very suitable for this work, was felt by the first promoters of these libraries, and by the legislature when the Act was framed. On this account, corporations were allowed to appoint "mixed" committees for the management of the libraries. This clause of the Act has worked beneficially for many libraries. Mr. Edwards holds that many towns "have profited by this clause," and he regards it as one of the "favourable circumstances" to which is owing the efficiency of the Birmingham free libraries, that they have been managed by a mixed committee. But is this contrivance sufficient to secure the good administration of these libraries? We think not. Valuable as the clause has been, experience proves that it is not adequate to secure effective management. No doubt it would have been more salutary had not the rating authority—the Town Council—controlled the funds. Mr. Edwards appears to be sensible of this failure, but he evidently does not like to speak out respecting Town Councils. ("Memoirs of Libraries," vol. ii. p. 560.) He suggests the *separate* election of at least a portion of the managing committee. We have not the least doubt that this suggestion of a *separate* election would be a great improvement. It would work a mighty change if a majority of the committee were so appointed. Such an election would constantly direct public attention to the working of the libraries, and secure for the people a direct interest in their operations. The men would be elected for a particular work, and some special fitness for this work would be required. Thus ratepayers would be led to fix upon candidates in reference to their qualifications for this particular duty. But then separate elections would involve considerable expense, and would probably bring much unprofitable excitement.

Would it not be far better to place Free Libraries under the management of the School Boards? Their superintendence by these boards would be quite in character with the other work of such bodies; and, strictly speaking, it is the proper place for the libraries. They are essentially educational agencies, and it is very desirable that all the educational institutions of a locality, that are of a strictly national character, should be managed by one body, by the Board elected for this kind of work, and chosen on account of the fitness of the members for these duties. It may be said that the members of School Boards are drawn from the same classes of society as are Aldermen and Town Councillors. True: but with these important differences: the members of School Boards are chosen for educational work, and on account of their interest in education and the spread of knowledge; and secondly, many persons of education and literary pursuit are elected on School Boards that would never think of entering a Town Council. In reference to the larger towns where the Free Libraries are well managed, no change need be made. It is highly probable that had School Boards been in existence when the Free Libraries Act was first passed, the management of these libraries would never have been given to Corporations, but have been devolved by the law on School Boards. If we felt concerned to argue this point at length, many considerations and facts might be urged in its favour. It appears to us very important, because, as some change in the management of these libraries is essential to their proper growth, this reform seems to be the most natural. It may be observed that in the United States and British North America, the Free Libraries are under the management of educational bodies, as committees or boards. In Canada, these libraries are in close connexion with the education department, and are managed by the same bodies that manage the schools. The law affecting Free Libraries is an education law. Dr. Ryerson, the great educationist of Canada, is the founder of the Free Libraries in that country, the organizer of the system and the author of the law on the subject. The same is true of some of the States of the American Union. The law regulating Public Libraries there is part of the School Law, and the fund from which they are partly supported is the fund from which Schools are supported. Full particulars will be found of these matters in Mr. Edwards's interesting volumes.

Whether any alteration in the law to secure the change now advocated can be obtained, or these institutions are to be allowed to go on in their unsatisfactory course, there is one thing most urgently needed, which we earnestly hope may be secured—viz., *the inspection of these libraries under the direction of the Education Department.* Mr. Edwards has repeatedly urged this in his different books. In France, where there are 300 town libraries, they are regularly inspected under the direction of the Minister of Public Instruction. In the States and in Canada, public libraries are inspected as parts of the educational system just as schools are. In connexion with inspection, Mr. Edwards contends for government aid, because these libraries are as much national institutions as schools. He and others seem to think that government aid and inspection should go together. We do not see the necessity for this connexion in institutions like free libraries. These libraries are truly public, and, as supported by the rates, national institutions, and there should be no difficulty in arranging for their inspection without grants from the imperial treasury. We are so anxious to foster local interest and local management in these libraries, that we do not desire to bring them into dependence on the department, or place them under the authoritative supervision of the government. We are satisfied nothing would effect so much good in the management of these libraries as inspection, and surely this might be accomplished without their being brought into such a dependence as would destroy local interest in their management.

We do not wish to be understood as objecting absolutely to public grants to free libraries, and perhaps these may be given in a way that will stimulate local energy and local liberality. We want to see zealous local action continued with a suggestive supervision from the central authority, in the shape of able reports and practical suggestions and recommendations. The visits of an inspector, and the circulation of his reports, would, we believe, put new life into all the operations of many of these libraries. At the present time, many of them are just in that condition into which English local institutions are too prone to run when left entirely to themselves—they want new vigour.

But whether any regular system of inspection may be ultimately procured in connexion with the Education Department or not, we think it most desirable that the department should at once promote an inquiry into the state and working of existing free libraries. Could not the department send a competent gentleman, either as inspector or commissioner, to visit these libraries and report upon them? There could not, surely, be any difficulty in arranging for a thorough examination of this kind. The managing committees and town councils ought to welcome such an inquiry, and court it. If a competent man could in this way visit all our free libraries, and examine into their constitution and working,—into their finances, the contents and characters of their collections,—and all details connected with their operations and effects, and then publish a full report, a mighty service would be rendered to the cause of free libraries and education. The country ought to have an able and searching inquiry and report of this kind, and nothing would tend more to improve these libraries than the publication of such a document. Perhaps some investigation of this nature should be made as a step preliminary to any change in the law, and then future legislation might be shaped according to the tenor of this report. If, therefore, permanent and systematic inspection cannot be obtained at once for these libraries, why should there be any delay of a full inquiry into their nature and working such as we have suggested? If Lord Ripon and Mr. Forster could be induced to look into this subject and institute such an inquiry as we have proposed, they would effect a great work for the improvement of these libraries, and also for the extension of the system, as well as for their multiplication throughout the country. We hope the time is not far distant when we shall have a good free library in every town in the kingdom.

Art. IV.—The Descent of Man.

The Descent of Man, and Selection in Relation to Sex.
By CHARLES DARWIN. In Two Volumes, with Illustrations.
London: John Murray. 1871.

WE are bound to apologize for having thus far delayed our notice of Mr. Darwin's latest work. Probably no work during the past year has so much attracted the attention of intelligent readers; assuredly not one has so well deserved it. Yet we feel convinced that those who are most competent to judge, who have studied Mr. Darwin's writings with the greatest diligence, who have best appreciated his facts and followed his arguments, will be the first to excuse us. The whole subject is so copious, so complex, so difficult, so varied in its aspects, and withal so suggestive, that one may well pause before venturing to pronounce a decided opinion upon it. Moreover, in his preface, Mr. Darwin has promised us yet another contribution to the same great topic, in the form of "an essay on the expression of the various emotions by man and the lower animals." For this, however, we shall not wait, but proceed forthwith to accomplish, as best we may, our long-protracted task.

Even our author's title-page must be read with care. He treats, in fact, of two subjects, which, though distinct, are closely connected with one another: (1) The Descent of Man, and (2) Selection in Relation to Sex. His book accordingly contains two Parts, which we shall discuss in turn.

The First Part may be regarded as one long attempt to show man's genetic relation to the rest of the animal world, in accordance with Mr. Darwin's views on the evolution of all organic beings.

Man is either an animal or not an animal. Those few naturalists who place him in a kingdom by himself, apart from the rest of the animal world, can only do so by finally disregarding those marks of resemblance in the structure and functions of his body to those of animals which at the outset, in their history of the subject, they must admit.

Those, on the other hand, who leave man in the animal kingdom, differ as to the rank to be assigned him there, from that of a species in one genus with the anthropoid apes to the more elevated position of a distinct province or even sub-kingdom. The founder of system, Linnæus, held the former view. With him man was only a species of the more extensive genus Simia. Let the unlearned reader note this, that he may see how possible it is to hold precise opinions as to the value of man's affinities to other creatures, without any reference to Darwinian controversies. Till within the last decade a majority of zoologists, following Blumenbach and Cuvier, have upheld man's title to the rank of an 'order.' Professor Owen proposed for his reception one of the four 'sub-classes' into which, having regard to cerebral characters, he divided the class of mammals. To this arrangement there are grave objections. By Professor Huxley man is held worthy to constitute a 'sub-order' of the modified Linnæan group Primates. In our own opinion, after a thoroughly eclectic and comparative review of all man's zoological characters, proper and common, the most just and useful estimate of man would seem to be that which allows him neither more nor less than the position of what is technically called a 'family.' Briefly, there are four families of Primates—(1) Man only; (2) the Catarrhines, or Apes, Monkeys, and Baboons of the Old World; (3) the Platyrrhines or Monkeys of the New World, with the exception of (4) the Marmosets. The Primates and Lemures may be regarded as two distinct sub-orders of the same ordinal group of mammals. Very similar views are expressed by Mr. Darwin, who justly hints that if "man had not been his own classifier, he would never have thought of founding a separate order for his own reception."

"As far as differences in certain important points of structure are concerned, man may no doubt rightly claim the rank of a Sub-order; and this rank is too low, if we look chiefly to his mental faculties. Nevertheless, under a genealogical point of view it appears that this rank is too high, and that man ought to merely a Family, or possibly even only a Sub-family. If we imagine three lines of descent proceeding from a common source, it is quite conceivable that two of them might after the lapse of ages be so slightly changed as still to remain as species of the same genus; whilst the third line might become so greatly modified as to deserve to rank as a distinct Sub-family, Family, or even Order. But in this case it is almost certain that the third line would still retain through inheritance numerous small points of resemblance with the other two lines. Here then would occur the difficulty, at present insoluble, how much weight we ought to assign in our classifications to strongly-marked differences in some few points,—that is, to the amount of modification undergone; and how much to close resemblance in numerous unimportant points, as indicating the lines of descent or genealogy. The former alternative is the most obvious, and perhaps the safest, though the latter appears the most correct as giving a truly natural classification."

Mr. Darwin's first chapter on "The Evidence of the Descent of Man from some Lower Form," is chiefly devoted to reviewing man's structure as bearing on his origin. So much has of late

years been written on the question—how far is man like and
how far unlike other animals, as to his form, parts, functions,
mode of development, and other zoological characters, that Mr.
Darwin does not deem it necessary to urge at length what to
most biologists will seem a foregone conclusion—that the body
of man is more like the body of certain apes than are these apes
to some other members of their own order. He lays particular
stress on three great classes of facts, the bearing of which is " unmistakeable." These are, the resemblances of homological structures in man and animals, the similarity of their embryonic
development to his, and the existence of rudimentary organs.
Many known facts and not a few new ones are admirably presented within the two sheets of printed matter to which this
chapter extends. We quote the following, by way of sample,
in hopes that the reader may be induced to seek the illustrative
figure referred to in the work itself:—

" The celebrated sculptor, Mr. Woolner, informs me of one little
peculiarity in the external ear, which he has often observed both in
men and women, and of which he perceived the full signification. His
attention was first called to the subject whilst at work on his figure
of Puck, to which he had given pointed ears. He was thus led to
examine the ears of various monkeys, and subsequently more carefully
those of man. The peculiarity consists in a little blunt point, pro-
jecting from the inwardly folded margin, or helix. Mr. Woolner made
an exact model of one such case. These points not only project inwards,
but often a little outwards, so that they are visible when the head is
viewed from directly in front or behind. They are variable in size and
somewhat in position, standing either a little higher or lower; and
they sometimes occur on one ear and not on the other. Now the
meaning of these projections is not, I think, doubtful; but it may be
thought that they offer too trifling a character to be worth notice.
This thought, however, is as false as it is natural. Every character,
however slight, must be the result of some definite cause; and if it
occurs in many individuals deserves consideration. The helix obviously consists of the extreme margin of the ear folded inwards; and
this folding appears to be in some manner connected with the whole
external ear being permanently pressed backwards. In many monkeys, which do not stand high in the order, as baboons and some species of macacus, the upper portion of the ear is slightly pointed, and
the margin is not at all folded inwards; but if the margin were to be
thus folded, a slight point would necessarily project inwards and probably a little outwards. This could actually be observed in a specimen
of the *Ateles beelzebuth* in the Zoological Gardens; and we may safely
conclude that it is a similar structure—a vestige of formerly pointed
ears—which occasionally reappears in man."

Several other particulars of great interest, gleaned by Mr.
Darwin from a variety of authentic sources, are given in the

same chapter. The whole mass of evidence adduced has led his mind to the following conclusion :—

" Thus we can understand how it has come to pass that man and all other vertebrate animals have been constructed on the same general model, why they pass through the same early stages of development, and why they retain certain rudiments in common. Consequently we ought frankly to admit their community of descent : to take any other view, is to admit that our own structure, and that of all the animals around us, is a mere snare laid to entrap our judgment. This conclusion is greatly strengthened, if we look to the members of the whole animal series, and consider the evidence derived from their affinities or classification, their geographical distribution and geological succession. It is only our natural prejudice, and that arrogance which made our forefathers declare that they were descended from demi-gods, which leads us to demur to this conclusion. But the time will before long come when it will be thought wonderful, that naturalists, who were well acquainted with the comparative structure and development of man and other mammals, should have believed that each was the work of a separate act of creation."

Turning now to man's mental powers, we find ourselves in a position of considerable difficulty. Mr. Darwin devotes two chapters to the " Comparison of the Mental Powers of Man and the Lower Animals." But the backward state of psychology will not permit us to distinguish man's mental powers with precision, and he would be a bold writer who should undertake to enumerate, much less define, the mental powers of animals. So that here the essential elements for exact comparison are wanting, and the subject is only susceptible of a mode of treatment which we must designate as vague, provisional, and contradictory. This is not the fault of Mr. Darwin.

Further, the whole matter is involved in a cloud of prejudice which, by a law of reaction unhappily too familiar to philosophers, has in its turn obscured and checked our thoughts. Independence and clearness of view very much above the average are necessary to him who would make any progress with these inquiries—nay, even to him who, without attaining to any height of discovery, would succeed in freeing his mind from vulgar errors. To some the statement that animals may reason seems almost profane. With many persons the word 'instinct' is a synonym for all the mental powers of animals and of these only, as ' reason,' on the other hand, is commonly understood to mean the sum total of the mental powers of man alone. But if these words are to have any meaning, the truer statement would be, that both instinct and reason are shared by man with many of the higher animals.

Mr. Darwin clearly shows that several animals possess the

faculties of Attention and Memory, together with some power of
Imagination. (He does not sufficiently distinguish this last from
Expectation, in Mr. J. S. Mill's sense of that term.) All of
those may be regarded as subsidiary to the reasoning powers
which such animals undoubtedly display. This is shown by their
capacity for progress, and by their use of tools and weapons.
Animals also use (inarticulate) language. They are not without
a sense of the beautiful. They are profoundly affected, like man,
by certain emotions—for example, that of curiosity. They imitate
the actions, not only of their own kindred, but sometimes of
other species, and finally of man himself. They "retain their
mental individuality." Perhaps a few animals possess a rudi-
ment of self-consciousness.

Mr. Darwin, in his second chapter, discusses all these topics
with his accustomed fairness. He starts with the admission that
man differs greatly in his mental power from all other animals,
and that "the difference in this respect is enormous, even if we
compare the mind of one of the lowest savages, who has no
words to express any number higher than four, and who uses
no abstract terms for the commonest objects or affections,
with that of the most highly organized ape." On the other
hand, all differences "of this kind between the highest men of
the highest races and the lowest savages, are connected by the
finest gradations. Therefore it is possible they might pass and
be developed into each other." In spite of these difficulties, Mr.
Darwin concludes "that there is no fundamental difference between man and the higher mammals in their mental faculties."
The whole chapter abounds in sagacious reasonings, and is worth
reading if only as a record of observations by the author and
other naturalists. We quote his account of Reason in animals:—

"Of all the faculties of the human mind, it will, I presume, be admitted that *Reason* stands at the summit. Few persons any longer
dispute that animals possess some power of reasoning. Animals may
constantly be seen to pause, deliberate, and resolve. It is a significant
fact, that the more the habits of any particular animal are studied by
a naturalist, the more he attributes to reason and the less to unlearnt
instincts. In future chapters we shall see that some animals extremely low in the scale apparently display a certain amount of reason.
No doubt it is often difficult to distinguish between the power of reason
and that of instinct. Thus Dr. Hayes, in his work on 'The Open
Polar Sea,' repeatedly remarks that his dogs, instead of continuing to
draw the sledges in a compact body, diverged and separated when
they came to thin ice, so that their weight might be more evenly distributed. This was often the first warning and notice which the
travellers received that the ice was becoming thin and dangerous. Now,
did the dogs act thus from the experience of each individual, or from
the example of the older and wiser dogs, or from an inherited habit,

that is, from an instinct? This instinct might possibly have arisen since the time, long ago, when dogs were first employed by the natives in drawing their sledges; or the Arctic wolves, the parent-stock of the Esquimaux dog, may have acquired this instinct, impelling them not to attack their prey in a close pack when on thin ice. Questions of this kind are most difficult to answer.

"So many facts have been recorded in various works showing that animals possess some degree of reason, that I will here give only two or three instances, authenticated by Rengger, and relating to American monkeys, which stand low in their order. He states that when he first gave eggs to his monkeys, they smashed them and thus lost much of their contents; afterwards they gently hit one end against some hard body, and picked off the bits of shell with their fingers. After cutting themselves only once with any sharp tool, they would not touch it again, or would handle it with the greatest care. Lumps of sugar were often given them wrapped up in paper; and Rengger sometimes put a live wasp in the paper, so that in hastily unfolding it they got stung; after this had once happened, they always first held the packet to their ears to detect any movement within. Any one who is not convinced by such facts as these, and by what he may observe with his own dogs, that animals can reason, would not be convinced by anything that I could add. Nevertheless I will give one case with respect to dogs, as it rests on two distinct observers, and can hardly depend on the modification of any instinct.

"Mr. Colquhoun winged two wild-ducks, which fell on the opposite side of a stream; his retriever tried to bring over both at once, but could not succeed; she then, though never before known to ruffle a feather, deliberately killed one, brought over the other, and returned for the dead bird. Colonel Hutchinson relates that two partridges were shot at once, one being killed, the other wounded; the latter ran away, and was caught by the retriever, who on her return came across the dead bird; 'she stopped, evidently greatly puzzled, and after one or two trials, finding she could not take it up without permitting the escape of the winged bird, she considered a moment, then deliberately murdered it by giving it a severe crunch, and afterwards brought away both together. This was the only known instance of her having ever wilfully injured any game.' Here we have reason, though not quite perfect, for the retriever might have brought the wounded bird first and then returned for the dead one, as in the case of the two wild ducks.

"The muleteers in S. America say, 'I will not give you the mule whose step is easiest, but *la mas racional*,—the one that reasons best;' and Humboldt adds, 'this popular expression, dictated by long experience, combats the system of animated machines, better perhaps than all the arguments of speculative philosophy.'"

We confess our inability to treat in a few paragraphs the subjects of language, also discussed in this chapter, and of ethics, to which the third chapter is devoted. These subjects, sufficiently vast in themselves, have their boundaries much enlarged when considered from the point of view of the derivative hypothesis. Mr. Darwin "cannot doubt that language owes its origin to the imitation and modification, aided by signs and gestures, of various natural sounds, the voices of other animals, and man's own instinctive cries." This is the famous *bow-wow* theory.

"The imitation by articulate sounds of musical cries might have given rise to words expressive of various complex emotions. As bearing on the subject of imitation, the strong tendency in our nearest allies, the monkeys, in microcephalus idiots, and in the barbarous races of mankind, to imitate whatever they hear deserves notice. As monkeys certainly understand much that is said to them by man, and as in a state of nature they utter signal-cries of danger to their fellows, it does not appear altogether incredible that some unusually wise ape-like animal should have thought of imitating the growl of a beast of prey, so as to indicate to his fellow monkeys the nature of the expected danger. And this would have been a first step in the formation of a language."

Mr. Darwin, contrary to what hasty thinkers might erroneously have anticipated, is no upholder of the "selfish" school of morals. With him, "the moral sense is fundamentally identical with our social instincts; and in the case of the lower animals it would be absurd to speak of these instincts as having been developed from selfishness, or for the happiness of the community."

"They have, however, certainly been developed for the general good of the community. The term, general good, may be defined as the means by which the greatest possible number of individuals can be reared in full vigour and health, with all their faculties perfect, under the conditions to which they are exposed. As the social instincts both of man and the lower animals have no doubt been developed by the same steps, it would be advisable, if found practicable, to use the same definition in both cases, and to take as the test of morality, the general good or welfare of the community, rather than the general happiness; but this definition would perhaps require some limitation on account of political ethics.

"When a man risks his life to save that of a fellow-creature, it seems more appropriate to say that he acts for the general good or welfare, rather than for the general happiness of mankind. No doubt the welfare and the happiness of the individual usually coincide; and a contented, happy tribe will flourish better than one that is discontented and unhappy. We have seen that at an early period in the history of man, the expressed wishes of the community will have naturally influenced to a large extent the conduct of each member; and as all wish for happiness, the 'greatest happiness principle' will have become a most important secondary guide and object; the social instincts, including sympathy, always serving as the primary impulse and guide. Thus the reproach of laying the foundation of the most noble part of our nature in the base principle of selfishness is removed; unless indeed the satisfaction which every animal feels when it follows its proper instincts, and the dissatisfaction felt when prevented, be called selfish."

Admitting that the differences, mental and bodily, between man and some animals are not such as to forbid the hypothesis of their descent from a common progenitor, Mr. Darwin proceeds, in his fourth chapter, to trace the manner of man's development. We do not think it necessary to analyse this chapter. The laws of the origin and development of man are presumably the same as those which govern the origin and development of other species. No doubt the conflict between these laws, and the more potent operations of some of them are, in his case, peculiarly interesting and are strikingly manifested when we come to study them in detail. But this would be to reopen the whole question of the origin of species.

How primitive man became civilized, especially by the development of his intellectual and moral faculties, and of the arts and institutions consequent thereon, is the subject of our author's fifth chapter. It is far too large and complex to be treated in the present article. The doctrine that civilized nations were once barbarous is an obvious consequence of Mr. Darwin's hypothesis. The opposite belief, that primitive man was civilized, urged by Archbishop Whately and again put forward by the Duke of Argyll, he does not think it necessary to refute, referring to the works of other writers for a full discussion of the subject.

"To believe that man was aboriginally civilized and then suffered utter degradation in so many regions, is to take a pitiably low view of human nature. It is apparently a truer and more cheerful view that progress has been much more general than retrogression; that man has risen, though by slow and interrupted steps, from a lowly condition to the highest standard as yet attained by him in knowledge, morals, and religion."

The stagnation, or what appears to be such, which the history of some peoples reveals, and the very unequal progress in civilization which the same nation may make at different periods, or at the same period among different sections of the population, tend much to complicate the subject of civilization in general. We know how different parts of the mental constitution of the same individual are liable to be affected in unequal degrees by the social and other conditions to which he is exposed. Hence arise some of the most noteworthy, though not always the most striking, points of disposition. For such inequalities, not harmonizing with those of our own minds, distract and mislead us in our estimate of the motives, and consequent interpretation of the actions of others.

Our author's views on man's affinities and genealogy, discussed in his sixth chapter, may easily be anticipated from what has been said. In short, the phylogeny of man, so far as our space permits, may be indicated by enumerating the following list of common progenitors—namely, the common progenitor of

1. Man and the Monkeys of the Old World.
2. All the Primates.
3. The Primates and Lemures.
4. The above and other 'disco-placental' mammals.
5. All placental mammals.
6. All mammals, placental and implacental.
7. Mammals and other vertebrate animals.

The phylogeny of the vertebrate animals is not easily discerned. From the time that Von Baer first pointed out the important characters which mark the Vertebrata at an early period in their embryonic development, almost every scientific zoologist has acknowledged the existence of a great gulf fixed between them and the higher invertebrates. But recently a Russian naturalist has made the startling discovery, since corroborated by others, that the free-swimming young of certain ascidians (the simplest in structure of all animals which are furnished with a distinct heart) exhibit structures which, in their relative position, resemble the highly characteristic nervous axis and dorsal chord of the Vertebrata; a primitive segmentation, like that of vertebrates, also shows itself. There is therefore some probability that ascidians and vertebrates had a common progenitor. This conclusion is strengthened when we consider the lowest and most aberrant of all vertebrate animals, the lancelet or Amphioxus. In this strange creature the heart is quite rudimentary, and no trace of an organ of hearing exists. Since the dorsal chord runs to the end of the pointed anterior extremity, while in other vertebrate animals it stops short close to where the young skull joins the spinal region, there is reason to infer that in Amphioxus all those important structures which, in other vertebrate animals lie in front of the termination of the notochord, are wanting. The brain of a lamprey, next to Amphioxus, the lowest vertebrate animal, more resembles the brain of man than it does that of the lancelet, or rather the scarcely modified anterior end of the nervous axis in this brainless animal. Lastly, the breathing apparatus of the lancelet is more like that of an ascidian than of a fish.

The affinities of the ascidians are very complicated. Placed by Milne-Edwards with the molluscoida, they are also allied to the true (or higher) molluscs, and even to the worms. No other invertebrate class has such diverse relationships with several groups, and this fact renders their possible connexion with vertebrates the more interesting.

In the seventh chapter, with which the First Part of his work concludes, Mr. Darwin considers the races of man, with a view "to inquire what is the value of the differences between them under a classificatory point of view, and how they have originated." After summing up the facts and arguments on both sides of the question, and pointing out the difficulties which impede its complete solution, he comes to the conclusion that the differences among men are not sufficient to justify the division of mankind into several species, and that the various races of man rather correspond, in systematic value, with what have been termed 'sub-species' in other departments of natural history.

It is certain that races may become extinct, and some, we know, are verging on extinction. In producing such extinction, untoward physical conditions, according to our author, have had little influence. But along with other causes, in the case of half-civilized nations, between whom the direct struggle for life is often strong, or when civilized nations clash with barbarians, their effect may possibly be more potent.

Mr. Darwin, in attempting to account for the origin of races, while admitting the existence of such causes as crossing, natural selection, and the direct action of the conditions of life, is of opinion that none of these are fully competent to produce such great results. Thus he is led to ask—what other causes are here in operation? Of these, neglecting the unknown agencies which produce spontaneous (or inexplicable) modifications, the most important is SEXUAL SELECTION, the detailed consideration of which occupies the Second Part of his work. This Part is nearly twice the length of the First. With the exception of its introductory and concluding chapters and one chapter on sexual selection in man, it is altogether devoted to a review of sexual selection and of the characters associated therewith in the several classes of the animal kingdom.

Sexual selection takes place whenever one animal mates with another of the opposite sex, preferring it to its fellows of the same sex. All acts of this kind, together with the conditions which of necessity immediately precede or accompany them, constitute the phenomena of sexual selection.

That sex which chooses must obviously have senses and a mind to perceive the differences which obtain among the individuals of the other. Hence two essential conditions of sexual selection, objective and subjective. We see also that powers of locomotion are necessary to bring the sexes into the neighbourhood of each other and thus afford due opportunity for the exercise of their respective abilities.

The act of sexual selection, apart from collateral circumstances and neglecting exceptional instances, may at once be described as the choice by the female of one out of many males of her own species. "The law is, that the male shall seek the female." Thus Kirby (as quoted by Mr. Darwin) wrote of insects, and might have written of most animals. But why is it so? Let us hear Mr. Darwin's answer.

"We are naturally led to inquire why the male in so many and such widely distinct classes has been rendered more eager than the female, so that he searches for her and plays the more active part in courtship. It would be no advantage and some loss of power if both sexes were mutually to search for each other; but why should the male almost always be the seeker? With plants, the ovules after fertilization have to be nourished for a time; hence the pollen is necessarily brought to the female organs—being placed on the stigma, through the agency of insects or of the wind, or by the spontaneous movements of the stamens; and with the Algæ, &c., by the locomotive power of the antherozooids. With lowly-organized animals permanently affixed to the same spot and having their sexes separate, the male element is invariably brought to the female; and we can see the reason; for the ova, even if detached before being fertilized and not requiring subsequent nourishment or protection, would be, from their larger relative size, less easily transported than the male element. Hence plants* and many of the lower animals are, in this respect, analogous. In the case of animals not affixed to the same spot, but enclosed within a shell with no power of protruding any part of their bodies, and in the case of animals having little power of locomotion, the male must trust the fertilizing element to the risk of at least a short transit through the waters of the sea. It would, therefore, be a great advantage to such animals, as their organization became perfected, if the males when ready to emit the fertilizing element, were to acquire the habit of approaching the female as closely as possible. The males of various lowly-organized animals having thus aboriginally acquired the habit of approaching and seeking the females, the same habit would naturally be transmitted to their more highly developed male descendants; and in order that they should become efficient seekers, they would have to be endowed with strong passions. The acquirement of such passions would naturally follow from the more eager males leaving a larger number of offspring than the less eager."

With the female it is otherwise. She "with the rarest exceptions, is less eager than the male."

"As the illustrious Hunter long ago observed, she generally 're-

* Prof. Sachs ('Lehrbuch der Botanik,' 1870, s. 633) in speaking of the male and female reproductive cells, remarks, "verhält sich die eine bei der Vereinigung activ, ... die andere erscheint bei der Vereinigung passiv."

quires to be courted;' she is coy, and may often be seen endeavouring for a long time to escape from the male. Every one who has attended to the habits of animals will be able to call to mind instances of this kind. Judging from various facts, hereafter to be given, and from the results which may fairly be attributed to sexual selection, the female, though comparatively passive, generally exerts some choice and accepts one male in preference to others. Or she may accept, as appearances would sometimes lead us to believe, not the male which is the most attractive to her, but the one which is the least distasteful. The exertion of some choice on the part of the female seems almost as general a law as the eagerness of the male."

When a strong pugnacious male succeeds in defeating his opponents of the same sex the female may easily content herself with the victor. She does not, however, invariably do so, though the exceptions are probably unfrequent. But should the males contend, in a more peaceful fashion, by the production of musical sounds, the display of ornaments, and such other like methods, the possession on her part of more refined selective powers becomes necessary. That the gentler sex among animals is often highly gifted in this respect seems more than probable. When we note, for example, the splendid colours of the males of many birds, and consider how sedulously, and with what wonderful adjuncts, they are displayed with increased effect during the season of courtship, can we doubt that one female for whose sake, since in her presence only, these gorgeous exhibitions take place, is capable of appreciating, at least, their general effect?

Exceptions to the ruling law of sexual selection take place when the female seeks the male of her own species, or when, as must occur with the parents of hybrids, she prefers the male of another.

We can easily see how important in regard to sexual selection is the relative proportion of the sexes, a subject which on other grounds claims our attention. A more extended acquaintance with facts is here much needed. Most of our statistics under this head refer to man or domestic animals. In their case we find it easier to obtain results, or even seek to modify them by a change of external conditions. Such facts, though not to be despised, are plainly less valuable, because less varied and more remote from the circumstances of unimpeded selection, than those affecting *feræ naturæ*. We have no means of estimating, in a vast majority of animals, which sex most abounds at birth. In the case of several species the males appear to predominate, but to this rule there are some exceptions. What determines the proportion of the sexes at birth—is another interesting question. Often, we must answer, unknown influences, whether internal, depending on mental and material constitution, or external, such as food and temperature, the action of which cannot in this connexion be ascertained.* Some of these influences may be constant, others variable. The period at which impregnation takes place and the circumstances of polygamous as opposed to monogamous unions are not here operating conditions. More potent is the relative age of the parents. Illegitimate births show an increased proportion of females. It would seem as if the sex of the more vigorous† parent were likely to be inherited.

> "Sectetur partem conclusio deteriorem,"

is not the rule in such cases, for love in its effects, as in its causes, is illogical. Noteworthy is the fact that with Jewish women the number of male births is very much above the Christian average.

"For our present purpose we are concerned with the proportion of the sexes, not at birth, but at maturity." Mr. Darwin has collected from a variety of sources all the accessible information on this head, and he sums up the results in a special supplement to his eighth chapter. It is known that with many animals the male is not only more exposed to danger than the female, but has a greater inherent viability, "for it is a well-ascertained fact that with man a considerably larger proportion of males than of females die before or during birth, and during the first few years of infancy. So it almost certainly is with male lambs, and so it may be with the males of other animals." We might therefore suppose that, with certain exceptions, the number of mature males must be less than that of females.‡ But our author is far too cautious to accept this conclusion unre-

---

* See, however, Falstaff's soliloquy on Prince John in *Henry IV.* Part 2.

† More vigorous, that is, at the period of fecundation.

‡ So that given M+F or M=F, the altered expression M—F might be worked out in different ways. Not only do males succumb to influences purely external or internal, as above stated, but they are also visited by a third class of catastrophes which cannot strictly be referred to either. We speak of dangers within the limits of their own species. The males of fishes are smaller than the females, who devour them freely. Baron De Geer saw a male spider which " in the midst of his preparatory caresses was seized by the object of his attentions, enveloped by her in a web, and then devoured—a sight which, as he adds, filled him with horror and indignation." Why are not these facts cited by those who believe in the existence of a great gulf fixed between men and animals? Uncivilized men, it is true, kill and eat their wives. Some civilized men kill but do not eat them, having so far lost the habits of their ancestors. But with no race of savages has a single instance occurred of a wife eating her husband. Mankind has never reached this lowest depth of animal degradation.

servedly. Practically, males are less numerous wherever polygamy obtains. Polygamy is unknown among the lower animals, and is only exhibited by those who possess obvious mental powers. Under ordinary circumstances it involves the exclusion of the weaker and less attractive males.

The practical disproportion between the sexes may arise from other causes. Thus in migratory birds the males first arrive and are ready to breed before the females. The females, when they begin to appear, since not all arrive simultaneously, are in the minority. Accordingly the males conteud for their possession. The females have therefore every opportunity for selection. Now those females which are most vigorous will, in their turn, have the first choice, for they will be ready to breed before their follows. They will also be able to rear the greatest number of offspring. So that, the best males uniting with the best females, the best and most numerous offspring will result. Allowing for the effects of inheritance and further variation, we begin to understand something of the part played by sexual selection. Let the above conditions be reversed, the males choosing the females, and a like result may easily be inferred.

In regard to animals with superfluous males or females, Mr. Darwin asks—"Could the sexes be equalized through natural selection?" He shows how in more ways than one equalization might be effected, directly or indirectly. The indirect action of natural selection will scarcely be felt where the disproportion between the sexes is slight. When it is greater, and natural selection has room to operate, the varying fertility of the same species becomes an important factor. A high degree of productivity is sometimes disadvantageous, in accordance with one aspect of the physiological law of individuation *versus* genesis; here natural selection may come strikingly into play, as both Mr. Herbert Spencer and Mr. Darwin have demonstrated. " In some peculiar cases, an excess in the number of one sex over the other might be a great advantage to a species, as with the sterile *females* of social insects, or with those animals in which more than one male is requisite to fertilize the female, as with certa n cirripedes, and perhaps certain fishes." These exceptional instances of ' imperative polyandry' are probably due to natural selection. " In all ordinary cases an inequality would be no advantage or disadvantage to certain individuals more than to others ; and therefore it could hardly have resulted from natural selection." We can only, in our ignorance, ascribe it to unknown conditions.

Let us now consider the differences on which sexual selection depends. These are chiefly of the kind called by Hunter secondary sexual characters—

"which are not directly connected with the act of reproduction ;

for instance, in the male possessing certain organs of sense or locomotion, of which the female is quite destitute, or in having them more highly-developed; in order that he may readily find or reach her; or again, in the male having special organs of prehension so as to hold her securely. These latter organs of infinitely diversified kinds graduate into, and in some cases can hardly be distinguished from, those which are commonly ranked as primary, such as the complex appendages at the apex of the abdomen in male insects. Unless indeed we confine the term ' primary ' to the reproductive glands, it is scarcely possible to decide, as far as the organs of prehension are concerned, which ought to be called primary and which secondary."

Apart from their mental powers, their habits and actions, the sexes of the same species may differ as to number, form, size, colour, and structure. They may also differ in their relations to time, as when one sex comes to maturity and acquires or loses certain characters sooner than another. Not all sexual differences have to do with sexual selection. We except such characters as are obviously correlated with the diverse modes of life of the two sexes, seen in some species.

The male more frequently than the female exhibits secondary sexual characters; and these, with other characters which may accompany them, are in him eminently variable. In accordance with the law of sexually limited transmission (as opposed to that of equal transmission) the male usually transmits the peculiarities he acquires to his own sex only. It also frequently happens that their appearance or more conspicuous development coincides approximately with the period at which sexual selection takes place, and this fact points to the probability that the characters in question first arose at the beginning of adult life. Again, these characters, accumulated and inherited from parent to child, tend still further to differentiate the male, who is thus ever subject to increased modification by means of sexual selection. The female remains more like the young of her own or the adults of allied species. In her, however, must be latent the secondary sexual characters manifest in her male parent. Otherwise, how could these be transmitted to her offspring when she is made to pair with a male belonging to a different species?

From our present point of view the animal kingdom is divisible into two groups, in one of which secondary sexual characters are of frequent occurrence, in the other usually absent. We commonly find these characters in mammals, birds, reptiles, batrachians, fishes, insects, and crustaceans—that is, in what zoologists term ' vertebrate' and ' arthropod' animals. Not all these exhibit them, some of the exceptions being very puzzling and suggestive of curious considerations. They are very obvious in man. They are wanting in the lowest animals (the 'Vermes' of Linnæus). Polygamy is favourable to their occurrence. Mr. Darwin asked Mr. Bartlett, Superintendent of our Zoological Gardens, whether the male tragopan (an exotic ally of the pheasants) was polygamous, and was much struck by his answer —" I do not know, but should think so from his splendid colours."

Our limits will not allow us to notice Mr. Darwin's account of sexual selection in each of the above classes. We can refer to one only, that of birds. This class is more interesting than any other, as illustrating the phenomena of sexual selection. The preferences and antipathies of birds are so wonderful and their opportunities for displaying them so varied, in consequence of the marvellous complexity and beauty of their secondary sexual characters, that " they appear to be the most æsthetic of all animals, excepting of course man, and they have nearly the same taste for the beautiful." It is therefore no wonder that Mr. Darwin devotes two hundred · pages, about one-fourth of his entire work, to these animals.

" Most male birds are highly pugnacious during the breeding-season, and some possess weapons especially adapted for fighting with their rivals. But the most pugnacious and the best-armed males rarely or never depend for success solely on their power to drive away or kill their rivals, but have special means for charming the female. With some it is the power of song, or of emitting strange cries, or of producing instrumental music, and the males in consequence differ from the females in their vocal organs, or in the structure of certain feathers. From the curiously diversified means for producing various sounds, we gain a high idea of the importance of this means of courtship. Many birds endeavour to charm the females by love-dances or antics, performed on the ground or in the air, and sometimes at prepared places. But ornaments of many kinds, the most brilliant tints, combs and wattles, beautiful plumes, elongated feathers, top-knots, and so forth, are by far the commoner means. In some cases mere novelty appears to have acted as a charm. The ornaments of the males must be highly important to them, for they have been acquired in not a few cases at the cost of increased danger from enemies, and even of some loss of power in fighting with their rivals. The males of very many species do not assume their ornamental dress until they arrive at maturity, or they assume it only during the breeding-season, or the tints then become more vivid. Certain ornamental appendages become enlarged, turgid, and brightly-coloured during the very act of courtship. The males display their charms with elaborate care and to the best effect; and this is done in the presence of the females. The courtship is sometimes a prolonged affair, and many males and females congregate at an appointed place. To suppose that the females do not appreciate the males is to admit that their splendid decorations, all their pomp and display, are useless; and this is incredible. Birds have fine powers of discrimination, and in some few instances it can be shown that they have a taste for the beautiful. The females, moreover, are known occasionally to exhibit a marked preference or antipathy to certain males.

If it be admitted that the females prefer, or are unconsciously excited by the more beautiful males, then the males would slowly and surely be rendered more attractive through sexual selection."

The plumage of birds, in connexion with secondary sexual characters and their transmission, is noted at much length by Mr. Darwin. He distinguishes six "Rules or classes of cases."

"I. When the adult male is more beautiful or conspicuous than the adult female, the young of both sexes in their first plumage closely resemble the adult female, as with the common fowl and peacock; or, as occasionally occurs, they resemble her much more closely than they do the adult male.

II. When the adult female is more conspicuous than the adult male, as sometimes though rarely occurs, the young of both sexes in their first plumage resemble the adult male.

III. When the adult male resembles the adult female, the young of both sexes have a peculiar first plumage of their own, as with the robin.

IV. When the adult male resembles the adult female, the young of both sexes in their first plumage resemble the adults, as with the kingfisher, many parrots, crows, hedge-warblers.

V. When the adults of both sexes have a distinct winter and summer plumage, whether or not the male differs from the female, the young resemble the adults of both sexes in their winter dress, or much more rarely in their summer dress, or they resemble the females alone; or the young may have an intermediate character; or again may differ greatly from the adults in both their seasonal plumages.

VI. In some few cases the young in their first plumage differ from each other according to sex; the young males resembling more or less closely the adult males, and the young females the adult females."

In the rare instances of the females being more conspicuous than the males, the habits and dispositions of the sexes are likewise transposed: the male sits on the eggs; the females are pugnacious. The disparity between the sexes in such birds, however, is never so extreme as when the male excels the female.

To show that the secondary sexual characters of birds are not causeless, Mr. Darwin appeals to their gradations. In this way he demonstrates how the beautiful and complex eye-like spots on the plumage of such birds as the peacock and argus pheasant may have been produced, the laws of variation and inheritance being also taken into account. His very ingenious explanation of these 'ocelli' is accompanied with several illustrations.

A few cases are cited by Mr. Darwin of differences between the sexes of birds which do not now appear to have any relation to sexual selection. Thus, the males of goldfinches have somewhat longer beaks than the females, and the two sexes do not commonly feed on the seeds of the same plant.

The author compares his views with those of Mr. Wallace and the Duke of Argyll in regard to the colours of birds as related to nidification and protection. We do not enter here into this controversy, no adequate discussion of which is possible without a lengthened analysis of the facts.

The fate of unpaired birds, the bachelors, old maids, widows and widowers of their kind, is also dwelt on by Mr Darwin. These constitute a reserve fund which is largely drawn on to recoup the losses caused by death. When one of a pair of birds is shot, we soon find the survivor in the company of a new mate, and this if the act of destruction be again and again repeated.

"These facts are certainly remarkable. How is it that so many birds are ready immediately to replace a lost mate? Magpies, jays, carrion-crows, partridges, and some other birds, are never seen during the spring by themselves, and these offer at first sight the most perplexing case. But birds of the same sex, although of course not truly paired, sometimes live in pairs or in small parties, as is known to be the case with pigeons and partridges. Birds also sometimes live in triplets, as has been observed with starlings, carrion-crows, parrots, and partridges. With partridges two females have been known to live with one male, and two males with one female. In all such cases it is probable that the union would be easily broken. The males of certain birds may occasionally be heard pouring forth their love-song long after the proper time, showing that they have either lost or never gained a mate. Death from accident or disease of either one of a pair, would leave the other bird free and single; and there is reason to believe that female birds during the breeding-season are especially liable to premature death. Again, birds which have had their nests destroyed, or barren pairs, or retarded individuals, would easily be induced to desert their mates, and would probably be glad to take what share they could of the pleasures and duties of rearing offspring, although not their own. Such contingencies as these probably explain most of the foregoing cases. Nevertheless, it is a strange fact that within the same district, during the height of the breeding season, there should be so many males and females always ready to repair the loss of a mated pair. Why do not such spare birds immediately pair together? Have we not some reason to suspect—and the suspicion has occurred to Mr. Jenner Weir—that inasmuch as the act of courtship appears to be with many birds a prolonged and tedious affair, so it occasionally happens that certain males and females do not succeed during the proper season in exciting each other's love, and consequently do not pair."

It may please our gentler readers to learn that the fierce

method of trial by battle does not always avail the combatants. Our author has "been assured by Mr. W. Kowalevsky, that the female capercailzie sometimes steals away with a young male who has not dared to enter the arena with the older cocks; in the same manner as occasionally happens with the does of the red-deer in Scotland."

Since young animals are more generalized than adults, probably resembling the early progenitors of their kind, and since the young of most birds are duller than their parents, or quite dull, "if we look to the birds of the world, it appears that their beauty has been greatly increased since that period, of which we have a partial record in their immature plumage."

Thus, by an overwhelming accumulation of facts, Mr. Darwin has established the importance of secondary sexual characters. These characters, though not exhibited by all, obtain in the majority, certainly in a very large number of the species of the animal world. They will doubtless be proved to exist in very many animals not yet examined in this connexion. They may very probably be acquired by other animals which do not now possess them. How far, in certain cases, it is within our power to aid or extend their production, is a problem, of very great interest, which judicious observations and experiments must decide.

We do not know how secondary sexual characters first arise. Perhaps they are the result of spontaneous modifications. They may be due to the direct influence of the outward conditions of life. This problem, which now appears so obscure, ought not to be deemed incapable of solution. It may well be imagined that at their dawning they are manifested so faintly as to require for their recognition every aid to minute and repeated investigations.

But when once produced, they become amenable to the laws of inheritance and variation. These laws are ever in action. We are not able to point to any characters able to escape their operation. So that secondary sexual characters, like others, will be intensified, accumulated, and transmitted from generation to generation. Moreover, they have, so to speak, within themselves, or related to them by a quite peculiar intimacy, a cause very capable of extending their sphere and promoting their utility—namely, sexual selection.

Sexual selection bears to secondary sexual characters a relation both of cause and effect. Given secondary sexual characters, sexual selection must follow, if we grant that one sex is able to perceive the differences which mark the individuals of the other. From observations of the habits of animals, especially during the season of courtship, it seems impossible to deny that they possess in various degrees this kind of mental power. Such inference is strengthened by the analogy of our own minds. An inhabitant of another planet, gifted with human intelligence, but without human desires, having watched both men and animals when in love, might surely ask—which is imitating the conduct of the other?

The marvellous diversities of habit which animals display, their repugnances and attractions, their curious behaviour towards one another, offer to our notice a crowd of striking phenomena. Much of what they do and think (for it is allowable to use this phrase) seems to us eminently natural. Their caprices, on the other hand, are sometimes quite unaccountable. In both respects they parody man, their observer. What we cannot explain in ourselves should not surprise us when we regard the actions of those whom, however active and intelligent our sympathies, we have not yet learned, never fully can learn, how to appreciate.

The student of sexual selection is not, *per se*, required to account for the intellectual and moral qualities of animals. These may be otherwise explained, and so explained must be acknowledged. Those animals which display secondary sexual characters are, in most cases, intelligent enough in other respects. If not so, the strongest and most typical of our unselfish desires is surely capable of utilizing to the utmost degree as much mental power as can be contributed towards its gratification. It may even react upon the higher nervous centres, and, other influences coming to its aid, the mental power of the species might thus become increased.

Sexual selections may transpose secondary sexual characters into primary, and *vice versâ*. It may even cause to become sexual characters not so originally, the master-passion love, with animals as with man, asserting its rights and acting on their material no less than on their mental constitution. For what else it can effect we refer to Mr. Darwin's book. He of course especially dwells on two kinds of results—(1) that sexual selection tends to enhance secondary sexual characters themselves, and (2) that it indirectly favours the transmission of variations not sexual, whenever these are associated with the former. Thus both, with all their proneness to further variation, are handed down to succeeding generations.

How extended is the view such considerations afford of the grand rôle which this agency performs in the scheme of organized nature.

" 'Tis love, 'tis love, 'tis love,
Which makes the world go round."

Mr. Darwin gives a wider meaning to these words. Yet, with modesty and caution all his own, he makes a temperate use of his discovery. For him sexual selection is but one out of many forces acting within and upon the living world, all tending towards one combined result.

In one sense selection is a less fundamental power than natural selection. Natural selection favours variation, and variation must first have furnished the materials on which sexual selection depends. Sexual selection, in its turn, by helping to transmit variations promotes them, and thus it acts along with natural selection, or rather, in many instances, begins where natural selection ends. Both have a destructive as well as a constructive operation. When males fight to the death for the possession of the female, sexual selection acts by destroying, and so far resembles in its results the more striking aspect of natural selection. But its ordinary effects are essentially peaceful and life-giving. It is a far higher power than natural selection, since it involves the element of mind, and aids the further development, while contributing to the transmission of mental qualities.

Doubtless, sexual selection has played an important part in the history of our race. Alike with savage and with civilized men its operation continues, though checked by various hindrances. The standard of beauty among men changes with time and place. Savages choose their wives and savage women esteem their husbands because of peculiarities which we regard as exaggerations or defects of characters already sufficiently hideous. With these characters are associated others, so that unconscious selection must also occur. And thus the characters which distinguish races were, in all probability, established.

Let us remember that sexual selection, as we now see it among men, has lost much of its ancient freedom of action. It still appears to predominate over artificial influences (between which and natural selection it holds a curiously intermediate place), but these retard if they do not otherwise diminish its operation. It must have acted much more strongly in early times, with us as with higher beings—

> " In der heroischen Zeit, da Gotter und Göttingen liebten,
>   Folgte Begierde dem Blick, folgte Genuss der Begier,"

than, "when man had advanced in his intellectual powers, but had retrograded in his instincts." According to our author, no other cause so potent has led to the differences which distinguish the races of men, and in a lesser degree man from the lower animals.

Our readers will now ask—has Mr. Darwin succeeded in proving his case, and is man descended from other animals?

Linnæus, we know, went further than Mr. Darwin in the view which he took of man's present zoological position. Successive anatomists have done their best to exaggerate every point of difference between man and the apes. The controversies thus provoked have led to a thorough and renewed investigation of the facts. These facts must be admitted in a sense very favourable to the reception of Mr. Darwin's opinions. Likeness in what we deem essential characters must ever strongly suggest relationship. The double meaning of 'affinity' (significant term) can no longer be neglected.

How primitive man arose from animal ancestors, and how he subsequently became civilized are two questions which cannot be separated from each other, particularly when we consider the origin of man's mental powers. It is more difficult to deal with these than with his bodily structure. Nor can we here employ a terminology so precise as that of anatomical science. But mental, like vital, phenomena obey the laws of gradation, variation, selection, inheritance, and accumulation. They also react powerfully on one another and their instrument, the nervous system. Hence any species which achieved early, though slight, superiority in this respect, would rapidly tend to surpass its fellows. Keeping in view the distinctions which obtain among men themselves, we may grant that man's possession of high mental qualities does not offer insuperable objections to the doctrine of his descent.

If man be descended from animals his genealogy cannot be doubtful. His nearest relations are the 'catarrhine' apes, and through these other vertebrates. As to the manner of his descent, the causes which have acted in the production of other species must have had their usual operation. The part played by sexual selection was probably, in his case, more effective.

The doctrine of man's descent from animals must stand or fall with that of descent in general. We cannot admit Mr. Darwin's hypothesis of the origin of species, and not apply it to ourselves. We cannot hold the intermediate view of man's body being the result of natural, his mind of supernatural, causes. Regarding the descent of man as a test of the Darwinian hypothesis, some will say that this hypothesis has been at once strengthened and weakened thereby. Admitting, as is obvious, man's case to be the most interesting, is it, on purely scientific grounds the best, the one most likely to yield exact results? It is indeed so important, that if we consider it as settled, the whole doctrine of development makes thereby a great step in advance, and we are introduced to the study of the genesis of all the higher mental phenomena.

Worthy of note is the position held by Mr. Darwin towards his own opinions. He is strongly convinced of their truth, yet he states them in moderate language. He feels more keenly than any one else the difficulties which surround him. He has altered some of his earlier beliefs, more especially in regard to the great importance of sexual selection. His work on this subject is a noble contribution to science, for the doctrine of development is truly independent of much that has been urged in its favour. The views of none of its supporters need be accepted in their entirety. An eminent palæontologist, now dead, compared it to the Duomo of Milan, so many years in building, that in process of time it underwent a change from a lower to a higher order of architecture. Mr. Darwin has distinguished himself above all his predecessors. Future investigators, grateful for what he has done, may elaborate his work still further, and carry it upwards towards its destined limits. The theory of development, when most truly expressed, will be the last of the grand series of facts which it must expound.

The case of man's descent does not yet admit of proof. The same may be said of the origin of any other species, of Mr. Darwin's hypothesis in general, and of the hypothesis of special creations, which it denies. Probability is the guide of life, and if it can be shown that the derivate hypothesis, applied to man, accounts for much that is otherwise inexplicable, that it colligates facts which the doctrine of special creations does not touch, that certain facts, which it does not explain are not inconsistent with it, that the objections to it are less formidable than those which the rival assumption must encounter, and that in truth it is worthy to be called an hypothesis, while that to which it is opposed is no hypothesis at all, but merely a confession that the subject is unknown and unknowable ;—if all this be so, then must we accept, for a time at least, Mr. Darwin's view of this great question as more probable and presumably more true than any doctrine which has hitherto been substituted in its stead. Common fairness suggests this course ; the interests of science demand it.

Let us hear the conclusion of the whole matter. He is a bold man who, testing Mr. Darwin's facts and arguments, believes in man's descent from the animal kingdom. He is a bolder who, resting on the evidence of ignorance, ventures to hold any other opinion.

Art. V.—The Scotch Education Settlement of 1872.

An Act to Amend and Extend the Provisions of the Law of Scotland on the Subject of Education. (6th August, 1872.)

FOR upwards of sixteen years attempts have been made to solve by legislation, directly or indirectly, completely or partially, three educational problems connected with Scotland: first, to give every child in that country the rudiments of knowledge; second, to destroy clerical ascendancy in the schools; and third, so to reconstruct the educational apparatus as to provide that ladder from the gutter to the University which, in the sixteenth century, was the ambition of John Knox, and in the nineteenth is that of Professor Huxley. During that time seven Bills have been before Parliament, and to quote from one of the ablest of Scotch members, who spoke in the course of the discussion on the second reading of the seventh and last, "Three generations of school-children have become men and women—many with no education of any kind, many with education of a most improper kind, and have become citizens not of that intelligent and orderly class which formed the pride of Scotland and a support to England, but ignorant citizens, such as we will before long have to account with for not having given them the advantages enjoyed by their forefathers." Of these, two have become law—that of 1861, which may be described as the first instalment of reform in the way of destroying ecclesiastical supremacy in the national schools by the abolition of tests for schoolmasters; and that of 1872, which aims at settling all the three problems to which we have alluded, and which there is every reason to believe is a settlement, so far as anything human, and especially anything parliamentary, can be considered a settlement. It is our purpose to inquire how far it can be said to implement its professions.

Scotsmen are fond of boasting of the excellence of their system of education as proved by the number of persons, juveniles and adults, who are in receipt of, or have received, the rudiments of knowledge. At the first blush, the boast seems justifiable. When the census was taken, in 1871, it was found that in Scotland, out of a population of 3,360,018 persons, 494,860 children of from five to thirteen years of age were in the receipt of education, giving a percentage of 14·72 of the population receiving education even at these early years. What the exact percentage of the population of all ages is, we do not know; but in 1861 it was 15·4, and there is every reason to believe that it is now greater. Taking this percentage as a standard of educational excellence, we find Scotland comparing very favourably with

other countries. Even in the German Empire, including all the
schools, gymnasia, and universities, the percentage is 15·0.
Taking the general ratio of scholars to the population, therefore,
the state of education is satisfactory. When, however, we come
to local details, we find something decidedly different. A Royal
Commission into the condition of education, which commenced
its labours in 1864, and concluded them in 1868, came to such
results as those—that 92,000 children were on the roll of no
school, and that in Glasgow alone little more than one-third of
the children of school age were then attending school. Even in
the rural districts, where the famous parochial system is in full
play, they reported a singular want of uniformity in educational
provision. In Selkirkshire the ratio of 1 to 5 of the whole population was found on the school-books of some schools; in Shet-
land, at once the most moral and most ignorant of Scotch counties, the ratio was 1 to 14. The state of the islands, such as the
Hebrides, may be imagined when we mention this fact, given by the
commissioners—that " in three populations of above 2000 souls
each, there were respectively only 26, 4, and 18 women able to
write their own names, or a total of 48 in a population exceeding 6000."

What the Education Act of this year has done with the view
of remedying this state of matters is to ordain absolute compulsion, after the Prussian model, not permissive after that of the
English Act. According to the Act, every parent is required to
provide elementary education in reading, writing, and arithmetic
for his children between five and thirteen years of age; default-
ing parents are to be prosecuted; and the fees of those whose
parents are unable, from poverty, to pay them, are to be paid by
the Parochial Board. Undoubtedly this will produce something
like educational equality over the country, for when it is ordained
that every child must be educated, the local boards are bound
to provide a sufficiency of educational machinery. With compulsion in education, it is unnecessary to say we have theoretically no sympathy. The *Westminster Review* has always
maintained, in spite of the present current the other way, that
for the State to educate is over-legislation, and that it is mere
impatience of imperfections, natural to our present civilization,
to ask it to overtake work which should be accomplished by the
spontaneous enterprise of a free people. Nor is there anything in
the past history and present condition of Scotch education to
shake our theory. It is true, as we have already seen, that the
educational machinery is badly distributed, and that in some of
the large towns and rural districts it has shown itself to be inadequate. But this simply proves that the old parochial theory—
the theory which maintained that one school was sufficient for a
district—was a short-sighted one, and that it was unable to meet

the emergency of a dense and daily increasing population on the one hand, and of a wide extent of almost uninhabited country on the other. With its numerous excellences, moreover, the parochial school system committed a grievous blunder in placing the teachers in a position of independence to their employers, that is to say, the parents of their pupils. A parish teacher had a fixed salary, in addition to what his professional energy could bring him in the shape of fees; and, besides, he was appointed *ad vitam aut culpam*—provided he were not drunken and immoral, he might draw his stipend annually, do almost no work, snap his fingers in the face of his employers, and yet retain his situation for life. The stock argument in favour of the parochial system is, that the competence and independence it offered, induced scholarly men to become parish teachers, and statistics of the number of young men who have gone directly from the parish schools to the national Universities, are triumphantly thrust in our face in support of that argument. We can perfectly understand men of considerable classical attainments finding it a luxury to train promising boys with an eye to the Church in Livy and Xenophon, but we can also understand their thinking it a drudgery and a bore to teach elementary reading, writing, and arithmetic, although so far as Scotland generally, and the average of their pupils in particular were concerned, it would have been better had they done the latter though lower work thoroughly, and left the former, in spite of its being higher, undone.[*] It is not, therefore, at all a matter for wonder that the Commissioners for 1868 should have to tell us that, in the Lowlands of Scotland, where the best parish schools are to be found, only 55 children between the ages of five and fifteen in every 100 born and living in the districts attend school, and that rather more than a fourth of the school buildings are unsuitable, and more than one-fourth of the teaching is indifferent and bad. When teaching was not left to the action of the ordinary law of supply and demand, when teachers were not allowed to be stimulated by the ordinary means to do the work for which they were appointed, it is not to be wondered at that indolence and bad teaching on the part of schoolmasters, indifference on the part of parents, and poor attendance in the case of children, should have been ascertained, when people left off singing the praises of the parochial-school system and began to investigate into its working.

The true cure for the evil would have been to have left the whole education field open to enterprise. Already adventure schools were, before the last Education Bill for Scotland was

---

[*] Since the above was written, Mr. Innes, in the course of a tour through Scotland has advised School Boards to see to elementary education, and the education of the poor first, and that of the better class afterwards.

introduced, springing up in the large towns to meet educational wants; and by far the most philosophical system of education tried in Scotland is that of the Merchant Company of
Edinburgh—an association of private individuals, who, having
under their control very considerable revenues, hitherto locked
up in hospitals for the education of the children of dead or de-
cayed members of their body, obtained the permission of Parliament to use these revenues freely, and have now devoted them
to the maintenance of a number of open schools, known as the
Merchant Company's schools, whose success, even although they
have been only a limited period in existence, has been already of
the most unequivocal character. But things have been differently
ordered. The State has decided to control the education of the
children of Scotland, and it has also decided to compel them to
be educated. If it is allowed to do the one thing, it may be as
well allowed to be logical, and do the other.

One result of the absolute compulsion of the Scotch Act is
worthy of notice, especially on account of the noise made on the
subject while the measure was in suspense. Under the Act,
teachers, instead of being appointed, as hitherto, for life, with a
fixed salary, in addition to what they may make by fees, are to
be appointed by local boards, and to continue in office during
their pleasure. At the same time no principal teacher of a public
school can be appointed who does not hold a certificate of competence from the Scotch Education Department. This was described and attacked, when it was first brought prominently forward, as leaving teachers to the operation of the law of supply
and demand, and Dr. Lyon Playfair, member for the Universities of Edinburgh and St. Andrews, and perhaps the ablest
of the critics of the measure, triumphantly reminded the Lord
Advocate for Scotland, its pilot through the House of Commons,
that Adam Smith does not apply the principle of supply and
demand to elementary education, but recommends that teachers
should partly be paid by a salary from the public purse and partly
by fees. The truth, however, is that, instead of that principle being
applied in the Act to elementary education, to the pecuniary detri-
ment of the teachers, it is deliberately violated to benefit their
purses. By the ordinary economic law, you are allowed to buy
in a certain market as you choose, and from whom you choose.
But the Scotch Education Act practically compels every one to
buy in the education market, and only to buy from certain persons—those, namely, holding a certificate of competence. Is it
not clear that such persons have the public virtually at their feet?
No one dare interfere with their monopoly of educational wares,
and yet every one must buy them. The danger here is clearly
not to the certificated teachers, but to the public; the former
have but to form themselves into a trade union, and they can

dictate their own terms. Yet, instead of our having, as we should have had, an agitation for free trade in teaching as in everything else, and for the protection of the public, we had actually, before the passing of the measure, a number of clergymen and of those half-clerical laymen who in Kirk Sessions, Presbyteries, Synods, and Assemblies, play the parts of Joshua and Hur to their clerical Moscses, going about the country denouncing the Bill, and endeavouring to get the sympathy of schoolmasters on the one hand, on the ground that the measure would give them inferior pay, and of the public on the other, because it would give them inferior teachers! Surely no better proof could be given of the necessity of emancipating education from the fetters of clerical delusion.

The second problem connected with Scotch education, the destruction of clerical ascendancy in the schools, the Act, which will soon come into operation, solves only in an imperfect way. Under the old parochial system, the central authority of the schools was vested in the General Assembly of the Church of Scotland, and the local authority in the parish ministers; while the inspectors were the ministers of the Presbyteries, and the rating for the support of the schools was confined to owners of land which yielded a certain annual rent, commonly called heritors. The parish teacher was paid by the same persons that paid the parish minister, was governed by him, inspected by him, and was—except to the extent of his being pecuniarily independent—virtually his servant. The Bill of 1861 altered matters a little; by the abolition of the tests for schoolmasters, men who were not members of the Church of Scotland might become parish schoolmasters. But down to the present time the parish schools have virtually been under the General Assembly, and through the systematic teaching of the Shorter Catechism have been made the feeders of the various Presbyterian bodies. The other sectarian schools which, especially on the formation of the Free Church in 1843, sprang into existence in great numbers, and in opposition to the parish schools, were entirely under the control of the churches to which they were attached; and the whole of the apparatus of elementary education in Scotland may, therefore, be said to have been till the present year in the hands of the Presbyterian clergy. That they have not been particularly successful in their management is admitted. The examinations of schools by clergymen are celebrated as being shams, laughed at by the more intelligent of the parents of the pupils, and despised by the teachers themselves; all that was necessary on the schoolmaster's part in many cases to insure flattery on the day of examination being to toady sufficiently long and earnestly to his minister.

The Act mends this unsatisfactory state of matters to this

extent, that it substitutes for the ministers and heritors, as the immediate governors and directors of schools, boards composed as in England, of persons elected by the ratepayers in the different parishes. No minister, in future, will be a member of a school board in virtue of his professional character, and a clerical monopoly of the management of national schools will, every day after the Act comes into force, become less and less of a possibility.

But the blunder has been committed in the Scotch, as in the English Act of handing over the "religious difficulty" to the local boards to be fought out there. Disapproving as we do, of education by the State, we must protest against the absurdity, even from the State education point of view, involved in this. The basis of a national system of education ought surely to be the teaching of those things about which all members of the nation agree, to the exclusion of those things about which there is any disagreement. The former are called secular; of the latter, the chief, comprehending, indeed, all the others, is religion. We are all agreed that two and two make four, that London is the capital of Great Britain, that M. Thiers is a Frenchman; and we are also agreed that the teaching of such things is requisite to the making of an intelligent citizen. But we are *not* all agreed that Jesus Christ was the Son of God; we are not even all agreed that a Personal God exists. Surely then, the rational thing for the State—in its capacity as educator—to do, would be to enact that only these things be taught in State-schools, about which all members of the State—all payers of education-rates, that is to say—are agreed, and that that thing about which there is so much disagreement should be left to the disagreeing bodies to teach as best they can. If we are to have a State education at all, it ought to be on the principle that secular teaching be afforded by the schools, and religious teaching left to the churches.

We should not have argued this matter at all, had not the opposition to what is known as the secular theory of education from those who are in favour of what they describe as unsectarian religious teaching been marked by conspicuous ability on the part of those in Scotland who urged it. The Bill which is now an Act, when it was introduced into Parliament, provoked, in so far as it dealt with the religious difficulty, a great deal of controversy, and at least three different views of the relations between religion and national education were urged by three parties. The first and noisiest of these parties consisted mainly of Church of Scotland Tories and Free Church Anti-Unionists, who wished to endow the teaching of Presbyterianism in the national schools of the future as in the parish schools of the past—with them it would now be out of date to argue. Diametrically opposed to these were the secularists, as they were called, who held that the teaching of religion should form no part of the school curriculum—to them, seeing we entirely agree with them, we need not refer.   Between them were the non-sectarians, who urged the exclusion of sectarian formularies from all national schools, and the limitation of religious teaching to the reading of the Bible at definite hours before or after the ordinary work, at which hours attendance should be voluntary. This limited religious teaching was subsequently described as the giving of "religious information."   As there is a possibility that non-sectarianism may be fallen back upon by some of the Nonconformist bodies in England, which, seeing that the English Act has virtually handed over the education of the country to the Church of England, yet despair of the realization of the secular theory—witness the discussions at the recent Conference of the Wesleyan Methodists, who to their cost, as they now experience, followed the lead of the Church in regard to the education question—it may not be amiss to consider the argument brought forward in support of this compromise.   It is thus that Dr. Wallace, well known as one of the foremost of the Liberal party in the Church of Scotland, and a persistent supporter of non-sectarian religious teaching in schools, reasons : " The State has no right, and so has no proper power," he says in one of his speeches on the subject, " to place any creed on any position of advantage as compared with any other creed, because it is bound to be equally the protector of all creeds; and therefore in its State schools, and through its delegate or representative, the State schoolmaster, it cannot conduct its religious education in such a way as to put it in the power of the adherents of any one creed to say that they have been wronged as compared with the adherents of another." In another speech he expresses the same truth in still pithier language : " The perfectly tolerant State has no theology; and having no theology, it can teach none. In its national schools, as represented by its national schoolmasters, it cannot, consistently with its own theory, preach any dogmatic theology whatever."   So far well ; this expresses at once very fully and very fairly the opinions of State-educationists who are also secularists.   But Dr. Wallace further says: " I do hold very strongly that in the State's education of as good citizens as it can get in the circumstances, there must be as good and thorough instruction in religion as possible, both because religiousness of disposition is, to my mind, an essential element in a good man and a good citizen ; and also because I am not able to see how any man can intelligently play his part as a good citizen in the community unless he possesses a competent and intelligent acquaintance with so stupendous a social force as religion must be allowed by all to imply." Again he says, that to "withhold information about so important a phenomenon as religion is anti-educational." He proposes to get out of his difficulty, and to reconcile his views of the State, as perfectly tolerant, with his belief that it is its duty to develop religiousness of disposition in those who are to be its citizens, by having religion taught impartially and historically, and not proselytizingly : "It seems to me that while the State is not at liberty to prescribe any one faith, it is still at liberty to describe all faiths. That is to say, it is able to give impartial information as to what are the constituent elements of the respective faiths that it may be useful for its subjects to know."

In this reasoning there are two fallacies—the one explicit, the other implicit. In the first place it is not possible to give impartial information of the kind—information at all events that would be accepted by the parents of school children as impartial, simply because what are merely beliefs to some people are facts to others. To the ardent theist, for example—we speak, of course, of the ordinary theistic parent—it is as much a fact that there is a God as that there is a place called London or a person of the name of Gladstone ; and he would be as much displeased by a non-sectarian teacher, while in the performance of his duty as a "describer of religion," telling his child that some people believe that there is a God and that other people believe there is not, as he would be by his cautiously stating that it is generally believed that Great Britain is an island. Here, indeed, we come to the great difference between the teaching of religion and the teaching of almost everything else. In the case of non-religious subjects, it is practically possible to separate facts from opinions ; in the case of religion it is not; and both parents and teachers must themselves be converted into comparative theologians before it would be either possible or desirable that children should be taught the rudiments of that most difficult of sciences, comparative theology. It may seem rather hard that religious instruction should be handed over to the sects, but it cannot be helped. At the best, none of the sects would accept impartial religious instruction as any instruction at all ; on the contrary, they would, one and all, consider it worse than instruction given by any opposing sect, and, just as two combatants unite their strength against any one who seeks to separate them, would, by a tacit agreement, endeavour to eradicate the effects of that instruction from the minds of its recipients.

In the second place, Dr. Wallace seems to think that what he calls "religiousness of disposition" cannot be developed in any other way than by the giving of religious information. Is this the case? Is there not such a thing as religion in common life? Are we not told, " Whether, therefore, ye eat or drink, or whatsoever ye do, do all to the glory of God ?" This means, not that we are to mumble an expression of thanks to God with every bite of food or sip of liquid we take—as if the Deity were like a silly girl who has no trust in her lover unless he pours flattery into her ears at every moment—but that we are to do everything, as well as we can, in the belief that the more we struggle to attain our ideal of manhood the more we satisfy the Divine will. In short, does not religiousness of disposition resolve itself ultimately into conscientiousness, and cannot this virtue be communicated in the course of elementary teaching—or rather is it not the essence of the relation between teacher and pupil, of the character both of him that gives and him that gets instruction? The thorough learning of a lesson in geography or history, and the thorough teaching of it, are both moral acts. It is the essence of bigotry to take things on trust, not to search the Scriptures, but to swallow them, or rather certain interpretations of them. It is the essence of good teaching to inculcate the taking of nothing upon trust; the successful pupil is he who disregards impressions and sticks to facts. In other words, it is quite possible that in the schoolroom there may be developed that fidelity to conscience which is the foundation of the highest philosophy and the truest religion, and which will serve, as the best criterion to the pupil, of truth and falsehood when the sects come to tout for his adherence. Under any circumstances, it cannot do other than good to obtain as good teachers as can be had of secular subjects. Good secular teaching means the inculcating of the scientific spirit, the sworn foe of superstition and sectarianism.

Even the confining of religious instruction in national schools to the reading of the Bible at certain hours—for this is what the religious information theory, if reduced to practice, would have come to—would have been a little more statesmanlike, and likely to be somewhat less mischievous than the relegating, as is done in the Act, of the religious difficulty to the School Boards. Eighty-six per cent. of the people of Scotland are Presbyterians, and this enormous majority has the power of erecting a Presbyterian School Board in every parish, and a Presbyterian School Board means the teaching of Presbyterianism in the school or schools of which it has the superintendence. Dr. Begg, the leader of the noisy agitators who during the discussion of the Bill predicted the handing over of Scotland to infidelity unless Presbyterianism formed a part of the ordinary school curriculum, has lately expressed his opinion that under the Act both the Bible and the Shorter Catechism will be taught in the national schools. He is probably right, and both Roman Catholics and Episcopalians, besides Unitarians and members of other non-Presbyterian bodies, will have to pay for the religious teaching of the children of those who have the good fortune to belong to the majority. In spite of this, however, it is by no means certain that there will be no dissensions among the Presbyterian bodies on the subject of education. Although the theological creeds of the Established Church and of the Dissenting Presbyterian bodies are substantially the same, their ecclesiastical differences have been of the bitterest character—their bitterness being, as a rule, in inverse ratio to the magnitude of the matter at dispute. All who are acquainted with the character of Scotchmen know that they will split religious hairs to the end of time, and that they import their differences into ordinary every-day life without scruple, or rather with zeal : there is scarcely a Town Council in the country that is not divided into two perpetually opposing bodies—Churchmen and Dissenters; if a superintendent of police is to be appointed, it is considered of the gravest importance to ascertain whether he is a Free Churchman or an adherent of the Establishment, a Unionist or an anti-Unionist.   School Board elections and the appointment of teachers under the Education Act will simply supply another field for those petty wranglings ; each sect will strive to have as many representatives as possible on the School Board, and although, by means of the cumulative vote, a stray person superior to sectarianism may be elected, his voice will not be heard amid the dissensions of fiery religionists, who, if they cannot get their own ecclesiastical polity taught in the schools, will at least endeavour to have teachers of their own shade of Presbyterian Blue appointed. Thus the religious difficulty, instead of being removed by the Education Act, will simply be made the cause of dissension in every village in Scotland.

Mr. Gladstone has therefore, through his fatal fondness for trusting to majorities however motley their description, rather than to principles however sound, committed a second educational blunder. After handing over the education of England to the Anglican Church, he has handed over the education of Scotland to the Presbyterian. The turn of Ireland and the triumph of the priests ought, according to the new theory of religious equality, to come next, and indeed next session. Last session, when speaking of the Dublin Trinity College Bill, the Premier said : " We have entertained and continue to entertain that belief, we are pledged to the belief, that it is an extreme hardship on that portion of the Irish population who do not choose to accept an education apart from religion that they should have no University open to them in Ireland at which they may obtain degrees; and we hold that this—call it what you like and

disguise it as you may—is the infliction of civil penalties on
account of religious opinions." Let Mr. Gladstone follow this
reasoning to its legitimate conclusions, and he will not only destroy the present national system of education in Ireland with its
united literary, separate religious instruction, but he will stop the
current of legislation which was promising to emancipate the
English Universities from clerical control. There is only one consolation in the event of his proving thus logical—he will ring the
death-knell of his own Government.

We come now to the third problem, which it is claimed for the
Education Act that it solves more or less thoroughly—namely,
the organization of Scotch education. Scotch schools may be
roughly divided into three classes—industrial or ragged-schools,
primary schools, and secondary schools. The two former aim at
teaching much the same thing; the rudiments of knowledge—the
one, to the children of the gutter, whose parents, that is to say,
are unable to pay for their education; and the other, consisting
of parish or private schools, to children whose parents can afford
school fees. Of these we need not speak at length; the absolute
compulsion of the Act will force School Boards to see to it, that
at least what have been called the "knife, fork, and spoon" of
education—namely, reading, writing, and arithmetic, will be given
to every child that comes within their statutory powers. It is
of the last—secondary, or as they are more commonly called,
burgh or public schools—that we would now specially speak.

Of late years these seminaries have stood between the
elementary schools and the Scotch Universities, and have been
the chief feeders of the latter. It is true that many parish
schoolmasters have sent pupils directly to the Universities, but
as a rule, of late at all events, the burgh-schools, like the Edinburgh High School, and the Aberdeen Grammar School, have
played the part of the Rugbys and Harrows of England to the
Scotch counterparts of Oxford and Cambridge. In all these
schools, with the exception of the two we have already mentioned,
not only are the higher branches of a public school education
taught, but also the most elementary subjects; in one room is to
be found a stripling from one of the Normal Schools teaching
the alphabet to thirty or forty children of six or seven years of
age, while in another a graduate of Edinburgh or Aberdeen
University, lectures to three or four lads of sixteen or eighteen
on Thucydides or conic sections. On the whole, this system has
been found to work well, and the Commissioners who some years
ago reported on the burgh-schools of Scotland, spoke most favourably of the manner in which they were conducted, and of their
educational results. But how are they likely to stand under the
new régime ? The Act sets apart eleven burgh-schools—those of

Aberdeen, Ayr, Dumfries, Edinburgh, Elgin, Glasgow, Hadding-
ton, Montrose, Paisley, Perth, and Stirling, and says:—

> "Such schools shall be deemed to be higher class public schools, and
> shall be managed by the School Boards accordingly, with a view to
> promote the higher education of the country."

Undoubtedly could the object aimed at be accomplished—namely,
the converting of these schools into seminaries where secondary
education alone is given, they, from their geographical position,
would serve as places of preparation for the Universities. But
can the School Boards afford so to convert them? The Act
indeed ordains that:—

> "A School Board having the management of any such school, shall
> so far as practicable and expedient, subject to the approval of the
> Board of Education, relieve the same of the necessity of giving elemen-
> tary instruction in reading, writing, and arithmetic to young children,
> by otherwise providing sufficient public school accommodation for such
> elementary instruction, so that the funds and revenues of such higher
> class schools, and the time of the teachers, may be more exclusively
> applied to giving instruction in the higher branches."

But will this be "practicable and expedient" in the eyes of the
members of School Boards in the burghs? Such Boards will have
three kinds of education to manage—industrial, primary, and
secondary, and to impose a rate for the maintenance of all three.
In all probability they will have to erect special schools for the
reception of those children whose parents cannot pay fees, and
whose fees must therefore be paid by the Parochial Boards.
Having incurred this expense, will they venture to burden the
ratepayers with the further cost of erecting distinct primary
schools, especially when there are in their midst institutions which
have hitherto done the work of supplying elementary instruction?
But even supposing that they were liberal enough to erect special
primary schools, where are the revenues for teaching what are
known as the higher subjects to come from? The endowments
of burgh-school teachers, whether from the "common good" of
burghs, or from private bequests, are so small that the income
of these teachers has been mainly composed of fees. The last
too have not been the fees derived from the classes in which the
higher subjects have been taught, but from those lower classes
to be found under the same roof with the pupils in classics and
mathematics; the primary teaching has supported the secondary.
Take away the fees of the lower, and it will be impossible for the
higher to maintain themselves. On this we may hear Dr.
Macdonald, Rector of Ayr Academy, one of the institutions
henceforth to be known as higher class public schools, and, from

his repute and experience, an authority on the subject of burgh schools. "Advanced classes, in Greek and Latin," he says, "must either be conducted out of the fees of the lower classes in the same or in other subjects, or given up altogether. The number attending them will always be so small, even in our best schools, that no fee which could reasonably be exacted would make them self-sustaining."

The higher subjects—we use the word in its conventional sense, for we have no objection to see Greek and Latin removed from their position as the gates to the universities—cannot, therefore, support themselves, and it cannot be expected that school-boards, already burdened with the support of industrial and primary education, will also endow secondary instruction to an extent that would induce men of scholarship to accept the post of a burgh school teacher. The State offers no assistance in the way of endowment. "The day, I fear, is past," says Dr. Macdonald, "when any statesman would propose to grant an endowment of the unproductive subjects from either imperial or local funds;" and he speaks truly. There is absolutely no prospect, therefore, that the Act will elevate the burgh schools. On the contrary, there is rather reason to fear two things, that, with more apparatus for elementary education in the rural districts, the contingents of pupils from these places which used to swell the rolls of burgh schools, and help materially to fill the purses of their teachers, will disappear, and that school-boards, in the interests of economy and of their constituents, will, instead of elevating the schools into higher class schools, make them merely elementary seminaries. The gentleman from whom we have already quoted has nothing better to fall back upon than private beneficence. "There are," he says, "those connected with the respective towns and counties who might have the heart, as they have the means, to do what is so much needed." We sincerely trust that his wishes will be gratified, and that the intelligent liberality of private individuals will do for the secondary education of Scotland what it is doing more and more every day for the universities. But is not this a confession of the complete inadequacy of the State education theory?

The Scotch Education Act of 1872 must, consequently, be considered a very aggravated piece of over-legislation, inconsistent and halting as such, certain to set the sects in Scotland more completely by the ears than they are even at present, another step in the descent of Mr. Gladstone from the healthy plateau of religious equality. That it will prove permanently satisfactory we cannot believe. But it will probably be accepted as a settlement for some time to come by the people of Scotland, who are nauseated with abortive bills and agitations that end in smoke, just as a traveller rests on a stone and is thankful, not because he feels the seat comfortable, but because it is the only one to be had, and he is thoroughly exhausted.

Art. VI.—France: her Position and Prospects.

THE rapidity with which France has recovered from the state of misery and destitution into which she was plunged after the war is the most remarkable phenomenon of the present time. If any prophet could have foretold to incredulous Europe at the period of her twofold desolation and destruction at the hands of the foreigner and her own sons, that within twenty months from the conclusion of peace with Germany and sixteen from the overthrow of the Commune she would be what we now see her, he would have been laughed to scorn as an idle dreamer. *Delenda est Gallia* was the burden of the self-satisfied British journalist; or if she ever might rise from her ruins, it would be by slow and imperceptible steps, and in ways alien to the character of her people, but which they must learn to practise if they would save their country from being blotted from the list of the Great Powers. The complacent moralist was able to connect by rigid links of cause and effect the crimes of France with the expiation she must offer. To what extremes of humiliation and suffering that might need to be carried was, perhaps, admitted to be uncertain, though there were some who did not hesitate to say that the sun of French greatness and prosperity had for ever set. The Latin race must make way for the Teutonic, and France would, ere long, sink to the condition of another Spain—a land of pronunciamientos, in which political power was the plaything of successive factions, each of them ruling for but a brief space, to be dispossessed in turn by its successor, in the same way as it had dispossessed its predecessor.

All the prophets prophesied falsely, and moralists and journalists were alike at fault. The depth of declension to which the country had apparently sunk has only rendered more noticeable her swift ascent. It is evident now that much as France seemed to have suffered, and great as appeared the exhaustion of her resources, there were in her reserves of strength that had not been even tapped. Her army has already been reorganized, so that she is able to present a force which, though far inferior to that of her great rival, is of by no means insignificant proportions, and begins to be formidable, both by discipline and admirable equipments. But the last and most eloquent symptom of French prosperity, as it is the last and most eloquent word of the session of the National Assembly, was the unexampled magnitude and success of her great loan. After making all deductions due to the conditions on which the loan was issued, after reducing by a third or a half, or even by two-thirds, the unprecedented figure of forty milliards, there remains a substantial and brilliant testimony both to the wealth of the country and to the extent of its credit, even among its enemies, which no analysis of circumstances can possibly explain away. Whatever her future may be, there cannot be any doubt that, though burdened with a debt that may well seem too heavy to be borne by any people, France is still capable of taking a prominent position among the nations. The perils before her are very great, and the dangers and difficulties she must encounter are numerous and severe. But in what she has done she has given a pledge of capacity to emerge safely from them all, and resume her place—if not as arbiter of peace and war on the Continent, yet as able to hold her own, and prove no insignificant enemy to any by whom she is likely to be attacked. It is not a little surprising to us that those who were so prompt little more than a year ago to call out *Finis Galliæ*, did not take the trouble to consider what had been the circumstances of the French people in the past. If they had done so, they would hardly have been so ready to predict her early dissolution, or her approaching permanent descent to the lowest place among the nations. For, in truth, this last and worst crisis has only been the last of a series of similar declensions, each of which was followed in turn by an ascent often to a higher pinnacle of greatness and glory than she had before known. During the whole fourteen centuries of its existence the old French monarchy scarcely knew twenty years of consecutive peace. Of all the peoples of Europe the French were most often, and for the longest periods, engaged in fighting; and what is a singular characteristic of their history, they were always apt to allow their enemies to obtain the advantage over them by superior organization, and by the greater assiduity with which they looked after their armaments and methods of military equipment and supply in the intervals of peace. The facile and mobile Frenchman of a thousand years ago was very much what he is to-day. No experience taught him prudence. In the long array of feudal, civil and religious, and foreign wars, by which his country was devastated in turn, he was the sport of impulse, the creature of circumstance, the spoiled child of nature, either jubilant over successes obtained by haphazard bursts of exceeding gallantry, or

downcast and disappointed under the sad reverses of his lot when
Fortune had turned her wheel the other way. Thus it rarely
happened that he employed the brief intervals of peace in making
systematic preparation for the next outbreak of war, though it
was sure never to be very far off at any time. The *inconditum
agmen* of the Gauls, of which Tacitus speaks, was the prototype of
the brave but loosely disciplined forces that fought so gallantly
and unavailingly at Wörth, on Spicheren heights, at Gravelotte;
and last of all—when the bands of discipline were yet further relaxed—on the fatal field of Sedan. The Gaulish hordes of the days
of Cæsar were innocent of discipline, lived by plunder, created
famine wherever they went, and died of hunger on the soil they
were appointed to defend. A like improvidence and recklessness
are observable in the wars with England half a dozen centuries
ago. The English forces that invaded France contrasted in a
marked manner with those by which they were opposed. Froissart
tells us how "the English lords bore along with them all things
necessary," and their well-trained bowmen, able to launch arrows
at two hundred mètres' distance that pierced iron armour, were
but feebly met by the untrained levies of France. These composed a confused gathering of municipal and feudal contingents,
or mercenary strangers, commanded by chiefs independent of
each other. Like Charles XII. of Sweden, Charles V. was
trained by experience of defeat, till he learned from the enemy
by being beaten how in turn to beat. He borrowed the organization of his foes, formed bands of archers on the model of theirs,
disciplined his cavalry, and by prudent changes in other branches
of the service, as well as improvements in tactics, he succeeded
in driving out the English from France. No sooner did his
death occur than the old process of disorganization recommenced.
Charles V. succeeded so far as he did through the energy with
which he inculcated the use of weapons that could be employed
at a distance in preference to those used in hand-to-hand en-
counters. But the great nobles did not love those bowmen who,
when massed together, might be more powerful than lords and
princes. They were disarmed, or only a few of them retained in
certain specially-privileged towns. The old methods of fighting
were to be alone relied upon, skill and training were treated as
of slight account, compared with individual strength and valour,
and the feudal cavalry regained the ascendancy. Soon had
France cause bitterly to rue the neglect of her military organization. Once more at Agincourt, as at Cressy and Poictiers, she was
taught how unavailing were courage and animal vigour, unless
wisely directed by trained intelligence, wielding instruments
prepared for their purpose. The romantic episode of Joan of
Arc followed. But her victories were no more the result of

unregulated enthusiasm than the recent victories of the Germans over the French. It was not by appeals to the fanaticism of religious faith alone that the heroine won her triumphs, but by the careful organization beforehand of the army of deliverance, composed of picked men, thoroughly equipped and disciplined. Profiting by this example, the States-General, in 1430, demanded the institution of a regular and permanent force, and though not realized at the time, their views were carried into effect some years afterwards, when companies of "free archers" were again constituted along with *compagnies d'ordonnance.* An effective force of 27,000 men was thus obtained, and placed under the command of experienced leaders—leaders also whose property made them feel they had "a stake in the country," and were directly interested in its defence. The old story was repeated. The trained forces were found capable of chaining victory to the French standards as their predecessors had done under Charles V. and Joan of Arc. Regular troops now became an institution in France, but owing to the temptations of poverty it was difficult to maintain their full efficiency in the days of piping peace. The tendency always declared itself, ere long, to let them drift away and decay in numbers and efficient training when the pressure of instant danger was removed. Consequently, when war broke out anew, France was unprepared, and as compulsory military service was only imposed upon the nobles, the recruiting of the army became matter of grave difficulty. Francis I. sought to overcome it by forming provincial legions, and Louis XIV. by instituting a regular militia, but these attempts were only partially successful. The efforts of the monarchy to institute a national army had similar issues, and of the 130,000, who under Louis XVI. constituted our effective force—says a recent writer—foreign mercenaries still counted a fifth of the whole. As usual, the French found out their deficiencies in discipline, armaments, and equipments when it was too late. "Part of our infantry," says the same writer, "were armed with pikes, when most of the other foot-soldiers of Europe were equipped with muskets; at Steinkirk the English Guards had flint-guns, when the French Guards still only bore the old matchlocks. At Rosbach we fired in haphazard fashion, each soldier advancing three paces from the ranks for the purpose, when the Prussians were firing in pelotons and battalions. The first State arsenals only date from Francis I., the first ambulances from Henry IV., our first military hospitals from Richelieu, our first military code from Louis XIV., and our first attempts at constructing barracks for the troops from Louis XV. Some of our kings and ministers indeed made great progress with our organization, but the good they did only lasted during their lives. Whenever death took them away their work disappeared along with them, and Louvois is almost the solitary instance of one who left permanent institutions behind him."

These facts and reflections we have preferred to borrow from a French writer, that it may be seen they are not in any way due to insular prejudice; and there can be little doubt that we have here the key to the disasters from which France is now suffering. The war of 1870, in fact, is only another instance of the perils to which the national character and disposition of the French has uniformly, at longer or shorter intervals exposed them for nearly two thousand years. The same excessive self-confidence; the same under-estimate of the capabilities of other nations; the same false security proceeding from the same ignorance of what was passing in the world outside of France, and infallibly resulting in the same unpreparedness that made the country an easy prey to an active and energetic enemy, have been witnessed over and over again, and receive fresh illustration from the German war. The time of trial having exposed the nakedness of the country, there succeeds a period of feverish activity during which excessive energy is put forth to repair the misfortunes due to culpable negligence. This has been the case with France hitherto, and it is the case with her now again. At the present moment she is in the stage of revival which succeeds that of her great depression and defeat, and events have proved that her strength and resources are sufficiently great to render it certain that she will, under moderately-wise guidance, emerge from the clouds that have covered her. Like another Phœnix she rises from her ashes with renewed beauty and freshness, indomitable in resolution, and determined to regain the place in Europe which has been lost to her, not less through the fault of the people themselves than through that of their rulers. Of course no casuistry can excuse the Empire for having left France unprepared, to be desolated and overborne by the foreign invader. The solitary claim which Napoleon III. could put forward to justify his rule was that he kept France in a position worthy of her military renown. If unable to maintain France as a martial power, the Empire was a swindle and a cheat, as events of course proved it to be. Yet it could never have left France thus defenceless if the French people themselves had not been first willing to be deceived. The slaves of names and cries, they never looked below the surface to see if the reality corresponded with the profession. Therefore it was possible for Napoleon to leave the country virtually without protection at the very moment *la grande nation* was priding itself on its prowess, and haughtily putting forward the claim to be accounted the first military State of Europe.

To the period of sure though sad awakening from false dreams succeeds the time of restless energy with a view to undo the past and to reinstate France in a position of pre-eminence. Consequently everywhere in France the one question that occupies the mind of the people is how they may make themselves equal with the Germans. And to that question there have been two main answers given, both articulately and instinctively, by the whole nation. The military organization of Germany, it is of course seen, has made the Germans what they are; therefore, to vie with them, France must, at whatever cost, reorganize her army. But the Germans are powerful as a military people because they are also an instructed people. Therefore, again, it is concluded, France must set her house in order in the matter of national education. The hour of misfortune is the time for penitence and confession of wrong-doing with the nation as with the individual. And France is eager to admit that the work of national instruction has been culpably neglected within her borders during the past. It must no longer be so in the future. Universal compulsory education, like universal military service, is demanded with one heart and one voice. The beginnings have been made in the work of military reorganization by the law on the subject passed by the National Assembly during its past session, and which comes into force on the 1st of January. We confess we are doubtful if this law will do all that is necessary to give the country such a force as it needs. But it applies the principle of universal service to the population; and the large sums voted by the Assembly at the bidding of the Government to enable them to fulfil the task of reorganization that is to be carried forward, prove that nothing in the shape of cost will be deemed too great a burden for the people to bear if only they see a prospect of the fulfilment of the object of their national desires. In regard to education, it is a noteworthy circumstance that the movement in favour of the compulsory principle is now almost co-extensive with the territory. Although the hand of the Roman Catholic clergy lies heavy on the departments, and clerical influence is actively and energetically exerted against all proposals of compulsion, the principle has made great way within a year. Last year the Councils-General were, as a rule, not favourable to it, and were stoutly opposed to secular and gratuitous education. Only in individual and what were accounted very Radical Councils, could a vote be obtained in favour of compulsion. Now the case is wholly otherwise. The majority of the Councils-General that recently held their sittings pronounced for the compulsory principle, though they still hang back from affirming the full Radical programme of compulsory secular and gratuitous education. In the hour

of misfortune France is wont to grow devout, and the influence
of the clergy finds full and free course. But though the mournful pilgrimages to the shrine of Our Lady of La Salette demon·
strate this, the clergy have not succeeded in spreading their
obscurantist, anti-educational ideas. There is, on the contrary,
every reason to believe that France is now prepared for a
more comprehensive Education Bill than she would have accepted
only a year ago. The bill of M. Thiers's Education Minister,
M. Jules Simon, would never have passed the National Assembly last session even if there had been time to discuss it.
The report of the Assembly Commission takes the very heart
out of the measure. The Commission substitute what they call
moral compulsion for actual effective legal compulsion, and
make many other changes—none of them for the better. Now,
however, that the Assembly sees how much in earnest the
country is on the subject, there is some probability of a satisfactory measure being permitted to pass. So that the delay
lamented by the friends of France at the time as a national misfortune in considering the Government Education Bill may not
improbably turn out, after all, to have been for the best.

The unanimity of the French people in favour of an adequate
military reorganization scheme, and the growing force of the
national demand for an effective Education Bill, are both
symptomatic of the earnestness with which the country has set
itself to the task of repairing its broken fortunes. We speak of
the country, meaning, of course, the mass of the population.
Yet we are aware it may be retorted that the country has simply
settled down to its old condition of stolid acquiescence in things as
they are, such as it manifested under the Empire, and now equally
exhibits under a Provisional Republic. All that has been done in
the way of active effort and preparation, it may be urged, has
been accomplished by the National Assembly, or rather by the
Government, in the leading-strings of the remarkable veteran who
plays upon the Assembly as on an instrument, and by playing
off one faction against another is able to mould the action of the
Assembly according to his will. What, it may be asked, has
France gained politically by the institution of a Provisional
Republic? She is still, as before, under personal government. So
long as the will of one man is the most potent force in the
country, initiating measures and only permitting such proposals
of others to become law as are agreeable to himself, what does it
matter though he be called king, emperor, or president? Is not
the National Assembly as deferential to M. Thiers as the Corps
Législatif ever was to Napoleon III.? It is true the Conservatives are numerically the most powerful party in it, but they
have not dared to, or they will not, exercise their power. They

gain nothing by trying a fall with the President, or rather they invariably gain a loss. They were resolved to thwart him in the matter of taxing the raw material, but in the end the energetic old man who sits in the presidential chair compelled them to unsay their professions and vote contrary to their vows. Sometimes the President coquets with the Left Centre and receives their full support, and at others he throws them over, and has his wishes registered for him by the docile Right. In every case the will of one man is the strongest force, and prevails in the end irrespective of all question of the drift of public opinion. So far as there is any intelligent public opinion in France, it pronounced decidedly against taxing the raw material or taking any step to return to the régime of protection. The vast majority of the Chambers of Commerce protested, the press was equally resolute, and manufacturing and mercantile France was almost of one mind, and uttered one voice on the subject. Nevertheless the tax on the raw material was voted by the National Assembly, and the Treaties of Commerce with England and Belgium—the first-fruits of the free-trade policy of the Empire —were "denounced" by the French Government with consent of the Assembly. Nor is that all. What more offensive exemplification of the intolerance of personal rule could be given than the prohibition of public celebrations of the overthrow of the Empire and the advent of the Republic? M. Thiers does not even hesitate to touch the press, and to announce to its writers that they must write in bonds, suppressing offensive comments upon the *personnel* of the Government, and avoiding attacks on the politicians of the Republic. The very efforts of the ministers or of M. Thiers to justify themselves in these proceedings show how feeble and false are their conceptions of liberty. M. Lefranc, the Minister of the Interior, issued a circular to the prefects throughout the country, in which he expounded the motives of the Government in forbidding memorial celebrations of the 4th September. France, said M. Lefranc, had need of rest, that she might bring to a prompt and happy end the important operation of the loan, and so hasten the liberation of the territory and consolidate the Conservative Republic. "You will then forbid," he says to the prefects, as if this were the most natural thing in the world, "all banquets and public gatherings, as well as those that, *though affecting a private character*, would none the less be public, or would run the risk of provoking agitation." The minister further admonishes the prefects to prevent the municipal authorities from giving any encouragement to such manifestations. If they may rightly claim a certain independence as to local matters, yet on questions that concern public order they are the subordinate agents of the Government. The terms of this circular are timid and hesitating. As the Government had resolved upon prohibiting the 4th of September celebrations, it would have been wise to have avoided argument if it had no better reasons to allege than those put forward. But was it entitled to interfere at all in the matter? It may be quite true that the 4th of September is a date of such fatal disaster to France, recalling as it does the defeat of her armies, that good taste should have dictated abstinence from all demonstrations. By glorying in and desiring festively to commemorate the fall of the Empire, which was contemporaneous with the defeat of Sedan, the French show the ineradicable vice of their character, their subordination of country to party, their readiness to forget the most terrible national misfortunes if they can glory over a defeated opponent. Wise Frenchmen were more inclined to observe the 4th as a day of mourning than a time for festive rejoicing. But that does not justify the interference of the Government with what no necessity connected with breaches of the peace or disturbances of public order. In this M. Thiers certainly acted as a personal ruler who set light store by the liberties of his subjects, and the ministerial attempt to justify the step must be proclaimed an egregious failure. The arguments employed only prove that the Government does not understand the true limits of public liberty. The assertion that it was desirable to show to France that a Republic can maintain order as well as any other form of Government is not convincing, and the admirers of M. Thiers had better fall back upon the plea that in the difficult circumstances of the moment a mistake should not be hardly judged. That a mistake was committed it seems to us has been practically admitted by the Government itself. It gave way before the threatened mutiny of M. Gambetta and his Republican followers. Not that there has been any open withdrawal of M. Lefranc's circular. So far from that, he wrote another letter when the celebration of the 22nd, instead of the 4th, was first spoken of. The second was virtually a repetition of the first. Very soon there were symptoms of gathering Republican wrath. M. Gambetta's organ, the *République Française*, declined to recognise the letter, which had nevertheless been sent to the various Prefects, as genuine, and persisted in alleging it was a forgery, as it had not been reproduced in the *Journal Officiel.* M. Gambetta himself indicated a like disposition. He was indeed compelled by his position to take action. He is much wiser than his noisy followers, but with a view to the future he must retain authority over his party, and occasionally do things of which he may not himself approve to humour them. Here, however, there was no doubtful action to be done. If the Republican leader acquiesced in such flagrant suppression of the right of meeting together and talking on national affairs, he would surrender everything. So M. Gambetta felt; and means were taken to suggest to the Government that while it might insist on preventing public gatherings that would be dangerous to order, it ought not to interfere with private dinner parties. The Minister of the Interior, under, doubtless, higher inspiration, accepted the way of escape thus opened up for him. He allowed it to be intimated that the Government had no intention of meddling with private meetings, notwithstanding the statement in the ministerial circular regarding gatheringsthat might "affect" a private character. M. Thiers evidently saw that this was a case in which it was necessary to some extent to give way. And the Government yielded with as much grace as possible, and thus M. Gambetta scored a triumph. There have been dinner parties on the 22nd of a private character, which in all except the name were public banquets, and at which much Republican rhetoric has been vented.* As it happens, the Government has avoided a danger by knowing when to yield at the right moment; and the manner in which it gave way saves it from loss of prestige in consequence with the multitude. Only those who scan matters a little closely perceive that M. Thiers has confessed that he is not infallible, and that his too zealous attempts to maintain order are apt to mislead him into stretching too far his authority as Provisional Dictator, which in fact he is so long as the form of France's constitution is not decided upon. It would have been wiser not to have interfered at the first, or, if it were deemed really dangerous to allow Republican eloquence to have free vent, to have left open the loop-hole for evasion which has been at length admitted when suggested by others.

In regard to the threatened attack on liberty of the press, we doubt if any better case can be made out for the ministry. We have been told, indeed, by the correspondent of a Paris paper, that M. Thiers was much annoyed at the credit given by the public to the rumour of an intention to institute a severe régime of avertissements and suppression against the press. He is stated to have declared, in talking on the subject, that he was, as he had always been, friendly to liberal principles; and in regard to the *Gaulois*, the paper specially inculpated, he had, at a council of the ministry, urged that its publication should not be interfered with.

---

* Although this is literally true, the most important of the expected banquets—at Paris and Chambery—were forbidden at the last moment, to the surprise and dismay of the Democrats. M. Gambetta, who was to have presided at Chambery, wisely yielded to the orders of the authorities, though protesting against them. The banquets that did come off—at Angers and elsewhere—were of minor moment. M. Gambetta's triumph is thus not so great as was expected.

Yet, at the very time he said this, the President indicated the
narrow limits within which he would confine freedom of the
press. He would permit absolutely free discussion, but the
organs of the press must not be guilty of abuse of public men,
as thereby authority would be brought into discredit, and disorder receive occasion to triumph. The crimes committed in
the name of order are as numberless as those done in the name
of liberty. No doubt order is a necessity for France—for its
credit, for the restoration of its wasted energies, for the repair of
its resources, for the success of the loan, and for the liberation of
the territory from the invader. But order without liberty is not
an end of which even a Conservative Republic can be proud. In
prohibiting the 4th and 22d of September meetings, in threatening
a war of repression against the press, and in the little incident at
Trouville, when the M M. Errazzu were arrested and condemned to
exile from France for shouting *Vive l'Empereur*, we see a tendency towards a maintenance of order by ways and means
utterly inconsistent with the education of a people in and for the
enjoyment of constitutional liberty. This much must be admitted against the President and his advisers.

Do we then allow that M. Thiers is simply another in the series
of personal rulers in, and over France? Is he, too, one of those
providential men who are always forthcoming when France requires them, and is he only continuing the Empire and its ways
under the name of a Republic? Although this is the accusation
the French Conservative papers bring against the President, we
should be loth to be compelled to believe it true. If it be, and
if no better is to be looked for, France must give up the attempt
to solve the problem of self-government. If at the very moment
she receives power over her own destinies, and the national
sovereignty is exerted, it is only exercised that she may place
herself and her people in bonds again to the arbitrary will of
one man, however serviceable and gifted, then indeed the
French nation must be declared incapable of free institutions,
and fit only to be ruled by a despot. But this is far from being
an accurate description of the state of France, of what she has
done, or of what she desires to do. We do not deny that M. Thiers
is often inclined to take too much upon him. He has repeatedly
stretched his influence with the Assembly, till it seemed as if it
would give way, though he has hitherto succeeded in all he has
undertaken. He practically declines to abide by the terms of
the Rivet constitution, by which the President was to hold aloof
from personal interference with the Assembly's debates. He is
ever eagerly rushing to the tribune to deliver impassioned
harangues ; and either by his eloquence, or by threats of resignation, he manages to control alike his enemies and his friends.
The history of the Assembly during its last session, from

November to August, demonstrates that the personal element is
much too strong a factor in the government of France to admit of
perfect constitutional liberty. But in judging of M. Thiers in
relation to the government and the political prospects of France,
it must not be forgotten that the present is avowedly a period of
provisional institutions. The last of her long series of revolutions
stripped France of all definitive constitution and form of rule.
She was without a ruler to represent the collective interests of
the nation, to be the organ of the national sovereignty, and while
representing the country in the view of foreign States to maintain
peace and order at home. Yet at the very moment she was
thus situated, the territory was overrun by a foreign foe, with
whom it was absolutely necessary to negotiate in order that terms
of peace and their faithful execution might be arranged for.
It was when in this naked, necessitous condition, bleeding at every
pore from the wounds inflicted on her, that the nation was appealed
to, to declare its will. There was this once a fair and genuine
appeal made to the country, to say what it wanted, and the
country responded by the election of a National Assembly, the
great majority of whom were monarchists. What France then
thought of was present relief. Peace must be made with the
enemy on any conditions, and as the Republic was identified
with war *à outrance* it was natural, under the reaction produced
by the failure of the Republic to do the impossible, and by the
sufferings under which the nation groaned, that a strongly conservative majority should be elected. The monarchists had the
very best chance in the concourse of circumstances of all that was
most favourable to them, that could be possible, and if they dared
not venture to vote a monarchy then it was certain they would
not dare to do so afterwards. They did not venture. The
Assembly made peace with the Germans at a heavy cost of
territory and treasure, and in order that France might not be
left utterly disorganized, it was essential that some form of
government for the administration of her affairs should be instituted. The monarchists, we have seen, could not venture to vote
a monarchy in face of the parties opposed to it, and the Republicans in turn had no chance of establishing a Republic in face
of the numerically powerful, if morally weak Conservative opposition. There was no possibility of course of the Empire, whose
déchéance was solemnly pronounced, and which was made the
scapegoat to bear away not only its own sins, but the whole inherited guilt of the French people into the wilderness of exile.
In such conditions the sole rational, as indeed the only possible
course was to declare a truce of parties, in order that a provisional
Government might be established which should be of no party, but
should devote itself to the great task of ruling well the country
so as to reconstitute its lapsed and broken administration, restore

its sunken credit, redevelop its material resources, give the nation time to reflect, and, as it were, retake possession of itself, and finally to prepare the means for the liberation of the territory from foreign occupation. This was the meaning of the celebrated pact of Bordeaux. That was a compact that proclaimed France more precious than all the parties in it, the national life of more moment than the ascendancy of any single faction, and patriotism a virtue greater than partisanship. M. Thiers received in solemn charge, as Chief of the Executive, the provisional régime that was consequently appointed, and undertook not to use his influence to further the ends of any party, but to look only to the interests of the nation, so that when the territory was liberated and the hour for the establishment of a definitive constitution had come, he might hand back the country to the Assembly somewhat healed of its wounds, somewhat revived from its deep declension, and somewhat restored to the possession of national life. When the Assembly some months afterwards made the Chief of the Executive, President of the Republic, fencing him round by the provisions of the Rivet constitution, that did not imply the termination of the pact of Bordeaux by the establishment definitively of a Republic, though the transaction was of a somewhat anomalous character. For it is hard to see how there can be a President of a Republic if there be no Republic of which he is the President. Nevertheless, the Conservative majority did not acquiesce in the Republic, but merely in its provisional institution as an avowedly temporary form of government, since some Government was indispensable. In fact the Assembly had no power to establish a definitive Government, for it was appointed itself for special ends, on the fulfilment of which it would naturally fall to be dissolved, in order that the country might anew take the decision of its destinies into its own hands.

It is easy, of course, to see that in all this there were the fertile seeds of confusion and dissension. And though nothing can excuse the undignified attitude of the Conservatives, the unworthy part they have often played in their numerous intrigues, their want of courage in maintaining their own principles, and the entire absence of political instinct among them, they have unquestionably been placed in difficult circumstances. The consequence has been those ever-recurring faction fights at Versailles between the Left and Right centres, between Radicals and Republicans on the one hand, and Legitimists, Orleanists, and Conservatives generally on the other. The scenes in the Assembly during any lively debate have been most discreditable, and if the conduct of affairs had been left wholly to be determined by the Assembly, the position of France at this moment could not have been what we see it. The Assembly, in fact, needed a master ; and it found one in the President of the Republic. The circumstances being what they were M. Thiers could not have discharged the primary duty he owed to his country, if he had shrunk from showing himself willing and able to master it.

The duties, both of the National Assembly and of the President and his ministers, were determined for them by the circumstances and wants of the country. What the country required, and what they have given her, was first of all peace, then security for life and labour, or the maintenance of order ; and finally a prudent administration of public affairs, so that the nation might repair its losses and have the opportunity afforded it of reconstituting and reorganizing its forces and developing its resources. There was here a sufficiently wide field for all parties to work in for the common good. Conservatives and Liberals, Legitimists and Republicans, Orleanists and Radicals, Left Centre and Right Centre—all sections in fact of political opinion, had scope and verge for the free exercise of energy in pursuit of these great ends. This was the policy recommended by the condition of the nation to men of all parties, if only they were patriots more than partisans. Pursued patiently to its legitimate issues, the Government and the Assembly would be able after a time to present France to herself, delivered from the foreigner, and reorganized in independent possession of her restored forces, when the sole duty she would have to discharge would be to settle the definitive régime under which she would choose to remain. How has the Assembly, how has the Government—which mainly means M. Thiers—fulfilled these important functions?

It is to the last session of the Assembly we must mainly look, to the conduct of the Government and the results of the deliberations of the deputies during it, for answers to these questions. Important work was doubtless done before, in the interval between the elections and last autumn. The Government had to face and put down the insurrection of the Commune, and however we may condemn sundry incidents connected therewith, and the exceeding harshness exhibited subsequently—as the Satory executions, for example, alike impolitic and injurious—it did its work effectively. If blunders were committed at the time, and if afterwards a certain stolid bloodthirstiness has been manifested, still let us bear in mind the exceeding gravity and difficulty of the situation. It is easy to pick faults and flaws in the attitude and dispositions of the executive. But in a struggle of life and death—and nothing less than national life and death were the issues—even the wisest of men might possibly do sometimes what he ought not to have done, and omit to do what he ought to have done. The task imposed by the

second siege of Paris was no matter of child's play, and it was
fulfilled. At least that much must be scored, with whatever
minor circumstantial abatements, to the credit of M. Thiers and
his colleagues. The enterprise attempted by the Commune
was directly at war with the existence of France as a constituted
nation. As Mazzini has shown, it would have split up France
into innumerable petty and individually independent centres,
whose existence would necessarily have overborne and suppressed
any possible collective life of the nation. Therefore there could
be no reorganization of France as a nation until the Commune
was got out of the way. It has been customary to inveigh against
M. Thiers and the Government because when the first attempts
at insurrection were made, they precipitately left Paris for Versailles. But it was well for France that they did. Only thus
could the national sovereignty of France have been preserved.
Had the Assembly remained with the Government in Paris, they
would both have infallibly been overpowered by force. That
done, no legal centre of authority would have existed. The
representatives of the people would have been overthrown, and
no representation of the whole of France would have survived.
Arbitrary force would have been established and made supreme,
as in all previous revolutions ; and the end must have been either
anarchy or despotism, as always happened in like circumstances
before. By the transfer of the Assembly and the Government
from Paris to Versailles, all that was avoided. Even although
there was insurrection in the capital, there was a centre of authority, a representation of the national sovereignty, outside the
capital. And as that was able to assert its supremacy and put
down its opponents, France was saved from the lawlessness or
the despotism which, alternately or together, had characterized
her revolutionary movements hitherto. Therefore it is, we say,
the existing Government accomplished a great work for France,
whatever may have been the particular and individual faults of
which it was guilty. To do this, to overthrow the Commune,
regain possession of Paris, and after that make such arrangements with the German conqueror as gave France the chance
of settling to quiet and steady industry, were no slight
achievements. We shall not attempt to follow the course of
the complicated and frequent negotiations with the Germans in
arranging the terms of the treaty, and after that was settled, in
negotiating for such modifications as might be obtained in regard
to the mode of payment of the war indemnity and the time of
evacuating the occupied provinces by the German army. These
negotiations were continued during the past session, and the
close of them then, though not bringing much benefit to France
in the shape of relaxation of the conqueror's harsh conditions,

has been a work that has fully employed the energies and required the vigilance and astuteness of the French Ministry. Passing from these matters, we come to look at the work done by the National Assembly during the session that was closed early in August. What are we taught by the doings and proceedings of the Assembly during its nearly nine months' session, and the doings and proceedings of the Government in connexion therewith in regard to the present political position and the future prospects of France?

The meeting of the National Assembly last December was eagerly looked forward to in the hope that it might bring to a close the excitements of party feeling and the frivolities of public discussion that too much occupied the recess. Would the Assembly prove moderate and wise enough to disengage the politics of France from the vain collisions of alternately aggressive and desponding factionists, in order to settle the view of the country upon the real interests that concerned her, and the due care for which was essential to the life of the nation? The speech in which M. Thiers opened the session was pitched in the right tone. The President, nothing concealing nor setting down aught in malice, strove to lay before the deputies a true picture of the state of the nation and its affairs, that thereby they might know the work that lay before them. It was, as M. de Mazade said at the time, a "serious, minute, and accurate exposition of the unfortunate condition of our country, of the trials it must still endure, and the difficulties that remain to be overcome; it was the courageous work of a faithful and indefatigable patriot who for ten months had borne the burden and heat of the day, who could certainly claim the honour of having been the first workman in this national reconstruction, undertaken amidst the double misery of foreign invasion and civil war—who felt that to bring this work to its end, 'there was still necessary much labour, fidelity, and devotion.'" M. Thiers sketched the various tasks in connexion with the national finances, military organization, and practical administration that required to be accomplished. Were not these the really important political questions offering a common field for action to all honest patriots? On this ground all the deputies might unite. Other questions that served as means of division must be held in reserve. In treating the one class, with the settlement of which was associated the fate of France, the deputies could, whatever their individual opinions, work together for the common good. But in order to that, they must consent to adjourn the others till a more convenient season. In them, as the source of national divisions, lay the root of danger. Too precipitate attempts to deal with them would only load the country in strife, possibly in civil war. That is to say, the source

of France's serious perils was French parties and their controversies. As M. Thiers himself said to the Assembly, "The
country in its totality, with a few slight exceptions, is wise; it
feels its disasters, and desires to repair them. . . . . Parties alone
would not be wise; from them alone is there anything to fear,
from them alone is it necessary to put you on your guard, and
against them you must arm yourselves with coolness, with
courage, with energy." Here the President put his finger upon
the real root of national peril. The successive revolutions that
have rolled over France, each leaving some smaller or larger
faction as its heritage, have bestowed a multitude of contending
parties on the country, each of which regards itself as the sole
source of salvation for France, and each of which is prepared to
vindicate its right to rule by force. In the turmoils and faction
fights occasioned by the conflicting claims of these opposing sections, the national interests that are common to all, for which
all ought to labour and to sacrifice, are pushed aside, while men
inflame themselves with party passions and rush furiously at
each others' throats to the sound of their respective war-cries.
No accommodation between them is possible except by sinking
the subjects that divide them from each other. Unfortunately
the past session of the Assembly has too often made this manifest.
At its very outset the storm was raised during a discussion on the
Budget by one of the deputies proclaiming from the tribune that
in royalty alone was there hope for France. This of course was
a direct defiance of the Republicans, who in turn shouted for
their favourite form of rule, and proclaimed the eternity of the
Republic, while a third section kept exclaiming for the Provisional Government. These fiery disputes, adorned by much
fierce rhetoric, have frequently recurred at Versailles, with the
result of exciting still further the passions of partisans and
wasting public time in profitless and mischievous wrangling, in
presence of the practical problems of the hour—the Budget, with
its enormously swollen dimensions, requiring an increase of 200
million francs in new taxes, the organization of the army, the
position of the Bank of France, the question of primary instruction, and, besides, the various matters of immediate concern
arising from day to day, that could be included in no programme.
While parties disputed, and the deputies were inflamed with
mutual antagonisms, France remained burdened and bound.
The foreigner was within her gates, and his armies had possession
of her territory. Yet even that does not suffice to allay the fury
of partisan hatreds, which burst forth at intervals in uncontrolled
volume, gathering force as they flow.

Such being the situation and the temper of parties in the
Assembly, there can be little doubt France has benefited from

the ascendancy which M. Thiers has been able to maintain over the deputies. Although we may chide the Right Centre for their inconsistencies in allowing themselves to be determined to courses of which they disapproved through the influence of M. Thiers, they very well knew that he was indispensable to the country. The threat of resignation always sufficed to bring them to his feet, even when they were most recalcitrant. The most lamentable consequence of this ascendancy has been the reimposition of protectionist duties—though the President disavows any wish to return to the old economical régime—and the termination of the commercial treaties. For the sake of France herself it must be regretted that she has abandoned the experiment of free trade. The results of her retrogression are not encouraging. Of course the duties on the raw material cannot be generally imposed so long as the country is bound by treaties with foreign States, and the new tariff, as the *Times* has pointed out, is mainly occupied with trifles such as gingerbread, cock's-feathers, and percussion-caps. In consequence they will yield a merely nominal sum this year, and the principle of free trade has been violated without any advantage in return. Not only so, but the general trade of France suffers as well; and as there are eighty-eight million francs of a deficit in the yield of the indirect taxes during the first half of the year alone, it will be a desperate work to balance the Budget. These probable results of a return to protection were pointed out at the time of the prolonged and repeatedly renewed debates in the Assembly on the subject. But the President was deaf to reason and remonstrance. At first the Assembly declined to obey the word of command, though backed by threat of resignation. But M. Thiers knows how to gain his ends by delay. The Assembly that refused the raw material taxes in January voted them in July. The Right Centre, indeed, which at the former date approved them, refused to vote them at the latter; but meanwhile the President had conciliated the Left, which before opposed, and with their assistance, though contrary to every principle previously professed by them, the pertinacious old man triumphed, and consummated the most grievous blunder of his presidential career. M. Thiers has also managed to have his own way in regard to military organization. The Assembly was bent upon universal compulsory service; M. Thiers was equally resolved upon laying the foundations of a thoroughly trained and efficient selected army. The one side trusted to numbers and patriotic enthusiasm, the other laid stress upon organization and long training. What has been actually decided upon is a compromise between the two, but a compromise in which the favourite ideas of the President will have scope for application. It is yet too

soon to judge the result. In consequence of the diverging views
between the President and Assembly there have been often
misunderstandings and quarrels between them. But necessity
has been laid upon both to bring these speedily to a close.
Each feels the other necessary to it. Born together, they cannot
be parted without mutual loss. The Conservative majority
dread a dissolution, for they are aware they will never be in such
numbers in a new Assembly as they muster in this one. The
Provisional Government of M. Thiers again, in the peculiar state
of the country which gives him such extraordinary powers, must
be greatly modified by a dissolution and the election of a new
Assembly. The present Assembly and the President have thus
common interests in each other; and however often the several
parties into which the deputies are divided may have desired the
overthrow of M. Thiers, or the curtailment of his power, they
have hesitated when the time of action came, as doubtful whether
in slaying their opponent they would not also slay themselves.
Thus the session has passed without a crisis. The President has
been skilful in playing off one party against another, and in
taking advantage of each in turn as it suited his purposes. In
doing this he has not acted unbecomingly or unworthily, but has
only carried out consistently the view that in his official capacity
he is of no party, but above all parties; that it is France, and
not any particular way of governing France, that ought to occupy
his thoughts; that he was bound to repair the ruins of the country,
and look to the maintenance of the national life and the national
sovereignty over herself, and that if he did this it would little
matter by whose aid he did it—whether of Radicals or Conser-
tives, Legitimists or Republicans.

What will be the upshot of the whole? At the present moment
there is a lull in the political struggle. Immediately after the
vacation began M. Thiers went to Trouville to study, and occupied himself hourly with the state of the country, and how to
keep it in the paths of prosperity while making diligent prepa-
tion for the possible eventuality of war. The deputies dispersed
to their own homes, and continued to testify their love for the
President by sending him multitudinous presents of game. The
Councils-General, though precluded from the discussion of politics, have exhibited a decided leaning in favour of the Conservative
Republic, and have conducted their debates in a sober business
fashion that augurs well for the future. These gatherings were
reinstituted by the Assembly, in the hope on the part of the
majority that they would show themselves Conservative in a
party sense, as under the Empire, whereas they have been
much more anxious that order and the interests of the nation
should be guarded, than desirous of furthering the prospects of

any particular party. The future of the Councils-General deserves to be watched with interest as furnishing the nucleus of local self-government. Public curiosity followed M. Thiers to Trouville, and vigilant correspondents surrounded him at every turn, all eager to find something of personal circumstance to report regarding him. But though the public has been inquisitive about the President, it has manifested too much of its old apathy in reference to the national affairs. It is this want of a healthy public opinion in France which is the source of greatest anxiety as to its future. Considering how but a short time ago it was exposed to the miseries of foreign invasion, and that part of the territory is still occupied by a foreign force; considering that it has suffered the horrors of civil war, that nearly its whole male population was under arms, and the ordinary commercial and industrial life of the nation was interrupted and arrested, it is marvellous how much has been accomplished in the way of restoration. Industry in all its branches has been reorganized, and happily the blessing of an abundant harvest has been added to France. The attitude of the people in at once setting themselves to repair the ravages of the past, and in manifesting how great their resources still are, inspired confidence in its future to outsiders; and we have therefore seen its credit established on a higher pinnacle than ever. It is but fair to state also, that French commerce has emerged with credit from its recent sore trials. It has manifested a scrupulous respect for its engagements which does it honour, and the unhesitating loyalty of the State to the engagements and contracts of its predecessors in the Government deserves to be equally signalized. To the foreign war succeeded the war of the Commune, and the Republic of M. Gambetta was followed by the Conservative Republic of M. Thiers; but throughout all changes the French nation has respected its various obligations. All this is matter for pride and congratulation to Frenchmen ; and were there only visible a more active and energetic public opinion, intelligently occupied with the great questions of the hour, and training itself to become capable of guiding the deputies who represent the nation, and influencing the Government, which is too prone to control the deputies, there might be much less anxiety for the future than we see cause for at the present moment. It is the culpable indifference of the mass of the bourgeoisie that gives the opportunity to parties to seize the direction of the national affairs whenever they have force enough at their disposal to make the venture. Had there been a firm and general expression of intelligent opposition to the imposition of the duties on the raw material, for example, M. Thiers must have given way. As it was, the opposition was confined exclusively to those directly concerned in trade and commerce, which enabled M. Thiers to denounce the petitions of deputations that came to Versailles to protest against recurrence to protection as instigated by selfish motives. The same fatal apathy and indifference to political considerations and to the state and prospects of the country gives the opportunity for that personal government which some of the Conservative newspapers declare is illustrated by M. Thiers as strongly and decidedly as ever it was by the Empire. In fact, so long as it continues, so long as the expression of the will of the nation directly through an educated public opinion, and indirectly through the press, is lacking or is only feeble and fitful, it is impossible for the government of the country to be carried on without an infusion of the personal element.

M. Thiers is well aware of this, and perhaps is not loth to exercise the influence which it is thus open to him to claim. He has done many things, as we have seen, that cannot possibly be reconciled with any view of constitutional liberty. The tendency to fetter the press, the prohibition of the 4th and 22nd of September celebrations, the importance attached to the Errazu manifesto at Trouville, the dismissal or "retirement" of Count Stoffel, and his action regarding the raw materials and the treaties of commerce are all so many exemplifications of a leaning towards the despotism of personal rule which no one denounced with greater energy in former days than the historian of the Consulate and the Empire. M. Thiers is reported to have said, not long ago, to one of his many "interviewers," that France had now passed beyond the phase of English Constitutionalism, and had entered upon the stage of American Republicanism. Surely this was one of the President's dry strokes of humour. The one grand merit, however, which may be fairly claimed for M. Thiers is, that he has known how to keep aloof from party intrigues. After the Assembly was first constituted, the Conservatives fancied they would, by supporting the Chief of the Executive, whose Orleanist proclivities of a former period they counted on, win an easy victory for themselves, and that by-and-by events might be so moulded that the *ancien régime*, or some branch thereof, should be restored. M. Thiers has refused throughout to lend himself to their designs. He was under obligation to try to heal the wounds of France, to co-operate with the National Assembly in obtaining the deliverance of the country from foreign occupation, and to maintain the Provisional Republic as provisional until the irresistible tendencies of events and the declared purpose of the nation pointed plainly towards a definitive form of Government. He was bound therefore to stand apart from all factions, to work with or to guide all parties in the tasks he and they had undertaken to do in common, but to abstain from

encouraging one or other of them in the promotion of principles
or projects that would excite division and let loose the dogs of
war. It is natural, it was indeed inevitable, that in doing this
he should make use of parties without committing himself wholly
to them. Only so could he combat the influence exerted for party
ends and to forward Monarchical or Republican intrigues. So
far then from regarding this playing fast and loose with parties as
a serious crime, it appears to us that in sometimes leaning on the
Right, and at another turning for support to the Left—not, observe,
in furtherance of the peculiar political and party ends of either,
but in order to get the essential work of the country done—
M. Thiers has honestly fulfilled his duty, as he has assuredly
displayed marked dexterity and astuteness.

For eighty-three years now France has been a prey to successive sections of revolutionists; that is to say, she has, during
that period, been ruled by Governments, each of which was
born of and was more or less supported by physical force. Not
one of the twelve different Governments that may be counted
during the period from 1789 to our own day, has been called
to rule by the spontaneously expressed wish of the nation.
They have all been usurpers, ruling by force and not by right;
and, striking the average, each of them we find has endured
only seven or eight years, when they were overthrown by the
same means as originally raised them to power. Besides the
attempts that were successful we need, to obtain a distinct and
adequate idea of the rôle which force has played in modern
French history, to include also the insurrections that failed—the
war of La Vendée, the attempt by the Girondins, the risings of
Lyons and Toulon, the rising of the Commune against the Convention on the 9th Thermidor, the Jacobin insurrection on the
2nd Prairial, and the Royalist one on the 12th Vendémiaire.
Then there were the Strasburg and Boulogne attempts later,
several futile risings after 1848, and during the existing Republic those of the 31st October, the 10th January, and last and
worst of the 18th March. Thus in all there have been fifteen or
twenty unsuccessful resorts to arms, and these added to the
successful revolutions, give us, in eighty years, no fewer than
thirty different insurrections, coups d'état, civil wars, &c., or an
average of one every three years. Three years of quietness or
repose has, during the period since the First Revolution, been
the average granted to France, and these were often troubled
years; for the plots and conspiracies that have proved abortive are
innumerable. Verily force has been enthroned in France, and
as it was arbitrary force, it had no stability, and was accompanied
by acts of violence and by crimes of the most sanguinary and
often tragic character. Can we wonder then at the instability

of French institutions, the restlessness of the French people, or
the anarchy and lawlessness to which the country has been a
prey ?   That, notwithstanding all, France should still stand with
unexhausted resources able to ask a remedy for the ills to which
the body politic is heir, is the most eloquent proof of her yet
unconsumed vitality.

We must draw rapidly to a close, but before doing so we
shall consider briefly this question of a remedy, and whether the
symptoms actually observable give any promise of a definitive
term having been put to past disorders and reigns of terror, to
material compulsion generally as the supremacy of arbitrary force.
France is no exception to other countries, and in order to have
stable institutions these must have historical roots, must have
grown out of the circumstances and conditions of the nation, and
must be capable of being the organs of the national will and
sovereignty.   The conditions under which they can be so are
the existence of an active public opinion, freedom of the press,
and representative responsibility.   Now these tests will exclude
the various forms of Monarchy and Imperialism.   Aristocratic
institutions have no longer any roots in French soil, and the
attempt to galvanize them into a feeble life-in-death in presence
of furious opposing parties, can only end in disaster and civil
war.   The Revolution, or rather the successive Revolutions of
eighty years, have utterly destroyed the possibility of a highly
organized society on the basis of aristocracy, after two centuries
of absolute monarchy had previously undermined it.   Besides,
any form of Monarchy could only now be imposed upon France
by force, and what is needed is a régime resting upon right.
The disease of French politics has been the employment of force,
and it is not curable upon the homœopathic principle of *similia
similibus curantur*, even though in only homœopathic proportions.   The same objection of course holds against any form of
Cæsarism, or military despotism, even though resting on the
palpable fiction of a vain *plébiscite*.   "The military régime,"
says Paul Janet, "bears within itself the principle of dissolution ;
condemned to war it perishes by war, and born of despotism it
begets anarchy."   If it be retorted that on several occasions the
country evidently desired the régime established since the Revolution, this may be admitted ; but the party that gained the
ascendancy went far beyond the warrant it had from the nation,
and sought to impose its own ideas on the latter without consulting it.   Thus, for example, as Janet says, in 1814 the country
certainly wished a reconciliation with the Bourbons, but it did
not wish the ascendancy of the aristocratic and sacerdotal idea.
In 1830 it wished the government of the middle classes, but *not*
a close oligarchy.   In 1852 it wished order, and perhaps did

not greatly love the Republic, but it did *not* wish military despotism. And on the 4th September, 1870, it wished a great effort in the national defence, but *not* that it should be made in the interest exclusively of any particular party. Perhaps the only period during the whole eighty-three years since 1789 in which France was mistress of herself, was from 1848 till the *coup d'état* in 1851—a sufficiently brief interval.

What was essayed then, France desires to see permanently established now. It is felt that, as M. Thiers said once, the Republic is the form of government that least divides the country. There is not in the rural districts any special preference for the Republic in the abstract, far less any vehement passion for it; but the experiences of the recent Councils-General prove that the rural districts acquiesce in the Conservative Republic as capable of maintaining order and as giving the opportunity of self-government. In the cities, again, the Democratic Republican party will submit to the maintenance of order by a Republic when they would revolt against the same work if attempted by a Monarchy. But if it seem evident that the Conservative Republic, such as France has provisionally instituted at the present time, is the most suitable form of government in the circumstances of the country, it does not follow that it is desirable to proclaim its definitive establishment immediately. At the moment we write, we observe a statement in the French papers, that as soon as the National Assembly comes together after the vacation, a scheme will be tabled by a group of the Left Centre embracing four propositions:—1. The definitive proclamation of the Republic; 2. The appointment of a Vice-President; 3. The creation of a Second Chamber; and, 4. The gradual and triennial renewal of the Assembly. This project, the *Patrie* says, has been submitted to M. Thiers, who is prepared to accept the second and third proposals, but wishes the adjournment of the first and the suppression of the fourth. This is very probable. Considering the advanced age of the President, it is obviously desirable that the chances of disturbance on occasion of his death should be guarded against by the selection of a Vice-President. We are doubtful of the feasibility of a Second Chamber in France. The materials for it are not forthcoming. However, if the Conservative interests of France will be conciliated by this step, there is no reason why the experiment should not be tried, so long as it is not attempted to call into being a feeble copy of an hereditary peerage. If by this means the Conservatives may be reconciled to the Republic, the experiment is worth trying, even though it should result, as it probably would, in the creation of a Senate that would have the name without the reality of power. It would, however, be un-

fortunate to raise the question of the definitive form of Government in the present Assembly, which was elected for quite other
purposes.   It will have enough to occupy it during the coming
session without that.   A hard task lies before it in preparing the
Budgets for 1873 and 1874, so as to make both ends meet, in perfecting the military reorganization scheme, in watching the commercial and economical interests of France in connexion with the
proposed new treaties of commerce, which we are glad to observe
the Government feel it will be necessary to negotiate, and last,
though perhaps most difficult of all, in passing a satisfactory Education Bill.   This will excite ecclesiastical and democratic passions
to the uttermost. The respective champions of secular and religious
instruction will fight the question out along the whole line, and we
wish we saw France well through the conflict.   To what intensity
of political passion this subject may give occasion, may be
estimated from what has lately passed at Lyons, where the re-
instatement of ecclesiastical teachers illegally dispossessed of their
offices, caused popular demonstrations that required the intervention of the military.   Before the Assembly can have completed
the tale of work thus lying before it, the time will have come
when, according to the treaty with Germany, France may negotiate
for the substitution of a financial for a territorial guarantee, and
obtain the final evacuation of the last of the occupied departments by the German troops.   When that is done, or in a fair
way of being accomplished, the work of the National Assembly
will be over, and the time for its dissolution will have come.

That in the meantime the more moderate and patriotic
members of the present Assembly are learning the much-needed
lesson of the necessity of preferring the interests of the nation
to the ascendancy of any one party in the nation has been lately
indicated by an incident of a gratifying character.   The letter
written by M. Casimir Périer to the French papers intimating
his conversion to Republicanism is a hopeful augury of good.
M. Périer, though personally in favour of Constitutional Monarchy, and known to be an Orleanist partisan, submitted, like
many other monarchists at the time of the pact of Bordeaux, to
the establishment of a Provisional Republic. He even consented
to work along with M. Thiers as a member of his Cabinet.   For
some time he continued Minister of the Interior, but a few
months ago difficulties in the Cabinet and differences with the
President led to his retirement, and M. Périer withdrew into
private life.   That he has not broken with his party from any
personal cause seems to be proved by the fact that he remains
on friendly terms with the representatives of the Orleanist
claims to the throne.   A short time ago he entertained the
Comte de Paris, who paid a few days' visit to him at his country

seat in the Isère. M. Périer's connexion with Orleanism is of an hereditary as well as a personal character, for his father was Prime Minister under Louis Philippe. Nevertheless M. Périer has avowed himself a Republican. The visit to him of the Comte de Paris having given occasion to many comments and remarks in the press, he lately wrote to declare that while remaining attached to the principles of Constitutional Monarchy he has definitively accepted Republicanism as the sole practicable form of government for France. In his letter he says, " I am one of those who remained faithful to Constitutional Monarchy so long as Constitutional Monarchy appeared possible on the only basis capable of rendering it acceptable and durable—an understanding between the monarchical parties and the two branches of the House of Bourbon, sanctioned by the assent of the country." But he has abandoned that hope, and looks to the early establishment of a Republic through " a parliamentary majority, in accord with the illustrious man to whom France owes such a debt of gratitude." The concluding sentences of the letter are so entirely in accord with the views we have sought to express that we give them. " In the course of nearly a whole century (writes M. Périer) of successive revolutions, all forms of government have been tried by turns except one—that of a regular Republic, loyally accepted by the majority of the nation, and carried on without too great restrictions on the one hand and without weakness on the other. This is the problem we have to solve; let us make the attempt courageously and honestly. For my part I pledge myself to it; and if some few consider it a sacrifice, I believe that on reflection they will find motives sufficient to determine them to it." That is to say, this distinguished Orleanist not only puts the interests of his party in abeyance, exhibits his readiness to acquiesce in the Republic as an unavoidable evil, and therefore resolves as it were to make a virtue of necessity by submitting to it; but he promises his active and energetic co-operation in the great work of rendering it acceptable to the country. Practical circumstances are stronger than abstract preferences. These remain the same, but France is more important than all parties in it; and in order to obtain a settled and well-ordered government in the only form that now seems possible, he will do all he can to facilitate the establishment of the Republic. Of course M. Périer's letter only binds himself. But his personal intimacy with the Orleans family is nevertheless a fact we need not lose sight of or leave out of account. The Comte de Paris has not renounced, nor is it likely he will renounce, the claims of his family to the throne of France. But we are warranted at least in believing that he does not view with displeasure, and that he will not visit with resentment, this seeming desertion by one of his chief supporters. Rather is it probable that, in the circumstances, the Comte de Paris regards the support of the Republic in the present state of France and the existing condition of its public opinion as a patriotic course, and does not disapprove the declaration of his friend and partisan. Above all, however, the step is significant as manifesting the tendency of moderate and patriotic Frenchmen, of, we believe, every party, to look at the present time to the necessities of the national position rather than to dream of winning party-triumphs. The more such a tendency prevails the more probable is the early establishment of a "regular Republic," which may be loyally accepted and supported by the great mass of the people. It is because public opinion among all classes is plainly more and more drifting towards this conclusion that the duty is imposed on those who love their country above their party to sink all considerations in regard to the latter, that they may obtain for the former settled institutions and a consolidated government. And if the same disposition as M. Casimir Périer has just exhibited be generally manifested, the work will prove a much easier one than lately seemed possible. When the time comes for the present National Assembly to be dissolved, which will probably be not many months hence, the nation will be called upon to elect a new Assembly for the distinct purpose of instituting a definitive Government and a regular Constitution.

During the interval the growing acquiescence in a Republican régime will, we may be sure—unless there should be some untoward interruption of M. Thiers' mission—increase. The form of rule that divides Frenchmen least, will be accepted by the country generally, as that which is best fitted to insure the maintenance of order. We believe M. Gambetta is right in calculating upon a Republican majority in the new Assembly, which will then have as its natural function the proclamation of a definitive Republic. The Republic sought and desired, however, will not be the Republic of abstract democratic enthusiasts, but a form of government which will maintain the rights of all classes of the population. It will be desired as a matter of sober business, because the people of France are convinced that any Government that needs an appeal to force to constitute it, or which would provoke appeals to force in opposition to it, would perpetuate the malady from which France has so grievously suffered since 1789. In any case, however, the task of establishing the Republic must prove an arduous one. It can only be established and maintained, as M. de Mazade has said, " by imposing restraints on itself, by creating institutions and habits which check the agitations incident to its nature." Much

has been already done under the guidance of M. Thiers to give a character of fixity of direction and design to the action of the Government, especially in regard to the foreign policy of the country. To impress upon the Provisional Republic the seal of a definitive institution will tax all the energies and wisdom of French statesmanship. M. Thiers is precluded by his position from directly hastening the end of the Assembly which must precede the establishment of a definitive Republic. As M. Barthélemy St. Hilaire has said in a letter written by him recently on the part of the President, in reply to the Councillors of the Saone et Loire, M. Thiers has solemnly promised from the tribune that he would take no part in a campaign in favour of dissolution should that question be agitated. Happily the campaign has not taken place. It is one of the symptoms of M. Gambetta's growing moderation that he should have discountenanced the idea of a campaign of that character, which was a few months ago certainly designed by the more extreme members of the Radical party. The *Republique Françzise* intimated the abandonment of the project, under, there is no doubt, the " inspiration" of M. Gambetta, and there has been since no attempt to revive it. But the end of the Assembly must come soon, and M. Barthélemy St. Hilaire does not feel precluded from contemplating the issue. After stating that M. Thiers is bound not to interfere in reference to that, he thus proceeds in his letter :—
" It is public opinion that ought to warn the Chamber that the time for convoking its successor has arrived. I do not doubt the Assembly will itself spontaneously feel that necessity when the evacuation of the territory shall be so near that it may be considered accomplished, and when the country, placed in a totally different situation from that in which the elections of 1871 were made, will perceive that it must make its voice heard directly in renewing its mandatories (*ses mandutaires*). The circumstances will then be so altered that the evidence of the change will be plain to all, and will attract an almost unanimous assent." The new National Assembly will come directly charged by the nation to fulfil its great mission. During the elections the direction of affairs will naturally continue with the present Government, under such conditions as the wisdom of the present Assembly may deem requisite. It would be absurd as well as dangerous to leave the country without a Government during the turmoils and excitement of a general election, fraught with such vital interests and issues, as some of the French Conservatives who fear the employment of the Government influence in favour of Republican candidates desire. M. Thiers's Dictatorship will, therefore, be continued for the present, and probably will also be extended under fresh constitutional checks

and guarantees by the new Assembly. So long as M. Thiers is
capable of holding the helm, all will probably go smoothly. The
hour of peril will be on his death, or resignation, or disconnexion
from public affairs from any other cause. Therefore it is that
a Vice-President is so essential. But the real successor of
M. Thiers, so far as coming events that cast their shadows before
enable us to judge, is unquestionably M. Gambetta. He alone
in France has made a reputation and gained a position
during late events. If he were guilty of grievous faults during
the war—as cannot be questioned—his countrymen will not
judge them harshly, because they remember they were committed under the impulse of a consuming patriotism. If individual energy could have saved France, his would have
done so. But her salvation in the circumstances of her lot
was impossible. The memory of the doings of the Government of the National Defence at Tours, therefore, does not discredit M. Gambetta, as the Conservative papers would fain believe,
but rather the contrary. And M. Gambetta's conduct since the
peace has established him further in the confidence of his fellow-
countrymen. He has shown the virtue, so rare with French
politicians, of patience. He can afford to wait, and he has
waited, and is waiting. He saw that acquiescence in, and support
of the provisional rule of M. Thiers as the sole possible form of
rule for the moment, was required of him, and he forgot irritating
antecedents and silenced strong prejudices in order to render
them. He was aware that the great want of the Republican
party was organization, and he has been seeking to organize it,
so that there may be men capable of filling the various offices in
connexion with local and general administration when the hour
for action comes. That self-control which has been so rare with
democrats, particularly of the enthusiastic southern temperament
of the ex-Dictator, M. Gambetta has proved that he possesses.
He has rarely opened his lips to speak in the National Assembly,
and his influence with it and the country when he did speak has
therefore been all the greater. He exhibited genuine tact in
declining lately to join his democratic brethren in the celebration
of the anniversary of the overthrow of the Empire, and in abandoning the more recent Republican festival rather than provoke
disorder. In addition to all, M. Gambetta is a true orator,
though of a different stamp from M. Thiers. His is the kind
of fervid, passionate temperament associated with powers of inexhaustible work and an indomitable energy of patriotic purpose,
that captivates Frenchmen. We are convinced M. Gambetta
has a great career before him if he continue to practise the
statesmanly reticence and self-control he has lately manifested.
We are much mistaken also, if M. Thiers does not think the

same thing. The "fou furieux" of eighteen months ago (as he called Gambetta), is the friend and councillor of to-day, as much as it is possible for one who is the leader of the Opposition to be the friend of the Head of the Government. When the sceptre drops from the necessarily relaxed grasp of M. Thiers, we believe it will be worthily held by M. Gambetta, freely chosen by the French people in the unimpeded and unfettered exercise of the National Sovereignty. The energy and exhaustless daring of the ex-Dictator will make him a formidable foe to the politicians who for party ends shall show themselves not unwilling to disturb public order by resort to force.

INDEPENDENT SECTION.

[Under the above title a limited portion of the Westminster Review is occasionally set apart for the reception of able articles, which, though harmonizing with the general spirit and aims of the work, contain opinions at variance with the particular ideas or measures it may advocate. The object of the Editor, in introducing this department, is to facilitate the expression of opinion by men of high mental power and culture, who, while they are zealous friends of freedom and progress, yet differ widely on special points of great practical concern, both from the Editor and from each other.]

Art. VII.—The Æsthetics of Physicism.

Force and Matter. By Dr. L. Buchner. Trübner & Co.

THE present paper is headed with the well-known name, and widely appreciated work of Dr. Buchner, not that there is any intention of offering criticism upon that treatise itself, but because it seems to contain the most concise, and at the same time, the most popular statement yet put forward of the reasons for regarding physical death as the termination of individual existence. So far as human reason, arguing from the facts of our present and past life, can arrive at any judgment at all on the subject, so far does this little work appear just in its conclusion that a self-conscious existence hereafter is an impossibility. To those persons who assume some higher mode of apprehending the phenomena of the universe, than that supplied by the reason, Dr. Buchner's logic will of course appear inconclusive. They stand upon a totally different plane, and from the nature of the case can never meet in argument. Whether or not any such modes have a real existence it is impossible to say : they are at all events self-evidently incognizable to reason, and as this must ever be the only medium by which truth can be demonstrated between man and man, it may be taken for granted that pure materialism is the only creed which a rational man can adopt. It is at least sound as far as it goes, and although the negative evidence, that we are utterly unable to perceive any psychic force in nature, or proof of a personal superintendence, does not give us the right absolutely to deny such possibilities, yet in the interest of truth, we are assuredly bound to abstain from their acceptance until their supporters can make them plain to the only arbiter between truth and falsehood, which we are sure we possess—the reason. With regard to this point we may say that Dr. Buchner here appears to overstep the limits of scientific argument, in that he endeavours to prove the unknowable to be also untrue—a position which seems on the face of it self-contradictory.

It is evident to all who watch the progress of modern thought that the gratuitous assumption of such modes of cognition as those above referred to, constantly decreases in repute as a justifiable method of founding an argument. Wherever this plan has been adopted, it is, under the influence of the more rigid and practical system of thought introduced by science, gradually dropping into disuse: for although science has in truth in no way increased our knowledge of logic, yet it has brought its necessity home to the most inferior intellects, and by this wide dissemination of its canons has caused it to be more generally appreciated than heretofore. Consequently no declaration of the hopes and attributes of humanity, which demands a higher sanction than that of the human understanding, receives the assent, though it is spared the denial, of persons averagely educated, and who are also bold enough to think for themselves. It is difficult to see how the soundness of this position can be called in question by any unbiassed person, and although of course spiritualists will differ *toto cœlo* from such a view of the case, yet it is impossible to avoid the conclusion that the sooner this position is recognised, and opponents as well as supporters set about modelling their institutions and laws on the hypothesis of its correctness, and on the certainty of its ultimate prevalence, the less violent and perilous will the work of reorganization be rendered. For as education advances, and it becomes more and more impressed upon the multitude that the evolution of man, with all his self-asserted wisdom and intellectual power, is, so far at least as man can ascertain, but an inevitable result of a vast chain of antecedent events, not proveably elaborated under supreme guidance, but probably simply from that uncalculating necessity of sequence inherent in the very existence of matter, so will there be changes innumerable in our modes of action and thought under all circumstances and upon all subjects. For all practical purposes the materialist formula is the only one to hand, and under its influence, life—political, social, and domestic—will be thoroughly revolutionized, let us say humanized. Humanized too will be every branch of art under the influence of this, the only creed which admits of demonstration. The fruit of the feelings, no less than that of the intellect, will be changed, and it is upon the point of contact between reason and the emotions (a convenient though not positively accurate division, inasmuch as ultimately human character is indivisible, and each part acts upon and through each), that it is proposed in the following essay to offer some remarks and speculations. Hitherto to the feelings, and through them to the imagination, the predominance has undoubtedly been given: in future it is believed the reason will be the ruler, and it is desired to form some conception of the general influence which this deposition from mastership to servitude will have upon the character of the servant.

To the new convert from mysticism there is doubtless something chilling—a horror-inspiring element, in the conviction that his mundane existence is all that he has to look for; and as his whole nature becomes inoculated with the belief that this conviction is founded upon inexorable logic, he feels at first that life is of little worth—that reality has too stern, too terrible a presence before which to permit himself the exercise of fancy, or to exhibit the possession of any other faculty than that of pure reason. He has been educated to believe in an eternal future existence, wherein enjoyment far transcending any which earth could afford would be his: to look forward to a mysterious state of being in which beauties ineffable would for ever surround him, in a spot where there should be no more sin, and no more sorrow; where toil would have ceased at the command of a supreme being of infinite love and infinite power; and where existence would be as it were one continuous thanksgiving, poured forth, not from any rigid sense of duty, but as a spontaneous tribute of unquenchable love. What wonder when such attractive, if rather misty fancies have been his ideal—impressed, be it remembered, with all the authority which the countless generations of the past have upon the present unit—that man should shrink in terror from the thought that all these conceptions must be laid aside as mere human imaginings if he is to be a follower of truth! Speaking in this connexion Professor Huxley has the following :*—

" As surely as every future grows out of the past and present, so will the physiology of the future gradually extend the realm of matter and law until it is co-extensive with knowledge, with feeling, and with action. The consciousness of this great truth weighs like a nightmare, I believe, upon many of the best minds of the day. They watch what they conceive to be the progress of materialism in such fear, and powerless anger, as a savage feels when during an eclipse the great shadow creeps over the face of the sun. The advancing tide of matter threatens to drown their souls; the tightening grasp of law impedes their freedom; they are alarmed lest man's moral nature be debased by the increase of his wisdom."

It was doubtless this species of despondency which induced Professor Wagner, while admitting the inevitable victory of the

---

* " Lay Sermons," p. 142, third edition.

materialist creed, to utter the mournful plaint referred to by Buchner in his concluding observations :*—

"The morality," said Wagner, "which flows from scientific materialism may be comprehended within these few words, 'Let us eat and drink, for to-morrow we die.' All noble thoughts are but vain dreams, the effusions of automata with two arms, running about upon two legs, which being finally decomposed into chemical atoms, combine themselves anew, resembling the dance of lunatics in a madhouse."

Now, much as all thinking men must deplore the use of such silly, inconsequent language by a man of undoubted ability and some authority, there is no difficulty in recognising the state of mind from which it springs ; and when the nature of the transition from a dreamland of untold bliss to the hard facts of life is taken into account, a feeling of genuine compassion for all—and they are many—who are involved in the same grievous trouble must arise. Rightly or wrongly, the misery is there, and at first it is well nigh intolerable. Bowed down by the vast incubus of superstition which has accumulated through ages, it is not possible to man by a simple effort of volition to cast off his load and become upright without much misgiving and sorrow. It would indeed speak ill for the honesty and stability of all human opinion if this were otherwise.

But we must not confine our view merely to the individual ; it is needful to look also at the national life, if the true character of any epoch is to be ascertained. Doubtless the feelings of individuals and nations are similar, and the former may be taken as a type of the latter in kind, but not in degree. The cumulative force of a national movement is greater than that of a simple aggregation of persons not bound together by any common ties. With the former enthusiasm or fear in one, beget enthusiasm or fear in another. With the latter each has to work out and ponder upon his problem for himself, and the emotions to which its solution gives rise are his exclusively. For those who inaugurated the present materialist revival, the master minds who have dared to look steadfastly on the face of truth, it may be—it usually is—possible to discern her unspeakable beauty, and so to yield her an unreserved and self-satisfied devotion. But it is not from such that the emotional tendencies evoked by any onward movement are to be learned. They indeed tell what they have seen ; but it is amongst the countless band of their followers, those who have not the ability or the bravery to explore for themselves, but have to learn their lesson at second hand, and even then imperfectly, from lack of that power, which

is the true seer's especial privilege, to comprehend a beauty
beyond description; it is amongst these that we must look for
the feelings and susceptibilities which a creed such as that of
which we are speaking, old as the world, yet new as to-day, will
excite. And we are convinced that the first effect upon nations
will not be other than upon the individual—namely, to create a
feeling of hopelessness, and lead them to echo the words,* "In
much wisdom is much grief, and he that increaseth knowledge
increaseth sorrow."

To this point, in England at least, we think that the development of the reason has already reached, and we shall endeavour
to exemplify our opinion by a very brief glance at the principal
works of the day of that kind which tend to draw forth the
emotions. Before proceeding, however, it will be well to observe
that we hold it to be axiomatic that æsthetic enjoyment, of
whatever degree, is always the exercise of the same faculty—nay,
as far as is known, there is no essential difference between even
mental and physical delights, for unless a mind be present it is
highly problematical whether even a passive delight can be
experienced. We cannot therefore draw any distinctions between
the emotional pleasure excited by a moral course and that called
forth by beauty. The only law which seems apparent on this
point is in æsthetics the analogue of that which is generally accepted in human action—namely, that as the course which is
most right contributes to the greatest happiness of the greatest
number, so the acme of æsthetic cultivation will be reached when
the greatest enjoyment is most widely distributed. As to any
difference between morality and beauty, we hold that there
is as high a morality discernible in a lofty work of art, of whatever kind, as there is beauty in the noblest deeds. The two are
simply different views of truth.

To return to the immediate subject. No one can have failed
to note the yearning fondness with which, when men have become despondent, even of their earthly future, they cling to
their past; and the intensely melancholy though genuine delight,
with which old people dwell upon the memories of their early
years! With how concentrated a force then should we expect
that this insatiable regret would hanker after those earlier traditions of a state of future happiness, the abandonment of which
matured age had rendered unavoidable in the interests of sincerity. In a stage of advancement yet lower than that we have
supposed, such as we believe the majority even of the present
generation, whose education has certainly tended rather to
emotional than rational development, has reached, when the

* Ecclesiastes i. 18.

spiritualist is unable to allay his doubts concerning the soundness of his creed, and is obliged, *nolens volens*, to consider the arguments of his opponents, what a deep and ever-present gloom these doubts throw over his whole existence! Inasmuch then as literature is the reflex of the popular mind, so will this gloom be found stereotyped upon the works of the day; and as poetry from its flexibility may be taken as a more delicate index of feeling than works of prose, we will endeavour to show how the influence spoken of has acted upon some of our greatest living singers.

To take the most celebrated first. Throughout Mr. Tennyson's works the shadow of an ever-present sorrow is observable. That this should be most remarkable in In Memoriam is not to be wondered at, considering the nature of the subject, and it is there that the origin of the sorrow is plainly enounciated (numbers 53 to 55). Although, in later verses, the author disclaims all doubts of the future, and asserts that his " Hope had never lost her youth ;" and although he urges that—

> " All is well though faith and form
> Be sundered in the night of fear,
> Well roars the storm to those that hear
> A deeper voice across the storm ;"

yet it is very questionable whether in his heart of hearts he does not feel that the wish was father to the thought, and that the doubts are still with him. How utterly vague and unsatisfactory in their mysticism, despite the noble, because purely human lesson of self-control and high morality which they convey, are the three concluding stanzas! But it is not in In Memoriam alone, but throughout his works that this nameless sorrow is apparent—a sorrow which, whatever be the subject, only seems to take therefrom—

> " The touch of change in calm or storm,
> But knows no more of transient form
> In her deep self, than some dead lake
> That holds the shadow of a lark
> Hung in the shadow of a heaven."

What could be more intensely sorrowful than the noble epic comprised in the Idyls of the King, and the Holy Grail? What than the tale of Enoch Arden? Each in its different kind relates the story of high human endeavour brought to nought—in the one case by treachery, in the other by circumstance. Even that exquisite little piece, the Miller's Daughter, is not free from the taint. Take, again, the wild dirge of passionate despair uttered to the crags of Ida by the forsaken Œnone ; or, once more, the dreamy, regretful song of the Lotus

Eaters. Where the poet speaks in the first person, as in those
sweet verses commencing " Flow down, cold rivulet," and
" Break, break," it is even more plainly apparent. Everywhere
the same sadness is found—a sadness which is not merely worn
as a garment, but is a very part of the poet as a poet, and which
because it so thoroughly accords with the feelings of those for
whom he sings, is doubtless to be regarded as one of his principal
attractions. It is the unavoidable influence of his time, wherein,
dreading the future, dreading even to scrutinize too closely its
hopes and its dangers, men love to lament over the grave of the
past.

But there are two poets of to-day, both of them of the highest
order, who perhaps even more than Mr. Tennyson may be taken as
representative of the age. It is now many years since the
Laureate began to write, and the movement towards materialism
has undoubtedly made a great advance during that period. It
is therefore from the works of those who have most recently
proved their right to the poet's crown, that the justest conception of the emotional bias of the time will be gained. These
two are Mr. W. Morris and Mr. D. G. Rossetti ; and we think
that a very brief glance at some of their productions will suffice
to confirm our view as to the delight which this generation takes
in steeping itself in sadness.

Who can read the introductory stanzas to the Earthly Paradise without feeling how heavy a cloud of melancholy hangs
over the poet's mind ? He confesses himself " the idle singer of
an empty day," " born out of his due time," and while in the
enchanter's chamber recalling fondly the seasons past and flown,
the reality was to him a winter time, and ever outside "piped
the drear notes of that December day." What can be more sad
than the whole groundwork of the poem :—A band of aged
wanderers, a gathering of aged colonists : these weary of the
work of life, those outworn in the vain quest for an earthly paradise : each waiting for, yet dreading death ; and each, to wile
away the time, remembering the others of many an old tale told
in the hopeful days of youth and early manhood ? Such is the
picture presented to us, and if we proceed with a further examination we find that almost all the stanzas intervening between
the several narratives are saturated with a vague sorrow. It is
the past alone which yields a congenial theme for the sad
heart to dwell upon : the present is filled only with thoughts of
former hopes and desires still unsatisfied. On this foundation
has Mr. Morris raised his fame—a fame which, from the intrinsic
merits of his poetry, the descriptive and narrative power, with
its ever-varying contrasts, the delicately-tender, yet faithfully-
elaborated expression of human sympathy everywhere discernible,

even amongst the cruel gods and goddesses, will long outlive the weak sentimentalism of to-day, and be dear to our sons and grandsons long after a sturdier and more untrammelled manhood shall have prevailed.

Now as to Mr. Rossetti. Again the same sorrow-cherishing spirit is found pervading almost every poem, whether expressed in the weird and hopeless misery of Sister Helen, the agonized remorse of the Last Confession, the heartfelt sympathy with the exiled Dante, the reflections on Jenny, or the exquisitely delicious sonnets of the House of Life. A love transfusing the whole being, a brief time of happiness, a parting, a life-long weariness haunted with the memory of the blissful past; this is the tale dimly and fitfully told in the House of Life, and we leave the surviving lover hopelessly bemoaning the barrenness of existence.

> "So spring comes merry towards me now, but earns
>   No answering smile from me whose life is twined
>   With the dead boughs that winter still must bind
> And whom to-day the spring no more concerns.
>
> "Behold this crocus is a withering flame;
>   This snowdrop snow; this apple-blossom's part
>   To breed the fruit that breeds the serpent's art.
> Nay, for these spring-flowers. Anon they face from them,
>   Nor gaze till on the year's last lily stem
>   The white cup shrivels round the golden heart."

More minute analysis is unnecessary, although the temptation to extend our remarks on this latter poem, so unique in its exceeding beauty, is very great. We must, however, adhere to our purpose—which is merely to point out how deeply the spirit of despondency has penetrated the hearts of those who may be called the most popular poets of the day.

The poet who appears to us most free from the fetters of the past is Mr. Swinburne, and we confess that on that account he has for us a peculiar attraction. He is more contented to take things as they are and make the best of them. His contempt for the gods of the past, and his scarcely less evident scorn for the man of the present—spite of the rich voluptuousness of expression and never-failing wealth of epithet with which they are conveyed—have no doubt greatly detracted from his popularity, and on this account he can scarcely be regarded as typical of the age, although we venture to prophesy that his poetry will constantly grow in favour as years pass on, and for a narrow, squeamish ideal of beauty we substitute a truer one, which knows not the word "sensuality" save as applying to sensual *excess* of any kind, even in the enjoyment of a fragrant bouquet.

If we turn to works of prose-fiction, we shall find that the same general tone prevails in a minor degree. It is not human gladness, but human sorrow that are principally depicted. Novelists, orthodox—for they cannot separate themselves from their age—and unorthodox alike delight to steep their characters in misery, and frequently to kill off the principal players at the finale. And why? Because it is the popular taste, and consciously or unconsciously they are ruled by the will of the people.

Here then is the limit of the first part of this paper—namely, the primary effects upon the feelings of a people of a growing materialism. True that we have only sought for these effects in the works of three leading poets, but a little consideration will convince the reader that these three are so far really typical of the time. That there are multitudes who escape the tendency we have described, who are naturally of a phlegmatic, unemotional temperament, or who have gained a better and a higher view of life than to regret the empty hopes which mysticism inspired, is of course beside the question. We speak only of the national mind; and although, as we are aware, a mere indication of the general truth of our views is afforded by the examples selected, yet it is sufficient for present purposes and can readily be further worked out by any who care to pursue the subject. The precise date at which the emotions will naturally assume a more hopeful and a more manly cast it is impossible to foretel; for many that date has already come, and every day adds to the number of those who not only adopt scientific truth as their sole reliable support, but who feel a genuine pleasure in having adopted it. The period we have treated of is that when reason is in conflict. It has lasted from the time of Galileo until now, but so numerous, so decisive have been the recent victories of reason over mysticism, that the result is no longer doubtful even to its adversaries.

II.

As time flows on, and the conviction that self-continuance after death is a thing utterly beyond the knowledge of human faculties becomes more fully realized, a healthier state of feeling than that described in the last section will assuredly supervene. Gradually but surely the old mystic creeds will lose every tittle of their authority and influence over men's minds, and the absurdity of the hopes they encouraged and of the terrors they inculcated will be simply a matter of memory. As regards the latter—though this was the easier because more pleasant lesson —their resolution may already be said to have taken place; and even most orthodox divines have come to admit that condemnation of His creatures to the most devilishly refined tortures

is in some measure inconsistent with the hypothesis of a beneficent Creator. A passive acquiescence in the inevitable will
probably be the spirit in which the bulk of mankind will receive the conviction that their mortal career is all they have
certainly to look for. The utter futility of praising or blaming
the existing order of nature because it is what it is, will be self-
evident, and men will act accordingly. We cannot expect that
the destruction of their spiritualistic fetters will be greeted with
joy by the majority. It will come upon them as release does
upon one who has spent long years in gaol : once more restored
to the world, his senses are staggered with the gift of freedom;
the beauty and variety of nature are to him simply a bewilder-
ment; his fellow-men a puzzle, involving his brain in the most
inextricable confusion. Fain would he return to the four strait
walls and the spider's webs of his prison-house: these at least
were not provocative of such intense, such maddening thought
as now surges within him. But the door is closed against him,
and he must therefore begin once more to learn the life of the
world, even as a little child. Here and there, indeed, where
men have been goaded by a sense of long-continued injustice,
and in the name of religion burdened by their fellows with artificial evils, excesses of the wildest kind may be foretold, and the
"red fool fury of the Seine" will be revived in all its horror.
But for morality there is no danger to be apprehended, not
being the fruit of any creed, but the sum of human experience.
Transmitted and consolidated from the earliest time, so that it
has become a portion of the man himself, it cannot perish with
those creeds, but will constantly become more noble and more
human in proportion as it is dissevered from the grotesque and
the untrue. That those who through the carelessness or wickedness of their fellows have been deprived of this their noblest
heritage will, with the awakening sense of their powers, lay
their protest against their sleek and self-complacent tyrants
before the tribunal of humanity, and that that protest will in
places be presented with much bloodshed and keen suffering, is
no more than can be anticipated. The cruel theft which generation after generation has countenanced and supported will
now meet with its punishment; but there is a sure hope for the
future in the fact that the robbed should be sufficiently awake
to wreak their vengeance even blindly upon the robbers.
Generally, however, we fully believe that the transition will be
effected in peace and almost imperceptibly. Reason having the
predominance, the feelings will naturally be under the gover-
nance of reason instead of its master, as in every recorded revolution of the past. The period at which this transition takes
place will be pre-eminently one of practical and material ad-

vancement. Those who have heartily accepted the position and are acting accordingly will of course be in the van. They will be filled with a deep sense of our past shortcomings as man to man, and under its influence their ever-present object will be to remedy that vast crowd of evils which were the inevitable crop of systems bolstered up by spiritualism, and to induce their race to act up to the highest standard which reason indicates. Of these, however, we must say more hereafter. The present is the place to speak of those who follow far behind them in the earnestness with which they have adopted the creed of nature, but who nevertheless must be regarded as the principal source from which a true conception either of the intellectual or emotional bent of the age is to be derived.

When an unpalatable truth has been forced upon a man's understanding, it is quite natural that in modifying or altering his previous plan of life—as he will do if he be true to himself—so far as its acceptance dictates, he should at first do so coldly, and more as a matter of moral necessity than from any increased enjoyment which his clearer light enables him to obtain from his actions. Bare fact and irrefragable demonstration are very frequently most unpleasant tutors even in the ordinary affairs of life. How much more so, then, when they are applied to the very highest hopes which the imagination of man has found itself capable of conceiving, and when they point out that, as far as humanity can form any judgment, those hopes are without warrant; and further, that as respects the form of the hopes themselves, their universally anthropomorphic character stamps them as mere etherealized pictures emanating from the anthropos. Yet this is in truth the lesson which science is already calling upon mankind to learn, and which at the period supposed will have been accepted by the majority. Under these circumstances it can be no matter of surprise that the imagination and susceptibilities, the creative and receptive parts of the human feelings, should be held in some disrepute, and their field of exercise be rigidly circumscribed. The outcome of this cold, unimpassioned feeling towards the new creed will, we believe, be increased action. Abandoning their dreams, men will, in self-defence, and to stifle their sense of the emptiness of existence, throw themselves boldly into the arena of human life. They will determine that their heart shall learn the lesson which their head has already learned, and, paradoxical as is the expression, their natural feeling will be a desire to alter the natural expression of their feelings; to forget regret, and truly to enjoy the life which is theirs with that end, in obedience to the behest of reason, taking upon themselves all noble tasks which a pure morality and a deep sense of the claims of man upon man shall suggest.

Reason has gained the victory, although the conquered feelings have not yet heartily accepted her rule. But the time has come, of which Huxley speaks, when the truth is recognised that[*] " Education has two great ends to which everything else must be subordinated. The one of these is to secure knowledge ; the other is to develop the love of right and the hatred of wrong." And how else could they be developed than by the rational control and guidance of the emotions, by transfusing men's hearts with the conviction that the love of right is a passion carrying with it the highest enjoyment of which human nature is capable ? The succeeding sentences in the speech from which we have quoted indicate what we believe will be the difference with regard to education between the present age and that of which we are endeavouring to form some idea :—

" With wisdom and uprightness a nation can make its way worthily, and beauty will follow in the footsteps of the two, even if she be not specially invited ; while there is perhaps no sight in the whole world more saddening and revolting than is offered by men sunk in ignorance of everything but what other men have written ; seemingly devoid of moral belief or guidance ; but with the sense of beauty so keen, and the power of expression so cultivated that their sensual caterwauling may almost be taken for the music of the spheres.

" At present education is almost entirely devoted to the cultivation of the power of expression and of the sense of literary beauty. The matter of having anything to say beyond a hash-up of other people's opinions, or of possessing any interior sense of beauty, so that we may distinguish between the godlike and devilish, is left aside as of no moment. I think I do not err in saying that if science were made the foundation of education, instead of being at most stuck on as a cornice to the edifice, this state of things could not exist."

Now although we differ from the learned speaker as to that sense of beauty which leads to " sensual caterwauling " being, in fact, a keen sense of beauty at all—unless, indeed, sensualism is itself to be conceived of as beautiful—yet we quite coincide with his view of the present education. Its result is, almost universally, refinement without solidity ; we gild and burnish the most ordinary earthenware, and pass it off upon each other as a vessel fashioned of pure gold. Every one is perfectly well aware of the sham, but it is not polite to speak about it, and to attempt to introduce sterling metal, be it only iron or copper, is a crime of the blackest dye, for how would the poor earthen pots come off in the crush ?

But at the age of which we are speaking, it is anticipated that a solid education will have been placed within reach of all, only we fear that the rebound from spiritualism and its various parasitical growths will, in a great measure, have quenched the desire to seek after the beautiful. The position will have been reversed, and solidity, without refinement in the sense of æsthetic susceptibility, will prevail. Now we hold that it is impossible that this susceptibility should be dormant without great loss to humanity. For we cannot, with Professor Huxley, imagine different kinds of sensitiveness, whether to beauty or virtue. In degree it will differ in different subjects, but the sense we regard as one, just as much as hearing or seeing is one. That the education we have had should have established a low standard alike of beauty and morality is not wonderful. The remedy, however, is not in vituperation of those who seize and revel in such delicia as are offered them, but in the endeavour to give them something better. The tangles of Neæra's hair and the wanton sports of Amaryllis do not, in themselves, give any great satisfaction: they are attractive only in contrast with the tinselled vanity of all the other baubles which it is customary to call "objects in life." There is about them something real, and a genuine, if lascivious enjoyment. Lay down a more lofty code of morality. Bring children up in the faith that true virtue and true beauty are one, and that where they appear as things apart the beauty is false and meretricious, and without doubt higher sensibilities will be called forth. For whatever may be said, sensualism, however deliciously tricked out, can minister only to carnality, and not to refined seeking after beauty, to which it is absolutely hostile.

A thirst for æsthetic enjoyment is, to our minds, one of the principal incentives to great and noble deeds; it confers upon duty and virtue that graciousness which renders them attractive for themselves, apart from the immediate value of their fruits. Now, much as reason may strive without the assistance of the feelings to adopt a rigid code of morality, and simply "because right is right to follow right," we may be very sure that her unassisted efforts will be found incomplete and unsatisfactory. The frigidity which attaches to a mere discharge of duty for the sake of duty, will render the effort too great for human weakness, and ultimately the emotions will surely re-acquire a limited influence. But unless our philosophers and teachers see this danger, and provide for the adequate cultivation of the æsthetic element in human character, not simply leaving the notion of beauty "to follow," to evolve itself, they are creating no insignificant barrier between themselves and their god. The suppression, however temporary, of a very powerful agent in all action, cannot fail to have an evil effect upon their work, and renders a reaction in the future as certain as the revolutions of the seasons.

As regards literature, should such a period as that supposed be brought about, there will be few who will read for the sake of the delicacy or sweetness of a book : for the actual information which it conveys only will a work be thought valuable. For the few, those whose temperament is such that æsthetic enjoyment is a necessity to their existence, the fact of reason having provided no place, will force them still to rely upon their old gods, the fanciful marvels of mysticism, with its gaudy portraiture and exquisitely refined falsity, or else on the poppy-crowned devil Sensuality, as the word is generally understood. In such a period all art will be held in light esteem by the multitude, and the consequence will be that the time will be barren of artists, painters, poets, and composers, save only those who minister to the above-mentioned few. At this time reason will, so to speak, have run into excess—not rationally, be it understood, but on account of the inexperience of the vehicle, humanity, through which it has to act, and because of its inability to act reasonably unless some other motive be superadded. Gloomy as this picture may appear, it seems to us that at present our civilization tends in this direction, and that any attempt to establish pure reason as the sole incentive to action must arrive at such a result. Nevertheless, even though such an intermediate chrysalis state should be needful to teach us the due relations of our reason and our emotions, we can but regard it as the forerunner of that more healthy ultimate condition when neither the one or the other will be permitted to reign irresponsibly, but when the former shall so have educated the latter by stripping the stage garments from the superstitions of the past and showing their naked monstrosity, that the purest virtue and the truest beauty shall afford the chiefest delight ; and on the other hand, when the emotions shall have gained the power so to influence reason, that its conceptions of the good and the true shall not merely be philosophical doctrines, but mainsprings of action, aiding all humanity in its enjoyment through life of every faculty which it possesses.

III.

Let us suppose now that a considerable time has elapsed, and that the nation consists, for the most part, neither of those who were first awakened to the vanity of spiritualism but who were unable to part with their shadow without terror and regret, nor yet of those their immediate successors who first perceived the paramount value of scientific materialism, and who on that account refused to allow either the feelings or the fancies begotten of these to have any place in the human economy. Let us imagine that a new generation of men has

arisen, by whom the spiritualistic hungerings of their grand-
fathers and the rationalistic pruderies of their fathers are equally
avoided; who have been educated to consider their reason the
sole arbiter between truth and falsehood, and who are therefore
accustomed to accept demonstrable facts as alone worthy of
credence; and who, on the other hand, possess feelings of refined
sympathy with their fellows, and whose impulses from judicious
cultivation tend naturally to the admiration of the most moral
as the most beautiful actions. As the contempt for the emotions
which pervaded the last period slowly and almost imperceptibly
wore away, so was reason brought to admit that they too were
an essential constituent in humanity, and being such were as
worthy of her consideration as any other source of human
action. Finding moreover that not only was it impossible to
eradicate this element but that if ignored or repressed it became
frequently productive of the greatest evils, whereas if kept under
due control it contributed largely not merely to the enjoyment
but to the direct utilities of life, men took to study this character of the race, and in the place of it proving, as had been
hitherto supposed, either an unamenable tyrant or a useless
slave, it has shown itself to be the most valuable assistant in
the grand work of educating mankind which reason has over possessed. On all sides its influences are visible, acting indeed everywhere rationally, but now for the most part almost as an inherited
instinct, but constantly with good effect. The above may seem
to many an exaggerated picture, and one which it is beyond
human nature, judging from experience, to realize. But it must
be remembered, in the first place, in what a field that experience
has been gathered—one overrun with weeds and poisonous plants
whose atmosphere is pervaded with heavy pestilential vapours;
and, again, that there is no predicable limit to the improvability
of mankind. When to these considerations is added the fact
that the tendency is decidedly in the direction indicated in the
foregoing pages, we cannot admit that our expectations are unfounded, although their realization may still be distant.

It was observed above that while under a recently established
materialism the attitude of most minds was a passive acquiescence in the inevitable, resulting in a plunge into every-day
work for the sake of stifling thought, that of some few, who had
been able to see truth in its naked beauty, was one of the highest
reverence for the actually existent. Those few are now supposed
to have long since passed; but not their work: that which was
their special characteristic is now to be seen in almost all. That
blind plunge into the work of reason, far from stifling thought,
has promoted it, and the work itself has gradually impressed man
with the nobility of work. For it is certain that any effort to

discharge a duty does carry with it a certain amount of self-satisfaction, and although a man may profess to despise this, and aver that he acts from pure reason, yet surely this is itself a wholly unreasonable course. The enjoyment is good, even as the work is good. Moreover it is observed that those who have most assiduously cultivated their minds, not storing them merely with scientific and practical knowledge, but also with poetry and art, developing their æsthetic faculties, are not only most susceptible to this self-satisfaction, but are also best fitted to enter into the feelings of others, and so to help forward the work of a complete universal education in which every faculty receives its due training. In addition to this it is found that the quality of emotional induction, if the expression may be applied, becomes in some so highly refined and so instantaneous in its action that they are able to conjecture with the most marvellous exactitude the course which people will adopt under given circumstances, and also to estimate characters from small indications with great promptness. Now these qualities are found invaluable in the work of the world, and it is beyond question that the rapid progress which will have been made in the age we are imagining will be due in a great measure to their cultivation.

But it is to the vast decrease in crime which will be a certain consequence of this highly developed susceptibility to nature's teachings, and to the great increase of average human happiness, that we would allude, rather than to the practical benefits which statecraft, diplomacy, or commerce may derive from a rational education of the emotions, although of course the two will act and react upon each other. This reverential feeling for all nature, and for himself as a part of nature, is undoubtedly the highest æsthetic enjoyment of which man is capable—it is the true worship of the beautiful, and there can be no greater stimulus to goodness and purity of life. Where reason weakly falters in its duty, as it ever will at times, this instinctive Reverence, which reason has fostered, will exercise an irresistible sway and render backsliding impossible. The same respect which each feels for himself he will feel for others, and thus so far as it is within his power, he will spare them the many humiliations which are inseparable from the social organization of to-day.

Not to extend our remarks farther, we will only ask whether, supposing our speculations are well founded, man can have any higher or more immediate duty than to examine each for himself whether scientific materialism is really the only true creed. For most surely if it fail, no other can supply its place. The true feeling of Reverence is totally incompatible with mysticism, and from the nature of the case must be opposed to any possible hypothesis of a supra-mundane authority. When the element of fear or of hope, the external command, is introduced, then the love of goodness for itself, the internal command, perishes.

We are aware that in many particulars our subject has been almost too cursorily discussed, yet we shall be content if we succeed in directing attention to the fact that although to the emotions are to be attributed the greatest evils which humanity has endured, nevertheless they are not in themselves unworthy, when freed from their self-created trammels, but are naturally capable of becoming the trusty and indispensable associates of reason. To act without feelings is impossible to man—it is a clear self-contradiction. It is for him to say whether he will attempt to deceive himself by professing to do so, or whether he will accept the necessity, and by due attention and effort endeavour so to refine and ennoble this part of his nature as to render it the champion of truth, instead of the guard of falsehood, a priceless blessing instead of a terrible curse.

R. H. ETTON.

CONTEMPORARY LITERATURE.

The Foreign Books noticed in the following sections are chiefly supplied by Messrs WILLIAMS & NORGATE, Henrietta Street, Covent Garden, and Mr. NUTT, 270, Strand.

THEOLOGY AND PHILOSOPHY.

THE author of "Jesus the Messiah"[1] discusses the personal history of Jesus Christ as it is contained in the New Testament, especially the Gospels. Anxious for the regeneration of Christianity on the basis of the pure doctrines taught by Jesus the Messiah, he presents the result of his studies in a volume of moderate size, which may be recommended as a good summary of conclusions critically arrived at. The writer evinces a competent acquaintance with the subjects handled, a spirit of honest inquiry, and a critical perception which is seldom applied to documents supposed to be sacred. The general tenor of his book, and most of his views, commend themselves to the thoughtful reader. He goes over ground often traversed of late, in his own independent way, exemplifying the exercise of a vigorous common sense in connexion with scholarship. The more works of this sort that appear, the better will it be for the cause of truth. The defects of the volume are small in proportion to its excellences. Fineness of critical tact and sagacity it does not show, but rather a blunt straightforward intellect, expressing itself in language less cautious than is desirable. Some chapters are inferior to the body of the book, such as those on the first state of man, where the view maintained is incorrect. That on the miracles of Jesus is beneath the subject, and elucidates nothing; while the copious discussion of the Messiah's resurrection, and the chapter on the Apostle Paul, cannot be accepted as successful. A weight is laid upon the Apostle's testimony which it will not bear. Nor can the view taken of the Book of Acts be considered a right one. The author sees truly and holds firmly the non-Johannean authorship of the fourth Gospel; but he applies to it epithets which are at least injudicious, such as "humiliating document," "mischievous document," "spurious document," &c. The unknown author is incautiously designated a forger. The language generally applied to him is too derogatory, leading us to infer a want of proper appreciation of the value of the Gospel. Perhaps the critic might have favourably omitted several digressions and expositions of texts; for in the latter department he does not excel. His interpretation of Matt. xvi. 18, 19 is wrong; and the assumption of the verses being an interpolation by one of the Eastern Churches in the dark ages perfectly arbitrary. In reading the work throughout, the wish was felt that the author had read some books with which he appears to be unacquainted, such as Keim's and Schenkel's, Baur's Kirchengeschichte, Zeller on the Acts, and Davidson's Introduction

---

[1] "Jesus the Messiah." London: Trübner and Co.

to the New Testament. These would have modified, enlarged, and
corrected his views.

In the "Life of Jesus Christ,"[1] by a member of the Church of England, a narrative is given harmonizing with the Evangelists while
endeavouring to explain them. The Gospel accounts are taken literally throughout. The volume is uncritical and worthless. The
author describes a miracle as "the product of a law, appertaining to
the world of spirit, introduced by Omnipotence, or by an agent or
factor qualified by Omnipotence to *override* certain laws belonging to
the region of physics." The temptation of Jesus is interpreted ob-
jectively, so that the devil carried the Redeemer away from the desert
through the air up to a battlement of the temple at Jerusalem.

The author of "The Papal Garrison,"[2] alarmed at the spread of
Popery and the insidious ways in which it is advancing, displeased too
with the feeble checks opposed to it by lukewarm Protestants, undertakes to show its dangerous strides. For this purpose, he adduces
numerous facts and statistics, the testimonies of its friends and the
admissions of its foes. The pamphlet overflows with Protestant zeal.
The tone is alarming. The urgency of the case is pleaded. All are
exhorted to stem the tide of idolatry which has set in. Many statements are calculated to arrest the attention of the reader, and the
historical facts adduced are instructive. The little book is worthy of
perusal, and should stimulate intelligent Protestants to oppose all
errors in religion, especially such as are strongly imbued with superstition. But the case is overdrawn; the authority often poor and ill-
chosen; the interpretations of Scripture prophecy erroneous. Individuals, too, are often charged with things of which they are guiltless.
The author's judgment cannot be commended, however sincere his intentions. He lacks enlightenment, knowledge of Scripture and of
Church-history, discernment of character, charity. His publication
needs sifting, as the chaff bears too large a proportion to the wheat.

"The Purpose of God in Creation and Redemption"[3] is a curious
book, setting forth the spiritual work supposed to be in progress in the
Church, and said to comprise a restoration of the gifts of the Holy
Spirit and of the ordinances of God's house. Proceeding from a
member belonging to "the one holy catholic and apostolic church," it
represents the views generally entertained by those who are sometimes
termed the followers of Mr. Irving. These are mystical to a large
extent, and founded in part on what is imagined to be unfulfilled prophecies in the Bible. The present is a time of confusion; the end approaches when all will be rectified. The millennium, with its antecedents and consequents, the future Jerusalem, the renovated earth,
the restored Jews, and such like topics, are dwelt upon, besides others
more largely doctrinal, such as justification. The writer shows a good
spirit, and seems to be an earnest, truth-loving man. But he has

---

[1] "The Life of Jesus Christ." By a Member of the Church of England. Vol. I.
From the Birth of the Saviour to the Death of the Baptist. London: Longmans.
[2] "The Papal Garrison." London: Wm. Hunt and Co.
[3] "The Purpose of God in Creation and Redemption : and the Successive Steps
for manifesting the same in and by the Church." London and Edinburgh: Thomas Laurie.

most erroneous ideas of the sense of Scripture, especially of the Old
Testament, which he converts into a huge type ; of the books of Daniel
and the Apocalypse, as well as of many other portions. His notions are
often chimerical. It is painful to meet with one whose mind is full of
strange fancies ; more painful still to observe the perverse way in
which they are identified with or derived from the sacred volume.

The object of the graduate who writes on St. Paul* is to sketch the
times in which the Apostle lived, the religious systems with which he
was brought in contact, the doctrine he taught, and the work he
achieved. This is done in a series of chapters with considerable ability
and vigour. The author has studied the subjects on which he descants
in a spirit of independence and impartiality. He has seized the leading
characteristics of the Apostle's times and teaching. He writes with
freedom, paints in graphic outline the scenes he wishes to present, and
exhibits an eloquence as well as beauty of description, which throws
an interest over his descriptions. The book has unusual excellence of
matter and style. The author thoroughly admires the Apostle, and
does him full justice in regarding him as the founder of modern Christianity, the man who saved it from becoming an offshoot of Judaism
with no permanent vitality. With him Paul is the impersonation of
all that is noble, disinterested, generous, large-hearted, intensely active
in humanity. The volume contains many just ideas well expressed
respecting the times and teaching of one who has influenced the world
for good, more than any man since his day. Its perusal raises the
Apostle of the Gentiles in our esteem ; and will help to correct some
false opinions which have been attached to his person or derived from
his writings. Perhaps it is too discursive and digressive. The writer
does not adhere to his themes with sufficient closeness, but is ever
diverging into topics collateral or having but slight relation to his
text. His materials might have been arranged more systematically,
and presented in a better shape. The outlines are general, bold,
rough, masterly, without the delicate shades and limitations which a
philosophical and subtle intellect would employ. The main defect in
the book is the assumption that the Pastoral epistles and that to the
Ephesians are authentic. This vitiates any delineation of the Apostle's
sentiments. The critical ability of the man who does not see the non-
authenticity of the Pastoral epistles is small. Connected with this is
the groundless supposition of a second Roman imprisonment. The
value of the work is also lessened by the inaccuracies that frequently
occur, which, though comparatively small, show either ignorance or
haste on the part of the writer. Indeed, his knowledge of Scripture
is neither full nor exact. Thus he thinks that Paul gave way in the
case of Titus ; that *Satan* is used in Hebrew with the article when it
denotes the superhuman adversary of man (contrary to 1 Chron. xxi.
1) ; that the communications made from the Almighty to the prophets
of the Jewish monarchy, the captivity and restoration, " were effected
by the instrumentality of the Word of God ;" that the last supper

* " Paul of Tarsus : an Inquiry into the Times and the Gospel of the Apostle
of the Gentiles." By a Graduate. London : Macmillan and Co.

narrated by Paul and that in the fourth Gospel are the same; that Junias (masculine) is Junia a woman, and spoken of as an apostle; that Marcion accepted a mutilated Gospel of *St. Matthew,* and that the language in 1 Timothy vi. 20 points to Jewish or semi-Jewish sects in Asia Minor. Nor can his Jewish knowledge be relied upon. Evil angels do not appear in Philo's writings, as he affirms they do. We also desiderate in the description of Paul's Christology a more definite account than that which is given. The Pauline ideas of sacrifice and atonement, of predestination, justification, &c., are unsatisfactorily handled or slurred over. In short, the author adds nothing to our knowledge of the Apostle or of his mental development. His interspersed reflections, however, are generally good and well expressed. From the noble example of the Jew of Tarsus he has caught inspiration, though it might have been calmer and more discriminating.

Mr. Sanday[*] professes to investigate the internal evidence furnished by the fourth Gospel on behalf of its authorship and authenticity. He goes through the document chapter by chapter, determining the exact value of the separate data, and then drawing his conclusions. Regarding the controversy as a drawn one as far as external evidence is concerned, he confines himself to the other branch of evidence. The result at which he arrives is, that the Apostle John wrote the Gospel in question, and that it bears throughout marks of an eye-witness. The book is written with a degree of calmness and candour, as well as a respectable acquaintance with the literature of the subject, which bespeak for it a favourable hearing. The author seems anxious to arrive at a conclusion logically deducible from the premises; but his argument, with all its appearance of fairness, is that of an advocate. He has not mastered all the literature of the subject, and his critical ability is small. Weak advocates, or the reasonings of weak advocates, are selected for refutation, while strong ones are passed over. The judgment of the writer seems so feeble that we suppose the present publication to be a first attempt at criticism. If so, it is a bold one for him, because the controversy is difficult and perplexing. One thing he sees clearly and brings out plainly—the discrepancies between the synoptists and the fourth Gospel. But in assuming throughout that the former are wrong, the latter right, he shows his prepossessions. This is especially observable in fixing the day of the crucifixion, while he argues in favour of the Johannean date against the synoptic one. The question of the Paschal controversy and its bearing on the Gospel's authorship does not seem to have been studied by Mr. Sanday, who contents himself with a few perfunctory observations derived from Steitz and Bleek. And it is puerile to meet Renan's position regarding miracles with the assertion, that the age of the Gospel miracles was a miraculous one, *sui generis,* wholly different from the present—signs and wonders being then in the air. The book must be pronounced a failure. It is impossible in the eye of sound criticism to hold that the Gospel was written by a Jew, that it is the most Jewish

---

[*] "The Authorship and Historical Character of the Fourth Gospel considered in reference to the Contents of the Gospel itself: a Critical Essay. By W. Sanday, M.A." London: Macmillan and Co.

book in the New Testament, and that it is historical rather than theological, ideal, symbolical, mystic. The problem discussed by Mr. Sanday is one for which his grasp is insufficient; so that he has only succeeded in making the difficulty of attributing the Gospel to the Apostle John more palpable. One who cannot discover proof in chapter xxi. that it was added to the Gospel by some other writer—who has "strong reason" to see in the Son of Thunder and the Apostle of love the same person—and to find the Christology of the Johannean discourses "fundamentally that of the synoptists and of Christ himself," is scarcely fit for the office of a New Testament critic at the present day.

The editors of a second series of essays entitled "The Church and the Age,"[7] tell us that it is intended to illustrate the position of the Anglican communion as a reformed branch of the Catholic Church; to discuss, from different points of view, various questions bearing upon the special circumstances of the present time; and to vindicate the capability of the Anglican Church for meeting the wants of each successive age without sacrificing her primitive faith, or abandoning the principles of her Apostolic constitution. The volume contains twelve essays, on the Church and pauperism, the American Church, the Church and science, systems of ecclesiastical law, the present and future relations of the Church to national education, the Church and the universities, toleration, the aspect of the Eastern Church towards the Churches of the Anglican Communion, the difficulties of a disestablished Church, the Christian tradition, dogma, and the co-operation of the laity in parochial councils. It is pitched on a High Church, orthodox key, and will be found somewhat heavy reading to all except such as take the same view of the Anglican Church. Some of the essays have little to do with the Church, or rather the Church should not meddle with the matters treated in them. This is the case with pauperism and with science, though the third essay is one of the best in the book. Those on national education and the universities breathe a narrow spirit, as does that on dogma. When a writer denies the possibility of religion without dogma, supposes that the distinction between the beliefs of conscience and dogmas is the result of "mental confusion," and that the cause of unity not less than the interests of charity demand the non-surrender of dogmas, he is manifestly bound in the fetters of Church authority. Perhaps the most interesting of the essays is that on the American Church, though we regret to see the same tone in it as in the rest. The most curious and the least valuable is that on tradition, in which some strange statements are put forth, such as that "the saints of all ages and the Church" have always "professed an interpretation of the Bible quite her own, which no stranger knoweth," independent of the literal criticism. Parables of truth and glory are found "beneath the letter." The entire volume lacks intellectual excellence and literary ability. The questions discussed in it are treated in a conservative spirit, that

[7] "The Church and the Age: Essays on the Principles and Present Position of the Anglican Church." Second Series. Edited by A. Weir, D.C.L., and W. D. Maclagan, M.A. London: John Murray.

resists any radical change in the principles or creeds of the Anglican Church, so that the writers aim at the impossible—the adaptation of the institution they belong to, while preserving it intact in all essentials, especially in the creeds and formularies, to the intelligence of the age.

The name of Thomas Scott, of Ramsgate,[*] is well known as that of one who has been employed for years in disseminating tracts, pamphlets, and books of a liberal tendency in theology. With great energy and perseverance he has pursued his mission to emancipate men from the dominion of orthodox creeds, and to promote rational views of religion, the Bible, man's future destiny, &c. &c. It is impossible that he has done no good; on the contrary, he must have led many to think, examine, and act as free agents under the moral government of God, instead of following the dogmas of priests or clerics. If he has issued his publications in rapid succession, and on a great variety of topics, guided by no fixed principle save that of demolition—the demolition of old faiths to make room for the introduction of a simpler one—if he has made himself obnoxious to the orthodox, he has pursued a course productive of benefit by encouraging the timid to speak out, and by putting in print thoughts that must have passed through serious minds in a variety of shapes. Multitudes owe their first conceptions of Bible fallibility to him. Not that we approve of all his pamphlets. A few of them, such as the flimsy one entitled "The Impeachment of Christianity," should not have appeared. One of his ablest publications is "The English Life of Jesus," a book formerly issued in six parts, from 1860 onwards, and now reprinted in a second edition, with slight alterations and additions. Here the Gospel history is minutely canvassed with a view of showing its want of credibility. In six chapters the biographies of Jesus given in the Gospels are analyzed with much acuteness and logical power. Few points are left untouched. The inconsistency of the narratives is shown with irresistible clearness and force. It is also proved that the documents on which certain dogmas of historical Christianity are founded contain legendary and fictitious accounts. The author does not shrink from carrying out his conclusions to their utmost extent, rejecting miracles,

* "The English Life of Jesus." By Thomas Scott. London: Trübner and Co. "Pleas for Free Inquiry." Part ii. "Some Observations on The Argument from Analogy." By M. A. Ramsgate: Thomas Scott. "On Religion." By a former Elder in a Scotch Church. Same Publisher. "A Dialogue by way of Catechism," &c. By a Physician. Part ii. Same Publisher. "On Public Worship." Same Publisher. "On Faith." By A. D. Graham and F. H. Same Publisher. "An Examination of some Recent Writings about Immortality." By W. E. D. Same Publisher. "A. J. Conversations." Edited by a Woman for Women. Part iii. Same Publisher. "Scepticism and Social Justice." By Thos. H. Bastard. Same Publisher. "Spiritual Pantheism." By F. H. J. Same Publisher. "On Church Pedigrees." By Rev. T. P. Kirkman, M.A., F.R.S. Part ii. Same Publisher. "The Impeachment of Christianity." By F. E. Abbot. Same Publisher.

the resurrection and ascension of Christ, as well as the historical character of the fourth Gospel. Perhaps he has carried his negative results too far in a few instances; while in others, such as the taxing of Cyrenius, he has not alluded to the plausible view of Zumpt, lately recommended in the *Quarterly Review*. But he is an acute reasoner; and the advocates of orthodoxy will find it difficult to meet his arguments fairly, or to overthrow them. The English Life of Jesus will confirm the general results which Strauss, Keim, and many others have arrived at. It will also serve to show the shallowness of Renan's criticisms regarding many particulars in the Gospels, and his vain attempt to uphold the authenticity of the fourth Gospel after a fashion of his own.

We have read the second part of what the author calls "Pleas for Free Inquiry" with much satisfaction. It deals with the argument from analogy in a way convincing to the thoughtful. Many educated people have perceived or felt the insufficiency of Butler's argument in favour of a Divine revelation. They have asked themselves, what is the use of a Divine revelation if it contain difficulties and mysteries similar to those inherent in the constitution and course of nature? Should we not expect it to solve some at least of these mysteries, to clear away some of the difficulties that meet us in nature, so that the path of human duty would be certain, God shining upon it with a light giving peace to the mind and conscience. The author of this pamphlet points out the legitimate scope and extent of the analogical argument. He shows how far it reaches, and where it fails as an evidence in favour of a miraculous revelation. His remarks are summed up under six heads, in which he proves that the general argument is so wide in scope as to apply to a great number of religions, not all of which, possibly not one, can be true in the sense of containing nothing but truth; that it is unsatisfactory in its mode of dealing with certain difficulties, such as the doctrine of eternal punishment, the alleged immoral commands of the Deity, &c.; that it fails to commend the probability of miracles; that it is fraught with danger to the doctrine of inspiration; that in all religions are to be found the same difficulties as there are in nature; and that Butler's argument is perfectly good in defence of a system of pure Theism—since all the objections which can be urged against such a belief can also be urged against the constitution of nature. No other publication exhibits such a condensation of pertinent, judicious, acute, and valid observations bearing upon Butler's analogical argument as the present brief pamphlet of fifty-seven pages. The strength and weakness of the argument are shown with great ability. We can only hope that many will listen to such a reasoner, and learn. That he is a scholar as well as thinker may be gathered from the numerous notes appended, which are usually pertinent.

The volume with the fanciful title, "The Garden and the City,"[*] appears to consist of sermons founded on parallels and contrasts in the Bible. The author has indulged his imagination with little advantage, for the ideas inculcated are curious, absurd commonplaces of ortho-

* "The Garden and the City, with other Contrasts and Parallels of Scripture." By the Rev. H. Macmillan, LL.D. London: Smith, Elder, and Co.

doxy; and the knowledge of Scripture displayed is usually superficial, often incorrect.

The sermons of the late Canon Melvill[10] on some of the less prominent facts and references in the Bible, are of the moderate evangelical type. The author, who was not a thinker but a popular preacher, belonged to the better class of the orthodox in the Church of England. The volumes contain nothing striking or peculiar, either in matter or style; but they are pervaded by good sense, and are not specially doctrinal. Many of the piously disposed may read them with profit.

Miss Sharpe has compiled "Outlines of Sermons,"[11] which will be useful not only to readers sympathizing in Unitarian doctrines, but to several preachers of the denomination. The sermons here presented are somewhat tame and dry, possessing few beauties of composition. They are neither eloquent nor profound. But they have a practical tone adapted to human life, and are fitted to edify readers of average intelligence, especially such as have little depth of spiritual feeling or glow of enthusiasm.

The editor of the *Hindoo Patriot* requested a graduate in the Government School at Calcutta to write a paper on the chief national festival of the Hindus of Bengal,[12] which he did accordingly. This has been published in a small volume, with notes and illustrations. The matter is curious, and may be studied with interest by those who inquire into ancient comparative mythology or religions.

The Commentary of Keil and Delitzsch on the Old Testament[13] proceeds apace, too hastily to ensure thorough or excellent work. Professor Keil has just published the portion of it relating to Jeremiah and the Lamentations, which represents the style of exegesis peculiar to that laborious scholar. Orthodox, superficial, dogmatic, he throws no light on the prophet, but resists views and criticisms not unfrequently which are undoubtedly correct. Thus the integrity of the Masoretic text of Jeremiah is maintained; an opinion which, though it has the countenance of Graf, is untenable. The 50th and 51st chapters are also assigned to the prophet himself; a view which few critics will approve. The part relating to the Lamentations is superior to the other; and the introduction to it especially is of higher merit. In it the Jeremiah-authorship is vindicated with considerable ability, in opposition to Thenius and Schrader. We do not agree, however, with his assertion of the originality of the present place which the Lamentations occupy in the third division of the Hebrew book.

---

[10] "Sermons on certain of the Less Prominent Facts and References in Sacred Story." By Henry Melvill, B.D. In 2 volumes. London: Rivingtons.

[11] "Outlines of Sermons, taken chiefly from the Published Works of Unitarian Writers." London: John Russell Smith.

[12] "Durga Puja: with Notes and Illustrations." By Pratapachandra Ghosha, B.A. Calcutta: printed at the Hindoo Patriot press.

[13] "Biblischer Commentar ueber das alte Testament." Herausgegeben von Carl F. Keil und Franz Delitzsch. "Der Prophet Jeremia und die Klaglieder." London: D. Nutt.

The ecclesiastical decisions of the Judicial Committee of Her Majesty's Privy Council within the last thirty years have been important in their bearings on the character of the English Church.[14] As precedents in future legislation they stand out distinctly; as documents embodying the results of great legal ability and calm interpretation of the Church's formularies, they attract the attention both of clerics and lawyers. The highest law functionaries of the land have been engaged in their composition. The six cases edited by Mr. Brooke are those of Gorham *versus* Bishop of Exeter, Liddell *v.* Western and Liddell *v.* Beal, Williams *v.* Bishop of Salisbury and Wilson *v.* Fendall, Martin *v.* Mackonochie, Hebbert *v.* Purchas, and Sheppard *v.* Bennett. The judgments in each are printed verbatim. The editor has prefixed a long introduction, partly historical, respecting the origin and jurisdiction of the Privy Council; and has also given in an appendix several notes illustrative of the separate cases or of particulars connected with them. The book, carefully compiled and edited, has a special interest for many, besides its value as a record of decisions vitally important to the Established Church. The chief cases are those affecting doctrines—viz, Gorham *v.* Exeter, Williams and Wilson in the matter of "Essays and Reviews," and Sheppard *v.* Bennett. The rest concern petty matters, such as postures, attitudes, rites, vestments, &c., which should not have been brought before the Council. The friends of toleration and liberty must have rejoiced at the decisions in favour of the essayists as well as of Gorham, where the principle of comprehension was wisely acted upon to its legitimate extent. Indeed, this principle seems to have influenced all the decisions. As there are distinct parties in the same church, no one should impose its meaning on the Articles and formularies to the exclusion of senses applied by the rest. We regret to find the absence in this volume of two cases as important perhaps as any it gives, those of Messrs. Heath and Voysey. Both turned on doctrines and opinions. The former seems a harsh judgment, contrary to the principle of comprehension. The latter, when put beside that of Purchas, seems unaccountable on the ground of equal and impartial justice. A very broad churchman is condemned; an Anglican who preaches the Romish doctrine of transubstantiation is acquitted. Great tenderness is shown to Mr. Bennett; little to Mr. Voysey. The two judgments can scarcely be harmonized, and one cannot but suspect a certain manipulation of the acting committee beforehand in Bennett's case, when he knows that Mr. Bernard, of Oxford, was put upon it the day before the sitting. In reading these judgments, the feeling is strong that articles, creeds, and formularies, to which every clergyman must subscribe on entering the Church, are hindrances to freedom, temptations to prevarication, pretexts for dishonesty. Those articles were set forth at first as subjects of belief, to which the incipient cleric should give his hearty assent and consent. In the plain meaning they bear, they are to be sub-

<hr />

[14] "Six Judgments of the Judicial Committee of the Privy Council in Ecclesiastical Cases, 1850-1872, with an Historical Introduction, Notes, and Index." Edited by W. G. Brooke, M.A. London: H. S. King and Co.

scribed without reserve. But if they are not consistent with each other, if their words be sometimes vague and ambiguous, they furnish a plausible excuse for evasion; a circumstance demanding their alteration or repeal. The public example set by men whose office is to inculcate religious duties, in not believing doctrines to which they subscribed at their entrance on office, though still reading in public the words expressing such doctrines, cannot be other than injurious.

An authorized report[14] of the proceedings of Nonconformists about education at Manchester, in January last, gives the speeches, papers, resolutions of the multitude assembled on that occasion. The leading tenet advocated was that the State should make provision solely for secular instruction, leaving the religious element to other and voluntary agencies. In this respect the Conference advocated a right policy. No comprehensive system of national education will be established in Great Britain till the State cease to meddle with the religious element and confine its operation to the secular. But the conference does not appear to have been conducted with calmness or dignity. Politics were introduced into the proceedings too freely; and the present liberal Government was threatened with a withdrawal of the support of Nonconformists. The occasion was ill-chosen. Mr. Forster's bill should have been allowed sufficient time for operation before an assault was made upon it; and he should have been spoken of in more courteous terms. The report shows the brethren to be deficient in intellectual ability and moral weight. There is a noisy shallowness about the speeches, an *ad captandum* spirit, a boastful declamation, which make an unfavourable impression on the reader. The reasoning indulged in is poor in texture, though pretentious enough. Plenty of zeal appears to have animated the chairmen, readers, and speakers; but we fear that if they could get their own views realized, and were exalted to power, intolerance and narrow-mindedness would prevail. It is a pity that the true basis of a national system of education should not have found worthier representatives.

The twenty-third volume of the Ante-Nicene Library contains a translation of books ii.—viii. of Origen's treatise against Celsus,[15] one of the most valuable early Apologies written by the Christians in defence of their religion. The work is rendered faithfully and accurately into English by Professor Crombie and his coadjutor, who add some notes and the originals of passages which are difficult or obscure. There are few places in which we should alter the translation except occasionally with relation to the expression or omission of the indefinite article before 'God' applied to Jesus Christ. A copious analysis of the contents, a life of Origen derived chiefly from Redepenning's

[14] "General Conference of Nonconformists, held in Manchester, January 23-25, 1872." Manchester: Alex. Ireland and Co.

[15] "Ante-Nicene Christian Library. The Writings of Origen." Vol. II. Translated by the Rev. F. Crombie, D.D.

[16] "Liturgies and other Documents of the Ante-Nicene Period." Edinburgh: T. and T. Clark.

work, and two good indices, the first of texts quoted or referred to, the second of principal subjects, increase the value of this scholarly volume. In the life of Origen prefixed to the volume we miss exact information about Celsus, of whom his Christian opponent knew nothing certain. The heathen philosopher was a Neo-Platonist, not an Epicurean, and was a contemporary of Origen's, whatever Tischendorf may say to the contrary. This is a point on which Baur, Bindemann, and Neander have thrown light. The twenty-fourth volume is occupied with curious liturgies translated by different persons, among whom Mr. Pratten, following his old calling, gives two pieces edited for the first time by Cureton, and translated by him too. The latter fact, however, is suppressed by Mr. Pratten, who says no more than that the text is found in the Spicilegium Syriacum. With these volumes the Ante-Nicene series terminates, forming a valuable library of early Christian literature. Though we cannot congratulate the publisher on the editorial judgment or superintendence of the work, nor on the competency of some translators, he deserves the thanks of all who are interested in this sort of literature. It is well for others than the learned to see that the early fathers of the Church were not critical scholars; that they were generally not orthodox in the sense of the Nicene creed, much less in that of modern symbols; and that their opinions must be sifted by the methods now applied to ancient documents. Their doctrinal views are interesting only historically. No authority attaches to them other than that inherent in their truth.

Dr. Steane's treatise on the doctrine of Christ developed by the Apostles" seems to present the substance of sermons preached or prepared years ago. The doctrines expounded in it are those of Puritan orthodox Calvinistic theology, now antiquated for thinkers. Forty years ago the dogmas here enunciated were commonly entertained in the Dissenting world: they have now lost their hold upon scholars. Those who have followed the current of Biblical exegesis and criticism will wonder at the self-complacency of a man who stereotyped his opinions long ago, and has since shut out modern light. Dr. Steane shows his ignorance of the Bible in its true sense, of the diversities in the Apostolic teaching, and the different degrees of authority attaching to the sacred writers. It is sad to see in a devout man the evidences of sleeping over the Bible for years, and ignoring the books which would have enlightened, enlarged, purified his mental vision. Thus in speaking of the evangelists he says, "The Holy Spirit used them as his amanuenses. The history is his in a more intimate sense than it is theirs. Their minds were taken under his immediate government, and they wrote nothing which had not his approbation; it may be said, which he himself would not have written."

Mr. Haweis's volume, entitled "Thoughts for the Times," consists

⁷ " The Doctrine of Christ developed by the Apostles: a Treatise on the Offices of the Redeemer and the Doxology of the Redeemed." By Ed. Steane, D.D. Edinburgh: Edmonston and Douglas.

⁸ "Thoughts for the Times." By the Rev. H. R. Haweis, M.A. London: H. S. King and Co.

of shorthand reports of various extempore sermons. The preacher discourses on very different subjects, such as the liberal clergy, God, the character and ethics of Christianity, the Bible, the Articles, the Lord's day, preaching, pleasure, sacrifice, the laws of progress, F. D. Maurice, &c. His papers are impregnated with a character of freedom and with a certain freshness which render them readable. The author seems to be a broad churchman who likes to speak openly on subjects which many of his brethren would be afraid to touch in the pulpit. But the essays are rather flimsy and superficial. Their author, evidently a poor theologian, speaks confidently on topics which he knows but imperfectly, or has never studied. With a little knowledge gathered from ordinary books, he utters jerky sentences in a style not distinguished for modesty or reverence. It is plain that he has got away from the sense of the articles intended by their framers, that he is far from being a calm teacher, and that he can speak at random about things demanding careful study. Thus, the fifth discourse is thickly strewn with incorrectnesses. In it the author asserts that Jesus Christ borrowed from the Talmud, that "His sermons were something like the sermons of the scribes, and yet different;" that the distinguishing character of the Sermon on the Mount is "an enthusiasm of love." Elsewhere he says that Erasmus "rejects" the epistle to the Hebrews, 2 Peter, and Revelation; whereas the truth is, that he merely denied the *Pauline authorship* of the first, and *the apostolic origin* of the last. But we have no space to point out the errors into which Mr. H. falls. He lacks information and accuracy on theological subjects. Instead of trying to say striking things, as "that Darwin would attribute half the misery of this world to original sin," and giving a shallow view of the Trinity by which it is simply explained away, he should adopt a sobriety of expression in harmony with the sacred subjects of which he speaks so confidently.

The argument delivered before the Judicial Committee of the Privy Council in the case of Sheppard against Bennett" is given pretty fully in an octavo volume recently published by Dr. Stephens, the learned lawyer who conducted the case with great ability and argumentative power. Combating very often the statements of the Dean of Arches, and quoting many authorities bearing on the points discussed, he exhibited a knowledge, tact, and logic not usual even in lawyers of high standing. As far as we can see, Dr. Stephens proved that the doctrine maintained by Bennett is contrary to the formularies of the Church of England. Why the judgment was such as it came forth it is not easy to explain, but it may be safely asserted that its effect on the church will be injurious. Comprehension is good: the wish to maintain it in an Established Church commendable; but we fail to see the justice of excluding

---

[19] "The Substance of the Argument delivered before the Judicial Committee of the Privy Council. By A. J. Stephens, LL.D., one of her Majesty's Counsel, in the Case of T. B. Sheppard against W. J. E. Bennett, Clerk. With an Appendix containing their Lordships' Judgment." London: Rivingtons.

Messrs. Heath and Voysey, while including the Romanizing Bennett.
The volume brings together many extracts and opinions which will be
serviceable to future theologians, as well as ecclesiastical lawyers.
It has also an excellent index.

Mr. Curteis has taken a good subject for the Bampton Lectures of
1871,* and his treatment of it is eminently conciliatory. After a
lecture on dissent in general, he passes in review six of the more important denominations now existing in England, the Independents,
the Romanists, the Baptists, the Quakers, the Unitarians, and the Wesleyans, sketching their origin and peculiar characteristics with competent knowledge and skill. The spirit in which the writer treats a
difficult and delicate subject, is both candid and charitable. Mr.
Curteis writes with the zeal of an educated churchman, who yearns
after the union of the people of England under a common banner, de-
ploring the secessions from the National Church which have taken
place in the past, acknowledging the good which the sects have done,
the mistakes committed by the Church, and the desirableness of a conciliatory spirit in order to win back the separatists. Were all clergymen animated by the same spirit as his, the bishops of the Church
especially, the sects would be weaker and less numerous than they
are. The volume may be commended to the perusal of Dissenters and
Churchmen alike, as an instructive survey of past dissensions, accompanied by large-hearted suggestions for remedying them in the
future. We fear, however, that neither the sects nor the Church are
yet disposed towards friendly overtures about Union, though it is
certain that there is more practical freedom for teachers of religion
within the National Establishment, than in any of the other
sects; and that her very creeds and formularies are more bearable in
practice, than those of the latter, where minorities often rule with
terrible severity. It is also certain, that the sects are declining, if
not in numbers of adherents, which is however probable, yet in intellectual strength, in theological learning, and doctrinal liberality.
They are noisy enough; but clamour is not the manifestation of
strength. It is natural for Mr. Curteis to think that the Church has
the apparatus within itself necessary to the wants of the age; and
that it can adapt itself to the intellectual as well as the spiritual
necessities of all. It is certainly a comprehensive, visible, organized,
educating society, though it has strangely failed to educate the people;
but whether it be possible for many "to discover the rich treasures
stored up for us in the Rituals, the lections from Holy Scripture, the
Creeds, the Hymns, the elaborate Synodal and hierarchical arrangements of our own Church," may be matter of doubt. And it is still
more doubtful whether Christ "intended to leave, or did actually leave
on earth an organized and visible society in which he has lodged his
commission to go and teach all nations, and has stored therein special
gifts of the Holy Ghost." Mr. Curteis must be aware of the fact, that

* "Dissent in its Relation to the Church of England. Eight Lectures preached
before the University of Oxford in the year 1871." By G. H. Curteis, M.A.
London : Macmillan and Co.

uniformity of ritual, creeds, and services in the Church, is not unity; that there are marked parties in the establishment, as distinct from one another as are Baptists and Wesleyans; and that the creeds they have subscribed are disbelieved by many clergymen. To allure the sects into the Church, that body must radically reform itself. And the first element in a real reform is by abolishing the creeds, and making religion undogmatic, so as to have a simple basis acceptable to the great majority of the population, leaving the preacher free to inculcate the spirit of Christianity as he thinks best. Hierarchism must be discouraged in all its forms; and the episcopate be chosen for other qualifications than political opinions, safe mediocrity of talent, quietude of temper, ignorance of theology. This powerful establishment should be simplified by a reduction of her cumbrous machinery and numerous rites amid which piety is often crushed. Comprehensive as the Church is, she needs greater comprehension in order to attract men of culture now generally alienated from her, and still more alienated from the external sects with their narrow creeds and ill-educated teachers.

The late Professor Maurice issued a second edition of his Lectures on Conscience," with a new Preface, just before he died. No change appears in their form or substance. They are readable productions, in which no analysis of what we call "conscience" is attempted, no new light thrown upon the faculty or rather that exercise of the reason so styled. But the writer makes some pertinent remarks on Bentham, Bain, and Jeremy Taylor; criticises Butler, and resolves the supremacy of conscience into the abdication of such supremacy on behalf of law proceeding from a lawgiver who has the right to govern. We do not think that he distinguishes properly between *conscience* and *consciousness*; or that his definition of the former, " that in me which says, I ought or ought not," conveys any exact idea of its nature.

The volumes of Professor Maurice on Moral and Metaphysical Philosophy," formerly published at different times, have recently reappeared in another shape, with a long preface in the form of a dialogue. The first volume contains ancient philosophy, and that of the first thirteen centuries of the Christian era; the second begins with William of Occam, terminating with Kant, Herder, and Jacobi. There are also some general observations on Stewart, Bentham, Coleridge, Mill's " Logic," and Hamilton's " Essay on the Unconditioned." The author did not attempt to give an account of systems and schools, but " to trace the progress of the thoughts that have contributed to form these schools and systems; to connect them with the lives of the men in whom they have originated ; to note the influence which they have exerted upon their times, and the influence which their times have exerted upon them." The work travels over a vast field, and shows how large the extent of Mr. Maurice's reading must have been. Yet

" "The Conscience : Lectures on Casuistry, delivered in the University of Cambridge, by F. D. Maurice." Second Edition. London : Macmillan and Co.
" " Moral and Metaphysical Philosophy." By F. D. Maurice. London : Macmillan and Co.

his genius was hardly fitted for metaphysics. In moral philosophy he was more at home, because he could expatiate there with greater freedom, indulging in that wealth of words he had at command. He wanted the exactness, clearness, precision, analytic acuteness, which metaphysics require. The work however is an instructive one, and will be of great use to students commencing a course of reading in philosophy. We could have wished, indeed, that the author had omitted many names and paragraphs, which have no real connexion with the subject; that he had compressed his materials into smaller compass; and discoursed less largely. Yet we miss names influential in their own times, or afterwards. Hutcheson of Glasgow, Abraham Tucker, Dalguy, Cogan, Isaac Watts, had more to do with philosophy than Erasmus, Reuchlin, Luther, and Melancthon. Nor is it fair to say no more of Dr. Thomas Brown than that Sir W. Hamilton denounced his popular lectures. In describing Jonathan Edwards's "Treatise on the Will," it should have been noticed, that the pith of the argument is in Collins's small "Treatise on Human Liberty," published in 1715; with which the American divine was probably acquainted. The Professor can invest dry topics with considerable interest. One thing is apparent, his fairness and candour. He loves to bring out the good features of a philosophy which he dislikes as a whole. Perhaps he is too much of a *doctrinaire* at times; putting his own ideas into the views of the man described. We need not specify the portions in which he is most successful. Probably the mediæval philosophy receives the best treatment. The ancient is scarcely handled satisfactorily. But the Professor is at home in characterizing Butler, Paley, Bentham, and Coleridge. Even Spinoza, difficult as he is to master, is ably delineated. The book deserves the attentive perusal of all that love to trace the progress of thought in the world, and the advancement of true knowledge, the knowledge of God and man. If it has the strong tinge of an earnest theologian, it is the production of one who tried to seek and promote truth in the genuine spirit of a philosopher.

The Bampton Lecture of Professor Mozley on Miracles[a] has reached a third edition. As the work was reviewed in the April number of the *Westminster* for the year 1866, it calls for no special remarks now. It remains the same in substance and form, an insufficient discussion of a difficult subject. The second edition and the third have long prefaces, contributing nothing, however, to the solution of the problem. The author speaks of an antecedent probability on behalf of miracles, which is formed by "original ideas, instructive impressions, and fundamental convictions of the mind;" of two ideas of the Divine Being, that of the Supreme Mundane, the impersonation of the causes at work in the visible world, and that of Him as moral Governor and Judge; and then assumes that if we entertain the former there is nothing for miracles to do; while in the latter, there is a reason for them; they "have a use as a guarantee to a Revelation, should it

---

[a] "Eight Lectures on Miracles, preached before the University of Oxford in the year 1865." By J. B. Mozley, D.D. Third Edition. London: Rivingtons.

please God to make known to us anything in His spiritual relations to us which we do not know by our natural reason." Here the author makes distinctions and assumptions perfectly arbitrary. Why should the idea of God, as a moral Governor and Judge, involve the antecedent probability of miracles? Does it do so? Certainly not. Since the first issue of his book, the lecturer does not seem to have studied the origin and date of the Gospels, else he would not continue to speak of "the contemporaneous date of the testimony" to the Gospel miracles, a statement disproved by historical criticism; or to assert, "that certain great and cardinal Gospel miracles possess contemporary testimony must be admitted by everybody;" which is precisely what those who have investigated the Gospel records in the fullest and fairest manner, refuse to admit. The evidence of eye-witnesses is wanting; for the Gospels recording the miracles are the product, in their present state, of the second century; none of them having been written—at least, as we have it—by Apostles or Evangelists in the first. As long as Dr. Mozley makes arbitrary statements which historical criticism disproves, he shows an utter incapacity to deal with the credibility of miracles. As long, too, as he continues to urge that miracles are necessary to a Revelation, he imperils his whole argument; for in that case, the existence of a Revelation will be denied by many, whose acceptance of it would powerfully tend to commend the fact.

Dr. Beard's book on Satan[14] is a well-timed production, intended to set forth the origin, period of composition, debasement, and decline of Satan as an historical existence. For this purpose he goes through such portions of history, profane and sacred, as relate to the idea, attributing it to the dualism of the East affecting later Judaism. He considers that many professional priests have found it useful, and look upon the extinction of the notion as a calamity to religion, because it would be ruinous to their interests. The work is a series of sketches meant for the general public rather than scholars. As such it will be productive of good, helping to dissipate a superstition which has no connexion with religion, but on the contrary, debases it. The autobiographical form hampers the author somewhat. The book shows evidence of reading, thought, and culture; though its statements and details are not always exact or precise. Neither are its interpretations of Scripture uniformly correct. In explaining antichrist or the man of sin, the author falls into error. The temptation of Christ is neither "a parable" nor "an allegory," in the proper sense of those words. "The fall" is not "an allegory in pictures." Dr. Beard also quotes Kuenen for some opinions which the Leyden Professor has since changed. Had he consulted the best German sources, omitted several ghost-stories and various quotations at the end of the work, which add nothing to its value, he would have done better. But though there is a want of scientific precision and accuracy in many places, as well as an useless accumulation of extracts; though the

[14] "The Autobiography of Satan." Edited by John R. Beard, D.D. London: Williams and Norgate.

subject is not presented in the best light, because the materials are thrown together somewhat loosely, without having been previously digested, the volume is a highly meritorious one.

The masterly commentary of Professor Tuch on Genesis" had been out of print for years before a new edition was undertaken by Dr. Arnold, who died before it had passed through the press, having committed the concluding portions to Professor Merx. A few notes from the author's copy are given by Arnold ; a few are subjoined by himself. The work is reprinted as it was. Merx has added a *Nachwort* of more than forty pages, containing a summary of the principal literary productions relating to the composition and date of Genesis since the first appearance of Tuch's book. The appendix may be useful to students and others ; but it is neither complete nor excellent. Professor Merx is scarcely competent to pronounce a summary opinion on the critical researches of men like De Wette and Ewald. The work should have been edited and supplemented by Professor Boehmer, whose acuteness and ability have been already shown in the department to which Tuch made so important a contribution.

The late Dean Alford had begun a commentary on the Old Testament," somewhat in the same style as that which he published on the New. As death interrupted his labours when he had proceeded no farther than the 25th chapter of Exodus, it has been thought fit to publish the part he completed. It was a mistake in the Dean to undertake such a work. He was not a Hebrew scholar ; neither had he the other qualifications necessary to a good interpreter of the Old Testament. All he could do was to make a respectable compilation from preceding writers ; taking care to keep in the main on orthodox ground. The volume, it need not be said, is far behind the results of recent criticism. Here and there a few unimportant concessions to those whom he calls rationalists appear, such as the existence of Elohistic and Jehovistic documents ; but he compensates for such admissions by dogmatic assertions levelled at the best critics. We observe also, that he ignores some of the ablest commentators and critics, restricting his attention to comparatively few, such as Knobel, Delitzsch, Kalisch, and Keil. Tuch does not seem to have been known to him, except through the pages of Kalisch. In the light of recent research nothing but an unfavourable opinion of the book can be given. It has little critical value, and abounds with mistakes. In the very first verse of Genesis, the Dean errs in saying that " the heavens and the earth" mean the universe. He adopts the wrong version of Genesis xii. 3, defending it by the wrong principle that the New Testament writers decide for us which senses of the Hebrew original should be adopted. His note on Exodus vi. 2-3,

---

" "Welland Dr. Friedrich Tuch's Commentar ueber die Genesis." Zweite Auflage besorgt von Professor Dr. A. Arnold nebst einem Nachwort von A. Merx." London : Trübner and Co.

" "The Book of Genesis and part of the Book of Exodus : a Revised Version, with Marginal References and an Explanatory Commentary." By H. Alford, D.D. London : Strahan and Co.

is misleading. And he does not hesitate to affirm that the dying Jacob spoke the words in Genesis xlix., as there recorded, although they are Jehovistic. Of course, the rendering of the authorized version in the 10th verse remains, incorrect though it be.

Dr. Phillips has recast his "Commentary on the Psalms,"[v] so as to make a new work, which bears a very favourable comparison with its predecessor. The respected President of Queen's College has been a diligent student of Hebrew, steadily encouraging the study of it in the university he belongs to, as far as he had opportunity. The new volumes are a good example of orthodox exegesis, moderate in tone, breathing a fair spirit, and assigning their due merits to critics of another school. The scholarship is also respectable, and the knowledge of Hebrew superior. The learning displayed is highly creditable to one who began his Hebrew studies at a time when German criticism had not penetrated into England, and was looked upon with much disfavour. The author, however, acknowledges his obligations to German scholars; to their grammars, lexicons, and commentaries, with which he is well acquainted. We are often at variance in opinion with Dr. Phillips, though he is a very sober expositor of the orthodox school. In the authorship and date of Psalms, their Messianic exposition, their application in the New Testament as authoritative, and in many other points, we hold that he is wrong. In the explanations of difficult words, such as *ben* (Psalm ii. 12); *caari* (Psalm xxii. 16); the reading *chasidcka* (Psalm xvi. 10); the rendering of lxxiii. 24, and innumerable others, we dissent. He assigns too many Psalms to David, assumes too many Messianic ones, and attaches too much weight to tradition. In passages and points of special difficulty, where critical ability and Hebrew learning of the highest order are required, or where orthodox views of inspiration come into play, he is very unsatisfactory, as in xlv. 7, where he repeats Hengstenberg's objections to the true rendering; though those objections show his grammatical knowledge to be at fault; and in the cix. Psalm, which is perversely supposed to contain Christ's denunciations of judgment on his enemies, on Judas first, and afterwards on the whole Jewish people. Yet Dr. Phillips's analyses of words are careful; and his work will help such as have not advanced far in their Hebrew studies or in critical research. Those familiar with the commentaries of Ewald, Hupfeld, and Hitzig, get into another and higher region, where the Psalms are seen in a truer aspect. If Dr. Phillips aids readers towards that, he confers a benefit.

Dr. von Hartmann[w] has already made a name for himself in the field of German philosophy. And justly so, for he has the true conception and spirit of a philosopher. A little volume of essays or treatises before us consists of seven papers which have already appeared in

[v] "A Commentary on the Psalms, designed chiefly for the use of Hebrew Students and of Clergymen." By G. Phillips, D.D., President of Queen's College, Cambridge. London: Williams and Norgate.

[w] "Gesammelte philosophische Abhandlungen zur Philosophie des Unbewussten." Von E. v. Hartmann.

different journals. The first is merely introductory, showing that the investigation of nature is inferior to philosophy in extent and importance. The second, treating of the necessary remodelling required by Hegel's philosophy seems to be the best, while maintaining Hegel's fundamental principle—viz., that the world-process is mere development, a logical development of the logical itself; in other words, logical or ideal *evolutionism*. He regards it as an error that Hegel also propounded *absolute* idealism, or *panlogism*. The argument is ably conducted, and commends itself to the reflecting mind. The third essay treats of Schopenhauer's philosophy, which in his opinion needs remodelling also. The fourth, entitled, Is the pessimist monism comfortless, conducts to dreary nihilism or nirvana, and contains reasonings which the highest nature of man resists. The remaining essays are of less importance, but worthy of study notwithstanding. Von Hartmann's style is excellent, as clear perhaps and lively as the subjects admit of. Some of his views are profound; many are shadowy and incorrect. He is a reformer of German philosophy, and the author of a new system derived in part from that of his predecessors in the same fruitful department. As he belongs, however, in the main to Schopenhauer's school, his leading ideas will have no permanent vitality.

Mr. Leifchild, impressed with the belief that the contemplation of nature in its various parts, properties, modes, and changes is a direct help to faith, has written a book* to commend and enforce such belief. He supposes that science, so far from being truly inimical to religion, illustrates in a most impressive manner the power, wisdom, and goodness of the Almighty Father whom to know is to worship. Aware that the tendency of some recent speculations in science is adverse to Christian faith, and regretting the fact, he undertakes to show their fallacy. What he insists upon is the fact, that a true conception of science and an adequate acquaintance with its latest discoveries, corroborate the fundamental principles of Christianity. The work, however, is not a systematic treatise on any branch of natural theology. It consists of certain subjects, selected and treated in such a way as to show their power of contributing to the great themes of religion. The author is well read in modern scientific books, and has evidently pondered over their contents with an anxious desire to understand and appreciate all they contain. He is also a religious man. His purpose is a good one. Has he succeeded in fulfilling it? To a considerable extent. His chapters are interesting. He comments on the philosophers to whose views he is opposed with vigour and acuteness. He is ingenious as well as discursive, fond of analogies and illustrations. An excellent littérateur in the department of science, he looks at nature with reverent eye. The chapters on the Infinite, the Absolute Being; and on the immortality of the human soul, are specimens of eloquent argumentation. All his strength is put

* "The Higher-Ministry of Nature viewed in the light of Modern Science, and as an Aid to Advanced Christian Philosophy." By John R. Leifchild, A.M. London : Hodder and Stoughton.

forth in chapters xi.—xiii., where the peculiar sentiments of Darwin, Wallace, and others are stated and combated. As to the first three chapters, they might be dispensed with. The two ministries of nature of which the author speaks are arbitrary distinctions. On "Ignorance" the ideas are commonplace. Yet we cannot say that the author is always successful, or that he contributes much to the solution of the great problems he touches on. His knowledge of the mental philosophers whom he contradicts seems to be inadequate. To Spinoza he does scant justice; or rather he has not studied him, except through Saisset. Has he ever considered the pantheistic ideas contained in some parts of the New Testament? And does not the author *preach* in the last chapter? Does he not indulge in fancy when he unfolds a spiritual pangenesis as an analogue to Darwin's natural pangenesis; descants on correlations of spiritual force; and makes divine goodness " a constant quantity in the universe?" He also employs "the universe" too lightly, and speaks of man as " the wonder and glory of it," which almost implies omniscience on the part of the speaker, and a forgetfulness of his own chapter on ignorance. The book lacks repose. The author's style is an excited one. He is too fond of fine writing ; and therefore the composition betrays artificiality, though it has boldness and strength. His book, with all its shortcomings, may be commended to educated readers as fitted to stimulate thought and give them some general notions of theories now current among men of science. The way in which an intelligent student turns aside the anti-Christian elements inherent in those theories may be seen here in fair outline, dictated by a true desire of knowing the Infinite in manifestation.

Some years ago Mr. Mahaffy translated Kuno Fischer's Commentary on Kant, accompanying it with numerous notes proving that he had been a diligent student of the philosopher's views. Intending to replace this by an independent work,[*] he has recently issued the first part of a first volume, together with the third volume, reserving the remainder for a future time. The former contains the two prefaces to the Critick, with remarks on their variations and consistency, Kant's Introduction, and the Transcendental Æsthetic, with a chapter on the modern sensual school by the editor; the latter has a translation of Kant's Prolegomena to any future Metaphysic, with four appendices containing translations of the principal passages in the Critick of the pure reason, altered in the second edition, and of part of the critical solution of the third Antinomy. Mr. Mahaffy has evidently spent great labour on his favourite philosopher, and presents a good claim to be considered his best English expositor. What he has done to make Kant's views accessible and intelligible to Englishmen is done well. He translates faithfully, simplifies the long, obscure sentences of the original, and adds valuable expositions or notes. That he is himself capable of philosophizing is amply shown by the fourth chapter of the

[*] " Kant's Critical Philosophy for English Readers. By John P. Mahaffy, A.M. Vol. I. "The Æsthetic and Analytic." Vol. III. " Kant's Prolegomena to any future Metaphysic." London : Longmans, Green, and Co.

first volume, where he tries to demonstrate that the Association school are wrong, discussing space, extension, and time with acuteness. Whoever wishes to master the philosophy of Kant, will find sufficient help in Mr. Mahaffy's publication, the best English exponent, if not the best in any language.

The late Professor Ueberweg's sketch of the History of Philosophy" is too well known to need commendation. It is divided into three parts or volumes, the first of which has reached a fourth edition, while the other two are in a third. The first is occupied with Greek philosophy ; the second with the patristic and scholastic period, including the mystics of the fourteenth and fifteenth centuries ; the third, which is the largest, surveys modern philosophy. The whole work gives the reader an idea of completeness. Prof. Ueberweg presents a clear, condensed, comprehensive outline of the different systems which have been propounded from the earliest to the latest time, so that the reader may be able to judge of their merits and defects, their characteristics and errors. We know of no compendium so satisfactory in all respects. The literature is very copious ; it is all but exhaustive. No book or dissertation bearing on the vast variety of subjects seems to have escaped notice. It may therefore be recommended to students of philosophy with all confidence as an admirable text-book, able to guide them with success through the difficult problems with which the acutest intellects in all ages have been anxiously occupied. An excellent index enhances the value of each volume.

Miss Cobbe's " Darwinism in Morals, and other Essays," are reprints from various reviews and magazines, so that they do not call for special notice. They are written with the author's usual ability on very various subjects. Her style is good, and her treatment of topics never dull. In morals she is a decided intuitionalist, opposed in that respect to philosophers of no mean ability. The first essay, strangely entitled " Darwinism in Morals," is sufficiently vigorous, and is probably considered by its author the most important in the volume ; but it is at times too vehement, narrow, one-sided. That on " Unconscious Cerebration " is much better. The book may be read with interest by intelligent students, though it will not convey much definite information, or help to settle them in a faith they can grasp with convincing evidence of its power over the heart. The author is an intelligent, devout Theist, who discusses more than she can master or throw new light upon.

" " Grundriss der Geschichte der Philosophie von Thales bis auf die Gegenwart." Drei Theile. Von Dr. Friedrich Ueberweg. Berlin : Siegfried Mittler und Sohn.

" " Darwinism in Morals, and other Essays." By Frances Power Cobbe. London : Williams and Norgate.

POLITICS, SOCIOLOGY, VOYAGES AND TRAVELS.

M. DE TOCQUEVILLE and Mr. Nassau Senior are names
gathering about them so much that the world will not
willingly let die, that Mrs. Simpson's works of further portraying in
these volumes at once her father and her friend, must have been a
pleasant as it is an invaluable labour. The notes of conversations which
she now publishes are unusually authentic, since one interlocutor
wrote them and the other revised them. Thus we are assured that
the opinions expressed in them are no hasty ones given in confidential
moments, but the grave and well-weighed views of astute political
thinkers, expressed at times when no official ties imposed caution or
reticence. Such talk is rare to hear, and of interest long after the
predictions contained in it are falsified or fulfilled. At the present
time most readers will turn with especial interest to the papers relating
to the period of M. Thiers' former political life and the beginning of
Louis Napoleon's reign. M. de Tocqueville's expectations a fortnight
after the *coup d'état* of 1852, were, that in a few years France would
free itself from "so rash and wrong-headed a man, surrounded, and
always wishing to be surrounded, by men whose infamous character is
their recommendation to him." It seemed even then impossible
that Louis Napoleon should ever settle down as a quiet administrator,
because the army which had been his tool must be kept in a better
humour than it was possible to keep it by mere decorations, and the
whole nation must have some substitute given it for the political
excitements of the foregoing forty years. A war with England was
commonly expected to satisfy both these requirements, but M. de
Tocqueville rather thought that Switzerland, Belgium, or Piedmont
was more likely to be attacked, and that England would in that way
only be drawn into the war. The French people were "insanely"
afraid of Socialism, and this fear threw them "headlong into the arms
of despotism;" and added to this was the fact that "Louis Napoleon
had the merit or the luck to discover, what few suspected, the latent
Bonapartism of the nation." M. Beaumont at that time expected,
what has now come in some measure to pass—to see France a republic
again; but M. de Tocqueville saw "no prospect of a French republic
within any assignable period." "We have found," he said, "that it
does not imply war, or bankruptcy, or tyranny; but we still feel that
it is not the government that suits us." M. Beaumont, speaking of
M. de Tocqueville's political career after his death, told Mr. Nassau
Senior that De Tocqueville was ambitious, and would gladly have been
a real minister to Louis Philippe, but that the King refused to allow
any of the necessary home reforms and improvements to be carried out,
and nothing would have tempted either Beaumont or De Tocqueville "to
sit in a Cabinet in which they were constantly out-voted, or to defend

---

[1] "Correspondence and Conversations of Alexis de Tocqueville with Nassau
William Senior, from 1834 to 1859." 2 vols. London : Henry S. King. 1872.

in the Chamber, as Guizot had to do, conduct of which they had disapproved in the Council." Early in his parliamentary life De Tocqueville learned that his desire to be an independent member crippled his power of action, and he allowed himself to be considered to belong to the Gauche, to whom, however, he was not even barely civil. He remained in parliament only in hope of some great change coming, and it was the short duration of the Constituent Assembly, and the hostility of the President during the Legislative Assembly, that, together with the state of his health, prevented his influencing the destinies of the Republic as much as his friends expected him to do. Some of the language in which Beaumont, in conversation with Senior, characterizes the impotency and glaring incompetence of Louis Philippe is sufficiently trenchant. " Louis Philippe would allow nothing to be done. If he could have prevented it we should not have had a railroad. He would not allow the most important of all, that to Marseilles, to be finished. He would not allow our monstrous centralization, or our monstrous protective system, to be touched. The owners of forests were permitted to deprive us of cheap fuel, the owners of forges of cheap iron, the owners of factories of cheap clothing. In some of this stupid inaction Guizot supported him conscientiously, for, like Thiers, he is ignorant of the first principles of political economy, but he knows too much of the philosophy of government not to have felt in every point that the King was wrong." No part of this interesting work is more interesting than the report of Beaumont's criticism of the first constitution under which Napoleon was appointed President. "That we gave the President too much power," said Beaumont, "the event has proved, but I do not see how, in the existing state of feeling in France, we could have given him less. The French have no self-reliance. They depend for everything on their administrators. The first Revolution and the first Empire destroyed all their local authorities and also their aristocracy. Local authorities may be gradually re-created, and an aristocracy may gradually arise, but till these things have been done the Executive must be strong. If he had been re-eligible, our first President would virtually have been President for life. Having decided that his office should be temporary, we were forced to forbid his immediate re-election." A remark of De Tocqueville's, made in 1853 may throw light on recent events. " It has always been said, and I believe with truth, that the revolutionary army of 1848 was mainly recruited from the 40,000 additional workmen whom the fortifications attracted from the country and left without employment when they were finished. When this enormous extra-expenditure is over, when the Louvre, and the new Rue de Tivoli, and the Halles, and the street that is to run from the Hôtel de Ville to the northern boundary of Paris, are completed—that is to say, when a city has been built out of public money in two or three years—what will become of the mass of discharged workmen?" Some pertinent observations are made in 1858, by an eminent Frenchman, mentioned as " L.," in Mr. Senior's journal, on the character of Louis Napoleon. " He is not satisfied with seeing the country prosperous and respected abroad. He wants to dazzle. His policy, domestic and foreign, is a policy of vanity and ostentation—motives which mislead every one, both in private and in public life. His great moral merits are kindness and sympathy. He is a faithful, attached friend, and wishes to serve all who come near him. His greatest moral fault is his ignorance of the difference between right and wrong; perhaps his natural insensibility to it, his want of the organs by which that difference is perceived—a defect which he inherits from his uncle." On the conversation being reported to De Tocqueville, he said that no one knew Louis Napoleon better than L., but that the latter had not dwelt enough on his indolence. " I am told that it is difficult to make him attend to business—that he prolongs audiences to kill time."

It is not often we have the pleasure of calling attention to more valuable compositions than the collected writings, or rather partial remains, of the late M. Charles Clavel. Young as he was when he died at Mentone, where he had resorted for his health, in the year 1862, it was not before he had exhibited a capacity for broad and con-nected thinking, apart from subservience to any existing authoritative types, which is not frequently found in men so young, regard being had to the depth and perplexity of the political topics involved. He proposed, had he survived long enough, publishing an exhaustive treatise on Education, and also a comparative Review of the œconomical and political institutions of the different nations of Europe. He had already contributed articles on different portions of these subjects to the *Economiste,* the *Journal of Geneva,* and the *Bibliothèque Universelle.* We have to thank M. Frederick Passy[2] for preventing the most precious of the surviving relics of M. Charles Clavel being lost to the world. The present work contains a touching and extremely interesting memoir of M. Clavel. He was born at Geneva in 1835, and lost his mother at the age of three years, and his father at the age of nine. A very agreeable picture is given of the opportunities for education at Geneva. It is said that without separating oneself from one's children, one can find for them all the resources of public education, and that " the friendships of early life, purified and fortified by the discernment and approbation of the family, disengaged on contact with the world without from that tendency to a vicious revolt which ferments more or less in the close atmosphere of colleges, possess something at once more frank, more serene, and more durable. They are more founded on choice and mutual esteem; they have, in their common objects, larger horizons, and interests more varied and more potent, and form a better and more real apprenticeship for life." In early youth, while yet conducting his studies, M. Clavel's aim became distinctly marked out before him, and he was true to it to the last; it was " the improvement of men through the improvement of education." Nevertheless, however ambitious this aim, his letters during his sojourn at Hamburg, Ulm, Göttingen and Berlin, show the modesty with which he conceived the want of proportion between the work of even the hardest-worked and the work to be done. Writing at the age of twenty from Göttingen to his guardian, he enumerated with some sadness the faculties which were lacking to him. " Happily,

---

[2] " Charles Clavel. Œuvres Diverses ; Education, Morale, Politique, et Littéra-ture. Avec une Notice." Par Frédéric Passy. Paris. 1871.

the will can supply many things; and it is with confidence that I do my utmost to replace by others, and by a good employment of those I possess, the faculties which have not been accorded to me. My ambition goes no farther than this: I aspire simply to be an 'honest' man, and to achieve some useful work." That he was an "honest" man in thought and work, and that he did achieve something, the contents of these volumes sufficiently establish. The essay on "l'Avenir de la Démocratie" is well worthy of serious study, and in it some of the most mature conceptions of the best English speculators will be found to have been independently arrived at. The limits of Government action are far more sharply marked than is common now-a-days, and especially by foreign writers; and the incapacity of a monarchical or aristocratical system to observe those limits, is severely animadverted upon. "The nature of an aristocracy is to pass the limits of its just power, and to exaggerate its mission, because it confers it upon itself." "The natural mission of Government has narrow limits; depositary as it is of the public force, it cannot, if it would continue just, employ that force for any other aims than those on behalf of which each of those in whose name it is exercised would be entitled, in default, to employ his own. Every man can compel his fellows to respect his rights, his property, his liberty; but he can compel them to do no more: the Government ought not to exercise in its own name any other power than that of personal defence. Its purpose is no other than to secure to each one the free use of his faculties, and the free possession of the fruits of his labour. . . . The Government which employs force (its only method of action) to constrain men to take itself as the regulator of their conduct, and of their ideas, and as the measurer of their interests, departs quite as much from its legitimate mission as the man who would endeavour to force another to work, to instruct himself, to think, and to regulate his interests in accordance with his own personal pleasure." The same unassailable principles are applied in a special case in another remarkable essay on "Education and the State," a topic which M. Clavel felt throughout to be one of transcendent importance. "This enfeebling," says he, "of individual forces by the intervention of the State has for its necessary consequence the indefinite prolongation of the habit of intervention. The more a nation has been long submitted to it, the more it loses its capacity of being sufficient for itself. People have often said that when once the State has given the people the means of knowing and tasting the advantages of education, the people will come to the point of loving and seeking it, and so grow capable of acquiring it by their own efforts. But there is nothing in it; history offers us no example of such a fact; it nowhere shows us that servitude is the best means of raising people to liberty. It is the same with education as with all the growing industries that the State tries to protect while it destroys them: they are feeble at first (it is said), we must support their first steps—it is the only means of making them capable of supporting themselves for a single day. But has not industry been invariably enfeebled by this protection? Every aid that is given to it has for its solitary effect to render it more dependent and more exacting." The Essay on the University of

Oxford shows a careful study of English institutions, and contains precious observations on modern higher education.

The expression "Self-Government" presents to an ordinary Englishman something of a less attractive or magnificent aspect than it does to a German philosophical politician and jurist like Dr. Gneist.[1] To an Englishman the expression is either another name for government by a House of Commons, as modified by the contingent advantages of "Trial by Jury" and the writ of Habeas Corpus, or else only calls to mind the stimulating topics of Select Vestries, Poor Rates, Provincial Justices of the Peace, Game Laws, and (till very recently) Church Rates. In this last sense of the expression "Self-Government," it is probable that the largest quantity of the abuses which have of late years, since the passing of the first Reform Bill, obstructed the progress of good government, have found a refuge. The whole policy of the "New Poor Law," was to strike a blow at "Self-Government" in this sense. The recent extension of the same policy as exhibited in the successive Public Health and Local Government Acts, has operated in the same direction. The multiplication of stipendiary magistrates, the efforts at reform of Local Taxation, and the increasing control exercised by the Executive Government over Education, Sanitary Provisions, Police, and even Lighting, Watching, and Sewage, all point to the rather low estimation in which prevalent political opinion in England is getting to hold some of the privileges of "Self-Government." We have already had occasion to draw attention to former editions of Dr. Gneist's very valuable work on "Self-Government in England." If an Englishman really wishes to get a sound and comprehensive view of the local institutions of his country, through which so much of the work of Government is actually (whether well or ill) accomplished, there is no one English work to which useful reference can be made. The different circumstances of Prussia and England at the present day may in some way account for Germans attaching so serious an importance to institutions which to Englishmen are rather topics of calm indifference, or even of humorous infidelity. The labour, research, and knowledge displayed in Dr. Gneist's work is nothing else than extraordinary. The history of the "Elements of English Self-Government," is given with great particularity and detail; the officials engaged in carrying out that Government, whether in the Parish, the Union, the District, or the County, carefully enumerated and described; the provisions for taxation and the administration of justice elaborately explained, and the effect of the most recent Acts of Parliament investigated and characterized. The English reader cannot fail to derive little less benefit from a diligent study of this work than the German reader, and the former will probably rise from a perusal of it with the sentiment that if the local institutions of his country are not too much idealized or exempted from central control, they may yet afford an useful refuge against Parliamentary or Government despotism.

The condition of the Criminal Law is probably one of the safest

[1] "Self-Government, Communalverfassung und Verwaltungsgerichte in England." Von Dr. Rudolf Gneist. Dritte, umgearbeitete Auflage. Berlin. 1871.

tests that can be applied to ascertain the character of a nation's political government. It is then no more than might have been expected to find French jurists and politicians, at the epoch of the recovery of the forms, at least, of political freedom in France, turning a wistful gaze towards the best devised Criminal Codes that the freest nations have originated. France indeed has a claim to rely upon any help to be gained in the matter of Law Reform from other nations, for to no nation is the modern world more indebted in this respect than to France herself, the entire recasting of her Criminal Law being one of the earliest results of the great Revolution, and the construction of her Five Codes one of its most lasting and beneficial achievements. Mr. Livingston's Code* is indeed well deserving accurate study, and will, it is hoped, amply repay the task of translating it into French—a task, the value of which is greatly enhanced by M. Charles Lucas's preface, and M. Mignet's historical notice of Mr. Livingston and his juridical labours. The Criminal Law of a nation must always bear a very close relation to the rest of the law, inasmuch as the general rights and duties of all members of the community, and more especially of official persons of all sorts, must first be carefully described before the sort of violation of them which is implied in a *crime* can be rendered intelligible. And yet it happens, as an historical fact, that Criminal Law is developed earlier than the rest of the law. But this is only a technical peculiarity, inasmuch as the rights and duties are presupposed to exist long before they become matter of national consciousness and juridical definition. Mr. Livingston's plan of distribution exhibits the relation of the different parts of the legal system with great distinctness. The arrangement of offences according to this plan follows the graduation suggested rather by the political importance than by the moral enormity of the offence. Thus, the first five classes of offences are those against (1) the legislative, (2) the executive, (3) the judicial authority, (4) public tranquillity, (5) rights of voting. Afterwards come offences against the liberty of the press, with respect to the use of the public coin, with respect to public roads, public health, and public morals. Then follow offences against religion and against reputation. Then the more familiar classes of offences against the person, against individual persons in their profession or trade, against civil and political rights and conditions, and lastly, against private property. The arrangement, which commends itself at a glance for its scientific character, may advantageously be compared with that of Bentham, of the Indian Penal Code, and of the English Criminal Law Commissioners, the last of which has not yet been adopted in practice.

Before the meeting of the late International Prison Congress, Mr. William Tallack was requested by the Howard Association to prepare a paper on the Defects of the Criminal Administration of Great Britain and Ireland, for distribution at the Congress and for circulation among prison authorities at home and abroad. This has been published in a

* "Exposé d'un Système de Législation Criminelle pour l'État de la Louisiane et pour les États-Unis d'Amérique. Par Edouard Livingston. Précédé d'une Préface par M. Charles Lucas, et d'une Notice Historique par M. Mignet." 2 tomes. Paris.

well-printed volume,[4] and forms a useful manual for those who are interested in the problems connected with the repression of crime and the reformation of criminals.

Among the advocates of the rights of the working classes few are more manly, frank, and thorough-going than Captain Maxse. In his pamphlet on the "Causes of Social Revolt"[5] the pernicious influences of the lecture-form in which it was originally composed are still to be traced. There is a manifest straining after sensational and rhetorical effect which detracts from the cogency of a very bold and striking plea on behalf of democracy, free thought, and free speech. Notwithstanding this drawback, which is inseparable from arguments prepared for the platform, Captain Maxse's little work may be commended to those who desire to master a clear and condensed statement of the aims and favoured means of the democratic party in our own country and our own day. The "platform" put forward by Captain Maxse includes four principal points: (1) Compulsory gratuitous secular education; (2) Land tenure reform; (3) The substitution of direct for indirect taxation; and (4) Electoral representative reform;—upon all of which except the first we find no difficulty in agreeing with him.

Never before has the "Labour Question" presented itself in such indisputable prominence as it has in the present year. The prevalence of strikes, the general rise of wages, the abnormal activity of production in certain industries, have in combination developed a state of things that makes workmen exult, appals capitalists, and gives economists a difficult problem to work out. The most painful and disheartening feature in the struggle is that capital and labour are fighting in the dark, dealing each other oftentimes deadly blows in the struggle, while there is on neither side a wish to wage an internecine warfare. Political economy might throw a peace-diffusing light over the scene of conflict, but this science has contented itself of late years with the barren discussion of abstract principles, instead of assisting in the diffusion of practical enlightenment. Mr. Thomas Brassey, M.P. has adopted another method of economic teaching in his unpretending but excellent little book, "Work and Wages."[6] This volume, the substance of which was originally intended to form a chapter in Sir Arthur Helps' life of Mr. Brassey the elder, grew in the process of its compilation, which was careful and elaborate, into a comparatively lengthy work, to which the author of "Friends in Council" has prefixed a preface. It is unnecessary to say that the son of the greatest of contractors is by no means disposed to deal harshly with the shortcomings of capitalists, but it is only just to add that Mr. Brassey is equally fair and kindly towards the workmen, "who possess especial claims on his sympathy and gratitude" by reason of the "honest and faithful services" rendered to his father during many years by vast numbers of that class. What is peculiarly wanted, however, in all discussions affecting the

. [4] "Defects in the Criminal Administration and Penal Legislation of Great Britain and Ireland, with Remedial Suggestions." London : F. B. Kitto. 1872.

[5] "The Causes of Social Revolt. A Lecture. Revised, with Notes." By Captain Maxse, R.N. London : Longmans. 1872.

[6] "Work and Wages Practically Illustrated." By Thomas Brassey, M.P. London : Bell and Daldy. 1872.

relations between labour and capital is, in the Baconian phraseology, "dry light," and this Mr. Brassey gives us. His statistics have been collected cautiously and exactly by persons who, not knowing the purposes for which they were to be published, the shape in which they were to be cast, or the connexion in which they were to stand, had no interest in falsifying or modifying the results of their inquiries. It would not be possible in a limited space to do justice to the striking and instructive accumulation of facts which Mr. Brassey has brought together. One or two points, however, may be noted—the one sustaining, the other apparently running counter to opinions that have been put forward frequently in this *Review*. Mr. Brassey most emphatically denies that a rise of wages necessarily increases the cost of labour. On the contrary he brings many interesting facts in support of his contention that according as wages are increased the efficiency of the workmen employed has increased also. In this conclusion we entirely agree. Of course there is a limit which the workmen cannot pass in demanding an addition to their wages without incurring the risk of driving the industry by which they subsist to foreign countries; but short of this limit, which is easily ascertained, the most highly-paid labour is beyond a doubt the most remunerative to the employer. The other point, on which we find Mr. Brassey in disagreement with us, refers to " partnerships of industry." He is of opinion that workmen who would be willing to participate in the profits of an undertaking in prosperous years, would not be prepared to share its losses and to have their wages reduced during a period of adversity. Again, in contracts, be contends, where one is remunerative and the other gives a loss, the labourers not being able to understand the difference of reward where the work done was the same, would insist upon an equal measure of wages in both cases, and so break up the principle of the industrial partnership. We admit the force of these objections, but we cannot consider them conclusive; at least it is unfair to reject the experiment on their account until it has been fairly tried.

Every traveller on the Continent, let alone every mercantile man, has a keen interest in the reform of the coinage of Germany. The traveller and the merchant suffer not only from the variety of the coinage they encounter, but from its quality. It has neither the excuse of antiquity nor the advantage of a recent scientific conception. It is then not surprising that some anxiety and alarm should be experienced on an attempted reform of the coinage of Germany in a false and vicious direction. An interesting pamphlet on the whole subject, by Moriz Mohl,[*] not only describes the state of the case as now presented in Germany, but furthermore gives some valuable information on the state of the coinage in other countries of Europe, and more especially on the history of the coinage of Great Britain. As to the last class of facts, the author has been largely assisted by the Report of the Commission of 1868. The general purpose of the pamphlet is to recommend a double standard of gold and silver, on the decimal system as used in France, both metals being for any

---

[*] " Ueber die Gefahr einer verfehlten Münz-Reform." Von Moriz Mohl. Stuttgart. 1871.

amounts legal tender. The argument is mainly directed against the mischievousness of making gold the only legal tender for sums above a certain magnitude. It is said, or implicated (on the authority, indeed, of English writers) that most of the poverty and miseries of England are due to the difficulties in the way of small retail dealers and customers procuring a sufficiency of silver coin. For, inasmuch as for sums above forty shillings silver is not legal tender, it can only be by vicious artificial means that the nominal value of silver coin can be kept generally capable of representing more than its metallic value. One sort of artificial means is to reduce its quantity far below what is really needed for the daily transactions of the vast number of small purchasers. In consequence of this a great loss is sustained by those least capable of bearing it. It appears that an exclusive silver coinage is employed in British India and in the whole of Southern and Eastern Asia, including from 700 to 750 millions of human beings. In Germany and Austria (up to the present time), Holland, and Scandinavia, silver is exclusively legal tender. In France, Italy, Belgium, Switzerland, Greece, and Spain, gold and silver are both legal tenders. So also in Russia, though in some respects greater favour is shown to gold. Thus, as the author points out, in every country on the whole continent of Europe, with the exception of Portugal and to a certain extent Turkey, either silver alone or silver and gold conjointly and equally, are legal tender. The pamphlet will well repay a careful perusal.

The subject of the "Conflict of Laws,'" or, as it is otherwise called, "Private International Law," according to the method in which it is at present almost of necessity handled, is probably the most dreary and repulsive topic in the whole region of law. There are, however, many reasons why it should gradually become the most important and interesting of all legal topics. If the intercourse of States by means of their citizens travelling for pleasure, curiosity, or profit is deserving of political encouragement, then it is no more than a natural consequence that each State should do its utmost to lend to the citizen of every other State sojourning in its territory, the advantages of its own legal system for the support of rights acquired or capable of being enforced elsewhere. The principle is clear and obvious. The difficulty commences when it is attempted to put it into practice. The legal rules which compose the National Laws of different States are so divergent and out of harmony with each other, that even were States ever so rational and courteous in their dealings with one another, the utmost difficulty must be experienced in ascertaining any general rules which are applied in all States for the purpose of enforcing rights wherever acquired or primarily available. Dr. Wharton has added a fresh treatise to the celebrated ones already dealing with the subject, and the title of his book sufficiently indicates that the only approach to systematization that the subject admits of is to be found in merely laying side by side with each other the doctrines dominant in the most important countries of the world on the various matters to

---

* "A Treatise on the Conflict of Laws, or Private International Law; including a Comparative View of Anglo-American, Roman, German, and French Jurisprudence." By Francis Wharton, LL.D. Philadelphia. 1872.

which the subject extends. In fact, each State has its own private system of Private International Law. The extreme interest attaching to the subject in itself will be sufficiently manifested from a survey of the materials of Dr. Wharton's work, which is very carefully elaborated, as it is of considerable bulk, though the recent editions of Story's "Conflict of Laws" have also reduced the predecessors to puny insignificance. Dr. Wharton discusses his topics in the following order:—Domicile, personal *status*, marriage and divorce, parental relations, guardianship, immovables, movables, obligations, successions and wills, practice, and criminal law. This is very nearly the arrangement of "Justinian's Institutes," and if not logically scientific, is probably about as convenient a one as could be suggested.

It is not of much service to discuss over and over again the doctrine of "consequential damages," as lately presented in its extreme form during one stage of the discussion of the claims arising out of the escape of the *Alabama*. In this form they were not capable of a moment's defence, and were, no doubt, never intended to be defended. They were little more than a species of exaggerated rhetoric, taking unfortunately, a very concrete and personal form. Nevertheless it is still instructive to recur to the mode in which the question has been generally discussed in England, and of which a good specimen is afforded by "Three Letters on the American Doctrine of Consequential Damages, by Saxe Brit."[16] Of course the first letter begins with a simple outrage on the method of analogous reasoning. "Jonathan Yank, of Yankstow, out yonder, had a quarrel not long since with his brother and co-heir, Jeff Yank, in the course of which Jeff killed some of the Yankstow deer. The brothers had hardly made matters up when my bailiff here at Dritworth received notice from Jonathan's steward that as the hounds with which Jeff had coursed were bought on the sly (when whelps) from one of my servants, Jonathan required me to pay for the deer which his brother had killed." The story is kept up to a great length, in which a fancied resemblance to some of the facts attending the late controversy and the circumstances of the claim for "consequential damages" is endeavoured to be sustained. It is curious to think how differently a fairly patriotic Northerner would present the facts, if he dabbled in like imagery. Jeff Yank would be transformed into the head of a desperate and organized gang of poachers, who had just abandoned, on a sudden, their respectable employment of being Jonathan's trusted keepers, and were now subsisting on the property of their late master. So far from the hounds being bought on the sly (when whelps) from one of Saxe Brit's servants, according to the other report of the facts, it would appear that Saxe Brit and all the neighbouring landowners had general notice of the formation of the gang, and a general understanding was come to among all who were friendly to Jonathan (and they all professed themselves to be so) that all dogs and other materials for sport were to be carefully secured and watched, lest by any means they might fall into the poachers' hands and enable them to keep themselves a

[16] "Consequential Damages: Three Letters on the American Doctrine." By Saxe Brit. London: Smith, Elder, and Co.

short time longer out of the hands of justice. Furthermore, Saxe Brit had special and personal notice, often repeated, that one or two of the gang were actually lurking about his premises, and doing their utmost to seduce his servants and procure from them some of their master's (not whelps, but) best trained hounds, wanting only to be taken to the cover and properly fed to be the cleverest hunters on the grounds. The rival story need not be pursued. It is sufficient to notice that this is the view of the whole transaction which the fact of the Geneva Arbitration establishes that both the English and the American nation have finally adopted. The last of the three letters contains a quantity of argument on the irrationality of the alleged claims for consequential damages, which either misrepresents the facts or loses sight of the principles on which any claim for damages can be sustained at all. Thus every one, including every American statesman, and even General Butler, confesses that there are some consequences too remote and indefinite or impalpable to be usefully made the subject of judicial investigation. Again, every statesman and lawyer in Great Britain and the States admits that a wrong-doer can with advantage be made responsible for consequences which he could never have foreseen and was only very indirectly concerned in bringing about. Where then the line is to be drawn between the sort of resulting mischief which can, and the sort which cannot usefully become subject matter of compensation, so far from being a question of noisy rhetoric, is one of the most perplexing ones in the whole field of judicial inquiry.

It is remarkable that while the American Government has been prosecuting the *Alabama* claims against England, it has been the defendant against very similar claims itself. We have received the opinion of the Mexican Commissioners in the Joint Claims Commission, under the Convention of July 4, 1868, between Mexico and the United States upon the claims made by Mexican citizens against the United States Government, for Indian depredations.[11] The Commissioner, Señor Palacio, refers frequently to the *Alabama* case, and argues that the neglect of the United States to protect Mexico against the incursions of Indian tribes was much more culpable than anything that had ever been alleged against England in the case of the Confederate cruisers.

Mr. Charles Harcourt Chambers has published a second edition of his "Phases of Party"[12]—a curiously absurd attempt to revive the pre-revolutionary Whig feeling of the last century as the political panacea for all the troubles of the time. Mr. Chambers complains in his preface of the "virulent attacks" which his first edition suffered at the hands of "the so-called Liberal papers." The book, however, is so tame and harmless that a conscientious Radical critic may be content to let it pass on its way to the butterman unscathed.

Dr. Birdwood has published a very able but passionate and preju-

---

[11] "Claims of Mexican Citizens against the United States for Indian Depredations." Washington, 1871.
[12] "Phases of Party." By Charles Harcourt Chambers, M.A. Second Edition. London : Longmans, Green, and Co. 1872.

dicial attack on Competition as applied to the Indian Services." With much of the author's criticism on the defects of mere examination as a test of fitness for public service, and on the dangerous tendency of "cram," we entirely agree: but the extravagant claims that he puts forward on behalf of the old officers of the Company, and the manner of their selection, is only a degree less ridiculous than his contention that Competitive Examination is breeding a class of "abandoned intellectual reprobates" in this country. Such exaggerations only repel those who wish to form sound and sober conclusions on a subject of great political importance. If the system of selection for the Indian Service is to be improved, it will be in spite of, not by means of Dr. Birdwood's intemperate advocacy.

An essay on "The Culture of the Observing Powers in Children,"[14] originally formed an introduction to Miss Youman's "First Book of Botany." It is edited separately by Mr. Joseph Payne, with some valuable notes, and a supplement extending the principle to the study of mechanics. Nearly two generations have passed away since a group of writers who made the minds of the young their especial study drew public attention to the necessity of training children to observe the more obvious natural phenomena which lay on every side of them. Some of us may remember "Eyes and no Eyes," in "Evenings at Home," and many can recall the pleasure they derived from Miss Edgeworth's "Frank," and "Harry and Lucy." But these judicious exertions bore little fruit. Books of "useful knowledge" for a time drove "Jack the Giant Killer," and "Little Red Riding Hood" from the field, but the principle of employing the physical sciences for educational purposes was imperfectly understood. It was, in reality, a system of "cramming," at an age when cramming is most injurious, and the fairy tale resumed its sway. We are now beginning to recognise the principle that a good education must aim at the harmonious development of the mental faculties in their natural order, and as from the first dawn of intelligence the child notes the *likeness* and the *difference* of objects, so the observing powers should be cultivated from the earliest age. For this purpose Miss Youman proposes that we should demand the introduction into primary education, in addition to reading, writing, and arithmetic, of "*a fourth fundamental branch of study, which shall afford a systematic training of the observing powers.*" The study of Botany is recommended as the best fitted for this purpose. We fully agree in this recommendation. The objects of the study are found by every roadside, and the elementary facts are easily learnt. We would add, that it should not only be taught in every school, but that every mother and every "nursery governess" (for a "nursery governess" should be an intelligent and sensible woman) should acquire enough botanical knowledge to lead children step by step to a familiarity with the vegetable life around them. It

13 "Competition and the India Civil Service. A Paper read before the East India Association." By George C. M. Birdwood, M.D. London: Henry S. King and Co. 1872.

14 "The Culture of the Observing Powers in Children." London: H. King and Co.

is the want of this early unfolding of the faculties which causes the results of school education to be so lamentably meagre. The child's true education should begin long before he enters the school-room. We cordially recommend this treatise, as well as Mr. Payne's supplement, to the notice of all who are interested in the training of the young.

The history of education must necessarily be constructed, even more than other history, out of very varied materials—biographical, ethical, physical, and political. The impulse given by individual original minds has been here more especially productive of lasting results, and of course religious and political revolutions have borne the most immediate and unmistakeable fruit. Dr. E. Kellner's[5] work on the history of education, though treated from a Catholic standpoint, is a good specimen of a valuable sort of work in this department. His method is rather biographical than anything else, though the biographical course is guided by a strictly philosophical conception. The whole work, which is sufficiently concise and compressed, consists of three volumes. The first volume relates to the whole history of education from Confucius and Pythagoras to Locke and Fénélon. The second volume commences with Rousseau, and concludes with a retrospective survey of all the previous history, and of the varied influences which in different countries and periods have directed the course of education. The last volume treats of the most modern materials, including a careful notice of Jean Paul Richter, Diuter, and Diesterweg, together with a summary of conclusions on what the writer takes to be the true relations of education to morality and religion.

A good reading book is one of the highest desiderata in education. It must not be too easy, or (as too frequently happens) silly and frivolous, or the mind of the learner remains simply without stimulus, or, what is worse, tired and irritated. It must not be too difficult, or the mind associates the accidental difficulty of the materials treated with the essential difficulties of learning to read, and so a disgust for study is generated which it is hard to get rid of. Dr. Bach's "Studies out of the Book of Nature,"[6] "for the more advanced young persons and their teachers," seems to us a peculiarly good specimen of a useful and attractive reading-book. The matter is miscellaneous and discursive, but it is solid, interesting, and scientifically disposed. A notion of the variety of the matter may be obtained from glancing at the chapters on the cockchafer, the "mammoth tree" of California—treated in all its descriptive, comparative, and botanical aspects; and on bees, "their natural history, their modes of life, and all that has to do with them." This last chapter is worked out with great care, and must afford an excellent series of reading-lessons.

One of those comprehensive and painstaking monographs for which Germany is so justly renowned—Herr Ignaz von Zingerle's "Manners,

---

[5] "Erziehungsgeschichte in Skizzen und Bildern mit besonderer Rücksicht auf das Volksschulwesen." Von Dr. E. Kellner. Zweite Auflage. Essen. 1869.

[6] "Studien und Landschafte aus dem Buche der Natur." Von Dr. M. Bach. Dritte Auflage. Köln. 1870.

Customs, and Opinions of the Tyrolese People'"[17]—has reached a "second and enlarged" edition. The author has been engaged for many years in the collection of legends, anecdotes, proverbs, and popular songs in the mountain region of his beautiful native land, the Tyrol. These he has published, arranged under different heads, according to their subject matter. The student of philosophy, of ethnology, of mythology, and of mere social life, will each find something of value in this interesting record of the simple, natural, and uncorrupted manners and faith of one of the few unsophisticated societies remaining in modern Europe. The value of the book is enhanced by the addition of an excellent index. The collection of nursery songs (Kinderlieder) is particularly rich and interesting, and in many of them the dialectic variations are peculiar.

When captive Greece subdued conquering Rome and bound her in the chains of learning, she chose at least a more generous mode of literary aggression than the science of France has adopted since the German victories. M. de Quatrefages' fierce attack upon " the Prussian Race,"[18] in which he attempts to avenge Sedan by proving the victors to be, not Germans, not even slaves, but Finns, with all the ferocious characteristics of their savage ancestry, appeared first in the usually sober pages of the *Revue des Deux Mondes*. A great part of M. de Quatrefages' brochure makes very entertaining reading, and his identification of the Esthonian Finns, Letts, and Courlanders with the pre-historic inhabitants of Europe in the glacial period has some real historical and scientific interest. But the whole argument is so governed by a preconceived notion that the Prussians are savages and should be denounced as such, that its argumentative value is diminished, and even as a piece of able invective it loses much of its force. Yet it would be unfair to ignore the strong points in the author's reasoning. The fact seems to be that Ethnology has hitherto in a great measure failed to recognise the blood-relationship of the masses in every country, and has taken account only of those of their masters. Language proves a delusive guide, for the conquered generally adopt the tongue of the conquerors; but physiology detects differences or resemblances where philology fails to see any. In this way doubtless the affinity of the modern Prussians and the Finns may be insisted upon, but when M. de Quatrefages proceeds to argue that because the Finns are treacherous, cowardly, and cruel, the Prussians must exhibit the same qualities, we are compelled to regard his work as an example of misplaced ingenuity, perverted learning, and an irrational spirit of revenge.

A very fine specimen of a valuable form of State paper is supplied by an authoritative abstract of the results of the Census of the Town

---

[17] "Sitten, Bräuche, und Meinungen des Tyroler Volkes." Gesammelt und herausgegeben von Ignaz v. Zingerle. Innsbruck. 1871.

[18] "The Prussian Race, Ethnologically Considered; to which is Appended some Account of the Bombardment of the Museum of Natural History, &c., by the Prussians, in January, 1871." By J. L. A. de Quatrefages, Member of the Institute (Academy of Sciences). Translated by Isabella Innes. London: Virtue and Co. 1872.

of Perth" for the year 1870. The thoroughness and comprehensiveness of the information conveyed must make the work of great service to the practical politician, and affords a useful example to English statesmen of an abbreviated catalogue of reliable facts which in this country could only be reached by poring over a number of scattered Blue-books. The whole population of Perth at the time of the Census consisted of 210,340 persons, dwelling in 5259 houses, 36,594 of the population being householders. The number and names of the streets, and the number of inhabitants in each for the several years 1870 and 1857 are carefully recorded, and in another extremely interesting table the houses in each street are classified according to the number of rooms they possess, varying from one room to more than eight. Special attention is given to the cases in which five or more persons occupy one room. There were 78,727, that is two-fifths of the whole population, living under these conditions, and of these 15,664 were living in cellars. As to education, half the female inhabitants could not write, and, excluding children under fourteen years of age, thirty-eight per cent. of women and nineteen per cent. of men could not sign their name. The religious and industrial statistics are carefully elaborated and of considerable interest.

Works upon our Indian Empire and our relations to the Indian people have been of late particularly numerous, and if the ignorance prevailing in England with regard to the affairs of India could be dispelled by books, the complaint would soon cease to have a foundation in fact. We have before us at present two volumes, written with the aim of enlightening England as to the condition of India, and both have a certain merit.

Mr. Robert H. Elliot, whose " Experiences of a Planter in the Jungles of Mysore" achieved a considerable success, has reprinted from *Fraser's Magazine*, with some additions, a number of discursive papers on our policy in India, which he entitles " Concerning John's Indian Affairs."[20] "John," of course, is our national representative, John Bull, and the fiction of "his Indian Estate" is rather wearisomely sustained throughout the greater portion of the book. As it is impossible to discuss Indian policy in the serious vein which Mr. Elliot affects under the allegorical form he chooses to assume, we find the allegory continually dropped and resumed, so that Mr. Elliot's well-meant attempt at enlivening a "heavy" subject results neither in amusement nor in clearness. For all this, Mr. Elliot talks very good sense, though his criticisms and suggestions must be taken with more than a grain of salt—for he belongs to the Positivist school, and believes in Mr. James Geddes, and in the incompetence of English rulers, especially those who govern from Downing-street, not from Calcutta. We are far from agreeing with Mr. Elliot's pessimist opinions, but we think it is an advantage that Englishmen who are interested in the affairs of our Eastern dependencies should not rely wholly upon the rose-coloured statements and predictions of officialism.

---

[19] "Vorläufiger Bericht über die Resultate der Pester Volkszählung von Jahre 1870."

[20] "Concerning John's Indian Affairs." By Robert H. Elliot. London: Chapman and Hall. 1872.

Mr. Elliot's book, notwithstanding many defects of form and style, gives the non-official view very ably and boldly.

Of a very different character are Mr. Braddon's sketches of " Life in India,"[11] also reprinted from *Fraser's Magazine*. Mr. Braddon avoids politics, or at most skims lightly over the surface of controversy; but his book, which is written in a lively, if somewhat loose style, supplies a decided deficiency in our Anglo-Indian literature. Guide-books enough we have, and solemn volumes of travels, and copious political disquisitions and handbooks to Indian polity; but except in Mr. Braddon's pages we know not where to look for a light, sketchy, and sufficiently accurate outline of the Anglo-Indian's daily life, his pleasures and his troubles, the people he meets and the people he rules. The general reader will glean a better notion of what life in India means and of what the work of an Anglo-Indian official is from Mr. Braddon's unpretentious sketches, than from many ponderous volumes of statistics and political controversy.

Major Morrison Bell's " Other Countries"[12] is one of those books of travel that alternately amuse and annoy the reader. Abounding in animal spirits and a familiar form of egotism, lavish in his distribution of petty scraps of various knowledge, chattering slang, retailing the oldest of " Joe Millers" and the most audacious of puns with the frankness of a schoolboy, Major Bell skips through two portly volumes, across India and Australia, China and Japan, Pacific and Atlantic America. If he does not give us much useful information, his travel talk is generally readable, and sometimes gives a better notion of the superficial aspects of the countries of which it gossips than works more elaborate and philosophic. It is difficult, however, to have patience at times with Major Bell, so disagreeable is the jargon ho writes in to eye and ear. It is not easy to tolerate an author who interpolates in a really entertaining description of a Japanese fête, the following stuff: " The gods were being fifed and drummed to, and—and it was awful jawlee. Don't sneer. Would you have snore—or whatever is the participle of the action whereby Darwin *dogmatises* on our early origin—had you lived with your grandfather's father's father, and taken part in the junketings of the good old days?"—and so on for half a page. In another place we find this kind of interesting and intelligent record of a day's amusement: " Home. Eat. The Black man. Debain. Dance. Another pair." But, at least, Major Bell spares us moral and political reflections—except of course when the enormities of American democracy have to be preached out in the official British tone.

Dr Semper,[13] in his sketches of human, animal, and vegetable life in the Philippine Islands, does not fail to exhibit the traditionary learning of German books of travel, while in some measure he distin-

[11] " Life in India." By Edward Braddon. London: Longmans, Green and Co. 1872.

[12] " Other Countries." By Major William Morrison Bell. Two Vols. London: Chapman and Hall. 1872.

[13] " Die Philippinen und ihre Bewohner." Von Dr. C. Semper. Würzburg. 1869.

guishes himself by the liveliness of his observations and style. One instance of this is his description of certain Holothuria or Trepangs, which inhabit the seas of the Philippines. The wonderful perfection and manifold variety of their organs is equalled by the numerous and astonishing peculiarities of their manners and customs. One will, in a few minutes, run away into formless slime, when exposed to the air; while another, getting angry with the hinder part of its body, throws it away and quietly lives without it, or makes another. Self-inflicted wounds in the skin it quickly heals, and makes new internal organs to supply the place of any that may be diseased; or, having lungs that are no longer fit to breathe, it turns its attention to breathing water instead through its gills. The volcanoes, coral reefs, and various races of the inhabitants are accurately and historically described, in relation both to each other and to the characteristic and violently opposed phenomena of the climate of the islands. In those regions it may seem to Englishmen strange to hear of a large section of the population who can almost without exception read and write.

Though it has been justly complained that Germany alone produced adequate works upon California, its attractions, resources, and brief but swiftly-flowing history, Mr. Player-Frowd [*] gives us a most useful and agreeable account of his personal experiences and the results of his inquiries into all that is special to that country. Avoiding the oft-told tale of the passage to the United States, a tour in Canada, and even the fresher one of a journey across the continent of America, Mr. Player-Frowd opens his sketch-book to us at Lake Tahoe, in the Sierras, "a volume of water suspended 6000 feet in the air, never varying in its height, never frozen over like neighbouring lakes, of such rarefied nature that wood sinks in it, and man cannot swim in it, the crater of an extinct volcano, fire substituted by water, fed by the everlasting snows, and full of great fish, bred heaven knows how." The water of this lake is to be taken to San Francisco, 200 miles off, supplying thousands of mining-claims and gardens on its way, and paying almost along every mile. The "big trees" have often been described, but Mr. Player-Frowd's vigorous pen adds something to the picture already familiar, as well as to that of the Yosemité Valley, "the greatest of California's attractions in point of grandeur of scenery." It is seven miles long, scarcely to be called a valley, but rather a rift in the earth; it varies "from one mile to ninety feet, with granite walls from 1000 to 4000 feet—that is to say, from one-fifth to three-quarters of a mile high;" the masses of rock standing isolated like giant obelisks, or cleft from top to base, with a clear, cold river at the bottom. "Let the reader conceive the most luxuriant vegetation and the extreme of barrenness, the softest carpet of moss and grassy lawns and great ferns and wild roses, alternating with the huge scathed rocks, where not even the lichen will cling, and then he will have a prosaic idea of the Valley of the Yosemité." The description of the Falls of the Yosemité, three times as high as Niagara at

---

[*] "Six Months in California." By J. G. Player-Frowd. London: Longmans. 1872.

the first fall, and half a mile high at the last, is too long to extract, and could only suffer from abbreviation. The warm springs of Calistoga and the geysers, the petrified forest, the black basalt ridge which for seventy miles shows the course of some ancient river, the banks of which were first filled by the lava stream and then worn away from their uncongenial occupant,—all these and many other attractions are set forth to tempt visitors from the worked-out fields of European travel. Under the head of "Mines and Mining" is a painstaking account of the past, present, and presumable future value of the principal gold and silver districts of California, together with a vivid picture of the chief modes adopted for getting gold out of the river-beds, mountain-sides, and rock, and for cleansing it from all impurities. In the earliest days the stream of a river was diverted at a sharp turn, and the bed was washed in "rockers" and "long Toms," or even by the hand in a pan; then came washing of the dirt in sluices of perhaps a mile in length, with various contrivances for bringing both water and quicksilver to bear upon the precious metal. "But the most powerful placer" (where the gold is mixed with dirt and not imprisoned in quartz) "mining agent is the hydraulic power. A stream of water is led to a small reservoir connecting with a hose of from 4 to 10 inches in diameter. This hose is made of very heavy duck, sometimes strengthened with iron bands. The nozzle is like that of a fire or garden engine, narrowing to its end. Two men hold it, the water is laid on, the nozzle is turned towards the side of a hill, and immediately it begins to melt away. Great care, however, must be taken not to bring too much of the overhanging cliff down at once." "It is incredible what this hydraulic power will perform. At Timbuctoo miles of the mountain's sides are washed away. The Yuba, into which run all the tailings or waste earth, has its bed raised seventy feet by this alone." It has been calculated that a cubic yard of gravel, containing on an average 27 cents of gold or more, may be washed by "hand for $15.00; by rocker for 4.00; by the Long Tom for 1.00; by the sluice for .34; by hydraulic washing for .06." One hydraulic mining company washed 224,000 cubic feet of dirt in six days, at a cost of $650, and cleared $3000. Rich as are the prospects of California, due to her mines, the intending emigrants from other countries are at least as much concerned, and have as much to rely upon in the more valuable agricultural facts and possibilities that are developing themselves within her boundaries. The first care bestowed by settlers upon cultivation was richly rewarded: in 1850-51 one man made a comfortable fortune by cabbages alone, while another made $10,000 a year by onions. But this abnormal state of things has given place to one in which all home needs are supplied, and in 1871, 8,583,124 cwt. of wheat and 389,526 cwt. of flour were exported. Other years have been more prosperous than this, the comparative poorness of which is due to a drought, the recurrence of which is provided against by improved methods of farming and irrigation. "The climate is peculiarly adapted for economical wheat culture. The farmer needs no barn, and in many parts he has neither a fence nor a drain to make." Next to the wheat trade in importance comes that

in wool. The native sheep produce only coarse wool; but foreign
sheep are bred, and in some parts crossed with the native sheep, with
marked success. In the first half of 1871 the export of wool was worth
$3,772,777. Californian blankets are unrivalled. After many dis-
couraging failures, owing to inexpert manufacture and unwise choice
of soils, the native wines are now of good quality, some as good as
good Rhône wines; 1871 bade fair to produce 8,000,000 gallons. The
cultivation of silkworms has, after many blunders, become a noticeable
industry, as has also that of sugar-beet, of the opium-poppy, and of
the olive. California is not likely to enter the markets of the world
as a purveyor of meat; her dry seasons are fatal to a very large trade
in beasts. As a sporting ground, too, it is growing less and less
attractive with every fresh advance of mining activity. Elk, antelope,
deer used to be common, and are now scarcely to be found. Bears of
various species and many common wild-fowl still may be shot. Nor
is the country more inviting to the botanist: with the exception of
the monster specimens of the red-wood-tree, there is little special to
be noticed, while the wild flowers are more remarkable for their abundance than for their variety, acres upon acres being covered with one
variety.

Mr. Shairp's "Up in the North,"** is in many respects a model of
what a book of travels ought to be. This pleasant little volume steers
a judicious course between the flippancy of Major Bell's incondite
gossip and the ponderous pomposity of Mr. Furley's political moraliz-
ings and trite sentimentality. Captain Hutcheson lately taught us to
"Try Lapland," so that Mr. Shairp's book is not quite the revelation
of an undiscovered field for the holiday-seeker of healthful pleasure
that he seems to consider it. In his modest preface he disclaims any
pretension either "to produce an elaborate disquisition on the moral,
social, or political condition of the Swedes or Laplanders," or "to dilate
learnedly on the fauna, flora, geology, or natural features of Sweden
or Lapland;" and, to say the truth, for neither of these tasks does Mr.
Shairp appear to be very well fitted. But the work which he has chosen
to do and for which his aptitude is undoubted, is quite important enough
to be well and carefully done. The personal character of a people who
are so near to us, not by geographical position alone, but by kinsman-
ship, as the Swedes, ought to be better known in England, and if the
attractions of Sweden as a field for travel were popularized, many
tourists would be glad to catch a glimpse now and then of the daily
life of our Scandinavian kinsfolk. It is true that the task which Mr.
Shairp puts aside as unsuited to his powers needs very urgently to be
undertaken by a competent person. The social and political condition
of the Scandinavian countries should be treated as Mr. Laing treated
them a generation ago, in works which, though now obsolete in their
statistics and in a part of their conclusions, are models in their kind.
With this serious labour Mr. Shairp, as we have said, does not busy
himself. He gives us instead the surface impressions which a cul-

---

** "Up in the North; Notes of a Journey from London to Luleå, and into
Lapland." By Thomas Shairp. London: Chapman and Hall. 1872.

tured and tasteful mind receives in passing through novel scenes,
whether of social life or of natural beauty. To such a mind Sweden
presents a strange aspect, yet in many ways not an unpleasing one.
Though nearer than some other lands much frequented by modern
tourists, the Scandinavian kingdom lies even less in the beaten track
than Russia. Probably the superior attractions of Norway for lovers
of the picturesque prevent the sister country from getting its fair share
of admiration. In Mr. Shairp at least Sweden does not find a cold-
hearted pilgrim. Stockholm he speaks of as the "most glorious town
of Northern Europe," and his enthusiastic description of the city as
he left it at sunset is well worth reading. The coast scenery pleased
him equally, and throughout Mr. Shairp seems to have done his
northward pilgrimage in a contented and joyful spirit. Perhaps
this may be accounted for by the fact that the fare, both in the inns
and on board the steamers, was at once cheap and excellent. The wines
were dear and bad, but the taste of a true Swede does not lead him to
wine-drinking. All day long spirits are tippled, and it is somewhat
horrifying to learn that though we are not the most temperate people
under the sun, the average Swede drinks just eight times as much
spirits as the average Englishman. In Northern Sweden and in Lapland the days without night, the purity of the air, and the simplicity
of the people charmed our author. But in the latter country he, like
other travellers, discovered that it was necessary to rough it. The
substantial fare and comfortable accommodation of the Swedish inns
gave place to bad food, and not always plenty even of that, with other
disagreeables of which the less said the better. Still, Mr. Shairp,
telling the truth and the whole truth fearlessly, does not despair of
tempting others to do as he has done. It should be added that he
appends to his book a table of expenses, which will be found useful by
any bold enough to imitate him in his journey "Up in the North."

Mr. G. W. Rusden, in an ably written historical preface, which
claims for Pitt the glory of being the true founder of the English
Colonies in Australia, dedicates to Mr. Anthony Trollope a pamphlet
on "The Discovery, Survey, and Settlement of Port Phillip,"[16] telling
a story of perseverance and daring of which Englishmen and Colonists
may alike be proud. We in the mother country know too little of
the history of our daughter nations, though their struggle ought to
be enrolled in the most shining pages of the annals of the Anglo-
Saxon race.

The pressure of each day's business and fresh excitement may well
be in danger of hiding from us the importance and interest of the visit
paid to this country by an embassy consisting of the foremost statesmen and politicians of Japan, and heralding one to be paid by the
Emperor himself to this and other countries. Foreign guests are so
little rare and so little thought about among us, that Mr. Lanman[17]

[16] "The Discovery, Survey, and Settlement of Port Phillip." By G. W.
Rusden. London: Williams and Norgate. 1872.
[17] "The Japanese in America." By Charles Lanman, American Secretary
Japanese Legation in Washington. London: Longmans. 1872.

does us, as well as the Japanese, good service by the publication of the volume before us. The first part of it consists of an account of the visit of the same embassy to America, and, in the verbatim reports of the speeches made on various occasions, contains sketches of the recent history of Japan, which are of the highest interest. A few years ago the present Emperor, aided by men who are now working under him, overthrew the usurping Tycoon, and inaugurated a new system of politics and of social and international relations. The chief ambassador says, in retrospect of these years: "Although our improvement has been rapid in material civilization, the mental improvement of our people has been far greater." The people knew no freedom or liberty of thought, but they learned their rightful privileges, and, though for a short time civil war ensued, the Daimios surrendered all their privileges, and "within a year a feudal system, firmly established many centuries ago, has been completely abolished without firing a gun or shedding a drop of blood." One of the first steps towards improvement was to begin to educate Japanese women, both by improved methods at home and by sending some to America. Railways, telegraphs, street-railways, docks, lighthouses, and the reconstruction of the army and navy, all speak for the efforts Japan is making to equal the nations which have had so great a start in the race of civilization. "Hundreds of the young nobility of Japan are being educated in their own country and in Europe." "Private schools are numerous throughout the empire, conducted by foreigners." "The Government schools at Yeddo contain about 1600 pupils, studying foreign languages." "During the last four years nearly one thousand young men of intelligence and ability have been sent abroad to study the languages, laws, habits, manufactures, methods of government, and all other matters appertaining to western civilization, the greater part of which is to be introduced into Japan." Marriages are now legal between class and class, and all the specific privileges of the nobles have been abrogated. The ancient penalties for professing or even listening to the teaching of foreign religions have been largely done away with, at the same time that Government support is no longer accorded to Buddhism, and the Buddhist priests have been officially advised to enlist as soldiers. It is rumoured that after this year no obstructions will be placed in the way of any variety of religious profession or teaching. The second portion of Mr. Lanman's volume consists of papers written by Japanese students in America, and collected by Mr. Mori, a young Japanese gentleman, *Chargé d'Affaires* in Washington, to whom the students commonly look as their protector and adviser. These papers are interesting in two ways. Some of them describe with great simplicity points of Japanese customs or history, and the rest show the impression produced by the forms of social life and of Christianity by which the young men are surrounded in America. One on the education of boys and girls together is particularly noticeable. The larger half of the book comes apparently from the pen of Mr. Mori, and is written for the information, with respect to American affairs, of those Japanese who have not visited America. In a sensible introduction he reminds his countrymen that they "Have been somewhat fascinated by what they have seen of the American government and institutions, and it is of the utmost importance that they should well consider the subject in all its bearings before adopting any of its features into their own form of government. The evils resulting from the misuse of freedom in America are among the most difficult to correct or reform. . . . . A prosperous, happy, and permanent Republican government can only be secured when the people who live under it are virtuous and well-educated." Others than Japanese will, however, look with interest to see what Mr. Mori, who, with a Japanese childhood, English education, and American residence, must be fairly unprejudiced, has to say on the official and political, commercial, religious, educational, literary, artistic and scientific, city, mining, frontier, factory, judicial, military, naval, and artisan life and institutions of the great Republic.

The historian of the future will have no reason to complain of scanty materials when he comes to deal with the war of 1870; for the crop of *mémoires pour servir*, "reminiscences," "experiences," and so forth, has been inconveniently exuberant, and is still growing. Among many more or less valuable contributions to our knowledge of this tremendous international crisis we must expect to meet with some worthless books, and in this class we must place Mr. Furley's "Struggles and Experiences of a Neutral Volunteer."[*] No doubt Mr. Furley's position as the representative in France during the war of the British National Society for Aid to the Sick and Wounded, and subsequently to the armistice as Chairman of the Paris branch of the Seed Fund Committee, gave him an opportunity of seeing the actual horrors and the immediate results of the conflict more closely and nakedly than even those able journalists who were generally attracted by the splendid and sublime side of war. But Mr. Furley neither possesses the literary skill required to present in an attractive form the record of his experiences, nor has he the good sense to subordinate himself to his subject. With painful minuteness he describes every step of his journeyings, but the omnipresent *Ego* comes between us and a clear view of his whole experience. In fact, Mr. Furley's particularity and his egotism become ineffably wearisome before we reach the end of his first volume; while, in the second, which professes to chronicle the rise and fall of the Commune, these uninviting characteristics are seasoned with the bitterest prejudice against the revolutionary party. Without attempting to extenuate the crimes which were perpetrated in the name of the Commune of Paris, impartial history will be compelled hereafter to confess that among the men who rose against the reactionist Assembly at Versailles were many inspired by the purest motives and the noblest ideas. To lump them altogether in exultant and almost brutal denunciation, as Mr. Furley does, can serve no cause whatever, nor, though the fashion may be appreciated by readers who account everything Republican utterly abominable, will candid men agree to brand as "cowards" the

---

[*] "Struggles and Experiences of a Neutral Volunteer." By John Furley. Two Vols. London: Chapman and Hall. 1872.

few leaders of the Commune, who, in the terrible days of May, succeeded in escaping the tender mercies of the Marquis de Gallifet and the other Versaillist heroes, and in finding a refuge, as so many royal, imperial, and noble fugitives have found before, on English soil. It would be unfair not to add that in Mr. Furley's description of Paris under the Commune, some scanty scraps of historical worth may be gathered by the diligent, and if they can be authenticated from other sources, may be used hereafter by the annalist of that fearful cataclysm; but it is weary work trying to sift the few grains of wheat out of the bushels of dusty and dreary chaff.

We have much pleasure in calling attention to a German Encyclopædia, which has many claims to recommend it, in preference to the few competing English ones. The "Allgemeine Real Encyclopädie"[m] has been in course of publication for some years, and the separate volumes have already run through several editions. The contributors are numerous and varied, including eminent professors in the universities. The subjects treated exhaust, apparently, the whole realm of knowledge, and the treatment is scientific and thorough. On referring to the topic "England," and more especially "English Literature," we find a tolerably, though not precisely, accurate account of the rise of the existing quarterly reviews, including that of the *Westminster Review*. "In 1800 there arose out of the impulse given by Sir W. Scott, the *Quarterly Review*, as the organ of the Tory party, and in 1824, the *Westminster Review*, which the renowned Bentham established as the organ of the Radicals. This same Bentham, an Utilitarian through and through, was the first of the fearless Reformers who opened the path of progress in legislation, and of freedom in the State."

SCIENCE.

PROFESSOR WITTSTEIN'S systematic course of Mathematics[1] is a fair specimen of a class of students' text-books which has almost innumerable representatives in France and Germany, but scarcely any in this country, where certain "standard works" are allowed to pass from generation to generation. On the Continent almost every competent teacher writes his own text-book; he infuses into the work his own individuality, and embodies in it generally a vast amount of educational experience. No wonder that an intellectual competition of this kind has produced many insignificant publications; but, on the other hand, the superiority of Continental, especially German, text-books on various branches of science must be referred to that fertility, and also to the enterprising spirit of their publishers. Professor Wittstein's work is well worth careful attention. The whole is divided into six

[m] "Allgemeine Real Encyclopädie, oder Conversationslexikon für alle Stände." Gänzlich umgearbeitete und mehr vermehrte Auflage. Regensburg.
[1] "Lehrbuch der Elementar-Mathematik." Von Dr. Theodor Wittstein. Hannover: Habasche Hofbuchhandlung. London: Nutt. 1872.

parts, forming three volumes; only five parts are before us, the sixth and last, on the geometry of the conic sections, has not yet appeared. The general plan of the work is to give not more nor less of the principal facts and applications of elementary mathematics than is really wanted by the majority of students; no superfluous introduction of mathematical niceties and artifices is therefore to be found, which the author justly thinks are required only by a few mature mathematicians who find food for their development elsewhere. The soundness of Professor Wittstein's experience in mathematical teaching is, however, particularly manifested in conveying throughout the whole book all information in such a manner to the student that he immediately sees the possibility of applying the scientific facts to some practical occurrences of every-day life. It is of course not difficult to proceed on the same plan in various portions of plane and solid geometry and trigonometry; but the manner in which the author has shown how even the results of the elementary portions of higher analysis may be rendered immediately useful in the solution of a variety of practical questions, has struck us as most admirable, and strongly to be recommended for imitation. The proofs are in many cases much better than those usually found in our own text-books. Take as an example the formula for the sum of an infinite number of terms in geometrical progression in which the common ratio is less than unity (part i. page 104), in which, instead of the usual—for the beginner—often obscure statements and algebraical transformations of our text-books, the infinite series is simply multiplied by the ratio, in the same manner in which the formula for a finite sum is found, and by subtraction the formula results at once, while the method conveys at once a clear notion of the nature of an infinite series. The geometrical proofs are always preceded by a condensed statement of the facts which form the supposition on which a theorem rests, and the conclusion to which the demonstration leads. We doubt very much whether this is an improvement in any geometrical text-book, nor do we think it altogether a good educational plan to place the enunciations of facts in algebra at the head of the demonstrations, in the time-honoured but scarcely commendable manner of Euclid.

The "Life of Richard Trevithick,"[1] by Mr. Francis Trevithick, is a genuine contribution to the history of scientific progress. The extension of the use of steam-engines owes undoubtedly very much to the extraordinary energy and the many-sided abilities of Richard Trevithick; the overflow of his practical designs has, however, rendered the task which the author has undertaken somewhat difficult. The thread of the story does not run on with the usual smoothness of biographies undertaken in a spirit of veneration for the object of the biographer. The technicalities to be detailed in relating the progress of the steam-engine are so dissimilar to the events in a man's life, that very naturally breaks occur in the whole which may appear discordant to many readers. On the other hand, those truly interested in the author's

[1] "Life of Richard Trevithick, with an Account of his Inventions." By Francis Trevithick, C.E. London: E. & F. N. Spon. 1872.

more scientific explorations will find in the work a mine of study and
information. In fact, the history of the life of the man has been made
subservient to that of the steam-engine. The work, true to this plan,
does not begin with the early days of Richard Trevithick, but with a
description and history of early Cornish engines, the life of the elder
Trevithick, and a short sketch of the labours of Smeaton and Watt,
preceding those of the author's hero. This is the really philosophical
procedure of the historian. In this manner the biographer of the first
Napoleon begins with a general sketch of the political and social state
of Europe, before he leads the man himself upon the stage which
he has shown to be well prepared for the labours of a particular
intellectual organization. The labours of Trevithick are sketched
throughout, analysed, and followed up in their further bearings with
the most faithful minuteness, extending, in the first volume before us,
up to about the year 1815. We cannot but think that even to the
most experienced in the history of science the work will be a source
of surprises, bearing in every chapter numerous proofs of how little is
usually known of the history of improvements, inventions, and applications of old scientific truths which are of daily use; and it is undoubtedly a special merit of Mr. Trevithick's book that he has kept
himself strictly aloof from personal criticism, and has allowed the facts,
with their documentary evidence, to speak for themselves. The work
is throughout illustrated in a manner highly creditable to the publishers.

We have already a very extensive literature on spectrum-analysis,
but very few attempts have hitherto been made to give a clear and
succinct account of the other branch of physics which has been
created during the past quarter of the century—viz, the mechanical
theory of heat.[1] The works which treat on the subject are usually
surrounded with a cloud of mathematical difficulties penetrable only
by those who have devoted long years of study to the higher func-
tional calculus; the works by Clausius, Zeuner, Briot, and others,
will, in spite of their intrinsic excellence, be quite unintelligible to the
majority of those who are in the best position to add by practical
labours to the further investigation and extension of the theory.
The work by M. Röntgen is therefore most welcome. It gives, in the
first place, a brief but very clear statement of the principles of the
dynamical theory of heat, a short history of their discovery, with a
description of the more important experiments by which the laws have
been established and the mechanical equivalent determined. The
author desires principally to enable engineers, in all technical applications of the principles of the theory, to become acquainted with the
methods of calculating the results to be expected from the performance
of various machines. Hence he discusses in detail—after completing
the theoretico-physical portion, and expressing the final facts resulting from it in as simple formulæ as possible—various well-known air
and gas machines, especially those of Ericson, Unger, Laubereau,

[1] " Die Grundlehren der mechanischen Wärmetheorie." Von Robert Röntgen.
Erster Theil. Jena: Hermann Costenoble. 1871.

Lehmann, Lenoir, and Hugon. In order to facilitate still more the
application of the formulæ for the non-mathematical reader, the work
contains very numerous problems and questions, which are worked out
in figures, with special reference to each kind of hot-air engine described.

M. Helmert's[1] work on the method of least squares has a very
practical, but in our opinion rather one-sided, aim. The application of
the method to geodetic observations has received too much attention
already, and the existing treatises fulfil all practical wants in this
direction. Very few of the writers on the subject seem to have ever
thought of the requirements of the physicist, although the extraordinary extension of observation in modern physics involves continually
the deduction of values from long and often discordant series, in which
cases the observer has to go himself through the difficulties which he
sees continually smoothened for the geodetic observer. It must, however, be conceded to M. Helmert that his work is not only thoroughly
complete and methodic, but much more intelligible than many other
works of great pretension which are usually studied on the subject.
The demonstrations are clear and, especially in the first portions,
thoroughly well explained; nor does the author claim from the reader
an acquaintance with the theory of determinants, a great advantage
to those who work practically but have not the time to study this
more modern branch of analysis. The difference between real and plausible errors is well maintained throughout, and on the investigation
into the most plausible errors more stress is laid than usually in text-
books on the subject. The great merit of this work lies, however, in its
numerical examples, which are exceedingly numerous, and well-selected;
after a careful perusal of most of them we may state it as our conviction that hardly a case can arise in which the worker in this special
branch can be at a loss for information on the particular method to be
pursued in his special case. As an addition, the author shows also the
application of the method to the purposes of interpolation, and he
thus strikingly points out the considerable difference in the meaning
of the results obtained by two applications of the method of least
squares.

Professor Wolfers[2] has published a German translation of Newton's
"Principia," with notes and explanations. We have compared a
great portion of the German text with the original, and find it a faithful
and clear translation, but unfortunately it is disfigured by exceedingly
numerous typographical errors, of which not one is indicated at the
end of the book, as is usually the case. We pity the German student
who reads Professor Wolfers' translation, and has no access to the
original. The translator has introduced an improvement in assigning
consecutive numbers to the theorems; they may be thus easily quoted
where they are alluded to. The notes are much inferior to those found

[1] "Die Ausgleichungsrechnung nach der Methode der Kleinsten Quadrate."
Von F. R. Helmert. Leipzig: B. G. Teubner, London: Nutt. 1872.
[2] "Sir Isaac Newton's Mathematische Principien der Naturlehre." Herausgegeben von Prof. Dr. J. Ph. Wolfers. Berlin: Oppenheim. 1872.

in many English editions of the " Principia." If we take them as a whole and compare them with what has been done collectively in this country for the elucidation of Sir Isaac Newton's great work, although in many instances they possess real merit, we cannot but regret that Professor Wolfers should not have paid more attention to the English editions, and embodied in his book many of the valuable notes and additions contained in them.

Professor Wolf's[6] Manual of Mathematics, Physics, &c., has reached the second part of volume ii. This part gives principally an outline of celestial mechanics, and of the physical constitution of the sun. We have already on a previous occasion pointed out the radical error committed by the author in filling the greater part of his work with nearly useless biographical sketches of all the thousands of men who have at various times " done something " in science. These sketches are given at the expense of real information which the man of science justly expects to find in the work. In the present part the physical constitution of the sun is treated on a single page, but the anecdotic and biographical statements, which convey a kind of further critical but certainly very meagre information upon the subject, fill no less than seven times that space. We cannot help thinking that Professor Wolf must be under a thorough misapprehension as to what students are in the habit of expecting in a " manual " of any branch of science.

Mr. Croll's pamphlet[7] on molecular motion is one of those theoretical speculations which are neither supported by any evidence of an experimental kind, nor based upon any observed facts of a special nature calculated to prove the probability of the particular theory promulgated. The theory does not proceed in total opposition to ascertained facts, and that is its whole merit. But what if Mr. Croll's views are the whole truth ? We are then quite as far as we were before Mr. Croll enlightened us.

In wholesome contrast with Mr. Croll's pamphlet, externally and internally, stands a stout volume published by Mr. Archer,[8] the Registrar-General of the Colony of Victoria in Australia, giving abstracts of specifications of patents applied for from 1857 to 1866. This volume refers exclusively to the working of metals, and is evidence of the vast amount of intellectual activity directed in the colony to the extraction of its mineral wealth. The appearance of the volume and the character of the illustrations compare very favourably with similar publications in this country.

The works of early man have never before been presented to modern readers under such gracious guise as in Mr. Evans' " Ancient Stone Implements of Great Britain."[9] Mr. Evans' book, though

[6] " Handbuch der Mathematik, Physik, Geodäsie, und Astronomie." Von Dr. Rudolf Wolf. Zürich : Friedrich Schulthess.

[7] " What Determines Molecular Motion ?—The Fundamental Problem of Nature." By James Croll. London : Taylor and Francis. 1872.

[8] " Abstracts of Specifications of Patents. Metals, Part I." By William Henry Archer, Registrar-General of Victoria. Melbourne : John Ferres, Government Printer. 1872.

[9] " The Ancient Stone Implements, Weapons and Ornaments of Great Britain." By John Evans, F.R.S., F.S.A., &c. 8vo. London : Longmans, Green, Reader, and Dyer. 1872

forming a single volume, exceeds in size what is usually called a manual, notwithstanding that it is a condensed and admirable summary of the whole subject. The very large number of woodcuts scattered through the text much increase its value for reference. They are so beautifully executed that others, beside anthropologists, may procure the work for their sake alone. In the choice of his materials, drawn from varied and extensive sources, the author shows both industry and skill. He begins with the description of implements the newest in date, proceeding gradually backward in time, until finally he arrives at the rude weapons which mark the dawn of the Palæolithic Period. Whatever may be thought of employing this reversed order in setting forth the whole history of our globe, as Sir Charles Lyell has done in his elementary works, there cannot be a doubt that Mr. Evans is right in thus treating the more limited period within his range. Not only by this method do we proceed from the better known to the less known, but the contrary procedure involves the difficulty of an uncertain starting point. The beginning of the ancient Stone Period is dubious, since, as our author well hints, implements older than any yet seen may be discovered. The frauds practised in the simulation of ancient implements, and the modes of detecting them, are noticed. By the use of a second and smaller type, Mr. Evans is enabled to give all required details, while his book at the same time is not rendered unsuitable to general readers. He succeeds also in explaining the larger views to which his researches point, more especially in his concluding chapter on the "antiquity of the river drift." We cite one passage :—

"Who, for instance, standing on the edge of the lofty cliff at Bournemouth, and gazing over the wide expanse of waters between the present shore and a line connecting the Needles on the one hand, and the Ballard Down Foreland on the other, can fully comprehend how immensely remote is the epoch when what is now that vast bay was high and dry land, and a long range of chalk downs, 600 feet above the sea, bounded the horizon on the south? And yet this must have been the sight that met the eyes of those primeval men who frequented the banks of that ancient river, which buried their handiworks in gravels that now cap the cliffs, and of the course of which so strange but indubitable a memorial subsists in what has now become the Solent Sea.

"Or, again, taking our stand on the high terraces at Ealing, or Acton, or Highbury, and looking over the broad valley four miles in width, with the river flowing through it at a depth of about 100 feet below its former bed, in which, beneath our feet, are relics of human art deposited at the same time as the gravels; which of us can picture to himself the lapse of time represented by the excavation of a valley on such a scale, by a river greater, perhaps, in volume than the Thames, but still draining only the same tract of country.

"But when we remember that the traditions of the mighty and historic city now extending across the valley do not carry us back even to the close of that period of many centuries when a bronze-using people occupied this island ;—when we bear in mind that beyond that period lies another of probably far longer duration, when our barbaric predecessors sometimes polished their stone implements, but were still unacquainted with the use of metallic tools ;—when, to the historic, bronze, and neolithic ages we mentally add that long series of years, which must have been required for the old fauna, with the mammoth and rhinoceros, and other to us strange and unaccustomed forms, to be supplanted by a group of animals more closely resembling those

of the present day ; and when, remembering all this, we realize the fact that all
these vast periods of years have intervened since the completion of the excavation of the valley, and the close of the Palæolithic Period, the mind is almost
lost in amazement at the vista of antiquity displayed."

The whole of this chapter is interesting. We concede to Mr. Evans
the merit of having produced the most complete, the most reliable,
and incomparably the best illustrated account of human art during
the Stone Ages which has yet appeared.

While Mr. Evans treats, almost exhaustively, a single group of an-
thropological facts, anthropology from the mental side, in all its bearings, is the subject of Herr Radenhausen's "Isis—Man and the Universe,"[18] the second edition of which is now completed. There is
scarcely a problem in human science, regarded from its most comprehensive point of view, upon which the accomplished author does not
touch. He discusses the psychological history of man, his progress in
morals and social relations, and the genesis and growth of religious
beliefs. By diligently reflecting on what seems most worthy of note
in the present and past states of mankind, Herr Radenhausen seeks
to construct a philosophy of the future. If he fail where no one has
hitherto achieved success, he must still be allowed the praise of des-
canting on the loftiest themes with much calmness, patience, and precision. His work, regard being had to its moderate price, and the
large amount of information concisely expressed, which it contains, is
well deserving the attention of our readers.

Herr Radenhausen's Isis is often quoted approvingly by Dr. Büchner,[11]
who has been engaged, contemporaneously with Mr. Darwin, in writing
a treatise on the origin of man. Such is the absorbing interest of this
subject that few will not ask, which of these two men of science has succeeded in setting it forth with most profit and satisfaction to his readers ?
Our verdict, on both counts, must be given unreservedly in Mr. Darwin's
favour. Dr. Büchner is well informed, and certainly displays much
skill in passing under review the details which would encumber a
feebler writer. He has a readable style and other qualities which
quite account for his popularity; nor can it be denied that he is prepared on all occasions to vindicate the necessity of using what he believes to be the one true method of scientific research. But he cannot
think profoundly—a fault of which, in spite of his ambition, we should
not now accuse him, were it not that he often wantonly disregards the
opinions of others. He is not, like Mr. Darwin, a genial writer; he
wants his sympathy and originality. Nor has he the gift of fairness
from its intellectual side, the power of imagining how his subject looks
to those regarding it from points of view other than his own. In
their account of man's bodily structure, affinities, and genealogy, there

[18] "Isis—Der Mensch und die Welt." Von C. Radenhausen. Zweite Auflage.
Halb-band, VII.-VIII. Post 8vo. Hamburg: Otto Meissner. 1872.
[11] "Man in the Past, Present, and Future." A Popular Account of the Results
of Recent Scientific Research as regards the Origin, Position, and Prospects of
the Human Race. From the German of Dr. L. Büchner, by W. S. Dallas, F.L.S.
8vo. London : Asher and Co. 1872.

is little to choose between Dr. Büchner and Mr. Darwin, since both draw largely on the published opinions of Professors Huxley and Ernst Haeckel. The advantages of style and method are with the English writer. On the far more difficult subject of the causes of man's origin and the theory of his descent, that is, (1) the true nature of the differences between him and animals, and (2) the laws, acting in concert or opposition, under which his evolution has taken place—Dr. Büchner has little or nothing to say, except what he might have gleaned from Mr. Darwin's earlier speculations. In consequence, Dr. Büchner leaves this part of the subject very much as it was before the "Descent of Man" was written. His view of the races of man is not only defective, but at variance with that of Mr. Darwin. The latter admits crossing as a possible factor of races, assigning little value to the direct action of the outward conditions of life. Not so Dr. Büchner, who thus finds himself involved in contradictions.

"Alterations of climate, change of dwelling-place or of external circumstances generally alter races, although never to such a degree as to make them quite unrecognisable; for a new race is never a simple product, but always a result of *two* causes—one represented by the *primitive race*, and the other by the *nature of the medium*. Hence two different races (for example, the Aryan and the Semitic) may both be very much altered in a foreign climate, and yet never become one and the same race. Overlooking this important point gave rise to many misconceptions and false opinions in the old controversy on the unity or plurality of the human species. Moreover, some races can thrive very well, even in foreign climates, and propagate their peculiarities: for instance, the Jews, the Canadians, the New-Hollanders, the European inhabitants of the Cape of Good Hope, &c."

Dr. Büchner is a polygenist, and quite misses the doctrine of sexual selection, so powerfully put forward by Mr. Darwin. Not content with discussing man's present condition and origin, Dr. Büchner enters upon the question of his future. Into this ultra-scientific field we cannot follow him. Mr. Darwin devotes about a page to such speculations. Dr. Büchner's third section, entitled, "Where are we going?" is the largest division of his work. It consists of a series of essays on Idealism, Materialism, Philosophy, Religion, Morals, Marriage, Woman, Education, the Family, Labourers and Labour, Capital, Society, Nationalities, Government, and things in general. (We cite these items backwards, to render their mutual connexion more intelligible.) Lastly, an appendix of "Notes, Explanations, and Additions" contains a large amount of interesting matter. The author is fortunate in his translator, Mr. Dallas, who does full justice to his meaning, while he disclaims accepting many of Dr. Büchner's crude and extreme opinions.

Dr. Büchner has a long note on Mr. Huxley's opposition to materialism, which ill accords with his own one-sided view of the subject. On the other hand, Mr. Stirling," in a new edition of his pamphlet,

" "As Regards Protoplasm." By James Hutchinson Stirling, F.R.C.S., and LL.D., Edin. New and Improved Edition, Completed by Addition of Part II., in Reference to Mr. Huxley's Second Issue, and of Preface, in reply to Mr. Huxley in "Yeast." 8vo. London: Longmans, Green, and Co. 1872.

"As Regards Protoplasm," again attacks Mr. Huxley, not only for being *de facto* a materialist, but also for misconceiving what his moral consciousness tells him in this connexion. Thus far Mr. Stirling.— *Dixit insipiens.* There is, however, no want of polemical vigour, combined with much learning and misplaced ingenuity, throughout his essay. Yet it is not worthy of serious notice. For while the true nature of protoplasm is a matter of the highest scientific importance, the errors in reference thereto which have clouded Mr. Stirling's mind can interest no one. Mr. Huxley is a philosopher, not a sophist, and may well abandon this controversy. A materialist in his thoroughgoing tenaciousness of facts, he is a spiritualist in not shutting his eyes to whatever lies beyond them. He knows too much to measure his own mind against the possibilities of nature.

Nor is Mr. Stirling the only writer on protoplasm and cognate matters with whom Mr. Huxley finds himself at issue. Like M. Milne Edwards in France, our great English biologist has had occasion, not long since, to review the history and indicate the present state of our knowledge of the vexed question of spontaneous generation. About the same time Dr. Bastian sought to re-habilitate the doctrine exposed by Redi, and with this intention devised a number of fresh experiments and renewed speculations. These he has since extended, reproducing the whole in a treatise entitled, "The Beginnings of Life."[13] Dr. Bastian has taken much pains with his subject, but his work bears evident traces of having been prepared in haste, amid many interruptions. It contains several repetitions, redundancies, inaccuracies, typographical errors, and quotations from second-hand sources. Dr. Bastian introduces several new terms. His book, we are sure, will largely be read, regard being had to the very interesting nature of the matter at issue, which deserves a lengthened discussion wholly impossible within our current limits. It is plain that there are five verbally possible modes in which living beings may originate, apart from the one made known to us from observation as the ordinary mode of the evolution of individual organisms. (For the various modes of asexual, as contrasted with sexual generation, which have been defined, are but so many stages in one continuous process of rejuvenescence.) These five modes are—(1) The appearance, *de novo*, of organisms without diminution of the surrounding stores of inorganic matter. This corresponds to special creation in its usual sense. (2) The appearance of organisms where inorganic, but not organic, matter exists (archebiosis of Bastian.) The inorganic matter, of course, must contain the ultimate, and, perhaps, some of the proximate constituents necessary to constitute the bodies of organisms, and might, therefore, require to be distinguished from other kinds of inorganic matter by a specially devised name. (3) The appearance of organisms in decomposing organic matter wholly belonging to organ-

---

[13] "The Beginnings of Life: being some Account of the Nature, Modes of Origin, and Transformations of Lower Organisms." By H. Charlton Bastian, M.A., M.D., F.R.S. In Two Volumes, Post 8vo. With Numerous Illustrations. London: Macmillan and Co. 1872.

isms diverse from those to which it gives rise; the amount and kind
of diversity must in each case be stated. (4) The production of organisms by the aggregation of others hitherto discrete. (5) The production
of organisms by the transformation of others, dissimilar to those which
are known to be related to them in the usual course of evolution. The
last three are the various modes of heterogenesis, and might indeed
be so expressed as to suggest the possibility of intermediate or critical
cases, scarcely distinguishing them from genesis proper. Dr. Bastian
admits all of these modes except the first. In considering the possibility of archebiosis, we must bear in mind—(1) The necessity of
cleanliness in its fullest physico-chemical signification. (2) The doctrine of latent life and the panspermic hypothesis, according to which
cognisable germs, ready to undergo development under favourable
circumstances, exist in most media. (3) The imperfections of the
best microscopes, suggesting the possible existence of still more minute
germs. (4) The range of temperature within which organisms can
live. (5) The production by our experiments of altered conditions,
so that the organisms are not really exposed to the influence of the
high temperature which surrounds them. Dr. Bastian is alive to
some of these sources of difficulty, but not to others. His experiments
must be repeated. His declarations on the frequent occurrence of
synthetic heterogenesis are wildly made. The wish is often father to
the thought, and Dr. Bastian admits very willingly what would have
staggered the faith of other investigators. Our knowledge of the
uniformity of nature makes us slow to believe that the same organism
should originate in two wholly different ways. We demur to most of
his conclusions, though we do not wish to speak lightly of what he has
long and seriously considered. Yet he ought to have considered his
subject still more seriously. He does not seem to realize how startling
are some of the statements which he makes, and how large a body of
evidence will necessarily be required before they can ever be confirmed.

Dr. Bastian's opinions on the nature of organisms, though not
supported by many advocates of the derivative hypothesis, militate no
less strongly against the assumption of special creations. Dr. Bree[14]
endeavours to support this assumption, in opposition to the views of
Mr. Darwin. But the strength of his convictions is not equalled by
his knowledge of scientific truths and methods. The doctrine of deri-
vation, under any form, is repugnant to him, and he objects, therefore,
not only to Mr. Darwin's hypothesis, but also to the milder views of
Professor Owen and Mr. Mivart on the same subject. He devotes
four chapters to a denunciation of "the physico-psychical argument"
of Mr. Herbert Spencer. Mr. Darwin's works on Variation under
Domestication and the Descent of Man, he notices at greater length.
Mr. Wallace, Professor Huxley, and Sir Charles Lyell are then called
to account as "supporters" of Mr. Darwin, while the late M. Flourens,
Professor Agassiz, and Professor Haughton are loudly praised for their

---

[14] "An Exposition of Fallacies in the Hypothesis of Mr. Darwin." By C. R.
Bree, M.D., F.Z.S., Post 8vo. London: Longmans, Green, and Co. 1872.

condemnation of Mr. Darwin's doctrines, copious citations being made from their writings. Dr. Bree does not understand Mr. Darwin, and he fails to understand whether others understand him. His book is not worthy of detailed criticism. It bears evident traces of having been written in haste; its style is flippant, and in some paragraphs weakly sensational. Undue allusion is made to personal topics, nor are other modes of bad taste wanting. Yet if any one were to cull from Mr. Darwin's works and the writings of others all the objections which appear to stand in the way of his hypothesis, and state these objections briefly with the utmost precision, adding any further objections which might suggest themselves, with such references to the literature of the subject and critical comments, whether in the way of refutation or confirmation, as seemed necessary, he would confer a real benefit on science, which no one would acknowledge more willingly than Mr. Darwin himself.

Could Mr. Darwin's or any other theory of the descent of organized beings attain perfection, a flood of light would thus be thrown on the very obscure subject of their mutual relations. The older naturalists unconsciously pointed towards this conclusion, when they used such phrases as *natural classification, essential* characters and true *affinities.* Ignorance of the nature, that is—the genealogy, of the objects classified is the great bar to unity of classification. The diversities of opinion which now perplex the student of systematic biology are felt less with plants than with animals. To remove, as far as possible, these difficulties, Professor Greene has drawn up three large sheets, "indicating the tribes, sub-orders, orders, and higher groups of the animal kingdom," in short, all divisions above the rank of families.[13] The tribes of insects, for want of space, are omitted. The author endeavours to maintain those groups which are thoroughly established, while at the same time he has not hesitated to alter the value or modify the limits of others, in accordance with the requirements of our advanced knowledge. In his choice of names, often no easy matter, he has done his best to reconcile the conflicting laws of priority, propriety, and notoriety. The exigencies of typography compel him to use a linear series, but he has added a "Table showing some of the affinities of the classes of the animal kingdom," in which their names are printed side by side in such a manner as to call to mind the more important of their cross relationships.

Whatever group of living beings we study soon brings us face to face with facts the interpretation of which involves questions suggesting more or less nearly the all-pervading doctrine of natural selection. The struggle for life between men and animals, so far as it concerns the former, is seldom noticed, yet we may see it taking place, with terrible directness, in such tropical countries as Hindostan. Within an area less than half that of the whole peninsula of India 11,416 persons died from snake-bites in 1869. This, with many other statements

[13] "Tables of Zoology, Indicating the Tribes, Sub-Orders, Orders, and Higher Groups of the Animal Kingdom; for Students, Lecturers, and others." By J. Reay Greene, M.D., &c., Professor of Natural History in the Queen's University in Ireland. London: J. and A. Churchill, 1872.

worthy of note, may be found in Dr. Fayrer's "Thanatophidia of India."[16] Dr. Fayrer's book, valuable no less to the physician than the zoologist, may be regarded as a special supplement to one section of Dr. Günther's more comprehensive work on the reptiles of British India. He treats of several important details beyond the limits of his predecessor. From a medical point of view we can only say that here, as in other cases, the better part of valour is discretion, since no remedy for snake-bites has yet been discovered. There are, however, hopes in this direction. Some of the facts confirmed or first mentioned by the author are curious. For example, one cobra's bite will not affect another, though fatal to a non-venomous snake. A poisonous snake may bite without allowing its poison to exude. Boys, as we might expect, are bitten more frequently than young girls; but the mortality is greater with women than with men. The number of species of venomous snakes is fortunately small. Of the cobra several distinct varieties are known. Numerous coloured plates, taken "from nature, most from life itself," at the School of Art in Calcutta, represent these and the other Thanatophidia described in Dr. Fayrer's volume.

> "Yet, spite of all this eager strife,
> This ceaseless play, the genuine life
> That serves the steadfast hours,
> Is in the grass beneath, that grows
> Unheeded, and the mute repose
> Of sweetly-breathing flowers."

These lines have been recalled to our mind by reading Dr. Forbes Watson's "Flowers and Gardens."[17] Very touching are the circumstances attending its preparation. We quote his preface in full:—

"The following papers have been written during a last illness, which has often made it impossible to examine the specimens I could have wished. In the primrose, for example, I have only been able to make out satisfactorily the drooping aspect of the leaf: how this combines itself with the more rigid character in the different stages of the leaf I do not fully understand. For the same reason many of the illustrations, especially in the chapters on gardening, have been selected as being the most ready to hand, rather than as the best. In my remarks on gardening, I have no wish at all to disparage the modern systems. My aim, chiefly, was to point out the faults of modern gardening, because its merits are such as it is impossible to overlook. Lastly, in many instances, my remarks bear more or less reference to the works of Ruskin, the greatest and best of art-teachers; but where I have consciously borrowed from him, I have said so. These papers are left in charge of a friend for publication."

Two days after he had written these lines Dr. Forbes Watson died. We are here, in some degree, reminded of Linnæus, whose "Philosophia Botanica," the most scientific and, as Rousseau felt, the most

---

[16] "The Thanatophidia of India. Being a Description of the Venomous Snakes of the Indian Peninsula, with an Account of the Influence of their Poison on Life; and a Series of Experiments." By J. Fayrer, M.D., &c. Folio. Coloured Plates. London: J. and A. Churchill. 1872.

[17] "Flowers and Gardens—Notes on Plant Beauty." By a Medical Man. Crown 8vo. London: Strahan and Co. 1872.

charming of his works, is said to have been composed during the intervals of relief from the attacks of a long and painful malady. Apart from science strictly so called, the influence of natural objects on our emotional life offers matter for much contemplation. A more inviting introduction to the study of plant beauty could not be found than Dr. Forbes Watson's legacy.

We believe that botany, rightly pursued, affords the best training for those entering on the study of nature, and desirous of cultivating at once their powers of thought and observation. Nevertheless, a good word may be said for geology, and by none better than Mr. Kingsley. Mr. Kingsley attracts us because of his frankness and simplicity, and because of the evident improvement which, at successive periods, marks his treatment of the same or kindred topics. His "Glaucus," with all its shortcomings, was a delightful book, and still higher praise must be accorded to his "Town Geology."[18] Here he discourses, in a series of lectures, of the soil of the field, the pebbles in the street, the stones in the wall, the coal in the fire, the lime in the mortar, and the slates on the roof. His last lecture, giving an account of Snowdon and the various geological agencies which have contributed to its present structure and form, is a highly successful piece of popular scientific writing. But the best part of the book is its preface, which is longer than any of the lectures, more general in its range, and contains a very noble protest in favour of the claims of natural knowledge.

This is a very remarkable essay[19] of thirty pages, containing more matter for thought than many a volume of three hundred. The author's chief purpose is to argue that, on the inexhaustible principle of doing all that lies in our power to lessen suffering, we are not only at liberty but bound to permit the deliberate ending of life in those to whom life has become hopeless in the future and intolerable in the present. Indeed, in the present essay the author confines himself to the special consideration of the pass to which men may be brought by disease, and to the way of relief by means of fatal doses of opium or chloroform. But it is pretty clear that the author knows well enough that this is but a small department of a greater inquiry into the whole morality of suicide, of the power, that is, of choosing life and death at our own hands. The present essay is a pilot-balloon, to be followed by the larger undertaking, and we thoroughly agree with the epigrammatic preface of the editor, Mrs. Crawshay, who says that there is "no reason why thought should not be directed to a very difficult and important subject. No question ever became clearer by no one thinking about it—indeed, except for religious topics, I never heard this plan proposed." We, who have no small experience of disease, are disposed to think that almost the whole importance of the Essay lies in its wider bearings, and that the number of cases of disease which need such a cutting of the thread are far fewer than may be supposed. It must be remembered that to make the ending of life jus-

---

[18] "Town Geology." By the Rev. Charles Kingsley, F.L.S., F.G.S., Canon of Chester. Crown 8vo. London : Strahan and Co. 1872.

[19] "Euthanasia." By S. D. Williams, Jun.

tifiable recovery must be wholly impossible, the patient's sufferings
exquisitely great, and the hopes and pleasures of life wholly out of
reach. Now are there in practice many such cases? All acute diseases in young persons must of course be excluded, as their recovery can
rarely or never be called impossible; organic diseases again in young
persons, such as aneurism, may perchance, in rare cases, be hopeless
and intolerable, but not often. The undulled sensibility which shudders at the pain, generally allows of so much hope and pleasure between the paroxysms as to make life more than tolerable, and indeed
acceptable. In old persons again, even chronic disease has its turns
of ebb and flow, so that it is hard to say when relief has become utterly
impossible; while, on the other hand, the duller sensibilities of age
make the inevitable mortal end to come gently. Fatal disease, in fact,
is rarely terrible in so far as bodily pain is concerned, and still more
rarely a terror without hope of mitigation. Now, the wider question
of the morality of suicide is opposed by many essentially unsound
arguments, theoretical and others, which no reader would expect to find
in the *Westminster Review*, and which, moreover, are well answered
in the pamphlet before us. It would have to be argued out on the
general ground of the bearings which the prevalence of suicide might
be said to have upon the wellbeing of society. To us the stronger
arguments would seem to lie in favour of its repression either by law
or by social opinion. Life to the looker-on seems to be a dark and
wretched state to thousands; and nothing tells more of the real vigour
and boldness of the author's thought than the power with which he
realizes and dares to expound the truth which presses so heavily on all
thoughtful men—namely, that life as a rule is not a happy thing,
commonly indeed a very miserable thing. Also that in the pursuit of
truth we seem to be divesting ourselves of all which seemed to explain
or to gild this misery, so that the progress of knowledge is the progress of "disillusionment," an insight into harder and crueller laws
as they seem to us, an insight which to many minds, as to Clough, for
example, made the further contemplation of the world almost intolerable. If then we reason on from the particular case of painful disease
to the more general principle in which it is included, and if thus reasoning we recognise the right of each and any to deal to himself death
or life according to the present apparent balance of individual happiness
and failure, we shall have to place "anæsthetics" in the way of more persons than we like to think about; life, it seems to us, will be cheapened,
encouragement to physical cowardice may be given, and the "paramount duty of lessening the amount of physical suffering in the world"
may find itself fulfilled by a few persons who calculate that the removal of sufferers may not only benefit the sufferer, but may also be
a mutual advantage.

When two persons arguing on the same subject argue consistently
from opposite points of view, the result is likely to be anything but
harmonious."* Such, it seems to us, have been the respective attitudes of lawyers and doctors in arguing on the legal relations of lunacy,

---

** "The Medical Jurisprudence of Insanity." By J. H. Balfour Browne, Esq.

whether such arguments are heard in the witness-box or read in the study. The medical men are extremely indignant at the narrowness of the lawyers, and the lawyers in their turn are no less severe upon the vagueness of medical testimony. Nor can we altogether side with our own profession of medicine in this matter, for we are bound to admit that medical men in discussing the legal relations of insanity, do often show themselves inaccurate and unpractical. But neither party is free from blame, and it seems to us that instead of lamenting the discrepancy it would be better to recognise the causes of it, and thus to clear the way for a reconciliation. The fact is, the two parties are aiming at different ends. The doctor makes what he calls a scientific definition of insanity, and claims immunity from legal responsibility for every person who may be included within such definition. The lawyer, on the other hand, ought to admit that he does not care whether a given person be, scientifically speaking, of disordered mind or not, but that he has to decide whether it is desirable in the interests of society to make such person, sane or insane, amenable to legal penalties or disabilities. Scientifically speaking, every criminal who has allowed one propensity to gain head at the expense of all other motives is so far insane, and the ungovernable imbeciles, so well discussed by Mr. Browne, are but extreme cases of such insanity. A perfectly sane man is as uncommon as a perfectly healthy man, nor can any fast line be drawn between sane and insane. On the other hand, it is the arrantest nonsense to say that many admitted lunatics are insensible to legal sanctions. Of many of them it is as true as of children, and no more. All men act from the strongest motive, and if legal threats can be shown to modify the actions of any person, sane or insane, it is for the good of society that such threats should in certain measure be held out. To take an extreme case: if it could be shown that homicidal maniacs, as a rule, feared the gallows more than they loved murder, then, sane or insane, it would be for the good of society to see them hanged. This is surely the whole answer to the vexed question of "legal responsibility." In making these remarks we are led away from Mr. Browne's volume, which we intended to praise highly. It shows a bold attempt to deal more freely with a difficult question, and one overlaid with heaps of nonsense; it is written by a good reasoner, and a man of breadth of culture; nor do we know of any book which can compete with it in the same department.

Nothing is more curious in the history of literature than the chance, for so it seems, which plays with the fortunes of books. It is seldom perhaps that a worthless book lives long, but how often do excellent books pass into oblivion only to be recovered, if recovered at all, by some historian of later times. These reflections are prompted by the wonder which comes over us as we turn Dr. Ross's pages,[21] whether his book is fated to live or die. So far as sheer excellence goes, and insight into new aspects of things, it deserves anything rather than oblivion, for it is long since the medical press has put forth anything of the same merit as a speculative treatise. We do not hesitate to say

---

[21] "The Graft Theory of Disease." By James Ross, M.D.

that Dr. Ross's theory, which is the application of Dr. Darwin's theory of pangenesis in a modified form to the facts of pathology, is, whether true or not, at any rate the best, if not the only theory upon which pathologists can presently work. It has fewer difficulties and more explaining power than any other hypothesis, and comes in well at a time when the foremost men of the profession have formally pronounced the "elimination," or humoralist hypothesis to be a failure and a snare. It is impossible for us in our present space to give our readers anything like a conception of Dr. Ross's argument; but we may shortly say that his thesis is, that the so-called "zymotic" diseases arise, not by a mere admixture of alien and injurious matter with the blood, nor again by the introduction and development in the body of zoological or botanical parasites, but by the grafting of new and different modes of growth upon the tissues. In the discussion of this hypothesis, Dr. Ross makes excellent use of the results of the best modern speculative thought—of the speculative conclusions of Darwin on Pangenesis, of the biological reasoning of Spencer—and so on. We venture to think that Dr. Ross has felicitously expressed opinions which have been floating in the minds of many, and which needed a prophet. We are paying no idle compliment, nor indeed are we specially congratulating Dr. Ross, but rather the whole of the medical profession, when we express our belief that sooner or later something like his hypothesis will become the basis of modern pathology. At the same time we do congratulate and compliment Dr. Ross very heartily, and we believe that if his admirable chapters had appeared as an address at one of our scientific congresses the author would have made a brilliant reputation. As it is his book must await readers, and we can scarcely doubt that it will find them.

The recent alarming increase of Rabies in England has induced Mr. Fleming to publish as a monograph[a] on the disease the materials he had collected to form part of a wider treatise. He appears to have collected his information from all available sources, English and Continental, and has produced a book which, while it contains little original observation, yet ably represents the present state of knowledge on the subject, and is a valuable contribution to the English literature of the disease. He gives first an interesting sketch of its history, from the distinct account of it by Aristotle, down to the most recent epidemics, or, as the author prefers to call them, unnecessarily it seems to us, epizootics. He agrees with most other writers on the subject, that rabies has occasionally, though perhaps only once in a thousand cases, a spontaneous origin. It is difficult otherwise to explain, not only certain individual instances, but also its occurrence among such animals as wolves, and its occasional sudden outbreaks in regions where it was previously unknown, and where no foreign importation could be traced, as in Peru in 1803. But of the conditions which can produce it, other

[a] "Rabies and Hydrophobia, their History, Nature, Causes, Symptoms, and Prevention." By George Fleming, F.R.G.S., M.A.I., President of the Central Veterinary Medical Society; Veterinary Surgeon Royal Engineers. London: Chapman and Hall. 1872.

than contagion, we know almost nothing. There is no evidence to show that it is contagious unless inoculated. Probably all warm-blooded animals are susceptible. The rate of human mortality in England has varied, since 1838, from 1 in 1802 to 30 in 1866. In France it is more common, the annual average is 102; in Prussia about 71. Recent observation has unfortunately not increased our knowledge regarding the curious "lyssi" under the tongue, alleged to exist, and to contain the virus, during the early period of incubation, by Marochetti in the early part of this century. They may possibly have some connexion with the popular delusion about a worm under the dog's tongue. Mr. Fleming calls especial attention to the character of the early symptoms in the dog. No furor or tendency to bite is present, but merely restlessness and perhaps even an increased manifestation of affection for its master; such manifestations are, however, as dangerous as is the bite of a later stage. In the dog, hydrophobia is never present. The account of the symptoms in other animals and man, and of the pathology and treatment, though full, unfortunately adds nothing to our knowledge or resources. In preventive measures alone can we hope for success in dealing with the disease. The isolation of suspected cases by a sanitary police organization, and the enforcement in districts, where the disease is epidemic, of efficient muzzling and the destruction of all stray and useless dogs, are the measures chiefly to be relied on. The whole chapter on the prevention of the disease is well worthy the careful consideration of our sanitary authorities.

Dr. John Ogle has collected, from various sources, an interesting series of facts illustrative of the "Hereditary Transmission of Structural Peculiarities"[13] in man and animals, and has added some remarkable instances which have come under his own observation. Several are examples of extensive collateral and vertical diffusion of congenital defects. It is conjectured that all such have, in the first instance, been acquired. Cases are narrated in which acquired defects in man as well as in animals have been transmitted to the offspring. Such transmission being possible, its rarity is a matter for surprise, perhaps also for congratulation. Other interesting examples are given of the supposed influence of maternal impressions, and of the relation between certain reproductive conditions in the lower animals.

The proper ventilation of dwelling-houses is a subject which, standing as it does midway between the provinces of public and private hygiene, has received far less systematic attention than its importance deserves. How to ventilate a house thoroughly without draughts is the great problem of house building; yet we still ventilate our mansions and our hovels on the same principle. In "Health and Comfort in House Building,"[14] Drs. Drysdale and Hayward describe an

---

[13] "On Hereditary Transmission of Structural Peculiarities." By John W. Ogle, M.D., F.R.C.P. Reprinted from the British and Foreign Med. Chir. Review for April 1872. London: Adlard.

[14] "Health and Comfort in House Building, or Ventilation with Warm Air by Self-acting Suction Power." By J. Drysdale, M.D., and J. W. Hayward, M.D. London: Spon. 1872.

attempt to discover and put in force the true principles of ventilation. They reject all schemes for immediate ventilation from the open air as inapplicable to the rigours of our climate, and all schemes for single-room ventilation as fragmentary and imperfect. Their problem is how to ventilate a house as a whole, with air at a temperature of 65°. The first point in their plan is that a central hall shall serve as the primary receptacle of the fresh air, which shall enter it through a simple warming apparatus, by which in cold weather it may be raised to the required temperature. For this purpose it is necessary that this central hall shall be separated from the open air by a double door, to the outer of which servants may have access without opening the inner one. Communications are made between the central hall and each room, say at the cornice. From the centre of the ceiling of each room a pipe conducts the foul air to a common foul-air chamber, which is in connexion with a suction apparatus. The draught in this is produced by the waste heat of the kitchen chimney (about seven-eighths of the whole), and is sufficient to draw the air through the rooms and the central hall. This air is not warm enough in cold weather to heat the rooms; for that purpose fires are to be employed as at present, any indraught from the chimneys being prevented by valves. Plans are given of two houses constructed on this principle. No difficulty was experienced in carrying out the details, and the result proved all that was desired. The authors consider that the expense need not be greater than of any ordinary well-built house, since compensatory saving may be effected through the lessened size of sleeping and living rooms, the air of which is thus constantly renewed. If this system can be worked with as little difficulty as the authors assert, it must be admitted that they have furnished a valuable contribution to practical hygiène.

Dr. Inman's pleasant, instructive, and very plain-spoken series of essays on the Preservation" and Restoration" of Health have reached the third and second editions respectively. The latter has received considerable additions, and appended to it is a review of Dr. Oldham's work on Malaria. With the peculiar views of that author on the nature of malaria Dr. Inman is in thorough accord.

A fifth edition has been issued of Dr. Dobell's small book on "Diet and Regimen."" It is prefaced by a justification of the author's own speciality and a denunciation of most other specialities, and consists of a number of selections from other productions of the author, chemists, wine-merchants, &c., together with a series of hygiènic aphorisms. Much of the information given is useful, but some is of very doubtful accuracy.

³⁵ "On the Preservation of Health ; or, Essays Explanatory of the Principles to be Adopted by those who Desire to Avoid Disease." By Thomas Inman, M.D. Lond. Third Edition. London : H. K. Lewis. 1872.

³⁶ "On the Restoration of Health ; being Essays upon the Principles upon which the Treatment of many Diseases is to be Conducted." By Thomas Inman, M.D., Lond. Second Edition. London: H. K. Lewis. 1872.

³⁷ "On Diet and Regimen in Sickness and Health." By Horace Dobell, M.D. Fifth and Revised Edition. London : H. K. Lewis. 1872.

In a translation from the French on " Change of Air and Scene,"[58] Dr. Donné, of Montpellier, gives us a pleasant outline of his rambles, during a long lifetime, amid the scenery and baths of France and some adjacent districts. After four brief chapters on what he terms the "hygiène of the seasons," he sketches a series of holiday tours among the Pyrenees, and then describes at length the various mineral springs of France, the Pyrenees, and Corsica. The constitution and ascertained efficacy of each spring is stated, and he depicts briefly but graphically, and from personal visits, the chief features of each place and of its neighbourhood. The book concludes with some remarks on sea-bathing on the different French coasts, on hydropathy, the hygiène of the lungs, teeth, eyes, &c., and with lists of mineral springs. The author's ideas of disease, from the glimpses we obtain of them, seem hardly those of the present day, and his belief in the value of the various waters rather extensive; but the information given is accurate, as far as we have tested it, and the book will form an interesting and useful addition to either the tourist's guide or the physician's handbook.

The position of homœopathic practitioners in the medical world is a natural source of annoyance to them, and of such complaints as find utterance in the pamphlets before us.[59][60] The exclusiveness with which they are treated is manifested among other ways, in the refusal of most physicians and surgeons of the regular school to meet homœopathists in consultation, for the purpose of giving them the benefit of their opinion upon the neutral grounds of diagnosis, or surgical and dietetic treatment. This refusal, much regretted by the homœopaths, is attributed by them to fear of the "rank and file" of the profession on the part of its leaders, and to the sinister influence of the medical press. Undoubtedly a powerful public opinion exists in the medical world, of which the journals are much more the exponents than the cause, against such consultations. But many men who thus refuse are as much above being influenced by the motive suggested, as they are above any need for its entertainment. Both the public opinion, and the individual refusal are, we believe, mainly due to two motives; first, to a desire to discountenance altogether, not an erroneous theory, but a system of therapeutics under which the public, it is believed, runs a greater risk than under the regular methods of treatment; and secondly, in the case of physicians, to a fear that such consultations would occasionally expose them to the painful liability of diagnosing diseases, which, they are convinced, the system they profess would cure, while under the homœopathic treatment, with which they must not interfere, recovery would be hopeless. Pro-

[58] "Change of Air and Scene. A Physician's Hints, with Excursions for Health amongst the Watering Places of the Pyrenees, France, &c." By Alphonse Donné, M.D., Rector of the Academy of Montpellier. London: King. 1872.

[59] "Modern Medicine and Homœopathy : an Address Delivered at the British Homœopathic Congress at Birmingham, 1870." By the President, Dr. J. J. Drysdale. London : Turner. 1870.

[60] "On the Need of Freedom of Opinion and of the Press in Medicine." Extracted from the *British Journal of Homœopathy* for April, 1872. London : Turner.

bably, however, by those who have the expression of professional opinion, it might with advantage be left to the individual judgment of those personally concerned, to determine whether their opinion of homœopathy and its practice, or their fear of such a contingency as that just alluded to, is such as to lead them to give or refuse to the section of the public under homœopathic care the fruit of their experience and skill. In those cases in which the name homœopathy is merely used as the cover for a practice in which there is no " homœopathy" at all, we believe that the authors of these pamphlets would be the first to approve, in the interests of a common honesty, the refusal of a consultation.

In " The Fallacies of Teetotalism,"[21] Mr. Ward contests the propositions of the United Kingdom Alliance in a series of counter-propositions, which may be thus summarized:—The State is not justified in interfering with domestic practices, except when such are inimical to the general welfare; this the use of alcoholic liquors is not, even in individual excess. The present law sufficiently protects legitimate, and punishes mischievous excess. Stimulants, alcoholic and other, have acted an important part in the civilization and intellectual development of mankind. Their moderate use is beneficial, because the Creator has made them pleasant to the taste and agreeable to the stomach. Forced abstinence would be exceedingly dangerous, both from its immediate effect, and because probably the ultimate result would be universal drunkenness and ruin. The Maine law, permissive or other, would unconstitutionally limit the liberty of the subject, prevent reasonable enjoyment, and endanger the advancement and happiness of Great Britain. These propositions are amplified and supported at considerable length and with no little energy. The old arguments against the Alliance are reinforced from history, poetry ,and science. They are advanced, however, with an acerbity which would only be justified by a much weaker cause, and a degree of exaggeration which is accounted for in their origin in newspaper polemics, but which diminishes the value of the work as a contribution to the cause it advocates.

In a small book on the " Causes of Heart Disease,"[22] Dr. Moinet has given an account of the morbid states that lead to cardiac affections, which is full, though by no means exhaustive of our present knowledge, and has added theoretical explanations of their mode of action. He insists strongly, and with reason, on the importance of degenerative processes, and believes that the co-existence of cardiac disease and emphysema is to be attributed quite as much to a common degenerative influence, as to the mechanical effect on the heart of the lung condition. But when he explains the affection of the fibrous tissues, and of some serous membranes, in rheumatism, by saying that the blood, charged with acid and fibrine, tends to stagnation,

[21] "The Fallacies of Teetotalism, Comprehending an Exposure of the False Doctrines of the United Kingdom Alliance, and of the Detestable Tyranny of the Maine Law, or Permissive Bill." By Robert Ward, Editor of the *North of England Advertiser.* London : Simpkin, Marshall and Co. 1872.
[22] "A Treatise on the Causes of Heart Disease, with a Chapter on the Reason of its Prevalence in the Army." By Francis W. Moinet, M.D., F.R.C.P.E. Edinburgh : Bell and Bradfute. 1872.

and in the unyielding capillaries of those tissues such stagnation takes place most readily, he ignores at least half the conditions of the problem he seeks to solve. Nor is his explanation of the prevalence of cardiac hypertrophy and aortic disease in the Army more happy. He believes it is due to the increased cardiac labour consequent on the maintenance for so long of the erect posture, and the exercise of the arms in that posture, the chief agent being the increased curvature of the arch of the aorta, by the weight of the heart, which augments the resistance to the passage of the blood. But this is to attribute the effect to influences which are in operation in quite one half of the human race, and certainly will not account for any greater prevalence of heart disease in a particular section.

Dr. Milner Fothergill's work on Cardiac Affections[3] is designed to introduce, in a systematic treatise, the results of recent research into the physiology and pathology of the organ. This has been done fairly well. The utility of the work would be increased, however, by more numerous references to the original sources of information. It is suited to the senior student and practitioner rather than to those commencing the study of the subject. The sections on treatment are particularly good, and appear to contain the results of much practical experience.

HISTORY AND BIOGRAPHY.

ALL Scholars and most literary men will welcome those writings[1] of the late Professor Conington which Mr. Symonds has recently edited. In the volumes before us they are preceded by a memoir from the pen of the Savilian professor. The life of John Conington was devoid of incident, but what little there was to say in a biography has been kindly and well said by Professor Smith. From this we learn that Mr. Conington was the son of a Boston clergyman; that he was educated at Rugby, where he was not always in favour with Dr. Arnold, and that after an unsuccessful attempt to transfer his affections from the Greek poets to jurisprudence, he was elected to the new chair of Latin at Oxford. He died in October, 1809, at a time when he had many literary projects in view which would, undoubtedly, have added to his high reputation, and have furthered the cause of scholarship. The distinctive mark of his excellence was, according to Mr. Symonds, his literary versatility. He approached scholarship, he says, from the point of view of literature rather than of philology. If he is known most widely as a scholar, these new volumes present to us the

[3] "The Heart, and its Diseases, with their Treatment." By J. Milner Fothergill, M.D., M.R.C.P. London: H. K. Lewis. 1872.

[1] "Miscellaneous Writings of John Conington, late Corpus Professor of Latin in the University of Oxford." Edited by S. A. Symonds, M.A., with a Memoir by S. H. Smith, M.A., LL.D., F.R.S., Fellow of Balliol College, Savilian Professor of Geometry. London: Longmans, Green, and Co.

other side of his character. Most will, however, be inclined to think
that it is as a scholar that Professor Conington claims attention. He
was strong in the power of arrangement and re-presentation rather
than in that of origination. Even in the present volumes what
is valuable seems to us to come from the scholar rather than from the
literary man. Take as an instance the first essay before us upon the
Poetry of Pope. We expect from the true literary critic a stream of
light which shall illuminate the whole of his subject, and exhibit the
characteristic unity of the entire range. Scholarship will throw
bright, and sometimes fantastic, but always desirable cross-lights
upon particular portions. And this is exactly what it has done in
this essay upon the poetry of Pope. We are not speaking against it :
it is gracefully written, it is instructive, it is even vigorous ; but
it lacks the systematic evolution of a subject which only the higher
literary ability can work out. In the essay upon the English
translators of Virgil, Professor Conington has had a more congenial
and happier field for his powers. Besides supplying the history of
the translations, he deals with the vexed question of the comparative
merits of prose and verse translations. But his essay leaves this
subject pretty much where it was. His conclusion is that English
verse is *per se* a better representation of Latin verse than English
prose, yet he advises men "who are neither Virgils nor Ciceros, but
simply men of culture with a good command over their own language,
and a good eye for the beauties of their author," to try the yet
unexhausted resources of prose. Professor Conington seems to us to
be speaking from two points of view. It is settled that an absolutely
adequate translation of a poem is an impossibility. If it be not so,
where is the perfect translation ? The question, then, is narrowed to
this issue : which form of translation is the less inadequate ? and this
must depend upon the audience for which the translation is designed.
Those who are ignorant of the original language will in most cases
prefer verse—though many even of these will believe that they gain a
truer knowledge of the original poem from a literal prose version.
Those who have a fair knowledge of the original will almost always
take the prose translation, Professor Conington's own renderings
will furnish an instance of this. Many scholars who have regarded
his poetical translation of Virgil with disfavour will admire and enjoy
the fidelity and felicity of the prose translation, which makes the
second of Mr. Symonds' volumes. There is another and smaller
audience to be considered. It consists of those who, being acquainted
with the original poem, experience a scholarly pleasure in observing
the manner in which the delicacies of one language can be represented
or compensated for in another. But this transfusion of beauties really
commends itself chiefly as an academic exercise. This is Professor
Conington's second point of view, and he is not careful to separate the
two. Perhaps the best article in the volume is the one which Professor Conington delivered as his inaugural address. The passage upon
the attitude of the true scholar, is admirable, and rises into enthusiasm as does the utterance of a man when he is speaking of his own
ideal standard. The first volume closes with two theological articles,

reprinted from the *Contemporary Review.* Professor Conington was of a religion which his biographer connects with the teaching of Dr. Arnold. For a short time, and for a short time only, he had sympathy with the spirit of free enquiry in religion. But a sudden and enduring change passed over the tenour of his thoughts. Professor Smith says: "For some weeks his mind was agitated and unstrung by the overwhelming consciousness of the terrors of the unseen world. He was unable to take any interest in, or even to give any sustained attention to, any subject not directly affecting the momentous questions which engaged his thoughts. He would not even read the New Testament in Greek, apparently because the very language suggested associations which, for the time, had become repugnant to him." This morbid condition of mind was not, however, permanent, though it left its mark upon him. Professor Smith adds: "It may be true to say that his mind was at all times too prone to dwell on the awfulness of eternity, and not ready enough to take comfort in the thought of eternal love." The second volume consists almost entirely of an English rendering of the works of Virgil. It is an admirable version, and well illustrates the principles upon which a prose translation should be made. We have already ventured to predict for it a wider and more appreciative audience than his verse rendering has yet met with. It is difficult to speak of the character of Professor Conington with impartiality. If he wanted breadth of view, he atoned for it by the intensity of his earnestness. His mind was tinged with the gloom of a one-sided theology, but was brightened by kindliness and a sincere love of truth. As a teacher he was most successful, drawing and attaching to himself by peculiarly close ties many of the promising young scholars of his University. And it is remarkable how he succeeded in connecting them with his own line of study. One of them, Mr. Nettleship, became his co-editor in his editions of Virgil and Persius. Most of the letters in the present memoir are to other pupils, and show the close terms of affection upon which they stood with him. We will conclude our notice with the following memorial lines (not in the memoir) by another distinguished pupil of Professor Conington:—

Cum quinto steterat vix quadragesimus annus;
lux brevis: an tantis plenior ulla bonis?
lux brevis: at puro non improvisa nec alto
flenda supervenit mors necopina viro.
at partem nostri tecum te detrahis ipse:
noster eras; sive te nos queror esse parum.
quos igitur tali junxisti foedere amantes,
hos non flete decet sed bene velle magis,
et colere atque alios simili pietate fovere
quos et amaturus tu modo vivus eras.

Those who are familiar with the versatility of Mrs. Oliphant will find without surprise that her "Memoir of the Count de Montalembert"" is a good biography. It is gracefully and tenderly written, for she

* "Memoir of Count de Montalembert, Peer of France; a Chapter of Recent French History." By Mrs. Oliphant. 2 vols. Blackwood and Sons.

knew and loved the character which she depicts; moreover we can allow much to a biographer even when the writer is not perfectly impartial. Montalembert was noble, enthusiastic, devoted and loyal to a losing cause, but—we cannot agree with Mrs. Oliphant when she says, " All that was best in France went with him to his grave." In spite of this she has given us a clear history of the life of the author of the " Monks of the West," and we rise from the perusal of the book with something of her love for the illustrious Montalembert. He was by birth half English or rather Scotch; his early education was conducted entirely by his Scotch grandfather, and his love and admiration of this country lasted through his whole life. At fourteen years of age he wrote in his diary an analysis of a work upon English law, and added: " Few works have produced so much impression upon me as this. It has convinced me of *what I had long suspected*, that England is the first nation in the world." Three years later he wrote again: "God and liberty—these are the two principal motive powers of my existence. To reconcile these two perfections shall be the aim of my life." Alas! his ideal of liberty was the Roman Catholic Church. At the death of his Scotch grandfather Montalembert joined his parents upon the continent. It was then he formed his friendships with Lacordaire, La Mennais, and Victor Hugo. But he still remained true to his Church. Later in life he visited Ireland and shared the hospitality of O'Connell, but the Liberator greatly disappointed his enthusiastic expectations. He had made his pilgrimage and had hoped to have discussed with becoming solemnity the great topics which engaged his own mind; he was shown into a drawing-room full of laughing Irish girls, and saw but little of O'Connell himself. As to his opinions they were earnest, but they were sudden and changeable. He was at first a warm supporter of Louis Napoleon, and regarded him as the saviour of society. He defended him as President, he approved his *coup d'État*, he voted for him as Emperor. Yet when the Prince Imperial was born, he expressed his surprise that Providence had thought fit to grant another male to the frightful race of Napoleon. But to the Church he remained always true. Nothing so struck the poet Rogers at his interview with Montalembert as the " immovable and cloudless faith which seemed to him the most enviable of all gifts." He willingly submitted his intelligence to the authority of the Church. When it was evidently the intention of the Pope to declare the doctrine of Papal infallibility, Montalembert said that he would do his utmost against it until it was proclaimed—and that then he would accept it. Yet his keenest suffering came from his devotion. His own daughter declared her wish to become a nun. " When his daughter avowed to him her intention it gave him a great shock," says Mrs. Oliphant. But it was still more painful for him to hear that he himself had inspired the desire. " She went to the bookshelf and sought out one of the volumes in which he had narrated the 'History of the Monks of the West.' 'It is you,' she said, 'who have taught me that withered hearts and weary souls are not the things we ought to offer to God.'" We have not found Mrs. Oliphant's book heavy reading, and those who are interested in the

life of Montalembert will peruse it with pleasure. With a little less
emotion and fewer tears, for literature is sexless, it would be permanently valuable. Perhaps it will be so as it is.

"The Life of Madame Lafayette,"[3] written by her daughter, presents a vivid picture of a noble and much suffering character. She
was born in 1759, and married at a very early age the Marquis of
Lafayette. In 1777 her husband carried out his plan of going to
America and joining in the War of Independence. The bitter opposition which he had to meet from his family in taking this step was not
increased by the weakness of his wife, and she was rewarded by the
glory and renown which he received upon his return. After the campaign of Virginia the conqueror of Cornwallis received every mark of
royal favour. When later Lafayette employed himself in obtaining
civil rights for the Protestants, Madame Lafayette received with the
greatest sympathy Protestant clergymen whom the carrying out of
this enterprise attracted to her house. She was religious, but her
religion was not too narrow to admit toleration when toleration was
almost unknown. Indeed in all the dangers incurred by her husband
for the zeal with which he supported every principle of justice and of
liberty against all parties, Madame Lafayette took her full share.
Nor was it long before she suffered. She was arrested and sent to La
Force in Paris. At that time sixty victims were falling daily, and
she expected continually to be herself summoned to the guillotine.
From La Force she was removed to Le Plessis, where she suffered all
the horrors of this mournful anticipation. At length, owing to the
unceasing exertions of the American minister, she was set at liberty.
After sending her son, George Washington, to America, she proceeded
to Vienna, where she obtained permission from the Emperor to share
the captivity of her husband, then for three years prisoner at Olmütz.
In this prison she voluntarily underwent all the hardships to which
her husband was subjected, and there she remained for three-and-
twenty months. But the confinement had undermined her health,
and when the illustrious exiles were liberated in 1797, Madame
Lafayette was in a precarious condition. Upon her recovery she devoted the remainder of her life to her family. She died on the
Christmas night of 1807. The present memoirs are family papers, and
are written with touching simplicity. The book has been printed in
Paris, and is not free from certain errors of the press and orthography,
but these do not impair the general interest of the affecting narrative.

The short sketch[4] which Sir F. Head gives of his friend the late
Sir John Burgoyne, is not intended to supersede the fuller information
which we are to expect from Sir John's son-in-law ; but it is a tribute
to the memory of the warrior who was intimately connected with much
of our recent military history. Sir John Burgoyne was the godson
of Fox, and entered the army at the age of sixteen. His career as an

[3] "The Life of Madame Lafayette." By Mdme. De Lasteyrie, her daughter.
Preceded by "The Life of the Duchess D'Ayen." Translated by Louis De
Lasteyrie. Paris and London : Barthès and Lowell.
[4] "Field-Marshal Sir John Burgoyne, Bart." By Sir Francis Head, Bart.
London : John Murray.

officer was marked by great personal courage and military ability. At the age of eighteen he was present at the surrender of Valetta, and subsequently at the siege of Rosetta in 1807. His letters so struck Sir J. Moore, that the general applied for Captain Burgoyne to be attached to his staff. He sailed with him to Portugal in 1808, and just missed the battle of Corunna. He was present at the siege of Badajoz, the siege of Ciudad Rodrigo, the storming of Salamanca, and was wounded at the siege of Burgos. At the battle of Vittoria and the storming of St. Sebastian he rendered assistance, and was severely wounded at the latter place. In 1815 he landed at Ostend, where he remained with the army of occupation until 1818. When the Russian war broke out he proceeded to the Crimea, and Sir F. Head contributes several interesting letters from the camp before Sebastopol. Popular clamour, however, attacked the old Peninsula generals, and Sir John was recalled. This slur upon his military character he bore in the true spirit of loyalty, nor were there wanting those ready to defend him. And after the fall of Sebastopol, he received the thanks of both Houses of Parliament for services in the Crimea. Other honours also crowded upon him, and when in January, 1869, after seventy years' service, he left the office of Inspector-General of Fortifications, a retiring pension of nearly the amount of his salary was granted him. This he did not long enjoy. Every one will remember that amongst the gallant crew who perished in the ill-fated turret-ship, the *Captain*, was the only son of Sir John Burgoyne. This loss shattered the energy and strength of the veteran, and he did not long survive it. In October of last year he died, and was buried in the Tower of London. Sir John Burgoyne was a brave soldier of the finest English type, a man who gave a freshness to the name of loyalty, and of whom Sir Francis Head says with truth, that "he lived without fear, and died without reproach."

Mr. Maurice's idea of making history a series of biographies is in many respects a good one, and this life of Stephen Langton[*] well opens the series. There have been other lives of Langton; there is one by Dr. Hook, in his "Lives of the Archbishops of Canterbury;" there is one by Dr. Newman, in his "Lives of the Saints," and there is one, we are told, by Mr. Martin Tupper. Mr. Maurice has not seen this latter work, but he thinks from what he has read of Mr. Tupper's works, that Mr. Tupper's conception of Langton would be sufficiently different from his to allow of room for both. In an introductory chapter, which is by no means without interest, Mr. Maurice traces the preparation of England from the time of the Conquest for the work which Stephen Langton was to do. Another chapter contains the life of Langton, until the time when Innocent chose him for the Archbishoprick. The remainder of the volume is devoted to his history in his work, until his death in 1228. Langton's early life is involved in obscurity. Where or when exactly he was born is uncertain, but in the last years of the 12th century, we find him at the University of Paris. There his chief friend was Lotherio Conti, a young Roman noble, distinguished for

* "Stephen Langton." By C. E. Maurice. London : Henry S. King and Co.

the grace of his manner and the purity of his life. When this young
nobleman became Pope Innocent III., Langton was called to Rome,
as Cardinal of the order of St. Chrysogonus, and Mr. Maurice thinks
that something of that practical statesmanship, that keen perception
of the thing that required to be done, which are Langton's great
claims on the gratitude of his countrymen, had already begun to show
themselves at the Court of Rome. The troubles which ensued upon
the consecration are well related, and the mean cunning of King John
is brought into bold relief. The interdict which Pope Innocent
placed upon the country; when "the frequent tinkle of the convent bell
no longer told the serf at the plough how the weary day was passing,
or guided the traveller through the forest to a shelter for the night,"
was followed by severer measures, which at length induced John to
receive Langton, and it was then that the real work of the latter
commenced. It was he who headed and guided the Barons in their
efforts to obtain the charter of rights, and first taught them, as Dr.
Hook says, to form a "House of Lords." The signing of the Charter
was not, however, the ending of the troubles; Langton was suspended
by the Pope, and even later, in the reign of Henry III., he received
letters from Rome in which he was severely rebuked. But he remained
firm to the principles which he set before him, and at a time "when
constitutional freedom was hardly known, when insurrection seemed
the only possible means of checking despotism, he organized and
established a movement for freedom, which by every act of his life he
showed to be in opposition to mere anarchy." The biography of such
a man may be well written more than once; it has not, however, been
better, or more instructively written, than by Mr. Maurice.

We pass into a very different atmosphere when we turn to Mr.
Planché's book.[*] Mr. Planché is as garrulous and sometimes as
amusing as the diarist Pepys, with whom he has much in common.
Like Pepys he is a great authority on questions of costume, and like
him, too, he is most happy in the society of the titled. Naturally he
recalls with pleasure Her Majesty's first *bal costumé* in 1842, when he
had the supreme happiness of being consulted as to the dresses which
were to be worn on that occasion. Let us bear the older writer first,
under date Feb. 3, 1664 :—

> "Then Mrs. Pickering did at my lady's command tell me the manner of a
> masquerade before the King and the Court the other day, where six women
> and six men in vizards, but most rich and antique dresses, did dance admi-
> rably and most gloriously. God give us cause to continue the mirth."

And Mr. Planché, May 12, 1842 :—

> "I need scarcely say with what pride and pleasure I placed my humble
> services at the disposal of those members of the Royal family who flattered
> me by their request. They were also readily given to such of the nobility as
> were personally known to me. . . . . The ball which I was enabled by
> the kindness of the Lord Chamberlain to witness was a magnificent sight, and
> a great success."

---

* "The Recollections and Reflections of J. R. Planché (*Somerset Herald*). A
Professional Autobiography." 2 vols. London : Tinsley Brothers.

Mr. Pepys was much struck by the farthingales of "some Portugall
ladys which are come to towne before the Queene. They are not
handsome, and their farthingales a strange dress."—May 25, 1662.
Mr. Planché is more gallant, but at Lisbon he too appears to have
been struck by "*le crinolin*." "It was really piteous," he says
(p. 187), "to see the condition of the costly dresses of the ladies as
they emerged from the place, to witness their despair as they
endeavoured to restore the crumpled skirts to something like their
pristine perfection." We must absolve Mr. Planché from the
charge of personal vanity, which is so amusing in Pepys, but we
confess that we are not interested in the three pages (vol. ii.
pp. 122-124) which relate how he and Mr. Young were in the
habit of "playing monkey" whenever they met "in public or
private," and we quite agree with him when he says, "To many
persons this may appear very silly and unworthy of a great trage-
dian." And here we have a word to say to the members of the
dramatic profession in reference to the character which is given them
by Mr. Planché. It seems (vol. ii. p. 26) that they are afflicted
with such extremely high spirits that they must give vent to them in
a manner which would qualify the members of any other profession for
a lunatic asylum. Mr. Planché says, not without a certain pride:
"Munden never saw me in the street that he did not get astride his
great cotton umbrella, and ride up to me like a boy on a stick." All
we can say is that it was very amusing of Mr. Munden, and quite
worthy of being "recollected" by Mr. Planché, but that it does not
raise our opinion of either. "Wallack and Tom Cooke," Mr. Planché
naïvely continues, "would gravely meet, remove with stolid countenance *each other's* hat, bow ceremoniously, replace it, and pass on
without exchanging a word, to the astonishment of the beholders."
Those who have not had the pleasure of knowing "Wallack and Tom
Cooke" may laugh at this, but they will not think more highly of
the profession to which "Wallack and Tom Cooke" belonged for this
instance of their "humorous and audacious pranks." And we fail
utterly to see the wit or humour which Mr. Planché finds in the
conduct of Mr. Meadows. "Meadows" it seems (who has not heard
of Meadows?) "would seat himself on the curbstone opposite my
house after we became neighbours, with his hat in his hand like a
beggar, utterly regardless of passing strangers, and remain in that
attitude until I or some of my family caught sight of him, and threw
him a halfpenny." We regret our inability to see the humour of these
jokes, because Mr. Planché assures us "that they were never pre-
meditated, but were the offspring of mere *gaîté de cœur.*" They
will, however, serve to explain our indifference to much of the society
with which Mr. Planché brings us into contact. His book is very
light reading, and is not wholly about actors. We catch glimpses of
such distinguished persons as the Emperor of the French, whom
Mr. Planché recognised by his breast-pin, the Marquis of Normanby,
the Earl of Cardigan, "whose only notion of mail was silver spangles,"
the "Hon. Frederick Byng (familiarly called Poodle)," and indeed
a host of other illustrious people. But we have not time to run

through the whole of these amusing volumes, which may be well read—and forgotten.

Mr. Spedding[1] continues his edition of the Letters of Lord Bacon. They are thoroughly and admirably edited. The commentary which accompanies and elucidates them leaves little for the reader to desire. But there are readers, it seems, from Mr. Spedding's preface to this sixth volume, who object to " the mass of comments which separate one paper from another." Such readers must indeed be hard to please, for Mr. Spedding has printed all that is really Bacon's in small pica, "and the mass of comments," being in a different type, may be easily omitted by those who do not need it. Most readers will, however, be grateful to Mr. Spedding for his concise and judicious remarks. Mr. Spedding is unnecessarily dissatisfied (p. 310) with the anomalous title by which Francis Bacon is popularly known. It is impossible for us now to speak of " Lord Verulam." We do not feel with Mr. Spedding that anything degrading attaches to the fact that the " ages " have fixed upon him one of the ugliest and most vulgar names—" a name associated with the poorest kind of joke." Mr. Spedding should have been above this feeling, and have left the paltry joke to those who could enjoy it; for after all it is only in England that this " poor joke " is possible. To the Germans he is, for some mysterious reason, " Baco," and with regard to the title, the Immortals do not need such decorations. The sixth volume contains the letters of three years, 1616–18. Not the least remarkable is the letter of advice to Villiers on the duties of a Favourite; but the most interesting portion is the correspondence which took place in reference to the quarrel between the Lord Keeper and the Earl of Buckingham. The whole volume brings the portrait of the great Chancellor before us as he was in life. But perhaps some reader will complain now, as before, of " the absence of the man, Francis Bacon," from the scene. Mr. Spedding can afford to let his complaints pass unnoticed.

The supplementary series of Despatches of the late Duke of Wellington[2] will be useful to the historical student as a work of reference. The present volume is chiefly valuable from a military point of view; it contains interesting statistics connected with the battle of Waterloo—papers on the manœuvring of cavalry, and on army expenditure. It embraces the period from 1812 to 1815, the most active and most important in the duke's life. It is at present without an index.

The Chronicles and Memorials of Great Britain and Ireland,[3] published under the direction of the Master of the Rolls, as they increase

[1] "The Letters and Life of Francis Bacon, with a Commentary Biographical and Historical." Vol. VI. By James Spedding, Honorary Fellow of Trinity College, Cambridge. London: Longmans, Green, and Co.

[2] "Supplementary Despatches, Correspondence, and Memoranda of Field-Marshal the Duke of Wellington." Edited by his Son. Vol. XIV. London: John Murray.

[3] "Matthæi Parisiensis Monachi Sancti Albani, Chronica Majora." Edited by Henry Richards Luard, M.A., Fellow of Trinity College, Cambridge. Vol. I. London: Longman and Co.

in number do not diminish in importance. We have this quarter five
volumes before us. The first is the St. Alban's compilation known as
the work of Matthew Paris. In a learned preface of some length
Mr. Luard discusses the authorship, and comes to a different conclusion
from any before adopted. Two other works, bearing the names of
Matthew of Westminster, and Roger of Wendover, are partially
identical with the work of Matthew Paris. Mr. Luard believes that
"Matthew of Westminster" is a transcript done in St. Alban's of the
earlier Corpus MS., which is called "Matthew Paris;" so, too, is
"Roger of Wendover." Now the Corpus MS. is very carelessly
written, "full of scribe's blunders, and occasional omissions." Mr.
Luard imagines this to have been the copy of an earlier compilation,
and the Wendover MS. again a copy of the Corpus MS. The main
question, then, is, who was the author of the original compilation?
Mr. Luard proves that Matthew Paris was the *corrector*, and not the
author, of the Corpus MS. He believes that he thus threw into the
shade the original author, whose name, like that of the author of the
"Life of Offa," passed entirely into oblivion. The book, which Mr.
Luard hopes will henceforth be called the "St. Alban's Compilation,"
is a very curious one. Legend and history, dates and facts, are
mingled together in a way which fairly earn for the compiler Lappen-
berg's title of "Verwirrer der Geschichte." In this edition Mr.
Luard strives successfully, as far as may be, to trace the various
statements to their source, and to distinguish the additions of the
corrector.

Our next record[10] contains the history of the monastery of St.
Alban's during the second abbacy of John Whethamstede, from 1452
to 1456. The authorship of this work is also called in question by
the editor. It has been attributed to Robert Blakeney and to
Whethamstede himself. Mr. Riley rejects these theories, and believes
the book to be a compilation made after the death of Whethamstede
by some now unknown hand. A summary of events, which are chiefly
domestic and monastic, is prefixed.

Our third chronicle[11] is excellently and fully edited by Mr. Williams,
and is especially valuable for the insight it gives into the period to
which it refers. But though the correspondence included in these
volumes belongs rather to the department of public history than to
the biography of the secretary, there are also several letters which
refer to the bishop's private affairs. There is, for instance, an amusing
correspondence between Bekynton and John Whethamstede, the
annals of whose abbacy Mr. Riley has edited. Readers of Mr. Riley's
book will know full well that Whethamstede was not over-scrupulous
in his efforts to improve the revenues of his already wealthy foundation. He wrote upon this occasion to Bekynton to ask his assistance

[10] "Registrum quorundam Abbatum Monasterii S. Albani qui saeculo xvmo floruere." Vol. I. Edited by H. T. Riley, M.A. Camb. and Oxf. London: Longmans and Co.
[11] "Official Correspondence of Thomas Bekynton, Secretary to King Henry VI. and Bishop of Bath and Wells." Edited by George Williams, B.D., Vicar of Ringwood. 2 vols. London: Longman and Co.

in a questionable transaction of mortmain, whereby his friend, John
Fray, Baron of the Exchequer, might grant a manor to the Abbey.
The covetous abbot, after a polite prelude, begs : " audacter pro
amico meo Johanne Fray, capitale Barone de Scaccario, intermedio,
rogoque fiducialiter quatenus ipsum juvare vellitis in sancto devotoque
proposito." But Bekynton replied in a tone of acid pleasantry. He
could not, he said, further his desire, since grants in mortmain were
universally odious. But he could and would correct the abbot's
Latin, although his own is not Ciceronian: " Rogo, pater, construe
Latinum hoc quod litteris mihi missis inscripseras: *Ipsum juvare
vellitis in sancto devotoque proposito suo.* ' Vellitis,' pater, quæ pars ?'
Si verbum hoc, declinando verbum *volo*, nullibi reperias ; quid prohibet
concludere quod incongrue sis locutus? Helas! pater, helas! ubi
ferula ? ubi virga ?" But for all that, Whethamstede carried his point,
and the manor of Baron Fray passed into the possession of the
monastery of St. Alban's. Bekynton was educated at Winchester and
New College, and became secretary to the king in 1438. In 1443 he
was consecrated Bishop of Bath and Wells, and died in 1464. Mr.
Williams describes him as a man of transparent simplicity of mind,
without pretensions to superior sanctity, but susceptible of strong
affections. We may add that he is very fortunate in his biographer,
and in the editor of his letters. A laborious and complete chrono-
logical table of his letters and documents renders reference to them
easy ; an appendix and index make the whole work useful and
interesting.

Our last Chronicle[12] is Professor Stubbs's edition of Walter of
Coventry. That curious history, like many others, seems to have had
a narrow chance of being anonymous. It was first discovered by
Leland, with the simple inscription, "Memoriale Fratris Walteri
de Coventria," which is all that is known of the author. From this
scanty information Leland constructed a biography which was subsequently enlarged by Bishop Bale, Pits, and other biographers, until we
learn that " Walter of Coventry was an English monk of the order
of St. Benedict, in the monastery of Coventry. He was born of honest
parents in the county and town of Warwick ; and having been by the
care of his friends consecrated as it were to God and the Muses,
having been diligently educated in piety and literary discipline, he
turned out a remarkably erudite man." Professor Stubbs has no
difficulty in demolishing this work of imagination: we are glad to record
his belief that there was such a person as Walter of Coventry. It is
unnecessary to add, since the book is edited by Professor Stubbs, that
it is well done.

Dr. Gladstone's book on Michael Faraday[13] is rather a study of the
man than a biography, and throws much light upon that pure and devoted character. Faraday seems to have possessed, besides the enthusiasm and perseverance which belong to all successful students of

---

[12] "The Historical Collections of Walter of Coventry." Vol. I. Edited by
William Stubbs, M.A. Longman and Co.
[13] "Michael Faraday." By J. H. Gladstone, Ph.D., F.R.S. London: Macmillan and Co.

science, a kindliness, geniality, and benevolence which attached to him
all with whom he came in contact. To Professor Tyndall he writes:
"The sweetest reward of my work is the sympathy and goodwill
which it has caused to flow in upon me from all quarters of the world."
But this kindliness was something very different from the vulgar
virtue of goodnature; Faraday knew how to be firm when occasion
required, and to rebuke what he knew to be wrong. His connexion
with the Spiritualists is an instance of this. The following is an extract of a letter to one of their professors, showing the manner in which
he could convey a rebuke.

"I beg to thank you for your papers, but have wasted more thought and
time on so-called spiritual manifestations than it has deserved. Unless the
spirits are utterly contemptible they will find means to draw my attention.
How is it that your name is not signed to the testimony that you give? Are
you doubtful even whilst you publish?"

Dr. Gladstone's study of Michael Faraday is deeply interesting, and
will be an acceptable supplement to the work of Dr. Bence Jones.
But most people know already that the great electrician, who was a
member of so many learned societies that the mere enumeration of
them occupies three pages, was a simple-minded, truth-loving, and
earnest man. For those who look upon science "as a milch-cow of
the field," whose "business is to calculate the butter she will yield," a
justification of Faraday's devotion to science will be found in the
chapters upon the value of his discoveries. To those who love science
as a goddess his devotion will appear in another and a nobler light.
But all who read Dr. Gladstone's book will agree with M. Dumas
when he says, "I have never known a man more worthy of being
loved, of being admired, of being mourned."

We have little to say of Mr. Cobbett's book[14] except that it will probably be very agreeable reading to the inhabitants of Twickenham,
and possibly to others who are interested in the Twickenham parishes.
We may, however, say this much, that it is a very good specimen of
a style of work which if it were more universal, might become of
national utility. If every clergyman in charge of a country or suburban
parish,—and most of them have leisure enough—were to write a history of his parish with the same care as Mr. Cobbett has shown,
marking the points of archæological and historical interest, the result
would be of some general value. Even a "list of Churchwardens from
1606" such as Mr. Cobbett gives, might be found useful.

Life in the Harem is generally supposed to pass in one monotonous
course of luxurious dulness. The lady who has written the present
Autobiography[15] shows however that intrigue and trouble may reign
within those closed doors. She was the daughter of a Frenchman,
and was born at Constantinople in 1813. She was married at an early
age to a gentleman in Lord Byron's suite, but from him she was soon
separated, and was shortly afterwards married to Kibrizli Pasha, and

[14] "Memorials of Twickenham." By the Rev. R. S. Cobbett, M.A. London: Smith, Elder, and Co.
[15] "Thirty Years in the Harem. The Autobiography of Melek-Hanum, Wife of Kibrizli-Mehemet-Pasha." London: Chapman and Hall.

entered upon the thirty years of which she gives us the history. We have neither space nor inclination to go through the events which she chronicles. It will be sufficient to say that after varied fortunes, oriental travels, and hair-breadth escapes, she left Turkey and came to Europe, where she has now been six years. These six years have been, she says, so many years of martyrdom and abject misery. We are promised another volume whose subject shall be the European vicissitudes. Perhaps the work will be more interesting than the present; it cannot be less so.

We will now take the three new volumes of the educational series, which Dr. W. Smith conducts. The first we shall notice is the "Student" edition of Hallam's Constitutional History." We must confess that we by no means like Dr. Smith's plan of adapting great historical works to this hand-book shape. We think it is injurious to the student, and unjust to the author whom he abridges, summarizes, and adapts. We admit that Dr. Smith is an editor both of experience and discretion, but in the interests of literature we protest against the "Student's Gibbon," the "Student's Hume," and the "Student's Hallam." If a man is a real student of Gibbon; of Hume, or of Hallam, he will be satisfied with nothing less than the originals. If he is "cramming" for an examination in either of these authors, let the implements he works with be known by their proper names, but let us cease from gibbeting great authors as accessories to this petty work. Dr. Smith says in his preface that he has brought the "Constitutional History into one volume by leaving out most of the notes at the foot of the pages, and by abbreviating some of the less important remarks;" but when we remember that Gibbon's great work slides telescopically into a volume of the same size, we have not much confidence in the Student's Hallam. We can trust Dr. Smith further than we can most editors, but we sincerely hope no other editor will adopt the plan of giving us great histories with the "less important remarks" omitted or abbreviated.

We have, however, nothing but praise for Mr. P. Smith's History of the East." Of its kind and for its purpose it seems to us admirable. We should like to see it in use in every school where ancient history forms part of the course. Mr. P. Smith has a way of enlivening by story and poetry the dullest records of history, that fixes them, as we know by experience, upon youthful minds. The present little volume is attractive both in style and appearance, and the letterpress is interesting and bright with illustrations, which add greatly to the knowledge of the text. We cordially commend it to all for whom it is designed.

We can also award much of the same praise to Mr. Bevan's smaller

16 "The Constitutional History of England." By Henry Hallam. Adapted for the use of Students, by W. Smith, D.C.L. LL.D. London: John Murray.

17 "A Smaller Ancient History of the East, from the Earliest Times to the Conquest of Alexander the Great." By Philip Smith, B.A. London: John Murray.

Manual of Ancient Geography." It is well and carefully written, and
the pupil who has gone through it will know more of ancient geography
than most schoolboys and some others do. Some of the illustrations
we have seen before in other works edited by Dr. Smith, but we are
not disinclined to see them again in this manual.

And since we are speaking of school-books, we may as well mention
here Miss Sewell's excellent little "Catechism of English History."[19]
Some of the answers seem to us rather long for catechetical instruction, but the chief points of civil and ecclesiastical history are well
seized and presented.

Two lectures have been wisely brought before a wider audience than
that for which they were originally designed. Mr. Freeman is too
well known to need general eulogy at our hands. The "Rede"
lecture,[20] which he has published, is marked by the usual characteristics
of its author—clear, decisive views, and vigorous out-spoken language.
It deprecates what we may term the provincialism of study, the
limiting the field of attention to a particular period which is marked
by the name "classical," and advocates a wider range of vision and a
broader horizon of thought. But Mr. Freeman is not, as we knew
before, an enemy of classical learning. The following passage will
illustrate his position, and his outspoken zeal.

"We are asked what is the use of learning languages which are dead? What
is the use of studying records of times which have for ever passed away? Men
who call themselves statesmen and historians are not ashamed to run up and
down the land, spreading abroad, wherever such assertions will win them a
cheer, the daring falsehood that such studies and no others form the sole
business of our ancient Universities. They ask in their pitiful shallowness,
What is the use of studying battles in which so few men were killed as on the
field of Marathon? In this place I need not stop for a moment to answer such
transparent fallacies."

We are also glad to see the publication of Mr. Forsyth's lecture.[21]
It sets forth in a popular style the history of ancient manuscripts.
Mr. Forsyth tells us very pleasantly what is known of the oldest
Biblical and classical manuscripts, and of the methods used by the
monastic copyists. He explains the wonderful way in which scholars
have made the palimpsests yield up their oldest treasures, and he
quotes once more the story of the discovery of the Sinaitic manuscript
by Tischendorf. Mr. Forsyth well brings out the fact that the oldest
MS. is still at an immense distance from the original author. The
whole subject is a lesson on the value of evidence, which is given
with great care by Mr. Forsyth. We are, however, ourselves able

[19] "A Smaller Manual of Ancient Geography." By the Rev. W. L. Bevan.
London: John Murray.
[19] "A Catechism of English History." Edited by E. M. Sewell. London:
Longmans, Green, and Co.
[20] "The Unity of History." The Rede Lecture. By E. A. Freeman, M.A.,
D.C.L. London: Macmillan and Co.
[21] "History of Ancient Manuscripts." A Lecture delivered in the Hall of the
Inner Temple. By William Forsyth, Esq., Q.C., LL.D., Treasurer of the Inn.
London: John Murray.

to correct one of Mr. Forsyth's recollections. He says: "I may mention a very amusing *jeu d'esprit*, which I once saw of the late Sir George Cornewall Lewis, who, to ridicule the fanciful conjectures of the Egyptologists, wrote in the old style, without any division between the words, the famous nursery rhymes:

"Heydiddlethecatsodthefiddleth
ecowjumpedoverthemoonthelit &c."

Now, as far as our recollection goes, the *jeu d'esprit* of Sir George, which was not a very novel one, was directed against the then recent interpretations of Etruscan monuments, especially those of Dr. Aufrecht. The nursery rhymes were certainly written with a more elaborate disguise than Mr. Forsyth gives them; but his little book, though not very profound, and, as we have sufficiently shown, popular in style, is one which will well repay perusal.

Our German works are not of great significance this quarter.

Herr Honegger's third and fourth volumes of the History of Culture[21] commence with the year 1832, Reform in England and the corresponding events upon the continent. They deal not only with the political, but the literary events of a period of about twenty years. The notices, embracing as they do several nations, are necessarily superficial, and do not seem to be very good or effective. In estimating English writers, for instance, Herr Honegger has not carefully weighed the relative importance of each. Thus his estimate of S. Warren, W. Carleton, and D. Jerrold occupy more space and claim greater prominence than his estimate of Thackeray or Browning. J. F. Cooper has a chapter to himself.

The two latest volumes of Dr. Dahn's learned work on the "Kings of the Germans,"[22] deal with the political history of the East Goths and the constitution of the West Goths. The fifth volume contains the history of the East Goths from the formation of the kingdom of Toulouse to the decline of the kingdom of Toledo (A.D. 375–711). The sixth volume deals more with the internal condition of the people, the social position of the different classes, and the royal prerogatives. An array of one thousand authorities (amongst which we observe only two English books) precedes this portion of the work.

The first volume of Herr Opel's history of the Low-Saxon and Danish war[23] (A.D. 1621–1623) brings down events to the resignation of Duke Christian of Hapsburg. The whole Protestant confederation had by this fallen away like a house of cards, and the Catholic hosts had penetrated to the very borders of Holland. Herr Opel relates with clear impartial detail the struggle between the Catholic and Protestant States.

Herr Dümmler has edited with great care the curious poem by an

[21] "Grundsteine einer allgemeinen Culturgeschichte der neuesten Zeit." Von J. J. Honegger. Bande iii. und iv. Leipzig.

[22] "Die Könige der Germanen. Nach den Quellen dargestellt." Von Dr. Felix Dahn. Bände v. und vi. Würzburg.

[23] "Der niedersächsisch-dänische Krieg." Von Julius Otto Opel. Halle. London: Trübner.

unknown Italian writer, which is called "Gesta Berengarii."[25] The text, which has a good and sufficient commentary, is preceded by essays upon Berengarius, his relation to Arnolf and Lambert, and the historical worth of the poem. The work concludes with a catalogue of the historical authorities for the period.

We must also be brief with our remaining books, most of which are in the form of pamphlets.

The Count Hermann von Wartensleben, a colonel on the General Staff of the South Army, traces the military operations in January and February, 1871.[26] The book is a complete history of the German military manœuvres, and has two good maps.

Dr. Oldham furnishes a historical account of the Ghazepoor district in the shape of a blue-book.[27] It is accompanied with maps, plates, inscriptions, and a good index.

Mr. Boult sends us, in a small pamphlet,[28] the results of his researches upon the subject of the "hide" of land. He derives the word from the Celtic *eid*, a tax or tribute, which in form of aids or subsidies is familiar in English history. He thinks that on the supposition that hides represent aids much which is otherwise incomprehensible assumes systematic relations.

Dr. Dyer has a very pretty quarrel with the Professor of Modern History at Cambridge. Mr. Seeley ventures to differ from Dr. Dyer's views respecting regal Rome, and Dr. Dyer proceeds to review[29] the Professor's arguments. The point in dispute is the amount of historical truth in Livy's account of early Roman history. Dr. Dyer has not only Professor Seeley, but also Niebuhr, Mommsen, and Sir G. C. Lewis against him. Dr. Dyer argues with much learning, some bitterness, and, as it seems to us, with little success. We must, however, be on our guard, for we notice that Dr. Dyer speaks of a former reviewer of his work as "a discredit to an otherwise well-conducted journal," and as a person whose "arrant nonsense and critical dishonesty he has been compelled to expose." We shall therefore stand aside and leave the battle to the principals.

Mr. Augustus Meves, *alias* Auguste de Bourbon, has collected and dedicated to the French nation and the European powers the correspondence between himself and the *Times*.[30] Like Dr. Dyer, Mr. Meves falls foul of the reviewers. He claims to be the grandson of Louis XVI., and the real heir of the Bourbons to the French throne.

[25] "Gesta Berengarii Imperatoris." Von Ernst Dümmler. Halle. London: Trübner.

[26] "Operations of the South Army." By Count Hermann von Wartensleben. Translated by Colonel C. H. von Wright. London: Henry King and Co.

[27] "Historical and Statistical Memoir of the Ghazepoor District." By Wilton Oldham, R.C.S. LL.D. Allahabad. At the Government Press. London: Trübner.

[28] "The Hide of Land." By Joseph Boult, F.R.S., B.A. Liverpool: T. Brakell.

[29] "Roma Regalis." By Thomas Dyer, LL.D. London: Bell and Daldy.

[30] "Louis XVII. versus the London Times." By Auguste de Bourbon, son of Louis XVII. London: Edward Stanford.

We will not pretend to decide the genealogical question, but we candidly confess that we agree with the *Times* in thinking the story "bungled and garbled," with "scarcely a page of clear and consecutive narrative."

Lord Hatherton shortly before his death entrusted to Mr. Reeve the memoir[u] which is now published. It contains an account of the occurrences which led to the dissolution of Lord Grey's administration. Until recently it could not be published from consideration to certain eminent statesmen. These are now no more, and it is satisfactory to learn that "the result of the perusal of these letters is alike honourable to almost every one concerned in these transactions." The reservation which Mr. Reeve makes has reference to the account given by Lord Brougham ("Autobiography," vol. iii. pp. 391 *et seq.*), but this, as Mr. Reeve says, was written when his memory was enfeebled by age.

BELLES LETTRES.

MR. BLACKMORE has made very considerable advances in the craft of novel writing since he gave us "Cradock Nowel." In many ways that was a very remarkable story. The plot was good, and well carried out. The chief characters were interesting. But the beauty of the book consisted in its descriptions of the New Forest scenery, which certainly have never been excelled. Mr. Blackmore, however, has in his present story,[1] where the scene is laid on the Glamorganshire coast, and partly on the north Devonshire coast, and partly on the open sea, left the descriptions in "Cradock Nowel" far behind. He paints with a far firmer hand. Every reader, too, of "Cradock Nowel" will remember that mimetic or ventriloquistic power which the author showed in his imitations of the New Forest dialect in the mouths of the foresters. Mr. Blackmore has put this power to the severest possible test. He tells the whole story, and it is rather an intricate one, by the mouth of an old Glamorganshire sailor. This is a feat which few novelists could perform with any degree of success. But Mr. Blackmore has accomplished it so successfully, that we never once throughout the nine hundred pages of narrative feel wearied with the old tar's yarn. The realistic quality which Mr. Blackmore shows, strongly reminds us of Defoe's best manner. David Llewellyn is as genuine a creation as Robinson Crusoe. Higher praise than this it is impossible to give. Mr. Blackmore has here shown real genius. What will, however, most probably prevent "The Maid of

---

Sker" taking the highest rank among novels are those two hideous
monsters, Parson Jack and Parson Chowne. We are not going into the
question, whether two such persons with their troop of naked savages,
did or did not live in Devonshire fifty or a hundred years ago. This is
not the point. It is a question of art. If we rightly remember, Mr.
Blackmore fell into a similar mistake in "Cradock Nowel." We then
pointed out in this *Review* Mr. Blackmore's tendency to follow Canon
Kingsley in his worst characteristics. The result of that tendency is
now shown in these two mistakes. They spoil a very beautiful story.
Of course there are plenty of people, who rate brute muscular strength,
especially in a person, far above any moral or intellectual quality. It
is useless to denounce the taste of the British public for these square-
jawed brutes, whose muscles always swell like the whip-cord which they
are so fond of using on any one physically weaker than themselves. We turn with pleasure from such monsters to Mr. Blackmore's
descriptions. There is a marked peculiarity about them. They are
not made up. Most of our novelists' descriptions might be taken from
the drop scenes of a theatre. They are all conventional. Mr. Blackmore, on the other hand, draws direct from nature. Here, for instance,
is a vivid description—

"The tide must have been pretty nigh the flood, and the moon was rising
hazily, and all the river was pale and lonely, for the brown-sailed lighters,
which they call the "Tauton fleet," had long passed by, when I heard a
silvery sound of swiftness cleaving solitude—the flight of a wedge of wild
ducks. I knelt in the very smallest form that nature would allow of, and
with one hand held a branch to keep the boat from surging. Plash they came
down, after two short turns, as sudden as forked lightning, heads down for a
moment, then heads up, and wings flapping, sousing and subsiding. Quacks
began, from the old drake first, and then from the rest of the company, and
a racing after one another. Under and between them all, the river lost its
smoothness, beaten into ups and downs, that sloped away in ridge and
furrow."—Vol. ii., pp. 60, 61.

This is a vigorous and truthful description. We recommend it to
our lady-novelists, and especially that lady who not long ago sent
her hero into a wood to shoot partridges, where he knocked them over
"like hail." Lastly we must not pass over Mr. Blackmore's humour.
It is quite refreshing to meet his quiet satire after the loud buffoonery
to which we are generally treated.

We are afraid to praise "Greville Landon"[1] as much as we should
like, as the praise would sound extravagant, and we should feel compelled to state at length our reasons, and for all of them we have no
space. The writer possesses something of the exquisite dramatic
power and humour of Jane Austen, and something, too, of the satiric
strength of Thackeray. And, like both those great writers, he thoroughly
understands the society which he describes. These are very rare
qualifications amongst modern novelists. We have often in these
pages complained that novelists constantly attempt to describe scenes

---

[1] "Greville Landon." A Novel by Piers Lisle. London: Chapman and
Hall. 1872.

of which they are entirely ignorant. Oxford is described by writers to whom "μαρ is just the same as δε." Noblemen are habitually represented as a sort of cross between a billiard-marker and a rat-catcher. Ladies are made to utter a slang which is partly Billingsgate and partly Haymarket. The author of "Greville Landon" falls into no mistake of this sort. Nor does he on the other hand commit the opposite error, and make his noblemen all millionaires, and his baronets admirable Crichtons. He thoroughly realizes the position of an English country gentleman, whether a nobleman or not. He understands that they have duties to perform as landlords, magistrates, and members of parliament. As a rule the average novelist imagines that he has described a peer of the realm by sticking a coronet on his head, and that he has created a statesman by placing the letters M.P. after his name. Further, too, the author of "Greville Landon" understands that English ladies and gentlemen are not totally uneducated, that amongst them are to be found more culture and more refinement than are, perhaps, anywhere else to be met in the world. Lastly, he has contrived to write a story without any of his characters breaking the seventh commandment. Now all this is a very great advance upon the ordinary novel of fashionable life. If any foreigner were to endeavour to form an idea of the English aristocracy from a study of the novels of "Ouida," Miss Braddon, Mr. Yates, and their followers, he would come to the conclusion that our noblemen were a set of fools, coxcombs and bigamists. In his picture of Lord Celadon the author has described a not uncommon type of the English nobleman. He is by no means a wealthy man, but yet is able to fulfil the duties of his station with a becoming liberality. Although naturally a Conservative, yet culture and contact with the world and other minds and other opinions, have softened down his prejudices. His son, Lord Lisle, is an equally good representative of the younger class of noblemen, who now really take an interest in social matters, and devote themselves to politics, and study Mill, Hare, and Fawcett. The ladies of the family are represented as refined, graceful women, with sufficient culture to take an interest in their husbands' and lovers' politics, and to enter into, and sympathize with their views. Now to draw such characters as these requires a very delicate touch. The author has certainly succeeded. We have only one or two very slight faults to find. We think that he paints Harley Grey's success with a little too much rose-colour. The Harley Greys, however witty they are, and however beautiful the poems which they write, do not find their way quite so easily as he does into Grosvenor Square. On the other hand the Rev. Father Gretch is drawn a little too coarsely. The author evidently dislikes him, and the religious school to which he belongs. But a novel is not the place to discuss theology. Besides, young ladies like Miss Delessert will regard their confessor as a martyr when he is held up to ridicule, and handled in the way in which Derthon treats Father Gretch. The scene is extremely clever, but as far as we can judge serves no purpose. Those who dislike Father Gretch and his views will regret that he was not kicked out of the house, whilst those who admire him will, as we have said, regard him as a martyr.

Time and the increasing good sense of mankind will more effectually deal with such priests than satire, however witty, in a novel. The minor characters are all most carefully drawn. The vulgar Greys and their house in Retford Street are capitally done. Equally good are the Pridelings and Villa Dante. Nor must we pass over the election scenes at Haddingford. Generally speaking the ordinary novelist describes an election from the outside. We are treated to an account of the brass bands, the appearance of the hustings, and the cat-calling and rotten-egg-throwing mob. But the author of " Greville Landon " leads us into the Committee rooms, and we hear the talk of the agents and the lawyers, and see the wire-pulling. He shows us the inside. So, too, with the law matters in the book. The author boldly takes us into chambers in Chancery Lane and Lincoln's Inn. We hear the whole question from the lawyer's point of view. And the author contrives to do this without ever being dull. Our interest grows as the story progresses. In conclusion we will merely say that if this is a first attempt at novel writing, the author, if he is only true to himself will most assuredly take a very high place among contemporary novelists. He can draw gentlemen and ladies. His middle-class characters are equally true. His yokels and labourers are not so good. His strength evidently lies in depicting social life, and surrounding it with that air of refinement and ease, which is seen to the best advantage in English country houses.

" Take Care Whom You Trust "[3] is a little too much occupied with clerical squabbles. We have no doubt that the book will be eagerly read in country vicarages and cathedral closes. The writer has apparently been behind the scenes. His portrait, however, of the Dean of Blankton is certainly not one which will be generally accepted as a fair representation of Deans. Whatever faults Deans may possess, vulgarity is not generally one of them. Some of the author's strictures upon church matters appear to us just, and his remarks upon the average training at an ordinary grammar school thoroughly sound. But these questions would be much better treated in the shape of an essay. If the writer would adopt a somewhat less slangy tone, he may succeed in writing a really interesting novel of clerical life.

" The Princess Clarice "[4] is no princess at all, and has nothing whatever to do with royalty. Instead of a princess there are, however, a great number of fops and coxcombs in the book. On reading the tale we discovered ourselves in exactly the reverse position to Saul, the son of Kish—we went out to seek a kingdom, and found only asses.

If the reader does not object to the somewhat " goody " tone of the book, he will find " Premiums Paid to Experience "[5] full of common

---

[3] " Take Care whom you Trust." By Compton Reade. London: Smith, Elder and Co. 1872.

[4] " The Princess Clarice. A Story of 1871." By Mortimer Collins. London: Henry S. King and Co.

[5] " Premiums Paid to Experience. Incidents in My Business Life." By Edward Garrett. London: Strahan and Co. 1872.

sense and sound morality. The author, too, has an eye for character. Thus he says of Mrs. Chance, "she sprinkled her discourse with French, as one peppers flavourless meat," and he describes the same lady as having an ideal cottage in the midst of meadows and woods, with bees and birds, but with "a mental reservation that it must be within five minutes reach of the Quadrant or the Bank." One of the best stories is, perhaps, the last. The fate of Percy Hare and the end of the Juanita Silver Mine may be read just now with some interest, when new mining companies are every day advertising that two and two make five. We can strongly recommend the book to all young people just beginning the world. The stories bear upon the everyday events of business-life. Many of them leave the impression that they have been drawn from actual experience. The great faults of the book are its slip-shod style, and a tendency to lecturing, which unfriendly critics might call by a harsher name.

We should be very sorry to seem to underrate by our short and most inadequate notice Mr. Palgrave's clever romance "Hermann Agha."[6] It is one of the few stories, which show real genius for story-telling and dramatic power. Mr. Palgrave seems to have drunk in some of the true oriental spirit of romance. He is a perfect master of style, and by his knowledge of Eastern manners and customs is enabled to throw over his story that charm of local colouring, which affects us almost as powerfully as in the Arabian Nights. And yet we confess to asking ourselves as we read the book, Will the tale be popular in England? In spite of its great merits, its dramatic power, and the great beauty of the writing, we fear that its charms will be thrown away. Mr. Palgrave will, however, have the satisfaction of knowing that by this book he has raised the standard of novel writing, and that it is sometimes the highest compliment to have only a few readers.

The real value of "Septimius"[7] lies in the fact that it shows us with what care a really great novelist works. Few writers understand that a novel is as much a work of art as a poem. Most novelists never revise a passage, or rewrite a line. Hawthorn worked on a very different principle. As may be seen from "Septimius," he would amplify a description to suit the circumstances, or would elaborate and polish it so as to produce a greater effect. Before, too, his characters were drawn, careful studies of them had been made. The same lesson, as we pointed out at the time, was to be learnt from the half-finished story, which Thackeray left. Both these great writers illustrate Carlyle's definition of genius, "an infinite capacity for taking pains."

"My Cousin Maurice"[8] is a very pleasant readable tale, written by some one who evidently has seen a good deal of the world. We are

[6] "Hermann Agha." An Eastern Narrative. By W. Gifford Palgrave. London: Henry S. King and Co. 1872.
[7] "Septimius." A Romance. By Nathaniel Hawthorn. London: Henry S. King and Co. 1872.
[8] "My Cousin Maurice." London: Sampson Low, Marston, Low and Searle. 1872.

taken here and there, to India, Ireland, and Germany, and the writer is evidently at home in each land. Some of the translations of German poetry are particularly well done.

"A Summer's Romance"[1] may be put into the portemanteau by any one thinking of going to Italy this winter. Miss Healy writes pleasantly, and appreciates both Italian scenery and character. The opening chapters, in which the disagreeable Lady Thurlow figures, are the weakest. The tale, however, soon improves. Miss Healy has had the good sense not to spin her story out into two or three volumes, but to compress all that is necessary into one. We wish other novelists would follow her example.

Everybody knows who Fifine is.[10] Her portrait is to be seen in every photograph shop-window in London and Paris. She is placed, too, in every possible attitude which even a professor of anatomy could desire. Our plain-spoken grandmothers would probably have called her not Fifine, but Fyefye. But one, whom Phœbus Apollo has thus deigned to honour, may surely find some favour from his chief poet. What, however, Euripides would say to Mr. Browning, is another question. We at all events are not disposed to quarrel with him. Theory is grey, and life is green. What, we should like to know, is Mr. Browning but the Fifine of poets? Does he not alternately charm, plague, and flirt with us wretched critics, till we are perfectly bewildered? Is he not always piping before us, shredding grammar, prosody, sense, and all such toys? Don't the Elvires of the world constantly say to us "What is it you can possibly see to admire in this Mr. Browning, with his pink and impudence? Why don't you like Tennyson, who is always musical? Or if you don't like Tennyson, why can't you read the good Tupper? But Browning!"—and Elvire clasps her hands, and looks more than she has brains to utter. The truth is, if we are to attack the Fifines, Mr. Browning must be the first to suffer. And this we take to be the meaning of his poem—it is an apology for himself and his poetry. Now we are going no further into the matter. It is not Fifine, but Fifine's dancing which we admire. And after this distinction, we proceed with a clear conscience. So far we have laughed. But it is a subject for the deepest regret that Mr. Browning should have cast his poem, dealing as it does with some of the most perplexing problems of human nature, those terrible difficulties, which in proportion—and this is the saddest part—as a man is endowed with a spiritual nature, beset him and hinder him and even altogether stop him, into such a form. The subject-matter of "Fifine at the Fair," would undoubtedly, treated as Browning could treat it, and as he has treated it here in many passages, have made the epic of the present day. We believe that he has put more substance into "Fifine at the Fair" than into any other poem. But for the ordinary reader it might just as well have been written in Sanscrit.

---

[1] "A Summer's Romance." By Mary Healy. London: Sampson Low, Marston, Low and Searle. 1872.

[10] "Fifine at the Fair." By Robert Browning. London: Smith, Elder and Co. 1872.

There are such breaks, digressions, involutions, crabbed constructions, metaphysical hair-splitting, that reading becomes a positive fatigue. On the other hand, a perfect anthology of beauties might be culled. If the duty of poetry has ever been fulfilled, it is by the prologue. Here the muse assumes her true office—to comfort us with hope, and to suggest that there may be possibilities which lie beyond the range of our philosophy. The epilogue is utterly unworthy of Browning. There is to our mind something akin to profanation about it. As to the main scope of the poem—the necessity of individual life and independent personality, for this of course is the moral, if we may use the hackneyed term—we need say nothing. We think, however, that the lesson might have been taught by a far better example than poor battered Filine. Lastly, Elvire is one of those tender, loving women who are the very salt and leaven of life.

We are always glad to meet Professor Blackie. Whether we agree with him or not, we always find him both original and instructive. He has the great merit of thinking for himself, and having the moral courage to proclaim his thoughts. But we have never been so glad to meet him as in the present volume of poems.[11] With the spirit of these poems we thoroughly agree. They are a protest against the luxury and effeminacy of the day. And never was a protest so needed. Careful observers have, not without reason, attributed all the recent disasters of France to the luxury and the morals of its capital. But Paris is fast migrating to London. *In Thamesim defluxit Orontes.* Professor Blackie, as an antidote, would recall us to Nature. And in making this appeal he does not ignore the conditions of the day. There is no raving, as in Ruskin, against political economy or factories. Professor Blackie feels the benefits of steam and gas, and newspapers, and even, we may suppose, quarterly reviews. But he feels that there are higher things than even the electric telegraph. He knows that man cannot live by bread alone. His cry is—

> "Shine on me, Sun! beneath thy clear strong ray
> To live and work is all the bliss I pray.—p. 29.

And again :—

> "And I am here, Time's latest product, Man,
> To work thy will, O Lord, and serve thy stately plan."—p. 92.

an aspiration which might be echoed, in its spirit, by members of any sect, even by Positivists. Professor Blackie recalls us then to Nature — to Nature, too, in her wildest and sternest aspects. It must not, however, be thought that in praising only the Scotch Highlands the poet is insensible to the softer beauties of southern scenery. In a most eloquent passage in his preface, Professor Blackie dwells with enthusiasm upon the long stretches of turf in our Midland and Western counties in England, our valleys full of apple and pear and cherry orchards, and our parks and leafy woods. But he reserves

---

[11] "Lays of the Highlands and Islands." By John Stuart Blackie, Professor of Greek in the University of Edinburgh. London: Strahan and Co. 1872.

all his poetry for his own Scotch mountains, for the wind-swept heather of moors where the curlew cries, for the black tarn and the thundering linn, and the grey peaks wreathed round with mist. He rightly thinks that scenes like these will help to strengthen our manhood, and brace our character. And it must be remembered that we are only just now beginning to learn the true use and the true beauty of our moors and mountains. For generations they have been regarded as the property of the sportsman. But the day will come, we are sanguine enough to think, when grouse-shooting and deer-stalking will be looked upon as the occupation of keepers and butchers, and not of gentlemen. The mountains and the moors, as all the earth is, are the property of the artist, the botanist, or the geologist; in a word, of all those who bring mind to explore the wonders and the beauties of Nature. To Nature then, especially as she is seen in Scotland, Professor Blackie invites us. As he writes,—

> "Men cut their manners as their clothes, by rule,
> But none grow strong in Nature's breezy school."—p. 158.

What Scotchmen, however, will say to Professor Blackie's enthusiasm about Nature we cannot pretend to guess. He has the boldness thus to conclude a sonnet to Loch Dan:—

> "If heaven be finer than thou art this day
> I know not, but with thee I'd rather stay."—p. 43.

We fancy, too, that the "unco' gude" will raise a howl at the following stanza in a poem on Braemar:—

> "Three churches in the village stand;
> This serves the State, and that is Free,
> The third doth own the Pope's command,
> And God in Heaven claims all the three."—p. 162.

Professor Blackie will have done a double service if he can spread both a love of Nature and a love of religious toleration. In the following sonnet we may see both united:—

"ARDLIN.

THE PULPIT ROCK.

> In sooth a goodly temple, walled behind
> With crag precipitous of granite grey,
> And by green birches corniced, which the wind
> Sowed o'er the ruin in random rich display.
> And for the roof the azure-curtained hall,
> Light-floating cloud, and broad benignant ray,
> And organed by the hum of waterfall,
> And plash of bright waves in the gleaming bay.
> And here's the pulpit, this huge granite mass
> Erect, frost-sundered from the mossy crown,
> And there the people sit on turfy grass,
> And here the fervid preacher thunders down;
> Go kneel beneath Saint Paul's proud dome, and say
> If God be nearer there, or here to day!"

In conclusion, we most strongly recommend this little volume of poems for its masculine good sense, its sustained elevation of tone, its passionate love of Nature, and its genuine sincerity.

As usual, our table is covered with some twenty or thirty little thin volumes of poetry. To criticise them all in detail is simply impossible There is a story told that some one asked a great living poet, to whom the poet nearly every morning brought a presentation copy of poetry, what he thought of the general character of such productions. His answer was that he was surprised at the high standard of poetry which many of them reached. And our verdict about them is much the same. But they unfortunately do not reach the highest standard. The poetical faculty, it must be remembered, is after all a common one. There is scarcely a parish in England where the curate has not published his " Stray Leaves," or his " Forget-me-nots," or where the teacher at the National School has not contributed to the Poets' Corner of the provincial newspaper. Such poets are as common as blackberries. We have amateur painters, amateur sculptors, amateur wood-carvers, but none of them in the same proportion as amateur poets. Many of the former are highly gifted artists. But they are modest. They never seek to obtrude themselves or their art upon the public. It is only the amateur poet who is noisy, and year after year persists in sending forth his wares. Let us take the very first volume which lies before us,—" The Violet Child of Arcadia,"[11] by the author of " Vasco." We can but repeat precisely the same general criticism which we passed a year or so ago upon " Vasco," and which the author has, we perceive, thought it worth his while to reprint at the end of the present volume. The pieces all show that the author possesses much cultivation. Beyond this they scarcely go. And how little cultivation avails towards making a poet when the greater gifts are wanting, we need not say. Friendly critics of course will see much more in these poems. But to what purpose? All the favourable criticism in the world will not save second-rate poetry, any more than hostile criticism will damn first-rate poetry.

Very much the same criticism may be passed upon Mr. Digby's " Ouranogaia."[13] Every canto shows tenderness of thought and cultivation of mind. But then on the other hand every canto shows such bald stuff as—

> " Then Marguerite of Burgogne so
> Made Peace, as old Historians show;
> Matilda, that great sage Empress,
> Did the same burning love express.
> Jean de Valois, Elizabeth,
> Thus, too, from men did ward off death."—Vol. ii., pp. 40-1.

This is about as poetical as a stockbroker's Share-list.

The Rev. S. J. Stone's poems" are of decidedly a higher quality than

<hr/>

[11] " The Violet Child of Arcadia." And other Poems. By the Author of " Vasco." London : Longmans, Green and Co. 1872.

[13] " Ouranogaia: Heaven on Earth." By Kenelm Henry Digby. London : Longmans, Green, Reader and Dyer. 1872.

[14] " The Knight of Intercession, and other Poems." By S. J. Stone, M.A. London: Rivingtons. 1872.

those in the two preceding volumes. They always too maintain the same level of excellence. We prefer the sonnets to the other minor poems. They show great command of language. We are afraid, however, that they will not make their mark, in spite of their many beauties.

Amongst the other volumes which show refinement and real poetical power, must be put Mrs. Clive's "Poems by V.,"[15] and Mr. Aubrey de Vere's Legends of St. Patrick."[16] Although we cannot go quite so far as the Quarterly Reviewer in his praise of the "IX. Poems," which Mrs. Clive has here reprinted, yet we think they display an intellectual power, which few poetesses have shown, and make us deeply regret that Mrs. Clive has not devoted her life to the cultivation of her really great talents. We can only here say that the new instalment is quite worthy of the "IX. Poems." They are marked by the same delicacy of thought, happiness of expression, and religious treatment, which won Mrs. Clive so many admirers for her previous volume. We must too, briefly dismiss Mr. Aubrey de Vere's "Legends of St. Patrick" with a word of praise, although we hardly like them so much as some of the writer's earlier poems.

Of course as usual there are a number of volumes about which in charity we should be glad to be silent. But silence is of no use. If we do not notice them, another copy is sure to be sent. If on the other hand we were to speak our mind, and say that the authors were howling idiots, we should be prosecuted. Do what we will, hit high or hit low, we can't please. Here, for instance, is the "Field of Rivalry."[17] What can we say to an author who begins his poem in this style—

> "O Albion beloved, thrice happy isle!
> With sons ingenious, astute, and hale."

Are we to say that he has an accurate ear, or are we to tell him to buy a rhyming dictionary? Perhaps we had better rewrite the lines for him. We would therefore suggest that they should run thus—

> "O Albion beloved for beer and ale,
> With sons who drink them either fresh or stale."

This couplet, at all events, is not only in good rhyme, but contains an undeniable truth, which is singularly appropriate just now when the New Licensing Act has come into force.

"Memories,"[18] for anything we know, may be written by the author of the "Field of Rivalry." It contains about as many pages and as much drivel.

"Hal and I"[19] is one of those would-be facetious poems, which simply oppress one with melancholy.

[15] "Poems." By V. Author of "Paul Ferroll." Including the "IX. Poems." London : Longmans, Green, Reader and Dyer. 1872.

[16] "The Legends of Saint Patrick." By Aubrey de Vere. London : Henry S. King and Co. 1872.

[17] "The Field of Rivalry. An Heroic Poem in Four Books. Written Midst the Nineteenth Century." By E. D. S. London : Longmans, Green and Co. 1872.

[18] "Memories. A Life's Epilogue." London : Longmans, Green and Co. 1872.

[19] "Hal and I." In Four Parts. By the Survivor. London : Elliot Stock. 1872.

It would be quite giving a wrong idea of Mr. Hales's "Longer English Poems,"* if we were to say, as he has done in his title-page, that it is "chiefly for use in schools." From whatever point of view we regard the volume, it is excellent. The selections are made with as good taste as Mr. Palgrave has shown in the delightful "Golden Treasury." The grammatical notes and the general scholarship place the book on the same level as Abbott's "Shakspearian Grammar," whilst for the introductory notices, with their keen appreciation of each individual poet, and the beauties and characteristics of his poetry, combined with a liberal spirit, we are at a loss to find a parallel. There is nobody that will not be the better for this most enjoyable volume. We have just now but one brief criticism to make. In his Introduction to L'Allegro and Il Penseroso, Mr. Hales remarks : "Milton is indeed not altogether at home in the poem describing the former. He distinguishes the sweetbriar from the eglantine, whereas they were one and the same. Larks do not visit even poets' windows to say good-morrow, but rather ' singing ever soar, and soaring ever sing ' " (p. 231). We will take first the question of the eglantine. If Mr. Hales will turn to Dr. Prior's excellent work on the "Popular Names of British Plants," he will find, amongst other valuable remarks, the following :—" In fact the name (eglantine) appears to be one of those which have had a double origin, having in the first place been given as *aguilen* to some prickly wild bush, in the south of France, and subsequently been transferred to a different plant, and modified by the Norman poets into *eglantier*, with the sense of a climber. The description of the eglantine by the writers of the fourteenth century does not at all accord with the sweetbriar." (First Edition, pp. 72, 73). Now it will be undoubtedly to this climbing plant, perhaps briony, honeysuckle, or wild clematis, to which Milton refers, and to which the epithet "twisted" is singularly appropriate, whilst quite out of place as regards the sweetbriar. A little research in the direction which Dr. Prior has indicated would soon clear up the matter. With regard to the lark, Mr. Hales a little further on, in support of his charge, proceeds to say—"The poet evidently means that the lark is to descend and perch for a moment upon his window-sill." Our view is that the eight lines about the lark simply mean to hear the bird ascend and descend. It is not true that the lark only sings when he soars, or soars when he sings. He also sings when he descends. We pity the man who has not, when lying in bed in dark spring mornings, even as early as February, heard the lark go up singing, until his song is almost hushed, and then suddenly come singing down again, seemingly almost close to the window, bidding one good-morrow. This we take to be the poet's true meaning. Once more, Mr. Hales's volume should be in the hands of all lovers of poetry.

Dr. Dircks has already established a reputation as a critic of poetry.

* "Longer English Poems. With Notes Philological and Explanatory. And an Introduction on the Teaching of English. Chiefly for use in Schools." Edited by J. W. Hales, M.A., &c. &c. London : Macmillan and Co. 1872.

His work "Nature-Study" attracted considerable attention. His present volume, "Naturalistic Poetry,"[*] is a sort of continuation of the former work. He here illustrates those principles which he laid down in "Nature-Study" by a reference to the sacred poetry of the last three centuries. We certainly think it would have been better if he had extended his field of observation. His work would thus have derived many advantages. As it is, however, "Naturalistic Poetry" is not without interest. We nowhere discover any partiality for this or that particular sect. Dr. Dircks judges each poet by his poetry, and not by his creed. Here and there, however, we venture to dissent from Dr. Dircks' criticism. Thus he calls a certain hymn of Cowper's "that fine, impassioned production, unsurpassed perhaps by any composition within the range of modern sacred poetry." This is indeed high praise. But when we turn to the hymn, we find it to be the well-known—

"God moves in a mysterious way,
His wonders to perform;
He plants His footsteps in the sea,
And rides upon the storm."

We will say nothing of the uncouth rhythm of the second verse, or the faulty rhyme of "way" and "sea." These are venial blunders. The offence consists in the utter bad taste of making God a kind of superior acrobat, walking on the sea and riding the storm.

"Goethe; his Life and Works"[**] is an unpretending little book, which performs a great deal more than it promises. The Americans have for a long time past been especially cultivating Goethe, in the same way as the Germans have been studying Shakspeare. Mr. Calvert's book may be used as a sort of introduction to Lewes's well-known "Life of Goethe." For the young it is perhaps even a safer guide. Mr. Calvert as a rule treads firm ground. His criticisms on Goethe's writings are especially what are needed for the young. He is careful to point out for them what a hard, indefatigable worker he was. Of course this may all seem commonplace enough, but it cannot be repeated too often for the young. And Mr. Calvert, if he does teach commonplaces, does not teach them in a commonplace way. His style is cultivated and graceful. One of the charms of the book is the way in which he illustrates his remarks by quotations taken from Goethe's own writings. We are tempted to give some of the reflections which Mr. Calvert has extracted from the Zelter correspondence:—

"Art, where it manifests itself through the highest artist, creates a form so powerfully vivid, that it ennobles and transforms any material."

"I have learnt immensely from Linnæus, but not botany. Except Shakspeare and Spinoza, I know none of the departed who has had such influence on me."

[*] "Naturalistic Poetry. Selected from Psalms and Hymns of the last Three Centuries. In Four Essays. Developing the Progress of Nature-Study in Connexion with Sacred Songs." By Henry Dircks, LL.D., M.R.S.L., &c. London : Simpkin, Marshall and Co. Edinburgh : William P. Nimmo. 1872.
[**] "Goethe ; His Life and Works." An Essay. By George H. Calvert. London : Trübner and Co. New York : Lee, Shepherd and Dillingham. 1872.

"Nothing is more natural than nature, which lies ever there where we don't look; we seek the horse on which we are riding."

"I have never concealed what a deadly enemy I am to all parody and travesty, but only on this account am I so, because this base brood pulls down the noble, the beautiful, the great in order to annihilate them."

If Goethe's first sentence were properly understood, we should not have quite so much nonsense talked about the Morality of Literature and Art. To Linnæus Goethe might have added perhaps Buffon's name. Many of us probably when reading a certain living naturalist have made a somewhat similar remark. The third sentence is very characteristic, and might be illustrated by plenty of parallel passages. The fourth extract the Americans would do well to lay to heart. American literature is just now poisoned with that comic writing which is also the curse of our own country. In conclusion, we can most strongly recommend Mr. Calvert's charming little volume as giving in a compact form an admirable account of Goethe's life and times, sound criticism on his principal works, and some excellent translations.

We cannot of course do more in this section than call attention to the new edition of Mr. Wedgwood's "Dictionary of English Etymology."[n] Mr. Wedgwood's general principles we described some years ago at full length in this *Review*. We can only now say that we have compared the present edition with our copy of the first, and find the misprints corrected, and a number of fresh words introduced, and a large amount of new matter. In the present edition Mr. Wedgwood has received the valuable assistance of the Rev. J. C. Atkinson, whose "Glossary of the Cleveland Dialect," is, without doubt, the very best glossary which we possess. Mr. Atkinson's knowledge of the local forms of words, especially in the north-east of Yorkshire, throws considerable light on many difficult points. "Everything has two handles, and beware of the wrong one," is especially applicable to etymology. Of course there will be great objections raised to many of Mr. Wedgwood's derivations. But the work is a great work, replete with varied learning, full of suggestions, and to which all future philologists, whether they agree or not with its conclusions, will be under the deepest obligations.

We have often wondered why Juvenal[n] has not appeared in the "Ancient Classics for English Readers." Probably most editors have felt the enormous difficulties of the task—chief amongst them the utter hopelessness of translating the satirist's fierce indignation. We in fact possess no translation of Juvenal, in the sense that Frere has translated Aristophanes. Mr. Walford does not tell us from what source his translation is taken. We suppose, however, that it is Gifford's. It is tolerably good, but then Juvenal is first-rate. And between tolerably good work and first-rate work lies the distinction which separates Juvenal from lesser men. Mr. Walford has done all

---

[n] "A Dictionary of English Etymology." By Hensleigh Wedgwood, M.A. Second edition. Thoroughly revised and corrected by the author, and extended to the Classical Roots of the Language. With an Introduction on the Formation of Language. London : Trübner and Co. 1871-2.

[n] "Juvenal." By Edward Walford, M.A. (Ancient Classics for English Readers). London and Edinburgh : William Blackwood and Sons. 1872.

in his power to bring Juvenal and his times within the comprehension
of the most uneducated English reader. His chapters on " Morals at
Rome," " Women at Rome," and " Town Life at Rome," are excellent.
But the prudery—for it is not Juvenal's reverentia—demanded by
modern society, takes the whole sting out of the satire. To the
English reader, who does not understand the allusions—and he cannot
possibly understand them—Juvenal's satire must be as flabby as dough.
Further, Mr. Walford evidently loves his author. He has carefully
noted those little flashes of humour by which Juvenal so often lights
up his pictures. Juvenal's humour has never been sufficiently taken
into account. The turbot scene, in the Fourth Satire, from which
Mr. Walford quotes, is one of the most humorous bits in any literature. But it is rather, perhaps, in little touches than in set scenes,
that Juvenal's humour is seen. Every one will rember the stroke by
which he describes the wild boar, as " animal propter convivia natum,"
which still holds good in England at Christmas; and the happy touch,
when he says, the noises in the streets of Rome "eripient somnum
Druso, vitulisque marinis,"· still true of London, if the seals in the
Zoological Gardens could but speak. But every satire is full of such
little bits, which irresistibly raise a smile, even when the mind is
wrought up to the highest pitch of indignation. The same peculiar
humour may be seen in two modern writers, Richter and our own
Carlyle. Further, we are glad to find that Mr. Walford has noticed
what has escaped so many critics—Juvenal's love of the country and
nature. The man who wrote these lines—

> " Quanto præstantius esset
> Numen aquæ, viridi su margine clauderet undas
> Herba, neu ingenuum violarent marmora tophum,"

paints in the spirit of a pre-Raphaelite artist, who might have read
" Modern Painters." In conclusion, Mr. Walford's little book has
given us real pleasure. We wish that we could think that it would
give the same pleasure to those for whom it is especially meant.
Juvenal's satire will fly over the head of the retired tradesman.
Gifford and rose-water is a poor substitute for the fire and vitriol of the
original. Probably a good poetical translation is impossible. We
think it however an open question whether or not a prose translation
is not the best medium for rendering verse, especially satire, from one
language to another. Of one thing we are certain, that a second-rate
prose translation is far preferable to a second-rate verse translation.
We live in hopes therefore of some day seeing a prose translation of
the greatest master of satire, which shall do him justice.

Whatever doubts we might have had as to the propriety of translating verse, and especially satire by prose, have certainly been dispelled by Conington's prose version of Persius.* Nothing can be

---

* "The Satires of A. Persius Flaccus." With a Translation and Commentary by John Conington, M.A., late Corpus Professor of Latin in the University
of Oxford. To which is prefixed A Lecture on the Life and Writings of Persius,
Delivered at Oxford by the same Author, January, 1855. Edited by H. Nettleship, M.A., formerly Fellow of Lincoln College, Oxford. Oxford: At the Clarendon
Press. 1872.

more admirable than the way in which the humour is caught, the turns of thought followed, the delicacies of language preserved, and the equivalents of each language opposed. The work is a marvel not merely of Latin, but of English scholarship. If any one wishes to see what good translation means, let them turn to the well-known Prologue—"Nec fonte labra prolui caballino." Then, if they are not satisfied, let them attempt to translate it—keep something of its melody, maintain its *calida junctura* of phrases, and above all preserve its sweetness with its delicate subacid of satire. This, however, is what Conington has done. But turn where we will, we perceive the same mastery. Now if any English reader is from henceforth ignorant of Persius, he has no excuse. All difficulties are smoothed. The vernacular is translated by the vernacular. Thus the well known lines—

> "Respue, quod non es; tollat sua munera Cerdo;
> Tecum habita; noris, quam sit tibi curta supellex."

read thus—"No, reject what is not you; let Hob and Dick take their presents back again; live at home, and learn how slenderly furnished your apartments are." Cerdo would of course be lost upon the English reader, but Shakspere's "Hob and Dick" will come home to him. Equally interesting to the English reader is the Lecture on the Life and Writings of Persius. Although that lecture was delivered as part of the duties of the Latin Professor in the University of Oxford, yet it appeals to an audience far beyond the University walls. Professor Conington possessed that genius which gives a world-wide interest to every subject which it touches. To praise the scholarship which the notes display would be a piece of impertinence. In conclusion, we must add that no fitter editor could have been found than Mr. Nettleship. We are quite sure that all scholars will rate his labours much higher than he himself has done in his very interesting preface.

Amongst reprints and second editions, we have to acknowledge the fourth volume of "The Works of Alfred Tennyson;"[20] "That Boy of Norcott's,"[21] the most characteristic perhaps of Lever's latest novels; three novels by Mr. Anthony Trollope,[22] well got-up and tastefully bound, and two other novels,[23] issued also by Messrs. Smith, Elder and Co., in tawdry yellow-and-red covers, after the vulgarest railway book-stall fashion.

[20] "The Works of Alfred Tennyson." Vol. IV. In Memoriam and Maud. London: Strahan and Co. 1872.
[21] "That Boy of Norcott's." By Charles Lever. A New Edition. London: Smith, Elder and Co. 1872.
[22] I. "The Small House at Allington." By Anthony Trollope. A New Edition. London: Smith, Elder and Co. 1872. II. "Framley Parsonage." By Anthony Trollope. A New Edition. London: Smith, Elder and Co. 1872. III. "The Claverings." By Anthony Trollope. A New Edition. London: Smith, Elder and Co. 1872.
[23] I. "Véra." By the Author of the "Hôtel du Petit St. Jean." A New Edition. London: Smith, Elder and Co. 1872. II. "In that State of Life." By Hamilton Aïdé. A new Edition. London: Smith, Elder and Co. 1872.

INDEX.

www.ingramcontent.com/pod-product-compliance
Lightning Source LLC
Chambersburg PA
CBHW022126020426
42334CB00015B/778